Instructor's Manual

Business Communication: Process & Product

Seventh Edition

Mary Ellen Guffey
Professor Emerita of Business
Los Angeles Pierce College

Dana Loewy
Business Communication Program
California State University, Fullerton

Australia • Brazil • Japan • Korea • Mexico • Singapore • Spain • United Kingdom • United States

For product information and technology assistance, contact us at **Cengage Learning Academic Resource Center, 1-800-423-0563**.

For permission to use material from this text or product, submit all requests online at **www.cengage.com/permissions**. Further permissions questions can be emailed to **permissionrequest@cengage.com**.

ISBN-13: 978-0-538-47324-8
ISBN-10: 0-538-47324-X

South-Western Cengage Learning
5191 Natorp Boulevard
Mason, OH 45040
USA

Cengage Learning is a leading provider of customized learning solutions with office locations around the globe, including Singapore, the United Kingdom, Australia, Mexico, Brazil, and Japan. Locate your local office at: **international.cengage.com/region**.

Cengage Learning products are represented in Canada by Nelson Education, Ltd.

For your course and learning solutions, visit **www.cengage.com**.

Purchase any of our products at your local college store or at our preferred online store **www.CengageBrain.com**.

Printed in the United States of America
1 2 3 4 5 6 7 14 13 12 11 10

CONTENTS

Letter from the Author 1

1 – GUIDE TO TEACHING MATERIALS 2

Ancillaries and Resources 2
Instructor's Manual 2
Instructor's Resource CD (IRCD) 2
Certified Test Bank 3
ExamView Testing Software 3
Triple-Option PowerPoint Presentation Slides 3
Transparency Acetate Lecture Outlines and Solutions 3
Expanded Video Collection 4
WebTutor 4
Aplia – Help With Homework 5
Business Communication Newsletter 5

Premium Web Site Support 5
Student Web Site 5
Instructor Web Site 6

2 – COURSE PLANNING 7

Learning Objectives 7

Classroom Tips 7
In the Beginning 8
During the Term 8
Near the End 9

Classroom Etiquette: An Instructor's Expectations 10

Including Grammar and Mechanics 11
Your Personal Language Trainer 11
Grammar and Mechanics Guide: C.L.U.E. 12
C.L.U.E. Proficiency Test Form A 14
C.L.U.E. Proficiency Test Form B 16
C.L.U.E. Proficiency Test Form C 18
Answers to C.L.U.E. Proficiency Tests 20
C.L.U.E. Proficiency Sentence Revision Keys 21

Speak Right! and Spell Right! 24

Possible Class Schedules 24
10-Week Course 25
11-Week Course 26
14-Week Course 27
16-Week Course 28
16-Week Course – With Oral Report Delivery 29

The Prebuilt Course – The Easy Way to Plan a Course 30
Introduction and Instructions 30
Schedule Overview 34
Syllabus 34
Syllabus – Orientation 35
Syllabus – Assignments 36
Grading in the Prebuilt Course 41
Prebuilt Course Grade Record 41

Delivering Your Course Online 43
Teaching Tips for Online or Hybrid Classes 43
Suggestions for Reducing Cheating in Online Classes 44
Creating a Community With Your Students 45

Using Textbook Features 45
Chapter Opening Case Studies 45
End-of-Chapter and Web Activities 46
Photo Essays 46
Ethics Checks 46
Documents for Analysis 46

Workplace Simulations 46

Assessing Writing Assignments 47
Revision 47
Correction Symbols and Comments 47
Six Assessment Methods 48
Assigned-Weights Method 48
Dual-Criteria Method 48
Check-Mark Method 49
0, 1, 2 Holistic Method 49
Contract Method 50
Workplace-Based Method 51
Assigned Weights Template for Grading Writing Assignments 51

Assessing Oral Presentations 53

Assessing Reports 55

Demonstrated Leadership Assessment 56

Strategies for Reducing Plagiarism 56

3 – VIDEOS, TEAMS, AND MORE 58

Video Discussion Guide 58

Video Library 1: Career Success Starts With Communication Foundations 59
Video Library 1: Intercultural Communication at Work 60
Video Library 2: Understanding Teamwork: Cold Stone Creamery 62
Video Library 1: Guffey's 3-x-3 Writing Process Develops Fluent Workplace Skills 63
Video Library 2: Writing Skills: The Little Guys 64
Video Library 1: Technology in the Workplace 65
Video Library 1: Smart E-Mails and Memos Advance Your Career 66
Video Library 2: Social Responsibility and Communication: Ben & Jerry's 67
Video Library 2: Persuasive Request: Hard Rock Café 70
Video Library 2: Innovation, Learning, and Communication: A Study of Yahoo 72
Video Library 2: Bad News: BuyCostumes 73
Video Library 1: Effective On-the-Job Oral Presentations 76
Video Library 1: The Job Search 77
Video Library 1: Sharpening Your Interview Skills 78

Classroom Collaboration and Teamwork 79

Collaboration Advantages and Disadvantages 79
Collaborative Assignments 80
Group Formation 82
Group Preparation Activities 82
Instructions in Small Group Processes 83
Instruction in the Writing Process 83
Analytical Report Group Activities 84
Performance Evaluation 85
  Assessing Individual Performance 85
  Assigning Group Grades 85
  References 86
Confidential Group Project Peer Evaluation Form 87

Teaching Business Etiquette 88

How to Use the Business Etiquette: Teaching/Learning Module 88

Teaching Formal Reports 89

Preliminaries 89
In-Class Assignments and Discussion 90
Project Proposal 90
Work Plan 92
Organization and Visual Aids 92
Documentation 92
Putting It All Together: Completing the Project 93

4 – LECTURE NOTES 94

Chapter 1 Lecture Notes and Teaching Suggestions 95
Chapter Synopsis 95
Learning Objectives 95
What's New in This Chapter 96
Lecture Outline 96
Lecture Transparencies and Solution Masters 104
Answers to Chapter Review Questions 105
Answers to Critical Thinking Questions 107
Activities 109
ZOOMING IN, Part 1: Led by Ambitious Indra Nooyi, PepsiCo Pushes Nutrition 116
ZOOMING IN, Part 2: Pepsico 117
ZOOMING IN, Your Turn: Applying Your Skills at Pepsico 118
Discussion Material for CAREER COACH: Sharpening Your Skills for Critical Thinking, Problem Solving, and Decision Making 118
Ethics Check Solutions 119
Photo Essay Solutions 121
Video Resources 121
Chapter Presentation Ideas 121

Chapter 2 Lecture Notes and Teaching Suggestions 123
Chapter Synopsis 123
Learning Objectives 123
What's New in This Chapter 124
Lecture Outline 124
Lecture Transparencies 134
Answers to Chapter Review Questions 135
Answers to Critical Thinking Questions 137
Activities 139
ZOOMING IN, Part 1: FedEx Office 145
ZOOMING IN, Part 2: FedEx Office 146
ZOOMING IN, Your Turn: FedEx Office 146
Discussion Material for CAREER COACH: Listening to Nonnative Speakers in the Workplace 147
Discussion Material for CAREER COACH: Perils of Casual Apparel in the Workplace 148
Discussion Material for ETHICAL INSIGHTS: Ethical Responsibilities of Group Members and Leaders 148
Discussion Material for PLUGGED IN: How to Form and Participate in Effective Virtual Teams 148
Ethics Check Solutions 149
Photo Essay Solution 150
Video Resources 150
Chapter Presentation Ideas and Extras 150

Chapter 3 Lecture Notes and Teaching Suggestions 155
Chapter Synopsis 155
Learning Objectives 155
What's New in This Chapter 156
Lecture Outline 156

Lecture Transparencies 162
Answers to Chapter Review Questions 162
Answers to Critical Thinking Questions 165
Activities 168
ZOOMING IN, Part 1: Costly Lessons for World's Largest Retailer 176
ZOOMING IN, Part 2: Wal-Mart in China 177
ZOOMING IN, Your Turn: Applying Your Skills at Wal-Mart 178
Discussion Material for CAREER COACH: He Said, She Said: Gender Talk and Gender Tension 178
Discussion Material for ETHICAL INSIGHTS: Overcoming Prejudice: Negative Perceptions of Muslims in the United States 179
Discussion Material for PLUGGED IN: Greenland and Iceland: The Most Connected Countries in the World? 180
Ethics Check Solutions 181
Photo Essay Solutions 182
Video Resources 182
Chapter Presentation Ideas 182

Chapter 4 Lecture Notes and Teaching Solutions 184
Chapter Synopsis 184
Learning Objectives 184
What's New in This Chapter 185
Lecture Outline 185
Lecture Transparencies 192
Solution Masters 192
Answers to Chapter Review Questions 193
Answers to Critical Thinking Questions 195
Activities 198
ZOOMING IN, Part 1: Suze Orman Preaches Financial Freedom in Simple Language 201
ZOOMING IN, Part 2: Suze Orman Preached Financial Freedom in Simple Language 202
ZOOMING IN, Your Turn: Applying Your Skills With Suze Orman 203
Discussion Material for PLUGGED IN: Using Technology to Edit and Revise Collaborative Documents 203
Ethics Check Solutions 203
Photo Essay Solutions 204
Video Resources 204
Chapter Presentation Ideas and Extras 204

Chapter 5 Lecture Notes and Teaching Suggestions 206
Chapter Synopsis 206
Learning Objectives 206
What's New in This Chapter 207
Lecture Outline 207
Lecture Transparencies 213
Solution Masters 213
Answers to Chapter Review Questions 213
Answers to Critical Thinking Questions 216
Writing Improvement Exercises 217
Activities 220

ZOOMING IN, Part 1: Once the Height of Hip, Gap Struggles to Stop Sagging Sales 223
ZOOMING IN, Part 2: Gap Inc. 223
ZOOMING IN, Your Turn: Applying Your Skills at Gap, Inc. 224
Discussion Material for PLUGGED IN: Seven Ways Computers Can Help You Create Better Written Messages, Oral Presentations, and Web Pages 224
Ethics Check Solutions 225
Photo Essay Solutions 225
Video Resources 226
Chapter Presentation Ideas and Extras 226

Chapter 6 Lecture Notes and Teaching Suggestions 227
Chapter Synopsis 227
Learning Objectives 227
What's New in This Chapter 228
Lecture Outline 228
Lecture Transparencies 232
Solution Masters 233
Answers to Chapter Review Questions 233
Answers to Critical Thinking Questions 235
Writing Improvement Exercises 237
Activities 239
ZOOMING IN, Part 1: Taco Bell Tweaks Menu to Rebuild Customer Base 247
ZOOMING IN, Part 2: Taco Bell 248
ZOOMING IN, Your Turn: Applying Your Skills at Taco Bell 249
Discussion Material for PLUGGED IN: Using Spell Checkers and Grammar/Style Checkers Wisely 250
Ethics Check Solutions 250
Photo Essay Solution 251
Video Resources 251
Chapter Presentation Ideas and Extras 251
Supplementary Lecture 252

Chapter 7 Lecture Notes and Teaching Suggestions 255
Chapter Synopsis 255
Learning Objectives 255
What's New in This Chapter 256
Lecture Outline 256
Lecture Transparencies 263
Solution Masters 264
Answers to Chapter Review Questions 264
Answers to Critical Thinking Questions 267
Activities 269
ZOOMING IN, Part 1: Twitter: From Obscure Tech Fad to Internet Sensation 277
ZOOMING IN, Part 2: Got Something to Tweet About at Work? Think Again 278
ZOOMING IN, Your Turn: Twitter 279
Discussion Material for PLUGGED IN: Cloud Computing 279
Ethics Check Solutions 280
Photo Essay Solutions 281
Video Resources 281

Chapter 8 Lecture Notes and Teaching Suggestions 282
Chapter Synopsis 282
Learning Objectives 283
What's New in This Chapter 283
Lecture Outline 283
Lecture Transparencies 289
Solution Masters 289
Answers to Chapter Review Questions 290
Answers to Critical Thinking Questions 292
Writing Improvement Exercises 294
Activities 295
ZOOMING IN, Part 1: Ben & Jerry's Uses Positive Letters to Sweeten Relations With Customers 299
ZOOMING IN, Part 2: Ben & Jerry's 299
ZOOMING IN, Your Turn: Applying Your Skills at Ben & Jerry's 300
Ethics Check Solutions 301
Photo Essay Solutions 302
Video Resources 302

Chapter 9 Lecture Notes and Teaching Suggestions 303
Chapter Synopsis 303
Learning Objectives 303
What's New in This Chapter 304
Lecture Outline 304
Lecture Transparencies 309
Solution Masters 310
Answers to Chapter Review Questions 310
Answers to Critical Thinking Questions 313
Writing Improvement Exercises 314
ZOOMING IN, Part 1: Passengers LUV Airlines—Even When Flights Are Late 321
ZOOMING IN, Part 2: Southwest Airlines 321
ZOOMING IN, Your Turn: Applying Your Skills at Southwest Airlines 323
Discussion Material for PLUGGED IN: Using Technology to Personalize Form Letters 323
Ethics Check Solutions 324
Photo Essay Solutions 324
Video Resources 325

Chapter 10 Lecture Notes and Teaching Suggestions 326
Chapter Synopsis 326
Learning Objectives 326
What's New in This Chapter 327
Lecture Outline 327
Lecture Transparencies 335
Solution Masters 335
Answers to Chapter Review Questions 336
Answers to Critical Thinking Questions 338
Activities 340
ZOOMING IN, Part 1: Hands on Miami 345
ZOOMING IN, Part 2: Hands on Miami 346
ZOOMING IN, Your Turn: Applying Your Skills at Hands on Miami 347

Discussion Material for ETHICAL INSIGHTS: What's Fair in Persuasion? Avoiding Common Logical Fallacies 348
Ethics Check Solutions 348
Photo Essay Solutions 349
Video Resources 349

Chapter 11 Lecture Notes and Teaching Suggestions 350
Chapter Synopsis 350
Learning Objectives 350
What's New in This Chapter 351
Lecture Outline 351
Lecture Transparencies 359
Solution Masters 359
Answers to Chapter Review Questions 359
Answers to Critical Thinking Questions 362
Activities 364
ZOOMING IN, Part 1: Pet Airways 371
ZOOMING IN, Part 2: Pet Airways 372
ZOOMING IN, Your Turn: Pet Airways 373
Discussion Material for PLUGGED IN: Staying on Top of Research Data 374
Discussion Material for ETHICAL INSIGHTS: Making Ethical Charts and Graphics 374
Ethics Check Solutions 374
Photo Essay Solutions 375

Chapter 12 Lecture Notes and Teaching Suggestions 376
Chapter Synopsis 376
Learning Objectives 376
What's New in This Chapter 376
Lecture Outline 377
Lecture Transparencies 383
Solution Masters 383
Answers to Chapter Review Questions 383
Answers to Critical Thinking Questions 386
Activities 387
ZOOMING IN, Part 1: Starbucks Perks Up: Recapturing the Soul of the Coffeehouse 401
ZOOMING IN, Part 2: Starbucks 402
ZOOMING IN, Your Turn: Applying Your Skills at Starbucks 403
Discussion Material for CAREER COACH: The Top Ten Tips for Designing Better Documents 403
Ethics Check Solutions 403
Photo Essay Solutions 404

Chapter 13 Lecture Notes and Teaching Suggestions 405
Chapter Synopsis 405
Learning Objectives 405
What's New in This Chapter 406
Lecture Outline 406
Lecture Transparencies 410
Solution Masters 410
Answers to Chapter Review Questions 410
Answers to Critical Thinking Questions 413

Activities 414
ZOOMING IN, Part 1: Writing Winning Proposals at Raytheon 415
ZOOMING IN, Part 2: Writing Winning Proposals at Raytheon 417
ZOOMING IN, Your Turn: Applying Your Skill at Raytheon 419
Ethics Check Solutions 420
Photo Essay Solutions 421
Chapter Presentation Ideas and Extras 421

Chapter 14 Lecture Notes and Teaching Suggestions 423
Chapter Synopsis 423
Learning Objectives 423
What's New in This Chapter 424
Lecture Outline 424
Lecture Transparencies 431
Solution Masters 432
Answers to Chapter Review Questions 432
Answers to Critical Thinking Questions 434
Activities 436
ZOOMING IN, Part 1: Apple's Steve Jobs and His Keynotes 441
ZOOMING IN, Part 2: Apple's Steve Jobs and His Keynotes 441
ZOOMING IN, Your Turn: Applying Your Skills at Apple Computer 443
Discussion Material for CAREER COACH: The 10/20/30 Rule for PowerPoint 443
Discussion Material for CAREER COACH: How to Avoid Stage Fright 443
Ethics Check Solutions 443
Photo Essay Solutions 444
Video Resources 444
Chapter Presentation Ideas and Extras 445

Chapter 15 Lecture Notes and Teaching Suggestions 446
Chapter Synopsis 446
Learning Objectives 446
What's New in This Chapter 447
Lecture Outline 447
Lecture Transparencies 456
Solution Masters 456
Answers to Chapter Review Questions 457
Answers to Critical Thinking Questions 460
Activities 461
ZOOMING IN, Part 1: Workplace Expert Liz Ryan Shares Job-Search Tips 464
ZOOMING IN, Part 2: Workplace Expert Liz Ryan Shares Job-Search Tips 465
ZOOMING IN, Your Turn: Applying Your Skills With Liz Ryan 465
Discussion Material for CAREER COACH: Network Your Way to a Job in the Hidden Market 466
Discussion Material for ETHICAL INSIGHTS: Are Inflated Résumés Worth the Risk 466
Ethics Check Solutions 466
Photo Essay Solutions 467
Video Resources 467
Chapter Presentation Ideas and Extras 467

Chapter 16 Lecture Notes and Teaching Suggestions 469
Chapter Synopsis 469
Learning Objectives 469
What's New in This Chapter 470
Lecture Outline 470
Lecture Transparencies 478
Solutions Transparencies 478
Answers to Chapter Review Questions 478
Answers to Critical Thinking Questions 481
Activities 483
ZOOMING IN , Part 1: Googling for Jobs 485
ZOOMING IN, Part 2: Googling for Jobs 486
ZOOMING IN, Your Turn: Applying Your Skills at Google 486
Discussion Material for CAREER COACH: Fighting Fear During Your Job Interview 487
Discussion Material for CAREER COACH: Let's Talk Money: Salary Negotiation Dos and Don'ts 487
Ethics Check Solutions 487
Photo Essay Solutions 488
Video Resources 489
Chapter Presentation Ideas and Extras 489

5 – SOLUTION MASTERS 491

Dr. Mary Ellen Guffey
Emerita Professor of Business
Los Angeles Pierce College
E-mail: m.e.guffey@cox.net
Web: www.meguffey.com

Dear Business Communication Instructor:

My coauthor Dr. Dana Loewy and I are proud to present the latest edition of *Business Communication: Process and Product.* This book brings you and your students one of the most effective teaching/learning systems on the market. Now recognized as the leading business communication textbook in this country and abroad, *Business Communication: Process and Product* continues to provide comprehensive coverage for students and unmatched support for instructors. Maintaining the position as the market leader means that many instructors found exactly what they wanted in this award-winning textbook from an author they knew and trusted.

In the Seventh Edition, we have retained all of the features that have made this textbook so successful. In addition to solid instruction in writing skills, which employers continue to demand, this edition provides cutting-edge coverage of digital tools and social media.

Most important for instructors, we present to you an edition aimed at making it easier for you to teach and easier for students to learn. What's easy about *BC:PP,* 7e?

- **Easy preparation.** A prebuilt course offers a comprehensive course plan with sample syllabi, assignments for each chapter, and grading plans. Lecture outlines, videos, PowerPoints, and transparency acetates further simplify course preparation.
- **Easy learning.** Students learn quickly from my signature writing process, model documents, and ample print and online activities to apply and reinforce concepts.
- **Easy Web site access.** Everyone with a new book has access to the companion site with many self-directed learning opportunities that extend the textbook.
- **Easy grammar review.** Simple grammar/mechanics exercises in every chapter present a structured review to guide students through all the rules.

A rich array of instructional resources supplement and support *Business Communication: Process and Product,* 7e.This Instructor's Manual contains many of the instructional support materials that provide the foundation for a dynamic and effective course. For publisher ancillaries, call your South-Western sales representative, call South-Western/Cengage Academic Support at 1-800-423-0563, or download them directly from www.meguffey.com.

My goal as an author has always been to provide you with quality teaching materials and to be the most accessible and active author in the field. I appreciate the confidence you have shown in making my books the leaders in their fields.

Sincerely,

Mary Ellen

GUIDE TO TEACHING MATERIALS

PART 1

ANCILLARIES AND RESOURCES

Business Communication: Process and Product, 7e, provides an exceptional collection of publisher ancillaries and author resources to make it easy for you to teach this course.

You may order all publisher items from your publisher's representative or by calling **South-Western/Cengage Academic Resources at 1-800-423-0563.** You may also download bonus teaching materials from the instructor's Web site at **www.meguffey.com.**

Instructor's Manual (ISBN 0-538-47324-X)

Following is an overview of the teaching materials in this Instructor's Manual. Invaluable to novice and veteran teachers alike, this Instructor's Manual provides exceptional teaching ideas and materials, summarized here and described in more detail in later pages.

- Prebuilt Course – The easy way to plan a course
- Complete lecture notes
- Course planning and classroom management tips
- Sample course schedules
- Teaching tips for online and hybrid courses
- Assessment/grading methods and rubrics
- Collaboration tips and activities
- Guide to grammar (C.L.U.E.) review
- Suggested answers for chapter review and critical thinking questions
- Suggested responses and solutions for case study questions and applications
- Transparency master solutions for nearly all e-mail, letter, and memo assignments
- Video discussion guide for "Building Workplace Skills" and "Bridging the Gap" video series
- Teamwork and collaboration suggestions
- Business etiquette module
- Procedures for teaching formal reports

Instructor's Resource CD (ISBN 0-538-47313-4)

In the Instructor's Resource CD (IRCD), you will find the following:

- Instructor's Manual, including solutions
- Instructor PowerPoint presentation slides
- ExamView Testing Software
- Print version of the certified test bank
- Transparency masters in Word and Adobe Acrobat pdfs

Certified Test Bank (ISBN 0-538-47316-9)

In our continuing effort to produce the most accurate and helpful test bank, questions for the Seventh Edition have been certified by outside professionals to assure correctness. Nearly 40 percent of the test bank questions are new. Every chapter now has 50 multiple choice questions, 40 true-false questions, 20 fill-in questions, and 5 essay questions. Our test banks provide feedback, and questions are identified by difficulty (5 = most difficult) and type (application, conceptual, or definition). As part of our Integrated Learning System, questions are identified by learning objective so that instructors can balance their tests appropriately. To aid in reporting compliance with accreditation standards, test questions are also labeled with AACSB competencies. To prepare students for unit tests and also to reward students, a few test bank questions appear in the chapter review quizzes at the student Web site.

New to this edition is a **test bank matrix** that identifies questions according to learning objectives. Instructors are able to organize tests more easily because they can quickly see the number of objectives, the types of questions, the number of questions in each section, and the difficulty of each question.

ExamView Testing Software (ISBN 0-53847313-4)

Free to adopters, ExamView enables instructors to create paper or online tests in minutes. All test bank questions are available through ExamView. You can customize a test, print multiple versions, or save tests for delivery via the Internet. You can track student results and view detailed item analysis. Test bank questions may be downloaded from **www.meguffey.com.** ExamView software, however, is available only on our Instructor's Resource CD. For technical support or assistance in creating ExamView tests, instructors may call the Academic Resources Center at 1-800-423-0563 (8:30 a.m. to 6 p.m. EST).

Triple-Option PowerPoint Presentation Slides (ISBN 0-53847313-4)

Our PowerPoint program for the Seventh Edition provides three versions of slides: (1) a classroom version for instructors, (2) a multimedia version for instructors, and (3) a plain student version. The multimedia version incorporates all the enhanced instructor slides but also adds links directly to video resources. The student version, with a different look from the instructor's slides, provides a condensed view with less content, fewer examples, and less emphasis on graphic presentation. The instructor's versions of the PowerPoint slides are available on the Instructor's Resource CD.

Transparency Acetate Lecture Outlines and Solutions (ISBN 0-538-47507-2)

Written by the authors, nearly 200 acetates summarize, supplement, and highlight course concepts. This transparency packet contains only acetates instead of a combination of acetates and masters. When instructors must teach in rooms without computer facilities, they can rely on our transparencies for chapter outlines, selected figures, enrichment material, and solutions to key problems. Because of the expense of the acetate package, we will send just one set to a school. However, we provide the entire set as transparency masters at **http://www.meguffey .com,** where instructors may download them as Word files. The Instructor's Manual also provides 150 additional transparency masters with solutions to nearly all e-mail, letter, and memo assignments as well as to most end-of-chapter writing improvement exercises. This totals **350 pages of transparency masters and acetates,** probably the biggest—and best—support package in the field! Nearly the same information that appears in the transparencies appears in the PowerPoint presentation slides.

Expanded Video Collection

For the Seventh Edition, we bring instructors and students a new video, "Technology in the Workplace." This video accompanies our new Chapter 7, "Electronic Messages and Digital Media." Illustrating appropriate and inappropriate use of technology in today's workplace, this fast-paced video is sure to stimulate class discussion as students learn how to use today's technology professionally. This new video joins the following Guffey video libraries from which instructors may choose:

Video Library 1 ***Building Workplace Skills*** **(ISBN 0-538-46836-X)** presents eight high-quality DVD videos made especially for Guffey books, introducing and reinforcing concepts in the Seventh Edition of *BC:PP*. These excellent tools boost learning by demonstrating chapter-specific material to strengthen students' comprehension and retention of key ideas.

Video Library 2 ***Bridging the Gap*** **(ISBN 0-538-46837-8)** presents six DVD videos taking students inside real companies such as Yahoo, Cold Stone Creamery, and Hard Rock Cafe. Nearly every video provides a structured writing assignment aimed at bridging the gap between the classroom and the real world of work. See the Video Discussion Guide for suggested responses to critical thinking questions, assignments, and solutions.

WebTutor (WebCT: 0-840-04707-X or Blackboard: 0-538-47431-9)

WebTutor is an interactive, Web-based student supplement that can be packaged with the textbook. Instructors can incorporate WebTutor as an integral part of the course, or students can use it on their own as a study guide. WebTutor for ***BC:PP*, 7e,** features the following:

- Chapter overviews with narrated slides
- Document demonstration problems
- Chapter review quizzes, with gradebook functionality
- Flashcards of key vocabulary
- Online testing and scoring
- Threaded discussion questions
- Video cases and video segments

WebTutor for either WebCT or Blackboard can be hosted on your campus or by South-Western/Cengage Learning. Learn more about WebTutor by calling your sales representative.

Aplia – Help With Homework

Aplia™ is an online, interactive tool that ensures students review fundamental grammar and mechanics and understand concepts presented in ***Business Communication: Process and Product,*** **7e.** Aplia improves learning by increasing student effort and engagement. Aplia is not automatically included with the Seventh Edition. If you would like more information, student pricing, or to see a demo, please contact Aplia at 888-858-7305 or email *info@aplia.com.* Aplia features include the following:

- Auto-graded, chapter-specific assignments that hold students accountable for reading and understanding the text
- Grammar and mechanics tutorials that help students improve key writing skills so that instructors spend less time reviewing and more time teaching advanced writing concepts

Business Communication Newsletter

Instructors using Guffey textbooks will find business communication teaching ideas, relevant current events, and a connection to the author in Dr. Guffey's quarterly Web-based *Business Communication Newsletter*. It contains news of interest in the business communication course as well as announcements of new textbook editions, teaching modules, writing improvement exercises, and bonus case studies with solutions. Visit **http://guffey.swlearning.com/newsletter** where the latest issue is always available. The newsletter site also contains archived newsletter issues, testimonials, and lists of schools where Guffey books have been adopted. To receive announcements of each quarterly issue, send an e-mail message (no subject line, no content) to ***join-guffeylist@lyris.dundee.net***. You will then receive a message confirming your registration.

PREMIUM WEB SITE SUPPORT

Two exceptional Web sites support *Business Communication: Process and Product,* 7e. Both are located at **www.meguffey.com.**

Student Web Site

Free to every student with a new book, the student site at **www.meguffey.com** presents unparalleled interactive self-help resources to expand and enhance student learning. Numerous resources assist students in developing basic grammar, mechanics, language, and writing skills. Other resources strengthen retention of textbook concepts, and still others develop listening, etiquette, and Internet skills. Students may also purchase access to this site if an access card did not come with their textbooks. The following resources are available at **www.meguffey.com**:

- **PowerPoint** slides (student version) summarize and illustrate chapter concepts.
- **Your Personal Language Trainer**, an interactive self-teaching resource, functions as a mini business English course reviewing grammar, punctuation, and usage while offering constructive feedback on student answers.
- **Chapter quizzes** with feedback will strengthen students' comprehension and retention of concepts and learning.

- **Speak Right!** helps students improve their pronunciation of difficult words.
- **Spell Right!** provides interactive exercises that help students improve their spelling skills.
- **Grammar/Mechanics C.L.U.E. Exercises** give students interactive practice drills with immediate feedback and answers using sentences that parallel principles in the textbook end-of-chapter exercises.
- **Sentence Competency Exercises** provide invaluable writing practice at the sentence level.
- **Flashcards** review key terms from the glossary so that students internalize vocabulary and concepts that are the foundation of their learning.
- **Documents for Analysis** allow students to revise the textbook documents online without rekeying.
- **New simulations with case-based scenarios** place students in workplace settings so they learn to apply their communication skills on the job as they react to real-world challenges.
- **Writing resources** include links to online writing labs.
- **Report Topics** provide an updated list of nearly 100 business report topics.
- **Bonus module, How to Write Instructions**, illustrates the creation of workplace instructions.

Instructor Web Site

Already the leading instructor support Web site, the Guffey site continues to get better! Located at **www.meguffey.com,** you will find an extraordinary collection of practical classroom teaching materials. To access our materials, instructors complete a Cengage Learning Instructor Request Form. Here is a partial sampling of the available resources:

- **Prebuilt course** makes it easy for instructors to plan a course by providing introduction, class schedule, syllabus, assignments, grading plan, and unit tests for *BC:PP, 7e.*
- **Downloadable supplements** mean that instructors have immediate access to the complete Instructor's Manual, PowerPoint presentations, certified test bank, lecture transparencies, solution masters, and video discussion guide.
- **Downloadable classroom teaching modules** on topics such as workplace etiquette, career strategic plans, listening, business plans, peer editing, informational interviewing, analytical reports, document design, confusing words, teamwork activities, and more.
- **Online teaching tips** including advice on introducing an online course, using WebTutor, setting up the course, handling the first week, evaluating chat, and including presentations.
- **Downloadable exercises** such as good/bad documents, confusing words, dangling/misplaced modifiers, supplementary cases, and many other handouts.
- **Downloadable Writing Improvement Exercises** help students improve control of active-passive voice, capitalization, commas, pronouns, and other writing problem areas.
- **Textbook information** provides product information about what is available.
- **Links to professional organizations** help instructors find conferences and associations.
- **Link to Dr. Guffey's *Business Communication Newsletter*,** which brings instructors quarterly issues with classroom teaching tips, news items, case studies, and author news.

COURSE PLANNING

Part 2

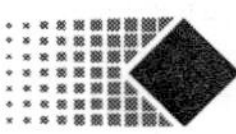

LEARNING OBJECTIVES

As students complete the textbook chapters, they will be able to

- Discuss and appreciate the importance of the communication processes and skills, critical thinking, and ethics in today's increasingly interconnected and digital workplace.
- Function successfully in teams and in meetings.
- Recognize and apply effective listening and nonverbal techniques in achieving successful professional and interpersonal interactions.
- Respect intercultural differences and be able to interact effectively in global and diverse work environments.
- Apply a 3-x-3 writing process in analyzing and solving communication problems.
- Demonstrate skill in composing and formatting professional e-mail messages, memos, and letters that deliver positive, negative, persuasive, and marketing messages effectively.
- Demonstrate skill in composing and writing well-researched proposals and formal reports that illustrate effective use of online information sources and appropriate documentation formats.
- Use social and digital media professionally.
- Display proficiency in grammar, punctuation, capitalization, style, and word use.
- Prepare and deliver an effective oral presentation appropriate for business audiences.
- Understand the employment search process, prepare customized résumés, and complete follow-up documents that impress employers.
- Identify and apply effective employment interview techniques.

CLASSROOM TIPS

Here are a few suggestions that may prove helpful to you as you begin your business communication course. If you have favorite teaching assignments or ideas that have proved successful, please send them to the author, who compensates for effective suggestions that can be shared with other instructors.

In the Beginning

- Distribute a syllabus on the first day of class. You look professional, and you provide needed information for purchasing books, evaluating course content, and planning study time. Make your syllabus as thorough as possible, including due dates for assignments. (See Dr. Guffey's "Prebuilt Course" in this Instructor's Manual or at http://www.meguffey.com.)

- Do something of value the very first day of class. First-day activities might include writing a letter to the instructor, making introductions, or analyzing communication styles.

- Prepare a check sheet of all assignments and due dates for the term. Distribute this check sheet to students the first week of class so that they can use it to keep track of their work.

- To help you learn the names of students as quickly as possible, take a digital snapshot of each one on the first day of class. Make a poster with their names below their pictures, and you will be able to learn their names more quickly.

- Encourage your students to write you a memo or an e-mail message introducing themselves. (See Activity 1.3, "Getting to Know You.") In addition to learning about your students as individuals, you will gain insight into their communication skills.

- Form permanent groups near the very beginning of the term. This will allow students to begin working closely with one another, collaborating on assignments and giving effective feedback.

- Introduce students to the computer lab early in the term so that they can use technology to complete assignments throughout the semester. Make sure that students have a working e-mail address that they can access from campus.

During the Term

- Strive to start class promptly. Some instructors begin with a short quiz to ensure punctuality. Others use *class starters*, such as motivational quotations, written bloopers, jokes about business communication topics, résumés, or other relevant topics. You might give students extra credit for pertinent class starters that they contribute.

- To maintain maximum interest level, plan to change activities several times during your class period. You may lose your audience if you spend your entire class period lecturing.

- Have students submit as many assignments as possible electronically, via e-mail, as attached files, on class discussion boards, to a class mailing list, and so on. This is how students will be communicating primarily in the workplace, and they need to practice now.

- Decide on an appropriate method of grading that suits you and your students. Talk to your colleagues to see what has worked for them. You may choose a traditional, behavioral, or criterion-referenced method. Take a look at the assessment methods outlined in this manual.

- Think about using a color other than red to grade/assess students' papers. Your goal is to avoid the appearance of bleeding all over their papers. Some students have an adverse reaction to red ink.

- Return graded student work as quickly as possible. The sooner work is returned, the sooner students can start applying your suggestions to future assignments.

- Have students regularly edit each other's work in small groups. This allows students to develop their proofreading skills, and they often learn from reading the work of others.

- Require students to submit rough drafts of all writing assignments. After they have received feedback from their classmates and from you, they can prepare a stronger final draft. Consider grading only the final draft, which motivates students and allows them to see measurable improvements in their writing.

- Use real-world examples as much as possible to illustrate your points. Encourage students to bring in their own real-world examples to share with the class, including newspaper articles, messages they have received at work, and so on. Students can be a great resource!

- Encourage students to write their names on the backs of their assignments. Not seeing the student's name enables you to grade the assignment objectively. You have no expectation of what that student "should" have written or earned as a grade. Only when you are ready to record a grade, should you turn over the sheet and identify the writer.

- Consider returning students' papers in individually labeled folders. This will allow you to keep each person's work organized and to return papers confidentially. This folder could also contain a grade record sheet on which students record their grades and track their progress.

- Create a class mailing list so that students can communicate with you and with one another between class meetings. You will find many mailing list activities in Part II of this instructor's manual to help you use the mailing list effectively.

- Create a class discussion board so that students can communicate with you and with one another asynchronously between class meetings. You will find many discussion board activities in the chapter teaching suggestions of this manual to help you use the discussion board effectively.

Near the End

- Learn whether your students would be interested in competing for awards and recognition. You might ask this as one of the questions to be answered in their introduction memos at the beginning of the term. Certificates of excellence could be awarded for the highest writing average, highest test average, best oral presentation, and so forth. Such certificates can be an impressive addition to an employment portfolio and résumé.

- Get feedback from students. Find out what they really liked about the course. Find out what they suggest for making it better. You can learn a lot from student feedback to make future classes even stronger.

- Consider having your students respond to the following scenario. The student's organization has paid tuition for this course. As the student completes the course, an executive in the organization asks for a letter. Write a letter to an executive in a real or imaginary organization explaining how this course made you more valuable to the organization.

As an instructor of business communication, consider joining the Association for Business Communication. This professional organization provides two publications with excellent articles, and it sponsors regional and international meetings where practical research and teaching methodologies are presented in top-notch sessions. For more information about ABC, visit **http://www.businesscommunication.org** or write to Dr. Betty S. Johnson, Executive Director, Association for Business Communication, P.O. Box 6143, SFA Station, Nacogdoches, TX 75962-6143.

CLASSROOM ETIQUETTE: AN INSTRUCTOR'S EXPECTATIONS

In addition to learning to use effective communication techniques, students must also develop a good work ethic. Establishing classroom etiquette rules and expectations early in the semester can help foster an atmosphere of respect and professionalism. You can have students develop these rules, or you can provide your own. You might also consider including your classroom rules on your course syllabus. Following are several etiquette rules and expectations you might consider incorporating into your classroom.

1. Please arrive at class on time or before the starting time. Please attend each class unless a good reason prevents it. If you must miss class, please inform your instructor ahead of time, by phone, by e-mail, or in person.
2. Please come to class prepared for the work to be done and in a positive frame of mind so that you are ready to learn. Please complete readings and other assignments on time. Bring all necessary course materials such as paper, pencil, required books, handouts, and notes.
3. Please try to be pleasant and positive in your classroom behavior. Show respect for all class members. Address legitimate grievances appropriately, preferably outside of normal class time. If you have a problem with the instructor, please try to solve the problem with him or her before appealing to a higher authority.
4. When responding to classroom questions, please do not interrupt a fellow student or the instructor. Take your turn. When you respond to another student's comment, please try to acknowledge the other's position. When responding, please try your best to call other class members by name.
5. Please treat the furniture and equipment in the classrooms and computer labs as if it were your own. Leave classrooms and labs as you find them, turning off equipment as necessary and pushing in chairs. Throw any trash away on your way out.
6. Most classes begin on time and end on time. If you need to know about schedule or assignment changes, please ask about them at the beginning of class. If you have a real need to leave early, please inform the teacher and leave quietly.

7. If before a night class, you need to eat, please do so before class, not during it. Please do not bring food and drink into the class if college rules forbid them. Throw away your trash. Under no condition is smoking or other tobacco use acceptable in the classroom.
8. You will do better if you are interested in the class, and the best way to be interested is to get involved. Talk to your friends about the material, and look for current applications or examples in newspapers or popular magazines and on the Web. If you can make connections between yourself and the course materials, you will be a happier and a better student.
9. Please come to class appropriately dressed. Unless the room is exceedingly cold, please take off your coat and hat.
10. Most of all, keep in touch with the class syllabus, the instructor, and your classmates. You will do better when you feel you are a real part of the class.

INCLUDING GRAMMAR AND MECHANICS

Business communication classes have a great deal of material to cover. Most of us feel that it's almost impossible to teach grammar, punctuation, and usage skills in addition to teaching business communication writing skills. One of our goals in *Business Communication: Process and Product,* therefore, is to make students responsible for learning or reviewing grammar/punctuation/mechanics—with a minimum of class time devoted to this review. To help students review these fundamental language skills, we provide two excellent resources: "Your Personal Language Trainer," a digitized, interactive tutorial, and the Grammar and Mechanics Guide, Competent Language Usage Essentials (C.L.U.E.), a printed review in Appendix A.

Your Personal Language Trainer

Written by the author, "Your Personal Language Trainer" is a remarkable self-teaching tutorial that reviews basic grammar and mechanics. It's available at **www.meguffey.com**, and it's free to all students with a new book. Students without a new book may purchase access at the site. This tutorial enables students to review an entire business English course—including grammar, punctuation, capitalization, and number style—at their own pace. Instead of using valuable class time to teach grammar, instructors can rely on Dr. Guffey to act as a personal trainer in helping students pump up their language muscles! "Your Personal Language Trainer" provides hundreds of sentence reinforcement exercises, all with immediate feedback and explanations for the best comprehension and retention.

Trainer Content. "Your Personal Language Trainer" is keyed to Appendix A, Grammar and Mechanics Guide (Competent Language Usage Essentials—C.L.U.E.) with these 11 sections:

- Nouns
- Pronouns
- Verbs
- Adjectives and Adverbs
- Prepositions
- Commas
- Semicolons & Colons
- Apostrophes
- Other Punctuation
- Capitalization
- Number Usage

Diagnostic Test and Language Profile. An interactive diagnostic test precedes the 11 learning workouts in "Your Personal Language Trainer." This online test has 66 questions that systematically cover all 11 learning workouts. Students receive a score from 0 to 100 percent in each of the 11 workouts, and they can compare it with the following scale:

95 to 100%	You have excellent skills in this category, but you should complete the workouts to be sure you understand and can explain the rules.
85 to 94%	You need a light review. The workouts can help!
75 to 84%	You need to refresh your memory of the rules by completing the workouts.
65 to 74%	You require careful study of the rules in the workouts.
0 to 64%	You need serious study and follow-up reinforcement in the workouts and your textbook. Consider buying and studying a reference manual.

Three-Step Workouts to Build Skills. Students should then complete the three-step Trainer workouts. These workouts provide rules plus exercises to reinforce learning.

- Step 1 involves a warm-up that reviews specific grammar rules. Students read the synopsis and take a quiz.
- Step 2 provides special sentences that focus on the target grammar area.
- Step 3 provides a quiz that measures how well students have pumped up their language skills. They can print a Fitness Certificate to submit when they complete this quiz.

GRAMMAR AND MECHANICS GUIDE
COMPETENT LANGUAGE USAGE ESSENTIALS — C.L.U.E.

In addition to "Your Personal Language Trainer," we provide a printed grammar and mechanics guide in Appendix A. Students will find 50 guidelines that review sentence structure, grammar, usage, punctuation, capitalization, and number style. These guidelines focus on the most frequently used—and abused—language elements. Presented from a business communicator's perspective, the guidelines also include realistic tips for application. Appendix A offers a list of 160 frequently misspelled words plus a quick review of selected confusing words. These words appear in many of the exercises.

The goal of our C.L.U.E. program is to present a reasonable package of language concepts that students can study and master. C.L.U.E. doesn't cover every language rule, each problem spelling word, or all confusing words. It is a selected group of common problem areas. If students conquer this body of guidelines and words, they will be able to meet with confidence about 95 percent of the grammar and mechanics problems that writers face.

Because the number of rules and words is limited, students will not feel that the goal is hopeless. The review exercises include only the principles and words covered in Appendix A.

How to Use C.L.U.E. Give students Proficiency Test Form A as a pretest. [This test is different from the Trainer diagnostic test, which students administer and evaluate themselves online.]

The C.L.U.E. Proficiency Test Form A has only 50 points and requires about 15 to 20 minutes to administer. Discuss it with students as they check their own papers. Caution them to be honest and accurate because they need to know how strong or weak their skills are. Use the first proficiency test as a pretest or base mark; collect and file it. Students who miss ten or more will have difficulty meeting minimum writing standards unless they improve their skills. These students are at risk and should be counseled individually.

At the beginning of your course, you may wish to devote one to three class sessions discussing the grammar/punctuation/mechanics principles in Appendix A. Tell students that they are responsible for mastering the 50 guidelines, plus learning the spelling and confusing words. Set a goal date, say eight to ten weeks into the class. At that time give a second test, Proficiency Test Form B. Students must pass with a minimum proficiency (which you determine).

If students wish to take another test to improve their scores, you could administer Proficiency Test Form C in two weeks. Encourage students to study so that they can improve their proficiency. Remind students that they are mastering a limited group of language guidelines and words. It is their responsibility to meet the minimum proficiency level.

What should you do if students do not meet your minimum proficiency? Actually, they will all improve—but perhaps not enough. Some instructors make language proficiency a portion of the final grade, say 10 to 20 percent. Another possibility is lowering a student's final grade one-half grade (or whatever you choose) if they do not meet the minimum proficiency. At least one research study confirms what many instructors have always known—learning can be substantially improved if motivated by grades. (See Bacon and Anderson, "Assessing and Enhancing the Basic Writing Skills of Marketing Students," *Business Communication Quarterly*, December , 2004, p. 451.) Students make much more effort to learn when graded on their final performance.

By devoting a small portion of class time to discussing the C.L.U.E. exercises, you help students review guidelines that are easily forgotten. Most students genuinely appreciate the challenge because they recognize their weaknesses and truly want to improve. Instructors will find additional downloadable C.L.U.E. exercises at **www.meguffey.com** in the category of "Exercises and Handouts." By the way, selected writing techniques (such as parallelism and misplaced modifiers) are not included in the C.L.U.E. program because they are treated in Chapters 4, 5, and 6.

Competent Language Usage Essentials (C.L.U.E.)
Proficiency Test Form A

Name ____ **Score** __________________

Grammar: In the space provided, write the letter indicating the word that correctly completes each sentence. Use only one answer for each question.

___ 1. If I (a) was (b) were you, I would take the job.
___ 2. Rachel showed me her iPad when she (a) come (b) came over last week.
___ 3. A list showing all the documents prepared for the attorneys (a) was (b) were missing.
___ 4. An executive's time and energy (a) has (b) have to remain focused on achieving corporate goals.
___ 5. How important (a) is (b) are salary, benefits, and job security to you?
___ 6. Please send all e-mails to (a) her and me (b) her and I (c) she and I.
___ 7. All the new equipment (a) seem (b) seems to be working satisfactorily.
___ 8. (a) Anyone (b) Any one of the computers may need to be replaced shortly.
___ 9. I would appreciate (a) you (b) your (c) you're sending the application immediately.
___ 10. The group of players, coaches, and fans (a) is (b) are booking a charter flight.
___ 11. Sixty days (a) is (b) are the period of the loan.
___ 12. Special reports must be written by (a) whoever (b) whomever has a sales problem.
___ 13. One of the men left (a) his (b) their tennis shoes in the locker room.
___ 14. The boss told Maria not to take the criticism (a) personal (b) personally.
___ 15. Every employee may have (a) their (b) his or her (c) his (d) her tuition reimbursed.

Mechanics: For each of the following sentences, select one letter to identify faults in
(a) Commas or semicolons
(b) Punctuation other than commas or semicolons (including hyphens and apostrophes)
(c) Symbols (including dollar and percent signs)
(d) Number expression (word or figure form)
(e) Capitalization

___ 16. The newly-passed legislation will affect taxes in Texas, California, and Michigan.
___ 17. Erics report, which was entitled "Living in a Digital World," caused a stir.
___ 18. Stockholders for IBM could attend the meeting or they could return their proxies.
___ 19. We are earning 42 dollars on every item; however, total sales are slow.
___ 20. The President of DataTech met with the Vice President to discuss the 9 percent dip in sales.
___ 21. If we receive all the figures we will sign the contract July 1 in our headquarters.
___ 22. The memo from our Human Resources Department is quite clear don't you think?
___ 23. All three collectors, by the way, specialized in antique german and dutch coins.
___ 24. When Alicia is absent, we have only 3 operators in our Customer Service Department.
___ 25. We ordered 15 Pentax Cameras to be awarded as prizes.
___ 26. Our interviewing team consists of these people: Ann Simms, Accounting, Tom Burns, Human Resources, and Carlos Santana, Operations.
___ 27. My graduating class is having it's ten-year reunion on June 10.
___ 28. The stockholders' meeting was heavily advertised, however, attendance was light.
___ 29. To improve their english, many Japanese students purchased the book entitled The Power of Language is Yours.
___ 30. Would you please send two copies of Invoice No. 39-5001?

Form A
Page 2

Confusing Words: In the space provided, write the letter of the word that best completes each sentence.

___ 31. Her (a) principal (b) principle concern was investment safety.
___ 32. The recent decline in prices will surely (a) effect (b) affect the entire market.
___ 33. Fidelity's brochure (a) assured (b) insured (c) ensured prospective investors that their money would be in good hands.
___ 34. Every new investor was given (a) complementary (b) complimentary concert tickets.
___ 35. Good researchers (a) sight (b) site (c) cite the sources of all references.
___ 36. After the theft everyone became more (a) conscience (b) conscious of equipment security.

Spelling: For each line of words indicate the letter of any misspelled word. If no word is misspelled, write (e). For each numbered item provide only one answer.

	(a)	(b)	(c)	(d)
___ 37.	accommodate	existence	excellent	feasable
___ 38.	neccessary	practical	sincerely	volume
___ 39.	efficient	independent	seperate	usable
___ 40.	argument	convenient	government	definitly
___ 41.	miscelaneous	occurred	receive	sufficient
___ 42.	budget	accross	consecutive	immediate
___ 43.	congratulate	committee	analyse	restaurant
___ 44.	similar	priviledge	offered	license
___ 45.	consistent	incidentally	equipped	becomming

Sentence Structure: In the space provided, identify any sentence fault by selecting one of the following letters. If the sentence is correct, select (d).

(a) Faulty pronoun reference
(b) Sentence fragment
(c) Comma splice (comma joining clauses inappropriately)
(d) Sentence is correct

___ 46. We've added more computers and printers, consequently we must update the wiring.
___ 47. Our office recycles paper and conserves energy because it helps save the environment.
___ 48. A number of stockholders who attended the meeting and expected to voice their opinions.
___ 49. Membership in the organization is voluntary; contributions and grants are the only means of support. This makes it difficult to continue a high level of support.
___ 50. Sales are increasing slowly, profits will respond soon.

Competent Language Usage Essentials (C.L.U.E.)
Proficiency Test Form B

Name ____**Score** __________________

Grammar: In the space provided, write the letter indicating the word that correctly completes each sentence. Use only one answer for each question.

___ 1. Kevin found it difficult to (a) chose (b) choose a color for his new truck.
___ 2. If Laura had (a) saw (b) seen the report, she might have caught the error.
___ 3. The company's full range of products and services (a) is (b) are offered locally.
___ 4. Only the production cost and the markup of each item (a) was (b) were known.
___ 5. Lying on the table (a) is (b) are the newspaper, two magazines, and airline tickets.
___ 6. Send updated contracts to (a) he and I (b) him and I (c) him and me (d) he and me.
___ 7. Most of the new equipment (a) appear (b) appears to be working well.
___ 8. (a) Everyone (b) Every one of the applicants presented a laser-printed résumé.
___ 9. Team members would appreciate (a) you (b) your responding to e-mails more promptly.
___ 10. A record of all dividends, rents, royalties, and pensions (a) was (b) were requested.
___ 11. Before you may rent a tandem bicycle, \$50 (a) is (b) are required as a deposit.
___ 12. Dr. Lee will see (a) whoever (b) whomever is next in line.
___ 13. The committee submitted (a) it's (b) its (c) their report yesterday.
___ 14. To reduce costs, management pushed for a settlement (a) quick (b) quickly.
___ 15. Every new employee should receive (a) his (b) her (c) his or her (d) their orientation packet.

Mechanics: For each of the following sentences, select one letter to identify faults in
(a) Commas or semicolons
(b) Punctuation other than commas or semicolons (including hyphens and apostrophes)
(c) Symbols (including dollar and percent signs)
(d) Number expression (word or figure form)
(e) Capitalization

___ 16. Our newly-hired supervisor was scheduled to see representatives from Hewlett-Packard, Xerox, and Canon.
___ 17. Jennifers presentation, which was entitled "How to Make Computer Graphics," was excellent.
___ 18. Employees at the Minneapolis-based plant could earn 5 percent interest or they could withdraw their funds for deposit elsewhere.
___ 19. Each office chair lists for 98 dollars; however, we expect to pay less.
___ 20. The Vice President and Marketing Director were called to the President's office.
___ 21. If both sides are in agreement the contract will be signed Monday, April 2.
___ 22. The positions in our Marketing Department were advertised last week weren't they?
___ 23. All nine investors, nevertheless, purchased European and latin American stocks.
___ 24. If I remember correctly, I sent only 4 e-mail messages in the morning.
___ 25. Our two-year-old Canon Copier is still running well.
___ 26. The committee selected three potential convention cities; Atlanta, Georgia; San Antonio, Texas; and Anaheim, California.
___ 27. TechTronics will move it's headquarters to Purchase, New York, within eight months.
___ 28. All customers' addresses must be accurate, therefore, we must check the list again.
___ 29. Because they spoke little spanish, many visitors purchased the book entitled <u>Speak Like a Native in Just Ten Days</u>.
___ 30. Would you please send two copies of IRS Form No. 1099?

Form B
Page 2

Confusing Words: In the space provided, write the letter of the word that best completes each sentence.

___ 31. Although it was only a (a) miner (b) minor event, management took notice.
___ 32. His (a) principle (b) principal problem was written communication.
___ 33. New taxation laws will (a) effect (b) affect all corporations.
___ 34. Each property owner must sign a (a) waiver (b) waver before construction can begin.
___ 35. Because security takes (a) precedence (b) precedents over all other factors, we're seeking safe investments.
___ 36. Each new customer was given 1,000 (a) complementary (b) complimentary checks.

Spelling: For each line of words indicate the letter of any misspelled word. If no word is misspelled, write (e). For each numbered item provide only one answer.

	(a)	(b)	(c)	(d)
___ 37.	absence	calender	convenient	interrupt
___ 38.	embarrass	dissatisfied	irrelavant	immediate
___ 39.	knowledgeable	ommission	prominent	questionnaire
___ 40.	recommendation	receive	volumn	writing
___ 41.	column	consecutive	familar	definitely
___ 42.	imediate	referred	separate	omitted
___ 43.	prevalent	noticeable	ninth	undoubtedly
___ 44.	business	acommodate	height	guarantee
___ 45.	February	usually	unecessarily	surprise

Sentence Structure: In the space provided, identify any sentence fault by selecting one of the following letters. If the sentence is correct, select (d).

(a) Faulty pronoun reference
(b) Sentence fragment
(c) Comma splice (comma joining clauses inappropriately)
(d) Sentence is correct

___ 46. The deadline is June 1, however we may receive an extension.
___ 47. Our specialists are trained in retirement planning, investment strategies, and working capital management. This explains our strength.
___ 48. Any number of investors who are looking for flexible leasing arrangements for new equipment.
___ 49. Rick suggested flexible work schedules for all who requested them and an extensive revamping of medical benefits. That was a big hit with all employees.
___ 50. The bond market is advancing slowly, the stock market is moving forward rapidly.

Competent Language Usage Essentials (C.L.U.E.)
Proficiency Test Form C

Name ______________________________ **Score** __________

Grammar: In the space provided, write the letter indicating the word that correctly completes each sentence. Use only one answer for each question.

___ 1. If you (a) was (b) were in my position, I'm sure you would do the same thing.
___ 2. Computer chips were (a) stolen, (b) stole last weekend from two warehouses.
___ 3. Here (a) is (b) are the complete list of names and addresses.
___ 4. Considerable time and money (a) was (b) were spent on publicity for the event.
___ 5. The president told Jeffrey and (a) I (b) me (c) myself that we would start Monday.
___ 6. Each of the classifications (a) contain (b) contains four parts.
___ 7. (a) Any one (b) Anyone of our 200 employees is eligible to win the prize trip to Hawaii.
___ 8. Although some checks were delayed, (a) yours (b) your's was delivered on time.
___ 9. One hundred dollars (a) is (b) are too much to pay for one parking ticket!
___ 10. A long line of applicants (a) is (b) are waiting to apply for the advertised jobs.
___ 11. The first new computer goes to (a) whoever (b) whomever is at the top of the list.
___ 12. I certainly appreciate (a) you (b) your responding to my e-mail messages so promptly.
___ 13. Someone on the women's team left (a) her (b) their purse in the locker room.
___ 14. All student learners were instructed to drive (a) careful (b) carefully near the school.
___ 15. Every graduate may pick up (a) their (b) his or her (c) his (d) her diploma today.

Mechanics: For each of the following sentences, select one letter to identify faults in
(a) Commas or semicolons
(b) Punctuation other than commas or semicolons (including hyphens and apostrophes)
(c) Symbols (including dollar and percent signs)
(d) Number expression (word or figure form)
(e) Capitalization

___ 16. The highly-regarded engineer was hired to work on water projects in Utah, Colorado, and California.
___ 17. Erika may compile the list of names and addresses of customers or Steven may do it.
___ 18. Tim Roths screenplay, which was entitled "Tattooed Teenage Aliens," made the rounds of Hollywood producers.
___ 19. We were offered fifty-three dollars a share; however, we are not ready to sell.
___ 20. If you return the entry form by June 15 you will be eligible to win $50,000.
___ 21. Both our President and Sales Manager were unhappy with the 2 percent sales dip.
___ 22. If the manager agrees, we will try to hire 2 temporary employees.
___ 23. Regulators feel, nevertheless, that the japanese yen and the european euro will remain strong in the currency market.
___ 24. Will you please send me a copy of Invoice No. 20-4991?
___ 25. All customers' addresses were checked, however, some still have incorrect zip codes.
___ 26. The need for Spanish-speaking teachers is discussed in the Board of Education's booklet entitled "Closing the gap: Language Skills across the Curriculum."
___ 27. The president returned from Europe, and immediately addressed Congress.
___ 28. On May 5th my boat and its trailer will be repainted.
___ 29. When we went fishing we caught a 20-pound Atlantic salmon at the privately owned lake.
___ 30. We brought some Ziploc Bags; however, we did not have enough to package all the items.

Form C
Page 2

Confusing Words: In the space provided, write the letter of the word that best completes each sentence.

___ 31. Our realtor promised to (a) apprise (b) appraise each prospective buyer of the unusual contract terms.
___ 32. Homeowners are (a) liable (b) libel for "attractive nuisances" on their property.
___ 33. If you (a) altar (b) alter any wording in the contract, you must initial the changes.
___ 34. Stacy had to consult her (a) conscious (b) conscience before resigning her position.
___ 35. Restaurant patrons receive a (a) complimentary (b) complementary glass of wine with their meals on Wednesday evenings.
___ 36. Dr. Myers considered himself a person of high (a) principals (b) principles.

Spelling: For each line of words indicate the letter of any misspelled word. If no word is misspelled, write (e). For each numbered item provide only one answer.

		(a)	(b)	(c)	(d)
___	37.	seperate	miscellaneous	truly	valuable
___	38.	accommodate	consistent	milage	occasionally
___	39.	column	convenint	mortgage	necessary
___	40.	apointment	committee	immediate	irrelevant
___	41.	occurred	opportunity	pamphlet	permenant
___	42.	automatically	Febuary	fourth	genuine
___	43.	criticize	definitely	desirable	serprise
___	44.	courteous	efficient	goverment	prominent
___	45.	libary	emphasize	ninety	therefore

Sentence Structure: In the space provided, identify any sentence fault by selecting one of the following letters. If the sentence is correct, select (d).

(a) Faulty pronoun reference
(b) Sentence fragment
(c) Comma splice (comma joining clauses inappropriately)
(d) Sentence is correct

___ 46. Employers usually have stacks of résumés from talented applicants, therefore your résumé must be flawless.
___ 47. A vehicle apparently ran off Kelton Road and struck the mail box as it attempted to get back on the roadway.
___ 48. Although few applicants among the most recent candidates had the proper qualifications for the opening in our Customer Service Department.
___ 49. Many students are completing internships, then they are more employable.
___ 50. Protesters released live cockroaches inside the White House on Friday, and they were arrested when they left and blocked a security gate.

Answers to C.L.U.E. Proficiency Tests

Form A

1. b
2. b
3. a
4. b
5. b
6. a
7. b
8. b
9. b
10. a
11. a
12. a
13. a
14. b
15. b

16. b
17. b
18. a
19. c
20. e
21. a
22. a
23. e
24. d
25. e
26. a
27. b
28. a
29. e
30. b or c

31. a
32. b
33. a
34. b
35. c
36. b

37. d
38. a
39. c
40. d
41. a
42. b
43. c
44. b
45. d
46. c
47. a
48. b
49. a
50. c

Form B

1. b
2. b
3. a
4. b
5. b
6. c
7. b
8. b
9. b
10. a
11. a
12. a
13. b
14. b
15. c

16. b
17. b
18. a
19. c
20. e
21. a
22. a
23. e
24. d
25. e
26. b
27. b
28. a
29. e
30. b or c

31. b
32. b
33. b
34. a
35. a
36. b

37. b
38. c
39. b
40. c
41. c
42. a
43. e
44. b
45. c
46. c
47. a
48. b
49. a
50. c

Form C

1. b
2. a
3. a
4. b
5. b
6. b
7. a
8. a
9. a
10. a
11. a
12. b
13. a
14. b
15. b

16. b
17. a
18. b
19. d
20. a
21. e
22. d
23. e
24. c or b
25. a
26. e
27. a
28. d
29. a
30. e

31. a
32. a
33. b
34. b
35. a
36. b

37. a
38. c
39. b
40. a
41. d
42. b
43. d
44. c
45. a
46. c
47. a
48. b
49. c
50. a

C.L.U.E. Proficiency Test Form A
Sentence Revision Key

16. The newly passed legislation will affect taxes in Texas, California, and Michigan. [b = punctuation error; do not hyphenate *newly passed* because *newly* functions as an adverb]

17. Eric's report, which was entitled "Living in a Digital World," caused a stir. [b = punctuation error; apostrophe missing in *Eric's report*]

18. Stockholders for IBM could attend the meeting, or they could return their proxies. [a = comma error; use comma to separate two independent clauses joined by the coordinating conjunction *or*]

19. We are earning $42 on every item; however, total sales are slow. [c = symbols, *$42* rather than *42 dollars*]

20. The president of DataTech met with the vice president to discuss the 9 percent dip in sales. [e = capitalization error; do not capitalize business titles]

21. If we receive all the figures, we will sign the contract July 1 in our headquarters. [a = comma error; insert comma following introductory dependent clause]

22. The memo from our Human Resources Department is quite clear, don't you think? [a = comma error; use a comma to separate a question added to the end of a sentence]

23. All three collectors, by the way, specialized in antique German and Dutch coins. [e = capitalization error]

24. When Alicia is absent, we have only three operators in our Customer Service Department. [d = number expression; use word form for numbers *ten* and under]

25. We ordered 15 Pentax cameras to be awarded as prizes. [e = capitalization; do not capitalize common nouns following brand names]

26. Our interviewing team consists of these people: Ann Simms, Accounting; Tom Burns, Human Resources; and Carlos Santana, Operations. [a = comma, semicolon error; use semicolons after department names to separate each name/department unit]

27. My graduating class is having its ten-year reunion June 10. [b = punctuation error; no apostrophe should appear in the possessive pronoun *its*. The numbers in this sentence are expressed correctly.]

28. The stockholders' meeting was heavily advertised; however, attendance was light. [a = comma, semicolon error; use semicolon before conjunctive adverb *however* because it joins independent clauses]

29. To improve their English, many Japanese students purchased the book entitled <u>The Power of Language Is Yours</u>. [e = capitalization error; capitalize *English* and *Is*. Teach students to capitalize all words in titles except short prepositions (with four or fewer letters) and articles (*a, an, the*).]

30. Would you please send two copies of Invoice No. 39-5001. [b or c; polite requests are punctuated with periods, not question marks. We expect action rather than an answer.]

46. We've added computers and printers; consequently, we must update the wiring.[c = comma splice; use a semicolon before the conjunctive adverb *consequently*]

47. Our office recycles paper and conserves energy because these efforts help save the environment. [a = faulty pronoun reference; replace vague pronoun (*it*) with clear reference (*these efforts*)]

48. A number of stockholders who attended the meeting and expected to voice their opinions were disappointed when they could not speak. [b = sentence fragment; write a complete sentence to replace the fragment]

49. Membership in the organization is voluntary; contributions and grants are the only means of support. These conditions make it difficult to continue a high level of support. [a = faulty pronoun reference (*this*) replaced by clear reference (*These conditions*)]

50. Sales are increasing slowly; profits will respond soon. [c = comma splice remedied with semicolon to join two independent clauses]

C.L.U.E. Proficiency Test Form B
Sentence Revision Key

16. Our newly hired supervisor was scheduled to see representatives from Hewlett-Packard, Xerox, and Canon. [b = punctuation; *newly hired* should not be hyphenated because *newly* functions as an adverb]

17. Jennifer's presentation, which was entitled "How to Make Computer Graphics," was excellent. [b = punctuation; *Jennifer's presentation* is a possessive construction requiring an apostrophe]

18. Employees at the Minneapolis-based plant could earn 5 percent interest, or they could withdraw their funds for deposit elsewhere. [a = commas; insert a comma before the coordinating conjunction *or* because it connects independent clauses]

19. Each office chair lists for $98; however, we expect to pay less. [c = symbols; use *$98* rather than *98 dollars* and omit the zeroes for even sums]

20. The vice president and marketing director were called to the president's office. [e = capitalization error; do not capitalize business titles]

21. If both sides are in agreement, the contract will be signed Monday, April 2. [a = comma error; use a comma after the introductory dependent clause]

22. The positions in our Marketing Department were advertised last week, weren't they? [a = comma error; use a comma to separate a question appended to a sentence]

23. All nine investors, nevertheless, purchased European and Latin American stocks. [e = capitalization error; capitalize proper adjective (*Latin*)]

24. If I remember correctly, I sent only four e-mail messages in the morning. [d = number expression; use word form for numbers *ten* and under]

25. Our two-year-old Canon copier is still running well. [e = capitalization; do not capitalize common nouns following brand names]

26. The committee selected three potential convention cities: Atlanta, Georgia; San Antonio, Texas; and Anaheim, California. [b = punctuation; use semicolons to separate city/state units]

27. TechTronics will move its headquarters to Purchase, New York, within eight months. [e = punctuation; do not use an apostrophe in the possessive pronoun *its*]

28. All customers' addresses must be accurate; therefore, we must check the list again. [a = comma, semicolon; use a semicolon before *therefore* when it joins two independent clauses]

29. Because they spoke little Spanish, many visitors purchased the book entitled <u>Speak Like a Native in Just Ten Days</u>. [e = capitalization; capitalize proper adjectives such as *Spanish*]

30. Would you please send two copies of IRS Form No. 1099. [b or c; use a period to punctuate a polite request]

46. The deadline is June 1; however, we may receive an extension. [c = comma splice; use a semicolon to join independent clauses]

47. Our specialists are trained in retirement planning, investment strategies, and working capital management. This commitment to training explains our strength. [a = pronoun reference; replace vague pronoun *This* with *This commitment*]

48. Any number of investors who are looking for flexible leasing arrangements for new equipment will find help at our new Web site. [b = sentence fragment; complete the sentence to remedy the fragment]

49. Rick suggested flexible work schedules for all who requested them and an extensive revamping of medical benefits. Those suggestions were a big hit with all employees. [a = faulty pronoun reference; replace vague pronoun *That* with *Those suggestions*]

50. The bond market is advancing slowly; the stock market is moving forward rapidly. [c = comma splice; use a semicolon to join two independent clauses]

C.L.U.E. Proficiency Test Form C
Sentence Revision Key

16. The highly regarded engineer was hired to work on water projects in Utah, Colorado, and California. [b = punctuation; do not hyphenate *highly regarded* because *highly* functions as an adverb]

17. Erika may compile the list of names and addresses of customers, or Steven may do it. [a = comma; use a comma to join two independent clauses]

18. Tim Roth's screenplay, which was entitled "Tattooed Teenage Aliens," made the rounds of Hollywood producers. [b = punctuation; add apostrophe to *Tim Roth's*]

19. We were offered $53 a share; however, we are not ready to sell. [d = number expression; write *$53* rather than *53 dollars*]

20. If you return the entry form by June 15, you will be eligible to win $50,000. [a = comma; use a comma after the introductory dependent clause]

21. Both our president and sales manager were unhappy with the 2 percent sales dip. [e = capitalization; do not capitalize business titles]

22. If the manager agrees, we will try to hire two temporary employees. [d = number expression; use word form (*two*) to express figures *ten* and under]

23. Regulators feel, nevertheless, that the Japanese yen and the European euro will remain strong in the currency market. [e = capitalization; capitalize proper adjectives such as *Japanese* and *European*]

24. Will you please send me a copy of Invoice No. 20-4991. [c or b; use a period to punctuate polite requests]

25. All customers' addresses were checked; however, some still have incorrect zip codes. [a = comma, semicolon; use a semicolon before the conjunctive adverb *however*; it joins independent clauses]

26. The need for Spanish-speaking teachers is discussed in the board of education's booklet entitled "Closing the Gap: Language Skills Across the Curriculum." [e = capitalization; capitalize all words in titles except short prepositions (four or fewer letters) and articles—capitalize *Gap* and *Across*]

27. The president returned from Europe and immediately addressed Congress. [a = comma error; omit comma before the conjunction *and* because it does not join independent clauses]

28. On May 5 my boat and its trailer will be repainted. [d = number expression; days following months do not use ordinal form (not *May 5th*), even though we may voice it]
29. When we went fishing, we caught a 20-pound Atlantic salmon at the privately owned lake. [a = comma error; use a comma to separate an introductory dependent clause from the sentence]
30. We brought Ziploc bags; however, we did not bring enough rolls to capture all events. [e = capitalization error; do not capitalize *bags*, a common noun following a brand name]
46. Employers usually have stacks of résumés from talented applicants; therefore, your résumé must be flawless. [c = comma, semicolon error; use a semicolon before the conjunctive adverb *therefore* as it joins two clauses]
47. A vehicle apparently ran off Kelton Road and struck the mail box as the vehicle attempted to get back on the roadway. [a = faulty pronoun reference; replace vague pronoun *it* with specific reference, *the vehicle*]
48. Although few applicants among the most recent candidates had the proper qualifications for the opening in our Customer Service Department, we were able to schedule two interviews. [b = fragment; make sentence complete or omit *Although* so that it no longer introduces a dependent clause]
49. Many students are completing internships; then they are more employable. [c = classic comma splice; two independent clauses must be joined by a semicolon]
50. Protesters released live cockroaches inside the White House on Friday, and the protesters were arrested when they left and blocked a security gate. [a = faulty pronoun reference; replace the vague pronoun *they* with specific reference such as *the protesters*]

SPELL RIGHT! AND SPEAK RIGHT!

In addition to a complete grammar review with "Your Personal Language Trainer," students will find further language resources at **http://www.meguffey.com.** "Spell Right!," an interactive program focused on 400 frequently misspelled words, and "Speak Right," featuring Dr. Guffey's voice to help students hear correct and incorrect versions of frequently mispronounced words.

POSSIBLE CLASS SCHEDULES

Veteran instructors realize that they cannot cover in one course everything that students need to learn about business communication. Instead, they focus on those topics they consider most important. Your objectives and the length of your course will determine how much time you can spend on various topics. Naturally, the focus and depth of coverage for a 10-week course stressing business correspondence will be different from that of a 16-week course that includes oral reports, written reports, and business correspondence. We present a variety of possible class schedules, all of which include time for testing. These schedules are meant to provide guidance; they are easily altered to fit your objectives.

10-Week Course
Business Correspondence and Employment Communication
Four 50-minute class meetings a week (40 class meetings)

For a 10-week course stressing business correspondence, you might elect to cover Chapters 1–11 and Chapter 16, while assigning Chapters 12–15 for reading only. If students have weak language arts skills, you may want to include more than one class period to review the C.L.U.E. program. The following schedule allows time for students to become proficient in writing e-mail messages, memos, letters, résumés, and cover letters. To include business reports or oral presentations, reduce the time spent on Chapters 1 through 10.

10-Week Course

Class Meeting	Chapter	Topic
1		Class orientation and introduction
2	C.L.U.E.	Review, practice, discussion
3	Chapter 1	Effective and Ethical Communication at Work
4-5	Chapter 2	Professionalism: Team, Meeting, Listening, Nonverbal, Etiquette
6-7	Chapter 3	Intercultural Communication
8		Review or testing
9-10	Chapter 4	Planning Business Message
11-12	Chapter 5	Organizing and Writing Business Messages
13-14	Chapter 6	Revising Business Messages
15		Review, testing, or in-class writing assignment
16-19	Chapter 7	Electronic Messages and Digital Media
20-22	Chapter 8	Positive Letters
23-25	Chapter 9	Negative Messages
26-29	Chapter 10	Persuasive Messages
30		Review, testing, or in-class writing assignment
31-34	Chapter 15	The Job Search, Résumés, and Cover Letters
35-39	Chapter 16	Interviewing and Following Up
40		Review, testing

11-Week Course
Business Correspondence, Short Written Report, and Employment Communication
Three 50-minute class meetings a week (33 total class meetings)

When a course has only 33 total class meetings (and some of those may be lost to holidays), the course must be streamlined. This schedule covers e-mail, digital media, letters, and memos adequately but treats report writing only lightly. Students might be expected to write one or two short reports. If the course is to include oral reporting, then you might reduce or eliminate the time spent on business reports and use that time for Chapter 14, Business Presentations

Class Meeting	Chapter	Topic
1		Class orientation and introduction
2	C.L.U.E.	Review, practice, discussion
3	Chapter 1	Effective and Ethical Communication at Work
4-5	Chapter 2	Professionalism: Team, Meeting Listening, Nonverbal, Etiquette
6-7	Chapter 3	Intercultural Communication
8		Review or testing
9-10	Chapter 4	Planning Business Messages
11	Chapter 5	Organizing and Writing Business Messages
12-13	Chapter 6	Revising Business Messages
14		Review, testing, or in-class writing assignment
15-16	Chapter 7	Electronic Messages and Digital Media
17-18	Chapter 8	Positive Messages
19-20	Chapter 9	Negative Messages
21-22	Chapter 10	Persuasive Messages
23		Review, testing, or in-class writing assignment
24	Chapter 11	Report and Research Basics
25	Chapter 12	Informal Business Reports
26	Chapter 13	Proposals and Formal Reports
27		Review, testing, or in-class writing assignment
28-29	Chapter 15	The Job Search, Résumés, and Cover Letters
30-32	Chapter 16	Interviewing and Following Up
33		Review, testing

14-Week Course
Business Correspondence, Short Written Report, and Employment Communication
Three 50-minute class meetings a week (42 total class meetings)

In a 14-week course with a total of 42 class meetings, you could cover e-mail messages, digital media, letters, memos, reports, and employment communication. If you prefer, skip written reports and focus on oral reporting. Even if you do not have students write reports, assign those chapters for reading and discussion. The model documents will always be helpful to students now and in their future business careers.

Class Meetings	Chapter	Topic
1		Class orientation and introduction
2	C.L.U.E.	Review, practice, discussion
3	Chapter 1	Effective and Ethical Communication at Work
4-5	Chapter 2	Professionalism: Team, Meeting, Listening, Nonverbal, Etiquette
6-7	Chapter 3	Intercultural Communication
8		Review or testing
9-10	Chapter 4	Planning Business Messages
11-12	Chapter 5	Organizing and Writing Business Messages
13-14	Chapter 6	Revising Business Messages
15		Review, testing, or in-class writing assignment
16-18	Chapter 7	Electronic Messages and Digital Media
19-21	Chapter 8	Positive Message
22-24	Chapter 9	Negative Messages
25-27	Chapter 10	Persuasive Messages
28		Review, testing, or in-class writing assignment
29	Chapter 11	Report and Research Basics
30-31	Chapter 12	Informal Business Reports
32-34	Chapter 13	Proposals and Formal Reports Submission of short report or proposal
35	Chapter 14	Business Presentations (read and discuss)
36-38	Chapter 15	The Job Search, Résumés, and Cover Letters
39-41	Chapter 16	Interviewing and Following Up
42		Review, testing

16-Week Course
Business Correspondence, Written Reports, and Employment Communication
Three 50-minute class meetings a week (48 total class meetings)

This 16-week course includes e-mail messages, digital media, memos, letters, reports, and employment communication, but it does not include oral report delivery. Because report writing generally takes considerable time for research and planning, you will want to have students choose their report topics and begin research early in the course.

Class Meetings	Chapter	Topic
1		Class orientation and introduction
2	C.L.U.E.	Review, practice, discussion
3	Chapter 1	Effective and Ethical Communication at Work
4-5	Chapter 2	Professionalism: Team, Meeting, Listening, Nonverbal, Etiquette
6-7	Chapter 3	Intercultural Communication
8		Test or review
Deadline for choosing written report topic. Research should begin this week.		
9-10	Chapter 4	Planning Business Messages
11-12	Chapter 5	Organizing and Writing Business Messages
13-14	Chapter 6	Revising Business Messages
15		Test, review, or in-class writing assignment
Written report checkpoint regarding research and final topic limitation.		
16-18	Chapter 7	Electronic Messages and Digital Media
19-21	Chapter 8	Positive Messages
22-24	Chapter 9	Negative Messages
25-27	Chapter 10	Persuasive Messages
28		Test, review, or in-class writing assignment
Report proposal due.		
29-31	Chapter 11	Report and Research Basics
32-34	Chapter 12	Informal Business Reports
35-36	Chapter 13	Proposals and Formal Reports
37		Test, review, or in-class writing assignment
38-39	Chapter 14	Business Presentations
40-43	Chapter 15	The Job Search, Résumés, and Cover Letters
44-47	Chapter 16	Interviewing and Follow Up
48		Test or review
Submit written report.		

16-Week Course
Business Correspondence, Written Reports, and Oral Report Delivery
Three 50-minute class periods a week (48 total class meetings)

The following 16-week course includes e-mail messages, digital media, memos, letters, business reports, and oral report delivery. To allow time for students to make oral reports in class, you may have to reduce the time spent on employment communication and other topics.

Class Meetings	Chapter	Topic
1		Class orientation and introduction
2	Chapter 1	Communicating in Today's Workplace
3-4	Chapter 2	Developing Team, Listening, and Etiquette Skills
5-6	Chapter 3	Communicating Across Cultures
7		Test or review
Deadline for choosing written/oral report topic. Research should begin this week.		
8-9	Chapter 4	Writing Process Phase 1: Analyze, Anticipate, Adapt
10-11	Chapter 5	Writing Process Phase 2: Research, Organize, Compose
12-13	Chapter 6	Writing Process Phase 3: Revise, Proofread, Evaluate
14		Test, review, or in-class writing assignment
Written report checkpoint regarding research and final topic limitation.		
15-16	Chapter 11	Business Report Basics
17-18	Chapter 12	Informal Business Reports
19-20	Chapter 13	Proposals and Formal Reports
21		Review, test, or in-class writing assignment
Report proposal due.		
22-24	Chapter 7	E-Mail Messages and Memos
25-27	Chapter 8	Positive Letters and Messages
28-30	Chapter 9	Persuasive and Marketing Messages
31-33	Chapter 10	Negative Messages
34		Test, review, or in-class writing assignment
35-36	Chapter 14	Business Presentations
37-39		Oral reports given by students Evaluations done by teacher and peers in class
40-42	Chapter 15	The Job Search, Résumés, and Cover Letters
43-45	Chapter 16	Interviewing and Following Up
46-47		Review requirements for written report
48		Review, testing
Submit written report.		

THE PREBUILT COURSE: The Easy Way to Plan a Course

by Dr. Mary Ellen Guffey

This Prebuilt Course is intended to help instructors organize a traditional basic business communication course for *Business Communication: Process and Product*, 7e. I know from experience how challenging it is to develop an effective and complete course, especially when the number of relevant topics and the array of supplements continue to grow. It's difficult to know what to assign, how much students should do, and where to find everything. This Prebuilt Course will include (a) instructions, (b) course schedule overview, (c) syllabus orientation, (d) syllabus assignments, (d) grading plan, (e) grade record sheet, and (f) unit tests.

Introduction and Instructions

The instruction section of the Prebuilt Course explains course content, the rationale behind course decisions, and how to use the various parts. This set of instructions, appearing here and also at **www.meguffey.com**, describes the course schedule overview, syllabus orientation, syllabus assignments, and so forth.

Course Schedule Overview. Shown on page 34, a course schedule outlines the course and tells how much time will be spent on each chapter. It also lists the days for testing.

Syllabus Orientation. The syllabus orientation on page 35 provides a template for you to use in preparing your syllabus to distribute to students. It includes a photograph of the textbook, contact information for you, course justification, a set of course objectives, and course policies. You can, of course, alter any of these to fit your course.

Syllabus Assignments. The list of Prebuilt Course Syllabus Assignments, beginning on page 36, is organized for a 15-week course that meets three times a week in 50-minute classes. However, you can adjust the class sessions to your course. If your course meets once a week, cover three class meetings from the syllabus. If your course meets twice a week, cover the material from three class meetings in two sessions. The syllabus shows what is to be done on every class day and what homework is to be assigned. You may decide to omit or deemphasize some chapters in the textbook. However, I recommend assigning all the chapters to be read even if they are not covered in lectures. Tests will cover all the chapter content. Tell your students that as college students they are expected to be able to read and internalize material even if it is not presented in lectures.

Emphasis on Writing Skills. This course focuses on developing writing skills, which are very important in all careers and which employers frequently say are lacking in graduates. The course also includes grammar and mechanics, but most of the grammar/mechanics review work is done by students outside of class using self-help online tutorial tools.

Course Content. This basic course includes the following:

- Communication foundations (organizational and workplace communication; team, listening, nonverbal, and etiquette skills; and intercultural communication).

- The writing process (writing techniques)
- Business correspondence (e-mail, digital media, letters, memos)
- Report writing
- Oral presentations
- Employment communication

This is a lot to cover in one 15-week course, and you may choose a different emphasis. If you prefer to spend more time on correspondence, you can eliminate the time spent on reports. If you prefer to focus on a long analytical report, you might not want to cover employment communication. You may not want to cover reports at all, focusing on oral presentations and employment communication. This Prebuilt Course is a basic course. You may alter it by giving more or less emphasis to any of the general areas shown.

First Class Meeting. Don't waste the first class meeting by handing out the syllabus and dismissing the group. You have precious few minutes with your class and much to cover. On the chalkboard or on a slide, give your name, course name, room number, and meeting times. Hand out the syllabus and discuss it briefly. Show a copy of the textbook.

Take this opportunity to have students write you a persuasive letter. I tell students that this is one of the few classes in which they will get their money's worth on the very first day. (Tongue in cheek: I'm not going to waste their tuition money by dismissing them!) I'm going to teach them a valuable lesson—how to write a personal business letter. I show the format of a personal business letter (with the writer's street address, city, state, zip, and date) along with a proper inside address (name of instructor, school department, school name, address) and proper salutation. I bring paper and writing tools to class and ask students to write a letter to me. I tell students that they are to assume that this class has a limited number of openings and only a select number will be admitted. This letter is to persuade the instructor to allow the writer to enter. Why should I admit this person to this class? In this letter students are to describe their background, discuss their educational and career goals, and evaluate their communication skills. Do they think their skills are (a) above average, (b) average, or (c) below average? I prepare a slide or transparency with the letter format and suggestions about what goes in the letter so that students have no excuse for not writing something.

This introductory letter, ungraded of course, gives you an excellent overview of your students and their weaknesses and strengths. You can also use it later in the course when you discuss persuasive letters. At that time you might return these letters and discuss how much students have learned about persuasive writing.

Grading Plan. This basic course includes my recommended grading plan and provides a template for using it.

Grade Record Sheet. The Grade Record on page 42 shows every graded assignment for the course. You can adjust the number of graded assignments upward or downward. Just be sure that every assignment is worth 100 points. For example, my Prebuilt Course has six memos and letters worth 100 points each. A report receives 300 points (3 segments), and an oral presentation is worth 200 points (2 segments). Distribute the Grade Record Sheet early in the course and discuss how it works.

Check-in Assignments. Some homework assignments can be checked in to indicate completion. They do not receive grades and merely tell you that the student completed the assignment. If a student completes 100 percent of the check-in assignments, the student's score would be 100 points. If 90 percent are completed, the student receives 90 points.

Testing. My Prebuilt Course calls for three unit tests and one final exam. Ready-made unit tests contain 50 items from the test banks (worth a total 100 points). The final exam, however, must be prepared by the instructor. I did not prepare a final exam because instructors may not cover written reports, oral presentations, or employment communication. Here are some possibilities for the final exam: (a) an objective test with 100 points, covering the entire course, (b) an objective test with 50 points covering Chapters 15 and 16 plus a writing assignment from Chapters 7-10, or (c) a letter or short report-writing assignment from one of the chapter activities. If you prefer to focus totally on writing and if you prefer not to give objective tests, use all of the unit test time for graded in-class writing assignments.

Grammar and Mechanics. This course includes a grammar and mechanics review. However, students complete nearly all of the review online in self-help sessions. At **www.meguffey.com**, they have a comprehensive grammar and punctuation tutorial program called *Personal Language Trainer*. They should also complete the Grammar/Mechanics C.L.U.E. end-of-chapter exercises online. I suggest giving three proficiency tests (located in the Instructor's Manual). If students do not pass one of them with at least 90 percent accuracy (or whatever level you set), the final grade of the student will be lowered ½ grade. This is an optional program, but research shows that students who are graded on improving a skill are more likely to improve than those who are not graded on improvement. Earlier in this Instructor's Manual, you can read more about how to include grammar/mechanics in your course with a minimum of class time devoted to it.

Calculating Final Grade. Students keep track of their assignments and grades on the Grade Record Sheet. On the last day of class, I allow class members to study for the final exam (or take a practice final) while I calculate final grades with each student individually. My Prebuilt Course has 18 graded segments. Students total their grades and divide by 18 to learn their course average. For the final exam, they can estimate their grade to give a close approximation of the final grade they will receive. You, of course, will calculate the final grade including the exact final exam grade. Because the final exam counts for only 100 points (unless you increase its value), it usually does not change the final average significantly. You can reduce or enlarge the number of graded assignments as necessary for your course. If your course has only 15 total grading segments, you divide the total number of points by 15. I have provided a grading scale, but you can alter the A – F points if you wish.

Calculating each student's final grade on the last day of class is a tremendous time-saver and stress reducer. I highly recommend this strategy!

Revising Assignments. Writing authorities recommend revision as an important technique in developing writing skills. You may want to allow students to revise a limited number of assignments, but only if significant changes are made. The second attempt can earn no more than 90 points. See the Instructor's Manual for a discussion on "Revision."

Alternate Assignments. You may alter the assignments in this Prebuilt Course for use in different sections or different terms of your course. Alternate activities are suggested for some chapters.

Converting the Instructor's Guide to a Student Syllabus. I have written the course schedule with assignments for instructors. To convert this multipage document to a student handout, you should make some changes. Read through the Class Activities column and remove or rephrase some of the items so that they are not instructions to you. Insert your class meeting dates in the first column below the class number:

Class 1
Sept. 9

Variations in Organizing Course. My Prebuilt Course is a basic course. However, you might want to add variations such as the following:

- Professional Development. Some instructors have students introduce part or all of new chapters for professional development points. See the Instructor's Manual for details on how one instructor does this.

- Treatment of Chapter-Opening Case Studies. Consider assigning the opening three-part case study to two- or three-student teams to present to class. See the Instructor's Manual for details on how to do this.

- Working With Teams. To develop team assignments, see the Instructor's Manual, which contains ideas for organizing and conducting classroom teams.

- Online Delivery. We provide extensive help with online delivery through our WebTutor Advantage and Aplia products. Learn more about using these products at www.meguffey.com or by talking with your sales representative.

- Overbuilt? If I have included more than you can cover with your class, don't hesitate to cut out some of the items I show. This is a very full class!

Teaching Tips. Here are a few classroom teaching ideas.

- Try to reserve five minutes at the end of each class to preview the homework assignment for the next class. Starting an assignment with the students motivates them to complete it out of class.
- Start with an easy writing task for the first graded assignment.
- Consider giving "name tents" to students on the first day of class. When they have a question, they raise their name tent. Displaying the name tents helps you learn their names. Have them make their own name tents in class on the first day.

- Prepare your grade book with an extra blank line between all student names so that you can cross out grades and replace with revised scores if you allow students to revise their assignments.
- Consider making class discussion part of the grading plan. However, this becomes very subjective and difficult to convert to number grades.
- Return tests and graded assignments at the end of the period unless you plan to use class time to discuss them. I have found that students focus better on the class lecture and discussion when graded assignments do not distract them.
- If you have extra class time, use the Writing Improvement Exercises, Good/Bad Messages, or handout worksheets from the Instructor's site. Never waste valuable class time!
- Use the last day of class to call each student to your side so that you can calculate the student's final grade with you. This eliminates an enormous amount of stress for all involved. And your grades are nearly finished with the help of your students! All you have to do is average in the final exam. Since the final exam counts as one 100-point segment, it usually affects the final grade very little. Students can estimate their final exam grade to extrapolate what final grade they will most likely receive.

Schedule Overview

The following assignment outline includes 42 class meetings for 50-minute classes, which is approximately a 15-week course. For courses that meet once a week, combine three of the classes shown. For courses that meet for two 150-minute classes, arrange three classes for that period of time. Here is a schedule covering 42 class meetings:

Class Meeting	Activity	Class Meeting	Activity	Class Meeting	Activity
1	Orientation	15	Chapter 6	29	Chapter 10
2	Grammar/Mechanics	16	Chapter 6	30	Chapter 10, Unit Test
3	Chapter 1	17	Chapter 6, Unit Test	31	Chapter 11
4	Chapter 1	18	Chapter 7	32	Chapter 12
5	Chapter 2	19	Chapter 7	33	Chapter 13
6	Chapter 2	20	Chapter 7	34	Chapter 14
7	Chapter 2	21	Chapter 8	35	Chapter 15
8	Chapter 3	22	Chapter 8	36	Chapter 15
9	Chapter 3	23	Chapter 8	37	Chapter 15
10	Chapter 3, Unit Test	24	Chapter 9	38	Chapter 15
11	Chapter 4	25	Chapter 9	39	Chapter 16
12	Chapter 4	26	Chapter 9	40	Chapter 16
13	Chapter 5	27	Chapter 10	41	Chapter 16
14	Chapter 5	28	Chapter 10	42	Review for Final Exam

Syllabus

On the next page is a syllabus template that you can use. Fill in your course information and alter any of the course information you wish. Because this is a general plan, you may want to change the course justification, course objectives, or course policies. Remember that all of these forms are also available at **www.meguffey.com** if you want to download them from there.

Syllabus — Orientation

Instructor: Your name
Office: Your office address
Telephone: Your telephone
E-Mail Your e-mail address
Office Hours: Your office hours
Course Name and Term: Your course name and term
Meeting Time and Place: Your meeting time and place
Textbook Web Site: http://www:thomsonedu.com/bcomm/guffey
Required Textbook: Guffey & Loewy: *Business Communication: Process and Product,* 7e
Other Requirements: Internet access and a working e-mail address

Course Justification

Developing excellent communication skills is extremely important to your career success, whether you are already working or are about to enter today's workplace.

Surveys of employers show that communication skills are critical to effective job placement performance, career advancement, and organizational success.

Employers often rank communication skills among the most-requested competencies. Communication skills include writing, reading, listening, nonverbal, and speaking skills.

Writing skills are more important than ever because technology enables us to transmit messages more rapidly, more often, and to greater numbers of people than ever before.

Flatter organizations demand that every employee be a skilled communicator. Communicating with peers, managers, clients, and customers who differ in race, ethnicity, gender, age, and lifestyle is commonplace and requires special skills.

The most successful players in the new world of work will be those with highly developed communication skills. The lectures, discussions, assignments, and exercises in this course are designed to improve your practical business communication skills.

Course Objectives

This course is designed to develop the following professional skills:

- **Written Communication**. You will develop or improve your ability to use clear, concise , and grammatically correct language as you employ appropriate formats in writing e-mail messages, memos, business letters, reports, citations, bibliographies, speech outlines, cover letters, and résumés.
- **Oral Presentation.** You will develop or improve your ability to select, organize, and effectively deliver information in a businesslike manner with appropriate language, articulation, nonverbal communication, and visual supporting materials. You will develop skill in using visual aids, handouts, and multimedia presentation materials.
- **Interpersonal/Team.** You will develop or improve your ability to listen; to contribute to team performance; to plan and participate in productive meetings; to use collaborative technologies; to understand and employ nonverbal skills to advance your career; to work in diverse environments, and to gain a competitive edge with professionalism and business etiquette skills.

Course Policies

- **Attendance.** As in the workplace, you must attend class and be on time. Roll call will be conducted the first five minutes of each class. If you are not present, you are considered absent or tardy. Two tardies equal one absence. Three absences reduce your final grade by one letter.
- **Late assignments.** Anything submitted late will receive only 50 percent of its total points. Being absent or late is not an excuse for submitting a late assignment.
- **Plagiarism.** Written assignments must be your original work. Please review the institution's definition of plagiarism and the resulting penalties.
- **Preparation.** An initial reading of all study assignments should be completed prior to the class period in which the material will be discussed.
- **Oral assignments** cannot be made up.
- **Cell phones.** All cell phones and beepers must be turned off during class.
- **Food and drinks.** No food or drinks may be brought to the classroom.

Syllabus — Assignments

Class	Instructor Guide to Class Activities	Student Homework for Next Class
Class 1 **[Insert dates]**	• Introduction of instructor. Present course orientation and syllabus. • Review textbook features. Discuss how to read the textbook. • Discuss importance of **ww.meguffey.com** site. Emphasize completing Communication Assessment (Activity 1.1) at site. • Students write persuasive letter: "Why I Should Be Allowed to Take Class"	**Homework for Class 2** Get textbook. **Web:** Activity 1.1
Class 2	• Discuss importance of communication skills and results of Activity 1.1 • Introduce the Grammar/Mechanics (G/M) C.L.U.E. program. • Give G/M C.L.U.E. Proficiency Test A from Instructor's Manual. Students grade their own papers. Discuss answers. • Briefly introduce *Personal Language Trainer* at **www.meguffey. com**. Consider collecting PLT printout of Step 3 (10-pt.) quiz to check in. • Introduce SpeakRight and SpellRight optional self-help online programs. • Introduce Grammar/Mechanics Guide, Appendix A. • Assign Text Chapter 1 and briefly preview. Emphasize studying Chapter Review questions and being prepared to discuss them in class.	**Homework for Class 3** **Text:** Chapter 1. ALWAYS study the Chapter Review questions and be prepared to answer them in class. **Web:** Grammar/Mechanics (G/M) Diagnostic Test at Personal Language Trainer. Also complete G/M C.L.U.E. exercise for Chapter 1.
Class 3	• **Chapter 1, EFFECTIVE AND ETHICAL COMMUNICATION AT WORK** • Present lecture using PowerPoint (or transparencies) and IM notes. • Call on students to answer selected chapter review questions. • If time, show video: *Career Success Starts With Communication Foundations.* • Begin Activity 1.3, Getting to Know You, in which students introduce themselves in class.	**Homework for Class 4** **Web:** For each new chapter, ALWAYS study the PowerPoint slides; and complete the review quizzes, flash cards, and online G/M exercises.
Class 4	• **Chapter 1.** Continue introductions, 1.3, Getting to Know You. • If time, discuss Activity 1.6, Who Me? I Won't Need to Write on the Job. • If time, discuss 1.8, Avoiding Misunderstandings. • Briefly preview Chapter 2.	**Homework for Class 5** **Text:** Chapter 2
Class 5	• **Chapter 2, PROFESSIONALISM: TEAM, MEETING, LISTENING, NONVERBAL, AND LISTENING SKILLS** • Present lecture using slides and IM notes. • Call on students to answer selected Chapter Review questions. • Optional: If time, discuss Ethics Checks, Photo Essay, and Critical Thinking questions. Consider discussing Career Application questions from Ethical Insights, Career Coach, and Tech Talk boxes. • Encourage students to take Dr. Guffey's Listening Quiz, Activity 2.10.	**Homework for Class 6** **Text:** Read and be prepared to discuss Activities 2.3, 2.4. **Web:** Take Dr. Guffey's Listening Quiz.
Class 6	• **Chapter 2** • Discuss Activity 2.3, Reaching Group Decisions, and 2.4, Resolving Workplace Conflicts. • If time, discuss Activity 2.15, Nonverbal Communication: Body Language. • Preview Activity 2.22, Guide to Business Etiquette. Students take preview quiz at Guffey Xtra. Instructor may elect to administer two posttests (see Teaching Materials at Instructor Web site). [Alternate class activities: 2.5, Groupthink; 2.6, Lessons in Teamwork; 2.14, How to be More Influential; 2.21 Nonverbal Communication Around the World.	**Homework for Class 7** **Text:** Due for Class 7, Activity 2.12, Career Listening Skills. Print list to turn in. **Web:** Guide to Business Etiquette (Activity 2.22). Take preview quiz. Study 17 etiquette topics. Chapter 2 PowerPoint slides Chapter 2 Review Quiz G/M Exercise 2

Class 7	• **Chapter 2.** Discuss Activity 2.12, Listening Skills Required in Various Careers. Collect student printouts to check in. • If time, discuss Activity 2.16, Universal Sign for "I Goofed." • If time, show Video Library 2, *Understanding Teamwork at Cold Stone Creamery*. • Briefly preview Chapter 3.	**Homework for Class 8** **Text:** Chapter 3
Class 8	• **Chapter 3, INTERCULTURAL COMMUNICATION** • Present lecture using slides and IM notes. • Call on students to answer selected Chapter Review questions and Critical Thinking Questions.	**Homework for Class 9** **Text:** Activity 3.1; Activity 3.13. Print analysis of letter weaknesses. **Web**: G/M Exercise 3 Personal Trainer Workouts for Nouns and Pronouns
Class 9	• **Chapter 3.** Show Video Library 1, *Intercultural Communication at Work.* Discuss video. • Discuss Activity 3.1, Intercultural Blunders. • Discuss Activity 3.7, Intercultural Proverbs. • Discuss Activity 3.13, International Letter. Collect printout and check in. • If time, complete Activity 3.5, Intercultural Gap, in class. [Alternate activities: 3.2, 3.4, 3.6, 3.14]	**Homework for Class 10** **Text:** Activity 3.2. Prepare for unit test. **Web:** Chapter 3 PowerPoint slides Chapter 3 Review quiz Flash cards for Chs. 1-3
Class 10	• **Chapter 3** • Check Activity 3.2, International Time. • Assign Chapter 4. • **Unit Test, Chs. 1-3.**	**Homework for Class 11** **Text:** Chapter 4 **Text:** Print answers to Activities 4.1 a–d; 4.2 a-d, 4.3 a-d, 4.4 a-d, 4.5 a-d, 4.6 a-d, 4.7 a-c.
Class 11	• **Chapter 4, PLANNING BUSINESS MESSAGES** • Present chapter using slides and IM notes. • Discuss selected items from Activities 4.1 to 4.7. • Collect printouts and check in. • At end of period, return unit test.	**Homework for Class 12** **Text:** Activities 4.10, 4.11, 4.12 **Web:** Chapter 4 PPT slides Chapter 4 quiz G/M Exercise 4 Personal Language Trainer, Adjectives and Adverbs
Class 12	• **Chapter 4**. Review the writing process. Consider showing video, *The 3-x-3 Writing Process Develops Fluent Workplace Skills.* • Discuss Activities 4.10 to 4.12. Students may work in pairs, discussing sentences and writing jointly, or they may work separately. • Discuss and revise together or in pairs 4.8, Document for Analysis. Consider showing transparency solution. • Briefly introduce Chapter 5.	**Homework for Class 13** **Text:** Chapter 5 Print answers to 5.1 a-d, 5.2 a-d, 5.3 a-d, 5.4 a-d, 5.5 a-d, 5.6 a-d, and 5.7 a-d. Be prepared to discuss 5.10, Collaborative Brainstorming.
Class 13	• **Chapter 5, ORGANIZING AND WRITING BUSINESS MESSAGES** • Present chapter using slides and IM notes. • Discuss selected student answers to 5.1 to 5.7. Collect printouts to check in. • Discuss 5.10, Collaborative Brainstorming or one of the other activities.	**Homework for Class 14** **Text:** Activity 5.12. **Web:** G/M Exercise 5 Personal Language Trainer, Commas
Class 14	• **Chapter 5.** Assign in-class writing in pairs or individually: 5.9 Document for Analysis. • Discuss Activity 5.12, Brainstorming Tips for Productive Sessions. • Briefly introduce Chapter 6.	**Homework for Class 15** **Text**: Chapter 6 Print answers to 6.1, 6.2, 6.3, 6.4, and 6.5 to be turned in.

Class	Activities	Homework
Class 15	• **Chapter 6, REVISING BUSINESS MESSAGES** • Present using slides and IM notes. • Discuss 6.1-6.5. Collect printouts to check in.	**Homework for Class 16** **Text:** Print answers to 6.6, 6.7, and 6.8.
Class 16	• **Chapter 6.** Discuss 6.6 – 6.8. Consider collecting printouts to check in. • In-class writing, Activity 6.6 and Document for Analysis 6.10. Show transparency solution for 6.10. Discuss how you would grade it if it were to be turned in. [Alternate activities: Documents for Analysis 6.11, 6.12, 6.13. Documents for Analysis appear at **www.meguffey.com** so that students do not have to rekey them.]	**Homework for Class 17** **Text:** Review for unit test. **Web:** G/M Exercise 6 Personal Language Trainer, Semicolons and Colons Chapter 6 PowerPoint slides Chapter 6 Review quiz Flash cards for Chs. 4-6
Class 17	• **Chapter 6.** Finish discussing chapter. Answer questions. • **Unit Test, Chs. 4-6**	**Homework for Class 18** **Text:** Chapter 7 Activity 7.1. Print list of weaknesses. Write and print revision of 7.1.
Class 18	• **Chapter 7, ELECTRONIC MESSAGES AND DIGITAL MEDIA** • Present chapter using slides and IM notes. • Call on students to answer selected Chapter Review and Critical Thinking questions. • Discuss 7.1. Consider showing transparency solution. • Return unit test.	**Homework for Class 19** **Text:** Activity 7.3. Rewrite and print Alex's responses. Activity 7.6. Write tweet. Activity 7.8. Print a summary of the podcast.
Class 19	• **Chapter 7.** Discuss 7.3. Collect and check in. • Discuss Activities 7.6 and 7.8. • Distribute copies of written assignment grading scale. Discuss. Students attach "Assigned Weights" grading rubric to every graded assignment.. Name of student writer appears only on back of grading rubrick. • Assign 7.2 to be **graded.**	**Homework for Class 20** **Text:** **To be graded:** Activity 7.2. **Web:** Chapter PowerPoint slides. Chapter Review quiz. G/M Exercise 7 Personal Language Trainer, Apostrophes, Other Punc.
Class 20	• **Chapter 7.** Collect 7.2. • Show video, Technology in the Workplace. Discuss video critical thinking questions. • Optional in-class writing practice: Activity 6.12, 6.13, or 6.14. Show transparency solution. • Preview Chapter 8 briefly.	**Homework for Class 21** **Text:** Chapter 8 Complete Activities 8.1 and 8.2 a-b. .
Class 21	• **Chapter 8, POSITIVE MESSAGES** • Present chapter using slides and IM notes. • Call on students to answer selected Chapter Review and Critical Thinking questions. • If time, discuss selected Writing Improvement Exercises, 8.1 and 8.2, a-b. • Return graded Activity 7.2. Distribute Student Grade Sheet to keep record.	**Homework for Class 22** **Text:** Activity 8.3. Print list of weaknesses. Print revision.
Class 22	• **Chapter 8.** Discuss Activity 8.3 weaknesses. Show solution. Students compare their revisions with suggested solution. Discuss. • In class discuss weaknesses in Activity 8.6. Revise if time. • Assign Activity 8.7 to be graded. [Alternate activity: Show Ben & Jerry's video and do writing assignment from video in class.]	**Homework for Class 23** **Web:** Chapter PowerPoint slides. Chapter Review quiz. G/M Exercise 8 Personal Language Trainer, Capitalization **To be graded:** Activity 8.7.

Class 23	• **Chapter 8** • Collect Activity 8.7 to be graded. • Discuss G/M C.L.U.E. and Personal Language Trainer exercises to be sure students are completing them outside of class. • Use remaining time for in-class **graded** writing assignment, **Activity 8.12**.	**Homework for Class 24** **Text:** Chapter 9 Print answers to Writing Improvement Exercises 9.1, 9.2, 9.3, 9.4 a-c.
Class 24	• **Chapter 9, NEGATIVE MESSAGES** • Present chapter using slides and IM notes. • Call on students to answer selected Chapter Review and Critical Thinking questions. • Discuss Writing Improvement Exercises 9.1 – 9.4. Collect and check in. • Discuss Document for Analysis 9.6. • Return graded Activity 8.12.	**Homework for Class 25** **Web:** Chapter PowerPoint slides. Chapter Review quiz. G/M Exercise 9 Personal Language Trainer, Number Use Activity 9.5. Prepare list of weaknesses.
Class 25	• **Chapter 9** • Discuss Activity 9.5 weaknesses. Revise together in class. • Assign Activity 9.13 as homework assignment to be graded. [Alternate activities: 9.7 – 9.29. Consider showing chapter videos and assigning video writing activity.]	**Homework for Class 26** **Text:** **To be graded:** Activity 9.13
Class 26	• **Chapter 9** • Collect Activity 9.13. • Arrange class members in pairs or in teams for peer editing (see IM). • Introduce Chapter 10 briefly.	**Homework for Class 27.** Revise Activity 9.13 based on peer comments. **Text: Chapter 10.**
Class 27	• **Chapter 10, PERSUASIVE MESSAGES** • Present chapter using slides and IM notes. • Call on students to answer selected Chapter Review and Critical Thinking questions. • Discuss Document for Analysis 10.1. Ask students to analyze weaknesses. • Assign 10.11 to be graded.	**Homework for Class 28.** **Text:** **To be graded:** Activity 10.11. **Web:** Chapter PowerPoint slides. Chapter Review quiz. G/M Exercise 10 Personal Language Trainer, Spelling, Confusing Words
Class 28	• **Chapter 10** • Collect Activity 10.11 to be graded. • Discuss 10.2 and 10.3. • Preview 10.22 to be graded. [Alternate activities: 10.10, 10.13, 10.15, 10.17, 10.18]	**Homework for Class 29.** **Text:** **To be graded:** Activity 10.22
Class 29	• **Chapter 10** • Collect 10.22 to be graded. • In-class writing Activity 10.4, 10.12, or another activity. Peer evaluate.	**Homework for Class 30.** Prepare for unit test, Chs. 7-10. Review PowerPoints, Web quizzes, flash cards.
Class 30	• **Chapter 10** • Finish discussion. Answer questions. • **Unit test. Chapters 7-10.**	**Homework for Class 31** **Text:** Chapter 11 Chapter PowerPoint slides. Chapter Review quiz G/M Exercise 11. Prepare for G/M C.L.U.E. Proficiency exam.

Class 31	• **Chapter 11, BUSINESS REPORT BASICS** • Present chapter using slides and IM notes. • Begin discussing report assignment. Report due Class 37. • Students select a topic (Activities 11.10-11.15; 12.12-12.29, or from list of Report Topics at student site). • Give G/M C.L.U.E. Proficiency Exam B. Must pass one test with 90 percent.	**Homework for Class 32** **Text:** Chapter 12 **Web:** Chapter PowerPoint slides. Chapter Review quiz. G/M Exercise 12 Select written report topic. Begin working on report project.
Class 32	• **Chapter 12, INFORMAL BUSINESS REPORTS** • Present chapter using slides and IM notes. • Discuss report assignment. • During class conduct individual consultations with each student about report topic and assignment. Other students work on their reports during class.	**Homework for Class 33** **Text:** Chapters 12 and 13 **Web:** Chapter PowerPoint slides Chapter Review quiz G/M Exercise 13
Class 33	• **Chapters 13, PROPOSALS AND FORMAL REPORTS** • Present Chapter 13 using slides and IM notes. • In-class: Activities 12.1 – 12.7.	**Homework for Class 34** **Text:** Chapter 14 Activity 14.12 **Web:** Chapter PowerPoint slides. Chapter Review quiz. G/M Exercise 14
Class 34	• **Chapter 14, BUSINESS PRESENTATIONS** • Present chapter using slides and IM notes. • Discuss in class Activity 14.12, Improving Design and Content of Slides • Discuss oral report assignment. Students may use their written report topic or select a new topic approved by instructor.	**Homework for Class 35** **Text:** Chapter 15. **Web:** Chapter PowerPoint slides. Chapter Review quiz. G/M Exercise 15
Class 35	• **Chapter 15, THE JOB SEARCH, RÉSUMÉS, AND COVER LETTERS** • Present chapter using slides and IM notes. • Discuss résumé writing.	**Homework for Class 36** Complete Activities 15.5, 15.6, and 15.7
Class 36	• **Chapter 15** • Discuss résumés and cover letters briefly. • During this period or subsequent one, analyze poor résumé and cover letter, Activities 15.1 and 15.2. Show revisions. • Begin student oral reports.	**Homework for Class 37** Written reports due Class 37.
Class 37	• **Chapter 15** • Written reports due at beginning of period. • Student oral reports.	**Homework for Class 38** Work on oral report. Review G/M exercises and Personal Language Trainer.
Class 38	• **Chapter 15** • Student oral reports. • Give G/M C.L.U.E. Proficiency Exam C. Must pass one test with 90 percent.	**Homework for Class 39** Prepare first draft of résumé and cover letter. Submit it with job advertisement.
Class 39	• **Chapter 16, INTERVIEWING AND FOLLOWING UP** • Rough drafts of résumé and cover letter due. • Student oral reports. • [If no oral reports are being given, select activities from Ch. 16 for in-class and homework assignments.]	**Homework for Class 40** **Web:** Chapter PowerPoint slides. Chapter Review quiz. G/M Exercise 16

Class 40	• **Chapter 16.** Present chapter using slides and IM notes. • Student oral reports. [If no oral reports are being given, select activities from Ch. 16 for in-class and homework assignments.]	**Homework for Class 41** Prepare final résumé and cover letter to be graded.
Class 41	• **Chapter 16** • Collect final draft of résumé and cover letter. • Conduct student oral reports or mock interviews. • If time, show video, *Sharpening Your Interview Skills.* IM discussion guide.	**Homework for Class 42** Review for final exam.
Class 42	• Calculate final grade. • Consider giving practice final exam.	**Prepare for final exam.**
	Final Exam Options (a) Objective test (100 pts.) covering entire course (b) Objective test (50 pts.) covering Chapters 15 and 16 plus a writing assignment from Chs. 7-10 (c) Letter or short report-writing assignment from one of chapter activities	

Grading in the Prebuilt Course

Consistency, fairness, and simplicity are the hallmarks of effective course grading. In this manual be sure to read the section on "Assessing Writing Assignments." You will find various grading methods described, thus giving you a choice of grading systems.

For the Prebuilt Course, I highly recommend my Assigned Weights Method. It enables you to give every writing assignment a number grade based on specific points earned in the assignment. This objective scoring system is effective in avoiding confrontations with students.

On page 52 you will find an Assigned Weights scoring sheet for business communication written assignments. I intentionally prepared it as a Word document so that you could easily alter any of the weights. ***(When you copy this form into your word processing program from our digital files on the Instructor's Resource CD or from http://www.meguffey.com, be sure to retain the source formats.)***

When you begin grading assignments, distribute many Assigned Weights scoring sheets (cut into quarters and printed on colored paper) to students. They attach one to every assignment. I always have the students write their names on the back of the scoring sheet so that I do not see the name and can be completely objective as I grade the assignment.

On page 54 you will find an Assigned Weights scoring sheet for oral presentations.

Prebuilt Course: Grade Record

Distribute a grade record sheet, shown on the next page, at the beginning of course or when you begin grading written assignments. This template has 18 graded assignments and can be altered to fit your course. You may prefer to have more or fewer assignments. Three objective unit tests are available. They may be downloaded from **www.meguffey.com.**

Grade Record

Name ______________________
Date ______________________

Keep printouts of your assignments and record your scores here.

Memos and Letters	Point Value	Your Grade
Chapter 7, Activity 7.2	100 pts.	________
Chapter 8, Activity 8.7	100 pts.	________
Chapter 8, Activity 8.12	100 pts.	________
Chapter 9, Activity 9.13	100 pts.	________
Chapter 10, Activity 10.11	100 pts.	________
Chapter 10, Activity 10.22	100 pts.	________
Report	300 pts.	________
Oral Presentation	200 pts.	________
Employment Communication		
Résumé	100 pts.	________
Cover Letter	100 pts.	________
Tests		
Unit 1 Test	100 pts.	________
Unit 2 Test	100 pts.	________
Unit 3 Test	100 pts.	________
Final Exam	100 pts.	________

Estimate your final exam grade to calculate your final average.

Check-in Assignments

Activities 2.12	________
Activity 3.13	________
Activities 4.1-4.7	________
Activities 5.1-5.7	________
Activities 6.1-6.5	________
Activities 6.6-6.8	________
Activity 7.3	________
Activities 9.1-9.4	________
Other check-in activities	________

If all assigned activities are checked in, you receive 100 pts.
If 90% are checked in, you receive 90 pts. and so forth.

Total ________

Divide total by number of 100-pt. segments (18)
Your Mathematical Average ________

A = 93 to 100%
B = 85 to 92%
C = 76 to 84%
D = 65 to 75%
F = 0 to 64%

Grammar/Mechanics (optional)

Your final grade will be lowered ½ grade (3.5 points) if you do not pass a grammar/mechanics proficiency test.

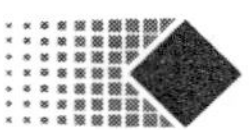

DELIVERING YOUR COURSE ONLINE

Many instructors are now teaching business communication in an online or hybrid format. *Business Communication: Process and Product,* 7e, provides many outstanding resources that can help you create an effective and pedagogically sound online course:

- **WebTutor** offers a content-rich teaching and learning aid that helps instructors easily create strong, interactive online classrooms using Blackboard or selected other platforms. Ready-made content includes flashcards, online quizzes, additional Web links, threaded discussions, and narrated PowerPoint presentations. In addition, WebTutor provides other important tools including a course calendar, synchronous chat, e-mail, and an asynchronous discussion board. Learn more about WebTutor at **http://www.cengage.com/coursecare/ cartridge/**
- **Premium Student Web Site** provides online access to an exceptional array of resources including Your Personal Language Trainer, Speak Right!, Spell Right!, PowerPoint chapter review slides, documents for analysis, grammar/mechanics C.L.U.E. exercises with answers and feedback, flash cards reviewing key terms, report topics, etiquette module, and other exciting learning tools.
- **Instructor's Web Site** provides online access to downloadable supplements, exercises and handouts, writing improvement exercises, and many teaching modules.
- **Sample Syllabi.** All business communication courses are organized differently. To see how a few other instructors have organized their online or Web-based business communication courses, send an e-mail to Dr. Guffey and request a list of sample syllabi.

Teaching Tips for Online or Hybrid Classes

If you are thinking about teaching business communication online, check with your college to find out what resources and training are offered to online instructors. You should also do research to learn about some of the best practices that others are using to make their online classrooms positive, interactive, and rich learning environments for online students. Here are a few proven best practices:

- Organize your online course materials so that students can easily navigate them and can clearly understand what is expected of them.
- Even when using publisher materials such as those provided with *Business Communication: Process and Product,* personalize and embellish them to add greater value and individuality to your course.
- Place a digital image of yourself in your online classroom so that students feel more of a connection to you. Encourage students to share digital photos of themselves.
- If you decide to have mandatory on-campus meetings (for orientation, exams, and so on), provide alternative accommodations for students who are unable to come to campus during required times.
- Develop a fun introductory assignment to help students get to know one another.
- Respond promptly to student questions, and provide prompt and constructive feedback for all assignments.
- Set firm deadlines to help students manage their time and stay on track. Provide regularly scheduled activities, and do not let students procrastinate.

- Don't expect that students can teach themselves. The active involvement of the instructor is essential.
- The student needs to feel connected to the online class. Provide ample opportunities for student-student interaction. Use the discussion board for class discussions, develop group projects, and plan other activities so that students work with one another.
- When communicating with students, it's important to do so in a respectful, positive way. Check the tone of all e-mail messages and discussion board postings before sending them. Also check your messages and postings carefully for accuracy and clarity before sending them. You are serving as role model in this course, and your grammar and spelling must be perfect!
- Invite and encourage online students to visit during your on-campus office hours.
- If a student has stopped logging on to your online classroom and is not responding to your e-mail messages, try calling the student. It's often this extra encouragement that can get an online student back on track.
- Consider taking an online class yourself. One of the best ways to learn what works and what doesn't is to take on the role of an online student.

Suggestions for Reducing Cheating in Online Classes

Even when following best practices, online instructors are naturally concerned about testing and security in their online classrooms. Without seeing the students in person, how can an instructor be sure that the student is actually completing his or her own work? Here are some tips you can use to combat cheating in your online classroom:

- Let students know exactly what you expect of them and inform them of any college regulations concerning academic honesty.
- The more interaction you have with students, the more you will become aware of their abilities and writing styles. Develop discussion board assignments that require students to interact regularly and frequently with you and with each other.
- Use a variety of assessment instruments in your course, and require numerous and regular assignments. The more required of students, the more difficult it would be for them to find someone else to complete the work for them. Grades in an online business communication course should be based on a variety of assignments (e.g., writing assignments, tests, participation, discussion board assignments, and so on).
- Change your assignments and tests from semester to semester so that students who have already taken your class can't share information with others.
- Do what's necessary to prepare your students well for tests and exams. Provide study guides, review sessions, and opportunities for students to ask questions on the discussion board. Encourage and help students set up study groups. Tell students exactly what to expect when taking tests (number of questions, types of questions, time allowed, etc.) prior to the test.
- Unless you give your tests in a monitored environment, you must assume that all tests you give are open book and open note. Write your test questions accordingly. Use questions that test students' application of knowledge. Make sure your questions are challenging, even if students are using their books. Include questions that come from your lecture notes and from classroom discussions.

Use the security features included with course management packages such as Blackboard to perform the following:

1. Deliver questions one at a time, where students must answer a question before moving on to the next question. Selecting whether questions can be revisited after they have been answered.
2. Set a time limit, but make it realistic for all students, including ESL students and those with learning disabilities.
3. Allow students to take the test only one time.
4. Make tests available for only limited periods of time.
5. Require students to enter a proctor password or IP mask address to access the test.
6. Release test scores and results only after the availability period is over. This will prevent students from taking the exam and then sharing answers with other students during the availability period.
7. Randomize the order that questions are released to students.
8. Create alternate questions so that students receive different question sets.

Creating a Community With Your Students

One of the most important things that online instructors must realize is that it is imperative for the instructor to establish and maintain early and regular communication with students and to provide ample opportunities for students to interact and communicate with each other.

USING TEXTBOOK FEATURES

Chapter Opening Case Studies

Each chapter opens with an introduction to a case study featuring a premier or significant organization or businessperson. These studies not only help students learn about real organizations and the problems they face, but the case studies also provide a context in which students can place the principles discussed in the chapter. Each case study has three parts. The first part introduces the organization, sets the scene, and builds interest. Critical thinking questions enable the instructor to guide class discussion so that students are able to relate the chapter concepts to a specific organization. The second part of the case study falls about halfway through a chapter and provides more specific information regarding the organization and some communication problem. Additional critical thinking questions require students to analyze what they have learned thus far and apply it to this organization. The last segment furnishes more information about a specific problem and sets up an application in which the students help to solve the problem.

Some of the applications require discussion only. Others require students to revise a document or produce a document. Many of the applications can be used for teams or for individuals, thus providing a flexible format for instructors. One instructor assigns each case study to a team of two or three students. The team analyzes the total case, answers the critical thinking questions, solves the application problem (if one is presented), and reports its findings to the class.

All case studies have discussion guides and application solutions. Instructors can find these guides and solutions in Part 3 of this manual under Chapter Teaching Suggestions.

End-of-Chapter and Web Activities

The seventh edition of *Business Communication: Process and Product* offers an enormous collection of activities that can be used for in-class discussion and reinforcement as well as for out-of-class assignments. In fact, no other business communication book offers the number or the variety of activities as those presented in *BC:PP,* 7e. In this edition more than 40 percent of all end-of-chapter activities are new or revised, thus providing instructors with fresh material. Instructors may choose from short, long, easy, and challenging activities. Nearly all activities have discussion guides or solutions provided in this manual. Selected activities are labeled **Web, Team, Intercultural, Ethics,** and **E-Mail.** These labels help instructors choose activities that develop specific skills.

Photo Essays

The photo essays bring business communication to life by demonstrating how concepts are applied in the real world. Each photo essay includes a critical thinking question that may be used to stimulate classroom discussion. Solutions may be found in the lecture outlines.

Ethics Checks

The ethics checks, located in the margins of the textbook, describe realistic ethical dilemmas and prompt students to choose the right course of action. Consider using these questions to spark interesting discussions about ethical issues. Suggested solutions are in the lecture outlines.

Documents for Analysis

Many chapters contain "Documents for Analysis." These documents are also available at **www.meguffey.com** so that students may edit and revise them without total retyping. Transparency solutions of the Documents for Analysis are available in this manual. For distance learning classes, a digital set of solutions is available for instructors at **www.meguffey.com.**

WORKPLACE SIMULATIONS

New to this edition are three simulation activities, located at the student site (**www.meguffey.com**), that help students transfer their skills to the workplace.

Writeaway Hotels Simulation encourages students to practice managing and writing e-mail messages. Designed as an in-class activity, the simulation works best for 12 to 25 students, each playing a role within the fictitious company, Writeaway Hotels. Within 30 minutes in a computer lab or classroom, students read, write, and respond to messages to each other. During a debrief discussion, students evaluate messages sent during the simulation. **Aggresshop** is a simulation that helps students apply principles of customer and internal communication in a retail environment. **Bank on Me** simulates a hiring cycle in which students participate in the recruitment and hiring process at a financial services company. All three simulations have complete instructions and instructor's guide at **www.meguffey.com**.

ASSESSING WRITING ASSIGNMENTS

Assessing and grading student performance is probably the least appealing aspect of teaching business communication. Although some instructors have developed "The Perfect Plan" for grading and are quite satisfied with it, others are still searching. To help those who are still searching, we present five methods for assessing student assignments.

Before examining these methods, you may want to consider these general ideas regarding assessment and grading.

- Be aware of your goal in assessment. Is your goal to judge the student's work and attach a number or letter grade? Or is your goal to help students improve their writing? Probably most of us try, to a certain extent, to accomplish both goals—without making the assessment task burdensome.
- Keep your grading plan as simple as possible—for your sake and the students' as well.
- Discuss your grading plan with students before they actually start working on their first graded assignment. Be sure they understand the nuances of your grading method, and explain your pet peeves regarding writing assignments. You may even want to have them submit this first graded assignment, give comments to help them improve it, allow time for revisions, and then have them resubmit it for a grade.
- Strive for objectivity. For example, ask students to write their names on the backs of assignments so that the grade is never influenced by their names.

Revision

Most writing authorities advocate revision as an important technique in developing writing skills. You may want to allow students to rewrite a certain number of assignments, which you will totally regrade, reducing the second grade by one letter. Some instructors allow students to write rough drafts that are not graded, followed by final versions that are graded. Other instructors allow assignments to be rewritten, assigning a grade no higher than a "C" to the second attempt. Whatever plan you choose, be sure to schedule deadlines for submitting revisions. Also be sure that your deadlines for rewrites give you ample time to evaluate these papers before the end of your marking period.

Correction Symbols and Comments

Resist the temptation to rewrite faulty student expression. Crossing out a student error and replacing it with a "quick-fix" is not nearly as effective pedagogically as allowing students to solve their own problems. Although comments that encourage problem solving require more time to write than "quick-fixes," such comments or symbols force students to analyze their writing fault and formulate their own revisions. See Appendix D in *Business Communication: Process and Product* for a list of correction symbols to use when grading papers.

Six Assessment Methods

Here are six possible methods for grading student assignments. They represent traditional, behavioral, holistic, and criterion-based methods.

1. ***Assigned-Weights Method.*** Each document is graded according to assigned weights. For example, the opening is assigned a weight of 10 points.

Category	Possible Points	Your Score
Opening, closing	10	_______
Strategy, organization	10	_______
Completeness, accuracy	10	_______
Tone, goodwill effect	10	_______
Clarity, coherence	10	_______
Overall effect, originality	20	_______
Mechanics	30	_______
Spelling (–5 pts.)		
Word choice (–5)		
Major error (–6)		
Minor error (–2 or more)		
Idiom, syntax, or other error (–2 to –12)		
Bonus Points		______
TOTAL POINTS		______

If you prefer to penalize more (or less) for mechanical errors, change the points deducted. See page 52 for a template using this method.

==

2. ***Dual-Criteria Method.*** Each assignment is graded on the basis of the following criteria:

Content (10 pts.)	Grammar/Mechanics (10 pts.)
Strategy	Appearance
Organization	Format
Coherence	Grammar
Tone	Capitalization
Clarity	Spelling
Reader benefit	Word choice
Opening, closing	Conciseness
Overall effectiveness	Writing technique

Every assignment starts out with 20 points. The instructor devises a method of deducting points for faults, for example, –2 for any content fault (or more, depending upon the severity of the fault), –1 for minor grammar/mechanical problems, and –2 for severe grammar/mechanical problems. Numbers may be converted to grades using this optional scale:

A = 18–20 points	C = 8–13 points
B = 14–17 points	D = 4–7 points

===

3. ***Check-Mark Method.*** Students may rewrite assignments as often as required to receive a check mark, which usually signifies "B" work. A student's grade is determined by the number of check-mark assignments completed during the marking period.

A = 15 check marks	C = 11–12 check marks
B = 13–14 check marks	D = 9–10 check marks

===

4. **0, *1, 2 Holistic Method*.** Similar to the checkmark method, this holistic method includes only three possible scores. Marilyn Dyrud, Oregon Institute of Technology, developed this plan which she says minimizes student complaints and reduces instructor drudgery. Students may rewrite assignments to improve their grades. For further discussion, see "Preserving Sanity by Simplifying Grading" appearing in *Business Communication Quarterly*, March, 2003, 78. Here is Professor Dyrud's assessment criteria for letters and memos:

2 An excellent letter/memo

- is mailable as is (requires no revision)
- follows format specs and assignment requirements
- is signed/initialed
- has no mechanical errors (spelling, punctuation, syntax)
- attends to the audience's needs
- maintains "you" attitude throughout
- uses positive terminology, even when delivering bad news
- is written with flair
- uses appropriate tone and is an asset to company image

1 An acceptable letter/memo

- may be mailed as is, but probably requires some revision
- follows format specs and assignment requirements
- is signed/initialed
- has some noticeable mechanical errors
- may inaccurately estimate the audience
- may not emphasize "you" attitude
- may include negative terminology

0 An unacceptable letter/memo

- is not mailable (requires a major overhaul)
- does not follow format specs and/or assignment requirements
- has noticeable mechanical errors
- uses inappropriate tone
- is not signed/initialed
- ignores the reader
- has negative terminology
- is a detriment to company image

==

5. *Contract Method.* At the beginning of a course, students sign contracts outlining the requirements that will determine their final grades. An example of such a contract follows:

CONTRACT

During the semester I would like to work for a grade of _________. I will complete the requirements stated below for this grade; if I fail to meet the requirements, I will contract down.

Proposed by ____________________________ Date ________________________

Approved by ___________________________ Date ________________________

C-Level

1. I will read the assigned material.

2. I will meet the basic requirements of the course, performing at a satisfactory level and handing in written assignments when due. I will rewrite any work that my instructor deems unsatisfactory and return it within one week.

3. I will make a positive contribution to the small-group activities.

4. I will take a final exam, performing at a satisfactory level, if my absences are excessive.

B-Level

1. I will complete all requirements for the "C" level.

2. I will make an oral report on ____
(some phase of communication that meets the instructor's approval).

3. I will interview a business executive on communication in his or her firm and write a report on the interview.
Name and/or title of executive ____
Name of business firm ____

4. I will perform at this grade level; that is, most papers will be satisfactory when turned in the first time.

A-Level

1. I will complete all requirements for the "B" level.
2. I will write a formal report.
3. I will work at this grade level throughout the semester; that is, an assignment will seldom, if ever, have to be rewritten.

---

6. ***Workplace-Based Method.*** This method allows you to use a rubric to grade students in a way that parallels how writing might be evaluated on the job. If you choose this method, you should give students a copy of the rubric at the beginning of the course and explain it in detail. The following workplace-based method is based on a grading plan developed by Mike Markel, author of *Technical Communication* (Bedford St. Martin's).

Grade	Description
A	Your supervisor would gladly send this message with no edits. This document would make you stand out among other employees. You might even get a raise or promotion!
B	Your supervisor would send this message with minor edits; document has a few grammatical, mechanical, and/or format errors.
C	This document contains several grammatical, mechanical, and/or format errors. It needs major editing before it could be sent.
D	This document shows some understanding of the assignment, but it must be completely rewritten before your supervisor would send it.
F	This document does not show an understanding of the assignment. It would put you in serious jeopardy on the job.

"Assigned Weights" Template for Grading Writing Assignments

On the next page you will find a template for possible use in grading student writing assignments. This "assigned weights" rubric is very effective in achieving objectivity in grading. It is also effective in avoiding student confrontation regarding writing weaknesses. You might wish to print this sheet on colored paper, cut it into quarters, and distribute a number of slips to each student. Each assignment turned in should be accompanied by one of the grading slips.
In downloading this from the Instructor's Resource CD or from **http://www.meguffey.com**, be sure to retain the source formats to be able to squeeze all of this onto one sheet.

BUSINESS COMMUNICATION ASSESSMENT
Assignment or page number ____________________

Staple this sheet to the upper left corner of the document. Write your name on the back of your document.

Category	*Possible Points*	*Your Score*
Opening, closing	10	_____
Strategy, organization	10	_____
Completeness, accuracy	10	_____
Tone, goodwill effect	10	_____
Clarity, coherence	10	_____
Fluency, written expression (parallelism, sentence unity conciseness, etc.)	10	_____
Overall effect, originality	10	_____
Mechanics	30	_____
Spelling, typo (–4)		
Word choice (–4)		
Major error (comma splice, run-on, fragment, subject-verb agreement, etc.) (–6)		
Minor error (–2)		
Idiom, syntax, other errors (–2 to –6)		
Bonus points		_____
Total Points (100 possible)		_____

BUSINESS COMMUNICATION ASSESSMENT
Assignment or page number ____________________

Staple this sheet to the upper left corner of the document. Write your name on the back of your document.

Category	*Possible Points*	*Your Score*
Opening, closing	10	_____
Strategy, organization	10	_____
Completeness, accuracy	10	_____
Tone, goodwill effect	10	_____
Clarity, coherence	10	_____
Fluency, written expression (parallelism, sentence unity conciseness, etc.)	10	_____
Overall effect, originality	10	_____
Mechanics	30	_____
Spelling, typo (–4)		
Word choice (–4)		
Major error (comma splice, run-on, fragment, subject-verb agreement, etc.) (–6)		
Minor error (–2)		
Idiom, syntax, other errors (–2 to –6)		
Bonus points		_____
Total Points (100 possible)		_____

BUSINESS COMMUNICATION ASSESSMENT
Assignment or page number ____________________

Staple this sheet to the upper left corner of the document. Write your name on the back of your document.

Category	*Possible Points*	*Your Score*
Opening, closing	10	_____
Strategy, organization	10	_____
Completeness, accuracy	10	_____
Tone, goodwill effect	10	_____
Clarity, coherence	10	_____
Fluency, written expression (parallelism, sentence unity conciseness, etc.)	10	_____
Overall effect, originality	10	_____
Mechanics	30	_____
Spelling, typo (–4)		
Word choice (–4)		
Major error (comma splice, run-on, fragment, subject-verb agreement, etc.) (–6)		
Minor error (–2)		
Idiom, syntax, other errors (–2 to –6)		
Bonus points		_____
Total Points (100 possible)		_____

BUSINESS COMMUNICATION ASSESSMENT
Assignment or page number ____________________

Staple this sheet to the upper left corner of the document. Write your name on the back of your document.

Category	*Possible Points*	*Your Score*
Opening, closing	10	_____
Strategy, organization	10	_____
Completeness, accuracy	10	_____
Tone, goodwill effect	10	_____
Clarity, coherence	10	_____
Fluency, written expression (parallelism, sentence unity conciseness, etc.)	10	_____
Overall effect, originality	10	_____
Mechanics	30	_____
Spelling, typo (–4)		
Word choice (–4)		
Major error (comma splice, run-on, fragment, subject-verb agreement, etc.) (–6)		
Minor error (–2)		
Idiom, syntax, other errors (–2 to –6)		
Bonus points		_____
Total Points (100 possible)		_____

ASSESSING ORAL PRESENTATIONS

Many instructors encourage peer evaluation of oral presentations. To guide your students in how to evaluate a presentation, you might wish to use a rubric such as that shown below. This descriptive evaluation system is helpful in teaching students what to look for and how to judge presentations. This rubric was developed by Kim Sydow Campbell, David L. Mothersbaugh, Charlotte Brammer, and Timothy Taylor at the University of Alabama. Notice that it assigns numeric values to various levels of performance.

A Rubric for Judging the Quality of an Oral Business Presentation

	1	2	3	4	5
Eye Contact	Essentially no eye contact. Reads continuously, glancing up only once or twice a minute. Stares at ceiling or consistently looks at slide screen	Somewhere between no and moderate eye contact.	Moderate eye contact. Either faces audience but refers to notes or slides occasionally (couple of times a minute) or turns body sometimes to screen.	Somewhere between moderate and continuous eye contact.	Continuous eye contact. Faces audience and refers to notes or slides less than once a minute. Rarely glances at slide screen or at part of room away from audience.
Body Language	Distracting. Sways, paces, or fidgets so that audience is distracted from presentation. Poor use of hands (in pockets, jingling keys, playing with pen).	Somewhere between distracting and neutral body language.	Neutral. Stands facing the audience. Occasionally uses hands and body movements appropriately, but may still be a little stiff or nervous.	Somewhere between neutral and engaging body language.	Engaging. Uses gestures (e.g., pointing with hands) and expressions to enhance the presentation. Speaker looks very comfortable and natural.
Voice Qualities	Poor. Halting, uneven pace. Can not hear all of the words due to mumbling, speaking too softly, speaking too quickly, or in a monotone.	Somewhere between poor and adequate voice qualities.	Adequate pace and volume. Speaks fairly clearly but lacks sufficient variations in vocal intonation for emphasis.	Somewhere between adequate and excellent voice qualities.	Fluid, natural delivery. Speaks moderately slowly with good vocal variety, articulation, and volume.
Command of Material	Poor. Struggles often to find words. Reads most of presentation.	Somewhere between poor and adequate command of material.	Reads less than once a minute, struggles occasionally to find words.	Somewhere between adequate and excellent command of material.	Excellent. Does not read from notes or slides. Expresses ideas fluently in own words.
Visual Aids	Ineffective. Overheads, slides, or handouts are hard to read, distracting, or inadequate for presentation.	Somewhere between ineffective and adequate visual aids.	Adequate. Readable overheads, handouts. Enhance presentation.	Somewhere between adequate and excellent visual aids.	Excellent overheads or slides. Easy to read, attractive, greatly enhance presentation.
Content	Poor. Purpose not clear, information disjointed or inadequate.	Somewhere between poor and adequate content.	Adequate. Information is usually relevant and appropriate to audience.	Somewhere between adequate and engaging content.	Engaging. Information is relevant to audience. Excellent details.

Source: "Peer Versus Self-Assessment of Oral Business Presentation Performance," *Business Communication Quarterly*, Volume 64, Number 3, September 2001, pp. 25–42. Reprinted with the permission of the Association for Business Communication.

Depending on what you emphasize in your class, you might wish to use the template shown on this page for grading student oral presentations.

ORAL PRESENTATION ASSESSMENT
Speaker's Name ______________________

Excellent	**10 points**
Above average	**8–9 points**
Average	**5–7 points**
Needs Improvement	**4 or below**

1. **Were the opening and closing clear and well planned?** _____
2. **Did the speaker help you remember two to four main points?** _____
3. **Were the speaker's movements and eye contact effective?** _____
4. **Were the visual aids effective and handled appropriately?** _____
5. **Was the presentation well organized, coherent, and obviously practiced before delivery?** _____

Total Points (50 possible) _____

On the back add a statement of praise and one pointer for improvement.

ORAL PRESENTATION ASSESSMENT
Speaker's Name ______________________

Excellent	**10 points**
Above average	**8–9 points**
Average	**5–7 points**
Needs Improvement	**4 or below**

1. **Were the opening and closing clear and well planned?** _____
2. **Did the speaker help you remember two to four main points?** _____
3. **Were the speaker's movements and eye contact effective?** _____
4. **Were the visual aids effective and handled appropriately?** _____
5. **Was the presentation well organized, coherent, and obviously practiced before delivery?** _____

Total Points (50 possible) _____

On the back add a statement of praise and one pointer for improvement.

ORAL PRESENTATION ASSESSMENT
Speaker's Name ______________________

Excellent	**10 points**
Above average	**8–9 points**
Average	**5–7 points**
Needs Improvement	**4 or below**

1. **Were the opening and closing clear and well planned?** _____
2. **Did the speaker help you remember two to four main points?** _____
3. **Were the speaker's movements and eye contact effective?** _____
4. **Were the visual aids effective and handled appropriately?** _____
5. **Was the presentation well organized, coherent, and obviously practiced before delivery?** _____

Total Points (50 possible) _____

On the back add a statement of praise and one pointer for improvement.

ORAL PRESENTATION ASSESSMENT
Speaker's Name ______________________

Excellent	**10 points**
Above average	**8–9 points**
Average	**5–7 points**
Needs Improvement	**4 or below**

1. **Were the opening and closing clear and well planned?** _____
2. **Did the speaker help you remember two to four main points?** _____
3. **Were the speaker's movements and eye contact effective?** _____
4. **Were the visual aids effective and handled appropriately?** _____
5. **Was the presentation well organized, coherent, and obviously practiced before delivery?** _____

Total Points (50 possible) _____

On the back add a statement of praise and one pointer for improvement.

ASSESSING REPORTS

REPORT ASSESSMENT

Before you turn in your report, study the categories in which it will be assessed. Turn in this sheet when you submit the report. At that time, sign the statement below.

My report contains no sentences or parts of sentences that are copied verbatim (word for word) from other writing without attribution.

Signed ____

Report format

Illustrates correct format
Displays headings appropriately
Shows neat overall appearance — 20 points _________

Report content

Achieves the purpose of the report
Contains sufficient data, supported by concrete detail
Includes relevant data
Shows evidence of sufficient research
Achieves overall effectiveness — 40 points _________

Report writing style

Shows good organization
Includes coherent and unified sentences and paragraphs
Uses transitions effectively
Attributes sources clearly and correctly — 20 points _________

Grammar and mechanics

Uses appropriate grammar
Contains conventional spelling
Shows proper punctuation
Includes correct capitalization — 20 points _________

Bonus points

Achieves exceptional merit — _________

TOTAL POINTS — 100 points _________

Comments

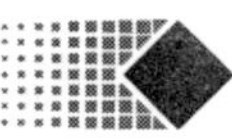

DEMONSTRATED LEADERSHIP ASSESSMENT

By Jo Koster Tarvers, Winthrop University

To make class participation more meaningful, you may wish to add a demonstrated leadership assessment to your syllabus as part of the course grade.

Students may earn 10 percent of their grade if they do the following tasks:

1. On assigned dates, they each present to the class a summary of concepts from the text and initiate a discussion of why these concepts are important for the skills they are currently learning.

2. Participate regularly in online class discussions.

3. At least three times during the semester, they each bring into class or to on-line discussions "real-world" examples from their own mail, work, reading, or discussions in other classes. They should use these examples to reflect on or illuminate the topics being discussed in class and use them to contribute to the discussion. They may raise such issues as grammar, rhetorical approach to business messages, current business communication practices, and business communication strategies.

4. On the last day of class, they each submit a short memo to the instructor explaining why they should get 10 percent credit for demonstrated leadership and the letter grade they think they earned. If they do not each submit a memo, they receive no credit.

Benefits to the Student

This assessment is more concrete than a general "class participation" grade for two reasons:

1. As students perform the tasks, they show the instructor and the class that they are thinking about what business communication professionals think about and contribute to the class's improved understanding of the issues of the discipline.

2. The assessment allows the instructor to talk about "demonstrated leadership" in letters of recommendation.

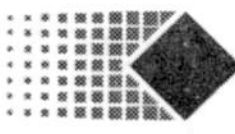

STRATEGIES FOR REDUCING PLAGIARISM

As many business communication instructors have learned, plagiarism has never been easier than it is today. Previously, students had to make an effort and spend some money to find a prepared research paper to turn in. But today the Internet has greatly simplified the task of appropriating material for research papers. In less than an hour, students can Google their way to an entire term paper by merely cutting and pasting selected passages. For those with more money than Internet skills, hundreds of online paper-mills or "cheatsites" provide papers in off-the-shelf or customized forms.

Clever instructors can, however, use a number of effective techniques to greatly reduce plagiarism in student papers.

- **Help students understand proper research practices.** Don't assume that students know what plagiarism is. Teach them by showing examples of an original text, a plagiarized version, and an acceptable paraphrased version. Create your own examples or use those appearing in Chapter 11 of Guffey's *Business Communication: Process and Product,* 7e, page 363. Other examples are available in the many Web sites devoted to plagiarism and its prevention.

- **Teach plagiarism from a coaching perspective.** Talk about plagiarism in class. Discuss good manual and electronic notetaking skills. Spend time explaining how to avoid "mistakes" that result in plagiarism.

- **Discuss the seriousness of plagiarism and its penalties.** Describe the consequences that plagiarists suffer. Develop knowledge of Web sites that sell assignments in your discipline and be sure your students are aware of your knowledge. Talk with them about how easy it is for knowledgeable instructors to use the Internet to locate character strings and their sources.

- **Monitor each step of the writing process.** Require students to turn in outlines, drafts, notes, and annotated bibliographies as part of an ongoing assignment. Monitoring is probably the single most important technique in preventing plagiarism.

- **Require students to save and submit Web pages.** One of the biggest attribution problems today is that of citing Internet references no longer available. To avoid this dilemma, ask students to save a permanent copy of a Web page (click "Save as" on Internet Explorer and save in a directory or print relevant pages).

- **Assign original topics.** Avoid repeating assignments used in previous classes, and don't allow popular topics that have a ton of prepared papers all ready to be purchased by writing- and ethics-challenged students.

- **Teach and grade citation techniques.** Explain how to quote individuals and sources and how to use APA, MLA, or your special citation format. Make the proper citation of sources a specific part of the research paper grade.

- **Consider using a commercial plagiarism detection service.** If your school is willing to foot the bill, subscribe to Turnitin.com. Students submit their papers to the service, which makes a "digital fingerprint" of the paper. It cross-references that fingerprint against its database of hundreds of thousands of papers. It also scours the Web searching for similar phrasing. Then it creates a custom originality report for each paper. Few students dare to plagiarize if they know their papers will be scrutinized electronically.

Although large schools assigning many term papers may find it worthwhile to invest in a service such as Turnitin.com, you can achieve excellent results without investing in an expensive service. Just implement the techniques discussed here—especially monitoring the entire writing process.

VIDEOS, TEAMS, AND MORE

Part 3

VIDEO DISCUSSION GUIDE

Two exciting video sets now offer a total of 14 videos to accompany Guffey's *Business Communication: Process and Product*, 7e. These 7- to 12-minute videos take students beyond the classroom to help build the communication skills they will need to succeed in today's rapidly changing workplace. Instructors may order them from Cengage, or students may view them directly at **www.meguffey.com.**

Video Library 1, *Building Workplace Skills,* eight videos that introduce and reinforce concepts in selected chapters of *Business Communication: Process and Product,* 7e. Made specifically to demonstrate chapter-specific material in *BC:PP,* these videos strengthen comprehension and retention of key ideas. Five videos were filmed in the stunning offices of a Boston financial firm. They bring to life and reinforce significant concepts in a way that the textbook cannot. For the Seventh Edition, we filmed a new video, *Technology in the Workplace,* which shows appropriate and inappropriate uses of digital technologies. Each video presents critical thinking questions to generate discussion and focus learning.

Video Library 2, *Bridging the Gap,* presents six videos transporting viewers inside real companies such as Yahoo, Cold Stone Creamery, and Hard Rock Café. Students are able to apply their new skills in structured applications aimed at bridging the gap between the classroom and the real world of work. Nearly all of these videos culminate in student writing assignments.

For each video we provide an instructors' discussion guide that includes a summary of the video, suggestions for use and discussion, and proposed solutions for any assignments. Below are the chapters where the videos seem most appropriate, but instructors may use them at any time they choose.

Chapter	Video Library	Video Title
1-3	1	Career Success Starts With Communication Foundations
2	2	Understanding Teamwork: Cold Stone Creamery
3	1	Intercultural Communication at Work
4-6	1	Guffey's 3-x-3 Writing Process Develops Fluent Workplace Skills
6	2	Writing Skills: The Little Guys
7	1	Technology in the Workplace
7	1	Smart E-Mail Messages and Memos Advance Your Career
8	2	Social Responsibility and Communication: Ben & Jerry's
9	2	BuyCostumes (Bad News Message)
10	2	Hard Rock Café (Persuasive Request)
10	2	Innovation, Learning, and Communication: A Study of Yahoo
14	1	Effective On-the-Job Oral Presentations
15	1	The Job Search
16	1	Sharpening Your Interview Skills

CAREER SUCCESS STARTS WITH COMMUNICATION FOUNDATIONS
Video Library 1
Chapters 1 to 3

Summary of Video

This video provides an overview of the concepts presented in Chapters 1 through 4. Cliff, Jackie, Ramon, and others discuss the importance of communication skills at Integrity Investments. The film illustrates the changing business world, flattened management hierarchies, the communication process, communication flow, ethics, listening, nonverbal communication, and other topics presented in Chapters 1 through 3.

How to Use the Video

This video can be used to introduce or review Chapter 1. It can also be used to review Unit 1, which includes Chapters 1 through 3. The film touches on nearly all of the concepts introduced in these chapters. It stimulates class discussion and reinforces key communication concepts.

Discussion Guide

The following critical thinking questions appear on the screen at the end of the film:

- **How is the world of work changing?**
  The world of work is changing because many businesses are now conducting global operations. Organizations are flattening management hierarchies so that managers are closer to employees. Many organizations are turning to teams to develop products and services and to conduct operations. Constantly evolving communication technologies change the tools and procedures of work. The workplace is also becoming more diverse, and more emphasis is placed on collecting, organizing, and communicating information

- **Why are communication skills increasingly important to your career success?**
  As organizations flatten their management hierarchies, decision-making is pushed downward. More and more employees, individually and as part of teams, exchange information as they function within teams and become part of decision-making processes. Because so much information is now exchanged by e-mail, writing skills are more important than ever. As our economy becomes increasingly information-oriented, those individuals who can communicate well will be in great demand.

- **What communication skills are most important for businesspeople and why?**
  All communication skills—reading, writing, speaking, listening and nonverbal—are important in today's information-based economy. Writing skills are increasingly important because of the emphasis on e-mail. Listening skills are important as subordinates listen for instructions from superiors and also as employees listen to customers. As employees are promoted into management, their writing, speaking, and listening skills become even more important and can often mean the difference between being promoted or passed over.

- **What communication skills would you like to improve?**
  Responses will vary for this question.

INTERCULTURAL COMMUNICATION AT WORK
Video Library 1
Chapter 3

Summary of Video

This video transports viewers into the offices of Clifton-Harding Associates (CHA), a small New York advertising agency. The company was founded by Ella Clifton and her husband Rob Harding. In meeting with a prospective Japanese customer, Ella and Rob, together with their dippy receptionist Stephanie, illustrate numerous clashes between American and Asian cultures, expectations, and etiquette. Ellen and Rob unintentionally insult their guest and, of course, lose the possible business contract.

What to Look For

Because this video moves fast and uses a documentary film-making style, it's necessary to watch and listen carefully. You can help students understand what is happening by explaining the context and introducing the characters briefly before showing the video. As students watch the film, they should make note of how many cultural misunderstandings take place in the meeting with Ella, Rob, and Stephanie.

Student Task

In class, discuss the following critical thinking questions:

- **Identify the cultural misunderstandings that occurred during Ken´ichi Takahashi's meeting with Rob, Ella, and Stephanie.**

  a. Upon arriving at Clifton Harding, Ken´ichi Takahashi was dismayed when no one greeted him. Similarly, he considered it rude when no one walked him to his cab at the end of the day.

  b. In the Japanese culture, casual business attire is still uncommon. Some Japanese companies frown on female employees who wear jewelry, very short skirts, or high-heeled shoes. Women with long hair and unprofessional attire may be treated as secretaries. Because of the way Ella was dressed, Mr. Takahashi did not take her seriously. In fact, he continuously looked to Rob for approval of Ella's recommendations during the meeting. Ella noticed this and was offended that he sought Rob's approval for her ideas.

  c. In Japan, the exchange of business cards is ceremonial and extremely important. Rob failed to show respect to Mr. Takahashi when he fiddled with the business card during the meeting. Ella correctly placed the card gently on the table in front of her.

  d. Rob offended Mr. Takahashi when he grabbed his hand for a two-handed handshake. The Japanese seldom shake hands and may be uncomfortable doing so. He further insulted him by slapping him on the back. It is inappropriate to pat a Japanese man on the back or shoulder. The Japanese greet each other by bowing. Bowing may include a small nod of the head to a long, 90-degree bow. If you are greeted with a bow, return the bow with one as low as the one received. Keep your palms flat to your thighs.

e. The Japanese consider it disrespectful to make derogatory remarks about competitors or one's own employees. While talking on his cell phone at the beginning of the video, Rob criticized the Mexican vendors for not working quickly. Mr. Takahashi considered this disrespectful.

f. Ella and Rob were confused when Mr. Takahashi did not react either positively or negatively to their proposal. They should have known that deals with the Japanese are usually not made during the first meeting. Furthermore, when Mr. Takahashi nodded his head during the presentation, Rob thought it meant he was approving the plan, prompting him to eagerly issue a contract. Instead, Mr. Takahashi's nodding simply meant that he was listening.

- **What suggestions would you offer Rob and Ella for improving their cultural competence?**
  To succeed in the global business environment, employees need to learn more about the culture in which they will be conducting business and modify their approach to business relationships. Rob and Ella could improve their chances of working successfully with Mr. Takahashi in the following ways.

  a. Study the Japanese culture and appreciate business traditions that are different from their own.

  b. Show tolerance and patience for cultural differences and accept other perspectives.

  c. Understand that Japan is a high-context culture which means that the Japanese place high value on interpersonal relationships, nonverbal expression, rituals, physical settings, and social settings.

- **At the end of the meeting with Mr. Takahashi, Rob assumed that Clifton-Harding Associates would be hired to develop an advertising campaign. In fact, Rob asked that a contract be prepared outlining their agreement. Do you think Mr. Takahashi plans to hire Rob and Ella's firm? Why or why not?**

It is highly unlikely that Mr. Takahashi will hire Clifton-Harding to create an advertising campaign for his company. Mr. Takahashi's relationship with Rob and Ella was jeopardized because of their lack of cultural sensitivity. Mr. Takahashi was insulted a number of times throughout the meeting, diminishing his trust and confidence in Rob and the rest of the staff.

UNDERSTANDING TEAMWORK: COLD STONE CREAMERY
Video Library 2
Chapter 2

Summary of Video
This video highlights teamwork at Cold Stone Creamery, a fast-growing ice cream specialty chain. It shows team members behind the counter but also provides the inside scoop through the insights of Kevin Myers, vice president, Marketing. Viewers see how teamwork permeates every facet of Cold Stone's corporate culture.

What to Look For
Tell students to watch for these items:
- Definition of the term *team*
- Six different kinds of teams
- Characteristics of effective teams
- Two broad categories of team roles

Student Task
In class, discuss the following:

- **How is the term *team* defined in this video? Can you offer a definition that is more specific?**
  The video defines *team* as "a group of workers with a shared mission and vision and collective responsibilities." Your textbook defines a *team* as "a group of individuals who interact over time to achieve a purpose." Students may suggest that a team is a group that focuses on a joint goal or product, such as a presentation, completing in-class exercises, writing a report, or creating a new design. Authors Katzenbach and Smith say that "a team is a small number of people with complementary skills who are committed to a common purpose, performance goals, and approach for which they are mutually accountable."

- **What six different kinds of teams were mentioned in the Cold Stone Creamery video? Can you provide examples of these teams based on companies with which you are familiar?**

  1. Formal team – members of a management team, such as the CEO, president, and vice presidents of any major company
  2. Vertical team – a manager and all the people whom he or she supervises
  3. Horizontal team – team members with different expertise at the same hierarchal level
  4. Special purpose team – members who come together for a specific project and are often disbanded after the project is completed
  5. Self-directed team – might include 5 to 20 multi-skilled members supervised by one of their own who rotate jobs to deliver a product or service.
  6. Global team – made up of members with different nationalities whose work spans multiple countries; could also be a virtual team using telecommunications to collaborate

- **What characteristics make for effective teams? In your experience with teams, do you agree or disagree?**
  This video discusses small size and diversity of members as effective characteristics. Small teams find it easier to reach decisions, share opinions, and ask more questions. Larger teams have more disagreements, less participation, and more demands on the group. Effective teams also need diverse members with different skill sets, thinking styles, and personal characteristics to help produce more innovative problem solutions.

GUFFEY'S 3-X-3 WRITING PROCESS DEVELOPS FLUENT WORKPLACE SKILLS
Video Library 1
Chapters 4 - 6

Summary of Video
This video combines narrative and role-playing to illustrate each phase of Guffey's 3-x-3 writing process. Students see four employees (David, Sarah, Jackie, and Cliff) as they go through each phase of the writing process. Rather than merely state the steps in the writing process, the video actually illustrates what happens in each step.

How to Use the Video
This film will be most useful to introduce Unit 2 of Guffey's *Business Communication: Process and Product.* It sets the stage for Chapter 4, but the video could be used for any or all of Chapters 4, 5, and 6.

Discussion Guide
The following critical thinking questions appear on the screen at the end of the film:

- **How can a process help a writer?**
  A writing process helps a writer by providing a skeleton of the process. The writer then has a description of what should be done at each stage. Following a writing process helps avoid writer's block. It enables writers to get started and to work efficiently and effectively.

- **Does the writing process always follow the same order?**
  The writing process does not follow the same order with each project. Often it involves looping back to a previous stage, such as thinking about your purpose and your audience. For example, if you are well along in the composition phase and then realize that your message may be read by the manager's boss, you might decide to go back to the first stage of thinking about what this secondary reader would expect in the message. The writing process is more nearly cursive than linear.

- **Why does revising take more time than any other part of the process?**
  Many writers record their ideas quickly and then spend the most time revising and polishing their writing. Important documents must be edited and proofread carefully to be certain they are clear, correct, and readable.

WRITING SKILLS: THE LITTLE GUYS
Video Library 2
Chapter 6

Summary of Video

The Little Guys Home Electronics specializes in selling and installing home theater equipment. In just 12 years, this organization has grown from a start-up company to an established business with annual sales of more than $10 million. The owners—Dave and Evie Wexler and Paul Gerrity—describe their goals, motivations, and experiences in making their business successful.

What to Look For

As they watch the video, students should be encouraged to look for the following:

- Good business practices that helped the owners launch a successful business
- Characteristics of successful entrepreneurs
- Reasons that some small businesses remain successful whereas others fail

Student Task

This video is intended to provide business students with positive role models as entrepreneurs. For this writing class, however, the video is useful to establish a context for a writing assignment. After watching the video, students are to summarize the reasons for the success of The Little Guys. Building on what they learned in this chapter, they are to compose a bulleted list with ten or more items. They should use this opening sentence: *The Little Guys Home Electronics business succeeded because the owners did the following.* They should add a title to the list they compose.

Class Discussion

The following questions will help students get started in writing a bulleted list.

- **How can you develop parallelism in a bulleted list?**
  You can develop parallelism by using the same grammatical construction for each statement. If one item begins with a past-tense verb, all items should begin with a past-tense verb. If the first statement begins with a noun, all statements should begin with nouns.

- **When items are listed vertically, how should they be capitalized? Should each item end with a period?**
  Each item listed vertically should begin with a capital letter. Each item should end with a period ONLY if that item is a complete sentence.

- **What is the difference between a bulleted list and an enumerated list (one with numbers)?**
  Most writers use numbered lists for items that represent a sequence, set of steps, or numbered items in a group. Bulleted items are for unrelated items that form no special order.

Proposed Solution

Why The Little Guys Electronics Business Succeeded

The Little Guys Home Electronics business is successful because the owners did the following:

- Believed they could provide home electronics better than big companies
- Recognized a niche market and moved quickly
- Had deep faith that they would succeed
- Were willing to risk failure and financial ruin because of their self-confidence
- Showed strong tolerance for ambiguity, a trait of most successful entrepreneurs
- Dedicated themselves to honest personal service
- Believed firmly that the future was within their control
- Made sacrifices and worked madly to take advantage of Christmas season sales
- Found unusual ways to finance their new business without giving up ownership to investors
- Maintained high energy level, putting in long hours to serve customers
- Started as "babes in the woods" but learned as they went along
- Refused to open more branches, preferring to focus their efforts on perfecting one store

TECHNOLOGY IN THE WORKPLACE
Video Library 1
Chapter 7

Summary of Video

Illustrating proper and improper use of today's technologies in the workplace, this video takes you to H. B. Jones, a small landscape design and supply firm. You will meet Elliott, the owner and founder, Helena, a competent office worker; James, East Coast manager; and Ian, an inept employee.

What to Look For

This fast-paced video gives you a glimpse of office workers using smartphones, computers, and other technologies on the job. Be watching for the attitudes of Ian, Elliott, James, and Helena toward their jobs and their use of company time. Who is using "Facespace" and why? Is James driving and accepting cell calls? Why does James complain about Elliott's e-mail and phone messages? This video moves so quickly that you may want to watch it twice to be able to answer these questions:

Class Discussion

- **Do you see significant differences between Helena's and Ian's use of social networking sites? Are their visits to Facespace legitimate?**

  Helena seems to use Facespace responsibly, but Ian posts messages and blogs about his late-night carousing and about his complaints of office colleagues and criticism of the company.

- **What efficiencies and inefficiencies do you detect in how each character uses his or her smartphone?**

  James seems to use his smartphone efficiently, but he should not be talking and driving at the same time. The boss, Elliott, uses the phone to call James, who is frequently on the road, but Elliott often repeats the same information that was sent by interoffice memo, thus wasting everyone's time. Helena tries to multitask by talking on the phone and typing messages at the same time, causing her to inadvertently reveal the surprise party being planned for Elliott.

- **Is the featured company a technologically functional workplace, or can it be called dysfunctional? Which remedies would you propose if you identify any shortcomings?**

  The featured company, H. B. Jones, fails to take advantage of today's technologies. It could use a wiki or internal Web site to post messages so that hard copy memos and frequent telephone calls were unnecessary. The employees have obviously not been trained in using smartphones efficiently and appropriately. The company may need an e-mail and smartphone policy outlining when and how employees should use the Internet and company equipment.

- **How would you describe Ian's and Helena's behavior upon entering the office in the morning?**

  Upon entering the office, Ian and Helena are both distracted by their headphones and earpods. Ian accidentally bumps into the boss, Elliott, and offers no apology or even recognition of his poor manners. Both Ian and Helena appear to be lost in their own digital audio worlds and not ready to focus on beginning their workday.

SMART E-MAILS AND MEMOS ADVANCE YOUR CAREER
Video Library 1
Chapter 7

Summary of Video
This video begins with Jackie reviewing Guffey's 3-x-3 writing process. Then Elaine and Sarah take us through the writing process by role-playing a scene in which Elaine is trying to write an important e-mail message to her boss, Bradford. We see what kinds of decisions are made in each step of the process. The video emphasizes significant e-mail dos and don'ts.

How to Use the Video
This video correlates directly with Chapter 8. Use it to introduce the chapter and spotlight the importance of e-mail messages.

Discussion Guide
The following critical thinking questions appear on the screen at the end of the film:

- **What are some e-mail catastrophes that you have heard about? How could they be avoided?**
  Students should be able to relate examples of e-mail disasters, such as sending a message to the wrong person or responding to an entire list of people rather than to the sender alone. To avoid disastrous e-mail catastrophes, writers must remember that e-mail creates a permanent record. They should avoid responding when angry. Your students will probably suggest many other techniques for avoiding e-mail catastrophes. Many of them have had first-hand experience with e-mail problems.

- **What do you think businesspeople mean when they say they have a "love/hate" relationship with e-mail?**
  Businesspeople love e-mail because it is a fast communication channel that requires little effort. They begin to hate it, however, when writing and responding to e-mail begins to cut into their daily work schedule. E-mail has become so easy to use that it is overused and misused. In addition, most of us receive many spam messages that clog the system and prevent us from focusing on important messages.

- **Why is it important to remember that e-mail is not like a telephone conversation?**
  Although it may seem like a casual phone call, every e-mail message produces a written record of what was written. The record appears not only on the writer's computer but also on the receiver's computer and on many servers and back-up systems along the way. E-mail messages have become the "smoking gun" in many lawsuits today. Prosecutors may demand computer records, and every e-mail message can be scrutinized as evidence in litigation.

SOCIAL RESPONSIBILITY AND COMMUNICATION: BEN & JERRY'S
Video Library 2
Chapter 8

Summary of Video
In this video we learn about Ben & Jerry's, the premium ice cream maker established in 1978 in Burlington, Vermont. The film pictures managers at Ben & Jerry's as they discuss six factors and issues affecting the company's potential for continuing success: demographics, political/legal issues, competition/economic factors, technology, and social change. We learn that although super premium ice cream is considered recession-proof and inflation-proof, Ben & Jerry's faces a number of challenges if it is to continue to be a profitable, as well as a socially responsible, business. In describing its commitment to the environment, we learn about a new package being developed for its ice cream.

How to Use This Video
The last portion of this short video focuses on its new packaging. As an environmentally conscious business, Ben & Jerry's redesigned its pint containers to use unbleached paper. This may seem like a small matter, but it involved developing an entirely new packaging material for

its ice cream. That packaging material had to please its marketing people, who wanted to show off their great label graphics. It also had to use paper that had not been bleached with chlorine. What's wrong with chlorine? Although it makes paper white, chlorine contains dioxin, which is known to cause cancer, genetic and reproductive defects, and learning disabilities. In producing paper, pulp mills using chlorine are also adding to dioxin contamination of waterways. Eventually, Ben & Jerry's found a new chlorine-free, unbleached paper board for its packages. That was the good news. The bad news is that the inside of the package is no longer white; the interior of the new packaging is now brown.

The video establishes a context for a writing problem in which students respond to a customer who is upset about the new packaging.

Student Task

Assume you have been hired at Ben & Jerry's to help answer incoming letters. Although you are fairly new, your boss gives you a letter from an unhappy customer. This customer opened a pint of Ben & Jerry's "World's Best Vanilla" and then threw it out. He saw the brown inner lid and sides of the package, and he decided that his pint must have been used for chocolate before it was used for vanilla. Or, he said, "the entire pint has gone bad and somehow turned the sides brown." Whatever the reason, he wasn't taking any chances. Although he had been a long-time customer, he now wanted his money back. His last comment was, "I like your stand on environmental and social issues, but I don't like my ice cream in used containers."

Write a letter that explains the brown carton, justifies the reason for using it, and retains the customer's business. The letter should be addressed to Mr. Adam W. Johnson, 4030 West Griswold Road, Phoenix, AZ 85051.

Discussion Guide

Help students understand this writing problem by posing the following questions:

- **In letters that grant claims and adjustments, the writer generally tries to rectify the wrong. Does a "wrong" exist in this case? Why or why not?**
  No wrong exists in this situation. The customer simply does not understand that the new containers have brown interiors.

- **Should you try to regain the confidence of this customer? How could that be done?**
  Yes, you should try to regain the confidence of this customer. You can do that by explaining why the interior of the new packaging is brown.

- **How could you learn more about the new containers so that you can answer this customer accurately?**
  As a new employee who needs information, you would probably first try to find it yourself before admitting your ignorance. A great way to learn about your company is to go to its Web site and read everything there. Another way to learn about what's happening to the company is to check the files and any literature, such as news releases, that may be available. You can also ask fellow employees and your boss.

- **Should you try to promote further business with this customer? How could that be done?**
  Yes, you should try to promote further business. You can include one or two coupons for free pints. You could describe new developments in flavors and activities at Ben & Jerry's.

- **How can you display the information to improve readability?**
  You can improve readability by listing some of the information.

Proposed Solution [Letter to Ben & Jerry's Customer]

Current date

Mr. Adam W. Johnson
4030 West Griswold Road
Phoenix, AZ 85051

Dear Mr. Johnson:

You'll find in this letter a coupon for a pint of Ben & Jerry's premium ice cream. We hope you will use it to try another pint of our "World's Best Vanilla," about which you wrote recently.

Please give it a second chance. The brown interior of the carton is actually our new packaging with unbleached paper. The outside of the container has a clay coat to make it look white, but the inside is a natural brown color. As you know, Ben & Jerry's has always been conscious of the environment. That's why we searched for a new packaging material. Most ice cream packages are made with a paper board that is treated with chlorine bleach. Bleach contains dioxin, which is known to cause cancer and is also a major contributor to toxic water pollution in many of our streams and rivers.

Our customers, we think, deserve the freshest and most wholesome product we can make. Although our new containers are brown inside, they deliver to you the same great-tasting ice cream. But now your ice cream no longer comes into contact with a package made with chlorine bleach.

As a long-time Ben & Jerry's connoisseur, you know good ice cream. Let us know if you don't agree that our "World's Best Vanilla" tastes great in its new package.

Sincerely,

Enclosure: Pint coupon

P.S. If you'd like to read more about this new packaging, visit our Web site at (http://www.benjerry.com). You can also learn about some of our sensational new flavors!

BAD NEWS : BuyCostumes
Video Library 2
Chapter 9

Summary of Video

BuyCostumes is the world's largest online costume and accessories retailer. Jalem Getz founded the business because he wanted to do something he enjoyed and to do it better than anyone else. BuyCostumes is a young business, and Getz uses his business plan as a road map for the managers in planning and assessing department progress and goals.

What to Look For

As they watch the video, students should be encouraged to look for

- Description and implementation of BuyCostumes' business plan
- Determination of the owner to be the best and to beat the competition

Student Task

BuyCostumes is proud of its extensive stock of costumes, its liberal return policy, and its many satisfied customers. But one day a letter arrived with a request that went beyond the company's ability to deliver. The customer said that he had ordered the Gorilla Blinky Eye with Chest costume. This popular gorilla costume comes with a unique gorilla mask, attractive suit with rubber chest, foot covers, and hands. The customer complained that the gorilla costume did not arrive until two days after his Halloween party. He planned an elaborate party with a gorilla theme, and he was extremely unhappy that he did not have his costume. He asks BuyCostumes to reimburse $300 that he spent on theme-related decorations, which he says were useless when he failed to receive his costume.

As a customer service representative, you checked his order and found that it was not received until 5 days before Halloween, the busiest time of the year for your company. The order was filled the next day, but standard shipping requires three to six business days for delivery. The customer did not order express or premium delivery; his shipping option was marked "Standard."

You showed the letter to Mr. Getz and said that this request was ludicrous. Mr. Getz, however, wanted to retain the customer's goodwill. Obviously, BuyCostumes was not going to shell out $300 for late delivery of a costume. But Mr. Getz suggested that the company would allow the customer to return the costume (in its original packaging) with a credit for the $134.99 charge. In addition, BuyCostumes would send a coupon for $20 off on the next costume purchase. Mr. Getz asks you to write a letter that retains the goodwill of this customer. Address your bad-news letter to Mr. Christopher King, 3579 Elm Street, Buffalo, NY 14202. Check <buycostomes.com> for more company information.

Class Discussion

- **In denying the claim of a disappointed customer, how should you begin the message?** Begin indirectly by expressing appreciation for the customer's order and letter. You might apologize if your organization was responsible for the problem.
- **Before delivering the bad news, what should you try to do?** You should provide reasons explaining what happened. Try to regain the customer's confidence.
- **How should the bad news be presented?** State the bad news objectively or imply it. To offset the bad news, consider offering a gift that might make the receiver feel better toward the organization.
- **How should the letter close?** The letter should close pleasantly and look forward to future business, offer best wishes, refer to gifts, or use resale information sensitively.

Proposed Solution

Current date

Mr. Christopher King
3579 Elm Street
Buffalo, NY 14202

Dear Mr. King:

Thank you for telling us of the late arrival of your Gorilla Blinky Eye With Chest Costume. Like you, we are disappointed that it did not arrive in time for your Halloween party.

In checking our records, we note that your order arrived five days before Halloween. This is the busiest time of the year for us, and our staff grows from 60 core employees to over 300 during this season. We were, nevertheless, able to ship your order the next day, which is our promise to all customers. We shipped your order according to the option you noted: Standard Shipping. This option requires three to six business days for arrival. Because the package was traveling from Wisconsin to Buffalo, New York, that apparently was not enough time.

We understand how disappointed you were at not having the gorilla costume for your Halloween party. Although we cannot repay the costs of the party, we will be happy to allow you to return the costume for a full refund of $139.99. Be sure it is returned in its original packaging. In addition, we enclose a $20 coupon toward the purchase of your next costume from BuyCostumes.

We are dedicated to providing the best possible service to our customers. If you need a costume by a specific date, please call our Customer Care Department (800-123-4567) to see if it's possible for us to deliver it in time. We invite you to visit our online catalog at <buycostumes.com> to see the exciting new costumes we are receiving daily.

Although BuyCostumes is the world's largest online costume and accessories retailer, we value personal relationships with customers like you, and we look forward to serving you again for all your costume needs.

Sincerely,

Your Name
Customer Care Representative

Enclosure

PERSUASIVE REQUEST: HARD ROCK CAFE
Video Library 2
Chapter 10

Summary of Video
Hard Rock Café has undergone much change in surviving over 30 years in the rough-and-tumble world of hospitality. Hard Rock International now has over 120 locations in 43 countries. To remain successful and overcome strong competition in the theme dining arena, Hard Rock must continue to evolve. Maintaining the prominence of its well-known logo around the world is one of many strategies it employs to distinguish its brand.

What to Look For
As they watch the video, students should be encouraged to look for

- References to the changes taking place at Hard Rock International
- Discussion of "brand control" and the problem of different logos

Student Task
As an assistant in the Hard Rock Corporate Identity Division, you have been asked to draft a persuasive message to be sent to the Edinburgh International Comedy Festival. In doing research, you learned that this festival is one of the three largest comedy festivals in the world, alongside Melbourne Madness Festival and Montreal's Just for Laughs Festival. An annual event, the Edinburgh International Comedy Festival takes over this Scotland city each autumn with stand-up comedy, cabaret, theater, street performance, film, television, radio, and visual arts programs. Some of the programs raise funds for charity.

The problem is that the festival is staging some of its events at the Hard Rock Cafe, and the festival is using outdated Hard Rock logos at their Web site and in print announcements. Your task is to persuade the Edinburgh International Comedy Festival organizers to stop using the old logos. Explain why it is necessary to use the official Hard Rock logo. Make it easy for them to obtain the official logo at <http://www.hardrock.net.official.logo>. Organizers must also sign the logo usage agreement. Organizers may be resistant because they have invested in announcements and Web designs with the old logo. If they don't comply by June 1, Hard Rock attorneys may begin legal actions. However, you need to present this date without making it sound like a threat. Your boss wants this message to develop goodwill, not motivate antagonism.

Write a persuasive e-mail message to Edinburgh International Comedy Festival organizer Barry Cook at <bcook@edinburghfestival.com>. Add any reasonable details.

Discussion Guide
Help students understand how to approach this writing problem by posing the following questions:

- **Why is it important for Hard Rock International to insist on one official logo? Why shouldn't event organizers be able to customize the logo to reflect the colors and lettering in their event announcements?**
  Establishing an official logo reinforces the brand identity for Hard Rock. Using different logos dilutes the recognition value of a brand. Hard Rock has developed one of the most recognized brands in the world. Maintaining its recognition value is very important in advancing the success of Hard Rock products, including cafes, casinos, and products.

- **Why is it a good idea to make this message a friendly persuasive request instead of a legalistic demand to achieve compliance?**
  The Edinburgh International Comedy Festival organizers probably have no idea that they are not using the official Hard Rock logo. After all, Hard Rock is merely providing a venue for a comedy charity event. The festival organizers may need only a gentle prod in the right direction, along with help in securing the official logo. Hard Rock prefers to secure compliance with goodwill rather than with clout.

- **What are the four components of a persuasive message?**
  (1) Gain attention, (2) build interest, (3) reduce resistance, and (4) motivate action.

- **What information can you use to complete each component of this persuasive request?**
  You might gain attention by complimenting the organizers on producing an exciting comedy program. You could then acknowledge that the Edinburgh International Comedy Festival is using a Hard Rock Cafe as one of its venues for its autumn festival. Build interest by explaining the importance of using the official Hard Rock logo, which is one of the world's most recognizable logos. Using the official logo would help viewers associate this well-known logo with their event. Reduce resistance by making it easy to download the official logo. Motivate action by summarizing the request. Use the end date of June 1 but don't make it sound like a threat. Conclude by repeating the main reader benefit.

Proposed Solution

TO: bcook@edinburghfestival.com
FROM: your_name@hardrock.identity.net
SUBJECT: Using the Official Hard Rock Logo

Mr. Cook,

Congratulations on offering exciting comedy programs at your annual Edinburgh International Comedy Festival.

Because some of your programs are offered at the Hard Rock Cafe, you will want to be using our official logo to identify this location. The Hard Rock logo is one of the most recognized logos in the world. You can build interest in your comedy offerings and associate your program with the high-energy Hard Rock Cafe by using our official logo instead of the out-of-date logos now appearing at your Web site and on printed announcements of your programs.

You may download the official Hard Rock logo at < http://www.hardrock.net.official.logo>. At that site you should also sign the logo usage agreement. Changing your images to the official logo is easy to do by inserting our electronic digital image into your Web pages or print masters.

Please change to the official Hard Rock logo before June 1, when Hard Rock will cease authorization of the use of old logos. It's easy to switch to the new logo and take advantage of the instant brand recognition that comes from it.

Your Name
Hard Rock Corporate Brand Identity

INNOVATION, LEARNING, AND COMMUNICATION: A STUDY OF YAHOO
Video Library 2
Chapter 10

Summary of Video
This film presents a quick look at a popular Internet company and how it solves some of its challenges. Yahoo is described as the Internet's most popular navigational service. Established in the early 1990s, it has become a comprehensive Internet portal offering many services in addition to its search tool function. The film features the young founders, David Filo and Jerry Wang, as well as other executives. One critical thinking question is presented: "How can a high tech company like Yahoo continuously innovate to achieve success in a highly competitive environment?" The film then answers the question by explaining that Yahoo has become a "learning" organization. It encourages employees to experiment, act independently, and solve problems. Its strategy includes rapid response to competition, creation of new services, and constant monitoring of Internet content.

How to Use the Video
Encourage students to view Yahoo as a place where they work. The film familiarizes them with some of Yahoo's managers and operating strategies. Instead of focusing on a macro approach to the company and its operating strategies, however, we want to take a micro approach and use this film as a context for a specific business communication problem: writing a request memo.

Student Task

After viewing the video describing the Internet company Yahoo, you are to assume the role of assistant to John Briggs, senior producer, who appeared in the video. John has just received a letter asking for permission from another film company to use Yahoo offices and personnel in an educational video, similar to the one you just saw.

John wants you to draft an e-mail message for him to send to the operations manager, Ceci Lang, asking for permission for VX Studios to film. VX says it needs about 15 hours of filming time and would like to interview four or five managers as well as founders David Filo and Jerry Yang. VX would need to set up its mobile studio van in the parking lot and would need permission to use advertising film clips. Although VX hopes to film in May, it is flexible about the date. John Briggs reminds you that Yahoo has participated in a number of films in the past two years, and some managers are complaining that they can't get their work done.

Write a persuasive memo or e-mail message to Ceci Lang, operations manager, asking her to allow VX Studios to film at Yahoo. Your request memo should probably emphasize the value of these projects in enhancing Yahoo's image among future users. Provide any other details you think are necessary to create a convincing request memo that will win authorization from Ceci Lang to schedule this filming.

Proposed Solution [Yahoo Memo]

To: Ceci Lang <clang@yahoo.com>
From: John Briggs <jbriggs@yahoo.com>
Date: Current
Subject: Scheduling of Educational Video
Cc:

Please authorize the filming of an educational video in the month of May. Although Yahoo has participated in a number of these filming sessions, we believe that these videos are well worth the effort because they strengthen our brand awareness among college students, an important market segment for us.

If we agree to participate in this project, VX will need to

- Shoot 15 hours of film here at Yahoo! headquarters in May.
- Interview four or five managers as well as David Filo and Jerry Yang.
- Set up its mobile studio van in our parking lot.
- Obtain permission to use selected film clips from our ad pieces.

Your authorization before March 20 will enable me to begin scheduling the interviews with the least disruption to our managers' working schedules. Thanks!

John

EFFECTIVE ON-THE-JOB ORAL PRESENTATIONS
Video Library 1
Chapter 14

Summary of Video

To learn more about applying Guffey's 3-x-3 writing process to the development of oral presentations, you see Ramon in the planning stages of his oral presentation to the board of directors for Integrity Investments. Ramon must persuade the directors that a paid time-off plan makes sense for Integrity employees. Ramon and Sarah brainstorm ideas in the prewriting stage of the writing process. Students see what is meant by anticipating the audience and focusing on a purpose. We see Ramon and Sarah go through all three phases of the process, including his successful presentation.

How to Use the Video

This video is especially instructive as an introduction to Chapter 14. It shows students how to implement the 3-x-3 writing process as they plan, research, and organize an oral presentation.

Discussion Guide

The following critical thinking questions appear on the screen at the end of the film:

- **How is the writing process useful in preparing an oral presentation?**
  The writing process provides a framework for developing a complete oral presentation. It guides the presenter in determining first the purpose of the presentation. It helps the presenter focus on profiling the audience and anticipating how the presentation can be adapted to that particular audience. The process leads the presenter through the organization, composition, and revision of the presentation.

- **What techniques can a speaker employ to overcome fear?**
  Presenters can overcome fear by preparing thoroughly and rehearsing repeatedly. They should breath deeply and try to convert their fear into enthusiasm for the topic. They can use positive self-talk to bolster themselves, and they can shift the spotlight from themselves to their visual aids. They should ignore stumbles, and feel proud when they finish.

- **Should every business presentation use PowerPoint? Why or why not?**
  PowerPoint can add pizzazz to a presentation, and its templates help some speakers organize their thoughts. Critics argue that it stifles creativity, forces thoughts into artificial overly simplistic bullet points, and reduces thoughtful expression. PowerPoint overshadows the speaker. However, PowerPoint has become the favorite tool of business presenters because it adds structure, sophistication, and efficiency to presentations. However, it should not be used for every presentation. Ask students to come up with some instances when PowerPoint would be a poor presentation medium.

THE JOB SEARCH
Video Library 1
Chapter 15

Summary of Video
At Clifton-Harding Associates (CHA), owner Ella Clifton realizes that she needs another employee to help run the business. She places a "blind" advertisement, to which her current employee, Stephanie, responds. Ella interviews a promising candidate, Yolanda, but during the process learns that Stephanie has lied on a résumé posted to a job site. In addition to the ethical dilemma, students see good and bad job-search and résumé techniques.

How to Use the Video
This film looks at the job search from two perspectives—the employer's view and the candidate's view. The film will be instructive when students are working on Chapter 15, "The Job Search, Résumés, and Cover Letters." Help students understand the fast-paced action by explaining that Ella is searching for a new employee and that Stephanie is hoping to land the new job and be promoted from her receptionist position. This office and these characters appeared in a previous video, "Intercultural Communication at Work."

Discussion Guide

- **What action should Rob and Ella take after learning that Stephanie lied on her résumé?** Student responses will vary. Some may want Stephanie to get a second chance. Others may state that she should be fired. Stress to students that distorting facts on a résumé is unethical and lying is illegal. Both can cause a person to get fired or destroy a career.

- **Yolanda prepared a functional résumé to deemphasize her limited work experience and promote her unique skills and potential for success in the new position. Which résumé format is best for you – the functional or the chronological? Why?**
Help students understand when to use a functional or chronological résumé. Functional résumés highlight skills and accomplishments and de-emphasize a negative employment history. Functional résumés are appropriate for recent graduates, candidates with gaps in their employment, who are entering a new field, or who have changed jobs frequently.

Chronological résumés are the most popular and list work history, starting with the most recent position. Recruiters favor the chronological format because such résumés quickly reveal a candidate's education and experience record. The chronological style works well for candidates who have experience in their field of employment and for those who show steady career growth.

- **Yolanda customized her résumé to best match the needs of the organization and the open position. She adjusted the career goal and placed emphasis on her foreign language skills to make her résumé stand out from the others. Describe the advantages of customizing a résumé instead of sending the same one to all potential employers.**

Customized résumés place special emphasis on a candidate's qualifications that best match those required in the targeted position. Because competition for open positions may be fierce, a customized résumé distinguishes a candidate from all others.

SHARPENING YOUR INTERVIEW SKILLS
Video Library 1
Chapter 16

Summary of Video
In this video you see the job search and employment interview of a recent college graduate, Betsy Chan. We follow Betsy as she finds a job advertisement and prepares for a job interview. The strength of this video lies in the interchange between the company interviewer and a typical applicant. It provides viewers with an inside look at how an actual interview takes place. It also gives viewers a chance to see how the interviewer and interviewee critique Betsy's interview.

How to Use the Video
This video was made to correlate with Chapter 16 in Guffey's *Business Communication: Process and Product*. It provides a perfect introduction to or review of the chapter.

Discussion Guide
The following critical thinking questions appear on the screen at the end of the film:

- **What did Betsy do well in her interview?**
  Betsy was enthusiastic and showed good nonverbal cues, such as smiling, nodding, and leaning forward. She was dressed appropriately and used good English in responding to questions. She seemed prepared to sell her strengths. She answered the "sell this pen" question very well. She demonstrated that she could "think on her feet."

- **What could she have improved?**
  Although we saw only parts of the interview, we didn't see much evidence that she had researched the company and was aware that it was a financial services (investment) company. She had occasional "Ummms" and "you knows" in her speech. At the end of the interview, she should have summed up her strengths and nailed down what would happen next.

- **How can a candidate prepare for an interview?**
  Job candidates should learn about the position, plan to sell themselves, prepare answers to possible questions, and be ready with success stories. They should research the organization so that they know about its field, service, or product. Candidates should study the organization's annual reports, catalogs, Web site, and possible brochures.

- **How can a candidate prepare for and respond to behavioral/situational questions?**
  Because behavioral questions are increasingly common in employment interviews, candidates should know how to answer them. Behavioral questions usually begin with "Tell me about a time when . . ."An easy response method involves the STAR plan. Describe a **S**ituation or **T**ask, tell what **A**ction you took, and explain the **R**esults. The best-prepared candidates will practice a STAR narrative for every bullet point on their résumés.

CLASSROOM COLLABORATION AND TEAMWORK

By Karen Sterkel Powell
and Mary Ellen Guffey

The widespread use of the team approach in business and industry includes teamwork in preparing written documents and oral presentations. Numerous studies reveal that businesses are increasingly dependent on teams to achieve their goals. Collaborative work is often necessary because rarely can one employee possess expertise in all areas of a business or industry. Thus, the knowledge of employees with specialized skills is required in preparing reports, memos, and presentations. Today's technology enhances collaborative efforts with hardware and software that assist teams in composing and revising documents.

Business communication instructors recognize the importance of providing their students with classroom experience in collaborative writing to prepare them for the demands of the workplace, as reflected in the research and publications on the topic.

The following sections describe the advantages and disadvantages of collaborative writing and present guidelines for implementing and managing collaboration in the business communication classroom.

COLLABORATION ADVANTAGES AND DISADVANTAGES

Collaborative writing projects result in advantages and disadvantages to the students and to you, the teacher.

Student Advantages. The advantages that students gain from teamwork projects include:

1. A better understanding of the course's concepts and their application in assignments. Group members have more knowledge and experience than an individual person and provide valuable feedback to each other during the writing process.
2. Efficiency in preparing assignments from sharing responsibilities.
3. The opportunity to earn higher grades.
4. The opportunity to learn to become a good team player by learning about group decision making and interpersonal skills. Learning to be an effective team player helps them perform successfully in class and in the workplace.
5. The development of a tolerance/appreciation of the opinions, personality types, and writing styles of others. This advantage is particularly important for students who will enter a work force that is highly diverse.

The disadvantages of collaborative writing for students include the following difficulties:

1. Handling conflicts that arise from different opinions, personalities, and approaches to the writing process, as well as writing styles.
2. Dealing with unequal member participation.
3. Managing time conflicts in scheduling group meetings.
4. Managing their own time and work load if the group project takes more time than an individual project. While group projects usually decrease the time spent on research and writing, they increase the editing, revising, and coordinating time. If a group does not work together well or if the writing skills are not fairly equal, some students will spend more time on the project than if they completed it on their own.
5. Earning a good grade at least equal to what they would earn on their own. Grades for a class are usually higher with collaborative writing; however, the grades of good students are sometimes negatively affected by group problems and the weak writing skills of other group members.

Instructor Advantages. The advantages that instructors gain from teamwork projects are as follows:

1. The opportunity to act as facilitator and coach for small groups, thus demonstrating to students how they will most likely be managed in the workplace. Students have an opportunity to observe your use of effective skills for managing groups.
2. The reduced grading time to accommodate increase in class enrollment.

The disadvantages are as follows:

1. Higher grades that may contribute to grade inflation.
2. Increased time demand for managing groups.

The advantages of collaborative writing for students and for you outweigh the disadvantages in the long run, as students are more prepared for writing and group experiences in the workplace. While you spend more time managing groups, this time is offset by reduced grading time. The grade-inflation concern can be minimized by using a combination of individual and group projects and by placing more weight for the course grade on individual projects.

The following sections provide suggestions for making collaborative writing valuable and enjoyable for students and for you.

COLLABORATIVE ASSIGNMENTS

The majority of business communication teachers use a formal analytical report or presentation for the collaborative assignment. However, cases involving letters, memos, and short reports can be used if class assignments do not include the formal report, or they can be used in conjunction with the formal report.

Short collaborative assignments might include writing:

1. A letter to a university committee or official about a problem the university has, such as parking, registration procedures, traffic congestion, and inadequate bike paths. Students should describe the problem and offer solutions.
2. A letter to a company inquiring about the company's policies on topics such as social responsibility and ethics.
3. A letter to a businessperson asking him/her to be a guest speaker for the class.
4. Abstracts of articles pertaining to communication topics, such as crisis communication, group communication, intercultural communication, nonverbal communication, and listening skills.
5. An informative report on a current communications or management issue.
6. An informative report about a student university organization, a student university committee, or a university office, such as financial aid, housing, student employment, or career services. This is a good way to acquaint lower-level students with the university's services and with opportunities for their involvement with organizations and committees.
7. A short analytical report that includes tables and graphs. To reduce research time, you can provide research sources or put them on reserve at the library. *Consumer Reports* provides product comparisons that could be used for this assignment.

Groups should select their topics with your approval. For lower-level classes with minimal business courses completed, the topics should be general, such as wellness programs, workforce diversity, sustainability, diversity, smoking in the workplace, or intercultural communication (see Activity 13.8 on page 453 in *BC:PP*, 7e, for an effective intercultural report assignment). For upper-level students, topics might include an analysis of a company and its environment, an investment analysis, a marketing plan for a new product, or an analysis of a computer information system for a company. You should check the proposed scope of the report to ensure that there is enough research and writing for a team project. Also, do not approve topics that have been difficult for previous students to research adequately.

Short collaborative assignments can be incorporated into the formal analytical report project. For example, students can prepare a proposal requesting permission to research the topic they have selected for the formal report. The proposal should explain why the topic is important to businesses, how they plan to gather the research, a preliminary outline, and a work plan showing tasks to be completed, along with a timetable for completion of the tasks, and who will complete the tasks.

Another short assignment with the formal report project could be a progress report detailing tasks completed, work in progress, problems encountered, and projected task completion dates. Incorporating a "problem encountered" section alerts you to problems that may delay the report. It also provides an opportunity for you to offer suggestions that may help the group solve the problems. Asking the students to include a section on their group's progress toward becoming a cohesive group could also alert you to some group problems so that you can intervene if necessary. The report can be prepared by the group or by individuals.

GROUP FORMATION

Groups of three to five members work best for collaborative writing, depending on the length requirement and complexity of the project. Most teachers report that three is the best number. Time conflicts for group meetings increase as groups become larger, as does the potential for a reduced level of participation by some group members. An odd-numbered group eliminates a tie situation when the group must vote to resolve differences. Students can choose their groups or be assigned to them. If they choose, you should give them some guidance in their selection, such as:

- Get acquainted with classmates early in the semester so that they make an informed decision. They should learn about others' personalities, work styles, time availability, and interests. However, caution them to avoid people with personalities very similar to their own, as one of the benefits of group work is the variety in personalities and work styles that others bring to the group.
- Discourage selecting good friends as group members, as they may avoid healthy conflict in order to maintain the friendship.

Allowing some time at the beginning of classes for this interaction will help students get to know class members and identify potential group members.

You can also assign students to groups. The assignment can be random or by some criterion, such as their major or concentration. If the class is an upper-level class, grouping by concentration allows the groups to select a topic pertinent to their concentration and to cover the topic in depth. Regardless of the method of assignment, some consideration should be given to the group composition in terms of gender and ethnic diversity. In addition, allowing groups to make some adjustments in their composition may be helpful if, for example, a group finds it has no common free time for group meetings. However, leaving some class time open for group meetings helps to alleviate some of these time problems.

Assigning students to a group can cause stress for the students and require more time for a group to become cohesive. Also, if the group experience and project turn out poorly, students may attribute that failure to you. Allowing the class to vote on whether they want to choose their group or be assigned may eliminate this situation.

After groups are formed, they should choose a leader or a chairperson. You should give the leaders a list of tasks they are expected to perform.

GROUP PREPARATION ACTIVITIES

You can enhance the opportunity for students to experience a successful, rewarding collaborative writing project by thoroughly preparing students for the project. Providing instruction about team processes before the project begins can help students avoid some problems and handle those that do arise.

INSTRUCTION IN SMALL GROUP PROCESSES

Problems related to small group processes include such issues as poor conflict management, personality differences, leadership issues, poor meeting management, poor division of labor, and public speaking anxiety. Therefore, students will benefit from instruction in the following areas:

- Small group development: stages (forming, storming, norming, and performing); building cohesiveness. Suggest they do something fun together to speed up this process.
- Small group roles: maintenance and tasks roles; functional and nonfunctional roles.
- Small group decision making: brainstorming; consensus building. Use some group exercises in class to reinforce these concepts.
- Conflict management: benefits of healthy conflict; supportive versus defensive communication; problem ownership; constructive criticism; avoiding Groupthink.
- Personality styles: strengths and weaknesses of different styles; appreciating other styles; assigning tasks compatible with styles. Give students a personality test, such as the Myers-Briggs Type Indicator.
- Active listening skills: discuss conversational styles and specific listening techniques appropriate for small groups.
- Meeting management: use of unstructured meetings initially to brainstorm and more structured meetings as tasks become more defined.

INSTRUCTION IN THE WRITING PROCESS

Problems in collaborative writing that are related to the writing process include lack of knowledge about the range and sequence of activities involved, poor division of labor, poor definition of task, as well as different agendas, competencies, and learning styles. You can assist students in learning the writing process in the following ways:

- Provide a report case that informs them of the activities required for the report, a list of the sequence of activities, and the due dates for completing the activities.
- Require students to seek your approval of their topic, work plan, and preliminary outline so that you can determine if the group has a good definition of their tasks.
- Discuss methods for dividing the tasks. Students most often use the horizontal model for division of labor where each student researches, writes, and edits a chapter or section of the report. However, businesspeople often use the stratified model, whereby the tasks are divided according to members' abilities. Thus, one member does the research, one writes the rough draft, one edits, and another prepares the visual aids and keyboards the report.
- Allow groups to choose the model they want to use based on their knowledge, skills, personality strengths and weaknesses. If they choose the horizontal model, suggest that they have one member act as the final editor of all sections so that they are consistent in voice and style throughout the report.

If interviews are conducted or surveys used to gather research, instruct students on the design of interview and survey questions and require them to get your approval before using the questions.

ANALYTICAL REPORT GROUP ACTIVITIES

Because collaborative analytical reports vary considerably in content, length, and complexity, the following list of activities can serve as a guideline for planning the sequence of activities involved in the report-writing process. These activities should appear on the report case students receive, along with due dates.

1. *Preliminary approval of report topic.* This step can be done informally since the goal is to ensure that in general the topic is all right and that another group has not already selected the topic. Having students write you a brief note about their topic should be sufficient. Consider requiring students to attach three current articles on the topic so that you can evaluate the feasibility of the topic.
2. *Proposal due, addressing report topic, research methods, work plan, and preliminary outline.*
3. *Group conference with instructor.* This conference will enable you to ask questions about the proposal and comment on the work plan and preliminary plan.
4. *Surveys, interview questions, and accompanying letters due.* Remind students that you must approve these items before they start gathering their research.
5. *Progress report due with final outline.* This report can be prepared by the group or individually. If it is a group report, ask them to include names of members who are doing each of the tasks. Refer to the previous discussion on progress reports under "Collaborative assignments." Requiring a progress report encourages students to complete their tasks and offers you an opportunity to monitor members' performance.
6. *Introduction section of report and visual aids for discussion section of report.* Requiring these items before students write the discussion section helps to ensure that the group has a well-defined purpose and problem definition. In addition, requiring the tables and graphs at this time forces them to consider carefully which information should be written in text format and which should be in visual-aid format. Return these items with suggestions for revisions, if necessary.
7. *Revised draft of introduction and draft of discussion, conclusions, and recommendations.* Ask group members to write their names by the sections they researched and wrote. This enables you to evaluate the performance of group members and encourages timely completion of the research and writing tasks. You can make some general comments about the draft and return it, but avoid extensive feedback on content, writing style, writing mechanics, format, and so on. If you give them this kind of feedback, the quality of the report they submit is actually just a reflection of how well you edit their rough draft of the report. Also, if you do this type of editing, students may believe that they only have to revise according to your comments, and they may get upset if you miss something for which you deduct points on the final copy of the report. In other words, you take away accountability for the quality of the report from the students.

   If you see some sections of the rough draft that look very poor, copy them before returning the draft. This will provide some documentation to justify lowering a student's grade. You do not have to return the drafts; you may want to keep them as evidence of individual contributions to the report. Ask the student to make a copy of the rough draft, and tell them that you will keep the copy they give to you.

8. *Final copy of the report, along with leader's or chairperson's report and peer evaluations.*
9. *Oral presentation of the report; each group member should use at least one visual aid.* You can grade the presentation on a group or individual basis. Peer evaluations are also very helpful but do not need to be used to calculate the group or individual grade. Videotaping the presentations provides meaningful feedback to the students and can be helpful in justifying a grade if a student challenges it.

PERFORMANCE EVALUATION

Business communication instructors want to give students a grade that reflects their writing ability, their contributions to the group's writing process, and their contribution to the group processes during the collaborative project. While no method guarantees this, some methods of gathering information about individual performances and methods for assigning grades will minimize injustices and increase the students' satisfaction with the grade assignment process.

Assessing Individual Performance

Several methods of gathering information about individual work are used by communication teachers. At least two or three methods should be used from the following list:

1. *Confidential peer evaluations.* These evaluations are an incentive to individuals to perform according to the expectations of their fellow groups members. Peer evaluations should focus on behaviors of group members rather than their traits. See page 87 for a sample of a group project peer evaluation form.
2. *Leader's or chairperson's report.* This report should detail the tasks or responsibilities completed by each member and provide a record of meeting dates, times, and attendees. You may also request minutes of meetings with group members sharing the responsibility for submitting these to you periodically so that you can identify the nonperformers.
3. *Student logs or journals.* Ask students to keep a log or journal about the group's activities, the group's small-group processes, and their feelings about other members' behavior and contributions, as well as their own. These should be submitted periodically to determine whether your intervention is necessary with the entire group or with just one member. Logs and journals also can be used to support peer evaluations.
4. *Class attendance record.* Take attendance on class days when instruction is being given on group processes, writing processes, and the report project, as students who are absent miss valuable information that helps them contribute effectively to the group project. Also, if group meetings are held during a class period, they miss that interaction with the group, increasing the out-of-class time required for group meetings.

Assigning Group Grades

Using a combination of group and individual grades increases the likelihood that the grade a student receives is an accurate reflection of his/her writing ability and contribution to the group and the assignment. Thus, a student's grade should be based on the score assigned to the written report and one or more of the evaluation processes described previously. Using a combination of evaluations helps provide you with a defensible and objective basis for assigning grades.

Some suggestions for using the combined evaluations follow:

1. Score the written report and give each group member the same grade. In addition, give a separate grade for each student's contribution to the report and to the group process based on the four evaluations discussed previously. For example, the written report may be worth 100 points, and the other grade may be worth 50 points. You need to establish the criteria for assigning this grade so that you have consistency from one student to another and to inform the students of the criteria.
2. Score the written report and add or deduct 10 points for individual members according to the evaluation they receive on the four evaluation items discussed previously. Criteria need to be established for the 10 points.
3. Score the written report and deduct points (no limit) for individual members according to the evaluations they receive on the four evaluations discussed previously. You should have some guidelines for deducting the points so that there is consistency in the deductions. For example, each low rating on the peer evaluation is –5 points; each missed meeting is –3; each missed class period is –3, and so on.

To minimize having to adjust grades for nonperformers, encourage groups to confront these students early in the project and set some guidelines for what the group expects from them, along with deadlines for completing tasks. If they do not meet the expectations or deadlines, the groups should consult with you. Giving groups the option of firing nonperformers from the group, with your approval, is an incentive to nonperformers to do what is required of them to stay in the groups. If members are fired, they should receive an "F" for the project or be given the option to do the report on their own for a significant deduction, such as 50 percent.

Numerous ideas and options are available for incorporating collaborative writing into the business communication class. The articles in the reference list provide additional valuable information on successfully implementing collaborative writing into your class.

References

Dufrene, D. D. & Lehman, C. M. (2005). *Building High-Performance Teams*, 2e (Cincinnati: Thomson/South-Western).

Markulis, P., Jassawalla, A. R., and Sashittal, H. (2006, Jan/Feb). The impact of leadership modes on team dynamics and performance in undergraduate management classes. *Journal of Education for Business, 81*(3), 145-150.

Nesbitt, P. & Bagley-Woodward, E. (2006, June) Practical tips for working with global teams. *Intercom*, 25.

Schullery, N. M. & Gibson, M. K. (2001, June). "Working in Groups: Identification and Treatment of Students' Perceived Weaknesses," *Business Communication Quarterly*, *64*(2): 9-30.

Snyder, L. G. (2010). The use of pre-group instruction to improve student collaboration. *Journal of Applied Research for Business Instruction*, *8*: 1.

Vik, G. N. (2001, December). "Doing More to Teach Teamwork Than Telling Students to Sink or Swim," *Business Communication Quarterly*, *64*, 112.

CONFIDENTIAL GROUP PROJECT PEER EVALUATION

NAME ______________________________ GROUP # _______ SECTION # _________

Rate each person in your group (including yourself) on the criteria indicated using the following scale: Excellent 4, Above Average 3, Average 2, Poor 1.

	Student 1	Student 2	Student 3	Student 4
Quality of contribution				
Quantity of contribution				
Creativity				
Turntaking (allowing all members to actively participate)				
Leadership				
Effort (time spent on project)				
Attitude toward group (cooperation, dependability, willingness to help others)				
Logistics (clerical-type duties)				
Attendance at meetings				
Preparation for group meetings				
Willingness to accept and complete tasks				
Completion of tasks on time				
Overall rating				

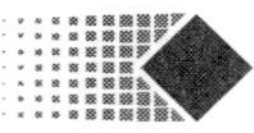

TEACHING BUSINESS ETIQUETTE

Many of today's students have little knowledge of what business etiquette involves and even less sense about how their manners affect their success on the job. To make it easier for instructors to teach their students the basic elements of business etiquette and workplace manners, we provide a relevant online teaching/learning module.

How to Use the Business Etiquette Teaching/Learning Module

Our module is made up of three parts: (a) a preview quiz at **www.meguffey.com**, (b) a 17-topic etiquette guide at the same place, and (c) three posttests in the instructor's section **http://www.meguffey.com**. Here are some suggestions about how instructors might use this module.

Preview Quiz. At the book companion Web site for students, we provide an interactive 17-point preview quiz made up of fairly challenging True-False questions regarding workplace situations that call for decisions involving etiquette. Answer checking is provided and each related etiquette topic is referenced; however, no explanations are given. Instructors may use this preview to whet the appetite of students and motivate them to read and study the related etiquette topics.

Etiquette Topics. After taking the preview quiz, students should read all 17 etiquette topics. They range from "Professional Image" to "Avoiding Social Blunders When Abroad." Instructors may want to discuss these topics in class and invite students to do further research on them. The posttests associated with the 17 topics divide them into three groups. Instructors may wish to give a posttest after each group has been studied or wait until all three groups have been covered before testing.

Posttests. Instructors may use the three posttests for assessment, motivation, and/or discussion. The posttests are not available at the Web site for students. We have limited the access to the posttests so that instructors will have greater control and flexibility in using them. Instructors teaching distance-learning classes may want to send the posttests to their students. Here are the topics covered in each posttest:

- Posttest 1 – Professional Image, Introductions, Networking, Workplace Manners, Coping with Cubicles, and Interacting With Superiors
- Posttest 2 – Manager's Manners, Business Meetings, Business Gifts, Business Cards, Dealing With Angry Customers, and Telephone Manners
- Posttest 3 – Cell Phones, E-Mail, Gender-Free Relations, Business Dining, and Etiquette Abroad

TEACHING FORMAL REPORTS

By Salvatore N. Safina
Lecturer, Department of English
University of Wisconsin-Milwaukee
in conjunction with Dr. Mary Ellen Guffey, Cengage/South-Western

In a meeting of business and technical communication instructors at the University of Wisconsin-Milwaukee, the following question was raised: "Do we need to teach the long report?" The question was tabled for further review. But my answer to the question is an unequivocal "yes." The formal report is, in my view, one of the most valuable learning experiences students of business communication come away from the course with. It helps students to hone their skills in managing a large project, researching, designing documents, and writing. That said, teaching the formal report from process to product is difficult; for instance, the process involves a considerable investment of time by instructors—both in and out of the classroom. Moreover, because most students have not had to undertake such a project, it can be frustrating—for both students and instructors. However, despite those drawbacks, I think the advantages for students far outweigh the disadvantages. In what follows, I will discuss, step by step, how I guide students through the formal report project.

Unlike many business communication instructors, I require each student to complete the formal report project individually. Additionally, students are allowed to choose from a list of topics (available at **www.meguffey.com**) divided into majors and/or areas of specialization; or, they may choose an analytical topic (yardstick, feasibility, justification/recommendation) from Chapters 11, 12, or 13 of *BC:PP*. If students do not wish to choose one of these topics, and decide they would like to develop one on their own, then they must first meet with me in person to discuss their proposed topic. My reason for choosing this route is based more on the realities of an urban commuter university than any theoretical position; however, I do believe that it gives all students a chance to learn from the process directly, even if the final product doesn't turn out as expected.

Preliminaries

I begin my discussion of the formal report project the very first day of class. I first point out to students that, because the project constitutes 25 percent of their final grade, they should begin thinking about it immediately. Then, I direct them to the three pages of the syllabus (on color-coded paper so they stand out) devoted to the following: (1) a set of detailed instructions for the project proposal assignment, which is students' first formal presentation of their chosen topic and preliminary research; (2) a set of detailed instructions for the formal report project itself, including the due date; and (3) a short list of possible topics from which to choose—in order for students to get a sense of the types of topics that are acceptable. (I also provide an electronic copy of the list and the syllabus on a course Web site) At this time I also inform students to check out one—or both—of the sample student reports on reserve at the university's library. Both reports were written by students who took my course in previous semesters, and both received an "A." These models give students a tangible example of what is expected of them and what students like them are capable of producing. After this, I encourage students to talk to me about their projects. I tell them how important communicating with me will be if their project is to be successful. And it's true. I can't stress enough how important it is to talk to students about this project. Face-to-face communication often alleviates potential problems in the future.

Before the first formal project related assignment (the proposal) is due, once or twice a week I will remind or ask students about their projects. At first, I'll make light of my reminders; as the semester draws on, though, I tend to make these reminders more serious. As I tell students: "Even if you spend 15 minutes to a half an hour a week doing preliminary research for this project, you will be in good shape when we begin the textbook coverage of formal reports." I find that it's very necessary to keep reminding students about the project, as they have other classes, papers, and projects to worry about.

Students generally begin making appointments to see me after the first four weeks of the semester. Others, however, need to be politely reminded. When students meet with me to present their topic ideas, I often ask a number of questions: "Why did you choose this topic?" or "Why is this topic meaningful or important to you?" or "How does this topic relate to your future career?" These are important questions because, believe it or not, even business-oriented students often have a tendency to choose topics that seem more geared toward research papers than formal reports. Or, they may look back on an English composition class and assume that, because it's an English course, the same kind of approach is expected. For whatever reason, these one-on-one sessions allow me to steer students in the right direction. I tell them, for instance, how important it is that they think of the report as being based upon a specific problem a business or organization is trying to solve. I explain that this is what business reports do: they solve problems or answer questions with a specific goal in mind.

Another common problem is objectivity. Often, students will have preconceived notions about how the report will pan out in the end. Or, in a case where a student has chosen to do a report on an on-the-job problem, often the student is clearly on one side of the issue and is emotionally invested. In these cases, I remind students that in most reports (at least, in my opinion, the most effective reports) writers should strive to be as objective and balanced as possible. They need to understand that their audience(s) will probably not look favorably on a report that, say, stresses only the benefits of a specific course of action.

In-Class Assignments and Discussion

Class discussion of the formal report project begins with students reading Chapter 11 of *BC:PP*. Two weeks are spent on this chapter alone because it helps to build a solid foundation for the rest of the report-writing process.

Project Proposal

The first formal report assignment students must complete is the project proposal, which allows students to demonstrate many of the skills learned in Chapter 11. This is a very detailed assignment, but it's an important one because it requires students to put their ideas on paper and begin thinking conscientiously about the project. In class, the first thing I do is "walk through" the assignment with the students. The proposal consists of two parts: an overview and preliminary research.

In the "Overview" section of the proposal, students are asked to explain the following:

1. Essential background information about the topic.
2. Purpose of the report, including an implicit—or explicit—problem question.
3. Audience(s) for the report (both primary and secondary).

In class, I tell students (and show them) that I will be asking the following questions about their report topics when I read the "Overview."

- Will the topic you've chosen be interesting or useful to you outside of the context of this course?
- Is the topic centered in a business or organizational context? Even if the topic is based on a "fictional" premise, could the report be generated in a "real life" business or organization?
- Will the topic ensure that there is going to be enough primary or secondary information or data to meet the report's page requirement?
- Will the topic require analysis?

In the "Preliminary Research" section of the proposal, students are asked to consider possible primary and secondary sources. For primary sources, students must locate two "experts" in their research areas. Then, they must record these experts' contact information and explain why each expert would be an appropriate source of information for their reports. Additionally, students are asked to consider two more ways of collecting primary data (other than interviews) and explain why these methods might contribute to their reports.

For secondary sources, students are asked to locate and present the following information using the MLA style: (1) a newspaper article, (2) two journal or magazine articles or abstracts, and (3) three Web sites, or Web-generated documents. Students are advised to use the databases available at the university's library, and they are also required to explain briefly how the sources they've found might contribute to their reports.

In discussing this part of the assignment, I show the students how to access the library's databases, and I do a practice search so they can see how to do it themselves.

While the benefits of this assignment are immense, students really struggle with it. Consequently, I allow enough time in class for students to ask questions about researching, presentation, etc. If all goes as planned, most students are able to use the overview information for the report's introduction (with some revision), and most use a good portion of their preliminary research materials.

On the day the assignment is due, I ask for volunteers to discuss their proposals. This discussion is probably one of the most fruitful of the semester for students. We take a "workshopping" approach to the discussion: I encourage students to ask questions about the report's purpose and audience; then, I ask students if they have any advice about research sources or how the report might be organized. As is often the case, many students will be doing similar reports, so this open forum is really a great chance for all of us to share ideas. In addition, I encourage students to use the course reflector I set up to solicit advice and share information. It's important, too, to thank student volunteers for sharing their ideas.

Work Plan

After I've returned their proposals to them, with advice about refining their topics, I then help students to prepare a work plan for the project. First, we look at sample work plans and discuss how they are organized and presented, and determine what their purposes are. Students almost always focus on the schedule; I in turn try to get them to focus on the purpose statement and the tentative outline. I tell them that these elements of the work plan, along with the sources and methods section, eventually will be a part of their reports. In other words, the more time spent on these things now will mean less time spent on these things when writing the report. Then, I have teams complete a case study or activity from Chapter 11 of *BC:PP* that requires them to complete a work plan. This is done so that students get practice before doing the "real thing." For comparison, I also provide them with a possible solution to the work plan on which they've been working. Having students complete the work plan also allows them, if necessary, to re-present their topics to me. It also gives me the opportunity to give them advice about organization, which, for many students, is a difficult aspect of composing the report.

Organization and Visual Aids

I try to combine these two difficult and time-consuming parts of the report project through a series of assignments taken from *BC:PP,* Chapters 11, 12, and 13. Consequently, each assignment not only requires students to evaluate, organize, and present data or information, but also to draw conclusions—and perhaps offer recommendations—based on an analysis of the audience and purpose. All of these assignments are completed in the computer lab. This is important—and necessary—so that I have the opportunity to help students create visual aids. After every assignment is completed, we discuss possible ways of presenting data or information, and discuss possible conclusions and/or recommendations. I also spend two weeks on this part of the process.

Because choosing visual aids is a stumbling block for many students, I also assign a variation of Activity 11.17 from *BC:PP*. Instead of having students choose four visual aids, for example, I ask them to choose three. In class, after I've discussed the various forms and functions of different visual aids, we then discuss this assignment itself. I first encourage students to take a "yardstick" approach to evaluating the visuals they will choose. Then, we discuss possible criteria for evaluating visual aids based on my previous discussion. By the time we've finished, students have usually come up with several criteria, so I ask them to use three or four in their assignment. This assignment is valuable because it helps students to become more aware about how visuals are used, and it also helps them to think about how their own reports will be put together.

Documentation

Experience has taught me that this is also an aspect of the report project that needs to be emphasized. Too often in the past I've seen examples of what could be considered plagiarism because I assumed students had learned proper documentation, citation, etc., in previous courses.

To rectify this problem, I spend most of an entire 50-minute class period explaining the finer points of documentation. Surprisingly, business students are generally interested in these details. In the computer lab, students are given random portions of articles from recent publications. Then, they are required to do the following:

- Present the publication information (MLA or APA style).
- Provide long, full-sentence, and partial phrase quotations from the source.
- Paraphrase a paragraph from the source.

After the assignment is completed, as a class, we look at possible correct and incorrect examples. It's imperative to show students an example of a paraphrased source that "crosses the line," and make it clear to them that this is plagiarism. I've found that spending this time in class is well worth the effort. I've had fewer and fewer problems with documentation since I began doing this.

Putting It All Together: Completing the Project

Although the syllabus contains detailed instructions for putting the report project together, I revisit it in class. I point out especially the submission requirements, and what must be included in the project packet. Of these, two are essential: (1) photocopies or originals of sources, and (2) a "dirty" rough draft of the report. I emphasize how important these items are for me to evaluate their projects fairly.

The final week of the course is spent "workshopping" drafts of the project. Aside from getting advice from their peers, I tell students that they must have specific questions in mind before coming to talk to me about their projects. Moreover, I extend my office hours the final week, encouraging students to come to me with questions about their reports. Because this is such a stressful time for them anyway, I go out of my way to be positive, patient, and understanding. I try to emphasize all of the hard work they've done already, and remind them about how much they have learned not only about researching, writing, and document design, but also about themselves. One week later, I get ready to read.

A list of possible report topics is available on the next pages and also at **www.meguffey.com.**

Lecture Notes

Part 4

Chapter 1 LECTURE NOTES AND TEACHING SUGGESTIONS

Effective and Ethical Communication at Work

CHAPTER SYNOPSIS

Today's workplace is undergoing significant changes including global competition, flattened management hierarchies, heightened ethical expectations, and the increased use of teams to accomplish organizational goals. In addition, new electronic technologies, flexible work environments, and a diverse workforce are creating dramatic changes in how and where we work. As the economy rebounds from its recent slump, job candidates and employees with excellent communication skills have the best chance of being hired and experiencing career advancement.

Communication, the transmission of information and meaning from one individual or group to another, has as its central objective the transmission of *meaning*. The process of communication is successful only when the receiver understands an idea as the sender intended it. Often, communication is impeded by barriers that distort the message. Students should recognize the types of barriers that interfere with communication and take steps to reduce them.

In this chapter, students will also learn how to compare and contrast internal and external functions of communication, formal and informal communication channels, and oral and written communication. This chapter concludes with a summary of the goals of ethical business communicators and provides practical guidelines for making ethical decisions and addressing wrongdoing in the workplace.

LEARNING OBJECTIVES

1. Understand the importance of communication skills in relation to career success, and explain the need for thinking critically and taking charge of your career.

2. Recognize significant trends in today's dynamic workplace and how these trends increase the need for excellent communication skills.

3. Analyze the process of communication and understand how to use it effectively.

4. Recognize barriers to interpersonal communication and examine specific strategies for overcoming those barriers.

5. Understand the internal and external functions of communication in organizations as well as compare and contrast the advantages and disadvantages of oral and written communication.

6. Examine critically the flow of communication in organizations and understand how to overcome typical barriers and respond ethically to office gossip.

7. Analyze ethics in the workplace, understand the goals of ethical business communicators, recognize and avoid ethical traps, and apply tools for doing the right thing.

WHAT'S NEW IN THIS CHAPTER

- Strengthened ethics coverage as suggested by reviewers in light of ethical lapses blamed by some for the recent economic downturn.
- Added more Ethics Checks, brief business scenarios with moral questions, so that students are better equipped to meet ethical dilemmas in the workplace.
- Presented new chapter-opening case study featuring PepsiCo's Indra Nooyi, one of the country's most powerful businesswomen and a role model to many.
- Related the importance of communication skills to finding a job in today's tight job market so that students recognize the value of this course and improving their business communication skills.
- Added new figures illustrating information flow in organizations, as well as examples of messages flowing downward and upward, so that students better understand the functions and flow of organizational communication.
- Introduced practical guidance in how to respond to workplace gossip.
- Updated as well as added new end-of-chapter activities that provide engaging opportunities to apply chapter concepts.

LECTURE OUTLINE

I. Communication Skills and You (p. 3)

Definition: *Communication skills* include reading, listening, nonverbal, speaking, and writing skills.

PowerPoint slides 1-3

A. The Importance of Communication Skills to Your Career Success

- Communication skills are critical to effective job placement, performance, career advancement, and organizational success.
- Employers often rank communication skills among the most requested competences.
- During times of economic recession when competition for jobs is intense, candidates with exceptional communication skills will set themselves apart from others with a unique competitive advantage.

B. Writing Skills Are More Important Than Ever

Writing skills are a necessary job skill:

- Technological advances enable us to transmit messages faster and to a greater number of people than ever before.

- Writing skills are necessary because many people work together from different physical locations, and they need to be able to communicate effectively together.
- Employees with excellent writing skills earn more than those with poor writing skills and have greater opportunities for advancement.

Lecture Tidbit

Kelly Guy, director of recruiting services for HumCap LP in Dallas stresses the importance of communication skills in the following statement: "If I have two engineers competing for the same job, the one with good communication skills will win out because they can do so much more." (Noble Sprayberry, "Tech skills + Communication Skills = More Pay," *The Cincinnati Enquirer*, August 6, 2006, p. J6.)

C. Communication Skills Must Be Learned

- Communication skills must be learned because we are not born with the abilities to read, listen, speak, and write effectively.
- This business communication textbook and course will help you develop the communication skills you need to thrive in a demanding work world.

Figure 1.1 How This Book and Course Can Help You Build Communication Skills

Let's Discuss

Why do you think writing has become so important to today's employees and employers?

Businesspeople today are doing more writing than ever before. E-mail, virtual teams, telecommuting, and participatory (collaborative) management all mean that more messages are being written.

II. Thriving as a Knowledge Worker in the Information Age (p. 5)

Definitions: *Knowledge workers* are individuals who get paid for their education and their ability to learn. *Information workers* describe those who work with information and technology. Knowledge and information workers deal with symbols: words, figures, and data.

PowerPoint slide 4

A. What Does This Mean for You?

- Knowledge and information workers can expect to be generating, processing, and exchanging information. These skills require employees to think critically, make decisions, and communicate those decisions.

B. Learning to Think Critically

- Thinking creatively and critically means having opinions that are backed by reasons and evidence and offering good ideas.

PowerPoint slide 5

C. Taking Charge of Your Career

- As an employee, you must be willing to continuously learn new skills that supplement the strong foundation of basic skills that you are acquiring in college. Training programs will help you learn new skills that will help you keep up with evolving technologies and procedures.

D. Finding a Job in Today's Tight Job Market

- Communication skills
- Strong work ethic
- Ability to work in a team
- Initiative

E. Using This Course to Advance Your Career

- This textbook and your instructor will help you develop superior communication skills that are so vital to your success as a businessperson. The resources available at http://www.meguffey.com will help you apply, reinforce, and perfect those skills.

III. Trends Affecting You in Today's Dynamic Workplace (p. 7)

- Heightened global competition
- Flattened management hierarchies
- Expanded team-based management
- Innovative communication technologies
- "Anytime, anywhere" and nonterritorial offices
- Increasingly diverse workforce
- Renewed emphasis on ethics

PowerPoint slides 6-8

Figure 1.2 Communication and Collaboration Technologies

Figure 1.3 Racial and Ethnic Makeup of U.S. Population, 1980 to 2020

Let's Discuss

Creating a diverse work environment makes good business sense. Why is it important to have diversity among senior levels of management?

Hiring managers recognize the importance of diversity among higher ranks of the organization. A management team made up of a diverse staff – including women and minorities -- helps companies attract and retain a diverse work force. Plus, it's important for minority and female employees to see role models whom they can go to for advice, counsel, and mentoring.

IV. Understanding the Process of Communication (p. 13)

Definitions:
Communication is the transmission of information and meaning from one individual or group to another.
The *sender* is the person with whom the message originates.
Encoding involves converting an idea into words or gestures that convey meaning.
Bypassing occurs when misunderstandings result from missed meanings.
A *channel* is the medium over which the message is physically transmitted.
Noise is anything that interrupts the transmission of a message in the communication process.
The *receiver* is the person for whom the message is intended.
Decoding means translating the message from its symbol form into meaning.

The process of communication:
- Sender has idea.
- Sender encodes idea in message.
- Message travels over channel.
- Receiver decodes message.
- Feedback travels to sender.

PowerPoint slides 9-11

Figure 1.4 The Communication Process

V. Overcoming Interpersonal Communication Barriers (p. 13)

A. Obstacles That Create Misunderstanding
- Bypassing
- Differing frames of reference
- Lack of language skill
- Distractions

PowerPoint slide 12

B. Overcoming Communication Obstacles
- Realize that communication is imperfect.
- Adapt the message to the receiver.
- Improve your language and listening skills.
- Question your preconceptions.
- Encourage feedback.

PowerPoint slide 13

VI. Communicating in Business Organizations (p. 175)

A. Understanding Internal and External Functions

- Internal communication includes exchanging ideas and messages with people inside the organization, including superiors, coworkers, and subordinates. E-mail is the most common form of written communication within an organization.
- External communication includes exchanging ideas and messages with those outside the organization, including customers, suppliers, the government, and the public. When you communicate externally, you may send letters on company stationery.

Figure 1.5 Functions of Business Communication

B. Shifting to Interactive, Mobile, and Instant Communication

- Technology is changing the way we communicate. Slower forms of communication, like memos and letters, are being replaced with interactive, fast-results communication, like e-mail, instant messaging, text messaging, smart phones, voice mail, cell phones, and wireless fidelity ("Wi-Fi").

Definitions:

Instant messaging is a type of communications service that allows you to create a private chat room to communicate in real time over the Internet.

Text messaging involves sending short text messages usually to a wireless device such as a cell phone or PDA.

C. Oral Communication

Advantages:
Can provide immediate feedback
Can be adjusted to audience
Can be delivered quickly
Provides nonverbal clues
Can generate warm feeling
Can produce forceful impact

Disadvantages:
Lacks permanent record
Expression may be careless or imprecise
May be inappropriate for formal or complex ideas
Does not promote easy recall

D. Written Communication

- Written communication includes most forms of business communication, including e-mail, announcements, memos, faxes, letters, newsletters, reports, proposals, manuals, presentations, and résumés.

Advantages:
Produces permanent record
Is convenient to distribute
May be economical
Promotes comprehension and recall
Allows precise and uniform expression
Gives audience flexibility in when and how to receive content

Disadvantages:
Leaves paper trail
Requires skill
Requires effort
Lacks verbal cues
Seems impersonal

PowerPoint slides 14-15

Figure 1.6 Comparing Oral and Written Forms of Organizational Communication

Let's Discuss
"If you are going to disagree with somebody, you certainly don't want to do it by email. You should never engage in a disagreement electronically," said Don Lents, chairman of Bryan Cave, an international law firm. "You want to do it face to face."

Do you agree or disagree with this statement?

Interpersonal communication is better than email when engaged in a disagreement because nonverbal cues conveyed by the sender's face and voice are unavailable with an email message. These nonverbal cues help the receiver decode the message accurately. Without nonverbal cues to support and reinforce the message, misunderstandings can easily escalate. E-mail saves time, but being there says more. [See Sharkey, J. (2010). Email Saves Time, but Being There Says More. *The New York Times*. Retrieved January 26, 2010 from http://www.nytimes.com]

VII. Improving the Flow of Information in Organizations (p. 19)

PowerPoint slide 16

A. Formal Channels

- **Downward Flow.** Formal channels of communication generally follow an organization's hierarchy of command. Information flowing downward moves from executives at the top of the organization through managers and onto lower-level employees. Downward communication includes policies, procedures, directives, job plans, mission goals, and motivation.

PowerPoint slide 17

- **Upward Flow.** Information flowing upward begins with nonmanagement employees and moves to management. This information, in the form of phone messages, e-mail, memos, reports, department meetings, and suggestion systems, guides managers in making decisions. Upward communication includes product feedback, customer data, progress reports, suggestions, problems, and requests for clarification.

  PowerPoint slide 18

- **Horizontal Flow.** Horizontal communication takes place among workers at the same level. This communication includes task coordination, problem solving, conflict resolution, idea generation, team building, and goals clarification.

  PowerPoint slide 19

- **Obstacles to the Flow of Organizational Information**
  Lack of trust, turf wars, fear of reprisal
  Uneven reward systems
  Closed communication climate
  Top-heavy organizational structure
  Filtering, prejudice, ego involvement
  Poor communication skills

Figure 1.7 Barriers Block the Flow of Communication in Organizations
Figure 1.8 Information Flow in Organizations
Figure 1.9 Policy Message From Management Flowing Downward
Figure 1.10 Information From Employee Flowing Upward to Management

PowerPoint slides 21-25

B. Informal Communication Channels

Definition: The *grapevine* is an informal channel of communication that carries organizationally relevant gossip.

- The grapevine can be a powerful, pervasive source of information, accounting for as much as two thirds of an employee's information.
- Studies demonstrate that the grapevine can be nearly 80 percent accurate, but it flows haphazardly.
- Follow these tips for handling gossip ethically:
  - Run, don't walk, away from anyone who starts to gossip.
  - End rumors about others.
  - Attack rumors about yourself.
  - Keep confidences.
  - Limit the personal tidbits you share about yourself; keep them light.
  - Avoid any form of coworker belittlement.
  - Build coworkers up; don't tear them down.

PowerPoint slides 20

VIII. Looking at Business and Ethics (p. 22)

A. What Is Ethics?

Definition: *Ethics* refers to conventional standards of right and wrong that prescribe what people should do.

PowerPoint slides 26-28

B. What Are Business Organizations Doing to Encourage an Ethical Culture?

- Adopting ethics programs
- Implementing ethics policies and procedures
- Establishing codes of ethics
- Appointing ethics compliance offers
- Instituting ethics training programs

C. What Are Schools Doing to Encourage an Ethical Culture?

- Revamping curricula to emphasize values reflecting the greater good and less on short-term profits
- Offering tools for responding to ethical dilemmas

D. Goals of Ethical Business Communicators

- Abide by the law.
- Tell the truth.
- Label opinions.
- Be objective.
- Communicate clearly.
- Use inclusive language.
- Give credit.

PowerPoint slides 29-30

F. Obstacles to Ethical Decision Making

- The false necessity trap
- The doctrine-of-relative-filth trap
- The rationalization trap
- The self-deception trap
- The ends-justify-the-means trap

B. Tools for Doing the Right Thing

- Is the action you are considering legal?
- How would you see the problem if you were on the opposite side?
- What are alternate solutions?
- Can you discuss the problem with someone whose advice you trust?

- How would you feel if your family, friends, employer, or coworkers learned of your action?

PowerPoint slides 31-34

Let's Discuss

What is the most ethical response to the following situation.

Assume that you have been hired as a telephone sales representative for a pharmaceutical sales company. You are expected to make 150 sales calls every day to doctor's offices across the U.S. to assess their interest for a new arthritis drug. Your newly hired colleague, who must also make 150 sales calls per day, secretly reveals to you that he dials the same number repeatedly so he can meet his daily goal. Your boss calls you into her office and asks your opinion on the performance of your new colleague. Do you share his secret?

Making ethical decisions can be challenging. Loyalty to both your boss and your colleague may create some confusion and uncertainty about how to respond to your boss's question. However, your goal is to be objective and tell the truth. Use the tools for doing the right thing on page 29 to help make an ethical decision.

Lecture Transparencies
(available in a separate packet and at http://www.meguffey.com)

Communicating in Today's Workplace Acetates	Transparency Number
Communication Skills and You; Thriving as a Knowledge Worker	1
Sharpening Your Skills for Critical Thinking, Problem Solving, and Decision Making; Trends Affecting You in Today's Workplace	2
The Communication Process—Basic Model	3
The Communication Process—Expanded Model	4
Obstacles That Create Misunderstanding; Behaviors That Overcome the Obstacles	5
Organizational Communication; Flow of Information	6
Obstacles to the Flow of Organizational Information; Responding to Gossip	7
Miscommunication in Product Evolvement	8
Message Distortion	9
Surmounting Obstacles to Effective Communication	10
What Is Ethical Behavior? Five Common Ethical Traps	11
Goals of Ethical Business Communicators, Tools for Doing the Right Thing	12

Solution Masters

		Page Number in This Book
1.11	Document for Analysis – Revision	491

Answers to Chapter Review Questions

1. **What does the expression *communication skills* include? (Obj. 1)**

   The expression communication skills includes reading, listening, nonverbal, speaking, and writing skills.

2. **In today's workplace can you expect to be exercising more or less control of your career? Why? (Obj. 1)**

   You can expect to exercise more control because you will probably be working for multiple employers. Jobs no longer guarantee lifetime employment or security.

3. **Who are knowledge workers? Why are they hired? (Obj. 1)**

   Knowledge workers are thinkers and planners who generate, process, and exchange information. They work with words, figures, and data. They are hired for their knowledge and ability to continue to learn.

4. **Fewer layers of management mean greater communication challenges for frontline workers. Why? (Obj. 2)**

   Frontline employees must participate in decision making, which requires skill in collecting, organizing, and disseminating information. Higher levels of communication skills are necessary.

5. **What technologies enable workers to have "anytime, anywhere" offices? (Obj. 2)**

   E-mail, instant and text messaging, file sharing, PDAs, fax, voice mail, smartphones, powerful laptop computers, satellite communication, wireless networks, and even Twitter have helped people conduct their business anywhere and anytime.

6. **What are the five steps in the communication process? (Obj. 3)**

   a. The sender has an idea.
   b. The sender encodes a message.
   c. The channel carries the message.
   d. The receiver decodes the message.
   e. Feedback returns to the sender.

7. **How can business communicators overcome some of the inevitable barriers in the communication process? (Obj. 4)**

   Communicators can overcome some barriers by (a) anticipating problems in encoding, transmitting, and decoding messages; (b) focusing on the receiver's viewpoint and frame of reference; and (c) asking questions that encourage feedback.

8. **What are the three main functions of organizational communication? (Obj. 5)**

   To inform, to persuade, and to promote goodwill

9. **Why is oral communication considered more effective than written communication? Why doesn't everyone use it exclusively? (Obj. 5)**

   Oral communication is considered more effective because it can provide immediate feedback, can be adjusted to the audience, can be delivered quickly, supplies nonverbal cues, may create a warm feeling, and is powerful. However, oral communication cannot always be used when individuals are separated. In addition, it does not provide a permanent record, may contain careless or imprecise expression, may be inappropriate for formal or complex ideas, and does not promote easy recall.

10. **Why is written communication important in business, and why doesn't everyone use it exclusively? (Obj. 5)**

    Written communication is important in business because it creates a permanent record, is convenient to distribute, may be economical, promotes comprehension and recall, allows precise and uniform expression, and gives audience members flexibility in when and how to receive the content. However, it cannot be used exclusively because it leaves a paper trail, requires skill and effort to produce, lacks verbal cues and warmth, cannot be modified based on audience feedback, and may seem impersonal.

11. **Compare formal and informal channels of communication within organizations. Which is more valuable to employees? (Obj. 6)**

    Formal channels of communication include such tools as e-mail, newsletters, official announcements, voice mail, and company videos. Informal channels of communication include the grapevine, which carries unofficial information. Employees would prefer to receive organization news through formal channels, which are more credible and reliable.

12. **Who is generally involved and what information is typically carried in downward, upward, and horizontal communication channels? (Obj. 6)**

    Downward communication usually moves from decision makers and managers to subordinates. It involves job plans, policies, and procedures. Upward communication usually flows from nonmanagement employees to management. It includes feedback, suggestions, product data, and customer information. Horizontal communication flows among workers at the same level. It includes messages that coordinate tasks, share information, solve problems, and resolve conflicts.

13. How can you control or respond ethically to office gossip? (Obj. 7)
Run away from anyone who starts to gossip.

a. End rumors about others.
b. Attack rumors about yourself.
c. Keep confidences. Be close-mouthed.
d. Limit the personal tidbits you share about yourself, and keep them on the light side.
e. Avoid any form of coworker belittlement.
f. Build coworkers up; don't tear them down.

14. What are seven goals of ethical business communicators? (Obj. 7)

a. Abide by the law.
b. Tell the truth.
c. Label opinions.
d. Be objective.
e. Communicate clearly.
f. Use inclusive language.
g. Give credit.

15. When you are faced with a difficult ethical decision, what questions should you ask yourself? (Obj. 7)

a. Is the action legal?
b. How would I see the problem if I were on the opposite side?
c. What are alternate solutions?
d. Can I discuss the problem with someone whose advice I trust?
e. How would I feel if my family, friends, employer, or coworkers learned of my action?

Answers to Critical Thinking Questions

1. Communication skills are frequently listed among the desired qualifications for job candidates. What do these skills consist of? How would you rate your skills? (Obj. 1)

Job listings frequently require excellent speaking and writing skills. However, communication skills also include nonverbal, listening, and reading skills. Student answers will vary regarding the rating of personal skills.

2. Recall a time when you experienced a problem as a result of poor communication. What were the causes of and possible remedies for the problem? (Objs. 3, 4)

Students' answers will vary but should include some of the following concepts:

- Incorrect/misleading word choice caused receiver to bypass intended meaning.
- Verbal message and nonverbal message did not agree.
- Hearing the message and listening to the message are entirely different.
- Too much noise or other distractions were present.
- Concentrating on evaluating the message rather than concentrating on the meaning of the message being communicated.

3. **Critics complain that e-mail is reducing the amount of face-to-face communication at work and this is bad for business. Do you agree or disagree? (Objs. 3–5)**

First, one must decide whether the assertion that e-mail is replacing face-to-face communication is a fact or an opinion. It might be difficult to prove that e-mail is indeed replacing face-to-face communication. Regardless, it is a fact that e-mail is rapidly becoming a prime communication channel. E-mail has many advantages including speed, ease, economy, and convenience. Yet, it has many disadvantages as well. It can be used casually, resulting in unprofessional messages. It produces permanent messages that can come back to haunt the sender. It contributes to information overload and productivity meltdown. It can carry viruses in attachments, and it is not private or secure. Moreover, it is difficult to be persuasive or to resolve conflict in an e-mail message. Angry tones, terse words, brusque manners, and even humor can all be incorrectly perceived by readers of e-mail messages. Face-to-face conversations help individuals reach consensus and avoid misunderstandings. Successful business communicators must work for the right balance in choosing communication channels.

4. **How are the rules of ethical behavior that govern businesses different from those that govern your personal behavior? (Obj. 7)**

This might be a tricky question because it suggests that a difference should exist between business ethics and personal ethics. In reality, no differences should exist. If students go astray in discussing this question, gently guide them to the following view.

Although any specialized activity or practice—whether business, sports, or entertainment—has its own distinctive rules and procedures, those rules and procedures should not violate one's personal moral principles. The ethics code that governs you and your family should not be at odds with the code that guides your behavior with customers, management, and competitors. Deceiving your family or lying to your friends should be no different from deceiving management or lying to customers.

It's been said by some that "businesses just don't have the same moral obligations as people do." It might be wise to point out to students that businesses cannot be divorced from the people who run them.

Businesses today are very concerned about hiring honest people. That's why many are using ethical dilemmas and critical incidents in interviewing techniques.

5. **Ethical Issue: Josh in the Accounting Department tells you that he heard from a reliable source that 15 percent of the staff will be released within 120 days. You would love to share this juicy news with other department members, for their own defense and planning. Should you? Why or why not?**

   It would be unwise to spread this rumor. The source is not reliable. In addition, if the organization had wanted employees to know, it would have made the announcement itself. Moreover, if the rumor is false, it will have needlessly upset other employees. Let the company take care of making announcements of this sort.

Activities

1.1 Online Communication Skills Assessment: How Do You Rate? (Objs. 1–3)

Encourage students to go to http://www.meguffey.com (click on Quizzes) and evaluate their communication skills using the interactive quiz. Reassure students that no matter what their scores, they can still succeed in your course. Encourage them to recognize their shortcomings in order to improve. After having them choose the traits they intend to work on immediately, encourage them to begin an action plan and record their progress in a journal detailing daily what they have done to improve their communication skills.

1.2 Collaborating on the Opening Case Study (Objs. 1–5)

This activity takes place over the entire semester. Student teams have a choice of one of the 16 three-part case studies in the textbook. Each team would fully research the company in the case study using outside resources, answer the questions presented, and prepare and deliver a group presentation about the company. This excellent long-term project would help students develop teamwork, research, writing, and presentation skills.

1.3 Getting to Know You (Objs. 1, 2)

This e-mail or memo is an excellent way to assess students' skills and, at the same time, get to know them. Don't grade this assignment, but be sure to write a friendly comment on all papers or in all e-mail replies to demonstrate that you have an interest in them as students and as individuals.

1.4 Small-Group Presentation: Getting to Know Each Other (Objs. 1, 2)

Decide whether you wish your class to (a) interview a group member and introduce that person to the group or (b) have each class member introduce himself or herself to the entire class. Class size may help you decide. Encourage students to consider this a casual introduction. However, it is a good opportunity for students to not only learn about each other but also start to develop speaking skills in front of a group.

1.5 Communication Skills: What Do Employers Want? (Obj. 1)

You could have students work in groups (possibly divide them by majors) to complete this activity. Provide poster board and a glue stick for each group to mount their ads. Then have a spokesperson from each group come to the front of the classroom to discuss their findings.

1.6 Language Skills: Who Me? I Won't Need to Write on the Job (Obj. 1)

a. Everyone writes in today's workplace—and probably more than ever in the past. In professional workplaces, e-mail has become the most important communication channel. Texting is less important. Regardless, all messages sent in the workplace must be businesslike and effective. This means they should be clear, concise, courteous, complete, and correct. They are indeed "real" writing and will require more skill and preparation than e-mail and texting to friends. What's more, as companies grow larger and become less cohesive, the written word becomes even more important. Because fewer people are working side by side, written messages replace face-to-face conversation. Those who can craft clear messages will be most successful.

b. Estimates suggest that nearly 90 percent of all business messages involve written communication. Conducting business in any field—even in technical and specialized areas such as information technology, accounting, engineering, marketing, hotel management, and so forth—involves some writing. "You can have the greatest technical skills in the world, but without solid communication skills, who will know and can understand?" said Kevin Jetton, executive vice president of the Association of Information Technology Professionals. [Jacobs, P. (1998, July 6). Strong writing skills essential for success. *InfoWorld*, 86.] Moreover, when individuals are promoted, their writing tasks will increase.

c. In the current work world of tightened budgets and economic downturn, only a few upper-level executives still have secretaries or administrative assistants who type their messages. Most managers and executives now write their own e-mails, memos, and letters.

d. Some companies employ technical writers to prepare manuals, documentation, and public documents, such as annual reports. Rarely, however, do these specialists write everyday messages (internal reports, letters, e-mails, memos) for employees.

e. Today's style, grammar, and spell checkers are wonderful aids to business writers. They can highlight selected trouble areas and occasionally suggest revisions. What they can't do, though, is organize and write the document and ensure its total accuracy. These tools are also not capable of catching all errors, especially commonly confused words and punctuation.

f. Books and computer programs can provide dozens of ready-made letters or pattern paragraphs for which businesspeople merely fill in the blanks. When these letters are appropriate and well written, they can be useful time-savers. Often, however, such letters are poorly written and ill suited for specific situations. Most messages demand that writers create their own original thoughts.

1.7 Customer Service: Tech Skills Not Enough (Obj. 1–3)

Service reps at any company must be totally familiar with its products and typical problems. On the telephone, service reps must exhibit good listening and speaking skills. In writing responses, they need to be able to spell and write clearly and concisely. Writing well requires training and practice. A trainer should consider adding writing skills to the training classes. A trainer might also include scenarios of typical chat sessions and demonstrate poor and good written responses.

1.8 Communication Process: Avoiding Misunderstandings (Objs. 3, 4)

a. Bypassing and poor language skills. The tournament committee member and Mr. Brooks attached different meanings to the expression "not concerned." One person thought that the expression expressed a negative reaction and actually a refusal. Mr. Brooks, however, thought "not concerned" meant that he would not receive any objection to the sale of his T-shirts. Perhaps the Louisiana communicator was trying to spare Mr. Brooks' feelings and his word choice was a form of politeness. However, more precise word choice would have avoided the resulting miscommunication.

b. Bypassing and frame of reference. The editor asked the staff to change the picture. He intended one meaning for the word, but the staff had a different meaning. Imprecise words often lead to bypassing and misunderstanding.

c. Bypassing. Tyson's interpretation of the word help differed from that of Alicia, resulting in miscommunication and resentment.

d. Lack of language skills. Does the sender mean the original price was 5 cents and now the price is increasing to 8 cents per copy? Or does the sender mean that the cost of each page will be raised 5 to 8 cents? If the latter is meant, which pages will cost 5 cents and which ones will cost 8 cents?

e. Bypassing and poor word choice. The pilot did not understand pull up, but he probably would have responded to the official term, climb. Perhaps the air flight controller suddenly realized the danger, and he blurted out the first thing that came to his mind.

f. Lack of language skills and frame of reference. These sentences appear to be word-for-word translations. Such translations are seldom accurate because every language has its own idiosyncratic rules for sequencing ideas. Moreover, synonyms are seldom equivalent.

g. Lack of language skills and frame of reference. The writing of these individuals shows poor sentence structure and poor word choice. Displaying such faulty skills in job application letters is humorous to readers but disastrous to job applicants.

Instructors please note: Nearly all of the preceding examples of miscommunication are a result of imprecise vocabulary and hurried communication. When people take the time to use precise words and exercise care in the communication process, much less confusion results.

1.9 Miscommunication in Organizations: Understanding the Boss (Objs. 3–6)

A number of factors contributed to this miscommunication. The message was delivered orally and at a busy reception when neither sender nor receiver was probably prepared for a serious personnel discussion. The CEO was unclear in his word choice, and apparently he and the vice president had differing perceptions. The CEO knew more about the sales rep than the vice president did, but the vice president was afraid to reveal his lack of knowledge. Fear, distractions, and perhaps ego involvement prevented clear communication. The vice president was remiss in not asking for clarification, and the CEO was remiss in failing to speak clearly and in not making sure his listener understood what he meant. Asking for feedback would have prevented the misunderstanding.

1.10 Differing Frames of Reference: E-Mail Cross-Cultural Misunderstanding (Obj. 4)

As business transactions become increasingly global, communicators must be alert to different cultures and the different frames of reference that affect all acts of communication. Savvy businesspeople recognize that people from different cultures will not think and act exactly as they do. Americans, Indians, and those in similar cultures have different ideas about what constitutes proper e-mail etiquette. Perhaps this misunderstanding could have been averted by including a request for feedback such as, "Please let us know that you have received this message and be so kind as to tell us when you will respond." Learning about other cultures and how to interact will become increasingly important to the success of American businesspeople and those from other countries. Students will learn more other cultures in Chapter 3 of this textbook.

1.11 Document for Analysis: Barriers to Communication (Objs. 3–5)

The memo written by the exasperated manager is less effective than it could have been because it uses a punitive, threatening tone. Its negative tone suggests a parent scolding a child. Instead of using a belligerent, disciplinarian tone, the writer would probably get better results if she tried to be more positive and encourage cooperation by focusing on how the receivers will benefit from cleaning the office. The memo also suffers from faulty grammar and poor organization. The tasks should be presented in a bulleted list so that they are easier to read and implement. The writer's lack of language skill and her lack of perception of the frame of reference in her receivers are barriers to communication in this message. The emphasis is on discussion of this memo. Students are not quite ready to write a revision, but you could show the following revision and use it to demonstrate what students will be learning to do themselves.

DATE: Current

TO: All Employees

FROM: Albertina Sindaha, Operations Manager

SUBJECT: IMPROVING OUR CLEANING ROUTINES

Because of custodial cutbacks, it is necessary for all of us to pitch in to clean up the department before leaving on Friday afternoons. This new procedure was to have started last Friday, but our first effort was not as successful as we had hoped.

Although some individuals cleaned their own areas, few departmental employees helped clean common areas. Once you have cleaned your own area, please help in the following tasks:

- Clean the copy machine area, including emptying waste baskets and organizing paper and toner supplies.
- Clean the office lunch room, including wiping the counters, cleaning the sinks, removing all food from the refrigerator, and cleaning the coffee machine.
- Straighten office supply shelves.
- If we can complete these tasks on Friday, we can return to a clean office on Monday. Please cooperate in this cleanup so that individuals do not have to be assigned to a specific cleaning schedule.

Note: All Documents for Analysis are prepared as transparency masters in the Solutions section of this manual.

1.12 Oral or Written Communication: Which Channel Is Better? (Obj. 5)

How should the following messages be communicated—orally or in writing? Explain the advantages and disadvantages of each.

a. At the request of the marketing manager, Roxanne has collected information about scheduling a promotional meeting for prospective customers at a hotel. How should she deliver her findings?

   Information flowing upward as feedback from employees should be in writing. The advantages include creating a permanent record, convenience in distribution, clarity of content, and ease of use by the receiver. The disadvantage is that a written message requires care in creation, is not delivered immediately, and may seem impersonal. The message would flow upward.

b. Richard, the information technology vice president, must tell employees about a new company blogging policy. He has two employees in mind who especially need this information.

Policies flowing downward from management to subordinates should be written. They produce a permanent record, are economical, promote comprehension and recall, allow precise and uniform expression, and give the audience flexibility in when and how to receive the content. Although he has two employees in mind, the policy should be directed to all employees.

c. As soon as possible, you need to learn from Carolyn in Document Imaging whether she can make copies of engineering blueprints. If not, you need her advice on how to do it.

When an immediate answer is required, the message should be delivered orally. In this instance, you may need to follow up with additional questions. Oral communication provides immediate feedback, can be adjusted to the audience, can be delivered quickly, supplies nonverbal cues, may create a warm feeling, and can be forceful. The message is traveling horizontally between coworkers.

d. As a manager in human resources, you must terminate three employees in a companywide initiative to reduce costs.

Messages as traumatic as termination should always be delivered in person. Oral communication provides immediate feedback, can be adjusted to the audience, supplies nonverbal cues, and shows greater compassion than a written message.

e. It wasn't your fault, but a check printing order for a long-time customer was mishandled. The checks are not ready, and the customer is mad.

Responding to an upset customer should always be done orally, if possible. The best procedure is to first call the customer and explain what happened. Oral communication allows you to show sympathy, express apologies, and suggest possible alternate solutions. Following the telephone call, it's wise to follow up with a written message confirming what was said orally. The written message clarifies the situation, creates a permanent record, and promotes comprehension and recall.

f. As chairman of the employee benefits committee, you have worked with your committee for several weeks evaluating several health plan options. You are now ready to convey the recommendations of the committee to management.

Explaining a committee's findings should be done in a written report traveling upward. Such a report provides a permanent record and is convenient to distribute. It provides precise and uniform expression. However, such a report lacks the immediacy of oral communication and cannot be adjusted to respond to the receiver's comments or questions.

1.13 Information Flow: What's Good and Bad About Gossip at Work? (Obj. 6)

Mr. Bender responded in an appropriate manner by going to the source and talking about the reason behind the gossip. Experts suggest seeking the source of malicious gossip and documenting what was learned or discussed.

Benefits of workplace gossip might include the following:

a. Managers can keep a pulse on what is happening by relying on information from employees who are known for spreading and knowing office gossip.
b. Managers can learn about morale, turnover, and productivity problems.
c. Managers can also plant news that they want spread. For example, if layoffs are approaching, managers might soften the blow by letting rumors start about future layoffs.
d. Gossip can also be helpful in building office friendships and building teamwork morale.
e. Gossip can benefit new employees who are learning office customs not covered in the official company handbook.

Negative consequences of gossip might include the following:

a. People who gossip are considered untrustworthy and may not be promoted.
b. Malicious, false gossip can create severe unhappiness and destroy careers.
c. Malicious gossip creates an ugly work environment forcing people to leave.
d. People who spend excessive amounts of time gossiping are a productivity drain on the company.
e. Companies that do not prevent malicious gossip may be sued for tolerating or condoning a hostile work environment.

1.14 Workplace Ethics: Where Do You Stand? (Obj. 7)

The Wall Street Journal Workplace Ethics Quiz provides an excellent starting point for a discussion about ethics in the workplace. The discussion can take place with the whole class or in small groups. What is interesting about this quiz is that it deals with issues that many of us face regularly in the workplace. You will find the results of The Wall Street Journal Workplace Ethics Quiz at the end of Chapter 1 in the textbook.

1.15 Ethical Dilemmas: Applying Tools for Doing the Right Thing (Obj. 7)

Students' responses will vary, of course. They should apply each question from the Tools list and
explain their answers in relation to the dilemma.

1.16 Ethics: Rival Chicken Chains Tempt Ethics in Taste Test (Obj. 7)

Students are faced with an ethical dilemma. Should they do what they think is right for the company and bolster its position by calling the El Pollo hot line with their praise of KFC chicken? Although it's not illegal, is it ethical, when they know that the hot line is intended for people who are not affiliated with a rival chicken fast-food restaurant? After hearing students discuss the case, you may wish to advise them that apparently some KFC employees did call the hot line. El Pollo Loco says that its caller ID showed some calls came from KFC headquarters in Louisville, Kentucky. In responding to El Polo allegations about the calls, KFC said, "We've been grilling our employees to see if anyone's done any undercover dialing. . . [but] it hasn't been a high priority." [Based on Jargon, J. (2009, May 9). Rival chicken chain calls out KFC, *USA Today*, p. B5]

ZOOMING IN, Part 1
Led by Ambitious Indra Nooyi, PepsiCo Pushes Nutrition

Critical Thinking

- **Indra Nooyi credited a college course in communication as an important step in her career. How do you think you could benefit from such a course?**

  A course in communication can help you sharpen your writing techniques and organizational strategies to compose clear, concise, and purposeful business messages. It will hone your presentation skills so that you can get your ideas across to large and small groups. It will build your confidence and skills with the Internet and digital communication technologies. It will teach you valuable team, intercultural, and etiquette skills. Finally, it will help you land the job of your dreams with the latest job-search, résumé-writing, and interviewing tips.

- **What skills do you think businesspeople need to succeed in today's workplace?**

  To succeed in today's workplace, businesspeople need technical skills in their fields. Increasingly, however, we hear that technical skills aren't enough. Businesspeople also need writing, speaking, listening, teamwork, etiquette, and people skills. Chapter 2 discusses "soft skills" in more detail.

- **How could emphasis on ethics and social responsibility improve profits and benefit a business?**

  For many corporations, social responsibility has become a big business. They feel that emphasizing ethics, being an admirable corporate citizen, boosting diversity in their ranks, and doing good works will bring them returns in the form of improved profits and better public relations. Consumers prefer businesses that respect the environment and produce goods ethically. Consumers have punished companies that have acted unethically. Students may be able to give examples of boycotts. Studies have shown that companies that act in a socially responsible manner and advertise that fact may be able to charge slightly more for their products. [See Trudel, R., & Cotte, J. (2008, May 12). Does being ethical pay? *The Wall Street Journal*, p. R4.] Consumers also prefer to deal with organizations that reflect their gender, culture, and social values. In addition, ethical organizations endure less litigation, less resentment, and less government regulation. Students will learn more about this topic later in Chapter 1.

ZOOMING IN, Part 2
PepsiCo

Critical Thinking

- **In communicating the changes in philosophy and practice within PepsiCo, should CEO Indra Nooyi and her management team use formal or informal channels of communication? Give examples of each.**

  Nooyi and her management team will probably rely most heavily on formal channels of communication. These would include directives, newsletters, announcements, videos, reports, and messages conveying her vision for achieving what is good for business with what is good for the world. She might use these channels in private discussions and chats with managers, employees, and customers. The company also promotes its goals through news releases, conferences, and interviews. By the way, Indra Nooyi is personable and comfortable with presentations and interviews. As part of the Cornell University eClips leadership series, she appears in 17 video segments available at **http://eclips.cornell.edu/entrepreneur.do?id=535.** These videos are a delight to watch! She answers questions and reveals her ideas on a range of topics from significant turning points in her career to giving feedback and the role of women in business.

- **In the midst of organizational changes at PepsiCo, what kinds of messages do you think will be traveling downward, upward, and horizontally?**

  Messages traveling downward will flow from management to workers. These messages would include job plans, policies, and procedures. CEO Nooyi and her management team would try to instill a sense of mission in achieving her goals of "Performance With Purpose." Messages traveling upward would include feedback from nonmanagement employees. Subordinate employees would describe progress in completing tasks, report roadblocks encountered, and suggest methods for improving efficiency. Messages traveling horizontally would include the exchange of information among workers at the same level. These messages would involve coordinating tasks, sharing information, solving problems, and resolving conflicts.

- **What kinds of barriers block the flow of communication in any organization undergoing change?**

  In any organization undergoing change, people are fearful of the changes that affect their jobs. Some of the barriers that might block communication are a closed communication climate, long lines of communication, lack of trust between management and employees, competition for power and status, turf wars, fear of reprisal for honest communication, differing frames of reference among communicators, lack of communication skills, and ego involvement.

You might ask students if they know anyone who has worked in an organization undergoing change. What experiences can they share? How did communication help or hinder the transformation?

ZOOMING IN, Your Turn
Applying Your Skills at PepsiCo

Students should be able to generate a list of skills and traits that lead to leadership success. Among them are reading, listening, speaking, writing, teamwork, and interpersonal skills. These skills would be sought in most job candidates. Hiring managers try to determine during job interviews whether job candidates have these skills. They judge the interviewee's speaking skills and ability to express ideas. They evaluate the candidate's facility in answering questions, some of which are behavioral with "what if" situations that test one's thinking skills. To test writing skills, some organizations give writing tests or ask for writing samples. For promotion, leaders must be able to think critically and express ideas in correctly written messages. Few business leaders today are promoted if they do not have excellent speaking and writing skills. Can these skills be taught on the job? Most business organizations expect new hires to come to them with good communication skills. Such skills are difficult to teach on the job, although some organizations send weak but promising trainees to seminars and courses to improve their writing skills. Management trainees can learn writing formats on the job, but actual writing skills are better taught and acquired with practice in a class intended for that purpose.

Discussion Material for CAREER COACH
Sharpening Your Skills for Critical Thinking, Problem Solving, and Decision Making

Students are asked to use their critical thinking and problem solving skills to guide EastCom Credit Union management in helping employees improve their wardrobes, perhaps with a monetary incentive.

1. **Identify and clarify the problem.** The problem is that management wants employees to dress professionally but worries that they may need funds to help them do so. One facet of the problem involves awareness of employee sentiments. What would the employees prefer? Another facet involves establishing a program that helps employees buy proper clothing.

2. **Gather information**. Management would probably conduct Internet and personal research to see what other similar financial institutions have done to ensure professional attire. More important, it should survey its own employees asking what suggestions they might have for a company-sponsored financial program to help them dress properly.

3. **Evaluate the evidence.** Feedback from employees should be evaluated by management. Do employees want to wear modified uniforms? Do they want to select and wear their own clothes? Would a clothing allowance help them purchase professional attire? When employees are asked for their opinions, they may provide additional ideas that management did not consider.

4. **Consider alternatives and implications.** Manages should discuss the employees' suggestions and also consider their own goals. Possible alternatives:
   a. Implement a dress code without any allowance for clothing.
   b. Implement a dress code supplemented with an allowance for clothing purchases.
   c. Require modified uniforms that the credit union provides.
   d. Require modified uniforms that each employee purchases, with or without a clothing allowance.
   e. Provide a clothing allowance of ___ dollars for the purchase of appropriate clothing.
   f. Provide a company loan for the purchase of appropriate clothing.

5. **Choose the best alternative and test it.** Managers had many alternatives. In a similar situation at a real company, management decided to provide a $300 allowance to be used by employees to upgrade their wardrobes or to maintain existing clothing with proper dry cleaning. Employees were also given two company collared shirts to be combined with slacks. [Based on Messmore, S. (2007, June 25). Clothes may not make the man, but they do make a difference at Wescom CU. *Credit Union Journal*, p. 4.]

Ethics Check Solutions

Ethics Check, Page 9
Too Connected?
Office workers use smart phones, e-mail, voicemail, and text messaging. Many are literally always on call and feel overwhelmed. What are the limits of connectedness? Is it fair to dodge an unpleasant call by sending it to voice mail or to delay answering certain e-mail messages?

Most of us would probably agree that it is not appropriate to take a call in the restroom, yet extreme forms of connectedness exist in the workplace. Trading partners may be on call in the middle of the night to accommodate their international counterparts in different time zones. Some office workers must be willing to reply to queries after hours and on weekends. The very concept of "after hours" is being eroded by instant communication. Although e-mail is an asynchronous messaging system because its reception cannot be controlled, the sender usually expects a response within 24 hours. Discuss with students the desire of some individuals to escape their "electronic leash."

Ethics Check, Page 14
Bypassing or False Advertising?

J. C. Penney produced a T-shirt emblazoned with a ferocious red and blue eagle beneath the words "American Made." However, a small label inside revealed that the shirt was made in

Mexico. In response to complaints that the slogan was deceptive, a Penney spokeswoman said that "American Made" referred to the actual person wearing the shirt, not to the manufacturer. Do you think this was a simple case of miscommunication?

Although J. C. Penney officials had one meaning for the slogan in mind, the T-shirt carried another meaning. Perhaps the slogan was just a little too clever. Certainly, company officials should have anticipated that wearers and others would expect the shirt to have been made in America so that both meanings would be accurate. It's embarrassing for companies to make faux pas such as this, but perhaps the company learned a valuable lesson in communication. Words and expressions can have many meanings. Slogans should be vetted with many people before they are used to represent a company.

Ethics Check, Page 22
Office Grapevine
Like a game of "telephone," the grapevine can distort the original message because the news travels through many mouths and ears at the office. Knowing this, can you safely share with even a trusted colleague something that you would not comfortably discuss with everyone?

Aside from the advantages and the general accuracy of the office grapevine, participating in this informal communication channel can spell trouble. Meaning can be distorted, and even colleagues we trust may mangle our words or reveal a secret, with which we entrusted them. On the other hand, savvy workers are able to work the grapevine to their advantage by purposely leaking their work-related accomplishments. Similarly, by tapping into the grapevine, they may be able indirectly to expose a coworker who clearly did wrong. Although honesty generally is the best policy, sometimes directness is not the smartest option.

Ethics Check, Page 26
Blurt Out the Truth?
While serving as an interviewer on behalf of your organization, you are expected to tell prospective employees that the firm is a great place to work. However, let's say you know that the work environment is bad, morale is low, and staff turnover is high. What should you do?

If the employment situation with your employer is that bad, you should probably be looking for another position yourself. However, if you must give a response, try to find something positive to say about the firm without lying. Are the benefits good? Are some supervisors better than others? Do employees find satisfaction in some tasks? If nothing positive comes to mind, sidestep the question by explaining that others might be better able to answer that question than you. Do not lie for your employer.

Photo Essay Solutions

Photo Essay, Page 9
Online communication and collaboration tools are critical in today's business world, especially for organizations that utilize virtual teams, telecommuting, and nonterritorial workspaces. Google Wave offers significant advantages over earlier messaging tools. Unlike e-mail, Google Wave enables multimember live messaging. In addition, Wave keeps track of group members' comments, assigned tasks, and contributions. The enhanced features facilitate effective online communication and significantly reduce the likelihood of communication-related project errors.

Photo Essay, Page 28
Like Bernard Madoff, many white-collar criminals start out with good intentions but lose their way. To avoid ethical lapses, professionals should ask themselves the following questions before deciding on a course of action: Is the action you are considering legal? How would you see the problem if you were on the opposite side? What are alternate solutions? Can you discuss the problem with someone whose advice you trust? How would you feel if your family, friends, employer, or coworkers learned of your action? The main idea is to follow the law and treat others as you would want them to treat you.

Video Resources

Instructors may show the *Communication Foundations* video from Video Library 1, *Building Workplace Skills*. This video illustrates how strong communication skills help students advance in today's challenging workplace. After viewing the video, students should be prepared to discuss critical-thinking questions. See the Video Discussion Guide provided in this Instructor's Manual.

Chapter Presentation Ideas

At times very simple exercises and discussion topics can drive home significant points. For instructors who have extra class time, we provide the following activity ideas.

1. *Importance of Communication Skills.* Bring to class a stack of classified ads from your local newspaper and/or printouts of job listings from employment Web sites such as Monster.com. Divide the class into small teams, and give each team several pages of ads. Have each team find as many references to communication-related skills as possible in the ads. When they are finished searching, have each team share its findings with the rest of the class. This is an excellent way for students to learn firsthand the importance of having good communication skills in the workplace.

2. *"Faked" Listening.* Have students share examples of times when they "faked" listening and how their lack of attention affected the situation. These instances may involve situations when students did not give their parents, teachers, or employers their full attention. Remind students that in their business lives, selective listening may result in serious consequences. When receiving directions for work assignments, they should take great care to listen actively and paraphrase the instructions given to them by their supervisor back to the supervisor. If

the supervisor accepts the paraphrase as accurate, the students may assume that they completely understand their work assignments.

3. *Emotional Interference.* Discuss with students how emotional interference can cloud their judgment. What would be the consequences of sending a coworker a negative e-mail message in the heat of anger, but then after cooling down, wanting to stop the individual from receiving the message? Or discuss the lasting consequences of an angry memo or e-mail message sent to a coworker or an angry voice-mail message left for a coworker.

4. *Noise as a Barrier to Communication.* Physical distractions (for example, *oral communication noise*—speaker's mannerisms, poor lighting, uncomfortable chairs, uncomfortable room temperature, or construction noise; *written communication noise*—poor letter format, inappropriate stationery, punctuation errors, misspelled words, and grammar errors) can take place during both written and oral communication. Have students discuss examples of these types of noise from their experiences or bring to class and discuss samples of written correspondence containing "noise."

Chapter 2 LECTURE NOTES AND TEACHING SUGGESTIONS

Professionalism: Team, Meeting, Listening, Nonverbal, and Etiquette Skills

CHAPTER SYNOPSIS

This chapter emphasizes the importance of soft skills and why they are becoming increasingly important in our knowledge-based economy. Soft skills include oral and written communications, listening proficiency, nonverbal communication, the ability to work in teams, and etiquette expertise. By developing soft skills, students will increase their ability to succeed in today's competitive work environment. With the increased use of teams in the workplace, it's particularly important for students to understand the roles of team members and how to contribute to the productivity of the team. This chapter also describes effective practices for planning and participating in virtual meetings. To familiarize students with technologies used to connect employees around the globe, chapter 2 also describes the tools used to connect virtual teams, including voice conferencing, videoconferencing, Web conferencing, instant messaging, blogs, and wikis.

Because listening is usually the least developed areas of communication, the chapter describes effective listening techniques and stresses that effective listening skills are essential for workplace success. Finally, the chapter stresses the importance of paying attention to and interpreting the meaning of what others are saying, both verbally and nonverbally, and gaining a competitive edge by demonstrating professionalism and business etiquette skills.

LEARNING OBJECTIVES

1. Explain the importance of professionalism, soft skills, and teamwork in today's workplace.
2. Understand how you can contribute positively to team performance, including resolving workplace conflicts, avoiding groupthink, and reaching group decisions.
3. Discuss effective techniques for planning and participating in face-to-face workplace meetings.
4. Describe effective practices and technologies for planning and participating in virtual meetings.
5. Explain and implement active listening techniques.
6. Understand how the functions and forms of nonverbal communication can help you advance your career.
7. Enhance your competitive edge by developing professionalism and business etiquette skills.

WHAT'S NEW IN THIS CHAPTER

- Focused chapter on professional workplace skills to help students make a smooth transition from the classroom to the business world.
- Revised three-part opening case study to reflect the current economic downturn and importance of professional skills and teamwork.
- Distinguished between face-to-face and virtual meetings, emphasizing the latter because virtual meetings reduce travel costs, lessen employee fatigue, and connect remote workers.
- Added instructions and Web screenshot illustrating the use of digital calendars to schedule meetings so that students will know how to use this electronic tool.
- Added Web screenshot to illustrate e-mail meeting summary template so that students see how savvy companies are using digital tools to summarize key points and note action items to monitor.
- Provided many tips and specific ground rules on how to plan and interact professionally during virtual meetings.
- Emphasized the importance of soft skills and professionalism in regard to being hired and promoted.
- Changed nearly 40 percent of the end-of-chapter activities to offer instructors fresh, relevant, and practical exercises for students to apply chapter content.

LECTURE OUTLINE

I. Becoming a Team Player in Professional Groups (p. 39)

- Hard skills refer to the technical skills in your field. Soft skills include both oral and written communication skills. Soft skills also include other competencies such as listening proficiency, nonverbal behavior, and etiquette expertise. Employers also value employees who are team players.

PowerPoint slides 1-3

II. Preparing to Work With Groups and Teams (p. 40)

A. Why Form Groups and Teams?

- Better decisions
- Faster response
- Increased productivity
- Greater "buy-in"
- Less resistance to change
- Improved employee morale
- Reduced risks

PowerPoint slide 4

B. Examples of Effective Teams

- Teams are effective in solving workplace problems and developing new products.

C. Virtual Teams

Definition: *Virtual teams* are groups of people who work interdependently with a shared purpose across space, time, and organization boundaries using technology.

D. Four Phases of Team Development

- Forming—members get to know each other and establish rules for working together
- Storming—members define their roles and plans for achieving goals; conflict may arise
- Norming—tensions subside, roles are clarified, and information is exchanged
- Performing—team reaches a state of high performance

PowerPoint slide 5

Let's Discuss

Four employees of a design firm have formed a team to plan a new business presentation to a prestigious client. The employees represent four areas of the business: design, production, finance, and marketing. The finance manager and marketing manager have a heated disagreement about the objectives of the presentation and the cost of the proposed marketing plan. Tension is so high that the team leader steps in to help address the conflict.

What stage of team development is this team experiencing?

This team is demonstrating characteristics of a team in the *storming* phase of development where conflict about the team's goals and members' roles may erupt. When this occurs, a good team leader will step in to set offer suggestions for getting the team back on track and progressing toward its goals.

Figure 2.1 Why Teams Fail: Typical Problems, Symptoms, and Solutions

E. Analyzing Positive and Negative Team Behavior

A team player showing positive behavior:

- Willingly establishes rules and abides by them
- Analyzes tasks and defines problems.
- Offers information and tries out their ideas on the group
- Listens actively
- Involves silent members
- Helps resolve differences and encourages a supportive environment

A team player showing negative behavior:

- Insults and criticizes others

- Wastes time by talking about irrelevant topics
- Disrupts with inappropriate comments and disruptive tactics
- Withdraws and refuses to participate in discussions

PowerPoint slides 6-7

Figure 2.2 Positive and Negative Team Behaviors

F. Six-Step Procedure for Dealing with Conflict

1. Listen.
2. Understand the other's point of view.
3. Show a concern for the relationship.
4. Look for common ground.
5. Invent new problem-solving options.
6. Reach an agreement based on what is fair.

PowerPoint slide 8

Let's Discuss

How should a manager address conflict that is a result of differences in culture, gender, age, or experience?

The more diverse the workplace becomes, the greater potential for conflict based on differences. Managers need to become more active listeners as opposed to just barking out orders. In addition to the strategies listed in the chapter, active listeners should ask open-ended questions such as, "Ty, when Jake suggested we send letters to all our customers about the cell phone recall, what was your reaction?" Then, the manager should let Ty speak without assuming she knows his answer and without passing judgment. (Steve Adubato, "Asking Right Questions Can Help With Conflict," *The Star-Ledger,* April 8, 2007. Retrieved May 22, 2007 from http://www.gale.com/BusinessRC/.)

G. Avoiding Groupthink

Definition: *Groupthink* describes faulty decision-making processes by team members who are overly eager to agree with one another. Effective teams can avoid groupthink by adhering to the following:

- Strive for team diversity—in age, gender, background, experience, and training.
- Encourage open discussion.
- Search for relevant information.
- Evaluate many alternatives.
- Consider how a decision will be implemented.
- Plan for contingencies in case the decision doesn't work out.

Let's Discuss

What are the advantages and disadvantages of groupthink in organizations?

Advantages: Groupthink reflects the team's desire for cohesiveness and harmony, a desirable trait for teams working toward a shared purpose.

Disadvantages: (a) Group members are reluctant to express opinions resulting in poorer decisions; and (b) group members fail to check alternatives, are biased in collecting information, and fail to develop a contingency plan.

H. Reaching Group Decisions

- Majority
- Consensus
- Minority
- Averaging
- Authority rule with discussion

PowerPoint slide 9

I. Characteristics of Successful Teams

- Small size, diverse makeup
- Agreement on purpose
- Agreement on procedures
- Ability to confront conflict
- Use of good communication techniques
- Ability to collaborate rather than compete
- Acceptance of ethical responsibilities
- Shared leadership

PowerPoint slide 10

III. Checklist for Developing Team Effectiveness (p. 47)

- Establish small teams.
- Encourage diversity.
- Determine the purpose, procedures, and roles.
- Acknowledge and manage conflict.
- Cultivate good communication skills.
- Advance an environment of open communication.
- Encourage collaboration and discourage competition.
- Share leadership.
- Create a sense of fairness in making decisions.
- Lighten up.
- Continually assess performance.

IV. Planning and Participating in Face-to-Face Workplace Meetings (p. 48)

PowerPoint slides 11-15

A. Deciding Whether a Meeting Is Necessary

- Only call for a meeting if the topic is important, can't wait, and requires an exchange of ideas.
- The real expense of a meeting is the lost productivity of the people attending.

B. Selecting Participants

- Decision-makers
- Those with information needed to make a decision
- Those responsible for implementing the decision

Figure 2.3 Meeting Purpose and Number of Participants

C. Distributing Advance Information

- Date and place of meeting
- Start time and end time
- Brief description of each topic, in order of priority, including the names of individuals who are responsible for performing some action
- Proposed allotment of time for each topic
- Any premeeting preparation expected of participants

Figure 2.4 Typical Meeting Agenda

D. Using Digital Calendars to Schedule Meetings

- Schedule meetings
- Check availability of attendees
- Keep track of daily activities
- Receive reminders of meeting times

Figure 2.5 Using Calendar Programs

E. Getting the Meeting Started

- Goal and length of the meeting
- Background of topics or problems
- Possible solutions and constraints
- Tentative agenda
- Ground rules to be followed

F. Moving the Meeting Along

- Encourage equal participation among participants.
- Avoid digressions and generate a "Parking Lot" list.
- Adhere to the time schedule and agenda.
- Summarize key decisions and check on agreement.

G. Participating Actively and Productively

- Arrive early.
- Come prepared.
- Bring a positive attitude.
- Contribute respectfully.
- Wait for others to finish.
- Keep your voice calm and pleasant, yet energetic.
- Give credit to others.
- Put the cell phone and laptop away.
- Help summarize.
- Express your views IN the meeting.
- Follow up and complete the assigned actions.

H. Handling Conflict in Meetings

- Encourage full discussion of issues.
- Reach consensus on a direction to follow.

I. Ending and Following Up

- End on time.
- Summarize decisions.
- Agree on who is responsible for action items and by what time.
- Distribute minutes within a couple of days after the meeting.

Figure 2.6 E-Mail Meeting Minutes

V. Checklist for Planning and Participating in Productive Meetings (p. 57)

Before the Meeting

- Consider alternatives.
- Invite the right people.
- Distribute an agenda.
- Use a calendaring program.
- Train participants on technology.

During the Meeting

- Start on time and introduce the agenda.
- Appoint a secretary and a recorder.
- Encourage balanced participation.
- Confront conflict frankly.
- Summarize along the way.

Ending the Meeting and Following Up

- Review meeting decisions.
- Distribute minutes of meeting.
- Remind people of action items.

VI. Using Effective Practices and Technologies in Virtual Meetings (p. 53)

PowerPoint slide 16

A. Audioconferencing

- *Audioconferencing* involves one or more people in a work area using an enhanced speakerphone to confer with others by telephone.

B. Voiceconferencing

- *Videoconferencing* combines video, audio, and communications networking technologies for real-time interaction.
- Videoconferencing reduces travel expenses, travel time, and employee fatigue.

PowerPoint slides 17, 18

Let's Discuss

What are the advantages and disadvantages of videoconferencing?

Advantages:

1. Videoconferencing allows people who are geographically spread out to collaborate and reach a decision.
2. Videoconferencing is more effective than conference calls because it allows participants to view facial expressions and body language.
3. Breakthroughs in video, audio, and broadband technologies create meeting experiences that are so lifelike that participants who are thousands of miles apart look like they're in the same room.
4. Videoconferencing reduces travel time, travel expenses, and employee fatigue.

Disadvantages:

1. Videoconferencing systems are expensive. Conventional videoconference rooms may cost $5,000–$80,000 per room.
2. Videoconferencing is still not better than face-to-face meetings.

C. Web Conferencing

- *Web conferencing* allows attendees to access an online virtual meeting room where they can present PowerPoint slides or share spreadsheets or Word documents, just as they might do in a face-to-face meeting.

PowerPoint slide 19

Figure 2.7 Web Conferencing
Figure 2.8 WebEx Conferencing on iPhone
Figure 2.9 Web Conferencing in Practice

D. Planning Virtual Meetings and Interacting Professionally

Premeeting Considerations:

- Decide which technology will be used
- Coach participants on using technology

- Set the time of the meeting using Coordinated Universal Time
- For global meetings, decide which language will be used.
- Distribute materials in advance

Ground Rules for Virtual Meetings:

- Explain how questions may be asked and answered.
- Turn off cell phones and smartphones.
- Don't multitask while participating in a virtual meeting.

Techniques for Collaborating Successfully in Virtual Meetings

- Be precise, give examples, and use simple language.
- Recap and summarize often.
- Confirm your understanding of what is being discussed.
- As a presenter, project an upbeat and strong voice.
- Encourage dialogue by asking questions and inviting responses.
- Allow time before or after the meeting for small talk.

PowerPoint slides 20-21

VII. Listening in the Workplace (p. 58)

A. Poor Listening Habits

Poor listening habits result from the following:

- Lack of training
- Competing sounds and stimuli
- Ability to process speech faster than others speak

Let's Discuss

Former Xerox CEO David Kearns learned that he should have listened to his employees before the company's disastrous launch of a new copier. "We could have told you it was a piece of junk," said one employee, "but you never asked our opinion." Why is it important to listen to colleagues and teammates in the workplace?

In the workplace, listening to teammates and colleagues vastly improves your ability to make good decisions. By listening to others, you tap into their experiences and insights about workplace issues resulting in better choices and decisions. (Fred Green, "Our Biggest Management Challenge: Communication," *Indianapolis Business Journal*, March 26, 2007. Retrieved May 22, 2007 from http://www.gale.com/BusinessRC/.)

B. Types of Workplace Listening

- Listening to superiors
- Listening to colleagues and teammates
- Listening to customers

PowerPoint slide 22

Figure 2.10 Listening to Customers: Comparing Trained and Untrained Listeners

VIII. Improving Workplace Listening

A. Ten Keys to Building Powerful Listening Skills

1. Control external and internal distractions.
2. Become actively involved.
3. Separate facts from opinions.
4. Identify important facts.
5. Avoid interrupting.
6. Ask clarifying questions.
7. Paraphrase to increase understanding.
8. Capitalize on lag time.
9. Take notes to ensure retention.
10. Be aware of gender differences.

PowerPoint slides 23-35

IX. Checklist for Improving Listening (p. 62)

- Stop talking.
- Work hard at listening.
- Block out competing thoughts.
- Control the listening environment.
- Maintain an open mind.
- Paraphrase the speaker's ideas.
- Listen between the lines.
- Distinguish between facts and opinions.
- Capitalize on lag time.
- Use memory devices.
- Take selective notes.

Let's Discuss

According to Thomas Friedman, author and foreign affairs columnist for *The New York Times*, "It's not just what you hear by listening that is important. It is what you *say* by listening that is important. It's amazing how you can diffuse a whole roomful of angry people by just starting your answer to a question with the phrase, 'You're making a legitimate point' or 'I hear what you say' and really meaning it."

Why do these phrases reduce barriers to communication?
Never underestimate how much people just want to feel that they have been heard. Once you demonstrate you have listened to them and respect their opinions, barriers come down and they become more willing to continue a healthy dialogue with you. Commencement address at Williams College Williamstown, Massachusetts, USA. Retrieved June 5, 2005, from http://www.humanity.org/voices/commencements/speeches/index.php?page=friedman_at_williams)

X. Communicating Through Nonverbal Messages (p. 63)

A. Functions of Nonverbal Communication

- To complement and illustrate
- To reinforce and accentuate
- To replace and substitute
- To control and regulate
- To contradict

PowerPoint slide 36

B. Forms of Nonverbal Communication

- Eye contact—maintain direct but not prolonged eye contact
- Facial expression—express warmth with frequent smiles
- Posture and gestures—convey self-confidence with erect stance
- Time—be on time; use time judiciously
- Space—maintain neat, functional work areas
- Territory—use closeness to show warmth and to reduce status differences
- Appearance of business documents—product careful, neat, well-organized messages
- Appearance of people—be well groomed, neat, and appropriately dressed

PowerPoint slides 37-38

Figure 2.11 Four Space Zones for Social Interaction
Figure 2.12 Sending Positive Nonverbal Signals in the Workplace

XI. Checklist for Techniques for Improving Communication Skills in the Workplace (p. 67)

- Establish and maintain eye contact.
- Use posture to show interest.
- Reduce or eliminate physical barriers.
- Improve your decoding skills.
- Probe for more information.
- Avoid assigning nonverbal meanings out of context.
- Associate with people from diverse cultures.
- Appreciate the power of appearance.
- Observe yourself on videotape.
- Enlist friends and family.

XII. Developing a Competitive Edge With Professionalism and Business Etiquette Skills (p. 68)

A. Professionalism Leads to Success

PowerPoint slides 39-41
Figure 2.13 Projecting Professionalism When You Communicate

B. Gaining an Etiquette Edge

- Use polite words.
- Express sincere appreciation and praise.
- Be selective in sharing personal information.
- Don't put people down.
- Respect coworkers' space.
- Rise above others' rudeness.
- Be considerate when sharing space and equipment with others.
- Choose the high road in conflict.
- Disagree agreeably.

Lecture Transparencies
(available in a separate packet and at http://www.meguffey.com)

Developing Team, Listening, and Etiquette Skills Acetates	Transparency Number
What Do Employers Want?	13
Preparing to Work With Groups and Teams	14
Four Phases of Team Development	15
Analyzing Positive and Negative Team Behavior	16
Six-Step Procedure for Dealing With Conflict	17
Methods for Reaching Group Decisions	18
Characteristics of Successful Teams	19
Duties of Meeting Leader	20
Duties of Meeting Participant	21
Virtual Meetings	22
Listening in the Workplace	23
Skillful Listening to Customers	24
Ten Keys to Building Powerful Listening Skills	25
Ten Misconceptions About Listening	26–27
Functions of Nonverbal Communication	28
Forms of Nonverbal Communication	29
Project Professionalism When You Communicate	30
Tips for Gaining an Etiquette Edge	31

Answers to Chapter Review Questions

1. **List seven reasons that explain why organizations are forming groups and teams. (Obj. 1)**

   Organizations are forming groups and teams for (1) better decisions, (2) faster response, (3) increased productivity, (4) greater buy-in, (5) less resistance to change, (6) improved employee morale, and (7) reduced risks for individuals.

2. **What are virtual teams, and how can misunderstandings among participants be reduced? (Obj. 1)**

   Virtual teams are groups that work interdependently with a shared purpose across space, time, and organizational boundaries using technology. Misunderstandings can be reduced by building credibility and trust in the beginning, establishing responsibilities, keeping track of information, and being patient and positive in responding to e-mail messages.

3. **Compare and contrast positive and negative team behavior. (Obj. 2)**

   Positive team behavior includes setting rules and abiding by them, analyzing tasks and defining problems, contributing information and ideas, showing interest by listening actively, encouraging members to participate, and synthesizing points of agreement. Negative behavior involves blocking the ideas and suggestions of others, insulting and criticizing others, wasting the group's time, making inappropriate jokes and comments, failing to stay on task, and failing to participate.

4. **What is *groupthink,* and how can it be avoided? (Obj. 2)**

   Groupthink describes faulty decision making reached by teams who are overly eager to agree. Teams suffering from groupthink fail to examine alternatives, are biased in collecting and evaluating information, and ignore the risks of the preferred choice. Groupthink can be avoided by choosing diverse team members, encouraging open discussion, searching for relevant information, and evaluating many alternatives.

5. **Why are team decisions based on consensus generally better than decisions reached by majority rule? (Obj. 2)**

   Consensus means that all members must agree to the decision. Although this method may require more discussion and more team time, it generally results in a fair decision that members are willing to implement. Decisions reached by majority rule leave some team members who object and who may sabotage the decision.

6. **If you are considering organizing a meeting, what should you do before the meeting? (Obj. 3)**

   You should (a) decide whether a meeting is necessary, (b) decide who needs to attend, (c) consider using a calendaring program to establish a schedule, and (d) distribute advance information including an agenda.

7. **List five behaviors you consider most important in participating actively in workplace meetings. (Obj. 3)**

   Students should select from among the following: (1) Arrive early, (2) come prepared, (3) bring a positive attitude, (4) contribute respectfully, (5) wait for others to finish, (6) keep your voice calm and pleasant yet energetic, (7) give credit to others, (8) put the cell phone and laptop away, (9) help summarize, (10) express your views IN the meeting and not afterwards, and (11) follow up on your assigned tasks.

8. **How is videoconferencing different from Web conferencing? (Obj. 4)**

   Videoconferencing combines video, audio, and communications networking technologies for real-time interaction. It is usually done in special videoconferencing rooms, some of which are very expensive. Web conferencing is similar to videoconferencing, but it is done from individuals' computers and may not involve video transmission.

9. **What techniques can make virtual meetings as effective as face-to-face meetings? (Obj. 4)**

   Effective virtual meeting techniques include (a) making sure all participants can use the technology; (b) establishing a uniform time, perhaps using Coordinated Universal Time (UTC); (c) distributing necessary materials in advance; (d) explaining how questions may be asked and answered; (e) controlling background noise; (f) avoiding multitasking during the meeting; (g) giving examples and using precise language; and (h) using "round the table" to encourage each participant to speak.

10. **According to experts, we ignore, forget, distort, or misunderstand 75 percent of everything we hear. Why are we such poor listeners? (Obj. 5)**

    Poor listening habits may result from lack of training, as well as the large number of competing sounds and stimuli that interfere with concentration. In addition, we are poor listeners because our minds are able to process speech much faster than people can speak.

11. **What are ten techniques for improving workplace listening? Be prepared to describe each. (Obj. 5)**

    (1) Control external and internal distractions, (2) become actively involved, (3) separate facts from opinions, (4) identify important facts, (5) don't interrupt, (6) ask clarifying questions, (7) paraphrase to increase understanding, (8) take advantage of lag time, (9) take notes to improve retention, and (10) be aware of gender differences.

12. List five functions of nonverbal communication. Provide an original example of each. (Obj. 6)

(1) To complement and illustrate. *Example:* Holding your hands apart to show the size of your netbook computer. (2) To reinforce and accentuate. *Example:* Clapping your hands to show approval. (3) To replace and substitute. *Example:* Yawning and covering your mouth to show boredom. (4) To control and regulate. *Example:* Letting your voice drop at the end of a statement signaling the completion of a thought. (5) To contradict. *Example:* Stating that you love your friend's new fragrance but holding your nose.

13. List ten techniques for improving nonverbal communication skills in the workplace. Be prepared to discuss each. (Obj. 6)

(1) Establish and maintain eye contact, (2) use posture to show interest, (3) reduce or eliminate physical barriers, (4) improve decoding skills, (5) probe for more information, (6) avoid assigning nonverbal meanings out of context, (7) associate with people from diverse cultures, (8) appreciate the power of appearance, (9) observe yourself on videotape, and (10) enlist friends and family to provide feedback on your body language.

14. Compare and contrast examples of professional and unprofessional behavior in regard to workplace speech habits and e-mail. (Obj. 7)

Unprofessional speech habits include speaking in uptalk, using *like* to fill in mindless chatter, substituting *go* for *said*, relying on slang, and letting profanity slip into your conversation. Professional speakers avoid anything that sounds uneducated, crude, or adolescent. Unprofessional e-mail behavior involves writing messages with incomplete sentences, misspelled words, IM slang, and senseless chatting. Professional e-mail messages are concise, correct, and concrete. They avoid sloppiness.

15. What five specific behaviors do you think would be most important in giving you an etiquette edge in your business career? (Obj. 7)

Students will choose five from among the following: (1) use polite words, (2) express sincere appreciation and praise, (3) be selective in sharing personal information, (4) don't put people down, (5) respect coworkers' space, (6) rise above others' rudeness, (7) be considerate when sharing space and equipment with others, (8) choose the high road in conflict, and (9) disagree agreeably.

Answers to Critical Thinking Questions

1. Harvard professor and team expert J. Richard Hackman claims that research "consistently shows that teams underperform despite all their extra resources."[i] How would you, as a critical thinker, respond to this statement? (Obj. 1)

A critical thinker might question a general statement claiming that "research shows" something. How many studies were involved? Who conducted the research? What is the writer's definition of *underperform*? What is meant by *extra resources*? Teams are generally thought to produce better results than individuals. Why would "research" show something contrary? If it is true that teams underperform, why do companies continue to form teams to investigate and recommend solutions to problems? A critical thinker could find much to dispute in this statement.

2. **Evaluate the following statement: "Technical proficiency has never been enough for professionals to grow beyond the staff level." Do you agree or disagree, and why? (Obj. 1)**

   Although the author, David Maturo, writing in *The Pennsylvania CPA Journal*, is referring to job candidates in technical fields, the statement is also true for nearly all job candidates. Employers are looking for "soft" skills that include communication, interpersonal, and team skills. In the accounting and other technical fields, a staff position is only a foot in the door. One writer observed that in technical fields, state-of-the-art knowledge has the half life of a gnat! (N. Johnson, "The Hard Truth About Soft Skills," *Computerworld*, March 20, 1999, p. 33). Technical skills in every field are short-lived because technology is constantly evolving; new programs, new tools, and new competencies are required.

3. **Why do executives and managers spend more time listening than do workers? (Obj. 5)**

   Before they can make decisions, executives must listen to feedback from supervisors, specialists, and others. They also listen to their bosses—boards of directors and owners—and they might also need to listen to customers, especially when handling serious complaints. Minds are like parachutes; they work well only when open. All three levels of workers should have good listening skills; but because the decisions coming from executives' listening may be more critical, their skills should perhaps be most highly developed.

4. **What arguments could you give for or against the idea that body language is a science with principles that can be interpreted accurately by specialists? (Obj. 6)**

   Although few would argue that body language does send silent messages, no scientific principles have evolved explaining exactly what those messages mean. Most researchers agree that nonverbal cues contain much information, but specifically what those cues mean is unknown. Authors Hickson and Stacks said, "The nonverbal message by itself may be ambiguous; in almost every instance it needs the verbal message to complete the process of communication" [(1993). *Nonverbal Communication.* Brown and Benchmark, p. 8]. Julius Fast, author of the precedent-setting *Body Language* [(1971). New York: Pocket Books, p. 14], stated that "nonverbal language is partly instinctive, partly taught and partly imitative." But it is not a science with principles that always hold true. Most communicators tend to believe nonverbal messages over verbal messages when the messages are in conflict. The Chinese have a profound proverb: "Be wary of the man whose belly does not move when he laughs." People who are sincerely laughing show it with their entire bodies, not just their faces.

5. **Ethical Issue: Rochelle is a good member of your team. However, you are disturbed that she is constantly promoting her Arbonne beauty products to other members of the team. She shows catalogs and keeps a supply of samples ready to distribute during lunch or after hours. Her desk smells like a perfume counter. During team meetings, she puts an order form on the table. As a team member, what should you do? What if Rochelle were selling Girl Scout cookies?**

   Selling for-profit items on company property is probably forbidden by your company. Rochelle is taking advantage of a captive audience. Even though most of the activity is taking place during lunch or after work hours, the activity could carry over into work time and could disrupt productivity. It would be wise for you to report the situation to your team leader, manager, or human resources representative. You should also check to see what the company's policy is on selling nonprofit items such as Girl Scout cookies.

Activities

2.1 Soft Skills: Identifying Personal Strengths (Obj. 1)

Your students should submit a list of four categories of soft skills. Encourage them to frame statements that will be useful when they prepare a résumé later in the course. For example, under "Thinking/problem solving," a student might write, "Learned new spreadsheet program and prepared cost projection for remodeling office," or "Learn new software applications quickly and with little training."

2.2 Team Effort: Denny's Hopes to Rock With All-Nighter Program (Obj. 1)

In persuading the marketing vice president that a team effort is needed to consider expanding Denny's All-Nighter program to the Southwest, students might mention some of the following points:

- A team of managers would bring wider experience to the decision. They would contribute more expertise and different perspectives.
- Should the decision be made to implement the program, the company would experience greater buy-in if the managers who approved the plan were the ones to implement it.
- The All-Nighter program would generate less resistance to change if the managers were involved in the decision.
- Overall morale among managers would be enhanced if they were invited to participate in this major decision.
- Responsibility for the decision is diffused, thus carrying less risk for a single individual making the decision.

2.3 Reaching Group Decisions: Majority, Consensus, or What? (Obj. 2)

More than one strategy may be appropriate for these situations. The author's recommendations follow.

a. Majority would work, but consensus would be better.

b. Majority

c. Authority rule with discussion

d. Consensus

e. Majority

f. Minority

g. Majority would work, but consensus would be better.

h. Minority

2.4 Resolving Workplace Conflicts: Apply a Plan (Obj. 2)

Students should apply the following six-step procedure: (1) Listen to each person's position. (2) Understand the other's point of view. Ask questions and paraphrase what you hear. (3) Show a concern for the relationship. Show an understanding of the other person's situation and needs. (4) Look for common ground. Strive to achieve a solution to which both sides can agree. (5) Invent new problem-solving options, if necessary. (6) Reach an agreement based on what's fair. Encourage students to role-play two or more of the scenarios.

2.5 Groupthink: Fastest Decision May Not Be Best (Obj. 2)

a. This group seemed too eager to make a quick decision. It failed to consider alternatives, and the chair was too invested in his recommendation.
b. The following conditions can lead to groupthink: team members with similar backgrounds, a lack of methodical procedures, a demand for a quick decision, and a strong leader who favors a specific decision.
c. Groups can avoid groupthink by striving for team diversity in age, gender, background, experience, and training. They should encourage open discussion, search for relevant information, evaluate many alternatives, consider how a decision will be implemented, and plan for contingencies in case the decision doesn't work out.

2.6 Lessons in Teamwork: What We Can Learn From Geese (Objs. 1, 2)

a. Lesson: Teams working as a unit can accomplish more than individuals working alone.
b. Lesson: Team members who recognize the effectiveness of team goals, procedures, and assignments strive to stay "in formation" because they realize that teamwork requires less energy and has better results than flying solo.
c. Lesson: Shared leadership and interdependence give each team member a chance to lead as well as an opportunity to rest. Team members should be prepared to lead when necessary.

d. Lesson: Team members can motivate leaders and fellow members with encouragement. Teammates need to make sure their "honking" is encouraging rather than discouraging.
e. Lesson: We all may need help from time to time. We should stand by our teammates in difficult times.

2.7 Evaluating Meetings: Effective or Ineffective? (Obj. 3)

Students may analyze the meeting by using the following template to conclude whether the meeting succeeded or failed.

Getting Ready for the Meeting

a. Was the meeting truly necessary?
b. Were the right people there according to the purpose of the meeting?
c. Was an agenda distributed?

Conducting the Meeting

a. Did the meeting start on time?
b. Did the meeting chair open with an introduction of the topic, a summary of topics, possible solutions, a tentative agenda, and/or a review of ground rules?
c. Did the chair provide suggestions for moving the meeting along?
d. Was conflict dealt with successfully? Did the chair keep control of the meeting? Did committee members making their points without attacking each other?
e. Was the decision made by consensus or by vote? Were minority views encouraged and tolerated?
f. Did the meeting end on time or whenever consensus was reached, according to the ground rules agreed on?

Ending the Meeting and Following Up

a. Were decisions reviewed, action items discussed, and/or schedule for completion established?
b. Were committee members reminded to follow through on action items?

2.8 Virtual Meetings: Improving Distance Meeting Buy-In (Obj. 4)

a. Setting a more reasonable start time for the Seattle office would have shown courtesy to the West Coast participants.
b. Asking participants to log on early helps to avoid delays in starting a virtual meeting.
c. Reminding participants of ground rules such as turning off or muting cell phones and not checking e-mail during a virtual meeting encourages people to focus and be more involved.
d. Using interactivity helps prevent group members from losing interest. A technique such as "round the table" would have elicited more active participation and discouraged multitasking on the other end.

e. Distributing materials prior to a virtual meeting allows participants to prepare questions and be more involved during the session.

2.9 Web Conferencing: Take a Quick Tour

This engaging video makes Web conferencing sound simple and easy.

Step 1. Schedule a meeting by using Outlook, the WebEx site, or IM.
Step 2. Meet your participants online. They do not need to have WebEx to join. They merely click a link in your announcement e-mail or IM. They can join the teleconference by computer or phone.
Step 3. Show and tell involves sharing your desktop with participants. You can show documents, presentations, or applications. Everyone sees the same thing at the same time.

Students may question whether WebEx is the best choice for small conferences. Perhaps other programs should be investigated such as Skype.

2.10 Rating Your Listening Skills (Obj. 5)

This listening quiz focuses attention on good listening techniques as presented in the textbook. Although some of the answers are obvious, an interactive quiz presents an alternative learning mode that can pique student interest and reinforce good habits.

2.11 Listening: Recognizing Good Habits (Obj. 5)

Students should be able to name five good and five bad listening behaviors. They should clearly identify the situation and participant for each item on their lists. This activity presents an excellent opportunity for you to make students more conscious of how listening habits differ in people around them. You should also be able to discuss techniques for improving poor listening habits.

2.12 Listening: Skills Required in Various Careers (Obj. 5)

Student teams should generate lists of listening and nonverbal cues that include some of the following: good eye contact, avoiding being distracted by others while listening, not interrupting, taking notes, paraphrasing instructions, asking pertinent questions in a nonthreatening manner, leaning forward, and showing empathy and compassion. *Critical listening* involves judging and evaluating what you are hearing. *Discriminative listening* is necessary when you must identify main ideas and understand an argument. Teams should generate different cues and behavior reflecting these forms of listening in relation to the professional role they are analyzing.

2.13 Nonverbal Communication: Recognizing Functions (Obj. 6)

Students should be able to list several examples for each of the following nonverbal functions:

- To complement and illustrate
- To reinforce and accentuate
- To replace and substitute
- To control and regulate
- To contradict

2.14 Nonverbal Communication: How to Be More Influential (Obj. 6)

At meetings you should sit at the end of the table if possible. If that is not possible, sit where you can make eye contact with the majority of the group. Make frequent eye contact with those at the meeting. Provide positive feedback to speakers through eye contact, nodding, and asking clarifying questions. In interacting with colleagues, you can make a good impression and become more influential with nonverbal signals such as eye contact; warm facial expressions; erect posture; being on time; maintaining a neat, functional work area; and being well-groomed, neat, and appropriately dressed.

2.15 Nonverbal Communication: Body Language (Obj. 6)

The following body movements do not necessarily mean the same thing when used by different individuals. Remember that to a certain degree nonverbal communication can be culture or subculture specific, and context always plays a major role when you interpret this type of communication. Students may have other interpretations, but these body movements can be construed to mean the following:

a. Whistling, wringing hands: nervousness or fear
b. Bowed posture, twiddling thumbs: boredom
c. Steepled hands, sprawling sitting position: contemplative or relaxed
d. Rubbing hand through hair: frustration or nervousness
e. Open hands, unbuttoned coat: relaxed
f. Wringing hands, tugging ears: upset or nervous

2.16 Nonverbal Communication: Universal Sign for "I Goofed" (Obj. 6)

This is a good exercise for teams. Suggest that team members take turns demonstrating each of the nonverbal messages described here. They should then discuss how effective each would be. Of course, some would be quite dangerous if they require taking your hands off the steering wheel. Be sure to discuss with students the difficulty of cultural implications. Although a gesture might be effective in one country, it might not work in another.

2.17 Verbal vs. Nonverbal Signals (Obj. 6)

Although this is a neat trick, it hardly proves that nonverbal signals are ALWAYS more meaningful than verbal signals. The truth is that nonverbal signals nearly always depend on context. That is, the situation, setting, and accompanying verbal signals are necessary to interpret nonverbal signals appropriately. Much nonverbal communication is ambiguous without verbal explanation to explain and interpret it. One conclusion that might be drawn from this demonstration is that visual aids (gestures demonstrating an action) can help or hinder a listener in following instructions.

2.18 Nonverbal Communication: Signals Sent by Business Casual Dress (Obj. 6)
This activity can be expanded into a research paper topic. A variation on this activity relies on student experiences. Instead of conducting interviews in the community, they can conduct a forum among students who work, asking them to comment on casual-dress policies in the jobs they have had. Activity 7.5 in Chapter 7 also relates to casual dress.

2.19 Body Art: A Butterfly on Her Neck (Obj. 6)
Acceptance of tattoos depends on many factors such as the office environment, the company, the geographic area, one's position within the company, the expectations of the company's management team, and the company's clientele. However, a career-conscious, ambitious person would probably advise a friend not to display the tattoo. Colleen Abrie, an image consultant, gave this advice: "If I worked in an administrative office and I got a tattoo and I was proud of it, I would go to the most senior person I could find and simply ask, 'Is it okay if I let it show?' I would go to my direct supervisor and find out if it's appropriate." [McCarty, M. (2007, January/February). Tattoos: Not just for sailors anymore. *OfficePro,* p. 26.]

2.20 Nonverbal Communication: Defining *Business Casual* (Obj. 6)
Team reports defining "business casual" will probably include some of the following information: Women should wear skirts, slacks, blouses, and jackets. Skirts should be no shorter than 2 inches above the knee. Hosiery should be worn in the fall and winter. No sandals or open-toed shoes, jeans, shorts, or hats. Men may wear khakis, dress slacks, polo shirts, button-down shirts, and jackets and ties (optional). Women should avoid leggings, spandex pants, casual and short shorts, ultrashort skirts, camisoles, sportswear T-shirts, jeans, sweats, athletic shoes, and thonglike flip-flop sandals. Men should avoid garish print sport shirts, sportswear T-shirts, sport team jackets, jeans, sweats, athletic "tube" socks, hiking boots, athletic shoes, and sandals. Activity 7.16 in Chapter 7 also relates to casual dress codes.

2.21 Nonverbal Communication Around the World (Obj. 6)
Students should be able to find a number of gestures and their meanings discussed at various Web sites. Here is one example: "The fingertip kiss, in which the tips of the thumb and fingers are kissed and quickly moved forward away from the face, is a sign of affection and may be used as a greeting in Sicily and Portugal. The fingertip kiss is not used often in Italy and the British Isles, but it is common in France, Germany, Greece, and Spain to signify praise" (J. S. Martin and L. H. Chaney, *Global Business Etiquette*, Praeger, 2006, p. 53).

2.22 Guide to Business Etiquette and Workplace Manners: Sharpening Your Skills (Obj. 7)
Students are encouraged to take the pretest and study the 17 business etiquette topics presented at the student Web site at **www.meguffey.com.** Instructors will find a complete

discussion guide titled "Workplace Etiquette Teaching Module" plus three posttests under *Teaching Modules* in the instructor's materials at **www.meguffey.com** To see the 17 student exercises, go to the student site and click "Business Etiquette Guide."

2.23 Business Etiquette: Mind Your Manners or Mind Your BlackBerry? (Obj. 7)

(a) Short policy statement:

In using a smartphone or other wireless device, be professional. Respect others.

(b) More complete policy:

- Turn your smartphone off or on vibrate. Keep it off the meeting table.
- Don't look at it during a meeting or conversation.
- Don't respond to a call, e-mail, or text during a meeting or conversation.
- If you are expecting an important call, let the person or meeting facilitator know in advance.
- Leave the room if you must take a call or respond to an e-mail.
- Shut the door quietly when you exit and enter the room.
- Apologize if you do interrupt the meeting.
- Use your e-mail "out of office" assistant and change your voice message to let people know you are not available.
- Post a sign if the organization has a "no cell phone" area or zone.

[Based on Harr, M. (n.d.). Smart phone etiquette—How smart are you? Retrieved June 25, 2009, from http://ezinearticles.com]

ZOOMING IN Part 1: FedEx Office

Critical Thinking

1. In what ways do employee work teams benefit organizations?

Employee work teams benefit organizations by bringing together people with different skill sets to solve problems. Teams may be able to respond faster and make better decisions than individuals. Team members, who may be closer to customers than managers, often bring practical, customer-oriented suggestions for improving productivity. Decisions that are arrived at by teams usually bring greater buy-in than those made by individuals. Organizations also benefit from improved employee morale when teams collaborate to solve problems and boost productivity.

2. Compare and contrast student and corporate work teams. In what ways are they similar and different?

Student and corporate work teams are similar in that both are formed with a purpose. Both usually have members with various skills, and both must learn to work together to achieve their purpose. Both require team members to cooperate and perform in their assigned roles.

One major difference is that team members in the workplace are less likely to be tolerated if they fail to perform or if they behave negatively.

3. **How could you make a positive contribution to a school or work team?**

   You can be a good team member by setting rules and abiding by them, analyzing tasks and defining problems, contributing information and ideas, showing interest by listening actively, encouraging members to participate, and synthesizing points of agreement.

ZOOMING IN Part 2: Fedex Office

Critical Thinking

1. **Why do you think workplace meetings are so disliked?**

   People hate to attend meetings because many are poorly planned and poorly run. They take up a huge amount of time in the workplace, thus preventing attendees from completing tasks that they often feel are more important. Meetings require that attendees listen to others who may be grandstanding, misinformed, or off topic. Meetings swallow chunks of time and may result in nothing concrete or meaningful.

2. **Do you think 15-minute stand-up meetings could be effective? Why or why not?**

   Short stand-up meetings can be effective in achieving specific and usually narrow purposes. They may be less effective in ironing out complex problems and reaching consensus on solutions. The success of any meeting, however, depends largely on the leader and the groundwork laid before the meeting.

3. **How can the attitude and behavior of attendees affect the success of a meeting?**

   If meeting attendees come with an unenthusiastic attitude, refuse to participate, and display negative body language, they will surely generate an unsuccessful meeting. When attendees arrive early, come prepared, and contribute respectfully, they contribute to successful outcomes. It's wise to remember that in the workplace, meetings are a reality. You can showcase yourself and boost your career by participating professionally and skillfully.

Zooming In, Your Turn: FedEx Office

Students are asked to prepare a list of suggestions for planning and interacting at virtual meetings. Instructors may also ask that this assignment be submitted as a memo. Shown here is a possible memo.

Date: Current
To: Daryl Thomas, Senior Manager, Sales Development and Education
From: Student's Name
Subject: Suggestions for Planning Virtual Meetings and Interacting Professionally

As you suggested, I am submitting this memo with suggestions for planning virtual meetings and interacting professionally during the meetings. These suggestions come from textbooks and Internet research into the topic.

Planning Virtual Meetings

- Be sure everyone understands the technology being used and can use it effectively.
- Schedule the meeting at a time convenient to all, regardless of time zones. Avoid spanning a lunch hour, holding someone overtime, or making someone arrive extra early.
- Limit the number participating; usually 12 is the maximum for effective virtual meetings.
- Distribute any documents before the meeting, and be sure participants know how to use online editing tools if documents will be revised.

Participating Professionally

- Take time before the meeting to develop camaraderie with small talk and personal conversation.
- Be precise in presenting ideas; give examples and use simple language.
- Encourage all participants to share in the discussion; don't have the leader do all the talking.
- Take turns. The microphone usually carries only one voice at a time.
- Identify yourself each time you speak.
- Make your points clearly but politely. Avoid the tendency to be overly frank because you don't see the other person.
- Do not multitask during virtual meetings.

I hope these suggestions are helpful in planning and conducting virtual meetings. If you would like to discuss these points or if you require further research, I would be happy to do so.

Discussion Material for CAREER COACH: Listening to Nonnative Speakers in the Workplace

You can have students take part in this discussion in the class as a whole or in small groups made up of both native and nonnative speakers. Encourage students to share their experiences of communicating in a second language, whether here in the U.S. or while traveling to another country. Also encourage students to share their experiences of communicating with a friend or coworker who speaks English as a second language. This discussion can be very eye opening to students, especially those who speak English as their native language. It is also a good introduction to Chapter 3, "Intercultural Communication."

Discussion Material for CAREER COACH: Perils of Casual Apparel in the Workplace

Students are asked to debate the proposition that business casual dress be the professional dress standard throughout the United States. To stage a debate, you might wish to follow some of the suggestions made by Dr. James Calvert Scott, "Business Casual Dress," Part 2, *Delta Pi Epsilon Instructional Strategies,* December 1999:

Divide your class into small groups of four to six students, each of which is assigned a number. Each group is given a set amount of time to prepare arguments both for and against the debate proposition. Just before the debate begins, each group selects two representatives to serve as its potential debaters. Two numbers are drawn, with the first corresponding group assigned to support the debate proposition and the second corresponding group assigned to oppose the debate proposition for a specified amount of time. The remaining class members serve as neutral judges, who listen carefully to the arguments offered by each debate team. After the presentations, questioning, and rebuttals, the debaters await the decision of the judges. The judges cast their votes in favor of the debate team that presented the more persuasive case. You can increase student involvement in this activity by having multiple groups debate the proposition either sequentially or simultaneously in different parts of the classroom or in a variety of nearby locations.

Discussion Material for ETHICAL INSIGHTS: Ethical Responsibilities of Group Members and Leaders

Students should enjoy this discussion because it is a common problem when students work as part of a small team in a classroom to complete a problem. Have students brainstorm about this problem in small groups and report their conclusions back to the entire class. Having this discussion early in the semester can help to avoid similar problems during the remainder of the semester.

Discussion Material for PLUGGED IN: How to Form and Participate in Effective Virtual Teams

Students discuss the reasons that virtual teams are becoming more popular and the advantages and disadvantages of virtual teams for employees and for employers. They may cover some of the following ideas.

- **Reasons for Popularity**

  The technology exists that makes virtual teams possible.
  They allow people located anywhere in the world to meet synchronously.

- **Advantages and Disadvantages for Employees**

  Advantages: Meetings can occur at any time that best suits the employees. Employees can engage in meetings with others from around the world without the time and expense of travel. Employees can develop their technology skills.

Disadvantages: Virtual meetings require that employees be excellent online communicators, which is not always the case. Employees may not be properly trained to use the technology. Members may experience feelings of isolation. Depending on the technology used, little or no opportunity to analyze nonverbal communication may exist. Members must work harder to develop understanding, commitment, and trust. Messages may be easily misinterpreted.

- **Advantages and Disadvantages for Employers**

  Advantages: Virtual meetings can be very cost-effective. Since traveling to another physical location is not necessary, employees do not have to be away from their offices. Virtual meetings can result in higher productivity and more motivated employees.
  Disadvantages: The initial technology and training costs can be high.

Students may also want to discuss the technological tools that make virtual meetings possible and the requirements for making virtual teams effective.

Ethics Check Solutions

Ethics Check, Page 45
Lazy Team Members, Anyone?
Teamwork is a staple in college classes today and usually works well for students and their instructors. However, occasionally a rogue member will take advantage of a group and barely collaborate. How do you deal with a student who does sloppy work, misses team meetings, and fails to respond to calls or e-mail?

Nonparticipating team members tend to be the most common complaint among students about teamwork. Instructors should establish clear ground rules for dealing with "flaky" group members, but leave the handling of such situations to the team members themselves, so that they may learn how to deal with difficult participants. A gradual approach should be encouraged ranging from warnings to action that is more serious. For instance, a smart policy is to allow the team to "fire" a noncompliant member who then has to work on another project by himself or herself. Gauging the state of the collaboration by asking students to fill out a confidential "teamwork evaluation form" is also helpful. Finally, the larger the student team, the more likely it becomes that someone will ride on the group's coat tails. Hence, it's a good idea to limit team size to 3–4 members. From the beginning, instructors should emphasize to students who form teams of three, for example, that their responsibility for the final document is 300, not 33.3 percent.

Ethics Check, Page 64
Impressing Your Instructor
Projecting a professional image begins in your business communication classroom and in other courses where your instructors evaluate your work and your participation. Imagine how a professor perceives students who skip classes, arrive late, forget homework, yawn with their tonsils showing, chew gum or eat, and doodle during class. What message does such nonverbal behavior send?

Even if told repeatedly, students often don't make the connection between behavioral guidelines they read about in their textbooks and their own practice in the classroom. They also tend to forget that they are being watched and evaluated as they will be in the workplace. Although the classroom is a training ground simulating workplace requirements and behavior, it ought to be taken seriously as a professional environment. Naturally, this means that instructors themselves need to lead by example.

Photo Essay Solution

Photo Essay, Page 40
Saving lives requires effective teamwork, and the emergency watercraft teams involved in 2009's "Miracle on the Hudson" included FDNY firefighters, NYPD police, Coast Guard personnel, and ferryboat captains. These rescuers were highly trained for water rescue and followed familiar procedures routinely rehearsed in rescue drills. In addition, the team members accepted shared leadership and displayed a strong sense of collaboration, not competition.

Video Resources

Instructors may also show the *Bridging the Gap* video from Video Library 2, *Understanding Teamwork: Cold Stone Creamery.* Instructors will find a complete discussion guide and activity solution for this video presented in this Instructor's Manual.

Chapter Presentation Ideas and Extras

For instructors who have extra class time, we provide the following activity ideas.

1. *Long-Term Group Roles.* To help your students gain a sense of the roles group members can play in a long-term project or task force, you may give them the following guides:

   TEAM PROJECT: JOB DESCRIPTIONS

   1. Manager, small group dynamics expert
   Conducts meetings effectively
   Delegates work appropriately and fairly
   E-mails the CEO (instructor) as required with team progress report or agenda and minutes
   Sets and distributes agenda
   Attends and contributes at all group meetings
   Participates effectively at group presentations
   Completes group assessment documents competently
   Follows up on group decisions

   2. Assistant Manager, small group dynamics expert
   Fills in for the manager
   Secures meeting rooms in a timely fashion
   Informs members of changes in a timely fashion
   Assists manager as needed, especially in following up group decisions

Collects and distributes minutes
Attends and contributes at all group meetings
Participates effectively at group presentations
Completes group assessment documents competently

3. Document Expert, word processing expert
Prepares final copies of documents effectively and on time
Collects copies of all group documents and files
Instructs group in word processing as needed
Attends and contributes at all group meetings
Participates effectively at group presentations
Completes group assessment documents competently

4. Multimedia Specialist, presentation software expert
Prepares audio-visual projects effectively and on time
Collects copies of all presentation software documents and files
Instructs group in presentation software as needed
Attends and contributes at all group meetings
Participates effectively at group presentations
Completes group assessment documents competently

5. Senior Researcher, print, Internet, electronic research expert
Organizes research projects effectively and on time
Ensures that research documents and files have appropriate formatting
Instructs group in research methods as needed
Attends and contributes at all group meetings
Participates effectively at group presentations
Completes group assessment documents competently

2. *Short-Term Group Roles.* When placing students in small, temporary groups in the classroom, assign them the following roles. Encourage students to adopt different roles in different groups or to rotate roles.

SMALL GROUP ROLES

1. Facilitator
Gets the task at hand or project started
Keeps group focused on the purpose
Keeps meeting running smoothly
Keeps members on task

2. Recordkeeper
Keeps a recording of the meeting
Reports the results of the group to the rest of the class

3. Timekeeper
Keeps track of time during the meeting
Helps facilitator keep meeting on track
Ends meeting on time

4. Encourager
Makes sure that all members are participating
Helps members deal with conflicts

3. *Parliamentary Procedure.* To help your students learn how to effectively manage and take place in productive meetings, you should introduce them to the basics of parliamentary procedure. Share the following the guidelines with them:

MINIMUM GUIDELINES FOR USING PARLIAMENTARY PROCEDURE

Running Meetings

1. Call meeting to order.
2. Read minutes of last meeting.
3. Hear reports of treasurer and other officers.
4. Process committee reports.
5. Consider old business.
6. Entertain new business.
7. Introduce program for meeting.
8. Adjourn meeting.

Making Decisions

1. Chair entertains new business in the form of main motion.
2. Member seconds main motion.
3. Main motion is debated with chair controlling discussion.
4. Chair calls for a vote.
5. Motion passes or is defeated.

Protecting Individual Rights

1. Appoint a knowledgeable, objective parliamentarian to enforce the rules.
2. Rise to a point of information if you do not understand discussion at hand.
3. Rise to a point of parliamentary inquiry to ask the parliamentarian about correct procedures.
4. Call for a division of the house if a voice vote is unclear.
5. Appeal the decision of the chair and ask members to vote on whether the chair is right.

GUIDES FOR AGENDAS AND MINUTES
Agenda

1. Specify date, place, starting time, and ending time.
2. Provide a statement of overall mission and purpose of the meeting.
3. Identify who will attend.
4. List the topics to be covered.
5. Identify the approximate amount of time for each topic.
6. Identify the premeeting action or reading expected of each member.
7. Distribute the agenda at least a week ahead of time.

Minutes

1. Provide date, time, and location of the meeting.
2. Maintain an objective tone (no editorializing).
3. Summarize when possible.
4. Express motions and amendments precisely.
5. Record time of adjournment, and if appropriate, the time of the next meeting.

4. *Class Discussion Board.* If you have set up an online discussion board for your class, set up private topic areas for the groups in your class. Here group members can asynchronously discuss group projects and other class assignments among themselves, without the entire class seeing their postings. These private areas also allow an excellent area for group members to share documents with each other outside of class. (See The Technology Link, Chapter 1, for information on discussion boards.)

5. *Listening and Nonverbal Communication Exercise.* The following paper-tearing activity is an interesting way to illustrate how important visual cues are in communicating. Which is more important—visual or spoken messages? What causes miscommunication?

Directions
Ask students to take a sheet of notebook paper (or distribute sheets of 8 1/2 × 11-inch paper). Tell students to follow four simple instructions—without looking at what anyone else is doing. Give the following instructions, and carry them out yourself. Pause just long enough after each command so that students can perform the action.

1. Fold your sheet of paper in half. Tear off the upper right-hand corner.
2. Fold it in half again, and tear off the upper left-hand corner. Fold it in half again, and tear off the lower right-hand corner.

When finished, ask students to hold up their sheets. Show yours as well. (By the way, your sheet will be most dramatic if you tear through several thicknesses with each corner tear command.) After observing the varying results of such simple instructions, lead a discussion focused on the causes of miscommunication. You might begin by saying, "If I'm a good communicator and you're good listeners, our sheets should all be the same. Right?"

What caused the miscommunication? Who is to blame? How could this communication transaction have been improved? To relate this exercise to the workplace, ask how managers giving instructions could improve the likelihood of success. How might listeners improve their comprehension? How should communicators react when miscommunication occurs? Who should be blamed?

Source: "Paper-Tearing Trick Teaches Lesson," *The Prior Report*, July 1992, p. 1.

---

[i] Coutu, D., & Beschloss, M. (2009, May). Why teams don't work. *Harvard Business Review, (87),* 5, 98-105. Retrieved June 1, 2009, from Business Source Complete database.

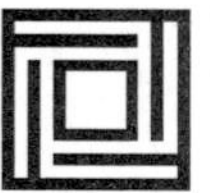

Chapter 3 LECTURE NOTES AND TEACHING SUGGESTIONS

Intercultural Communication

CHAPTER SYNOPSIS

As businesses go global and the world market place becomes increasingly international, employees will likely experience the rewards and challenges of working in a culturally diverse workplace. More than ever employees will be presented with opportunities to work alongside coworkers representing different cultures and interact with customers outside U.S. borders. To equip your students to succeed in this type of culturally rich work environment, they will need to develop intercultural proficiency including an awareness of their own culture, how it differs from others, and methods for improving communication techniques.

Chapter 3 helps students prepare for successful intercultural communication by presenting the characteristics of culture including the concepts of individualism, formality, communication style, and time orientation. The chapter explains the effects of ethnocentrism, tolerance, and patience in achieving intercultural proficiency and identifies techniques for improving nonverbal, oral, and written communication in intercultural settings. Students will investigate intercultural ethics and methods for coping with business practices broad. They will explore the challenges and benefits of working in a diverse workplace. Suggestions for thriving in an intercultural environment will help students succeed in today's global village.

LEARNING OBJECTIVES

After studying this chapter, you should be able to

1. Understand how three significant trends have increased the importance of intercultural communication.

2. Define *culture,* describe five noteworthy cultural characteristics, and compare and contrast five key dimensions of culture including high and low context.

3. Explain the effects of ethnocentrism, and show how tolerance and patience help in achieving intercultural proficiency.

4. Apply techniques for improving nonverbal and oral communication in intercultural settings.

5. Identify techniques for improving written messages to intercultural audiences.

6. Discuss intercultural ethics, including business practices abroad, bribery, prevailing customs, and methods for coping.

7. Explain in what ways workforce diversity provides benefits and poses challenges, and how you can learn to be sensitive to racial and gender issues.

WHAT'S NEW IN THIS CHAPTER

- Added several end-of-chapter social media assignments to ensure that students acquire business-relevant technology skills.
- Updated three-part Wal-Mart case study as well as created fresh critical thinking questions and assignments for each part to broaden students' perspective on intercultural issues.
- Designed a new figure showing how McDonald's is adjusting its menus around the world to suit local tastes reinforcing the concept of intercultural adaptability.
- Prepared a new Tech Box displaying population figures in various countries around the world side by side with percentages of Internet access to help students see beyond their own limited vantage points.
- Included a provocative Ethical Insights feature to invite students to discuss a controversial case of stereotyping and prejudice toward Muslims in the United States.
- Provided two current Spotlights on Communicators shedding light on relevant chapter content.
- Created two new Ethics Checks and Ethical Issue for critical thinking and discussion, thus further strengthening the focus on ethics throughout the chapter.

LECTURE OUTLINE

I. The Increasing Importance of Intercultural Communication (p. 79)

PowerPoint slides 1-3

A. Globalization of Markets

U.S. companies have expanded into global markets because of:

- The desire to increase revenue outside U.S. markets
- Passage of favorable trade agreements such as GATT and NAFTA
- Growing middle class in foreign countries such as China
- New transportation methods
- Advanced information technologies

Figure 3.1 Fries With Your Shrimp Burger?

PowerPoint slide 4

B. Technological Advancements

- Fast, reliable planes speed delivery of products overseas.
- Internet communication and online commerce occurs instantaneously across time zones and continents.

PowerPoint slide 5

C. Intercultural Workforce

- Increased immigration and the increasing number of foreign-born persons make intercultural communication increasingly important.

PowerPoint slide 6

II. Culture and Communication (p. 83)

Definition: *Culture* is the complex system of values, traits, morals, and customs shared by a society.

A. Characteristics of Culture

- Culture is learned.
- Cultures are inherently logical.
- Culture is the basis of our self-identity and community.
- Culture combines the visible and invisible.
- Culture is dynamic.

PowerPoint slide 7

Lecture Tidbit

McDonald's has adapted its menu and services to appeal to customers in foreign markets. For example, restaurants in Australia and France have coffee lounges that feel like Starbucks. In China, children can substitute corn for fries in their Happy Meals. Because drive-through windows are not popular in some traffic-choked cities, fleets of McDonald's motor scooters deliver burgers and fries to customers in Shanghai, Cairo, Taipei, and Manila. (Michael Arndt, "Knock Knock, It's Your Big Mac," *BusinessWeek*, July 23, 2007, p. 36.)

B. Dimensions of Culture

- Context (the stimuli, environment, or ambience surrounding an event)
- Individualism (an attitude of independence and freedom from control)
- Formality (level of emphasis on tradition, ceremony, and social rules)
- Communication Style (different oral and written communication styles)
- Time Orientation (time as a scarce or unlimited resource)

PowerPoint slides 8-17

Figure 3.2 Comparing Low- and High-Context Cultures

C. Stereotypes, Prototypes, Prejudices, and Generalizations

Definitions: A *stereotype* is an oversimplified behavioral pattern applied uncritically to groups.

A *prototype* is a mental representation based on general characteristics that are not

fixed and rigid but open to new definitions.
Prejudice is a rigid attitude based on erroneous beliefs or preconceptions.

PowerPoint slides 18-22

III. The Benefits of Intercultural Proficiency (p. 87)

PowerPoint slides 23-24

A. Avoiding Ethnocentrism

Definition: *Ethnocentrism* is the belief in the superiority of one's own race.

- Ethnocentrism causes us to judge others by our own values.
- Ethnocentrism can be reduced by increasing cultural sensitivity.

PowerPoint slide 25

B. Bridging the Gap

- **Tolerance.** Improve tolerance by practicing empathy.
- **Saving face.** In high-context cultures, *save face* and strive for harmony in relationships.
- **Patience.** Display patience and when talking with people from other cultures. Recognize that periods of silence are used for reflection and contemplation.

PowerPoint slide 26

Let's Discuss

Why is it important to understand cultures other than our own?

According to the Business Roundtable paper released in March, 2007, 20 percent of U.S. jobs are tied to international trade, a percentage expected to grow in coming years. Much of this growth will come from China, India, and Japan. Given this landscape, the business community is in serious need of a workforce that can understand cultures other than its own. (John Castellani, "Overcoming Our Language Barriers," *The Cincinnati Enquirer*, June 17, 2007, p. E1.)

IV. Effective Communication in Intercultural Settings (p. 90)

A. Successful Nonverbal Communication in Intercultural Environments

- Nonverbal behavior includes eye contact, facial expressions, posture, gestures, and the use of time, space, and territory.
- Hand gestures may have different meanings in different cultures. Use them cautiously.
- Become aware of your own use of nonverbal cues to increase sensitivity to variations in other cultures.

Lecture Tidbit

Don't use a lot of hand gestures when communicating to an intercultural audience. A thumb's up and the OK sign are obscene in places like Brazil, Australia, Spain, and the Middle East. (Mary Brandel, "Culture Clash," *Computerworld*, February 26, 2006, p 26.)

B. Techniques for Achieving Intercultural Competence

- **Descriptiveness.** To minimize misunderstanding, use concrete and specific feedback instead of judgmental feedback.
- **Nonjudgmentalism.** Avoid being judgmental to broaden your cultural competence.
- **Supportiveness.** Demonstrate positive support for others with head nods, eye contact, facial expressions, and physical proximity.

Figure 3.3 Basic Expressions in Other Languages

C. Successful Oral Communication in Intercultural Environments

- Learn foreign phrases.
- Use simple English.
- Speak slowly and enunciate clearly.
- Observe eye messages.
- Encourage accurate feedback.
- Check frequently for comprehension.
- Accept blame.
- Listen without interrupting.
- Smile when appropriate.
- Follow up in writing.

PowerPoint slides 27-30

Let's Discuss

English is a compulsory subject for all Chinese elementary school students; more than 200 million Chinese children study English. By comparison, only about 24,000 U.S. elementary children study Chinese. Why would it be helpful for more U.S. students to study the Chinese language?

As a 2006 report by the Committee for Economic Development notes, "businesses require employees with knowledge of foreign languages and cultures to market products to customers around the globe and to work effectively with foreign employees and partners in other countries." Because China has become an important economic partner with the United States, students who anticipate working with Chinese customers or colleagues should develop a familiarity with frequently used Chinese greetings and phrases. (John Castellani, "Overcoming Our Language Barriers," *The Cincinnati Enquirer*, June 17, 2007, p. E1.)

D. Effective Written Messages to Intercultural Audiences

- Consider local styles.
- Observe titles and rank.
- Use short sentences and short paragraphs.
- Avoid ambiguous expressions.
- Strive for clarity.
- Use correct grammar.
- Cite numbers carefully.
- Accommodate the reader in organization, tone, and style.

Figure 3.4 Typical Data Formats

E. An Intercultural Letter That Misses the Mark

- Effective, intercultural messages avoid slang, idioms, imprecise words, unclear abbreviations, and confusing dates.

Figure 3.5 Ineffective Intercultural Letter

Figure 3.6 Effective Intercultural Letter

F. Checklist for Improving Intercultural Proficiency and Communication

- Study your own culture.
- Learn about other cultures.
- Curb ethnocentrism.
- Avoid judgmentalism.
- Seek common ground.
- Observe nonverbal cues in your culture.
- Use plain English.
- Encourage accurate feedback.
- Adapt to local preferences.

V. Ethics Across Cultures (p. 95)

A. Business Practices Abroad

- Ethical codes of conduct should guide an employee's ethical behavior in other cultures.

Figure 3.7 Corruption Perceptions Index

B. Laws Forbidding Bribery

- The Foreign Corrupt Practices Act of 1977 prohibits payments to foreign officials for the purpose of obtaining or retaining business.
- Sarbanes-Oxley Act of 2002 forbids off-the-book bribes.
- Treaty by the Organization for Economic Cooperation and Development (OECD) bans the practice of bribery of foreign government officials.

C. Whose Ethics Should Prevail?

- Although world leaders agree that bribery is wrong, they do no agree on ethical behavior.

D. Making Ethical Decisions Across Borders

- Broaden your view.
- Avoid reflex judgments.
- Find alternatives.
- Refuse business if options violate your basic values.
- Embrace
- Don't rationalize shady decisions.
- Resist legalistic strategies.

PowerPoint slide 31

VI. Advantages and Challenges of Workforce Diversity (p. 99)

A. Dividends of Diversity

- **Consumers.** A diverse workforce is better equipped to meet the needs of a varied consumer base.
- **Work Teams.** Diverse work teams are better innovators and problem solvers.
- **Business Organizations.** Businesses that foster a diverse workforce experience positive employee relationships and increased productivity.

B. Divisiveness of Diversity

- A diverse workforce may cause divisiveness, discontent and clashes and result in lost productivity.

C. Tips for Improving Communication Among Diverse Workplace Audiences

- Seek training.
- Understand the value of differences.
- Don't expect conformity.
- Learn about your cultural self.
- Make fewer assumptions.
- Build on similarities.

PowerPoint slide 32

Lecture Transparencies
(available in a separate packet and at http://www.meguffey.com)

Communicating Across Culture Acetates	**Transparency Number**
Increasing Importance of Intercultural Communication; Characteristics of Culture	32
Dimensions of Culture	33-34
High-Context and Low-Context Cultures	35
Proverbs Reflect Culture	36
About Stereotypes, Prototypes, Prejudices	37
Improving Communication with Intercultural Audiences	38
Making Ethical Decisions Across Borders	39
Tips for Capitalizing on Workforce Diversity	40

Answers to Chapter Review Questions

1. **Why is intercultural communication increasingly important, and what must business communicators do to succeed? (Obj. 1)**

   In a global marketplace, communicators will need to become aware of their own culture and how it differs from others. Thus, they will be able to overcome obstacles such as misunderstandings stemming from cultural differences. The workers of tomorrow may have employers, coworkers, or clients from other countries.

2. **Why is geographical location virtually irrelevant for many activities and services today? (Obj. 1)**

   Geographical location is nearly irrelevant because of high-speed, high-capacity, and relatively low-cost communication methods, along with improvements in transcontinental transportation.

3. **Describe five major dimensions of culture. (Obj. 2)**

   1. Context describes the stimuli, environment, and ambience surrounding an event.
   2. Individualism refers to the degree to which independence and freedom from control are valued.
   3. Formality describes the emphasis placed on tradition, ceremony, and social rules.
   4. Communication style refers to the manner in which people communicate. High-context cultures rely less on words and more on context than do low-context cultures.
   5. Time orientation describes the emphasis placed on time. Is it precious and not to be wasted, or is it an unlimited and never-ending resource?

4. Briefly, contrast high- and low-context cultures. (Obj. 2)

People in low-context cultures (Germans, North Americans, Scandinavians) tend to prefer direct verbal interaction, understand meaning at one level only, are less proficient in reading nonverbal communication, value individualism, emphasize linear logic, use "logic" to express ideas, say *no* directly, communicate in highly structured messages with many details, and stress the literal meaning of words. People in high-context cultures (Chinese, Japanese, Arabs, South Americans) tend to prefer indirect verbal interaction, understand meanings embedded at many sociocultural levels, are more proficient in reading nonverbal communication, value group membership, emphasize spiral logic, use more "feeling" to express ideas, talk around the point, avoid saying *no*, communicate in simple but ambiguous messages, and use fewer words but understand the context of a situation.

5. How is a *stereotype* different from a *prototype*? (Obj. 3)

A stereotype is an oversimplified behavioral pattern applied uncritically to groups. A prototype describes mental representations based on general characteristics that are not fixed and rigid but are open to new definitions. Stereotypes are fixed and rigid; prototypes can be changed as a result of observation and experience.

6. Name techniques for bridging the gap between cultures and achieving intercultural proficiency. (Obj. 3)

a. Practice tolerance by being open-minded and by showing empathy, which means to see the world through another's eyes.
b. Help others save face, especially in high-context cultures where social harmony and saving face are prized.
c. Embrace patience, a mark of tolerance. Don't finish nonnative speakers' sentences, and accept silence as an opportunity for reflection.

7. When interacting with people who do not use your language, why is it important to learn the words for please, yes, and thank you rather than relying on gestures? (Obj. 4)

Gestures and other forms of nonverbal communication are ambiguous. One can't be certain of their meaning. Learning a few words shows respect, engenders goodwill, and improves understanding.

8. What should you assume about the level of proficiency in nonnative speakers of English? (Obj. 4)

The level of proficiency may be limited among nonnative speakers of English. Americans abroad should not assume that people who speak English always understand what is being said.

9. Describe five specific ways you can improve oral communication with someone who speaks another language. (Obj. 4)

1. Learn some phrases in the listener's language.
2. Use simple English, including short words and sentences.
3. Speak slowly and enunciate clearly.
4. Observe eye messages so that you are more likely to know when a listener is lost.
5. Encourage accurate feedback. Check frequently for comprehension.
6. Accept blame if a misunderstanding occurs.
7. Listen without interrupting. Smile!
8. Follow up conversations in writing.

10. Describe at least five ways you can improve written communication with someone who speaks another language. (Obj. 5)

1. Adopt local formats and observe titles and rank.
2. Use short sentences and short paragraphs.
3. Avoid ambiguous expressions.
4. Strive for clarity. Avoid words with many meanings. Clarify meanings.
5. Use correct grammar.
6. Cite numbers carefully.
7. Accommodate the reader in organization, tone, and style.

11. What categories of ambiguous expressions should be avoided because they could confuse readers for whom English is not a first language? (Obj. 5)

Ambiguous expressions include slang, idioms, imprecise words, unclear abbreviations, and confusing dates.

12. Are there laws forbidding bribery in the United States, and are they effective in stopping corruption? (Obj. 6)

The United States has taken the global lead on corruption by passing the Foreign Corrupt Practices Act of 1977. It prohibits payment to foreign officials for the purpose of obtaining or retaining business. However, the law applies only to U.S. companies. The Sarbanes-Oxley Act of 2002 forbids off-the-book bribes. American law does permit payments not exceeding $500 that may ease the way for routine government actions, such as expediting a visa request.

13. List seven techniques for making ethical decisions across borders. (Obj. 6)

1. Broaden your view of values and customs in other cultures.
2. Avoid reflex judgments in regard to what is immoral, corrupt, primitive, or unworkable.
3. Find alternative solutions instead of caving in to government payoffs.
4. Refuse business if the options violate your basic values or those of your firm.
5. Conduct all relations and negotiations as openly as possible.
6. Don't rationalize shady decisions with statements such as, "This is really in the company's best interests."
7. Resist legalistic strategies that are legally safe but ethically questionable.

14. Name three groups that benefit from workforce diversity and explain why. (Obj. 7)

1. *Consumers* benefit because a diverse workforce can turn out the specialized goods and services they want.
2. *Work teams* benefit from workforce diversity because they are less inclined toward groupthink. Heterogeneous teams are thought to turn out richer, more creative ideas.
3. *Business organizations* benefit from workplace diversity because they endure fewer discrimination lawsuits, fewer union clashes, and less government regulatory action. Moreover, diversity can improve productivity and profits.

15. Describe six tips for improving communication among diverse workplace audiences. (Obj. 7)

1. Seek training. Look upon diversity as an opportunity, not a threat.
2. Understand the value of differences. Diversity in problem-solving groups encourages independent and creative thinking.
3. Don't expect conformity. Differences can enrich and expand creative opportunities.
4. Learn about your cultural self. Strive to understand what makes you react as you do.
5. Make fewer assumptions. Don't assume that everyone is like you.
6. Build on similarities. Look for areas in which you and others agree. Look for common ground.

Answers to Critical Thinking Questions

1. Queen Elizabeth of England once said, "Stereotypes wither when human contacts flourish." What does this statement mean? Have you found this to be accurate in your own experience? (Objs. 1, 3)

Astute students will recognize that ignorance and lack of contact with people not like us tend to engender aversion and even hate. Once we learn how other cultures function and meet individuals from formerly "exotic" locales, most of us temper their preconceived notions. However, it is also likely that some students will argue the opposite: Sometimes knowing "the other" is not a guarantee of friendly relations. Stereotypes and prejudice bloom despite acquaintance or a deeper knowledge. Examples: In former Yugoslavia the ethnic factions mingled and coexisted in close proximity before launching a bloody Balkan war in the 1990s. German Jews in the 1930s and 1940s were persecuted although they had been loyal and profoundly assimilated into the general population. And, closer to home, few would deny that despite the rich cultural diversity in the United States and a great degree of interaction between ethnic groups, prejudice and racism continue to plague us.

2. English is becoming the world's business language because the United States is a dominant military and trading force. Why should Americans bother to learn about other cultures? (Objs. 1, 2, and 7)

Nearly every large U.S. company today is part of a global market, whether it wants to be or not. Any American company ignoring the global market is in danger of being swallowed up by foreign competition. Even small U.S companies are looking beyond our borders for business. Some of our trading partners may speak English, but as a second language. Moreover, although they speak our language, they do not share Euro-North American culture. For our products and services to compete on a global basis, Americans must understand what motivates people in other cultures and must use this knowledge to become more economically successful. Americans must also learn more about other cultures to be able to work and live with people from our own increasingly diverse subcultures. We need to learn that all cultures have validity. Students can expect to work for organizations that sell to, buy from, or have partners or subsidiaries or a head office in foreign lands. They can expect their coworkers to come from a number of cultures.

3. **Cultural expert John Engle complained that his American students resist references to cultural generalizations. He asserted, "Thoughtful generalizations are the heart of intercultural communication, allowing us to discuss meaningfully the complex web of forces acting upon individuals that we call culture." Do you agree or disagree? Why? (Objs. 2, 3)**

   Generalizations are indeed necessary to discuss the vastly different cultures within our own country and certainly abroad. Professor Engle said that American students are very uncomfortable when generalizations are made about cultures. "Faced with cultural differences, their tendency is to oscillate between a flaccid we-are-the-world universalism—'people are people everywhere'—and its unexpected corollary, the certitude that any generalization constitutes stereotyping." He says it is hard to discuss culture with American students who are trained to see every story as an individual one. Professor Engle wisely made the following observation:

   Culture studies helps us see that knowing the world better is knowing the self better. Coming to understand the cultural weight that each of us carries, and to empathize with the different loads borne by others, is finally to enrich and liberate the individual self (John Engle, "Culture's Unacknowledged Iron Grip," *The Chronicle of Higher Education*, February 2, 2007, p. B16).

4. **We are told to overcome our natural tendency to show ethnocentrism, judging other cultures by our own values. Does this mean we should accept actions we find abhorrent in other world regions as a mere manifestation of the indigenous culture? Provide examples to support your answer. (Objs. 3, 6)**

   The question whether culture should be observed from a value-neutral perspective or allow an ethical judgment is vexing. Students should realize that to some degree ethnocentrism is natural and unavoidable. Our environment shapes us and makes us what we are. However, a stubbornly ethnocentric view becomes pernicious when we make snap judgments without knowing other cultures and arrogantly believe in our own superiority over others in all things. A more productive approach may be to note the distinctness of other cultures and retain an openness as well as curiosity. This chapter provides guidelines on how to deal with intercultural ethics.

Grasping another culture fully takes a lifetime and, as we know, culture changes over time. Ethics and the law change too. Students could be reminded in this context that slavery, for example, was always wrong, in all its manifestations although it was the law of the land and even some of the Founding Fathers unfortunately owned slaves. Slavery was not just a "cultural" trait. The persecution of the Jews was never morally right although the Nazis saw to it that it was legal when they passed their infamous Nuremburg Laws to justify genocide. More recently, we may find public executions and stoning abhorrent and do not have to condone them if they run counter to our sensibilities. Nor are we obligated to ignore the poor human rights record of the People's Republic of China despite our strong trade ties.

5. Some economists and management scholars argue that statements such as "diversity is an economic asset" or "diversity is a new strategic imperative" are unproved and perhaps unprovable assertions. Should social responsibility or market forces determine whether an organization strives to create a diverse workforce? Why? (Obj. 7)

Thomas A. Kochan, one of the most respected human resources management scholars in the country, said that his five-year study shows that "there are no strong positive or negative effects of gender or racial diversity on business performance." He went on to say that "the diversity industry is built on sand. The business case rhetoric for diversity is simply naïve and overdone." Although employers spend billions on diversity programs, little evidence can be provided to show improved business performance, financial results, or accountability (Fay Hansen, "Diversity's Business Case Doesn't Add Up," *Workforce*, April 2003, 28).

Other critics of diversity programs assert that market forces, not social engineering, should determine whether a firm strives to select employees whose characteristics mirror those of the general population. For example, if customers of your products are new mothers, it makes sense to have a sales force that understands and speaks their language. If companies are forced to hire individuals who do not necessarily represent their customers, then the costs that result (miscommunication and the time spent sorting out misunderstandings) may not be worth the social gains. (See Bob Filipczak, Rebecca Ganzel, and others in "A Market Solution for Diversity?" *Training*, June 1998, 14.)

Supporters of diversity programs argue that workplace diversity is a positive force, even a source of competitive advantage. Arguments supporting diversity programs appear in this chapter. Students should be aware, however, that documenting financial or performance results for diversity programs is difficult. Should social responsibility take precedence over bottom-line results?

6. Ethical Issue: You know that it's not acceptable to make ethnic jokes, least of all in the workplace, but a colleague of yours keeps invoking the worst ethnic and racial stereotypes. How do you respond? Do you remain silent and change the subject, or do you pipe up? What other options do you have in dealing with such a coworker? Consider whether your answer would change if the offender were your boss. (Objs. 6, 7)

Answers will vary. Students will probably realize that they will have to choose their battles wisely; in other words, sometimes they may want to signal to the bigot that they disagree. However, in some situations silence or a change of topic may be the most opportune strategy, especially when dealing with superiors. Power relationships may influence how we respond in such situations, yet most of us would probably prefer to work in environments that are not racist and would try their best to find companies where such behavior is frowned upon and explicitly disparaged by policies.

Activities

3.1 Trouble on a Global Scale: Analyzing Cultural Blunders (Objs. 1–3)

a. The American visitor broke three major rules of etiquette during the meeting with his Middle Eastern business partner. Showing the soles of shoes is considered an insult. So is refusing hospitality in the form of a cup of coffee. Finally, the left hand is viewed as unclean; therefore, the guest should have used his right hand to distribute materials.
b. For the Japanese, brainstorming is difficult because their culture teaches them to be deliberate. Decisions are made at a slower pace to ensure the "right" answer. Although such deliberation is frustrating to Westerners, the upside is that people do things carefully and well. To generate ideas and to coax people to express themselves and take risks, companies might consider offering incentives; a promotion; or training in leadership, public speaking, confidence, and English. (Rochrock, V. Culture clash. EBSCO database)
c. The chief of protocol on the Czech side should have done his or her homework. Eager to show off the host country's specialty—rabbit—the Czech delegation ignored the visitors' customs and dietary habits. Food and eating rituals are important cultural markers and respecting them ensures harmonious relations. The lack of preparation and poor choice of dish for the banquet could be interpreted by the guests as insensitive, uncaring, and offensive.
d. Americans should try to understand that in high-context cultures, business transactions are more hierarchical. Consensus is often required; thus many people may be involved in decisions. The Americans should probably yield to their foreign colleagues. After all, how hard is it to copy someone on a memo or e-mail message? The extra effort is necessary to achieve harmony.
e. Face-saving is important in China. People frown on psychological counseling because it admits weakness and loses face. Chinese culture also values harmony. People would prefer to discuss workplace harmony than workplace conflict. In addition, China is a collectivist culture; meeting in groups is more acceptable than one-on-one counseling.

3.2 Mastering International Time (Objs. 1–5)

a. Students will find a number of definitions. UTC stands for "Coordinated Universal Time." It represents the international time standard and replaces GMT (Greenwich Mean Time or Greenwich Meridian Time). UTC is midnight in Greenwich, England, which is located at 0 degrees longitude. Everything east of Greenwich is later in time; everything west is earlier.
b. The notation 13.00 indicates 1 p.m. The 24-hour clock is a universal convention of time-keeping in which the day runs from midnight to midnight and is divided into 24 hours, numbered from 0 to 23. A 12-hour clock starts at 12 midnight and runs until 12 noon. Then it starts at 1 p.m. and runs to 12 midnight. A 24-hour clock runs from 00:00 (12 midnight) until 23.59 (11:59 p.m.) and then starts again at 00.00 (midnight). The United States is one of the few industrialized countries to use the 12-hour clock. Instructors should encourage students to become familiar with the 24-hour clock.
c. Probably the best times to talk are 5 or 6 p.m. in Indianapolis, which is 7 or 8 a.m. in Osaka.
d. Probably the best times are 7 or 8 p.m. in Atlanta, which is 8 or 9 a.m. in Singapore.

3.3 The World is Atwitter – Hot New Medium Opens up Countries and Cultures (Obj. 1)

To benefit fully from the *follow* function, students and instructors should open a Twitter account. The account can be set up allowing varying degrees of privacy. The short training video is helpful in jumpstarting competent use. Students should recognize that unless they follow a recognizable and legitimate news organization such as CNN, the origin and identity of a source is murky. Twitter has spawned impostors. A case in point: As the *Los Angeles Times* reported, Bill Gates of Microsoft fame recently had his office deny that he is the @billgates on Twitter. Ashton Kutcher, an early adopter and Twitter phenomenon, also prompted a number of fakes. Students who speak foreign languages can explore international tweets. As the post-election protests in Iran showed, Twitter has become a powerful and speedy global communication tool. We will explore how Twitter can be used by businesses and how it affects today's world of work in Chapter 7.]

3.4 Global Economy (Obj. 1)

Students should find articles related to global markets and trading in print newspapers and magazines or on the Internet. You may wish to have them make written or oral presentations.

3.5 Intercultural Gap at Resort Hotel in Thailand (Objs. 1–4)

Managers and employees alike would benefit from a training course centered on intercultural issues. Foreign managers should be taught about Thai culture so that they better understand their values and behavior. Thai employees should be encouraged to take complaints, urgent requests, and deadlines seriously. However, managers might have difficulty implementing this behavior. You would probably not aim to change either the Westerners' or the natives' cultures. Instead, the goal should be to teach each group about the other's culture. It might also be best to teach problem-solving techniques in regard to specific situations. In looking at the big picture, one imagines that guests enjoy the smiles and might be willing to be patient in regard to having requests filled immediately. An actual training program for the hotels in Phuket centered on four topics: smiles and greetings, talking and listening, answering and anticipating, and resolving problems.

3.6 From Waterloo, Wisconsin, Trek Bicycles Goes Global (Objs. 1, 3, and 7)

What broad lessons can other entrepreneurs learn from Trek's international experiences?

a. Large markets are available outside the U.S.
b. Don't assume that the way a product is advertised, packaged, and distributed here will work similarly across borders.
c. Test the language for all advertising and packaging with local cultures to assess its effectiveness and impact.
d. Research a country's culture to better understand how to market successfully.
e. Be prepared to adjust your manufacturing, distribution, and advertising to appeal to local markets.
f. Look for ways to improve your product based on the feedback from international markets

3.7 Interpreting Intercultural Proverbs (Objs. 2, 3)

Here are some interpretations and values associated with the following proverbs:

North American Proverbs
- *An ounce or prevention is worth a pound of cure.* (Practicality, logic, linear thinking)
- *The squeaking wheel gets the grease.* (Individualism, speaking out, aggressiveness)
- *A bird in the hand is worth two in the bush.* (Practicality, immediate rewards)
- *He who holds the gold makes the rules.* (Power, individualism, aggressiveness)

Japanese Proverbs
- *A wise man hears one and understands ten.* (Context and experience expand the meaning of one word to many levels.)
- *The pheasant would have lived but for its cry.* (Modesty, reticence, aversion to individualism)
- *The nail that sticks up gets pounded down.* (Modesty, reticence, aversion to individualism)

German Proverbs
- *No one is either rich or poor who has not helped himself to be so.* (Individual responsibility)
- *He who is afraid of doing too much always does too little.* (Individualism, action orientation)

Other proverbs that students might mention or that you might mention to students:

- *Time is money.*
- *Don't cry over spilled milk.*
- *Cleanliness is next to godliness.*
- *Take care of today, and tomorrow will take care of itself.*
- *Don't count your chickens before they are hatched.*
- *If at first you don't succeed, try, try again.*
- *Waste not, want not.*
- *What you see in yourself is what you see in the world.* (Afghan)
- *Who tells the truth is never wrong.* (African)
- *There is more wisdom in listening than in speaking.* (African)
- *The wind does not break a tree that bends.* (African)
- *Between the beginning and the end there is always a middle.* (Brazilian)
- *An ant may well destroy a whole dam.* (Chinese)
- *A book holds a house of gold.* (Chinese)
- *Of all the stratagems, to know when to quit is the best.* (Chinese)
- *When the sun rises, it rises for everyone.* (Cuban)
- *Better to ask twice than to lose your way once.* (Danish)
- *There is no pillow so soft as a clear conscience.* (French)
- *Don't bargain for fish which are still in the water.* (Indian)
- *Every tear has a smile behind it.* (Iranian)
- *To him that watches, everything is revealed.* (Italian)
- *A little axe can cut down a big tree.* (Jamaican)
- *Fall seven times, stand up eight.* (Japanese)
- *Pray that you will never have to bear all that you are able to endure.* (Jewish)
- *Lower your voice and strengthen your argument.* (Lebanese)
- *There is more time than life.* (Mexican)
- *There is no shame in not knowing; the shame lies in not finding out.* (Russian)
- *A man is judged by his deeds, not by his words.* (Russian)
- *A book is a garden carried in the pocket.* (Saudi Arabian)
- *Be slow in choosing a friend but slower in changing him.* (Scottish)
- *When in doubt who will win, be neutral.* (Swiss)
- *He who gets up with anger, sits down with a loss.* (Turkish)
- *Two heads are better than one.* (Turkish)

3.8 Negotiating Traps (Objs. 2–5)

a. Since Americans are so legalistic, they are usually more concerned about the letter of the law rather than the spirit of the law. Therefore, they assume that contracts are inviolate. Other cultures, such as the Japanese, consider contracts as a good starting point for discussion and further negotiations, the results of which do not necessarily need to be written.

b. Because individuals in other cultures, Asian in particular, want to get to know people on a social basis before they begin their business relationships, the wheels of business grind more slowly there. The Thais have an expression *mai pen rai* that, loosely translated, means "never mind." If something wasn't completed today, maybe it will be completed tomorrow. Americans must realize that they have to tailor their business practices to the countries with which they wish to do business.

c. If American businesspeople want to gain the respect of foreign business partners, one sure way is speaking their language. Mastering only a few phrases at first will demonstrate a great respect for them and their culture. Since language translation is not an exact science, having a working knowledge of both the language and culture will give these American businesspeople the confidence that ideas are being interpreted correctly.

d. Someone who is speaking English did not necessarily learn English as his or her first language. It is important to understand that even one who appears to speak fluent English may not understand slang, idioms, jargon, and other specialized language. It is important to speak clearly in plain language, avoiding words that may be misinterpreted.

e. The saying that "rank has its privilege" is very true, especially in Asian cultures. Knowing the chain of command and giving the proper deference at each level is of utmost importance. If their strict rules of conduct are not followed, someone could lose face in front of employees who are not considered peers. So they should become astute observers of social and business customs and pattern behavior accordingly. Also the status of women in the company is something to be concerned with. Since business representatives have only one opportunity to make a good first impression, they shouldn't destroy their chances by committing a serious social faux pas for which they and their company will not be forgiven.

3.9 Learning About Other Countries (Obj. 4)

a. **Australia:** With a handshake standing an arm's length apart.

India: With the *namaste*, which is formed by pressing the palms together below the chin and nodding the head. To show respect, a slight bow is added.

Japan: If you are greeted with a bow, return the bow with one as low as the one received. Keep your palms flat to your thighs.

Korea: With a slight bow and a handshake, for men.

Netherlands: With a warm and hearty handshake for both men and women.

Spain: With a brief but firm handshake.

b. Australia, Canada, India, and the United Kingdom

c. In France, people may be greeted with a handshake or a kiss. Depending on the region, the number of kisses varies from two to four. The intensity varies from a lip-smacking smooch to an air kiss. In Spain, if the people have a personal relationship, they may embrace or touch cheeks while exchanging an air kiss.

3.10 Calling iPhone or iPod Touch Owners: Pick up a Few Foreign Phrases (Objs. 3, 4)

Not every student will own an iPhone or iPod Touch, but the popularity of these devices is growing. Students who have them could be asked to demonstrate the applications. The audio can be played back, and the spelling may be viewed on the screen. The pro versions currently range in cost from $1.99 to $9.99 and are immensely useful for travel and the learning of simple phrases that the program provides.

3.11 Tracking Facebook's Explosive International Growth (Objs. 1, 7)

Keeping up with Facebook's staggering growth is a challenge. The latest numbers cited here were collected in 2008 by the social networking powerhouse itself and show that in absolute numbers the fastest-growing contingent of Facebook users comes from the United Kingdom, Chile, and Colombia. Heading the 25 top countries outside the United States was again the UK, followed by Canada and Turkey. Students are encouraged to write to mail@insidefacebook.com to obtain data for the 90 countries in which Facebook appears. Bilingual students can be especially helpful in comparing the social networking sites in various languages and could be asked to look for signs of localization, similarities, and differences.

3.12 Examining Cultural Stereotypes (Objs. 1, 3)

This activity drives home the limiting nature of stereotypes, even the positive ones. Very few of us are comfortable representing our entire culture, although others may perceive and designate us as "ambassadors" of our country of origin. Students may find some stereotypes flattering, but most will recognize that they are ambivalent at best. Few Jewish students, for example, would enjoy being called "good with money" because it's an old anti-Semitic prejudice couched in positive language. Likewise, being seen as a "Latin lover" is a mixed blessing, and not all Asian students are studious and nerdy. Students should also recognize that we may be amused by positive and even negative stereotypes leveled at others, but we may react with less humor once the barbs of prejudice are pointed at us.

3.13 Analyzing a Problem International Letter (Obj. 5)

The letter is poorly organized, poorly written, and overly casual; but let's just focus on the difficulty it might cause readers unfamiliar with our language.

a. Slang: "royally turned off," "put down our customers"
b. Idioms: "on-again/off-again haggling," "take the bull by the horns"
c. Two-word verbs: our good name to "keep up" (instead of "maintain"), "fire off" (instead of "send")
d. Sports idioms: "playing ball with us," "score big," "give it your best shot," "in the running"
e. Ambiguous words: "shoddy merchandise"
f. Acronym: "ASAP"
g. Confusing date: "3/8" instead of March 8.

h. Dangling participle: "By playing ball with us, your products . . . ."
Possible revision: "By acting as our supplier, you and your products will enjoy wider distribution."
i. Informality: Uses first name in salutation. Might be offensive to reader.

3.14 Dropping in Anytime: Avoiding Ambiguous Expressions (Obj. 5)

Idioms: by leaps and bounds, crossing bridges before coming to them, grin and bear it, with flying colors, putting the cart before the horse, getting lost in the shuffle

Slang: getting the "hang" of it; get the "drift"; "cool"; "bad" (when it means the opposite); just "ballpark" it; "chew" on that (think about it); a "no brainer"; "butt" in or out; a real "worm"; a geek; "hella"; "props"

Acronyms: ASAP (as soon as possible), OSHA (Occupational Safety and Health Administration), PIN (personal identification number), ZIP (Zone Improvement Plan), FAQ (frequently asked question), COLA (cost-of-living adjustment), RAM (random-access memory).

Sports references: hit a grand slam, go to bat for someone, ballpark figure, step up to the plate, make a slam dunk.

Abbreviations: FYI (for your information), BTW (by the way), ISP (Internet Service Provider), DJ (disc jockey), HMO (health maintenance organization), VIP (very important person).

Jargon: Microspeak expressions, a lexicon from former Microsoft employee: "disambiguate" (to clarify); "EOM" (end of message); "facemail" (technologically backward means of communication; involves walking to someone's office and speaking face to face); "generating content" (writing); "net it out" (boil it down); "push back" (respond forcefully to an unfavorable answer); "touch skin" (a meeting arranged to communicate in person); "weasel text" (intentionally stilted or murky text).

Two-word verbs: hold back (withhold), take back (return), come to an agreement (agree), shut down (close), figure out (calculate), mark down (reduce).

3.15 *Baksheesh, Mordida, and Kumshah*: Making Grease Payments Abroad (Obj. 6)

a. Your company would be prohibited from making cash payments to government officials involved in making decisions regarding a contract for your firm. This is a bribe and could be prosecuted. The most prominent case of this kind occurred in 1995. Lockheed Martin plead guilty to making a corrupt $1 million payment to an Egyptian legislator in return for assistance in obtaining a contract for the sale of three aircraft to Egypt. Lockheed paid a fine of $24.8 million. A former Lockheed official involved in the bribe was sentenced to 18 months in prison. Students should be warned to avoid any payments made in cash. Always work "in the fresh air" with legitimate records that form a permanent money trail.

However, the request to update agricultural research in Pakistan may be legitimate. Although your firm may not be able to make direct private payments, you might be able to offer additional expertise to assist in agricultural research. Perhaps nonmonetary public service benefits could replace payoffs and satisfy the needs of the government.

b. This is an actual case. The vice president of an aircraft parts company was convicted for, among other things, using his Diner's Club card to charge the honeymoon present.
c. The government considered this "collection service fee" a bribe and convicted the official.
d. In another real case, the Justice Department investigated a company giving gifts to officials who regulated their industry. If a company cannot earn the contract with superior products and service, it is safer to move on. Beware of any requests to keep payments quiet.
e. When goods are waiting to be unloaded at docks in foreign ports, the Federal Corrupt Practices Act allows "grease" payments. It considers these "routine governmental actions" and does not prohibit them.
f. Hiring the relative of a government official involved in transactions with your company is actionable, according to the FCPA. In the 1980s individuals were prosecuted in the Pemex case even though the payments did not go directly to the official involved.

3.16 Investigating Gifts, Gratuities, and Entertainment Limits (Obj. 7)

Students will find many interesting specific restrictions. For example, BlueCross BlueShield of Illinois limits gifts, gratuities, or favors at a "nominal value of $50 or less." Its Code of Conduct further states, "The value of all gifts received in one year from all business sources must not exceed $150. Entertainment and meals offered or received by employees as part of legitimate business activity are not included in the $50 gift limit, but must be within the boundaries of reason and moderation." Generally, raffles and prizes that are part of an outside business activity are not considered gifts. (BlueCross BlueShield of Illinois Code of Conduct at http://www.bcbsil.com/code/code_gifts.htm)

3.17 Investors Try to Push All-White Board to Diversity (Obj. 7)

In this role-playing exercise, one student should argue for the benefits of diversity. A diverse staff is better able to read trends and respond to increasingly diverse world markets. Specialized goods and services are more likely to be developed by diverse teams who are similar to the markets they serve. Teams can generate more creative and effective problem-solving techniques. Business organizations with diversity programs and diverse staffs suffer fewer discrimination lawsuits, fewer union clashes, and less government regulatory action. Most important, a diverse staff can improve employee relations and boost productivity. The other student in the pair might argue that diversity creates divisiveness, conflict, and prejudice.

3.18 What Makes a "Best" Company for Minorities? (Obj. 7)

A quick online search will lead students to the *Fortune* article at http://money.cnn.com/magazines/fortune/bestcompanies/minorities/. Students can use the information on this site to supplement the list provided in the book.

ZOOMING IN Part 1: Costly Intercultural Lessons for World's Largest Retailer

Critical Thinking

- **In its international expansion policy, Wal-Mart followed the advice of Harvard business professor Theodore Levitt, whose famous 1983 book *The Globalization of Markets* advocated standardization, not localization: "Gone are accustomed differences in national or regional preference." Whereas conventional multinational companies adapted to "superficial and even entrenched differences within and between nations," truly global firms sought to "force suitably standardized products and practices on the entire globe."[i] Should companies stick to a standardized approach or adapt to local markets?**

  Many analysts believe that multinational companies with a proven business model, such as Wal-Mart's discounting strategy, will be most successful if they implement the techniques that made them successful. For Wal-Mart, this would mean copying the efficiencies of Wal-Mart's single-story supercenters and Wal-Mart's buying and selling techniques. Levitt believed that globalization would eventually overcome national differences. Other marketing veterans say that multinational companies must adapt to local customs and tastes. Tolerance and patience are required to forge a new culture that is adaptive, flexible, and accommodating. This question has no right or wrong answer. Its goal is to make students think about the significance of culture in the increasingly global business environment.

- **What domestic and global changes are taking place that encourage the international expansion of companies such as Wal-Mart?**

  Like Wal-Mart, many domestic as well as multinational companies are expanding their operations overseas. This expansion is largely motivated by a desire to increase profits. To do this, companies need to expand. As domestic markets mature and growth declines, companies look abroad to develop new markets. Favorable trade agreements have fueled this expansion along with technological advances in communication and transportation. It is easier to send products overseas, and it is easier to manage far-flung enterprises because of advances in transportation and information technologies. Another important trend is the growth of middle-class consumers in other countries. These consumers want and can afford the kinds of items that Americans enjoy.

- **What other U.S. businesses can you name that have merged with foreign companies or expanded to become multinational in scope? Have you heard of any notable successes or failures?**

  Students should be able to name many U.S. companies that are multinational in scope, such as Johnson & Johnson, Disney, McDonald's, GM, Intel, Microsoft, Coca-Cola, IBM, General Electric, and Citigroup. Nearly every large company is now multinational in scope. Not all of them are enjoying success in their global ventures. One notable international merger involved Daimler (Mercedes Benz) and Chrysler. Many called the merger a colossal mistake, insisting that the German parent company badly overestimated the strength of the Chrysler brand. In the end, Daimler sold Chrysler. Another problematic international expansion involves Disneyland Park near Paris (formerly known as Euro Disneyland), where attendance and revenues are disappointing. This open-ended question encourages students to think about many familiar companies that are no longer domestic.

ZOOMING IN Part 2: Wal-Mart in China

Critical Thinking

- **How do Chinese and Americans differ on key dimensions of culture as described in this chapter?**

  Speaking generally, most observers agree that Japan represents a high-context culture whereas America represents a low-context culture. Japanese people tend to be more formal and to prefer indirect verbal interaction. They value group membership rather than individualism, which Americans champion. Americans favor straightforwardness and are considered more aggressive. Japanese value humility while Americans see nothing wrong with "tooting one's own horn." Americans value logic, written instructions, and contracts. People in high-context cultures put faith in the context of a situation and in their feelings or interpretations.

- **In what ways does Wal-Mart's strategy in China compare to its misadverntures in South Korea, Germany, and Japan?**

  The retailer seems to have researched consumer tastes and living conditions very closely and accommodated the Chinese consumers' preferences. Unlike its lost opportunities in South Korea, Wal-Mart responded nimbly to the Chinese market's desire for a novel shopping experience. It did not impose its unchanged business model on the Chinese. Rather, it has provided a pleasant environment and high-quality goods while also catering to the Chinese palate and way of life.

- **How can Wal-Mart and other multinational companies overcome the cultural barriers they face when expanding into other countries?**

  In bridging the gap between widely divergent cultures, companies must often learn new attitudes and behaviors. Wal-Mart should probably not expect to impose its routines on Japanese employees. It might be more effective to adapt these routines to local preferences. The "10-foot" rule (approaching any customer within 10 feet and offering assistance) makes sense in the United States. In Japan it might not immediately work. Over time, however, it may become more acceptable. In moving into other cultures, multinational companies need to develop tolerance and patience. They also must learn how important it is to save face for local managers and employees.

ZOOMING IN, Your Turn: Applying Your Skills at Wal-Mart

Wal-Mart is struggling with image problems at home and abroad, mainly due to its bottom-line, cost-cutting approach, its conservative human resources policies, low wages and lack of health insurance, and what some perceive as corporate hubris. At the same time, since at least 2005, Wal-Mart has embarked on a campaign to burnish its tarnished image. Whatever its motives, the company has launched some significant green initiatives and encouraged others to collaborate on making global consumption more sustainable. Thanks to its sheer size, Wal-Mart is in a good position to effect genuine change. It can pressure suppliers to adopt its sustainability mandates. How should the news about green initiatives be spread? Students should consider starting a Facebook page and suggest that the corporate Web site provide links to social media including Twitter to help "publish" the positive news and press releases on the Web as soon as they happen.

Discussion Material for CAREER COACH: He Said, She Said: Gender Talk and Gender Tension

Students are asked to discuss whether men and women do indeed have different communication styles. You might wish to ask your students to conduct their own studies on this question by observing men and women for one week. In the workplace, in classrooms, in casual surroundings—do the interpretations of Tannen and Grey seem valid? Your students will probably agree that some of the observations are valid, but much depends on the situation and the position of power of the individual speaking. Men in low power positions (for example, when one talks to his boss) can be deferential, indirect, and better listeners. Conversely, women in charge can be assertive, direct, and authoritative.

Which style is more appropriate for today's team-based management? Some theorists believe that as we move away from authoritative, hierarchical management methods toward consensus-building participative management strategies, some of the female communication techniques are more appropriate. Others say that we should avoid "knee-jerk reactions" and train people to make a clear distinction between communication habits and personality traits. Everyone, both male and female, should be taught the most successful techniques required by the situation. We should encourage the interchangeable use of those styles depending on need. Forget about masculine and feminine stereotypes, says Jayne Tear, gender dynamics specialist. Instead, teach everyone the best listening, conversation, and consensus-building techniques. It's not a male-female thing, she says.

For interesting classroom activities involving gendered conversational styles, see Louise Rehling, "Improving Teamwork Through Awareness of Conversational Styles," December 2004, *Business Communication Quarterly*, 475–482.

Discussion Material for ETHICAL INSIGHTS: Overcoming Prejudice: Negative Perceptions of Muslims in the United States

This topic is potentially incendiary and should be handled with tact. Nevertheless, some of the most engaging subjects are those that incite passions. They prove that discomfort with "the other" is common, and that preconceived notions remain even in very diverse societies such as ours. In the workplace, prejudice can be toxic. It is no coincidence that Mansoor's classroom is filled with business professionals who were sent there by their employers for diversity training.

Chances are that at least some of the students in your classes are Muslim. The subject may make some of them feel uncomfortable because their faith causes them to be in the spotlight. Others may be eager to share their experience with prejudice, especially if they embrace the Islamic concept of modesty and wear items of clothing that identify them as Muslims.

The brief facts listed in the scenario show that many of the gut-level responses the average person in the United States associates with a minority may be based on misinformation, ignorance, and fear. Students may find it heartening that several witnesses to the bagel shop incident chose to leave in protest and that at least one assailed the presumptive bigot in the bakery. Perceptive students may recognize that the scenario is far from specific to the Muslim minority but that it recalls Jim Crow, discrimination against Jews, South Africa under apartheid, and other racial and ethnic bigotry.

Responses to the discussion questions will vary, but they could include the following answers: Empathy vs. fear of the other may explain the different reactions in the bagel shop. Most people are able to identify with those who suffer injustice, even if they appear "foreign" or "exotic." The collective shock of 9/11 and subsequent violence in Iraq, Afghanistan, Pakistan, and Iran have contributed to a negative image of Muslims—not just radical Islam—around the world, but particularly in Western countries with sizable Muslim immigrant communities.

The hijab is not only a cultural and religious symbol, but it is also highly political. In Turkey and Tunisia, two Muslim countries that have banned the headscarf in public places, wearing the hijab is an act of defiance and protest. It signifies strict adherence to Islamic law. Women being forced to cover their heads (as in Iran, for example), and women forced to forego the hijab (most recently in France and Germany for civil servants) in each case lose their freedom of religion and right to self-expression. The defenders of human rights argue that forcing Muslim women to choose between their jobs and their religion is inhumane. Supporters of bans attribute oppression to Islamic dress and advocate what they see as empowerment.

Workplace tensions—and conflict due to prejudice is no exception—almost always affect productivity. They also poison the work atmosphere and may disrupt team cohesion.

Discussion Material for PLUGGED IN: Greenland and Iceland: The Most Connected Countries in the World?

The Central Intelligence Agency (CIA) runs a Web site that is a treasure trove of intercultural information. It gives you access to country comparisons and profiles as well as important statistics. For example, you can learn about economies, governments, ethnic groups, or telecommunications around the world. Likewise, BBC News in the United Kingdom compiles reliable facts about various nations. Using Google, locate *CIA World Factbook Iceland* (*Greenland*) or *BBC News Country Profiles*. Try to find answers explaining why North European nations are so Internet friendly.

The Scandinavians, with Greenland and Iceland at the top, are the world's most avid Internet users relative to their populations. Not surprisingly, Internet access correlates strongly with wealth. The strong economies in Northern Europe and the cold climate that leaves few outdoor options during the long winter may explain the high penetration. Despite their relatively small populations, Finland (think Nokia), Sweden, and Iceland are high-tech locations in Europe.

Examine the table *Internet Use Around the World*. For example, in China 22.4 percent of the people have Internet access. Relate that percentage to the population figure. What can you say about the likely development in the future? What conclusions can you draw about Internet use worldwide? How can you explain the low Internet penetration for Asia as a whole?

The potential for the growth of Internet access in China and Asia as a whole is huge. Only about a quarter of the world's population have Internet access, reflecting a very uneven distribution between haves and have-nots. At nearly a billion people, Africa shows a low Internet penetration rate of 5.6 percent, but signs of growth are evident. Between 2000 and 2008, the number of users on that continent grew 1,100 percent. Assuming peace and stability in the poorer regions of the world, Internet use is likely to grow.

Visit *Internet World Stats* (http://www.internetworldstats.com/stats.htm) and weigh population figures against Internet usage; for example, compare Africa, Europe, North America, and Asia. Study user growth between 2000 and today. By clicking the links for the continents, you can view individual countries. How could businesses use this statistical information? Which types of business could benefit the most?

The individual country statistics are revealing. The small but highly developed and population-dense country of Japan closely matches the United States in Internet access as opposed to populous China, where only about a fifth of the people are connected. Again, the correlation between per-capita use and wealth is significant. These statistics would benefit businesses with a global reach that wish to market products or services in foreign countries, tech and IT companies perhaps most of all.

Ethics Check Questions

Ethics Check, Page 74
Cultural Change: From the Dinner Table to the Drive Through
The advent of mass mobility by automobile in the 1950s and increasing numbers of women joining the workforce have led to the dramatic rise of the fast-food industry. Middle-class families no longer gathered around the dinner table but became used to snacking on the go. Now many critics blame the fast-food franchises for making us fat. Are these businesses responsible for Americans' expanding waistlines?

The discussion will probably center on individual responsibility versus corporate social responsibility. The other dimension of this subject involves a profound transformation of the American family and our social fabric. A mobile society with two breadwinners has developed needs and habits that are radically different from those of a traditional "nuclear family." To illustrate the dynamic nature of culture, introduce other examples of profound cultural change, showing, for example, how computers and the Internet have transformed business and our everyday lives. For instance, e-commerce didn't exist some 25 years ago.

Ethics Check, Page 84
Culture Change: From "Sexist" to Gender-Neutral Language
Just a generation ago, businesspeople were *businessmen*, letter carriers were postmen, and flight attendants were stewardesses. A sea of change in language now dictates gender neutrality to avoid type casting. In business, the honorific Ms. Is used for all women, regardless of their marital status. Does language reflect just the current culture, or does it have the power to effect change?

Introduce examples of other changes in language use that were the result of conscious efforts to reflect equality between genders or were designed to show greater respect of minorities: The evolution of epithets for blacks, from *Negro* to *African American*, or the movement away from the dominance of the male gender—from *manpower* or *mankind* to *staff* and *humankind*. Perceptive students will perhaps recognize that language carries meaning beyond what it denotes on the surface and that it mirrors our biases and prejudices. You could discuss connotations of words as varied as *terrorist*, *insurgent*, *rebel*, or *freedom fighter*, often applied to the same group of people by different constituencies. Bias-free language is discussed in Chapter 4.

Ethics Check, Page 89
The World's Worst Tourists: Rude, Arrogant, Stingy, and Monolingual
You may have heard about the so-called "ugly American," the demanding, ethnocentric traveler who finds fault with all that is different abroad. But a recent survey among 4,500 hotel owners worldwide suggests that the least liked tourists come from France. The "best tourists" are the Japanese followed by the British and the Germans. What may account for such perceptions?

In past surveys, U.S. tourists actually ranked close to the top in popularity but were judged the worst dressed. Although the Reuters story does not disclose the full details of Expedia's latest TNS Infratest study, several Internet outlets have quoted the story and attempt to explain the reasons behind France's poor showing: Apparently close to 90 percent of the French vacation at home and may, therefore, lack flexibility abroad, appearing demanding. Because they are used to service charges being included in restaurant bills, they leave small tips. Finally, their lack of foreign language skills makes them seem arrogant. Discerning students with travel experience will recognize the parallels between some aspects of this behavior and stereotypical perceptions of Americans abroad.

Photo Essay Solutions

Photo Essay, Page 83
Understanding the characteristics of Chinese culture has been invaluable to marketers of Crest toothpaste. Knowledge of China's tea tradition led Procter & Gamble to develop tea-flavored Crest, now the company's best-selling variety. Understanding the self-identity and community aspects of China's youth culture led marketers to select Chinese pop star Li Yuchun as Crest's celebrity spokeswoman. Finally, recognizing that culture is dynamic has given Procter & Gamble confidence that Chinese consumers can be persuaded to use toothpaste, even though China has not historically shared American attitudes on hygiene and beauty.

Photo Essay, Page 100
Multinational corporations are increasingly seeking workforces that reflect the diversity of their customer bases. A diverse staff working in global markets will naturally possess intercultural proficiencies such as the ability to identify intercultural trends, communicate effectively with international business partners, and develop messages tailored to diverse audiences. Fisher-Price, for example, has become a successful marketer of Dora the Explorer and other bilingual toys. The company's English tagline "Play. Laugh. Grow." is changed in Hispanic markets to read "Play With Them. Laugh With Them. Grow With Them." (Juega con ellos. Pie con ellos. Crece con ellos.). This subtle change in message formulation shows that Fisher-Price is cognizant of Latino values that stress parental involvement and the importance of playing alongside children. The ability to recognize and respond to the needs of diverse consumer segments is one of many dividends of diversity.

Video Resources

Instructors may show the *Intercultural Communication at Work* from Video Library 1, *Building Workplace Skills*. This video demonstrates the importance of understanding different cultures in today's global workplace. After viewing the video, students should be prepared to discuss critical-thinking questions.

Chapter Presentation Ideas

For instructors who have extra class time, we provide the following activity ideas.

1. *Cultural Differences.* If students have lived in other countries, ask them to relate cultural differences they noticed regarding social customs or business customs. For instance, in Thailand wearing white could indicate the recent loss of a loved one. Touching children on the top of the head is frowned upon because it interferes with their spirits, and killing insects goes against Buddhist beliefs.

2. *Empathy Development.* Sometimes students understand intellectually the concepts of culture and the differences among cultures but emotionally approach interculturalism egocentrically, i.e., in terms of *us* and *them*. To help students take broader perspectives, the instructor can stress empathy through listening and sensitivity to nonverbal language through interviewing and role-playing to help reinforce the skills developed in Chapters 2 and 3.
3. *Travel and Culture.* Ask students if they have traveled to a country outside the United States. Have them share their experiences. What cultural differences did they notice? How did they feel being an "outsider"? Ask students who are new to the United States to share their experiences. Getting students to open up about differences and feelings can help students better understand and respect intercultural differences.

---

[i] Smith, J. (2007). The perils of prediction. *World Trade, 20*(1), 39-44. Retrieved July 20, 2009, from Business Source Premier database.

Chapter 4 LECTURE NOTES AND TEACHING SUGGESTIONS

Planning Business Messages

CHAPTER SYNOPSIS

Chapter 4 introduces a systematic process for creating business messages and oral presentations. The 3-x-3 writing process, introduced early in the chapter and illustrated in Figure 4.1, describes three steps in the writing process: prewriting, writing, and revising. The goals of Chapter 4 are to describe and illustrate the first step of the writing process (prewriting) with special attention focused on analyzing, anticipating, and adapting to audiences. While some students may resist the planning steps because they seem too time-consuming and unnecessary, you will want to stress the importance of empathizing with their audiences and moving from sender-focused ("I/we") to receiver-focused messages ("you"). Poor planning often results in sender-focused messages that alienate readers with insensitivity, bias, or negative attitudes.

Remind students that innovative companies use teams to achieve their objectives; therefore, it is important to learn the strategies for preparing team-written documents and become familiar with cutting-edge technology used by teams to share information and responsibilities. Chapter 4 thoroughly covers both of these topics.

LEARNING OBJECTIVES

1. Identify four basic principles of business writing, summarize the 3-x-3 writing process, and explain how a writing process helps a writer.
2. Recognize the components of the first phase of the writing process (prewriting), including analyzing your purpose, anticipating the audience, selecting the best channel, and considering how to adapt your message to the audience.
3. Effectively apply audience benefits, the "you" view, and conversational but professional language.
4. Effectively employ positive and courteous tone, bias-free language, simple expression, and vigorous words.
5. Understand how teams approach collaborative writing projects and what collaboration tools support team writing.
6. Summarize the legal and ethical responsibilities of business communicators in the areas of investments, safety, marketing, human resources, and copyright law.

WHAT'S NEW IN THIS CHAPTER

- Reorganized the chapter to introduce the writing process earlier so that students immediately grasp the three-phase process and its importance in planning business messages.
- Strengthened Figure 4.1 describing the writing process so that it is more specific and contains more details to enhance student comprehension.
- Expanded the discussion of channel selection by adding media richness theory.
- Added a new figure and discussion illustrating customer live chat so that students recognize the importance of communication skills in expanding technology applications in the workplace.
- Updated discussion of student collaboration tools including Google Docs and revised commands for Word 2007 Comment and Track Changes functions.
- Provided all new chapter review and writing improvement exercises so that instructors have a fresh set of these popular chapter reinforcement and application exercises.
- Added new Document for Analysis and new case study featuring Burger King regarding its channel selection for delivering news to its franchisees.

LECTURE OUTLINE

I. Understanding the Writing Process for Business Messages (p. 112)

PowerPoint slides 1-2

A. Starting With the Basics

- **Purposeful.** You will be writing to solve problems and convey information.
- **Persuasive.** You want your audience to believe and accept your message.
- **Economical.** You will try to present ideas clearly but concisely.
- **Audience oriented.** You will concentrate on looking at a problem from the reader's perspective instead of seeing it from your own.

PowerPoint slide 3

B. Following the 3-x-3 Writing Process

- Prewriting: Analyzing, Anticipating, Adapting
- Writing: Researching, Organizing, Composing
- Revising: Revising, Proofreading, Evaluating

Figure 4.1 The 3-x-3 Writing Process

C. Scheduling the Writing Process

- Phase 1 (Planning): About 25% of the time
- Phase 2 (Writing): About 25% of the time
- Phase 3 (Revising and Proofreading): About 45% for revising and 5% for proofreading

PowerPoint slides 4-6

Let's Discuss
Why do good writers spend most of their time on Phase 3 of the writing process?

The third phase of the writing process is the most time consuming phase of the 3-x-3 writing process because it involves revising and proofreading your message. Revising means improving the content and sentence structure of your message. Proofreading involves correcting its grammar, spelling, punctuation, format, and mechanics. During Phase 3, you will revise the message for clarity, conciseness, tone, and readability; proofread for correct spelling, grammar, punctuation, and format; and evaluate the message to see if accomplishes your goal.

II. Analyzing Your Purpose and Selecting Your Channel (p. 115)

A. Identifying the Purpose

- Why am I sending this message?
- What do I hope to achieve?

B. Selecting the Best Channel

- How important is the message?
- How much feedback is required?
- How fast is feedback needed?
- Is a permanent record necessary?
- How much can be spent?
- How formal is the message?

C. Switching to Faster Channels

- E-mail is the preferred channel of communication in corporations.
- Faster options of communication include live chats, Web sites, and instant messaging.

Figure 4.2 Choosing Communication Channels
Figure 4.3 Live Chat Connects Service Reps and Customers

Let's Discuss
What is the best communication channel for the following situations?

1. You want to persuade a colleague to apply for an open sales position in the territory that you manage.

   If you expect *your colleague to resist or to have many questions about the new sales position, plan to meet in person. You can be much more persuasive in a face-to-face meeting than through other channels of communication. If you can't meet in person, a phone call would also be appropriate.*

2. You need to update your manager on the results of a sales presentation with a new client.

   Report the results of the meeting in an e-mail to provide a permanent summary. When composing the message, be aware that your message may be shared with others in the organization.

3. As a travel agent, you need to contact hundreds of clients and tell them that an increase in fuel costs will force the cruise line to increase its fees.

   Write a letter because it provides a written record of correspondence sent outside of your organization.

III. Anticipating the Audience (p. 116)

- Profile the audience so you can tailor the message to your readers or listeners.
- Determine the tone of the message and select a channel.
- Consider secondary audiences.

PowerPoint slides 7-13

Figure 4.4 Asking the Right Questions to Profile Your Audience

Let's Discuss

Andrea, who answers customer service calls for an insurance company, is preparing an e-mail message to her supervisor requesting that she be transferred to the accounting department.

Who is her primary audience? (Andrea's supervisor)
Who is the secondary audience? (supervisor of the accounting department)

IV. Adapting to the Task and Audience (p. 118)

PowerPoint slides 14-17

Figure 4.5 Customer Response Letter

A. Developing Audience Benefits

- Emphasize benefits to the audience.
- Focus on the needs of your audience and demonstrate empathy.

B. Cultivating the "You" View

- Focus on the receiver.
- Emphasize second-person pronouns (*you, your*). Instead of "We need you to work on Saturday," try this: "By working on Saturday during the open house, you may surpass your sales goals for the quarter."
- Avoid overusing *you* or your message may appear to place blame and cause ill will.

Let's Discuss
Which of the following two sentences reflects the "you" view?

We will present strategies for handling difficult customers in Friday's training session.
OR
You will learn strategies for handling difficult customers during Friday's training session. ***("You" view)***

You must log off the network on Monday from 8:00 a.m. until noon for system maintenance.
OR
The IT department is upgrading the network to improve your search capabilities. Therefore, the network will be unavailable Monday morning from 8:00 a.m. until noon. ***("You" view)***

C. Being Conversational but Professional

- Use warm, friendly, and informal writing.
- Keep your messages professional and do not use IM abbreviations, slang, sentence fragments, and chitchat.

Figure 4.6 Levels of Diction

D. Expressing Yourself Positively

- Find positive ways to express your ideas to avoid angry reactions from your audience. Avoid words like *complaint, criticism, defective, failed, mistake*, and *neglected.*

E. Being Courteous

- Soften the tone of your message by using a courteous tone and words like please and thank you.

F. Choosing Bias-Free Language

1. **Avoiding Gender Bias**
Use neural, inclusive expressions and avoid sexist language.

firefighter	instead of *fireman*
letter carrier	instead of *mailman*

2. **Avoiding Racial or Ethnic Bias**
Indicate racial or ethnic identification only if the context demands it.

A sales manager	instead of *A Korean sales manager*
A graphic designer	instead of *A Hispanic graphic designer*

3. **Avoiding Age Bias**
   Specify age only if it is relevant, and avoid expressions that are demeaning or subjective.

   The receptionist retired. instead of *The older receptionist retired.*
   a woman instead of *little old lady*

4. **Avoiding Disability Bias**
   Unless relevant, do not refer to an individual's disability.

   The applicant instead of *the handicapped applicant*

Let's Discuss
How should the following sentences be revised to reflect bias-free language?

The female doctor (*doctor*) studied the chart.
The workmen (*workers*) removed the shattered glass.
The stewardess (*flight attendant*) closed the emergency door.

G. Using Plain Language and Familiar Words

- Use strong verbs and concrete nouns to provide more specific information to your audience.

H. Employing Precise, Vigorous Words

Figure 4.7 Improving the Tone in an E-mail Message

PowerPoint slides 14-17

Let's Discuss
How should the following sentence be revised to professional writing?

Hang loose until I get back to you	*I will answer your questions by the end of the day.*
He kept his cool during the crisis.	*He remained calm during the crisis.*
She ran out of gas at the end of the speech.	*She was tired by the end of the speech.*

I. Checklist for Adapting a Message to Its Audience

- Identify the message purpose.
- Select the most appropriate form.
- Profile the audience.
- Focus on audience benefits.
- Avoid gender and racial bias.
- Avoid age and disability bias.

- Be conversational but professional.
- Express ideas positively rather than negatively.
- Use short, familiar words.
- Search for precise, vigorous words.

PowerPoint slides 18-22

V. Writing in Teams (p. 124)

A. When Are Team-Written Documents Necessary? Collaboration on team-written documents is necessary for projects that are (1) big, (2) have short deadlines, and (3) require the expertise or consensus of many people.

B. Why Are Team Documents Better? Collaboration improves the quality of the document, builds camaraderie among team members, enhances understanding of the organization's values and procedures, strengthens communication, breaks down functional barriers, and enhances buy-in.

C. How Are Team Documents Divided? Teams work closely together in Phase 1 (prewriting) of the writing process. Team members generally work separately in Phase 2 (writing), when they conduct research, organize their findings, and compose a first draft. During Phase 3 (revising) teams may work together to synthesize their drafts and offer suggestions for revision.

PowerPoint slides 23-24

D. What Online Collaboration Tools Support Team Writing?
- E-mail
- Mailing lists
- Discussion boards
- Instant messaging
- Blogs and wikis
- Groupware and portals

E. What Tools Work Well for Student Collaboration?
- Google Docs & Spreadsheets
- Writeboard™
- Microsoft Word

Figure 4.8 Track Changes and Comment Features in Team Documents

V. Adapting to Legal and Ethical Responsibilities (p. 128)

PowerPoint slides 25-28

A. Investment Information

- Avoid misleading information, exaggeration, and half truths.

B. Safety Information

- Warn consumers of risks in clear, simple language.

Lecture Tidbit

Wary manufacturers sometimes state the obvious in their warning labels to avoid being sued. Some of the more humorous safety labels found by Dr. Steven Parker, WebMD, are shown below. (S. Parker, "Helpful" Safety Tips From Product Warning Labels," *WebMD*, July 12, 2006. Retrieved August 1, 2007, from http://blogs.webmd.com/healthy-children/2006/07/helpful-safety-tips-from-product.html.)

On a child-sized Superman costume:
"Wearing this garment does not enable you to fly."

On a hair coloring product:
"Do not use as an ice cream topping."

On a scooter for children:
"This product moves when used."

On a pair of bicycle shin guards:
"Shin pads cannot protect any part of the body they do not cover."

On a flushable toilet brush:
"Do not use for personal hygiene."

On an electrical drill:
"This product not intended for use as a dental drill."

On a box of rat poison:
"Warning: has been found to cause cancer in laboratory mice."

On a sign at a railroad station:
"Beware! To touch these wires is instant death. Anyone found doing so will be prosecuted."

C. Marketing Information

- Avoid statements that falsely advertise prices, performance capability, quality, or other product characteristics.

D. Human Resources Information

- Avoid subjective statements in evaluating employees; describe job-related specifics objectively. Also avoid promissory statements in writing job advertisements, application forms, and offer letters.

E. Copyright Information

1. **Four-Factor Test to Assess Fair Use**
   - Purpose and character of the use, particularly whether for profit.
   - Nature of the copyrighted work.
   - Amount and substantiality of portion used.
   - Effect of the use on the potential market for or value of the copyrighted work.

   PowerPoint slides 29-30

2. **How to Avoid Copyright Infringement**
   - Assume that everything is copyrighted.
   - Realize that Internet items are NOT in the "public domain."
   - Observe fair-use restrictions.
   - Ask for permission.
   - Don't assume that a footnote is all that is needed.

Lecture Transparencies
(available in a separate packet and at http://www.meguffey.com)

Writing Process Phase 1: Analyze, Anticipate, Adapt Acetates	**Transparency Number**
Business Writing; 3-x-3 Writing Process	41
Analyzing and Anticipating; Selecting the Best Channel	42
Adapting to Task and Audience	43
Developing Reader Benefits and "You" View	44
Negative Expressions and Their Hidden Messages	45
Writing in Teams; Writing Process	46
Adapting to Legal and Ethical Responsibilities	47
Four-Factor Test to Assess Fair Use	48

Solution Masters

	Page Number in This Book
4.1 Audience Benefits and the "You" View	492
4.2 Conversational but Professional	493
4.3 Positive and Courteous Expression	493
4.4 Bias-Free Language	494
4.5 Plain Language and Familiar Words	494
4.6 Precise, Vigorous Words	495
4.7 Legal Language	495
4.8 Document for Analysis—Revision	496

4.9	Burger King and the $1 Double Cheeseburger	497
4.10	Channel Selection	497
4.11	Analyzing Audiences	498
4.12	Copyright Confusion: Myths and Facts	499

Answers to Chapter Review Questions

1. Why do you think business writing differs from school essay writing? (Obj. 1)

Business writing has different goals from school essay writing. Business messages deliver information and may be persuasive. They have a purpose, are economical, and focus on the audience. The goal is to deliver information concisely and clearly. School essays are usually intended to display learning, exhibit creativity, confirm research, express feelings, and complete an assignment. Many writers think that business messages are easier to compose because they respond to situations that require practical expression.

2. List the three phases of the writing process and summarize what happens in each phase. Which phase requires the most time? (Obj. 1)

a. Prewriting includes analyzing, anticipating, and adapting.
b. Writing includes researching, organizing, and composing.
c. Revising includes revising, proofreading, and evaluating.

The most time is spent on revising.

3. What six factors are important in selecting an appropriate channel to deliver a message? What makes one channel richer than another? (Obj. 2)

a. Importance of the message
b. Amount and speed of feedback and interactivity required
c. Necessity of a permanent record
d. Cost of the channel
e. Degree of formality desired
f. Confidentiality and sensitivity of the message

A richer channel is one that permits more interactivity, feedback, verbal cues, and visual cues. Conversation is a rich channel; a business letter is a lean channel.

4. How does profiling the audience help a business communicator prepare a message? (Obj. 2)

Profiling the audience helps a business communicator determine the level of language, the degree of formality, and the most appropriate delivery channel to use. Thinking about the audience also helps the communicator anticipate whether the receiver's reaction will be positive, neutral, or negative.

5. **What is meant by "audience benefits"? (Obj. 5)**

   Writers who recognize audience benefits try to put themselves in the position of the reader. How is this message going to save the receiver money, time, or effort? The message should be written so that it develops benefits for the audience, if possible.

6. **When is the "you" view appropriate, and when is it inappropriate? (Obj. 5)**

   The "you" view is appropriate when it focuses on audience benefits. It is inappropriate when it is used to manipulate or when it conveys a sense of blame. (*You neglected to include necessary information.*)

7. **Why is it OK to use instant messaging abbreviations (such as BTW) and happy faces in messages to friends but not OK in business messages? (Obj. 3)**

   To sound credible and to be taken seriously, you need to project a professional image. This means writing clear, concise, and focused messages. Not everyone immediately comprehends abbreviations, and happy faces (emoticons) are not businesslike.

8. **What is wrong with using expressions such as *you claim, complaint, criticism, defective, failed, mistake, and neglected?* (Obj. 4)**

   These expressions create a negative impression. "You claim" suggests that you don't believe the receiver. Strive for more positive expressions.

9. **What is wrong with the following statement? *Pertaining to the above-referenced infraction, all employees are herewith warned by the undersigned not to install private software on company computers.* (Obj. 4)**

   This statement is overly formal, uses unfamiliar words, generates a negative tone, and sounds harsh. Such messages are less effective than messages that use a more conversational tone, familiar words, and a positive tone.

10. **What is bias-free language? List original examples. (Obj. 4)**

    Bias-free language avoids gender, race, ethnicity, age, or disability expressions that might be hurtful or stereotype people. Bias-free language strives to be inclusive rather than exclusive. It eliminates words that focus attention on exclusions. Examples: *physician* rather than *female doctor*; *new teacher* rather than new *Asian teacher.*

11. **Why should business writers strive to use short, familiar, simple words? Does this "dumb down" business messages? (Obj. 4)**

    Using short, familiar, simple words increases the likelihood that business messages will be understood. Because writers are not trying to impress readers and listeners with their extensive vocabularies or broad knowledge, their messages make sense. The goal is to be clear—not impressive.

12. What is jargon, and when is it appropriate for business writing? (Obj. 4)

Jargon is specialized or technical language. Use it only when the audience will understand.

13. What are the advantages and disadvantages of team-written documents? (Obj. 5)

Team-written documents may combine members' expertise and ideas to develop a better product. Team members buy in to the project when they share in its development. However, shared documents can be frustrating because of the difficulty in identifying different versions of a document and knowing who made what comment or change. Combining formats is difficult, and slackers may cause team resentment.

14. Under copyright law, what does fair use mean? (Obj. 6)

Fair use describes conditions under which one may copy original copyrighted material. Courts apply four factors: (a) the purpose and character of the use, particularly whether it is for profit; (b) the nature of the copyrighted work; (c) the amount and substantiality of the portion used; and (d) the effect of the use on the potential market for or value of the copyrighted work.

15. What kinds of works are protected by copyright laws? (Obj. 6)

Copyright laws protect words, charts, graphs, photos, music, or anything created privately and originally after 1989.

Answers to Critical Thinking Questions

1. Why do you think employers prefer messages that are not written like high school and college essays? (Obj. 1)

Businesspeople prefer messages that are purposeful, persuasive, economical, and audience-oriented. This kind of writing is often different from essay assignments that required descriptions of feelings, displays of knowledge, and adherence to a word count. Employers want messages that are clear, concise, and focused.

2. A wise observer once said that bad writing makes smart people look dumb. Do you agree or disagree, and why? (Objs. 1–4)

Bad writing conveys the impression that the writer is uneducated, uncaring, unintelligent, or all three. In business, bad writing not only makes the writer look dumb but also leads to misunderstandings, missed profits, and lost jobs.

3. Discuss the following statement: "The English language is a land mine—it is filled with terms that are easily misinterpreted as derogatory and others that are blatantly insulting. . . . Being fair and objective is not enough; employers must also appear to be so." (Obj. 4)

4. Why do you think that writing in a natural, conversational tone is difficult for many people? (Obj. 3)

Many writers tend to become formal, unnatural, and distant when they put words on paper. They seem to undergo a personality change when they pick up a pencil or approach a keyboard. Perhaps this is a result of composition training in schools. Students learned to develop a writing style that impressed their instructors. They were rewarded when they used big words, complex sentences, and abstractions, even if their ideas were not altogether clear. After leaving school, some writers continue to use words that inflate ideas, making them sound important and intellectual. Instead of writing as they would speak in conversation, they construct long and complex sentences, and the expression of their thoughts becomes confusing. Other people are poor writers simply because they haven't been trained. Still others inflate language to disguise empty thoughts or to hide the facts.

5. Ethical Issue: Peter Whitney, an employee at Wells Fargo, launched an Internet blog to chat about his life, his friends, and his job. After criticizing some of his coworkers in his blog, he was fired from his job handling mail and the front desk. Whitney said, "There needs to be clearer guidelines. Some people go to a bar and complain about workers. I decided to do it online. Some people say I deserve what happened, but it was really harsh. It was unfair. Do you agree or disagree, and why?

Some students will agree that the firing was harsh and unfair because Wells Fargo had no blogging policy. But other students will recognize that employees are generally retained on an "at-will" policy, which means they can be fired at will. Many students will argue that companies should communicate blogging rules to employees. IBM created guidelines stating that employees make it clear that they are speaking for themselves and not on behalf of IBM. They should not use ethnic slurs, personal insults, obscenity, and so forth.

Writing Improvement Exercises

4.1 Audience Benefits and the "You" View (Obj. 3)

a. To prevent you from losing money in third-party check transactions, our credit union no longer cashes such checks presented by our members.
b. To have your orders processed more quickly and efficiently, please fill out your customer information at this Web site.
c. You may use your iPhone discount for the next 30 days at our electronics center.
d. All your work-related travel expenses will be reimbursed under our new policy.
e. Congratulations! You have been selected to enter our management trainee program!
f. So that you may continue to buy name brands at discount prices, we offer only store credit on returned merchandise.

4.2 Conversational but Professional (Obj. 3)

a. As you requested, we are sending your printer toner and supplies to your Oakdale office.
b. Please tell me whether your representative will be visiting before June 1.

c. Please submit your departmental budget before January 1.
d. Although we've fallen behind somewhat in the schedule, we don't have to begin anew.
e. We urge you to approve the agreement by voting yes.
f. She didn't have the nerve to criticize him to his face.

4.3 Positive and Courteous Expression (Obj. 4)

a. Customers with membership cards receive a 10 percent discount.
b. We can process your claim if you send us a letter from your doctor showing that he or she treated your injuries.
c. By following each requirement, you will receive your $50 rebate.
d. We will pay you once you complete the job satisfactorily.
e. In the message you left at our Web site, you explain that you returned a headset.
f. The first 25 customers will be able to purchase our special netbook computers.

4.4 Bias-Free Language (Obj. 4)

a. Applicants for firefighter positions must submit medical reports signed by their physicians.
b. All employees are entitled to see their personnel files.
c. All servers are covered under our new benefits package.
d. A salesperson would have to be very skillful to sell those condos. OR: Salespeople would have to use all their skills to sell those condos.
e. Serving on the panel are a veterinarian, a doctor, two businesspeople, and a CPA.
f. All conference participants and their spouses (or partners) are invited to the banquet.
g. How many working hours are required to complete the project?

4.5 Plain Language and Familiar Words (Obj. 4)

a. Please find out whether we must continue our current contract despite troubling profits.
b. He guessed that the car (or truck) was not working because of a broken gasket.
c. Because we cannot check all cash payments, we must end the contract.
d. The contract requires that management continue the retirement plan.
e. 'll talk with Mark about using (addressing?) his staff.
f. One party cannot leave the contract early without a good reason. (Plain English version)

4.6 Precise, Vigorous Words (Obj. 4)

a. applaud
b. include, recipient
c. complicated, create
d. glitch, retrieve
e. (a) examining, studying, analyzing (b) useless, deceptive, unethical
f. (a) eliminate, reduce (b) balance, cut, repair
g. (a) explained, declared, suggested (b) qualified, experienced, proficient

4.7 Legal Language (Obj. 6)

a. reviewed or studied
b. facilitate
c. evaluate, assess, or analyze

Activities

4.8 Document for Analysis: Improving the Tone of E-mail Messages (Objs. 3-5)

NOTE: Solutions in the form of transparency masters are available in this manual.

4.9 Channel Selection: Burger King and the $1 Double Cheeseburger (Obj. 2)

Burger King Holdings Inc. should have considered (a) the importance of the message, (b) the amount and speed of feedback required, (c) necessity of a permanent record, (d) cost of the channel, (e) degree of formality desired, and (f) confidentiality and sensitivity of the message. This message was important, but little feedback was expected or encouraged. Management probably did not want to hear responses after receiving a second negative vote. Apparently, no permanent record was necessary, and a recorded phone message was fairly cheap. No formality in the message was necessary, and the message was not especially confidential or sensitive because the promotion had been discussed openly for some time. Management might have been exhibiting its unhappiness at the vote by using a cheap channel that allowed no feedback. It might have used e-mail, but that might have elicited responses, which management apparently did not seek. If management expected to try a third time to push this promotion, it might have used e-mail.

4.10 Channel Selection: Various Business Scenarios (Obj. 2)

a. If this request is likely to be refused and you wish to be quite persuasive, talk to Crystal in person. Otherwise, use the telephone. Any other channel would probably be too slow—unless you know that Crystal answers her e-mail immediately.
b. A wiki would work well as an information repository where members can add, remove, and edit content about the progress of the project.
c. If all the team members are online, you could use instant messaging to see whether they are available. Sending an e-mail is also possible, but it is slower and problematic. You won't know whether the message was received.
d. Schedule a personal conversation with each one.
e. Most global transactions such as this are conducted by fax, which is cheap and fast and provides a written record. E-mail would also be appropriate if you have the customer's address.
f. Write a letter because it provides a written record of correspondence sent outside of your organization.
g. Because considerable data will be involved, you would write a report to be submitted to the president, who might be familiar with the topic. However, you would also include enough background information to inform secondary readers such as the board of directors or management council. Your tone would be professional and fairly formal.

4.11 Analyzing Audiences (Obj. 3)

a. Because the primary reader is your sales manager, you should know what kind of communication format and content he expects. But he may not know much about the customer and specifically what the customer is demanding. Because the manager is familiar with the business, you can use jargon or references that outsiders might not understand. You can expect the receiver to be receptive to prospective new business; perhaps he's willing to make concessions to please this new customer. However, you should also remember that the sales manager may wish to forward your message to a higher executive, so you should be sure to fill in details and use fairly formal language.
b. The primary reader will probably be a busy human resources director, an educated, experienced individual who may be deluged with applications. Because the job is advertised, you would expect the reader to be neutral or positive toward your letter. Because your relationship is professional, your tone should be formal, yet friendly.
c. The audience will be all municipal water users, with a wide range of language abilities represented. The audience knows little about the technicalities of water chemistry and delivery. You would use plain English, adopt a conversational yet professional tone, and show courtesy.
d. The primary reader is your boss, but a secondary reader may be your boss's superior, if further approval is sought. The relationship is both personal and professional. Since your boss probably has no knowledge of the computer class, you would want to describe the class in detail and offer well-planned reasoning explaining why your proposal would benefit both the company and you. You might expect a negative response.
e. A targeted audience of executives means that you have some expectations about their income, education, status, and interests. You can use language that educated readers would comprehend. Because readers probably know little about shared ownership of jet planes, you will have to provide persuasive arguments and data. You might expect to overcome a negative response.

4.12 Copyright Confusion: Myths and Facts (Obj. 6)

Students are asked to decide whether the following statements are true or false. Actually, all are totally or mostly false. This is an excellent opportunity to clarify misinformation about copyright. The following discussion (reprinted with permission) is based on "10 Big Myths About Copyright Explained" by Brad Templeton (retrieved May 22, 2010, from http://www.templetons.com/brad/copymyths.html).

a. **If it doesn't have a copyright notice, it's not copyrighted.**
False. This was true in the past, but today almost all major nations follow the Berne copyright convention. For example, in the USA, almost everything created privately and originally after April 1, 1989, is copyrighted and protected whether it has a notice or not. It is true that a notice strengthens the protection, by warning people and by allowing one to get more and different damages, but it is unnecessary.

b. **If I don't charge for it, it's not a violation.**
False. Whether you charge for something can affect the damages awarded in court, but that's the main difference under the law. It's still a violation if you give it away—and there can still be serious damages if you hurt the commercial value of the property. There is an exception for personal copying of music, which is not a violation; however, courts seem to have said that this exception doesn't include wide scale anonymous personal copying, as done with Napster.

c. **If it's posted to the Internet, it's in the public domain.**
False. Nothing modern and creative is in the public domain anymore—unless the owner *explicitly* puts it in the public domain. The author/owner would have to say something very specific, such as "I grant this to the public domain."

d. **I can always argue that my posting was just fair use.**
False. The "fair use" exemption to U.S. copyright law was created to allow things such as commentary, parody, news reporting, research, and education about copyrighted works without the permission of the author. This exemption is vital so that copyright law doesn't block your freedom to express your own works. However, you just can't appropriate other people's works. Intent and damage to the commercial value of the work are important considerations. Fair use generally involves a short excerpt and almost always is attributed. Facts and ideas can't be copyrighted, but their expression and structure can. You can always write the facts in your own words!

e. **If you don't defend your copyright, you lose it.**
False. Copyright is effectively never lost these days, unless explicitly given away.

f. **If I make up my own stories, but base them on another work, my new work belongs to me.**
False. U.S. copyright law is explicit in that the making of what are called "derivative works"—works based on derived from another copyrighted work—is the exclusive province of the owner of the original work. This is true even though the making of the new works is a highly creative process. If you write a story using settings or characters from somebody else's work, you need that author's permission. This means that nearly all "fan fiction" is arguably a copyright violation. If you want to publish a story about Harry Potter or Lord Voldemort, you need Scholastic's permission. However, many holders of popular copyrights turn a blind eye to "fan fiction" or even subtly encourage it. A major exception involves criticism and parody. The fair use provision says that if you want to make fun of something like *Harry Potter and the Sorcerer's Stone*, you don't need permission to do so.

g. **They can't get me; defendants in court have powerful rights!**
False. Copyright law is mostly civil law. If you violate copyright, you would usually be sued, not charged with a crime. "Innocent until proven guilty" is a principle of criminal law, as is "proof beyond a reasonable doubt." Sorry, but in copyright suits, these conventions don't apply. Decisions depend on which side and set of evidence the judge or jury accepts or believes.

h. **Copyright violation isn't a crime or anything, is it?**
Actually, in the 1990s in the United States, commercial copyright violation involving more than 10 copies and value over $2,500 was made a felony. However, it's unlikely that you could get someone thrown in jail for posting your e-mail message. Courts have much better things to do.

i. **It doesn't hurt anybody. In fact, it's free advertising.**
It's up to owners to decide whether they want the free ads or not. If they want them, they will be sure to contact you. Don't rationalize about whether it hurts the owner or not. *Ask!* Usually that's not too hard to do.

j. **They e-mailed me a copy, so I can post it.**
To have a copy is not to have the copyright. All the e-mail you write is copyrighted. However, e-mail is not secret, unless previously agreed. This means that you can *report* what an e-mail message said. You can even quote parts of it to demonstrate. However, somebody who sues over an ordinary message would almost surely receive no damages because the message has no commercial value. However, if you want to stay strictly within the law, you should ask first. Keeping private correspondence private is courteous and honorable, of course.

ZOOMING IN, Part 1:
Suze Orman Preaches Financial Freedom in Simple Language

Critical Thinking

- **Whether one is writing a book, making a speech, or composing a business letter, why is it important to anticipate the audience for the message?**

  Anticipating the audience for a message helps you shape the message. Picturing a typical reader enables you to know what kind of language and strategy to use. Will the reader be neutral, positive, or negative toward your message? Who is the primary reader of the message? Who else might see or hear the message? What is your relationship with the reader? How much does the reader already know about the subject? An effective communicator anticipates the audience and is ready to adapt the message accordingly.

- **What does writing an effective financial help book have in common with writing an effective business message?**

  An author of an effective financial help book and an author of an effective business message go through a similar conceptual process. They are both writing purposeful, reader-oriented messages. Effective writers analyze their audiences and adapt their messages to that audience. Effective writers do not write for themselves; they write for the benefit of the reader. They think about how they can shape the message to be appealing to the reader. They try to put themselves in the shoes of their readers. Most good business writers also strive to be persuasive and to use language economically. That is, they don't waste words.

- **Why is it important to follow a writing process?**

  Following a writing process benefits the writer in many ways. If you follow a process, you are less likely to procrastinate because you know what you must do, and it is easy to get started. A writing process helps you organize ideas into a conceptual framework. Even short messages are easier to write if you first make notes about what you want to cover. Following a process enables you to gather necessary information and organize it systematically. You can write more quickly, and you are less likely to forget something importance if you have an outline. Once you are familiar with your writing process, all assignments become easier and the final product is better.

ZOOMING IN, Part 2: Suze Orman Preaches Financial Freedom in Simple Language

Critical Thinking

- **When writing, what are the advantages and disadvantages to multitasking?**

  Multitasking means doing more than one thing at a time. Some people can listen to music or half-watch TV at the same time they are writing. Some people don't mind interruptions from messaging buddies. However, any activities that take your mind away from focusing on your message will delay the completion of the project and may reduce its effectiveness. When Suze Orman hires people to work on a project, she insists that they clear their schedules of other jobs. "I'm not saying they can't multitask, just not on my time. The people who multitask, I think, do everything to mediocrity at best. While they are getting a lot done, they are getting it done in such an inefficient way that they usually have to do it again." (W. Wallis and S. Steptoe, "The Case for Doing One Thing at a Time, *Time South Pacific*, January 1, 2006, p. 50.) Students will have interesting thoughts on their own abilities to multitask. The major advantage is that they might get more done; the disadvantage is that the product may be inferior. Recent neurological studies suggest that no one can truly multitask, that is, complete two cognitive tasks simultaneously. Apparently our rains aren't designed to achieve that. Even the supposed multitaskers are switching back and forth momentarily while attempting the impossible.

- **Suze Orman is known for using simple, familiar language to express complex ideas. Does a business writer lose credibility when using this kind of language?**

  Expressing ideas in simple language gains credibility for the writer because it takes real skill to do so. Explaining complex ideas in simple language is especially challenging. That's why Suze Orman is applauded for her ability to present financial information in terms that most people can comprehend. Business writers are encouraged to use simple language and familiar words because their goal is to *express* rather than *impress*. Using simple language, however, doesn't mean giving up a precise word for a less precise one.

- **Why does it make sense for a business writer to express ideas positively instead of negatively?**

  Saying things positively rather than negatively usually conveys more information. For example, *We cannot fill your order unless you send us your size specification* does not sound as helpful as *We can fill your order as soon as you send us your size specification.* Positive messages convey good feelings and build customer goodwill.

ZOOMING IN, Your Turn: Applying Your Skills With Suze Orman

Students will write a one-page memo explaining why college students have debt. They will probably mention school expenses, student loans, credit card expenditures, car insurance, car payments, and so forth. Submitting a writing sample is a common practice for positions in which language skills are important. Students will find this experience beneficial in preparing them for real-world job requirements.

Discussion Material for PLUGGED IN: Using Technology to Edit and Revise Collaborative Documents

Divide students into three groups. If students do not have access to Microsoft Word, encourage them to use computers in school labs. Students should learn how to use the **Comment** feature by editing Activity 4.1. Have them submit a printout of one or more pages showing their comments. Compare the activity solution to student revisions and discuss their editing in relation to what they learned in this chapter.

Ethics Check Solutions

Ethics Check, Page 114
Essays for Sale

Web sites with playful names such as Cramster, Course Hero, Koofers, and Spark Notes provide ready-made solutions and essays for students. Do such sites encourage cheating and undermine the mental sweat equity of day-to-day learning?

Students can probably name many more Web sites that provide essays and solutions to old exams. Some might argue that professors should not assign essays that can easily be purchased online, and instructors should not recycle old tests that can circulate. But realistic students will recognize that those who simply copy solutions or purchase essays are hurting themselves at exam time. One professor said, "Part of what's valuable about homework is that it gives you a safe space to practice and struggle."

Supporters of such sites say that using these sites is not cheating. For instance, in a *New York Times* article, "Psst! Need the Answer to No. 7? Click Here," one student said that when a professor returns homework and doesn't explain why the student got an answer wrong, such sites provide the missing feedback. Additionally, Aaron Hawkey, Cramster's chief executive officer, says that such sites can't take exams for students. Critics argue that such sites encourage scholastic dishonesty and undercut the effort that creates learning.

Ethics Check 2, Page 130

Poster artist Shepard Fairey created a popular "Hope" poster of Barack Obama from a striking photo he saw on the Internet. Freelance photographer Mannie Garcia cried foul and demanded licensing fees, which Fairey refused. Are items on the Internet free for the taking if they have been changed a little?

Technology makes it easy to lift Internet items, tweak them, and claim the result is yours. Typically, this causes no trouble. But in the case of this popular money-making poster, we are reminded that just because something can be done doesn't make it right. The photographer Mr. Garcia said, "This part of this whole story is crucial for people to understand: that simply because it's on the Internet doesn't mean it's free for the taking, and just because you can take it doesn't mean it belongs to you." [Crovitz, L. G. (2009, March 16). The fine art of copyright. *The Wall Street Journal*, p. A17.]

Photo Essay Solutions

Photo Essay Page 127
Farmers can use online collaboration tools to assign tasks, share files, message, and track deadlines. The partners at Stranger's Hill Organics began using Basecamp because they held other jobs and couldn't meet in person to manage the 81-acre farm. The tool enabled the group to make team decisions about crop conditions, daily farm chores, and marketing. Workers at the farm receive tasks through Basecamp and post updates using a laptop in the farmhouse. Managers check in remotely at any time to see progress on specific tasks—such as fixing a leaky barn roof. Basecamp makes Stranger's Hill Organics a functional business by bringing together partners who otherwise would not be able to collaborate.

Video Resources

Instructors may show the *Guffey's 3-x-3 Writing Process* video from Video Library 1, *Building Workplace Skills.* The video illustrates each phase of the writing process and is a useful introduction to Chapters 4, 5, and 6, all of which present writing techniques. After viewing the video, students should be prepared to discuss critical-thinking questions.

Chapter Presentation Ideas and Extras

For instructors who have extra class time, we provide the following activity ideas.

1. *Audience Analysis.* Have students complete Activity 4.3 in class. Divide the class into small groups of two or three and assign each group two or more items from Activity 4.3 to analyze. After 10 minutes or so as time permits, have each group report its analysis and justify it. The multiple analyses will help students remember the key questions in Figure 4.4. These questions force writers to consider their audience each time they plan a message.

2. *The "You" View.* Have students complete Activity 4.5 in class one sentence at a time. Let the students revise each sentence to reflect the reader's perspective (1–3 minutes). Ask students to share their revisions with the group. Let them negotiate a revision if they disagree. Be sure that each student offers a revision of one of the sentences as the activity progresses. The class exercise helps to reinforce the concept that writing in business is often collaborative and the product of negotiation within teams.

3. *Planning With a Deadline.* Give students approximately 20 minutes to write a simple letter. Be sure to make a point of telling them that they must have it completed in the allotted time. Naturally, some of them will suffer writer's block, and that is just what you want to happen. Their problems with writer's block will be a springboard to your discussion regarding writing under pressure.

   After the exercise, ask students to describe briefly how they composed; i.e., what they did first, second, and so forth. Did some begin by outlining, asking questions about audience, considering the reader's point of view, or writing immediately without planning? Ask students if they are satisfied with the results (the draft of the letter). This follow-up exercise makes them conscious of how they attack writing assignments. Close by reviewing how planning methods discussed in the chapter really work, if internalized.

   Since students will have to write under pressure in the business world, they should start forming and practicing good composing habits. Not all good writers plan in the same way, but they all have methods of planning that work for them. For example, tell them that they don't always have to start at the beginning of the letter. They could conceivably write the last paragraph first. The important thing is to get something down. They can always revise later.

4. *Samples of Messages.* Have students bring in samples of letters, memos, and other messages that are sender-and/or receiver-oriented. Was the focus of the writer effective? How would they improve these letters? Direct mail solicitations are very useful for this exercise.

5. *Group Writing.* Ask students to describe a group writing project with which they were involved. Did they like the collaborative process? What were some of the good and bad experiences they had while working on this assignment? How could the whole process have been improved? If given the choice, would they be willing to collaborate again?

6. *Writing Checklist.* To help students internalize the important points of this chapter, have them develop a checklist for the documents they will be writing for this class as well as when they become employed in the future. Then they should refine this with each succeeding chapter. You could even give them a quiz grade for a refined/perfected checklist at the end of the course.

Chapter 5 LECTURE NOTES AND TEACHING SUGGESTIONS

Organizing and Writing Business Messages

CHAPTER SYNOPSIS

This chapter explains how to carry out the second phase of the writing process: researching, organizing, and composing. First, before writing, a businessperson collects relevant information, which helps the writer shape the message to the receiver. Students may expect research to be complicated. Remind them that at times researching can be informal and involve looking at the previous correspondence, talking to your boss, or searching the company files. More formal research might include performing tests and collecting data, interviewing people, or searching secondary data sources. Help students grasp the many facets of the word *research*.

Second, the writer organizes the collected information into direct or indirect patterns, anticipating the audience's reaction. If the audience will be pleased, interested, or neutral, the writer should use the direct pattern. If the audience will be uninterested, displeased, or hostile regarding the message, the writer should use the indirect pattern. To introduce the process of organizing, help students see its two parts—generating ideas and selecting patterns according to their purpose. First, through brainstorming, outlining, cluster diagrams, or the like, students develop the data and ideas needed to compose the first draft. Then, students select an appropriate pattern to use—direct for receptive audiences or indirect for unreceptive audiences.

Finally, the writer composes the first draft. The chapter concludes by reviewing ways to compose effective sentences and paragraphs. As you present the composition process, suggest to students that drafting and revising are two separate steps of the composing process. First, they should get their ideas down on paper quickly (perhaps through *freewriting*) without worrying whether the draft is perfect. Once they have created a substantial draft, then they can revise, using effective sentences and paragraph patterns as explained and modeled in the chapter.

LEARNING OBJECTIVES

1. Apply Phase 2 of the 3-x-3 writing process, which begins with formal and informal methods for researching data and generating ideas.

2. Explain how to organize data into lists and alphanumeric or decimal outlines.

3. Compare direct and indirect patterns for organizing ideas.

4. Compose the first draft of a message, avoiding sentence fragments, run-on sentences, and comma splices as well as emphasizing important ideas, avoiding misplaced modifiers, and using active and passive voice effectively.

5. Compose effective paragraphs using three classic paragraph plans as well as applying techniques for achieving paragraph coherence.

WHAT'S NEW IN THIS CHAPTER

- Strengthened discussion of effective sentences by adding coverage of fragments, comma splices, and run-ons so that students will avoid this common set of writing faults.
- Expanded discussion of active voice and passive voice and added figure illustrating use of each to help business communicators better understand how to implement these tools effectively.
- Added Ethics Check feature about bloggers who use their writing skills to endorse products for pay.
- Streamlined coverage of techniques that build paragraph coherence.
- Revised 100 percent of the Chapter Review and Writing Improvement Exercises to give instructors and students fresh reinforcement material.
- Prepared new Document for Analysis to enable students to apply many writing techniques covered in the chapter.

LECTURE OUTLINE

I. Gathering Information Through Research (p. 138)
Before collecting data, ask these questions:

- What does the receiver need to know about this topic?
- What is the receiver to do?
- How is the receiver to do it?
- When must the receiver do it?
- What will happen if the receiver doesn't do it?

Figure 5.1 Guffey's 3-x-3 Writing Process

PowerPoint slides 1, 2

A. Formal Research Methods

- Access electronically (Internet, databases, CD, DVDs)
- Search manually (books, magazines, journals).
- Go to the source (consumers).
- Investigate primary sources (interviews, surveys, questionnaires, focus groups).
- Conduct scientific experiments (measure variables using control groups).

PowerPoint slide 3

B. Informal Research Methods

- Look in the organization's files.
- Talk with your boss.
- Interview the target audience.
- Conduct an informal survey.

PowerPoint slide 4

Lecture Tidbit

Researching for information today is vastly different from the past when business organizations and writers relied on libraries, encyclopedias, and experts. Today, the Web offers a vast amount of information that can dramatically shape decision making and corporate strategy.

For example, company executives are increasingly monitoring blogs to gather market information about customer satisfaction with its products and services. Blogs pushed Dell and Apple into recalling millions of laptop computers after the fire risk of its laptop batteries was exposed. Engadget, a gadget news blog, posted photos of a Dell notebook that had caught fire in Singapore. Its comment: "We'll keep posting these until we see a recall or a solution, so please Dell, treat 'em right." (S. Hamm, "The Battery Recall: A Win for the Web," *BusinessWeek*, August 30, 2006. Retrieved June 20, 2007, from http://www.businessweek.com.)

C. Generating Ideas by Brainstorming

- Define the problem and create an agenda that outlines the topics to be covered.
- Establish time limits, remembering that short sessions are best.
- Set a quota, such as a minimum of 100 ideas.
- Require every participant to contribute ideas, accept the ideas of others, or improve on ideas.
- Encourage wild, "out of the box" thinking. Allow no one to criticize or evaluate ideas.
- Write ideas on flipcharts or on sheets of paper hung around the room.
- Organize and classify the ideas, retaining the best. Consider using cluster diagrams, discussed shortly.

D. Collecting Information and Generating Ideas on the Job

- A cluster diagram captures the ideas that are generated during a brainstorming session.
- Similar ideas are grouped together and sequenced to form subclusters.
- Writers of well-organized messages group similar ideas together so that readers can see relationships and follow arguments.

Figure 5.2 Creating Cluster Diagram to Generate Ideas for Old Navy/Gap Recruiting Brochure

Figure 5.3 Organizing Ideas From Cluster Diagram Into Subclusters

II. Organizing Ideas (p. 141)

PowerPoint slides 5-7

A. Using Lists and Outlines

- Scratch list—a quick list of topics to cover
- Outline—ideas organized into a hierarchy using the alphanumeric or decimal system

Figure 5.4 Two Outlining Formats

Figure 5.5 Typical Major Components in Business Outlines

Let's Discuss

How is an alphanumeric outline different from a decimal outline? (Obj. 2)

An alphanumeric outline uses roman numerals (I, II, III), capital letters (A,B,C), and numbers (1,2,3) to divide a topic into main and subpoints. A decimal outline uses numerals (1.0, 2.0, 3.0) for main points and decimal numbers (1.1, 1.2, 1.3) for subpoints so that every item is related to the overall theme.

PowerPoint slides 8-12

B. Organizing Ideas Into Patterns

Business messages follow either the direct pattern, with the main idea first, or the indirect pattern, with the main idea following explanation and evidence.

Figure 5.6 Audience Response Determines Pattern of Organization

C. Direct Pattern for Receptive Audiences

- Places the main idea in the first or second sentence of your message followed by details and explanations
- Saves the reader's time
- Sets a proper frame of mind
- Prevents frustration

PowerPoint slide 13-14

D. Indirect Pattern for Unreceptive Audiences

- Explanation precedes main idea
- Respects the feelings of the audience
- Facilitates a fair hearing
- Minimizes a negative reaction

PowerPoint slide 15

Let's Discuss

If you are being told bad news, would you prefer to have it delivered directly or indirectly? What factors would affect your choice?

Many Americans prefer to hear bad news delivered indirectly, which is the opposite of a blunt announcement. The choice might be affected by the severity of the news, whether it touched the receiver personally, and the relationship between the communicators.

III. Composing the First Draft (p. 147)

PowerPoint slides 16

A. Recognizing Basic Sentence Elements

- Complete sentences must have subjects and verbs and must make sense.
- Clauses have subjects and verbs, but phrases do not.
- Independent clauses may stand alone; dependent clauses cannot stand alone.

B. Avoiding Three Common Sentence Faults

- Fragment – a broken-off part of a complex sentence
- Run-on (Fused) sentence – a sentence containing two independent clauses without a conjunction or a semicolon
- Comma-splice sentence – two independent clauses joined by a comma

Let's Discuss

Identify the common sentence faults that appear in the following sentences:

1. The company president scheduled a meeting for this afternoon we suspect an announcement about his replacement.
2. Because presentation software offers illustrative slide effects.
3. Adam plans to write a blog about his safari to Africa, his wife will e-mail video and photos.

1. Run-on sentence
2. Fragment
3. Comma splice

C. Preferring Short Sentences

- Strive for sentences that average 20 words.
- Reader comprehension drops as sentences become longer.

D. Emphasizing Important Ideas

- Use vivid words.
- Label the main idea.
- Place the important idea first or last in the sentence.

- Place the important idea in a simple sentence or in an independent clause.
- Make sure the important idea is the sentence subject.

E. Managing Active and Passive Voice

Active voice: subject is the doer of the action
Example: *Staples shipped our order for office supplies today.*

Passive voice: subject is acted upon
Example: *The office supplies were shipped by Staples today.*

- Use the active voice for most business writing.
- Use the passive voice to emphasize an action or the recipient of the action.
- Use the passive voice to de-emphasize negative news.
- Use the passive voice to conceal the doer of an action.

Figure 5.7 Using Active Voice and Passive Voice Effectively

Let's Discuss

Why is the active voice preferred for business writing?
The active voice reveals the doer of the action immediately. It creates efficient, concise, and simple messages.

Does it seem unethical to use the passive voice to conceal the doer of an action? (An error was made in the report.)
Many people use the passive voice to be tactful.

F. Avoiding Dangling and Misplaced Modifiers

- A modifier dangles when the word or phrase it describes is missing.
  Example: *By advertising extensively, all open jobs were filled quickly.*
- A modifier is misplaced when the word or phrase it describes is not close enough to be clear.
  Example: *Any student has full online privileges who is enrolled in the college.*

IV. Drafting Powerful Paragraphs (p. 153)

- Well-constructed paragraphs discuss one topic.
- Paragraphs may be composed of three different types of sentences: main, supporting, and limiting.
- Paragraphs may be organized into three plans: direct, pivoting, and indirect.

PowerPoint slides 17-31

A. Using the Direct Paragraph Plan to Define, Classify, Illustrate, or Describe

- Most business messages use this paragraph plan because it clarifies the subject immediately.
- Use the direct paragraph plan to define, classify, illustrate, or describe.

B. Using the Pivoting Paragraph Plan to Compare and Contrast

- The pivotal plan is useful in comparing and contrasting ideas.
- Notify the reader in the turn in direction by using but or however.

C. Using the Indirect Paragraph Plan to Explain and Persuade

- The indirect paragraph plan is appropriate for delivering bad news.
- The paragraph starts with the supporting sentences and concludes with the main sentence.

D. Building Paragraph Coherence

1. Sustaining the key idea (repeating a key expression or using a similar one)
2. Using pronouns (using familiar pronouns such as this, that, these, and those)
3. Dovetailing sentences (linking the idea at the end of one sentence to an idea at the beginning of the next)
4. Showing connections with transitional expressions (using verbal road signs to help the receiver anticipate what's coming, reduce uncertainty, and speed up comprehension)

Figure 5.8 Transitional Expressions to Build Coherence

PowerPoint slides 32-40

E. Composing Short Paragraphs for Readability

- Short paragraphs are more attractive and readable than longer ones.
- Paragraphs with eight or fewer lines look inviting.

F. Checklist for Composing Sentences and Paragraphs

For Effective Sentences

- Avoid common sentence faults.
- Control sentence length.
- Emphasize important ideas.
- Apply active- and passive-voice verbs carefully.
- Eliminate misplaced modifiers.

For Meaningful Paragraphs

- Develop one idea.
- Use the direct plan.
- Use the pivoting plan.
- Use the indirect plan.
- Build coherence with linking techniques.
- Provide road signs with transitional expressions.
- Limit paragraph length.

Lecture Transparencies
(available in a separate packet and at http://www.meguffey.com)

Organizing and Writing Business Messages Acetates	**Transparency Number**
Formal Research Methods; Informal Research, Idea Generation; Organizing Data	50
Audience Response Determines Pattern of Organization—Direct Pattern	51
Audience Response Determines Pattern of Organization—Indirect Pattern	52
Creating Effective Sentences	53
Drafting Effective Paragraphs	54

Solution Masters

	Page Number in This Book
5.1 Sentence Elements	500
5.2 Sentence Faults	500
5.3 Emphasis	501
5.4 Active Voice	501
5.5 Passive Voice	502
5.6 Dangling and Misplaced Modifiers	502
5.7 Paragraph Organization	503
5.8 Paragraph Organization and Revision	504
5.9 Document for Analysis – Revision	505

Answers to Chapter Review Questions

1. **Compare the first phase of the writing process with the second phase. (Obj. 1)**

The first phase includes	The second phase includes
a. Analyzing	a. Researching
b. Anticipating	b. Organizing
c. Adapting	c. Composing

2. **For routine writing tasks, what are some techniques for collecting information data and generating ideas? (Obj. 1)**

   Informal research methods include looking in company files, talking with your boss, interviewing the target audience, conducting an informal survey, and brainstorming.

3. Name seven specific techniques for a productive group "brainstorming" session. (Obj. 1)

a. Define the problem and create an agenda that outlines the topics to be covered.
b. Establish time limits, remembering that short sessions are best.
c. Set a quota, such as a minimum of 100 ideas. The goal is quantity, not quality.
d. Require every participant to contribute ideas, accept the ideas of others, or improve on ideas.
e. Encourage wild, "out of the box" thinking. Allow no one to criticize or evaluate ideas.
f. Write ideas on flipcharts or on sheets of paper hung around the room.
g. Organize and classify the ideas, retaining the best. Consider using cluster diagrams.

4. What is the difference between a list and an outline? (Obj. 2)

A list is merely a group of topics. An outline is a list of topics arranged in a hierarchy with main topics and subtopics so that readers see relationships among the topics.

5. What are the major components in a letter or memo? (Obj. 2)

The major components in a letter or memo are (a) opening, (b) body, and (c) close.

6. What are the major components in an analytical report? (Obj. 2)

The major components in an analytical report are (a) introduction/problem, (b) facts/findings, (c) conclusions, and (d) recommendations (if requested).

7. Why do many readers prefer the direct method for organizing messages? (Obj. 3)

The direct method involves starting a message with the main idea immediately. Many readers prefer the direct method because it saves time, sets a proper frame of mind, and reduces frustration.

8. When is the indirect pattern appropriate, and what are the benefits of using it? (Obj. 3)

The indirect method is appropriate for bad news, ideas that require persuasion, and sensitive news, especially when being transmitted to superiors. The benefits of using the indirect method include (a) respecting the feelings of the audience, (b) encouraging a fair hearing, and (c) minimizing a negative reaction.

9. What is the primary difference between the direct and indirect patterns of organization? (Obj. 3)

The primary difference is the position of the main idea. In the direct pattern, the main idea comes first followed by details. In the indirect pattern, the main idea follows the details, explanation, and evidence.

10. List four techniques for emphasizing important ideas in sentences. (Obj. 4)

a. Using vivid words
b. Labeling the main idea
c. Placing the important idea first or last in the sentence
d. Placing the important idea in a simple sentence or in an independent clause

11. When should business writers use active-voice sentences? Passive-voice sentences? Give an original example of each. (Obj. 4)

Most business writing should use active-voice verbs. Passive-voice verbs are useful (a) to emphasize an action or the recipient of the action, (b) to de-emphasize negative news, and (c) to conceal the doer of an action. Active-voice example: My team and I researched and wrote a report. Passive-voice example: A report was researched and written by my team and me.

12. What's wrong with this sentence? After reading it carefully, the proposal doesn't interest us. (Obj. 4)

This sentence suffers from a dangling modifier. After the introductory verbal phase, a logical subject must follow. The proposal did not read itself. You can avoid dangling modifiers involving introductory verbal phrases by always including a logical subject. Ask the question, *Who?* or *What*? following the introductory verbal phrase.

13. What is a topic sentence, and where is it usually found? (Obj. 5)

A topic sentence states the main idea of a paragraph. In business messages the topic sentence usually appears first in a paragraph. However, it can also appear in the middle or at the end of a paragraph depending on the organizational plan.

14. Describe three paragraph plans. Identify the uses for each. (Obj. 5)

The most frequently used plan for business messages is the direct plan. It begins with the main idea followed by supporting sentences. A variation may include one limiting sentence followed by sentences that support the main idea. The direct plan is useful for defining, classifying, illustrating, or describing.

The pivoting paragraph begins with a limiting sentence followed by the main and supporting sentences. This plan is useful for comparing and contrasting.

The indirect plan begins with supporting sentences and concludes with the main sentence. This plan is useful for building a foundation of ideas and drawing a conclusion from it or for delaying bad news until after explaining the reasons causing it.

15. What is coherence, and how is it achieved? (Obj. 5)

Coherence exists when one idea leads logically to another; sentences are coherent when they stick together. To achieve coherence, (a) sustain a key idea, (b) use pronouns and demonstrative adjectives (this, that, these, those), (c) dovetail sentences, and (d) use transitional expressions.

Answers to Critical Thinking Questions

1. Why is cluster diagramming considered an intuitive process whereas outlining is considered an analytical process? (Obj. 1)

Cluster diagramming calls for us to jot down ideas without censoring or evaluating them. By freely using our imaginations, we allow intuition to take over; that is, we are governed by only logical processes. Outlining is a methodical, analytical process. It involves ordering items into a hierarchy. Cluster diagramming is free form, thus promoting a shower of ideas, some usable and many unusable. Postponing judgment on this flow of ideas acts as a stimulant to our creative processes.

2. Why is audience analysis so important in the selection of the direct or indirect pattern of organization for a business message? (Obj. 3)

Audience analysis is extremely important because it helps you decide whether the receiver will react positively or negatively to your message. Help your students develop the habit of always thinking of the audience first. Ask them to put themselves in the place of the receiver. If Lisa, who sits in the first row, were receiving this message, how would she feel? If the news is going to upset her, it might be better to break it softly. Most business messages, of course, are not sensitive and should be handled directly. But occasionally, especially when bad news is concerned, the indirect method may work better.

3. How are speakers different from writers in the way they emphasize ideas? (Obj. 4)

Speakers have an array of nonverbal cues that can be used to express many more emotions and nuances of meaning than are possible in writing. A speaker can raise an eyebrow, lower her voice, utter a sigh, wipe her hand across her brow, or tap her fingers on the table. Each of these cues sends a message that the receiver reads and interprets. A writer has only words. And words have many meanings. Some speakers emphasize ideas by raising their voices, speaking more slowly, or using facial, arm, or hand motions. Writers emphasize ideas by using vivid words, labeling the main ideas, and positioning the important idea strategically (at the beginning or end of a sentence, in an independent clause, and with few words surrounding it).

4. Why are short sentences and short paragraphs appropriate for business communication? (Objs. 4, 5)

Business readers want to see the main idea immediately. Short sentences and paragraphs convey ideas quickly and are more readable than longer ones.

5. Ethical Issue: Discuss the ethics of the indirect pattern of organization. Is it manipulative to delay the presentation of the main idea in a message?

All good writers practice empathy. Since the indirect pattern is used when receivers will be uninterested, unwilling, displeased, or hostile toward the message, they certainly will not be pleased to receive the communication. Although you may not be able to give them exactly what they want, you may have alternatives that will partially satisfy them. Encouraging receivers to read and understand your entire message is very important under these circumstances. Beginning with an explanation followed by alternatives is not manipulative; when bad news is involved, this indirectness shows courtesy and consideration. Delaying the main idea is not unethical unless the intent is to deceive.

Writing Improvement Exercises (Transparencies available)

5.1 Sentence Elements (Obj. 4)

a. DC – you
b. IC – interviewer
c. P
d. DC – they
e. IC – results
f. P
g. DC – people
h. P

5.2 Sentence Faults (Obj. 4)

a. Fragment. Revision: Because 90 percent of all business transactions involve written messages, good writing skills are critical.

b. Fragment. Revision: The recruiter requested a writing sample even though the candidate seemed to communicate well orally.

c. Comma splice. Revision: Major soft-drink companies considered a new pricing strategy. They tested vending machines that raise prices in hot weather.

d. Run-on. Revision: Thirsty consumers may think that variable pricing is unfair; they may also refuse to use the machine. *OR:* Thirsty consumers may think that variable pricing is unfair. They may also refuse to use the machine.

e. Comma splice. Revision: About half of Pizza Hut's 7,600 outlets make deliveries; the others concentrate on walk-in customers. *OR:* About half of Pizza Hut's 7,600 outlets make deliveries. The others concentrate on walk-in customers.

f. Run-on. Revision: McDonald's sold its chain of Chipotle Mexican Grill restaurants. The chain's share price doubled on the next day of trading.

g. Fragment. Revision: Private equity players are betting they can breathe new life into old brands, which explains why Golden Gate Partners paid millions for defunct retailer Eddie Bauer. **Note:** This long sentence could also be broken into two shorter sentences.

5.3 Emphasis (Obj. 4)

a. b
b. b
c. a
d. a
e. b
f. a
g. a
h. a
i. b

5.4 Active Voice (Obj. 4)

a. The manager gave employees their checks at 4 p.m. every Friday.

b. McDonald's tried new spices and cooking techniques to improve its hamburgers.

c. My boss designed our new company logo.

d. The CEO commended the managers with the most productive departments.

e. The leader asked all team members to brainstorm for 10 minutes.

5.5 Passive Voice

a. A computational error was discovered in the company's tax figures.

b. Your order for ten monitors will be shipped June 15.

c. The accounting statement was not submitted on time.

d. Deceptive diet advertisements by weight-loss marketers were targeted [by the Federal Trade Commission].

e. Corporate and financial information is being stolen by thieves using data-stealing malware on the Web.

5.6 Dangling and Misplaced Modifiers (Obj. 4)

a. By advertising extensively, our company filled all open jobs quickly.

b. Correct. The understood subject is you (To apply for early admission, [you] submit your application by November 1.)

c. After leaving the midtown meeting, Angela discovered that her car would not start.

d. Walking up the driveway, the detectives immediately spotted the Hummer parked in the garage.

e. No matter how silly they seemed, the manager's rules were to be observed by all staff members.

f. To complete the project on time, the team established a new deadline.

g. Acting as manager, Mr. Lopez hired several new employees.

h. In our boardroom Michelle Mitchell presented a talk about workplace drug problems.

5.7 Paragraph Organization (Obj. 5)

a. Which sentence should be the topic sentence? 5

b. Which sentence(s) should be developed in a different paragraph? 4

c. Which supporting sentences should follow the topic sentence? 1, 2, 3, 6, 7

d. Responses will vary.

5.8 Paragraph Organization and Revision (Obj. 5)

a. Pizza Hut is considering launching a new product called "The Extreme." It will be the largest pizza on the market. With double the cheese and double the toppings, it will target the X and Y Generations. These are the fastest growing segments in the fast-food market. This population segment has been successfully targeted with the "extreme" strategy in other areas. However, we feel that the "extreme" strategy has not been developed fully in the fast-food market. The same target audience that would respond to an extreme product also reacts to low prices. Therefore, we plan to price this new pizza at $19.99.

b. A common problem in PowerPoint involves lost sound and video files. When you move the presentation to a network folder or send it to someone else, it has no sound. However, you can solve this problem by keeping your sound and video files together. Create a new folder for your presentation and copy the sound and video files to that folder before you put them in your presentation. When you move the presentation to the network, move the entire folder. As a result, you will always have your sound files ready for use with your presentation.

c. A number of high-level positions are available to current employees. These positions are in production, marketing, and administrative support. If you are interested, come to the Human Resources Department to see the list showing positions, qualifications, and job descriptions. Many of the jobs are now open. Therefore, you should apply immediately. Interviews must be scheduled within the next two weeks.

Activities

5.9 Document for Analysis: Weak E-Mail Message (Objs. 3–5) The "Document for Analysis" exercises appear at http://www.meguffey.com so that students may edit and revise them without total retyping. Solutions in the form of transparency masters are available in this manual.

Dangling modifiers: Sentences 3, 11, 17
Passive voice: Sentences 1, 4, 5, 11, 12, 13, 17
Fragments: Sentences 8, 14, 16

Suggested Revision

Dear Mr. Gibbons:

[1]You probably chose Body Fitness Center here in Scottsdale because it is one of the top-rated gyms in the Southwest. [2]Our principal goal has always been making your workouts enjoyable. [3]To continue to provide you with the best equipment and programs, we need your feedback.

[4]Body Fitness provides an outstanding program with quality equipment and excellent training programs. [5]However, we could give more individual attention to our customers if we could extend our peak usage time. [6]You have probably noticed that attendance at the gym increases from 4 p.m. to 8 p.m. [7]We wish it were possible to accommodate all our customers on their favorite equipment during those hours. [8]Although we can't stretch an hour, [9]we would like to make better use of the time between 8 p.m. and 11 p.m. [10]With more members coming later, we would have less crush from 4 p.m. to 8 p.m.

[11]To encourage you to stay later, my partner and I are considering adding security cameras for our parking area. [12]We may also add cameras for some inside facilities. [13]We have given this matter a lot of thought, [14]although Body Fitness has never previously had an incident that endangered a member.

[15]Please fill in the attached interactive questionnaire, [16]which will give us instant feedback about scheduling your workouts. [17]By completing this questionnaire, you will help us schedule workouts and training sessions to give you exactly the equipment and trainers you prefer.

Cordially,

5.10 Collaborative Brainstorming (Obj. 1)

Be sure students realize that this is a serious assignment and that you will be asking them to submit their results. If you will give them about 10 minutes to work in groups for three or four days, they will have time to prepare and present their findings to the class. Since students dislike completing an activity without receiving a grade, you may want to give them a quiz grade on this. To help them stay on task, be sure to roam the room while they are working. You might want to combine this activity with 5.4 below to have students compare the effectiveness of these two techniques.

5.11 Individual Brainstorming (Objs. 1, 2)

Be sure students realize that this is a serious assignment and that you will be asking them to submit their results. If you will give them about 10 minutes to work individually for three or four days, they will have time to prepare and present their findings to the class. If you do not have time for each student to present, have each student submit his or her findings in writing. You might want to combine this activity with 5.3 above to have students compare the effectiveness of these two techniques.

5.12 Brainstorming Tips for Productive Sessions (Obj. 1)

Students will find many "tips" articles if they conduct a Google or database search. Each student outline should look something like the following:

Outline

I. Before your brainstorming session
   A. Select a leader.
   B. Define your problem.
   C. Create an agenda.
   D. Set time limits.
   E. Set quotas.
   F. Select your group and announce a session.
   G. Circulate background information.

II. During your session
   A. Review the problem and background information.
   B. Establish ground rules.
      1. Each participant must contribute ideas, accept ideas of others, or improve on ideas.
      2. No one may criticize or evaluate any idea.
      3. No one will hold back ideas.
      4. The group will encourage wild, out-of-the-box thinking.
      5. The goal of the session is quantity, not quality.
   C. Take detailed notes.

III. After the session
   A. Allow time for the incubation of further ideas.
   B. Type and circulate all the ideas generated.
   C. Organize or classify the ideas in some fashion for later evaluation.
   D. Evaluate the ideas and choose the best.

5.13 Collecting Primary Information: Research Interviewing (Obj. 1)

Students will generate a number of responses to these questions. The goal of this activity is to encourage students to develop their speaking, interviewing, summarizing, and outlining skills.

5.14 Brainstorming: Are Ethics Programs Helpful? (Obj. 1)

Depending on their level of business experience, students will have definite opinions about whether ethics codes are effective. You might wish to get them started by citing typical ethical lapses: stealing office supplies, lying about absences, misusing company resources. Managerial employees may be guilty of accepting presents, meals, or performance tickets in return for favors to vendors. You might ask students to download some ethics codes and bring them to the discussion.

5.15 Researching, Brainstorming, and Organizing: Student Loans (Objs. 1-3)

Searching the Web and databases, students will find many articles about burgeoning student loan debt. They should produce a final outline with a title, an introduction, and some of the following strategies for avoiding, reducing, and repaying student loans:

STRATEGIES FOR AVOIDING, REDUCING, AND REPAYING STUDENT LOANS

I. Introduction
   A. Demographics of student borrowers
   B. Current overall picture for nation as a whole
   C. Individual student situations

II. Strategies for avoiding student loans
   A. Apply for financial aid
   B. Attend community college for first two years of degree program
   C. Secure private loans; have parents fund schooling
   D. Negotiate with college for lower fees

III. Strategies for reducing student loans
   A. Finish school early
   B. Shop for campus-specific discounts (such as taking classes during off-peak hours)
   C Shop for lowest and best loans
   D. Refinance loan rates

IV. Strategies for repaying loans
   A. Take a job with a federal agency that helps pay off loans
   B. Consolidate all debt for a lower rate
   C. Stretch out student loans for lower payments

Based on Smith, C. (2009, May 9). Crushing student debt draws takeover plan. *The Pittsburgh Tribune-Review*. Retrieved August 3, 2009, from InfoTrac College Edition database; Bonnici, J. & Scherban, D. W. (2006, November). How to turn marketing students into millionaires: Decision making for personal wealth management. *Journal of Financial Services Marketing, 11*(2), 125-130; Schembari, J. (2003, November 9). I'm NOT going to pay a lot for this education. *The New York Times*, p. 4A.27; Importance of federal student aid continues to grow. (2003, October 23). *Black Issues in Higher Education,* 13; Kristof, K. M. (2003, September 14). More grads struggling to repay loans. *Los Angeles Times*, p. C3.

ZOOMING IN Part 1: Once the Height of Hip, Gap Struggles to Stop Sagging Sales

Critical Thinking

- **In what ways would research (gathering information) be important to Gap and Old Navy in getting their customers back?**

  Research is important to the Gap, Old Navy, and all decision makers. Companies that are struggling generally seek ways to turn around their fortunes. They want to know what is wrong and how to fix it. Gap and Old Navy would probably gather information from customers, product managers, field researchers, and competitors to learn what procedures and fashion mix they need to become successful again.

- **Why is it important for Gap managers, as well as other business communicators, to gather all necessary information before making management decisions?**

  Before making management decisions, businesspeople must gather all necessary information. Most decisions are then communicated through writing or presentations. Before beginning to write, business communicators should have completed all their research. If new information emerges, it often changes the writer's perspective and strategy. To save time in the long run, it is always better to complete all research before beginning to write.

- **What techniques can business communicators at Gap and other companies use to generate ideas for new products as well as to improve business processes?**

  Business communicators often must generate ideas for projects or to solve problems. One of the best ways to generate ideas is by brainstorming. This chapter provides techniques for effective brainstorming.

ZOOMING IN Part 2: Gap Inc.

Critical Thinking

- **When a business communicator responds to an inquiry, such as a letter about human rights violations among contractors, is "research" necessary?**

  Of course! Form letters would be inappropriate, especially for an organization such as Old Navy or the Gap. They pride themselves on their senses of social responsibility and doing the right thing. Research is necessary before answering any inquiry or starting any project. Research merely means collecting information. Informed decisions cannot be made without solid facts. Gathering information is the first step in solving any problem.

- **What are the differences between formal and informal research?**

  Long reports and complex business problems typically require some use of formal research methods. Formal research might include a serious review of all literature (printed and electronic) available on a topic. It might also involve scientific experiments to test various alternatives to solving a problem. Informal research is generally necessary for routine tasks, such as answering letters, writing memos, and preparing informational reports. Informal research involves looking in the files, checking the company Web site, talking with management, perhaps interviewing the target audience, and brainstorming for ideas.

- **What are the advantages and disadvantages of brainstorming with groups?**

  Proponents of brainstorming say that it is a productive and powerful method of generating ideas. It is especially effective for solving problems that one person may not be able to solve alone. Group brainstorming enables many individuals to share their ideas, a process that may stimulate unusually creative solutions. Critics say that brainstorming groups produce fewer and poorer quality ideas than the same number of people working alone. Brainstorming also takes time, which might be better used with individuals working separately. But even critics say that if people are going to use brainstorming techniques, they should do it with the most effective techniques.

ZOOMING IN Your Turn:
Applying Your Skills at Gap, Inc.

Because most students know the Gap and Old Navy retail outlets, they probably have definite opinions about shopping there. Students should be able to generate many ideas about improving the fashion mix, changing the stores, and generating positive publicity about its social responsibility principles.

Discussion Material for PLUGGED IN:
Seven Ways Computers Can Help You Create Better Written Messages, Oral Presentations, and Web Pages

Have students complete this activity individually or in teams and discuss the results in class. What software programs are best for creating documents? Which ones are best for designing and producing professional presentations and Web pages? What are some of the drawbacks of each one for business communicators?

Ethics Check Solutions

Ethics Check, Page 146
How Sweet It Is
The makers of artificial sweetener Equal sued competitor Splenda because the latter claimed that Splenda was "made from sugar." In reality, Splenda's core ingredient is made from sucralose, a nonnutritive synthetic compound manufactured in laboratories. Although Splenda contains a sugar molecule , sucralose is not the same as sucrose, the technical name for pure table sugar, despite its similar-sounding name. Is it unethical for companies to intentionally advertise using wording that would confuse consumers?

Of course it is unethical for companies to intentionally use words that deceive consumers. Attorneys for Splenda claimed it had never deceived consumers, but a French court ruled that it had intentionally confused consumers with its advertising. Eventually the makers of Equal and Splenda settled their case out of U.S. courts with what is said to be a huge settlement going to Equal. However, Splenda went on to lead in sweetener sales, and Equal lost a large segment of the market.

Ethics Check, Page 154
Blogging for Pay
One single mother earned nearly $500 a month by putting her writing skills to use on "opps" (opportunities) at PayPerPost.com. This site pays consumers to write favorable comments in blogs about specific products. Is it ethical for bloggers to hide their motivation and affiliation when rating products?

Students will doubtless feel that failing to reveal the monetary motivation for product endorsements is unethical. However, is this any different from Procter & Gamble's payment to a novelist to include references to its Cover Girl products, or Coca-Cola's payment to *American Idol* to have former host Paula Abdul sip from a Coke-branded cup during a show? In regard to PayPerPost, its CEO, Ted Murphy, said, "We are betting on the ethics and morals of the bloggers themselves. If someone really hates a product, to make $5, will they say something positive? It really comes down to the blogger being honest with its audience." [Frazier, M. (2006, October 30). Want to build up blog buzz? *Advertising Age*. Retrieved August 7, 2009, from InfoTrac College Edition.]

Photo Essay Solutions

Photo Essay, Page 139
Research data developed by buzz-tracking firms like Nielsen BuzzMetrics enable business communicators to better align their messages with known market preferences. Communication professionals with access to timely business intelligence can harness the power of consumer-generated content to gauge audience receptivity and to craft persuasive messages.

Photo Essay, Page 142
Negative events and bad publicity require business communicators to craft written responses using indirect patterns. The indirect approach is favored for ideas that require persuasion or when a company has sensitive news that predisposes an audience to be unreceptive or hostile. The indirect strategy shows sensitivity to readers, helps soften the impact of bad news, and minimizes a negative reaction.

Video Resources

Instructors may show the *Guffey 3-x-3 Writing Process* video from Video Library 1, *Building Workplace Skills*. The video illustrates each phase of the writing process and is a useful introduction to Chapters 4, 5, and 6, all of which present writing techniques. After viewing the video, students should be prepared to discuss critical-thinking questions.

Chapter Presentation Ideas and Extras

For instructors who have extra class time, we provide the following activity ideas.

1. *Cluster Diagramming vs. Outlining*. Give students the same topic to consider or a problem to solve. Ask half the class to use cluster diagrams and half the class to use regular outlining techniques to organize their thoughts. At the end of ten minutes, see which method has resulted in the generation of more ideas. You will probably find that students feel less restricted when they use the cluster diagram method for outlining because it tends to increase the free flow of ideas, especially for visual learners.

2. *Independence vs. Collaboration*. Give students another topic or problem to consider. Have half the class work alone. The other half of the class should be divided into groups of three or four. At the end of ten minutes, see who has generated more solutions or ideas. You should find that those who collaborated have generated many more options. If you intend to include some collaborative writing work in your course, laying the groundwork here will help to make team writing more meaningful for your students.

3. *Direct and Indirect Patterns*. Ask students when they would consider using the direct pattern or the indirect pattern. Can they think of situations when using the direct approach for bad news would be appropriate? Why do good business writers prefer the indirect pattern for bad news?

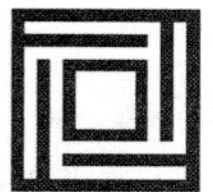

Chapter 6 LECTURE NOTES AND TEACHING SUGGESTIONS

Revising Business Messages

CHAPTER SYNOPSIS

Students often resist the work of significant, substantial revision in favor of proofreading, so you may wish to spend enough time on this chapter to emphasize that all three—revising, proofreading, and evaluating—are important. They must operate in concert for any written communication to be successful. Writing requires greater precision than speaking because a speaker can get instant feedback and correct misunderstandings. Writers do not have the luxury of instant feedback and reply.

To help students understand that individuals at all levels of an organization need to be clear and precise when writing, allow them to critique actual business letters. Also, encourage students to make a habit of proofreading each other's papers. Psychologically, we don't want to find errors in our own work, but we can often find errors in someone else's work. Because we are certain of our intended meanings, we fail to see how a message actually does read. On the job, businesspersons have only one opportunity to help their company make a good first impression. The first impression made by their correspondence can either help their organization make money or lose money, earn goodwill or lose it. Writers need to commit the time it takes to make this first impression a positive one.

LEARNING OBJECTIVES

1. Complete business messages by revising for conciseness, which includes eliminating flabby expressions, long lead-ins, *there is/are* and *it is/was* fillers, redundancies, and empty words.

2. Improve clarity in business messages by keeping the ideas simple, dumping trite business phrases, dropping clichés and slang, unburying verbs, and controlling exuberance.

3. Enhance readability by understanding document design including the use of white space, margins, typefaces, fonts, numbered and bulleted lists, and headings.

4. Recognize proofreading problem areas and apply effective techniques to proofread both routine and complex documents.

5. Evaluate a message to judge its success.

WHAT'S NEW IN THIS CHAPTER

- Revamped opening Zooming In case study to update this feature, which leads to the popular revision exercise "Applying Your Skills at Taco Bell."
- Reorganized coverage of revision techniques to improve chapter flow and enhance coverage of revision techniques.
- Expanded coverage of document design so that students learn about white space, margins, typefaces, and fonts to prepare them for today's workplace where they will be expected to design effective, readable messages.
- Added Figure 6.1 showing students how to make revisions manually and digitally because writers today increasingly edit on screen.
- Added Figure 6.2 comparing typefaces so that students recognize font personalities and appropriate use.
- Added Figure 6.3 with before/after illustrations showing how the readability of an e-mail message can be greatly improved with document design.
- Added Figure 6.5 showing revisions on PDF files because many messages today are exchanged in this format and revisions must be done using markup software.
- Provided 100 percent new Writing Improvement Exercises offering fresh opportunities to apply and reinforce chapter content.

LECTURE OUTLINE

I. Applying Phase 3 of the Writing Process (p. 163)

- The final phase of the 3-x-3 writing process focuses on revising, proofreading, and evaluating.
- Some experts recommend devoting about half the total composition time to revising and proofreading.

Definition: *Revising* means improving the content and sentence structure of your message.

PowerPoint slides 1, 2

Let's Discuss

Revision is the most important part of the writing process

Most students cannot articulate the difference between revising and proofreading. Before showing the PowerPoint definitions, be sure to conduct a class discussion to generate interest and stimulate critical thinking about these concepts.

II. Revising for Conciseness (p. 164)

- Use the fewest words possible to make your message easy to understand and to save the reader's valuable time.

A. Eliminating Flabby Expressions

Instead of this	Try this
In addition to the above	*Also*

Figure 6.1 Revising Manually and Digitally

PowerPoint slide 3

B. Limiting Long Lead-Ins

Instead of this	Try this
This memo is to inform you that we accept your bid.	We accept your bid.

PowerPoint slide 4

C. Dropping Unnecessary *there is/are* and *it is/was* Fillers

Instead of this	Try this
There were three messages in his inbox.	He had three messages.

PowerPoint slide 5

D. Rejecting Redundancies

Instead of this
She expressed *serious interest* in renting the new office.

Try this
She expressed interest in renting the new office.

PowerPoint slide 6

III. Revising for Clarity (p. 167)

- Clear messages are immediately understood, simple, and conversational.

A. Keep It Short and Simple

- Apply the Kiss formula: Keep It Short and Simple!

Instead of this
The purpose of this e-mail is to notify staff members that you will not be able to park in the parking lot while it is being repaved next week.

Try this
While the parking lot is being repaved next week, please park on Elm Street.

PowerPoint slides 7-8

B. Dumping Trite Business Phrases

<u>**Instead of this**</u>	<u>**Try this**</u>
every effort will be made	we'll try
in accordance with your wishes	as you wish

C. Dropping Clichés and Slang

<u>**Instead of this**</u>	<u>**Try this**</u>
make a bundle	earn more money
fit the bill	solves a problem

PowerPoint slides 9-11

D. Unburying Verbs

<u>**Instead of this**</u>	<u>**Try this**</u>
take action on	act
perform an analysis of	analyze

PowerPoint slide 12

E. Controlling Exuberance

- Avoid sounding unprofessional by overusing words such as *very, definitely, quite, completely, really,* etc.

  PowerPoint slide 13

IV. Designing Documents for Readability (p. 170)

A. Employing White Space

- White space is the empty space on a page.
- Increase white space with headings, bulleted or numbered lists, and effective margins.

B. Understanding Margins and Text Alignment

- Business letters and memos usually have side margins of 1 to 1 ½ inches.

C. Choosing Appropriate Typefaces

- Serif typefaces have small features at the ends of strokes.
- Sans serif typefaces are widely used for headings and signs.

Figure 6.2 Typefaces with Different Personalities for Different Purposes

D. Capitalizing on Type Fonts and Sizes

- Font styles are a mechanical means of adding emphasis to your words (all caps, bold, and italic).

E. Numbering and Bulleting Lists for Quick Comprehension

- High-visibility numbered or bulleted lists improve readability and skim value.

PowerPoint slides 14-23

F. Adding Headings for Visual Impact

- Headings help writers to organize information and enable readers to absorb important ideas.

PowerPoint slide 24

V. Proofreading (p. 173)

Definition: *Proofreading* involves correcting grammar, spelling, punctuation, format, and mechanics.

PowerPoint slide 25

A. What to Watch for in Proofreading

- Spelling
- Grammar
- Punctuation
- Names and numbers
- Format

Figure 6.3 Using Document Design to Improve E-Mail Readability
Figure 6.4 Proofreading Marks

B. How to Proofread Routine Documents

- Look for typos and misspellings.
- Search for easily confused words, such as *to* for *too* and *then* for *than.*
- Read for missing words.
- Study for inconsistencies and ambiguous expressions.
- Look for factual errors.

PowerPoint slide 26

C. How to Proofread Complex Documents

- Set the document aside for at least a day.
- Allow adequate time to proofread carefully.
- Be prepared to find errors.
- Read the message at least twice—once for word meanings and once for grammar and mechanics. For very long documents (book chapters and long articles or reports), read a third time to verify consistency in formatting.

- Reduce your reading speed and concentrate on individual words rather than ideas.
- For documents that must be perfect, enlist a proofreading buddy.
- Use standard proofreading marks, shown in Figure 6.1, to indicate changes.

PowerPoint slides 27-33

D. How to Proofread and Revise PDF Files

- Soft proofing involves using Adobe Acrobat markup tools, which enables collaborates in distance locations to proof each other's work electronically.

VI. Evaluating (p. 176)

Definition: *Evaluating* is the process of analyzing whether your message achieved its purpose.

Figure 6.5 Proofreading and Marking PDF Files
Figure 6.6 Partially Revised First Draft

PowerPoint slide 34

VII. Checklist: Proofreading, Revising, and Evaluating

- Eliminate flabby expressions.
- Avoid opening fillers and long lead-ins.
- Shun redundancies.
- Tighten your writing.
- Keep the message simple.
- Avoid trite business phrases.
- Don't use clichés or slang.
- Unbury verbs.
- Control exuberance.
- Improve readability through document design.
- Proofread for correctness.
- Evaluate your final product.

Lecture Transparencies
(available in a separate packet and at http://www.meguffey.com)

Revising Business Messages Acetates	**Transparency Number**
Revising Tips	55–56
Designing for Readability	57
Proofreading; Evaluating	58
Basic Proofreading Marks	59

Solution Masters

	Page Number in This Book
Applying Your Skills at Taco Bell - Revised Memo	507-508
6.1 Flabby Expressions	509
6.2 Long Lead-Ins	509
6.3 *There Is/Are* and *It Is/Was* Fillers	509
6.4 Redundancies	510
6.5 Empty Words	510
6.6 Trite Business Phrases	510
6.7 Clichés, Slang, and Wordiness	511
6.8 Buried Verbs	511
6.9 Lists, Bullets, and Headings	511
6.10 Document for Analysis—Revision	513
6.11 Document for Analysis—Revision	515
6.12 Document for Analysis – Revision	516
6.12 Alternate Revision for 6.12	517
6.13 Document for Analysis—Revision	518

Answers to Chapter Review Questions

1. **How is proofreading different from revising? (Objs. 1, 4)**

   Proofreading involves correcting grammar, spelling, punctuation, format, and mechanics. Revising consists of improving the content and sentence structure of a message.

2. **Why should business writers strive for conciseness? (Obj. 1)**

   Concise messages save time and money. Business audiences prefer to receive messages that are direct, clear, and concise.

3. **What's wrong with expressions such as *due to the fact that* and *in view of the fact that*? (Obj. 1)**

   Although familiar, these are flabby expressions. Replacing them with because makes a message more concise.

4. **What is a redundancy? Give an example. Why should writers avoid redundancies? (Obj. 1)**

   Redundancies are expressions that repeat meaning or include unnecessary words. Example: *combined together*. Writers should avoid redundancies because they are wordy.

5. **Why should a writer avoid the opening *I am sending this e-mail because we have just hired a new manager, and I would like to introduce her*? (Obj. 1)**

   The opening phrase, *I am sending this e-mail because*, says the obvious. It is a long lead-in and needlessly delays getting to the real message. Omit it.

6. **Why should writers avoid opening a sentence with *There is* or *There are*? (Obj. 1)**

   Expressions such as *there is/are* and *it is/was* are fillers that delay getting to the point of the sentence.

7. **What is a buried verb? Give an original example. Why should they be avoided? (Obj. 2)**

   A buried verb is one that has been converted to a noun expression, such as *provide an explanation* rather than *explain.* Buried verbs slow the reader, increase sentence length, drain verb strength, and muddy the thought.

8. **Why would a good writer avoid this sentence? When it arrived, I read your message and am now replying. (Obj. 2)**

   This sentence says the obvious and wastes the reader's time. The fact that the writer is responding acknowledges that the writer received the message and has read it.

9. **What are five document design techniques that business writers can use to enhance readability? (Obj. 3)**

   Design techniques include the appropriate use of white space, margins, typefaces, numbered and bulleted lists, and headings.

10. **How can writers increase white space to improve readability? (Obj. 3)**

    To increase white space, use headings, bulleted or numbered lists, short paragraphs, and effective margins.

11. **What is the difference between serif and sans serif typefaces? What is the preferred use for each? (Obj. 3)**

    Serif typefaces have small features at the ends of strokes. Sans serif are clean fonts without such features. Serif typefaces are often used for body text. Sans serif fonts are popular for headings, titles, signs, and material that does not require continuous reading.

12. **What are five specific items to check in proofreading. Be ready to discuss methods you find useful in spotting these errors. (Obj. 4)**

    Writers should check spelling, grammar, punctuation, names and numbers, and format.

13. In proofreading, why is it difficult to find your own errors? How can you overcome this barrier? (Obj. 4)

Many writers struggle with proofreading because they read what they thought they wrote. In addition, psychologically we prefer not to find our own errors. To overcome these obstacles, develop a mind-set of expecting to find errors. Congratulate yourself when you do!

14. List four or more effective techniques for proofreading complex documents. (Obj. 4)

Following are techniques for proofreading complex documents:

1. Set aside the document for a day.
2. Proofread a printed, double-spaced copy.
3. Allow adequate time to proofread.
4. Be prepared to find errors.
5. Read the message twice—once for word meanings, once for grammar/mechanics.
6. Reduce your reading speed.
7. Have one person read to another.
8. Use standard proofreading marks to indicate changes

15. How can you overcome defensiveness when your writing is criticized constructively? (Obj. 5)

It's natural to be defensive. But try to consider this criticism valuable advice. Look upon this training as skill development. Writers, like athletes, need pointers that speed improvement.

Answers to Critical Thinking Questions

1. Is the revision and proofreading process different for short and long documents? Can you skip revising if your message is brief? (Objs. 1, 4)

Even the shortest of messages should be revised and proofread. Long messages, of course, get the full treatment. This is the time when you can refine and enhance the expression, check facts, and reorganize, if necessary. You can also see how the ideas relate to each other, improve readability, and correct errors. Even short messages require a quick reading before printing or sending. You will save yourself embarrassment and miscommunication by taking the time to revise and proofread. A member of Congress had a staff member retype a letter cowritten by two parents' organizations. The letter urged Congress to vote against school voucher programs for the District of Columbia. The original was fine, but the new version was riddled with grammatical errors and typos. In explaining the lapse, a spokeswoman said, "It was an issue of haste and proofreading." [Spell check. (2003, August 11). *U.S. News & World Report*, p. 6.]

2. Would you agree or disagree with the following statement by writing expert William Zinsser? "Plain talk will not be easily achieved in corporate America. Too much vanity is on the line." (Objs. 1-5)

It is unfortunate that few executives have taken specialty writing courses such as business communications. Some of them believe they are much more impressive when they use big words, long sentences, and convoluted reasoning. Because their egos affect their oral and written communication, even simple ideas sound difficult. Zinsser says, "Executives at every level are prisoners of the notion that a simple style reflects a simple mind. Actually a simple style is the result of hard work and hard thinking; a muddy style reflects a muddy thinker or a person too lazy to organize his or her thoughts."

3. Because business writing should have high "skim value," why not write everything in bulleted lists? (Obj. 3)

Although listing items in bulleted or enumerated lists does improve readability, excessive use of such lists prevents the achievement of other business writing goals. Business writing must be purposeful, goal oriented, and conversational. Achieving a friendly, conversational tone is difficult or impossible in a bulleted list. It's also difficult to be persuasive or to convey a "you" view in lists. Bulleted lists are valuable to improve "skim value," but they are appropriate only when used occasionally in presenting related ideas. Used excessively, they begin to look like laundry lists and turn off readers.

4. Conciseness is valued in business. However, can messages be too short? (Obj. 1)

Of course, messages can be too short. Although conciseness is valued, messages must be clear. If that means adding extra verbiage to explain, then a message may be longer. Persuasive and sales messages are necessarily longer than routine business memos and e-mails. Messages should be as long as necessary to be clear and effective.

5. Ethical Issue: What advice would you give in this ethical dilemma? Lisa is serving as interim editor of the company newsletter. She receives an article written by the company president describing, in abstract and pompous language, the company's goals for the coming year. Lisa thinks the article will need considerable revising to make it readable. Attached to the president's article are complimentary comments by two of the company vice presidents. What action should Lisa take?

Lisa is in a difficult, sensitive position and needs to be cautious about handling this situation. All of her options involve risk. She could ask the president for permission to revise the article, but this action could anger her boss and endanger her position.

She could seek the advice of one of the vice presidents, but both of them seem to be protecting the status quo. If her interim position will last only a short time longer, she may want to "forget" the article and allow her successor to handle this situation. "Forgetting" to publish the article is the least acceptable because Lisa is portrayed as weak and unable to make difficult decisions.

Writing Improvement Exercises

6.1 Flabby Expressions (Obj. 1)

a. Although we lost the contract, we must now move forward.

b. Because prices are falling, we will invest soon. [*OR:* Because prices are falling, we will invest March 1.]

c. We cannot fill the order until payment is received for previous shipments.

d. Generally, we would not accept the return; however, we will probably make an exception in this case.

6.2 Long Lead-Ins (Obj. 1)

a. I received your e-mail and its attachments.

b. We will observe Monday as a holiday.

c. Your homeowners' coverage will soon expire.

d. The loss of laptops endangers company security.

6.3 *There is/are* and *It is/was* Fillers (Obj. 1)

a. Many businesses are implementing strict e-mail policies.

b. The CEO must approve the plan.

c. You must update several Web pages.

d. The manager says that many employees did not return the health surveys.

6.4 Redundancies (Obj. 1)

a. Because the proposals are identical, we need not check each item.

b. All requests for iPods and BlackBerrys were combined in our proposal.

c. The office walls were painted beige.

d. Our supervisor requested that team members return to the office.

6.5 Empty Words (Obj. 1)

a. He scheduled the meeting for 11 a.m.

b. Because of the surprising response, the company expanded its gift program.

c. I will distribute your proposal immediately.

d. Are you aware that our budget has a deficit of about $100,000?

6.6 Trite Business Phrases (Obj. 2)

a. As you request, we will no longer send you e-mail offers.

b. Thank you for considering our plea for community support.

c. As you request, we are sending the original copies separately.

d. Enclosed is a check for $700.

6.7 Clichés, Slang, and Wordiness (Obj. 2)

Note: Acceptable student responses may vary from the suggested responses.

a. Although our last presentation failed, we are sure our new presentation will be well received.

b. Out team must be willing to think creatively when developing marketing ideas that capture attention.

c. As usual, our competitor has made an underhanded claim that we think is unfair [*OR*: devious, false, undeserved].

d. If you refer to the budget, you will see provisions that prevent overspending.

6.8 Buried Verbs (Obj. 2)

a. Ms. Nelson appraised the home's value.

b. Web-based customer service reduces overall costs.

c. Management recommended abandoning the pilot project.

d. The board of directors will consider the contract at its next meeting.

6.9 Lists, Bullets, and Headings (Obj. 3)

a. Security Plus specializes in the following preemployment background reports:
   - Professional reference interviews
   - Criminal reports
   - Driving records
   - Employment verification
   - Credit information

b. A high-powered MBA program costs hundreds of dollars an hour. Our program covers the same information:
   - Starting a business
   - Business plans
   - Taxes
   - Marketing feasibility studies
   - Employment benefits plans
   - Licensing requirements

c. On-site GuruGeek computer technicians provide fast, affordable solutions to residential and small business clients including the following popular offerings:

   - **Antivirus security.** Our GuruGeek technician can protect your computer against viruses, worms, and spyware as well as help you avoid e-mail attacks, identity theft, and malicious hacker programs.
   - **Wireless networking**. We can help you share Internet access through a single wireless router so that many computer users use the same network.
   - **Data backup and recovery.** Our technicians focus on helping small businesses and home users protect their data without investing a lot of time and energy.

Activities

6.10 Document for Analysis: Ineffective Customer Letter (Objs. 1-5)

Weaknesses

1. Begins with long lead-in (*This is to inform you that*)
2. Includes wordy expression (*that will be beginning* instead of *that will begin*)
3. Fails to use side headings to improve readability.
4. Buries verb (*change in how the calculation* instead of *change in how we calculate*)
5. Uses redundant expressions (*exactly identical, absolutely essential)*
6. Buries verb (*make an explanation* instead of *explain*)
7. Uses wordy expression (*in the event that* instead of *if*)
8. Fails to use bullets to list two reasons in paragraph 3
9. Uses wordy expressions (*every effort will be made, by the date of, at that point in time*)
10. Uses trite expression (*please do not hesitate*)
11. Includes general wordiness throughout

Revision

Current date

Mr. Michael Chatham
329 Sycamore Street
Pikeville, KY 41605

Dear Mr. Chatham:

We are changing your World Bank Card Agreement. These changes will be effective for all billing periods beginning on or after February 3.

How Your APR Will Change
We are increasing your variable APR (annual percentage rate) for purchases. Your APR will be identical to the U.S. Prime Rate plus 10.99 percent with a minimum APR of 16.99 percent.

Default APR
All of your APRs on all balances may automatically increase to the default APR if you default under any card agreement you have with us if

- You do not make the minimum payment when due
- You make a payment that is not honored

The default APR takes effect as of the first day of the billing period in which you default. We may lower the APR for new purchases or cash advances if you meet the terms of all card agreements that you have with us for six billing periods.

Right to Opt Out
To opt out of these changes, call or write us by March 31. Include your name, address, and account number in your letter. If you opt out of these changes, you may use your account under the current terms until the end of your current membership year or the expiration date on your card. We will close your account at that time. You must then repay the balance under the current terms.

Please take advantage of your World Bank Card revolving line of credit and all the benefits and services we offer you.

Sincerely,

Note: Based on a real credit card message, this letter definitely employs the direct strategy.

6.11 Document for Analysis: Poorly Written E-Mail Message (Objs. 1–5)

Weaknesses

1. Begins with long lead-in (*I am writing this message because*).
2. Includes trite expression (*pursuant to your request*).
3. Suffers from wordy fillers (*there might be* and *There were several points*).
4. Includes empty words (*on the subject of* and *of an important nature).*
5. Converts verbs into nouns (*give consideration to*) and (*to make an illustration*).
6. Fails to use bulleted list with category headings to improve readability for four items.
7. Concludes with redundancy (*elaborate and expand*) and wordy compound preposition (*subsequent to*).

Revision

To: Marcy Love <marcy.love@sokia.com>
From: Shelton Matthews <shelton.matthews@sokia.com>
Cc:
Subject: Improving Presentation Techniques

Marcy,

As you requested, I attended a seminar about presentation techniques. You suggested that I might learn tips to share with other staff members, especially those who use PowerPoint. The speaker, Gary Dixon, made several important points to help speakers avoid putting listeners to sleep in what he called a "PowerPoint slumber party." Our staff members might consider the following:

Create the message, not the slide, first. Only after preparing the entire script should you think about how to illustrate it.

Prepare slides with short lines. Your slides should have only four to six words per line. Short lines encourage people to listen to you and not read the slide.

Don't put everything on the slide. If you put too much on the slide, your audience will be reading Item C while you are still talking about Item A.

Think in terms of headlines. What is the main point? What does it mean to the audience?

Please let me know whether you want me to expand on these points after the next staff meeting.

Shelton

6.12 Document for Analysis: Poorly Written Response Letter (Objs. 1–5)

Weaknesses

1. Says the obvious *(We have received your request for information.)*
2. Uses trite business phrase (*as per your request)*
3. Fails to use conversational language (*the undersigned)*
4. Transforms verbs into nouns (*improvement of security* instead of *improving security*; *make a decision* instead of *decide; make a recommendation* instead of *recommend; obtain protection* instead of *protect*)
5. Uses wordy phrases (*due to the fact that , because of the fact that)*
6. Suffers from redundancies (*first and foremost, last and final*)
7. Fails to express conciseness (*in all probability* instead of *probably; areas that are to be protected* instead of *protected areas; initiate a verbal discussion* instead of *discuss)*
8. Fails to use familiar words (*contemplate* instead of *think*)

Current date

Mr. DeJuan Wilson
Fairfield Associates, Inc.
4290 Park Avenue
Fairfield, CT 06435

Dear Mr. Wilson:

At your request I am sending you the attached materials about improving security in your business. To improve your after-hours security, you should first decide what must be protected. You are probably concerned about your electronic equipment and about company data.

Because we feel you will want to protect both equipment and data, we can suggest a number of prudent steps to deter crime. First, install defensive lighting. Our lighting expert can design both outside and inside lighting. Second, post security signs. Amateur thieves are often deterred by signs on windows and doors. Finally, install space alarms. These sensors look down over protected areas. The sensors can activate bells or lights, thus scaring off intruders.

After reading the enclosed materials, please call me at (385) 259-1380 to further discuss protecting your business.

Sincerely,

Enclosure

Alternate Revision for 6.12

Current date

Mr. DeJuan Wilson
Fairfield Associates, Inc.
4290 Park Avenue
Fairfield, CT 06435

Dear Mr. Wilson:

At your request, I am sending you the attached materials about improving security in your business. To improve your after-hours security, you should first decide what must be protected. You are probably concerned about your electronic equipment and about company data.

Because we feel you will want to protect both equipment and data, we suggest the following three steps to deter crime:

1. **Install defensive lighting**. Our lighting expert can design both outside and inside lighting.

2. **Post security signs**. Amateur thieves are often deterred by signs on windows and doors.

3. **Install space alarms**. These sensors look down over protected areas. The sensors can activate bells or lights, thus scaring off intruders.

After reading the enclosed materials, please call me at (385) 259-1380 to discuss further protecting your business.

Sincerely,

Enclosure

Note: Enumerated paragraphs may be indented or typed flush left.

6.13 Document for Analysis: Poorly Written Response (Objs. 1–5)

Weaknesses

1. Suffers from long lead-in (*This message is an opportunity to*).
2. Includes flabby phrase *(at this point in time* instead of *now.)*
3. Could be written more concisely (*available only to firms that were larger* instead of *available only to larger firms*).
4. Lacks parallelism (*monthly payroll, quarterly taxes, and records related to personnel matters* instead of *monthly payroll, quarterly taxes, and personnel records*).

5. Includes empty words (*matters of a safety nature* instead of *safety* and *can be reduced by a significant degree* instead of *can be significantly reduced*).
6. Uses redundancies (*basic fundamentals* instead of *fundamentals* or *basics*).
7. Includes fillers (*There are many* and *There is also.)*
8. Uses flabby phrase (*In view of the fact that* instead of *Because*).
9. Suffers from noun conversion (*make an analysis* instead of *analyze*).
10. Includes another wordy phrase (*Whether or not* instead of *whether).*
11. Includes redundancy (*return back* instead of *return).*
12. Lacks parallelism (*return to the basics of running your business and improvement in* instead of *return to the basics of <u>running</u> your business and <u>improving</u> profits).*

Revision

Current date

Ms. Monique Faria
Grey Wolf BioSolutions
4210 Geddes Road
Ann Arbor, MI 48105

Dear Ms. Faria:

Thank you for your interest in employee leasing through Enterprise Staffing Services. Small businesses like yours can now enjoy powerful personnel tools previously available only to larger firms.

The employee leasing concept allows you to outsource personnel duties so that you can focus on the fundamentals of running your business. You can reduce many administrative burdens such as monthly payroll, quarterly taxes, and personnel records. Expert guidance in the areas of human resources, compliance, and safety is available. Because we have extensive experience, your employer liability can be significantly reduced. You can be assured that our entire staff will assemble a plan that will save you time and money as well as protect you from employee hassles and employer liability.

Whether you offer no benefits or a full benefits package, Enterprise Staffing Services can analyze your needs and help you return to the basics of running your business and improving profits. Please allow me to call you to arrange a time to meet and talk about your specific needs.

Cordially,

6.14 Learning About Writing Techniques in Your Field (Objs. 1–5)

This activity could be one of the best possible for convincing students that writing is very important to their future success. Be sure to have students either present their findings orally or write a detailed memo or e-mail message. You will be amazed how businesspeople reaffirm everything you have said to the students. Because students have interviewed professionals who have reaffirmed the importance of writing, they will have an even stronger desire to master writing. To save students frustration, you could keep a list of businesspeople who are willing to be interviewed.

6.15 Searching for Deadwood (Objs. 1, 2)

This activity provides an entertaining way for students to locate "deadwood" phrases on the Web. Consider consolidating all of their findings into one comprehensive list to give out to the class to help them with their future writing assignments.

Students may work individually or in teams on this activity. Individuals may locate ten deadwood phrases (and their preferred substitutes) not included in the textbook. Examples:

Deadwood Phrase	**Substitute**
a majority of	*most*
a sufficient amount of	*enough*
be deficient in	*lack*
by a factor of two	*two times, double, twice*
equally as well	*as well, equally well*
has been proved to be	*is*
in no case	*never*

Some of the Web sites students may find include the following:

Technical Writing—Deadwood Phrases: http://www.klariti.com/technical-writing/Deadwood%20Phrases.shtml
Verbal Litter (U.S. Senate): http://thomas.loc.gov/cgi-bin/query/z?r105:S10JY8-55:

If the instructor chooses a longer assignment, have students work in teams to collect many deadwood phrases, amassing a Dictionary of Deadwood Phrases.

6.16 Conciseness Is Hard Work (Objs. 1, 2)

You may want to suggest to your students that they prepare a table, such as the following for recording what they hear in completing this assignment:

Conciseness Principle	Source	Medium	Violation
Remove Fillers			
Delete Long Lead-ins			
Eliminate Redundancies			
Reduce Compound Prepositions			
Purge Empty Words			

Lead the discussion in the direction of finding out which errors were most common, which medium seemed to carry the most errors, and which source was the biggest violator. You could also ask such questions as:

In your opinion, does conciseness matter more in written or spoken word? Support your answer.

When you're communicating, do you find yourself focusing on being concise more when you're writing or when you're speaking?

While written words can be edited and revised to be more concise before sending them to the receiver, what's your best tool for making your spoken words concise? [Suggested answer: Preparation. For example, before placing an important phone call, jot down a brief outline of what you need to say or ask. Before giving a speech, prepare your remarks so you can identify what's most important and delete what would lead to rambling (remember the Abraham Lincoln quotation).]

Did you notice any types of conciseness errors that show up in speaking that do not appear in written communications? [Suggested answer: Fillers such as *uh*, *ya know*, *like*, and *um* are unique to spoken communication.]

6.17 Communicating With a Nonnative English Speaker

Students will find excellent Web advice on communicating with nonnative English speakers. Here are ten good ideas:

1. Speak clearly but don't turn up the volume.
2. Don't cover or hide your mouth; listeners will want to watch as you pronounce words.
3. Don't use baby talk or incorrect English, which is confusing.
4. Enunciate clearly and avoid running words together (*Are you gonna come?).*
5. If asked to repeat, change a few key words. Try simple synonyms.
6. Write things down. It's easier to understand written language than spoken language.

7. Speak a little more slowly than usual and use gestures.
8. In making requests, avoid using politeness techniques (*Would it be possible . . . , I was wondering if you could . . .*). Instead, *Please do . . . .*
9. Don't agree to anything until you know that you have communicated effectively.
10. Avoid the temptation to correct a speaker or listener.

(Adapted from How to Communicate With a Non Native English Speaker. Retrieved April 17, 2007, from http://www.wikihow/com/Communicate-With-a-Non-Native-English-Speaker)

6.18 How Plain Is the English in Your Apartment Lease? (Objs. 1–3)

Apartment leases are a part of most people's lives. Renters have problems with maintenance, appliances, security, and cleaning deposits. This activity requires students to study rental agreements, most of which are difficult to read. Your class members will probably be relieved when they learn why their leases are difficult to understand. This real activity is quite meaningful and should give students a better idea of the need for plain English and how to achieve it. You might consider having an attorney speak to your class about common problems with leases. Some campuses have specialists with Student Legal Services who will come to your class and discuss leases. One of the biggest problems with student leases is that remaining roommates are liable for all payments when one roommate moves out.

ZOOMING IN Part 1: Taco Bell Tweaks Menu to Rebuild Customer Base

Critical Thinking

- **When new ideas must be generated and sold to management, what role does communication skill play in the process?**

  Even if someone has excellent, creative ideas for a new product or strategy, those ideas will be unappreciated unless they can be expressed effectively. Strong communication skills are necessary for employees and entrepreneurs to explain their ideas to others when support is needed to proceed.

- **Do you think the Taco Bell culinary product manager will be making an oral or a written presentation of new menu ideas?**

  The Taco Bell culinary product manager will undoubtedly write a report that will be distributed before or after an oral presentation. Ideas presented to managers must be carefully thought out and well documented.

- **Why is a writing process helpful in developing a presentation of new ideas?**

  Both novice and veteran writers benefit from following a writing process. If you know the structure of what should go in the introduction, body, and closing of a report or a presentation, the task becomes immeasurably easier.

ZOOMING IN Part 2: Taco Bell

Critical Thinking

- **Based on what you learned in this chapter, what specific advice can you give about keeping a message clear? Should a business message be conversational?**

  Keep the message simple. Resist the urge to show off or be fancy. Use simple words and active-voice verbs. Avoid negative, indirect, and pompous language. Although you should sound professional, you should also be warm and friendly. Unless you know your management team is rigidly formal, use a conversational tone. That means including occasional contractions and first person pronouns (*I, we*). Sound as if you are talking to someone in a friendly conversation. Avoid legal terminology, technical words, and third-person constructions (*the undersigned, the writer*).

- **Why is conciseness important, and what techniques can be used to achieve it?**

  Conciseness is important because wordy writing takes longer to read and longer to understand. In business, time is money. Most executives are very busy people, and they resent wasting their time reading wordy writing. Concise writing means removing opening fillers (*there is, it is*, etc.), redundancies (*first and foremost, each and every*), compound prepositions (*by means of, due to the fact that*, etc.), empty words, and long lead-ins (*this memo is to inform you that. . .*).

- **Would you advise the culinary chef to be direct with her ideas? What advice can you give for improving the directness and readability of a business message?**

  If readers are expected to be supportive of the ideas to be presented, the sender should use a direct strategy. Moreover, to avoid dull writing, writers should strive to express ideas directly. One bad habit is transforming verbs into nouns (*bring about a reduction in* instead of *reduce*). Business writers also should avoid tired and trite phrases such as *as per your request* and *please do not hesitate to . . . .* Readability is enhanced by expressing ideas in parallel construction (*working, playing, and studying*) and by using graphic highlighting to spotlight important ideas. Some of the best techniques for graphic highlighting include using bulleted lists, enumerated lists, headings, capital letters, underscores, boldface, and italics.

ZOOMING IN Your Turn: Applying Your Skills at Taco Bell (Transparency solution available)

Date: Current
To: Taco Bell, Executive Council
From: Erin Jackson, Culinary Product Manager
Subject: Fast-Food Trends and Menu Options

As you requested, I am submitting the following ideas based on my observation and research about eating trends in fast-food restaurants. Below is a rough outline of possible concepts to upgrade Taco Bell's menu. This memo summarizes the findings to be presented at our next meeting.

Mexican cuisine is increasingly popular from coast to coast, and in a depressed economy our restaurants can offer value as well as tasty food. From my first-hand experience gained as a chef and from current research, I have observed numerous eating trends. Below are four that are of interest as we rethink the Taco Bell menu.

Current Eating Trends

- **Low-fat, healthful choices**. With as many as one in five U.S. consumers on a diet, our menu should reflect low-calorie, healthful options that still taste good.
- **Spices**. Consumers are appreciating more highly spiced foods and hot sauces. Spicy Thai and other ethnic dishes are growing in popularity.
- **Freshness**. As consumers become more knowledgeable and more discriminating, they are demanding fresher ingredients.
- **Tasty food but at low prices**. In an economic downturn, consumers are looking for value meals that don't break their budgets.

Given the increasing acceptance of Mexican cuisine and the rich array of flavors and textures, we have many possibilities for expanding our menu. Although my full report contains additional trends and menu ideas, I will concentrate below on four significant concepts.

New Menu Concepts

- **Spicy grilled items**. Selections might include chicken marinated in lime juice, chipotle-rubbed ahi tuna served with cranberry-mango salsa, and Volcano Beef Burrito served with Lava sauce.
- **Fresco menu.** I suggest that we offer an entire menu of ten or more items that cater to dieters and health-conscious customers. The Fresco menu might include Crunchy Beef Taco, Grilled Steak Taco, Blazing Bean Burrito, and Ranchero Chicken Soft Taco. These low-calorie, low-fat items will contain fewer than 10 grams of fat but be tasty, filling, and inexpensive.
- **Self-serve salsa bar**. We could offer exotic fresh salsas with bold flavors and textures.

- **Fruit-flavored frozen drinks.** Mango and strawberry-flavored frozen beverages topped with strawberries could be sweetened with sucrose rather than high-fructose corn syrup for an appealing, inexpensive, low-calorie selection.

I would be happy to discuss these ideas with you in greater detail and to demonstrate them in the kitchen. Thanks for this opportunity to work with you in expanding our menu to ensure that Taco Bell remains tops in Mexican cuisine.

Discussion Material for PLUGGED IN: Using Spell Checkers and Grammar/Style Checkers Wisely

Have students complete this activity and discuss the results in class. What settings do students find are most useful for them? When checking their own documents, what kinds of spelling and grammatical errors do their spell checkers and grammar/style checkers find? What kinds of spelling errors is the spell checker not programmed to find? What kinds of grammatical errors is the grammar/style checker not programmed to find? Do students take the spelling checker's and grammar/style checker's advice at all times? Why or why not? Does a spelling or grammar/style checker eliminate the need for careful proofreading?

Ethics Check Solutions

Ethics Check, Page 173
Costly Writing
Bad writing can be expensive: A Philadelphia lawyer was charged with malpractice to the tune of $6.6 million for drafting a poor commercial lease. The judge in Los Angeles said the draft was "inartfully written and done so in a confusing fashion, which lends itself to ambiguities and disagreements." Can you think of other situations when writing can be deliberately or accidentally misleading and cost money?

Students may come up with examples involving the small print in contracts and agreements. They may also be reminded that, for example, on the Internet, most Web surfers simply click "I accept" on terms of use without ever reading them—sometimes inviting spam or allowing their personal data to be shared with third parties. Careless writing also wastes time in the workplace when recipients cannot be sure they understood the intent of a message.

Ethics Check, Page 176
Overly Helpful
Students may visit writing centers where they receive useful advice and help. However, some well-meaning tutors take over, revising documents until they don't resemble the original student work. Instructors worry that the resulting documents amount to cheating. Yet in the workplace today, writers must collaborate, and drafts go through multiple revisions. Individual authorship is often not relevant. How much revision is acceptable in a college setting? How much in the workplace?

The line must be drawn at rewriting the original copy. Well-trained tutors know the difference between gentle, competent guidance and assuming control over the tutee's paper. The students also needs to take responsibility for their writing and should want to learn from each writing center visit instead of seeking "quick fixes." In the workplace, prompt and creative responses to feedback and text modifications will be expected. Writers cannot hide behind their collaborators but must share the responsibility for the final product.

Photo Essay Solution

Photo Essay, Page 168
Due to industry specific language, pharmaceutical companies, technology firms, biotech companies, accountancies, hospitals, and other specialized businesses face enormous challenges in producing messages that are clear and conversational.

Video Resources

Instructors may show the *Bridging the Gap* video from Library 2, *Writing Skills: The Little Guys*. Instructors will find a complete discussion guide and activity solution for this video presented in this Instructor's Manual.

Chapter Presentation Ideas and Extras

1. *Proofreading*. To give students a realistic experience revising and proofreading, provide several letters to proofread. Students should be encouraged to mark anything they believe to be a mistake. (Be sure the letters have various types of mistakes in them.) Then use transparencies to show them the errors. This would also be an effective way to introduce proofreading marks.

2. *Revision.* Have students revise at least one or two of the letters that you discussed in the previous activity. Then make transparencies of their letters to aid in the discussion of revising.

3. *Letter Collection.* For courses that emphasize letters and memos, have students start a letter collection. You will need to decide the number as well as the types of letters to include. If you have been saving sample letters yourself, you may be able to help students start their collections. This is always good for their morale.

4. *Proofreading Practice.* Since students need to have the maximum practice in proofreading both routine and complex documents, have samples of each so that you can provide this necessary practice.

Supplementary Lecture

Measuring Readability

Formulas can measure how easy or difficult a message is to read. Two well-known formulas are Robert Gunning's Fog Index and the Flesch-Kincaid Index. Both measure word and sentence length to determine readability. The longer a sentence is, the more difficult it is to read. If you are using a current version of Microsoft Word, the software will calculate a readability score for any passage you highlight. Word shows a "reading ease" score as well as the Flesch-Kincaid grade-level score. A score of 10, for example, means that the passage can be easily read by a person with ten years of schooling.

The foggier a message is, the higher its reading level is. Magazines and newspapers that strive for wide readership keep their readability between levels 8 and 12. *USA Today* is 10.6, *The New York Times* is 12.6, [Neuharth, A. (1990, October 12). Why Washington is lost in the fog. *USA Today*, p. A13] and *People* magazine ranges between 8.4 and 11.2. By occasionally calculating the Fog Index of your writing, you can ensure that you stay within the 8 to 12 range. Remember that long words--those over two syllables—and long sentences make your writing foggy.

Readability formulas, however, don't always tell the full story. They cannot measure how complex the content is, whether the topic is appropriate for the audience, whether the message was designed attractively, or whether the vocabulary is at the right level for the audience. Readability tests cannot assess the context in which the message will be used. Readability tests would not reflect whether a document contains gender, class, or cultural bias. They would not reveal whether the material appears in a form and font style that is easy or hard to read. One might also guess that that interest and prior reader knowledge are important in determining whether a document is readable and understandable.

Although readability formulas provide a rough estimate, those based solely on word and sentence counts fail to measure meaningfulness. Even short words (such as *skew, onus,* and *wane*) can cause trouble if readers don't recognize them. More important than length are a word's familiarity and meaningfulness to the reader. In Chapter 4 students learned to adapt their writing to the audience by selecting familiar words. Other techniques that can improve readability include well-organized paragraphs, transitions to connect ideas, headings, and lists.

Applying the Fog Index to Determine Readability

One way to calculate the "readability" of a document is by applying the Gunning Fog Index. Use the following letter to apply the Fog Index:

> Dear Mrs. Lawrence:
>
> [1]Yes, I can meet with you Thursday, April 3, at 10 a.m. to discuss <u>possible</u> ways to finance the purchase of a new home in San Diego. [2]Before we meet, though, you might like to <u>consider</u> two <u>possible</u> plans.
>
> [3]The first plan finances your purchase with a swing loan, which has a fixed <u>interest</u> rate for a short <u>period</u> of time. [4]A second plan requires you to <u>refinance</u> your present <u>residence</u>. [5]We have located five programs from three <u>different</u> <u>institutions</u> that would do this. [6]Enclosed is a <u>summary</u> of these five plans. [7]I look forward to seeing you Thursday to find a way for you to own a home in San Diego.
>
> Sincerely,

To manually calculate the Fog Index for the preceding business letter, follow these steps:

1. **Select the passage.** Choose a continuous passage of between 100 and 130 words.
2. **Count the total words.** Count numbers, dates, and abbreviations as separate words. Our business letter sample has 110 words.
3. **Count the sentences.** Count all independent clauses separately. For example, *He applied, and he was hired* counts as two sentences. Our sample has seven sentences, marked with superscript numbers.
4. **Find the average sentence length.** Divide the total number of words by the number of sentences (110 divided by 7 equals 16 words).
5. **Count the number of long words.** A word is long if it has three or more syllables. Exclude (a) capitalized words, (b) compound words formed from short words (*nevertheless*), and (c) verbs made into three syllables by the addition of *-ed* or *-es* (*located, finances*). In our sample the long words are underlined.
6. **Find the percentage of long words.** Divide the number of long words by the number of total words (10 divided by 110 equals .09 or 9 percent).
7. **Add the results.** Add the average sentence length (16) and the percentage of long words (9). The result is 25.
8. **Multiply.** Multiply by 0.4 (25 times 0.4 equals 10). The reading level of this letter is 10.

The reading level of this short letter is 10. This level indicates that the reader needs ten years of schooling to understand the letter. Your goal should be to keep your writing between the levels of 8 and 12. Two factors that most influence reading level are sentence length and word length.

Instructors may ask students to compare the reading levels of several publications. Have them calculate the Fog Index for short passages from local newspapers, a business document (letter, memo, report), an insurance policy, or two of their college textbooks. Discuss in class the appropriateness of the reading levels for each document.

Students can have fun with this exercise as they determine the readability of a variety of documents, including textbooks, local newspapers, business documents, magazines, and even Web sites. Your students can determine readability manually using the process outlined in the text, or they can key passages into a word processor and use the built-in readability measurement tool. Have students discuss the various readability levels they find. Why are specific documents written at specific levels?

Additional Application: Computing the Fog Index

a. Compute the Fog Index for Activity 6.10 (Document for Analysis) **before** you revise it.
b. Revise the letter reducing its length and improving its readability. Eliminate redundancies, wordiness, and trite expressions. Use simple, clear words. Shorten sentences.
c. Prepare a clean copy of the revised letter.
d. **After** revision, calculate the Fog Index.
e. Compare the before and after versions and discuss their readability.

Chapter 7 LECTURE NOTES AND TEACHING SUGGESTIONS

Electronic Messages and Digital Media

CHAPTER SYNOPSIS

Although office workers still send paper-based messages, the exchange of information in organizations today is increasingly electronic and mobile. E-mail continues to be the lifeblood of businesses today, but instant messaging is gaining popularity.

Any applications that do not require a human presence (e.g., certain training videos) lend themselves to podcast recordings that users can stream or download on demand. Blogs help businesses to keep customers, employees, and suppliers informed and receive feedback. Wikis enable far-flung team members to share information and build a knowledge base, and can be used to replace meetings, manage projects, and document projects large and small.

Facebook, MySpace, and Twitter allow firms to share company news; exchange ideas; and connect with customers, employees, other stakeholders, and the public at large. Companies may boost their brand recognition and provide a forum for collaboration by participating in established social networks or by creating their own in-house communities. The downsides of social media participation are productivity losses, fallout from inappropriate employee posts, leaking of trade secrets, and angry Internet users.

Professional networking sites such as LinkedIn help companies and job seekers to connect. Really simple syndication and social bookmarking allow users to navigate the huge resources on the Internet. RSS feeds are time-savers because they allow businesspeople to monitor many news sources in one convenient online location. Social bookmarking sites such as Digg, Del.icio.us, and Reddit help users search, organize, share, and store bookmarks on the Web. The use of all digital media requires professionalism and caution because they create permanent records.

LEARNING OBJECTIVES

1. Describe the role digital media play in the changing world of business in contrast to traditional paper-based messages.

2. Meet professional e-mail standards for usage, structure, and format; and follow the rules of netiquette and other best practices.

3. Explain how business professionals communicate by instant messaging and texting.

4. Identify professional uses of podcasts, blogs, and wikis; and describe prudent policies to protect authors of electronic content.

5. Understand business uses of social and professional networking sites as well as RSS feeds and social bookmarking.

WHAT'S NEW IN THIS CHAPTER

- Created a new chapter dedicated solely to digital media to acquaint students with the latest trends in workplace communication technology.
- Emphasized business uses of digital media so that readers will recognize their professional, rather than social, applications.
- Updated coverage of e-mail with special focus on format and message components to ensure that college graduates understand how business messages differ from personal e-mail messages.
- Introduced discussion of blogs, instant messaging, text messaging, podcasts, blogs, wikis, and social networking so that students see how these communication channels function in the workplace and comprehend the risks associated with their use.
- Covered RSS feeds and social bookmarking sites to help readers to share and manage information online efficiently.
- Inserted a new three-part case study about Twitter to pique interest, expose some of the risks of technology use, and relate the textbook to today's digital world.
- Provided a Plugged-In feature about cloud computing so that students glimpse future trends.
- Prepared three new Documents for Analysis, including one transcript of a live IM exchange for revision, to reflect the great variety of workplace digital communication today.
- Added two new Ethics Checks relevant to electronic communication to highlight moral quandaries presented by modern technology on the job.
- Included five Spotlights on Communicators, all of whom are commenting on cutting-edge technology in the workplace and provide up-to-date guidance to readers.
- Presented end-of-chapter activities for students that reinforce the use of new digital media.

LECTURE OUTLINE

I. How Organizations Exchange Messages and Information (p. 188)

Increasingly, information is exchanged electronically and on the go. You will be expected to collect, evaluate, and exchange information in clearly written messages, whether electronic or paper-based.

PowerPoint slides 1-4

A. Communicating With Paper-Based Messages

- Business letters
- Interoffice memos

B. Communicating With Electronic Messages

- Electronic mail
- Instant messaging
- Text messaging
- Podcasts
- Blogs
- Wikis
- Social networking

Lecture Tidbit

How have Twitter and Facebook changed business communication? These new services make communication *more frequent and informal*. Twitter, for example, allows users to send 140-character messages to people who have subscribed to see them, called followers. So instead of sending an email to friends announcing that you landed a new job, you can just tweet it for all the people who have chose to "follow" you to see. [See Vascellaro, Jessica, E. (2009). Why Email No Longer Rules; and What That Means for the Way We Communicate. *The Wall Street Journal.* Retrieved October 12, 2009, from www.wsj.com].

II. Preparing and Composing Professional E-Mail Messages (p. 190)

PowerPoint slide 5

A. Analyzing the Components of E-Mail Messages

1. Subject Line—summarizes the central idea
2. Opening—reveals the main idea immediately
3. Body—explains and justifies the central idea
4. Closing—presents action information, summarizes the message, or offers a closing thought

Figure 7.1 Formatting an E-Mail Message

PowerPoint slides 6-11

B. Applying E-Mail Formats

- Guide Words—e-mail address or receiver's name plus e-mail address
- Greeting—Dear Leslie, Leslie, Hi, Greetings
- Body—just cover one topic, single space, don't use all caps, maximum three screens in length
- Complimentary Close and Signature Block—name, e-mail address, and contact information

C. Composing Professional E-Mail Messages

- Compose e-mail messages carefully. Once they have been sent, they cannot be retrieved.
- E-mail messages are permanent and searchable.

Let's Discuss

Bryan Cave, chairman of an international law firm, said, "You should never engage in a disagreement electronically. If you are going to disagree with somebody, you certainly don't want to do it by e-mail. You want to do it face to face."

Do you agree or disagree?

Although today's students are more comfortable with electronic communications, face-to-face meetings allow employees to read the other person's body language and other social signals that may communicate confusion, misunderstanding, or anger. In texting and e-mails, you can't always gauge reactions and misunderstandings may occur. .

[See Sharkey, J. (2010). Email Saves Time, but Being There Says More. *The New York Times.*Retrieved January 26, 2010, from http://www.nytimes.com.]

D. Checklist for Writing Professional E-Mail Messages

Subject Line

- Summarize the central idea.
- Include labels if appropriate.
- Avoid empty or dangerous words.

Opening

- State the purpose for writing.
- Highlight questions.
- Supply information directly.

Body

- Explain details.
- Enhance readability.
- Apply document design.
- Be cautious.

Closing

- Request action.
- Provide a goodwill statement or a closing thought.
- Avoid cliché endings.

Figure 7.2 Using E-Mail Safely and Smartly

PowerPoint slides 12-20

Lecture Tidbit

Employees and executives continue to send off careless e-mails, which later get them fired or sent to jail. Harry Stonecipher, CEO of the giant aircraft company Boeing, lost his job because of alleged explicit romantic e-mails sent to a colleague. In fact, one in five companies has fired an employee for e-mail abuse. Avoid the pitfalls that others have fallen into by following the guidelines presented in this chapter.

III. Using Instant Messaging and Texting Professionally (p. 178)

A. How Instant Messaging and Texting Work

- Use a public IM service, such as AOL's Instant Messenger.
- IM communication is exchanged between two computers that are linked by severs or handheld devices such as the iPhone.
- Texting requires a smartphone or PDA, and users are charged for the service.

Figure 7.3 Instant Message for Brief Fast Communication
Figure 7.4 Texting and Instant Messaging with iPhone

B. Pros and Cons of Instant Messaging and Texting

Pros:
- Real-time communication with colleagues anywhere in the world
- Allows people to share information immediately and make decisions quickly
- Includes group online chat capabilities
- Offers a low-cost substitute for voice calls
- Avoids phone tag and eliminates downtime associated with telephone conversations
- Offers presence functionality – coworkers can locate each other online

Cons:
- Reduces worker productivity
- Creates risk that private company records will be accessed by hackers
- May be the source of evidence in lawsuits
- Creates driving hazards when users text while driving

PowerPoint slides 21-22

Let's Discuss

What is your employer's policy for using instant messaging and texting at work?

As the chapter suggests, employees should learn the company's IM and texting policies and follow them while at work. Some students may not know their company's policies, so this question may prompt them to investigate them.

C. Best Practices for Instant Messaging and Texting

- Learn company's IM policies.
- Don't text or IM while driving.
- Make yourself unavailable when trying to meet a deadline.
- Separate business from personal contacts.
- Keep messages simple.
- Don't use IM or texting to send confidential information.
- Don't IM or text anything that could damage your reputation or your company's.
- Keep texting to a minimum.
- Keep your presence status up-to-date.
- Reduce use of jargon, slang, and abbreviations.
- Use good grammar and proper spelling.

IV. Using Podcasts or Webcasts, Blogs, and Wikis for Business (p. 200)

A. Business Podcasts or Webcasts

- The words broadcasting and iPod combined to create the word podcast.
- Podcasts can extend from short clips of a few minutes to 30-minutes or longer digital files.
- News organizations and media outlets podcast radio and TV shows.
- Podcasts encoded as MP3 files can be downloaded to a computer, smartphone, or an MP3 player.

B. Creating a Podcast

- Decide whether to record one podcast or a series.
- Download software.
- Obtain hardware.
- Organize the message.
- Choose and extemporaneous or scripted delivery.
- Prepare and practice.
- Publish and distribute your message.

Figure 7.5 GreenTalk Radio Podcasts

PowerPoint Slide 23

C. Professional Blogs

- A blog is a Web site with journal entries written by one person.
- Businesses use blogs to keep customers and employees informed and to interact with them.

D. How Companies Use Blogs

- Public relations, customer relations, and crisis communication
- Market research and viral marketing
- Online communities
- Internal communication and recruiting

E. Tips for Creating a Professional Blog

- Identify your audience.
- Find a home for your blog.
- Craft your message.
- Make "blogrolling" work for you.
- Attract search engines by choosing the right keywords.
- Blog often.
- Monitor the traffic to your site.
- Seek permission from your employer.
- Avoid inappropriate topics.

PowerPoint slides 24, 25

F. Wikis and Collaboration

Businesses use wikis for the following purposes:

- Share information between headquarters and satellite offices.
- Collect and disseminate information to large audiences.
- Facilitate feedback before and after meetings.
- Sharing information among team members.
- Document large and small projects.
- Provide templates for report.

Effective wiki contributors follow these guidelines:

- Show respect.
- Avoid improper or ambiguous language.
- Don't attack or criticize another contributor.
- Don't "troll" and post provocative comments online.
- Pay attention to correct grammar and spelling.
- Verify your facts.
- Follow the guidelines for contributors.
- Give credit where credit is due.

Figure 7.6 Creating a Wiki With Google Sites and Google Docs\\

PowerPoint slides 26, 27

V. Negotiating Social and Professional Networking Sites (p. 206)

A. How Businesses Use Social Networks

- For brainstorming and teamwork
- To boost their brand image
- To provide a forum for collaboration

Figure 7.7 Big Companies Rule on Facebook: Netflix

B. Potential Risks of Social Networks for Businesses

- Productivity losses
- Loss of trade secrets
- Risk of attracting wrath of huge Internet audiences
- Embarrassment over inappropriate and damaging employee posts

C. Tips for Using Social Networking Sites and Keeping Your Job

- Use caution in sharing sensitive information, especially risqué photographs.
- Don't share information online that you would not share openly in the office.
- Avoid snubbing coworkers by not accepting friend requests or blocking users for no apparent reason.

D. Harnessing the Potential of Professional Networking Sites

Business-oriented networking sites are used for:
- Recruiting
- Networking

Figure 7.8 Adobe Systems Jobs on LinkedIn
PowerPoint slides 28, 29

E. Sharing Information Through RSS Feeds and Social Bookmarking

- RSS (really simple syndication) allows users to monitor many news sources from one convenient location.
- RSS is a data file format and the documents are called feeds or channels.
- Feeds increase traffic to syndicated Web sites because they can be indexed in search engines.
- Social bookmarking helps users search, organize, manage, and store bookmarks on the Web with the help of metadata – that is, information tags or keywords.

Figure 7.9 Social Bookmarking Sites
PowerPoint slides 30-33

VI. Checklist: Using Electronic Media Professionally: Dos and Don'ts (p. 211)

Dos

- Learn your company's rules.
- Avoid or minimize sending personal e-mails, IM messages, or texts from work.
- Separate work and personal data.
- Be careful when blogging, tweeting, or posting on social network sites.
- Keep your virus and malicious software protection current.
- Pick strong passwords and vary them.
- Keep sensitive information private.

Don'ts

- Don't send, download, print, or exhibit pornography, sexually explicit jokes, or inappropriate screen savers.
- Don't open attachments sent by e-mail unless they come from a trusted company source.
- Don't download free software and utilities to company machines.
- Don't store your music library and photos on a company machine, and don't watch streaming videos.
- Don't share files and avoid file-sharing services.

Lecture Transparencies
(available in a separate packet and at http://www.meguffey.com)

Electronic Messages and Digital Media Acetates	Transparency Number
Preparing and Composing Professional E-Mail Messages	61
Formatting E-Mail Messages	62
Smart E-Mail Practices	63-65
Top Ten Mistakes that Can Sabotage Your Career	66-67
Using IM and Texting Professionally	68
Using Podcasts or Webcasts, Blogs, and Wikis for Business	69
Creating a Professional Blog	70
How Businesses Use Wikis	71
How Businesses Use Social Networks	72
Tips for Using Social Networks and Keeping Your Job	73

Solution Masters

	Page Number in This Book
7.1 Document for Analysis—Revision	519
7.2 Document for Analysis—Revision	520
7.3 Document for Analysis—Revision	521
7.4 Choosing a Holiday Plan	522
7.5 Reaching Consensus About Holiday Attire	523
7.6 Learning to Write Superefficient Tweets	525
7.7 Practicing Your Professional IM Skills	525
7.8 Analyzing a Podcast	525

Answers to Chapter Review Questions

1. What is Web 2.0, and how has it changed the way users engage with information? (Obj. 1)

Web 2.0 is a dynamic, interactive environment, not a repository of passively consumed information. Users are empowered, active participants who create content, review products, and edit and share information.

2. Name and describe the two prevailing technological trends today. (Obj. 1)

Mobile communication and cloud computing are the two main tech trends today. Mobile communication means that workers are untethered to office desktop computers. Instead, they are free to share information anytime and anywhere with smartphones, PDAs, netbooks, and laptops. Cloud computing describes the storing and accessing of data and software applications in remote network clusters called clouds. Information and software programs are not stored locally on computer hard drives or other memory devices, but rather, on remote servers online.

3. List and concisely describe at least six electronic communication channels used most commonly by businesspeople today. (Obj. 1)

1. E-mail: The channel of choice in business today, gradually replacing paper memos and letters in many instances.
2. Instant messaging: More interactive and immediate than e-mail; users chat in real time by logging on to an IM service.
3. Text messaging: Very brief messages sent from cellular phones using SMS protocol.
4. Podcasts: Digital media files, either audio or video, that can be streamed or downloaded on demand.
5. Blogs: Web sites containing public journal entries, or posts, with feedback added by readers.
6. Wikis: Public or private Web sites enabling users to collaboratively create, post, edit, and access information; helpful for project management.

4. List and briefly describe the four parts of typical e-mails. (Obj. 2)

Typical e-mails have four parts: (a) an informative subject line that summarizes the message; (b) an opening that reveals the main idea immediately; (c) a body that explains and justifies the main idea; and (d) a closing that presents action information, summarizes the message, or offers a closing thought.

5. Suggest at least ten pointers that you could give to a first-time e-mail user. (Obj. 2)

Students should list at least four of the following:

1. Get the address right.
2. Avoid misleading subject lines.
3. Be concise.
4. Don't send anything you wouldn't want published.
5. Don't use e-mail to avoid contact.
6. Never respond when you are angry.
7. Care about correctness.
8. Resist humor and sarcasm.
9. Limit any tendency to send blanket copies.
10. Use design to improve the readability of longer messages.
11. Consider cultural differences.
12. Double-check before hitting the Send button.

6. How can you use instant messaging and texting safely on the job? (Obj. 3)

Before using instant messaging on the job, check with your supervisor. Follow any company policy rules regarding its use. Don't send anything you would not want published. Use it as a professional business tool, not as a time to chat casually with friends.

7. Name at least five reasons some organizations forbid employees to use instant and text messaging. (Obj. 3)

1. IM and texting can be distractions in addition to the telephone, e-mail, and Web browsing.
2. Privileged information and sensitive company records may be revealed through public IM messaging and intercepted by hackers.
3. Phishing schemes, viruses, malware, and IM or text spam can be introduced.
4. Tracking and record keeping may be necessary to comply with legal requirements.
5. IM and texting have been implicated in traffic accidents.
6. Inappropriate uses of IM and sexting (sending sexually explicit pictures or texts) could lead to a hostile work environment and lawsuits.
7. Like e-mail, IM and texting are subject to disclosure and can become evidence in lawsuits.

8. How can you show professionalism and respect for your receivers in writing business IM messages and texts? (Obj. 3)

Beware of jargon, slang, and abbreviations, which, although they may reduce keystrokes, may be confusing and appear unprofessional. Respect your receivers by using good grammar and proper spelling and by proofreading carefully. Keep your presence status up-to-date so that people trying to reach you don't waste their time.

9. Describe the process of creating a simple podcast. (Obj. 4)

a. Decide whether to create a one-time podcast or a series on a related subject.
b. Download recording and editing software such as Audacity, ePodcast Creator, or Gabcast.
c. Obtain hardware such as a microphone and other audio equipment. Find a recording room that's shielded against noise.
d. Organize the message and build in some redundancy.
e. Choose extemporaneous (free) or scripted delivery.
f. Prepare and practice before recording.
g. Publish and distribute your message on your Web site, in a blog entry, or on a social networking site. Consider using an RSS feed.

10. Explain why companies use blogs. (Obj. 4)

Companies use blogs to keep customers, suppliers, and employees informed and to interact with them. Through blog entries, companies can potentially reach a far-flung, vast audience. Blogs can also elicit unbiased consumer feedback.

11. What is a wiki, and what are its advantages to businesses? (Obj. 4)

A wiki is a Web site that employs easy-to-use collaborative software to allow users to create documents that can be edited by tapping into the same technology that runs the well-known online encyclopedia Wikipedia. Wikis are a valuable collaboration and project management tool that can be used across time zones and vast geographic distances.

12. Name a few of the potential risks that social networking sites may pose to business. (Obj. 5)

Managers fear productivity losses, compromised trade secrets, the wrath of large Internet audiences, and embarrassment over inappropriate and damaging employee posts.

13. What do employment and hiring experts recommend to young job seekers who wish to connect with companies on LinkedIn and other professional networking sites? (Obj. 5)

Hiring experts say that about three quarters of U.S. companies view professional networking sites, primarily LinkedIn, as indispensable recruiting tools. They recommend that job seekers keep their profiles "clean"—that is, free of risqué photos, profanity, and negative comments. Instead, job candidates are encouraged to highlight awards, professional goals, and accomplishments.

14. What is really simple syndication (RSS), and why is it helpful? (Obj. 5)

Really simple syndication, or RSS, is a fast and easy way to search and manage information. RSS is a data file format capable of transmitting changing Web content. RSS documents are called feeds or channels, and they can be read most efficiently with a Web-based feed reader (aggregator), an easy-to-use software application. Feeds alert subscribers to up-to-the-minute blog entries, news items, videos, and podcasts.

15. Explain the role of social bookmarking sites such as Digg, Del.icio.us, Reddit, StumbleUpon, and Squidoo. (Obj. 5)

Social bookmarking sites help users search, organize, manage, and store bookmarks of their favorite content with the help of metadata; that is, information tags or keywords. If you are publishing a Web site or a blog, you will want your readers to share your information with others and provide links to your online presence. As a result, your ranking in search engine keyword queries will rise.

Answers to Critical Thinking Questions

1. How could IM be useful in your career field? Does IM produce a permanent record? Do you think that common abbreviations such as *lol* and *imho* and all-lowercase writing are acceptable in text messages for business? Will the use of shorthand abbreviations as well as creative spelling negatively affect writing skills? (Obj. 3)

Students should be able to generate ideas on how instant messaging will be useful in their career fields. Yes, IM does produce a permanent record. Any IM conversation transmitted electronically establishes a digital record. Many IM users also regularly save their messages. In regard to abbreviations, remember that business messages—even instant messages—may be shared with others. Don't include abbreviations that are unprofessional and confusing. They do not save time if someone has to stop and think about what they mean. The last question on whether shorthand abbreviations and creative spelling will affect the writing of workers should generate interesting student observations.

2. Tweeting, texting, and quickie e-mailing all may foster sloppy messages. Author Mark Garvey argued, "In business, in education, in the arts, in any writing that takes place outside the linguistic cul-de-sac of our close friends and relatives, writers are expected to reach for certain standards of clarity, concision and care."[i] What did Garvey mean? Do you agree? (Objs. 2, 3)

Garvey is talking about the difference between messages to friends and serious writing. Do you agree that there are two kinds of writing? Which kind is appropriate in the workplace? How is it different from tweets and instant messages? [See Garvey, M. (2009). Stylized: A Slightly Obsessive History of Strunk & White's The Elements of Style. New York: Simon & Schuster.]

3. **Why are lawyers and technology experts warning companies to store, organize, and manage computer data, including e-mails and instant messages, with sharper diligence? (Obj. 2)**

   Storing, organizing, and managing computer data with diligence will avoid lawsuits, costly litigation, and poor worker productivity. Computerized information has increasingly become critical in all types of lawsuits. New guidelines for cyber discovery, which took effect December 2006, now make retention even more critical. If a company in a lawsuit protests that it cannot produce needed evidence, the court may allow outsiders to prowl through company digital records with unexpected and possibly expensive or embarrassing results. [See Kabay, M. E. (2007, February 6). E-mail retention policies. *Network World.*] E-mails and instant messages can be used in court. Companies are finding that even when messages are deleted, they can be recovered by experts and used by opposing attorneys in lawsuits. Although the files of most companies do not contain dangerous information, having to produce old records is laborious and expensive. Moreover, companies are learning that casual language can lead to misinterpretations. If casually worded and potentially damaging messages are retrieved for lawsuits, companies could suffer severe consequences.

4. **Discuss the ramifications of the following statement: *Once an e-mail, instant message, text, or any other document leaves your hands, you have essentially published it.* (Obj. 2)**

   As soon as a written document or digital file leaves your hands, it has actually been "published." Anyone may read it, copy it, and distribute it to others. Many business and other writers fail to consider what can happen to their written words. An e-mail intended for a colleague is seen by the boss, a text message gets sent to the wrong person, an IM log is shared with a competitor, a casual first draft of a performance evaluation circulates on the e-mail system. Sensitive messages that could cause trouble for you or your organization should probably not be put into print or entrusted to digital media. Every message should be written with the knowledge that it may travel much farther than originally intended. Nothing can expunge a poorly written e-mail or a text sent in anger.

5. **Ethical Issue: What Internet behavior could get employees fired? Do employees deserve broad Internet access on the job—if they are responsible? Should employers block access to Web sites? If so, what kind? (Objs. 2, 3, 4, and 5)**

   Employees can be fired for any Internet use prohibited by their employer. Companies can fire employees for viewing offensive content, sending inappropriate e-mail, or opening unsafe content. Students will quickly see that defining "responsibility" is the key issue in responding to the question of broad Internet access on the job. What is responsible behavior? Who defines it? One bad apple can ruin privileges for everyone else. Many companies do allow employees to send personal e-mail messages, and some even allow online shopping, if not done excessively. But students should know that more than three quarters of all companies are monitoring their employees' Internet activity, and two thirds use filtering software to block inappropriate Web sites [Dubie, D. (2007, May 7). Majority of tech execs watch employee Web use. Network World. Retrieved January 3, 2010, from http://www.networkworld.com/news/2007/050707-employee-web-use.html]. What kinds of Web sites may be blocked? Consider adult content, gambling, illegal activities, racism, abortion or antiabortion advocacy, and activist groups. What about cultural institutions (including galleries and museums), educational institutions, gay and lesbian issues, health information, hobbies, job search, news, personals, political groups, religion, restaurants, search engines, sex education, shopping, sports, and travel sites?

Activities

7.1 Document for Analysis: Jumbled E-Mail Message (Obj. 2)

Weaknesses:

- Uses a poor subject line that doesn't summarize the topic clearly.
- Fails to begin by telling the receiver exactly what is being requested.
- Masses all information into one bulky paragraph.
- Does not make it easy for reader to comprehend information quickly.
- Uses wordy expression (*due to the fact that*) and trite ending (*Don't hesitate to call* . . . .)
- Fails to include a deadline for returning the information.

To: Greta Targa <greta.targa@gamma.com>
From: Jim Morales <jim.morales@gamma.com>
Subject: Need You to Confirm the Gamma Fall Training Conference Speakers
Cc:
Bcc:

Please send e-mails to the following speakers to confirm their dates and topics for the Gamma Fall Training Conference in Miami:

Date	Speaker	Topic
Tuesday, November 12	Nicole Gold nicole.gold@etc.com	Using E-Mail and IM Effectively
Wednesday, November 13	Anthony Mills tony.mills@sunbelt.net	Leading Groups and Teams

Because we must print the program by September 1, please send me the confirmation information by August 15. Thanks for helping to make this one of the best training sessions ever.

Jim
[Include full contact information]

Note: Students may choose a different organization of speaker data such as the following:

Tuesday, November 12: Nicole Gold (nicole.gold@sunbelt.net) "Using E-Mail and IM Effectively"

Wednesday, November 13: Anthony Mills (tony.mills@sunbelt.net) "Leading Groups and Teams"

7.2 Document for Analysis: Poorly Organized E-Mail (Obj. 2)
Weaknesses:

- Fails to summarize message in a clear subject line.
- Does not immediately reveal the purpose of the message in the opening.
- Suffers from wordiness and stream-of-conscious expression.
- Shows no sign of thoughtful organization.
- Fails to use headings or listing techniques for three recommendations.
- Ends with cliché and confusion instead of clear statement regarding what is to be done.

Revision:

To: Mitchell Moraga <mitchell.moraga@media.com>
From: Eleanor Hutchinson <ehutchinson@media.com>
Subject: Suggestions for Preventing Workplace Violence
Cc:
Bcc:

Mitchell:

As you requested, I am submitting the following report with suggestions for preventing workplace violence in our organization. These ideas resulted from the November 3 Workplace Issues conference that I attended as our company representative. Kit Adkins, the presenter, provided many excellent ideas, which I will summarize in three categories.

- **Prescreen Applicants**. Wise companies, said Ms. Atkins, do not offer employment until a candidate's background has been checked. Just the mention of a check often makes a candidate with something to hide withdraw.

- **Recognize Red-Flag Behavior.** Companies should train managers to recognize signs of possible workplace violence. Some of these include a rise in petty arguments with coworkers; extreme changes in behavior, statements indicating depression over family or financial problems; bullying or harassing behavior; and bringing a firearm to work or exhibiting an extreme fascination with firearms.

- **Develop Reporting Procedures.** Companies should prepare a good employee handbook that outlines what employees should do when they suspect potential workplace violence. Include a system for anonymous notification.

The recommendation that I think is most feasible is prescreening of job candidates. Please let me know by November 15 whether you want me to do more research on prescreening techniques and present a full conference report at our December 3 management meeting.

Ellie

[include full contact information]

7.3 Document for Analysis: Instant Messaging at Local Auto Dealer (Obj. 3)

The flaws in this IM exchange are many. Just to name a few, Alex is unprofessional, too informal, folksy, and chatty. He does not show the customer respect and asks inappropriate questions or makes improper comments, for example, by inquiring about Mr. Rhee's name and country of origin or by making a contemptuous remark when the customer asks about fuel-efficiency. The rep's entries are full of typing mistakes and colloquialisms or slang. Unsuited as they are in any customer-service situation, they are particularly unlikely to be understood by a customer with limited English skills. The informality of the rep would probably annoy most customers inquiring about luxury cars by live chat. As a sales rep, Alex must tolerate the customers' quirks and mistakes, but he himself should represent his employer better by producing professional, courteous, friendly, and error-free replies. The revision could be done in class as a short exercise or sent by e-mail, as appropriate.

Revision:

Sales Rep: Hello, I'm Alex. Welcome to Harkin BMW of Glendora! How can I help you?

Customer: ??

Sales Rep: I am here to help you online. Do you have any specific questions?

Customer: I want buy car.

Sales Rep: May I have your name first?

Customer: Jin Bae Rhee

Sales Rep: What kind of a car would you like? New or pre-owned?

Customer: BMW. 2011 model. for family, for business.

Sales Rep: A new car, then. All right.

Customer: What car you have?

Sales Rep: We have some new models that may interest you. What did you have in mind?

Customer: I want green car, low mileage, less gasoline burn.

Sales Rep: You would like a fuel-efficient car, one that uses less gas than most vehicles, right? You are not asking about a green-colored car, correct?

Customer: ?

Service Rep: We offer a full lineup for you, the 3, 5, 6, or 7 series. Or are you interested in an X3 or X5? A Z4 convertible?

Customer: 760 sedan?

Service Rep: We may get those in again, but right now they are not in stock. We can offer you two 550i, one for $68,695 and one for $71,020.

Customer: European delivery?

Service Rep: If you are interested in European delivery, I will gladly refer you to our delivery specialist. In case we are disconnected, may I have your phone number and e-mail address?

Customer: i prefer not get a phone call yet... but 299-484-9807 is phone numer and jrhee@techtrade.com email

Service Rep: Thank you. We will call you back today or contact you by email. Is there anything else I can do for you?

7.4 Choosing a **Holiday Plan (Obj. 2)**

To: **All Employees**
From: **Student's name and e-mail address**
Subject: **Floating Holiday Options**
Cc:
Bcc:

Would you prefer (a) an individual floating holiday or (b) a companywide uniform floating holiday?

Because we're genuinely interested in developing a holiday plan that pleases as many people as possible, we'd like your response below.

In the past we've allowed 11 holidays plus one floating holiday, agreed on by companywide ballot. Now, though, we'd like to offer you the possibility of an individual floating holiday. You would be able to choose the date you wish to take, subject to staffing needs within your departments. If several requests are made for the same date, employment seniority would govern.

In your reply e-mail, please return only this part to me, and check the plan of your choice (use an X):

___ I prefer to retain the current policy of a uniform floating holiday.

___ I prefer an individual floating holiday, subject to the provisions described above.

To have your choice counted, return this form to Human Resources by January 25.
Student's name

Student's electronic signature and contact information

7.5 Reaching Consensus About Business Attire (Obj. 2)

To: Michael Harding <Michael.Harding@schilling-voigt.com>
From: Student's name and e-mail address
Subject: Your Request for Reaction to CEO's Inquiry Regarding Casual Dress
Cc: [Other team members' names and e-mail addresses]
Bcc:

At your direction, our team of interns consulted literature and discussed the casual-dress policy questions posed by CEO Laughton. Here are our reactions to the first five questions in his e-mail request.

ACCEPTABLE WEAR FOR WOMEN ON CASUAL-DRESS DAYS. After reading a number of articles and discussing the matter among ourselves, we concluded that acceptable wear for women included the following: slacks, skirts, and ankle-length pants along with coordinating blouses or wool or cotton sweaters and flat leather shoes. To be avoided are leggings, Spandex pants, casual and short shorts, ultra short skirts, camisoles, bared midriffs, halter tops, tank tops, sportswear tee-shirts, jeans, sweats, athletic shoes, and thong-like "flip-flop" sandals.

ACCEPTABLE WEAR FOR MEN ON CASUAL-DRESS DAYS. For men, business casual means khakis, chinos, or gabardine trousers and a collared shirt, either polo-style or button-down. Ties are optional, with wool or cotton sweaters, trousers, and loafers with dark, coordinated trouser socks. To be avoided are garish print sport shirts, sportswear tee-shirts, sport team jackets, jeans, sweats, athletic "tube" socks, hiking boots, athletic shoes, and sandals.

RESTRICTIONS ON BODY ART AND PIERCING. We believe that body art and piercing should not be visible. Tattoos covered by clothing are not a problem. In regard to body piercing, we believe that one set of traditional pierced earrings for women is appropriate. Eyebrow and other piercing to display jewelry of any sort are out of place in a conservative environment such as Schilling & Voigt.

SUPERVISORS REACTING TO INAPPROPRIATE CLOTHING. If someone comes to work in offensive, tasteless, revealing, or sloppy clothing, we think that a supervisor has the right to send the employee home to change. We would hope that the dress code is specific enough to prevent this occurrence.

DEFINITION OF CASUAL ATTIRE. Although it is difficult to define "casual attire," we think that a specific dress code spelling out what is acceptable and what is unacceptable should function as the definition that staff members at Vanderbeck & Associates understand and follow. It is critical that the dress code define specifics, as we did in our previous remarks.

ADVANTAGES AND DISADVANTAGES OF DRESS CODE. Proponents of casual dress say that it improves employee communication by removing symbols that dictate differences between people. Casual dress brings comfort, increased camaraderie, and improved productivity. Casual clothes cost less than more formal clothes and therefore represent a saving for employees. As a result, a casual dress policy is a cheap "perk" for companies to offer.

Critics say, however, that casual attire forces employees to have two wardrobes, creates confusion about what is appropriate to wear, contributes to sloppy work, and makes people feel uncomfortable or less presentable in professional situations. Casual dress also damages the image of professionals in the eyes of clients.

Please let us know if you need any more information about business attire.

Best regards,
Student's Name

Student's electronic signature including full contact information

7.6 Twitter: Learning to Write Superefficient Tweets (Objs. 1, 4, and 5)

Students may enjoy this activity because it invites their creativity in a familiar area. After the extremely brief music reviews, students can be asked to tweet about relevant business topics of the day. They could also tweet about unparalleled customer service they received or about a negative experience.

Examples:
AllComm's customer service is super responsive. They often don't know the answer, but hold times are short. Call center is based in the U.S. (140 characters with spaces)

I'm having Internet problems, and MineNet isn't picking up the phone. Customer service is awful. Anybody having issues with the Internet? (137 characters with spaces)

7.7 Instant Messaging: Practicing Your Professional IM Skills (Obj. 3)

This activity can also be accomplished with the help of Blackboard's chat function, but Yahoo, Skype and the other IM tools are often more versatile and sophisticated or have a more pleasant interface. It's important that all students download the same client because not all of the software is designed to work together. Yahoo and Windows Live Messenger are compatible, however. Once students install the software on their computers, distribute their tasks. Various options can be chosen. Two or three students could role play while the rest of the class is also logged in but only watching. The IM dialogue could be projected to a screen where available. Students in the class could take turns responding to hypothetical business situations.

Short instructor-generated guidelines could assign specific roles, say, playing a customer who has a question about a product. He or she will IM a customer service representative who will need to improvise, showing professional courtesy. Therefore, only minimal notes, scripts, or instructions should be provided.

A post-training question-and-answer session could serve as a group activity involving the whole class. The "training" could rely on the content of a chapter in this textbook or a business article that was assigned to the class. The leader—either the instructor or a student volunteer—fields questions from all logged-in participants. He or she has to maintain order and ensure turn-taking. The participants must wait their turn and ask professional, relevant questions. Other one-on-one or group scenarios are possible.

The log of the IM session can be saved and downloaded for subsequent analysis.

Examples:
Scenario 1: Potential customer (Student 1) accesses AB company's Web site looking for information about XYZ. Customer service representative (Student 2) is to greet the visitor, ask if he/she needs help, and offer information.
Scenario 2: Software user (Student 1) contacts CDE company for help with a particular feature of the program. Representative (Student 2) provides advice. The instructor should select a simple scenario such as, for instance, setting up and securing a router or asking questions about a computer game.

7.8 Podcast, Twitter, Texting: Analyzing a Podcast (Obj. 4)

E-mail responses to this assignment would enable students to respond to the assignment more fully and in greater detail. However, practicing professional texting or tweeting by making the messages very concise yet informative is also a valuable skill. Summarizing is often not the students' strong suit and this activity may provide playful practice.

If you are understandably reluctant to give away your cell phone number, consider asking the students to text to your e-mail address or to tweet to your Twitter account. Here are instructions on how to open a Twitter account: Go to **http://www.twitter.com**. You don't need to register to search for and view tweets in your Internet browser, but you should open a Twitter account to enjoy the full benefits of the free service. Also, students will need to be able to follow you and for that purpose they will need your Twitter user ID. Signing up is quick and intuitive. Execute the onscreen directions and watch the brief instructional video clip, if you like. You will be able to follow not only friends and family, but also news, business updates, film reviews, sports, or receive and share other up-to-the-minute messages.

Example of a tweet or brief text message:
(Excerpted from Grammar Girl, who is attempting a "quick-and-dirty" definition of the object of a sentence; see **http://grammar.quickanddirtytips.com/who-versus-whom.aspx**)

I love you. You are the object of my affection and my sentence. It's like a Valentine's Day card and grammar mnemonic all rolled into one. (138 characters with spaces)

7.9 Podcast: Turning Text to Video in a Jiffy (Obj. 4)

Although strictly speaking, students are not producing a podcast, Article Video Robot playfully introduces them to a machine-aided media tool. You could assign the type of writing students need to do, such as informational, persuasive, or instructive (e.g., how to create a podcast; how to demonstrate the safety of small cars; and how to search for a job). Note that beyond the trial version, the distribution of the content may require a fee or a subscription.

7.10 Blog: Analyzing Nuts About Southwest Blog (Obj. 4)

The tone of the guidelines is friendly, irreverent, and deliberately not worded like the typical "fine print." The language is conversational and the writers present themselves as rank-and-file crew members and other employees. The purpose of the blog is addressed in the excerpt cited in the activity: "We want to build a personal relationship between our Team and you," meaning the passenger. The blog is inviting discussion and participation. Southwest Airlines is known for its irreverence and jocular banter in the cabin and among the ground crew. The airline has a loyal following and boasts low employee turnover. In fact, a few years ago, the U.S. Marine Corps and Southwest teamed up to exchange training tips. The military was interested in adopting some of the successful strategies the airline had initiated.

7.11 Blog and Wiki: Reviewing Fortune 500 Business Blogging Wiki (Obj. 4)

This assignment allows for a variety of activities. Students could be asked to evaluate an unreviewed blog verbally or in writing. They could also analyze the blog review by an independent blogger either verbally or in writing—in memo form, by e-mail, or as a blog entry. Additionally, Blackboard, Facebook (see Activity 7.13), or another course management site could be used to post the student reviews for feedback and comment by the class.

7.12 Creating a Twitter Group (Obj. 4)

This Twitter assignment requires that students write ultrabrief tweets on a predetermined topic or communicate freely in 140 characters or fewer without abbreviations and grammatical errors on the Tweetworks Web site. In the absence of an Internet connection, this task can also be completed in MS Word, which has a character count function.

Students need individual Twitter accounts for this activity, and you should create a Tweetworks group for the class to monitor activities effectively. The group would then function much like a bulletin board, only with a strict limit of 140 characters. Students practice writing professional, well-considered tweets on a topic of your choice or freewrite within the confines of the character restriction.

7.13 Social Networking: Building an Online Community on Facebook (Obj. 5)

A business communication Facebook site could be a useful tool to teach students the responsible use of social networking. The public setting of the site would demand that they behave like the future business professionals they aspire to be. You have control over which features to allow, such as photo or video sharing. The wall feature lends itself to being used as a bulletin board for the sharing of unusual and stimulating business-related news items. Because students are used to social networking and could easily link to the class site from their personal Facebook pages, they may be more inclined to contribute to the virtual class than they do in face-to-face sessions. The chat function in Facebook that enables logged-on participants to communicate could serve as a discussion board in real time and give you a chance to offer virtual office hours or answer assignment-related questions.

7.14 Social Networking: Preparing a Professional LinkedIn Profile (Obj. 5)

The LinkedIn activity allows students truly to grasp the distinction between their personal social networking pursuits and this career and recruiting site. Creating a profile is quick and easy. You do not need to completely fill in your profile to view students' pages. Reviewing even a large number of profiles should not consume much time. Revisions and critiques could be assigned to small student groups or pairs of students to save time.

7.15 E-Mail Simulation: Writeaway Hotels (Obj. 2)

The Writeaway Simulation encourages students to practice managing and writing e-mail messages. Designed as an in-class activity, the simulation works best for 12 to 25 students, each playing a role within the fictitious company, Writeaway Hotels. Within 30 minutes in a computer lab or classroom, students read, write, and respond to messages to each other. During a debrief discussion, students evaluate messages sent during the simulation. A complete instructor's guide for this simulation activity can be found at **www.meguffey.com**.

ZOOMING IN Part 1: Twitter: From Obscure Tech Fad to Internet Sensation

- **In what ways have social media and "real-time Web" changed how Internet users communicate? Have services like Twitter improved the way we exchange information?**

  Social media and "real-time Web" are about immediacy in an always-on, fast, and simple manner if not strictly in real time. Twitter and related services have drawn lots of "eyeballs" to their sites and that in itself represents a value to investors and businesses. How exactly the social media will shape our communication remains to be seen. Nevertheless, it's already evident that Twitter has evolved from mundane updates about what users had for lunch to a much more sophisticated tool. Communicating in 140 characters or less does not allow for much nuance, but it's invaluable as a lightning-fast distribution channel of news and status updates. Part three of Zooming In focuses on which businesses are using Twitter and how they do so. Whether Twitter will prove useful to a larger number of mainstream adopters remains to be seen. Many users and businesses in particular are watching from the sidelines to see whether some value to their bottom line will emerge from the new media.

- **What trends have facilitated the emergence of social media, specifically Twitter?**

  Increasingly ubiquitous Wi-Fi networks, smartphones, and other hardware along with online software applications have enabled the explosive growth of social media including Twitter. Perhaps Twitter is an expression of our ever-faster culture by allowing users instantly to share information online with family, friends, and even strangers because it's increasingly more difficult to find the time to connect face to face.

- **What could be advantages and drawbacks of using Twitter for business?**

  Some of the advantages are low cost; ease of monitoring the image of one's company; potentially broad reach of company information; flexibility as well as speed of response to customers; and a sense of immediacy and connectedness.

  The following may be some of the disadvantages: The 140-character limit does not allow for clarification, nuance, or detail. The new medium is still untried and may not work for certain industries as well as it does for others. You may want to ask students how communicating virtually compares to face-to-face interaction, whether they believe that anything is gained or lost in electronically mediated communication, or what percentage of their interaction with friends and family is virtual.

ZOOMING IN Part 2: Got Something to Tweet About at Work? Think Again

- **How do you explain the amazing lapses of judgment apparent in the tweets included in Zooming In, Part 2, on p. 200?**

  As is the case with e-mail and other digital media, Twitter users are lured into a false sense of privacy online. Some bloggers disregard the fact that they aren't just journaling for themselves and a few close friends. Twitterers and members of social networking sites may forget that not only their friends and followers are privy to their exploits. When Cardinal Roger Mahoney's e-mail account was hacked and messages leaked a few years ago, the clergyman was outraged at the breach and asserted the belief that his e-mail was "private." Unfortunately, at work when we use our employer's hardware and software and are on the clock, we have no reasonable expectation of privacy. The courts have consistently sided with employers, except in a few recent cases involving companies lacking clear disclosure of employee monitoring.

- **How widespread is the use of Twitter among your friends, and how do they benefit from the service?**

  Answers will vary, but students may cite as benefits being in touch in real time and communicating instantaneously from anywhere. A Pew Internet survey concludes that "Twitter users engage with news and own technology at the same rates as other Internet users, but the ways in which they use the technology—to communicate, gather and share information—reveals their affinity for mobile, untethered and social opportunities for interaction."[ii] The benefit of Twitter is that it enhances the opportunities for the kind of interaction that this group prefers. As the Pew Internet survey further reports, young people like to vent their complaints about companies, forward interesting tidbits, share ideas, document events, chat, and flirt. Some of these activities can potentially cause problems, of course.

- **What are the most effective ways to warn young people about the dangers to their careers that lurk online?**

  This is a difficult question but because young people are often not open to admonishments from their elders, they may be more willing to listen to appeals from peers. Despite tech savvy, many young people do not know or choose to ignore potential repercussions of their online conduct. Risking one's career may be a strong enough incentive to exercise caution. This consequence is so severe that it may have a deterrent effect. Popular culture will catch up as stories about dismissed twitterers and unlucky job losses will make the rounds. Parents and educators should also discuss the hazards of reckless online behavior.

ZOOMING IN, Your Turn: Twitter

Results will vary. Students will visit **http://twitter.com** and key the search term **Coca-Cola** in the search box. It is advantageous to preface the search term by the so-called **hashtag** represented by a pound sign to identify **#Coca-Cola** as a tweet topic. Searches including hashtags are likely to be more productive and targeted than those without. The search function can be enhanced by selecting **advanced search** and choosing appropriate key terms or excluding irrelevant ones. The search parameters also allow the user to indicate the "attitude" of the tweet as positive or negative, if known or identifiable.

In a randomly conducted search, for example, one result may turn up a twitterer linking his or her message to a 1985 commercial featuring Bill Cosby as he introduces Coke Classic. Another result may alert others to Coke's recent PR blunder in the UK, when students and parents were stunned by racy pop-ups in a Facebook app advertising Dr. Pepper. Another tweet may advertise "51 uses for Coca-Cola" around the house--removing stains and loosening rusty screws are just two examples. Scanning the many long lists of Coca-Cola-themed tweets, the students will easily gain an understanding of where the short announcements are trending.

Discussion Material for PLUGGED IN: Cloud Computing

Chances are that students are using Google Docs, Yahoo, or Gmail. They may be familiar with Picasa, Flickr, and other photo-sharing applications on the Web. If students bring up file-sharing networks, they should be warned that file sharing is taboo in the workplace and could lead to prosecution.

When compiling a list of disadvantages, students may identify the potential dependency on providers and their pricing as well as technical glitches. Easy access and convenience may be perceived as advantages. Users don't need to carry pictures or store them on a computer; rather, they can show them on their portable devices. They can immediately share their photos and other information with their friends and family, even from afar.

Security breaches are likely, despite encryption software and best efforts of the hosting companies. Ironically, if encryption is employed so that only the owner can decrypt the information, the data can be lost irretrievably if the user loses the password. The greater the convenience, the greater is also the risk. Allowing Web access from any computer and sharing with a group of users pose the most significant risk. Information can always be disclosed to third parties or determined hackers.

Clearly, not all information is created equal. Family photographs "leaked" on the Internet are not as significant a breach as confidential company data. Embarrassment and worse could result from unwanted exposure of sensitive earnings or merger information to prying eyes.

Experts say that convenience and productivity will always win over security risk. Outages and potential security threats may be the price we will have to pay for staying connected anytime and anywhere.

Ethics Check Solutions

Ethics Check, Page 193
Hiding Blind Copies
Some workers use *Bcc* (*blind carbon copy*) to copy their friends and colleagues on e-mail when they do not want the recipient to know that a third party will also read the message. Based on the "netiquette" discussed in this chapter, do you believe that hiding copies from the recipient is harmless and acceptable?

Today's writers should use *Cc* to reveal openly all recipients of a message. Violating this practice can become quite risky in the workplace if, for example, one of the hidden recipients accidentally shows knowledge of the content transmitted in the e-mail. Such lapses could lead to embarrassment and worse.

Ethics Check, Page 204
Fired for Blogging
Former flight attendant Ellen Simonetti was fired by Delta Air Lines for posting on her blog "Queen of Sky" photos showing her in uniform. Simonetti claims that her dismissal violated her free-speech rights and was an act of sexual discrimination. She has been fighting her firing since 2004, parlaying her fame into a book and even a few talk show appearances. Whose rights take precedence, the employee's or the employer's?

In 2003 Simonetti began to document her life and work experiences in her blog without mentioning her airline by name. Her case was widely publicized as a now-classic example of employee rights to express their views about their work experience and their employers' rights to limit them. In a 2008 article in *Mental Floss* magazine [Palan, E. (2008, May 29). Seven people fired for blogging. *Mental Floss.* Retrieved October 31, 2009, from http://www.mentalfloss.com/blogs/archives/15329], Erica Palan writes about Simonetti and six other bloggers who were fired by their employers for material deemed inappropriate, even though the content was created on the bloggers' own time and coworkers or the employers were not mentioned explicitly by name. Similarly, Virgin Atlantic fired a cabin crew that was joking about faulty jet engines and maligning passengers on the Internet. Encourage students to consider how and why workers' rights to free expression may be curtailed in the workplace.

From the employers' point of view blogs and social networking sites can turn into a nightmare. Companies typically discipline and fire workers for online indiscretions, but as happened in the Simonetti case, the dismissed workers can turn around and sue or, worse yet, turn their cause into a career.

Ethics Check, Page 208
Social Media Help Spread Errors Like Wildfire
Electronics retailer Best Buy recently offered a 52-inch flat-screen TV worth $1,799.99 for $9.99 on its Web site. Within hours bloggers and Twitter users posted jokes about this "steal," and some insisted that Best Buy honor the advertised price. The company quickly corrected the online pricing error and would not accept orders at the incorrect price. Was Best Buy obligated to honor the offer?

A company does not have to honor an innocent mistake, such as an obvious typo or misprint resulting in a glaring error in pricing, for example. Businesses make mistakes and they generally shouldn't have to bankrupt themselves to take responsibility for posted errors. Legally, advertisements and other promotional materials are generally considered invitations to bargain, and are not contracts. A few consumers take advantage of costly mistakes and hope to extract some advantage from them. However, using strikingly low prices and declaring them erroneous to generate publicity and viral buzz are deceptive practices. Internet posts suggest consensus that repeated incidents represent deceptive intent whereas an occasional error is most likely innocent. Companies react in different ways to potentially expensive blunders. The immediacy and speed of today's media heighten the problem of erroneous advertising. Someone is going to see the mistake and can potentially broadcast it within seconds to thousands, even millions, of people.

Photo Essay Solutions

Photo Essay, Page 191
Schultz's short statement in his closing paragraph is effective because it concisely summarizes the entire message. Appropriate closings to memos typically include a summary of the message; action information, dates, or deadlines; or a closing thought.

Video Resources

Instructors may show the *Technology in the Workplace*, Video Library 1, for a humorous look at the appropriate and inappropriate uses of workplace technology. Instructors may also show *Smart E-Mail Messages and Memos Advance Your Career* from Video Library 1, *Building Workplace Skills*. This video presents a demonstration of how to use e-mail skillfully and safely. After viewing the video, students should be prepared to discuss critical-thinking questions.

---

[i] Garvey, M. (2009, October 31). Fifth years of simplicity as style. *The Wall Street Journal*, p. A19.

[ii] Lenhart, A., & Fox, S. (2009, February 12). Twitter and status updating. *Pew Internet & American Life Project*, p. 5. Retrieved February 15, 2010, from http://www.pewinternet.org

Chapter 8 LECTURE NOTES AND TEACHING SUGGESTIONS

Positive Messages

CHAPTER SYNOPSIS

Positive messages—whether e-mails, interoffice memos, or business letters—carry important, but usually routine information. In this chapter you will learn to apply the 3-x-3 writing process to positive messages that are intended for both internal and external audiences.

E-mail is appropriate for short, informal messages for both internal and external audiences. Interoffice memos are appropriate for internal messages that are important, lengthy, or formal. Business letters are appropriate for external messages that you will send to customers, vendors, government officials, and others. Letters are important when you must make a permanent record is required, when confidentiality is critical, when formality or sensitivity are essential, and when a persuasive presentation is important.

As a business or professional person, you will be delivering many routine messages both orally and in writing. Although many principles taught in this chapter apply to both oral and written communication, the main focus will be on positive written messages. You will learn more about oral presentations in Chapter 14.

Positive messages are those that follow the direct strategy because you expect the response to be receptive or neutral. Therefore, most positive messages begin with the good news or neutral news immediately. In this chapter you will learn to write direct messages that request action or information, and you will learn to respond to requests. One of the most important parts of the chapter includes how to write clear step-by-step instructions. You will also learn how to make claims and how to write adjustment messages. In addition, you will study how to write goodwill messages that convey kindness, thanks, and sympathy. If you are like most people, you hate to write thank-you notes or sympathy messages. But this chapter teaches you how to do it and provides excellent models. Finally, this chapter closes with suggestions for modifying international messages to accommodate readers from other cultures.

As you are writing, remember this sage advice: "One universal constant about business writing in this era of electronic marvels: Your reader doesn't have enough time to do everything he or she needs to do. When you write a document to busy readers, you are in effect asking them to donate to you a portion of their time. They know they will have to make up that time later on. That's why they will not permit you and me to waste it." (Chambers, D. *The Agile Manager's Guide to Writing to Get Action*. Bristol, Vermont: Velocity Business Publishing, p. 11.)

LEARNING OBJECTIVES

1. Apply the 3-x-3 writing process to creating successful positive messages, including e-mails, interoffice memos, and business letters.
2. Understand the appropriate use of e-mails, interoffice memos, and business letters.
3. Compose direct messages that make requests and respond to inquiries.
4. Write messages that clearly explain step-by-step instructions.
5. Prepare messages that make direct claims.
6. Create adjustment messages that regain the confidence of customers and promote further business.
7. Write special messages that convey kindness and goodwill.
8. Modify international messages to accommodate readers from other cultures.

WHAT'S NEW IN THIS CHAPTER

- Reorganized chapter to combine positive e-mails, interoffice memorandums, and business letters in one place so that students can recognize similarities in content and strategies regardless of channel choice.
- Explained the primary uses of interoffice memos and how they differ from e-mail messages so that students can make appropriate choices in selecting channels for these important workplace messages.
- Discussed the significance, primary functions, and value of business letters, regardless of the popularity of e-mail.
- Added discussion of how to write messages that describe instructions, a common workplace task.
- Illustrated the difference between indicative verbs and imperative (command) verbs to help readers prepare instructions.
- Prepared new case studies and exercises for two thirds of the end-of-chapter activities, thus providing fresh opportunities for students to apply their skills.

LECTURE OUTLINE

I. Successful Positive Messages Start with the Writing Process (p. 220)

PowerPoint slides 1-3

- **Phase 1: Analysis, Anticipation, and Adaptation.** Determine your purpose, visualize your audience, and anticipate the reaction to your message.

- **Phase 2: Research, Organization, and Composition.** Collect information and make a list of the points you wish to cover.
- **Phase 3: Revision, Proofreading, and Evaluation.** Revise for clarity and proofread for correctness.

Figure 8.1 Analyzing Ben & Jerry's Customer Response
Figure 8.2 Applying the Writing Process to an E-Mail
PowerPoint slides 4-6

II. Positive Messages: E-Mails, Memos, and Letters (p. 223)

A. Comparing E-Mails and Memos

E-Mails

- Appropriate for short messages (setting appointments, giving updates, requesting information, etc.)

Hard-Copy Memos

- Offer a permanent record or formality
- Provide quick recognition of sender and receiver

B. Preparing Interoffice Memos

- Begin with guide words (*Date, To, From, and Subject*)
- 1-inch top and bottom margins
- 1.25-inch left and right margins
- Single-space the message; double-space between paragraphs

Figure 8.3 Interoffice memo that Responds to a Request
PowerPoint slides 7, 8

C. Understanding Business Letters

- Offer a permanent record
- Are confidential
- Carry a sense of formality and importance
- Deliver persuasive, well-considered messages

Figure 8.4 Formatting Direct Request Business Letter in Block Style
PowerPoint slides 9, 10

III. Routine Request and Response Messages (p. 227)

A. Creating Request Messages

- Start with the main idea first.
- Start with a question or a polite command.

- Provide details of the request in the body of the message.
- Close with appreciation and an action request.

PowerPoint slides 11-24

B. Responding to Requests

- In the first sentence of a direct response letter, deliver the information the reader wants.
- In the body of the response, supply explanations and additional information.
- Try to promote the organization and products.
- In concluding a response message, refer to the information or to its use.

Figure 8.5 Customer Response Letter
PowerPoint slides 25-28

IV. Checklist: Writing Direct Requests and Responses (p. 231)

Requesting Information or Action
- Open by stating the main idea.
- Explain and justify the request.
- Request action in the closing.

Responding to Requests
- Open directly.
- Supply additional information.
- Conclude with a cordial statement.

V. Instruction Messages (p. 231)

- Divide the instructions into steps.
- List the steps in the order in which they are to be carried out.
- Arrange the items vertically with bullets or numbers.
- Begin each step with an action verb using the imperative (command) mood rather than the indicative mood.

Figure 8.6 Interoffice Memo Delivering Instructions
PowerPoint slides 29-32

VI. Direct Claims (p. 233)

Definition: A *claim* is a letter your write as a customer to identify or correct a wrong.

- Written claims are taken more seriously and establish a record of what happened.
- Straightforward claims use a direct approach.

A. Opening With a Clear Statement

- Open the letter with a clear statement of the problem or with the action you want the receiver to take.

B. Explaining and Justifying a Claim

- State the facts logically, objectively, and unemotionally.
- When service is involved, state the names of individuals spoken to and dates of calls.

C. Concluding a Claim With an Action Request

- Close with a summary of the action requested and a courteous goodwill statement.
- Submit written claims promptly.

Figure 8.7 Direct Claim Letter
PowerPoint slides 33-36

VII. Adjustments (p. 236)

Definition: An *adjustment* is a written message that favorably responds to a customer's claim.

- The three goals of the adjustment include (a) rectifying the wrong, if one exists; (b) regaining the confidence of the customer; and (c) promoting further business.

A. Revealing Good News in the Opening

- Reveal the good news immediately.
- Don't start your letter with a negative statement.
- Announce the good news enthusiastically, without a grudging tone.

B. Explaining Compliance in the Body of an Adjustment Letter

- Seek to rebuild faith in your company by complying with the request.
- Avoid negative words and keep your message positive.

C. Deciding Whether to Apologize

- The majority of adjustment letters contain an apology.
- Apologize if it seems natural.

PowerPoint slides 37-42

Lecture Tidbit

Apologies can diffuse an emotional situation. Akio Toyoda, the grandson of the world's largest automaker Toyota, apologized profusely for the defects in some Toyota vehicles that caused some automobiles to accelerate out of control. "I am deeply sorry for any accidents Toyota drivers may have experienced. Again, I sincerely regret accidents," Toyoda said when appearing before the House oversight committee. [Ahrens, F. (2010, February 25). Toyota president apologizes under fire from U.S. officials. The *Washington Post*. Retrieved July 23, 2010, from http://www.washingtonpost.com/wp-dyn/content/article/2010/02/24/AR2010022404915_2.html?sid=ST2010022304826.

Why do apologies like this one build customer goodwill?

D. Using Sensitive Language

- Retain customer goodwill by avoiding negative language.
- Do not use negative words, blame customers or your colleagues, or make unrealistic promises.
- Rebuild customer confidence by including resale information.

E. Showing Confidence in the Closing

- Close the letter positively and confidently.
- In the closing, show appreciation, a desire to be of future service, or promote a new product.

Figure 8.8 Customer Adjustment Letter

IIX. Checklist: Direct Claim and Adjustment Messages

Messages That Make Claims

- Begin directly with the purpose.
- Explain objectively.
- Conclude by requesting action.

Messages That Make Adjustments

- Open with approval.
- In the body win back the customer's confidence.
- Close positively.

IX. Goodwill Messages (p. 241)

- Send goodwill messages promptly.
- General guidelines:
  1. Selfless
  2. Specific
  3. Sincere
  4. Spontaneous
  5. Short

PowerPoint slides 43-48

A. Expressing Thanks

- Send a thank-you letter to extend thanks or show appreciation to the following:
  1. Customers for their orders
  2. Hosts and hostesses for their hospitality
  3. Individuals for kind gestures
  4. Customers who complain

- Open directly with the purpose of your message.

Figure 8.8 Thank-You Letter for a Favor

B. Responding to Goodwill Messages

- Always respond to notes of congratulations or other goodwill messages.

PowerPoint slide 49

C. Conveying Sympathy

- Refer to the death or misfortune sensitively.
- Praise the deceased in a personal way.
- Offer assistance.
- End on a reassuring note.

X. Checklist for Goodwill Messages

A. General Guidelines: The Five Ss

- Be selfless.
- Be specific.
- Be sincere.
- Be spontaneous.
- Keep the message short.

B. Giving Thanks

- Cover three points in gift thank-yous.
- Be sincere in sending thanks for a favor.
- Offer praise in expressing thanks for hospitality.

C. Responding to Goodwill Messages

- Respond to congratulations.
- Accept praise gracefully.

D. Extending Sympathy

- Refer to the loss or tragedy directly but sensitively.
- For deaths, praise the deceased.
- Offer assistance.
- End on a reassuring, positive note.

XI. International Messages (p. 243)

- The organization, format, and tone of letters to foreign correspondents should be adapted to meet the cultural requirements of the reader.

Lecture Transparencies
(available in a separate packet and at http://www.meguffey.com)

Positive Letters and Messages Acetates	Transparency Number
Successful, Positive Messages Start With the Writing Process	73
Comparing Typical Positive Messages	74
Formatting Hard Copy Memos	75
"Before"—Ineffective Routine Request	76
Critical Thinking Questions	77
"After"—Improved Request	78
Formatting Business Letters	79-80
Routine Requests for Information or Action	81
"Before" – Ineffective Routine Request	82
Critical Thinking Questions	83
"After" – Improved Request	84
Direct Response Messages	85
Instruction Messages	86
Direct Claims and Complaints	87
Adjustment Messages	88
The Five Ss of Goodwill Messages	89

Solution Masters

	Page Number in This Book
Applying Your Skills at Ben & Jerry's	526
8.1 Direct Openings	527
8.2 Writing Instructions	527
8.3 Document for Analysis—Revision	529
8.4 Document for Analysis—Revision	530
8.5 Document for Analysis—Revision	531
8.6 Document for Analysis—Revision	532
8.7 Seeking a New Look for the Company Web Site	533
8.8 Heading to Las Vegas	534
8.9 Restaurants Join Obesity Fight	536
8.10 Response: Luxury Hotels Embrace Signature Scents	538
8.11 Arranging Interviews for Environmental Architect/Designer	540
8.12 New Process for Purchase Requests	541
8.13 Cell Phone Use and Texting While Driving	542
8.14 Describing a Workplace Procedure	544
8.15 How to Be Safe at Work	544

8.16 Writing Clear Instructions 546
8.17 Protesting Unexpected Charges 548
8.18 Short Door for Tall Player 549
8.19 The Real Thing 550
8.20 Barking Mad With Happypets.com 551
8.21 But It Doesn't Work! 552
8.22 Responding to Short Doors for Tall Player 553
8.23 We Can Restretch But Not Replace 555
8.24 Pigeon Problems 556
8.25 Backing Up "No Surprise" Offer 557
8.26 Thanks for a Favor: Got the Job! 558
8.27 Thanks for the Hospitality: Holiday Entertaining 559
8.28 Personalizing Group Greeting Cards 560
8.29 Responding to Good Wishes: Saying Thank You 561
8.30 Extending Sympathy: To a Spouse 561
8.31 Negotiating a Cool Deal With a Chinese Supplier 562

Answers to Chapter Review Questions

1. **Into what three content categories can most business messages be organized? What group will make up the bulk of your messages? (Obj. 1)**

   Business messages may be organized into three categories: (a) positive messages communicating straightforward requests, replies, and goodwill; (b) negative messages delivering refusals and bad news; and (c) persuasive messages including sales pitches. Positive messages make up the bulk of a business communicator's messages.

2. **How can you save the reader's time and make your business message easy to comprehend at a glance? (Obj. 1)**

   Use bullets, asterisks, lists, headings, and white space to improve comprehension and readability.

3. **What kinds of messages are sent as are interoffice memos? (Obj. 2)**

   Interoffice memos are useful for important internal messages that require a permanent record or formality. They are useful to deliver procedures, official policies, reports, and long internal documents.

4. **When is it important to send a business letter rather than an e-mail? (Obj. 2)**

   Business letters are important when a permanent record is required; when confidentiality is critical; when formality and sensitivity are necessary; and when a persuasive, well-considered presentation is essential.

5. **What are the most emphatic positions in a message, and what goes there? (Obj. 3)**

The most emphatic positions in a message are the opening and closing. Writers should put their most significant statements in those positions.

6. **What should you include in the closing of a request message? (Obj. 3)**

The closing of a request should tell courteously what is to be done and include an end date (with an explanation) if the date is important. Appreciation should also be expressed.

7. **How should instructions be written? Give a brief original example. (Obj. 4)**

Instructions should be divided into bulleted or numbered steps listed vertically in the order in which they are to be carried out. Each step should begin with an action verb in the imperative (command) mood. Example: 1. Read the book. 2. Study the chapter. 3. Take the test.

8. **What is the imperative mood, and why is it important to use it in writing instructions? (Obj. 4)**

The imperative mood involves action verbs that give commands. In preparing instructions, writers use the imperative mood for clarity and conciseness. When all steps in a procedure begin with an action verb, readers comprehend more quickly.

9. **What is a claim? When should it be straightforward? (Obj. 5)**

A claim is a request by a customer to correct a problem. The customer may request a replacement, refund, new product, credit to his or her account, correction of an error, free repairs, free inspection, or cancellation of an order. A straightforward claim is one to which you expect the receiver to readily agree.

10. **Why should a direct claim be made by letter rather than by e-mail or a telephone call? (Obj. 5)**

Most organizations take a claim letter more seriously than an e-mail or a telephone call. In addition, letters establish a record of what happened and the claim.

11. **What is an adjustment message? (Obj. 6)**

An adjustment message is a company's favorable response to a customer's claim.

12. **What are a writer's three goals in composing adjustment messages? (Obj. 6)**

In an adjustment letter, the writer tries to (a) rectify the wrong, if one exists; (b) regain the confidence of the customer; and (c) promote further business.

13. **What are five characteristics of goodwill messages? (Obj. 7)**

Goodwill messages are selfless, specific, sincere, spontaneous, and short.

14. **What are four groups of people to whom business communicators might write letters of appreciation? (Obj. 7)**

Business communicators might write letters of appreciation to (a) customers for their orders, (b) hosts and hostesses for hospitality, (c) individuals for kindnesses performed, and (d) customers who complain.

15. **What are three elements of business letters going abroad that might be modified to accommodate readers from other cultures? (Obj. 8)**

Writers may wish to modify the organization, format, and tone of letters going abroad. Foreign correspondents may be offended by the directness and conversational tone of typical American writing. Following the format style of the receiver's country is wise.

Answers to Critical Thinking Questions

1. **Are the writing skills that are required for sending business e-mails and text messages different from those required for writing interoffice memos and business letters? Explain. (Objs. 1, 2)**

Any message sent in business should be clear, correct, and concise. The same skills are required to write clear e-mails, text messages, memos, and business letters. Regardless of the delivery channel, business messages should not contain misspellings, incomplete sentences, grammatical errors, confusing abbreviations, all caps, or all lowercase letters. Although the same good writing skills are required for all business messages, it may be challenging for some writers to transition from social e-mail habits to business e-mail etiquette and business-letter writing formats.

2. **In promoting the value of letter-writing, a well-known columnist recently wrote, "To trust confidential information to e-mail is to be a rube." What did he mean? Do you agree? (Obj. 1)**

A rube is an unsophisticated person. The columnist meant that educated, knowledgeable people today know that e-mail is notoriously unsafe for confidential information. Nearly everyone agrees that e-mail is unsafe for confidential information, yet it is so convenient that people go on sending messages that can be embarrassing and dangerous if and when revealed.

3. **Why is it important to regain the confidence of a customer in an adjustment letter? How can it be done? (Obj. 6)**

   Unhappy customers have, naturally, lost some degree of confidence in the company and its products or services. Regaining that confidence and reestablishing good feelings is crucial for future business. Regaining confidence requires more than a general form-letter statement, such as "We apologize for any inconvenience this has caused." When possible, companies should provide specific explanations of what is being done to rectify the conditions leading to the product failure or dissatisfaction. Warm, simple, and sincere language helps, too. Many companies extend coupons for free products or services so that customers will give the company a second chance.

4. **How are American business letters different from those written in other countries? Why do you suppose this is so? (Obj. 8)**

   American business writers appreciate efficiency and directness. American letters tend to be rather informal, compared with those in many foreign countries. All of these elements reflect the culture and values of North Americans. North Americans generally are straightforward and hate to waste time. They get right to the point and consider ritual and formality to be senseless and unnecessary. Naturally, cultures that put more value on ceremony, courtesy, decorum, patience, and relationships have different expectations about how letters should be developed. Moreover, letters are formatted differently in other countries. Before sending any letter abroad, it's wise to learn local preferences.

5. **Ethical Issue: Assume that you have drafted a letter to a customer in which you apologize for the way the customer's account was fouled up by the Accounting Department. You show the letter to your boss, and she instructs you to remove the apology. It admits responsibility, she says, and the company cannot allow itself to be held liable. You are not an attorney, but you can't see the harm in a simple apology. What should you do? Refer to the section "Tools for Doing the Right Thing" in Chapter 1 to review the five questions you might ask yourself in trying to do the right thing.**

   In this instance it's probably better to follow the instructions of your superior. Ethically, you are not obligated to apologize. The letter may have sounded warmer with a sincere apology, but it can still be worded so that it retains goodwill. If you apply the "Tools for Doing the Right Thing" (from Chapter 1), you would respond to these questions. (1) Is the action legal? Yes, of course it is legal to write a letter that does not include an apology. (2) How would you see the problem if you were on the opposite side? From a management position, you can understand that an apology might suggest a responsibility for the incident and might conceivably be dangerous in establishing liability. (3) What are alternate solutions? One alternative is to omit the apology but word it so that the letter is warm and sincere. (4) Can you discuss the problem with someone whose advice you trust? You might wish to do this, but in this instance it might seem more like complaining rather than seeking a workable solution. (5) How would you feel if your family, friends, employer, or coworkers learned of your action? Most would probably not support your view (that an apology is necessary). In this instance, it would appear best to do as the supervisor directs.

Writing Improvement Exercises

8.1 Direct Openings (Objs. 1–7)

a. Liberty Bank would deeply appreciate your answers to a few questions to help us learn about developing an internship program.
b. Please answer the following questions about your voice recognition software program.
c. Yes, we do offer our European-style patio umbrella in colors: cream and forest green.
d. Yes, I would be happy to talk about online résumés at your business management club May 2.

8.2 Writing Instructions (Obj. 4)

a. To order from our Web site, follow these steps:

1. Find the items you want in the catalog.
2. Add the items to your shopping cart.
3. Proceed to checkout.
4. Create a new account.
5. Enter a shipping address and shipping method.
6. Provide payment information.
7. Review and submit your order.

b. To make a YouTube video, you should do the following:

1. Obtain a video recording device such as a cell phone, webcam, or camcorder.
2. Decide whether you want to make a video blog, comedy skit, how-to video, or travel video.
3. Keep the video to 10 minutes or less for traditional YouTube membership accounts.
4. Record in the daytime for good light quality.

c. To make double-sided copies, do the following:

1. Place Side 1 of the original facedown on the document glass.
2. Close the document cover.
3. Select the required quantity.
4. Press Start.
5. Remove Original 1, and insert Original 2 facedown on the document glass.
6. Close the document cover.
7. Remove the copy of Original 1 from the output tray and insert it facedown in the paper bypass tray.

Activities

8.3 Document for Analysis: Direct Request (Obj. 3)

Weaknesses

1. Begins with a wordy, indirect opening.
2. Positions the action request and deadline in the first paragraph instead of at the end of the message where readers expect to find such information.
3. Uses a long lead-in (I am writing this note to ask for your help); buried nouns (had the expectation instead of expected and make a reduction instead of reduce); wordy expression (each and every day); and other wordiness.
4. Organizes message poorly and rambles instead of writing concisely.
5. Uses excessive superlatives (extremely, actually, exceedingly).
6. Fails to list questions in concise, clear, and parallel form.
7. Does not conclude with an end date, reason, or expression of appreciation.

Revision

To: Amsoft Manager List
From: Stella Soto <stella.soto@amsoft.com>
Subject: Answering Questions to Address E-Mail Problem
Cc:
Bcc:

Managers,

Please help us address the problem of excessive e-mail by answering the questions below. Your ideas will assist us develop a plan that should benefit your staff, yourself, and our organization.

Everyone expected e-mail to be a huge productivity tool. However, its excessive use cuts into work time. One study found that the average office worker spends two hours a day on e-mail. In our organization we may be spending even more than this. It's difficult to get any work done because of countless e-mails every day. Your responses to the following questions will help us focus on the problem.

1. About how many e-mail messages do you receive and answer personally each day?
2. About how many hours are your staff members spending on e-mail each day?
3. How could we reduce the volume of e-mail within our own organization?
4. Do you think that e-mail is being used excessively by our employees?
5. What do you think of a weekly e-mail-free day, such as Friday?

I look forward to your advice in controlling e-mail and improving productivity. Your written responses to these questions by May 5 will help me prepare for our supervisory committee meeting May 10, when we will discuss this problem. Many thanks!

Stella Soto
Vice President, Operations

8.4 Document for Analysis: Direct Response

Weaknesses

1. Fails to provide a meaningful subject line.
2. Does not begin with a statement explaining why he is writing.
3. Presents disorganized information in dense paragraphs.
4. Makes no effort to list important items to improve readability.
5. Fails to use parallel language.
6. Does not end with an action request. What does he want the receiver to do? By when?

Revision

MEMORANDUM

Date: March 4, 2010

To: Trevor Kurtz, CEO

From: Emily Lopez-Rush

Subject: Report on Instant Messaging Symposium

Because many of our employees are using instant messaging, you asked me to attend the March 2 Instant Messaging Symposium sponsored by Pixel Link. It was a most informative meeting, and I learned some information that should help us decide how to handle instant messaging in our organization.

The symposium leader, Jason Howard, discussed the benefits, risks, providers, and costs involved in using instant messaging in the workplace. Let me summarize his major points:

- Instant messaging is here to stay. Over 80 million workers now use the technology and the number is increasing steadily.
- Its primary advantages are speed, documentation, and cost savings.
- Its principal disadvantages are spam, security, control, and possible loss of productivity.
- The major consumer IM providers are AOL Messenger, MSN Messenger, and Yahoo Messenger.
- Misuse of IM will result in productivity deterioration, but appropriate use will have positive results.
- For maximum security, many organizations are investing in enterprise-level IM systems and adopting employee guidelines.
- Costs range from $30 to $100 per user license, depending on functionality.

I would be happy to elaborate on these points. Please let me know by March 13 whether you want me to make a presentation to the next management council meeting on March 25.

8.5 Document for Analysis: Direct Claim (Obj. 5)

Weaknesses

1. Fails to use proper salutation (*Dear Ms. Cholston*).
2. Opens with long lead-in (I am writing this letter to inform you that).
3. Does not describe a desired action in the opening.
4. Uses argumentative, belligerent tone.
5. Includes wordy and outdated expressions (in view of the fact and inasmuch as).
6. Closes with a cliché instead of asking for action by a specific date.

Revision

Current date

Ms. Melanie Cholston, Manager
Nationwide Car Rentals
1325 Commerce Street
Dallas, TX 75202

Dear Ms. Cholston:

Please reimburse my company $49.43. This amount was charged for a tank of premium gasoline when I returned a rental car to your branch in Houston June 26.

On June 23 I rented the car at the Dallas-Ft. Worth International Airport. Because its gas tank was nearly empty, I filled it. I assumed your policy required car rental customers to fill the tanks when they received their cars. Therefore, when I returned the car in Houston, I purposely left the tank nearly empty. However, your attendant filled it up and charged me for it. Surely your company does not provide cars with empty tanks and then expect customers to return them with full tanks.

Enclosed are a copy of the signed rental agreement and a receipt showing my payment of $426.50 (which includes $49.43 for gas). You may either credit my company card, or you may send a check for $49.43 made payable to my company. If you issue a VISA credit, please send a copy of the transaction to me at Criterion Enterprises, 402 North Griffin Street, Dallas, TX 74105.

We have not regularly used Western Car Rentals in the past, but your good service and competitive rates encourage me to give you our repeat business.

Sincerely,

Enclosure

8.6 Document for Analysis: Instructions

Weaknesses

1. Uses poor subject line.
2. Starts with a long lead-in (This message is to let you know that . . .)
3. Fails to begin with a summary of the main idea.
4. Does not explain need for new procedures concisely.
5. Fails to enumerate steps in describing the instructions.

Revision

To: Sam Oliver <sam.oliver@stcc.edu>
From: Alexandra Tutson <alex.tutson @stcc.edu>
Subject: New Online Instructions for Reporting Equipment Repairs
Cc:
Bcc:

A new procedure for submitting equipment repairs will speed the process by enabling us to better track your request. We are transitioning from using the printed "Equipment Repair Form" to a more efficient online database system. Please begin using the following new procedure immediately:

1. Log on to http://www.BigWebDesk.net.
2. Select the kind of repair you need: AudioVisual, Mac, PC, or Printer.
3. Select "Create New Ticket" to begin the process of data entry for your specific problem.
4. Fill in the information required.
5. Print the ticket and attach it securely to the equipment.

The warehouse truck driver will pick up and deliver the equipment as before. If you have questions, call Sylvia at Extension 255 or write her at sylvia.freeman@stcc.edu. We look forward to providing you with efficient pickup and repair service.

Alexandra Tutson, Manager
Operations and Facilities
alex.tutson@stcc.edu
(813) 355-3200, Ext. 230

ZOOMING IN Part 1: Ben & Jerry's Uses Positive Letters to Sweeten Relations With Customers

Critical Thinking

- **Have you ever written a letter or sent an e-mail to a company? What might motivate you to do so? Would you expect a response?**

  Most students have probably never written to a company. They might be motivated to do so if a product or service is unsatisfactory, if they need information about a product or service, or if they want to provide feedback (positive or negative) about products and services. If a customer takes the time to write to a company, that customer naturally expects a response.

- **If a company such as Ben & Jerry's receives a fan letter complimenting products or service, is it necessary to respond?**

  Companies thrive on customer approval. Of course a company would want to respond to a complimentary letter or e-mail message. Many companies not only respond, but they try to reinforce the bond with the customer by including samples or coupons for free products. Responding promptly and appropriately to inquiries results in loyal customers.

- **Why is it important for companies to answer claim (complaint) letters immediately?**

  Customer complaints generally are called claim letters because they make some claim on the company. The customer may want money back, repairs made, credit given, or simply an apology. When things go wrong and unhappy customers write, most companies respond immediately. Prompt company responses send a nonverbal message that the complaint is taken seriously. Moreover, companies generally try to fix problems before they grow into lawsuits. Most organizations sincerely want to please their customers. They explain what went wrong and how they are correcting the situation so that it won't be repeated. They strive to regain the trust of the customer.

ZOOMING IN Part 2: Ben & Jerry's

Critical Thinking

- **When customers write to Ben & Jerry's for information and the response contains both positive and negative news, what strategy should the respondent follow?**

  If a message contains both positive and negative news, the positive news should be presented first and it should receive the most emphasis. Don't let the negative news become the focus of the letter. Sandwich the bad news between the good news and a goodwill ending (such as giving free product coupons).

- **If a customer writes to complain about something for which Ben & Jerry's is not responsible (such as ice in frozen yogurt), should the response letter contain an apology? Why or why not?**

  Customers like to hear apologies, even if the company is not at fault. An apology raises the customer's feelings of self-worth and shows the humility of the company. If an apology generates no liability, you may decide to include one. But don't overdo it. Apologize early and quickly, and avoid using clichés to do so. Concentrate on something positive, such as the company's exceptional quality and service.

- **Why is letter-writing an important function for a company like Ben & Jerry's?**

  Letters are a primary means of promoting goodwill. Answers to inquiries cement relationships with customers. Equally important are letters that provide feedback about products. Companies like Ben & Jerry's often receive good ideas for new flavors and products, as well as valuable feedback about how well a product is received.

ZOOMING IN Your Turn: Applying Your Skills at Ben & Jerry's (Transparency solution available)

Current date

Ms. Cora Nicol
246 Falls Overlook Drive
Niagara Falls, NY 14109

Dear Ms. Nicol:

SUBJECT: YOUR LETTER ABOUT BEN & JERRY'S PRODUCTS

You're absolutely right in expecting an ample number of cookie and chocolate chunks in your Ben & Jerry's ice cream. Like you, we are disappointed when a product doesn't meet your expectations—or ours.

Although we work hard and long to get the right amount of chunks, nuts, and cookies in each pint, our chunking equipment is not always as consistent as we would like it to be. However, you can be sure that I will report your remarks to our production personnel so that they can redouble their efforts to maintain the proper ratio of chunks to ice cream.

You also inquire about the possibility of our producing a sugar-free ice cream. Ben & Jerry's did experiment with such a product, but it was far below our taste standards. Rather than compromise the excellent reputation we have achieved for premier ice creams, we decided to abandon our efforts. Any product we offer must meet our founders' and our customers' discriminating tastes.

We appreciate learning that you share our efforts to achieve peace in the world. We also appreciate your writing so that we can make amends to you. Because your satisfaction is very important to us, we are enclosing a check for $3.49, the estimated cost of a pint of ice cream. We hope that with your next pint we can regain you as a satisfied customer.

Sincerely,

Ethics Check Solutions

Surprising the Boss, Page 225
Kyra M. uses e-mail for nearly all messages. She is ecstatic over a new job offer and quickly sends an e-mail to her manager announcing that she is leaving. He did not know she was looking for a new position. Is this an appropriate use of e-mail?

E-mail is wonderful for many announcements, but it is totally inappropriate for something as serious as resigning a position. Such an announcement deserves a face-to-face talk followed by a formal resignation letter that identifies the last day of employment and expresses appreciation for the opportunities given. A resignation letter strives to leave a good impression. No e-mails here!

Stretching the Truth, Page 229
A magazine publisher sends you a letter saying that you should renew your subscription immediately to ensure continued delivery. Your subscription is paid for at least a year in advance, but nowhere in the letter or magazine label does your subscription end date appear. How far can a writer go in stretching the truth to achieve a purpose?

Magazine publishers and their sales agents regularly send misleading messages to subscribers telling them that their subscriptions are about to run out. Many publishers do not include the subscription end date to inform subscribers when the subscription will end. At one time helpful reminder letters were legitimate because they were sent close to the time subscriptions were running out. Today, however, desperate magazine publishers use this ploy to trick subscribers into long-term renewals. Clearly, it is unethical for letter writers to stretch the truth to achieve their goals. Consumers must keep their own records and be wary of all renewal requests and suspicious invoices.

Ethics Check, Page 234
Renting or Buying
Lucky U.S. consumers enjoy among the world's most generous merchandise return policies. No wonder, perhaps, that some customers presumably buy a video camera or a dress for a special event and afterwards return the product, no questions asked. Is this so-called "renting" or "wardrobing" wrong? Do retailers invite such behavior with their liberal policies?

Most Americans would probably agree that such practices are unethical and wrong. Competition is tough and consumers have high expectations of retailers. Surprisingly perhaps, abuse in the form of "renting" or "wardrobing" is rare, accounting for about 1 percent of retail returns, says receipt-fraud expert Mark Hilinski. About 20 to 25 percent of annual sales transactions result in returns—legitimate and otherwise. Hilinski acknowledges that this particular minority is more brazen than it was even five years ago and that some customers today feel entitled to return merchandise for any reason. Thoughtful students will realize that if more consumers resorted to abuse, the policies would have to be changed or prices raised to offset the losses to retailers.

Photo Essay Solutions

Photo Essay, Page 234
Businesses write adjustment letters to rectify a wrong, regain customer confidence, and promote further business. An effective adjustment letter opens with good news, explains the company's compliance with a claim, offers an apology as necessary, uses sensitive language, pledges fair compensation, and closes confidently.

Photo Essay, Page 242
Sympathy notes, whether handwritten or typed on stationary, should refer to the misfortune sensitively and directly, praise the deceased in a personal way, offer general assistance, and end on a positive and reassuring note.

Video Resources

Instructors may show the *Social Responsibility and Communication: Ben & Jerry's* from Video Library 2, *Bridging the Gap*. The video establishes a context for a writing problem in which students respond to a customer who is upset about the new packaging. Students are required to write a letter to a long-time customer explaining the reasons behind the new packaging.

Chapter 9 LECTURE NOTES AND TEACHING SUGGESTIONS

Negative Messages

CHAPTER SYNOPSIS

Breaking bad news is a fact of business life. Employees of every company from the highest to lowest will give bad news of some sort almost every day. Often the recipients of bad news do not take kindly to it, no matter how justified or necessary it is. The critical questions many business communicators ask themselves daily are these: How can I deliver bad news clearly and yet retain my recipient's goodwill? How can I avoid creating legal liability or responsibility? Am I being fair? Offering strategies to help business communicators find answers to these questions is the crux of Chapter 9.

This chapter focuses on applying the 3-x-3 writing process, including distinguishing between when to use the direct strategy and the indirect strategy for bad news messages. The direct strategy works best when the bad news is not damaging, when the receiver may overlook the bad news, when the receiver prefers directness, or when firmness is necessary. The indirect strategy is better when the bad news is personally upsetting, when the bad news will provoke a hostile reaction, when the bad news threatens the customer relationship, and when the bad news is unexpected. Students will learn to refuse typical requests, as well as how to handle bad news with customers and within organizations. In addition, the chapter compares strategies for revealing bad news in other cultures.

LEARNING OBJECTIVES

1. Describe the goals and strategies of business communicators in conveying negative news effectively, including applying the writing process and avoiding legal liability.

2 Decide whether to use the direct or indirect strategy in conveying negative news.

3. Analyze the components of effective negative messages, including opening with a buffer, apologizing, conveying empathy, presenting the reasons, cushioning the bad news, and closing pleasantly.

4. Describe and apply effective techniques for refusing typical requests.

5. Explain and apply effective techniques for handling bad news with customers.

6. Understand and apply effective techniques for delivering bad news within organizations.

7. Compare strategies for revealing bad news in other cultures.

WHAT'S NEW IN THIS CHAPTER

- Reorganized chapter to give more emphasis to the possible use of the direct strategy for delivering bad news so that students can use either direct or indirect strategy depending on the context.
- Revised opening three-part case study with current information about Southwest Airlines and its use of emerging channels such as blogs and social sites to communicate with customers.
- Streamlined the goals in communicating negative news to make them easier to comprehend and retain.
- Added specific real-world examples, including bad-news situations for Microsoft and Amazon.com, to illustrate how the writing process is applied to the delivery of negative news.
- Added coverage of managing negative news on Facebook, Twitter, and other Web sites to enable readers to be able to deal with unhappy customers in cyberspace.
- Added new section announcing rate increases and price hikes including a blog model document to show students that companies today are using new channels to deliver negative news.
- Streamlined the checklists for conveying negative news into one comprehensive list so that students have all the tips in one handy list.
- Changed 60 percent of the end-of-chapter activities so that students and instructors have new or fully revised activities to apply their skills in relation to new chapter content.

LECTURE OUTLINE

I. Conveying Bad News Effectively (p. 257)

PowerPoint slides 1-3

A. Establishing Goals in Communicating Negative News

- Explain clearly and completely.
- Project a professional image.
- Convey empathy and sensitivity.
- Being fair.
- Maintain friendly relations.

PowerPoint slide 4

B. Applying the 3-x-3 Writing Process

1. **Analysis, Anticipation, and Adaptation**
    - If the disappointment will be mild, announce it directly.
    - If the news is serious or personal, choose words that show respect and protect the reader's ego.

2. **Research, Organization, Composition**
    - Gather information and brainstorm ideas.
    - Select the best reasons to include and eliminate weak ones.
    - Flesh out each of the four sections as you compose your first draft.

3. **Revision, Proofreading, and Evaluation**
   - Look at the problem from the receiver's position.
   - Is the message clear without being too blunt or too subtle?
   - Proofread for format, punctuation, and correctness.

   PowerPoint slides 5-9

C. Avoiding Legal Liability in Conveying Negative News

1. **Abusive Language**

   Definition: *Defamation* is the legal term for any false statement that harms an individual's reputation. When the abusive language is written; it is called *libel*; when spoken, it is called *slander.*

   - To be actionable, abusive language must be (a) false, (b) damaging to one's good name, and (c) published (written or spoken within the presence of others).
   - Electronic transmissions are considered to be "published."

2. **Careless Language**
   - Careless language includes any statement that could be damaging or misinterpreted.

3. **The Good-Guy Syndrome**
   - Avoid the temptation to use words that make you feel good but are legally dangerous.
   - Your words, decisions, and opinions are assumed to represent those of your organization.
   - Beware of promises that can't be fulfilled.

Let's Discuss

What's the difference between slander and libel?

Libel is abusive language that is written; slander is abusive language that is spoken.

PowerPoint slides 10-12

II. Examining Negative News Strategies (p. 261)

A. When to Use the Direct Strategy
- When the bad news is not damaging
- When the receiver may overlook the bad news
- When the organization or receiver prefers directness
- When firmness is necessary

B. When to Use the Indirect Strategy

- When the bad news is upsetting
- When the bad news will provoke a hostile reaction
- When the bad news threatens the customer relationship
- When the bad news is unexpected

PowerPoint slides 13-15

Let's Discuss

What are the writer's primary and secondary goals in communicating bad news?

Primary goals are (1) to make the receiver understand the bad news, (b) to have the receiver accept the bad news, and (c) to maintain a positive image of the writer and his or her organization. Secondary goals are (1) to reduce bad feelings, (b) to convey fairness, (c) to eliminate future correspondence, and (d) to avoid creating legal liability or responsibility.

III. Analyzing the Components of Effective Negative Messages (p. 263)

A. Buffer to Open Indirect Messages

- Best news
- Compliment
- Appreciation
- Agreement
- Facts
- Understanding

PowerPoint slides 16-17

B. Apologizing

- Apologize if you or your company erred.
- Apologize sincerely.
- Accept responsibility.
- Use good judgment.

C. Conveying Empathy

- Convey empathy, the ability to understand and enter into the feelings of another.

D. Presenting the Reasons

- Explain clearly.
- Cite reader benefits, if plausible.
- Explain company policy, if relevant.
- Choose positive words.
- Show that the matter was treated seriously and fairly.

PowerPoint slide 18

E. Cushioning the Bad News
- Position the bad news strategically; avoid the spotlight.
- Use the passive voice.
- Accentuate the positive.
- Imply the refusal.
- Suggest a compromise or an alternative.

PowerPoint slides 19, 20

F. Closing Pleasantly
- Forward look
- Information about alternatives
- Good wishes
- Freebies
- Resale or sales promotion

PowerPoint slide 21

Let's Discuss

Does bad news travel faster and farther than good news? Why?

Students will probably respond that bad news does travel faster and often farther than good news. Why? Good news is not as interesting and doesn't always provoke action. Bad news often makes people angry, and they wish to vent their anger or seek revenge by broadcasting their news.

IV. Refusing Typical Requests (p. 268)

A. Rejecting Requests for Favors, Money, Information, and Action

1. Rejecting Requests for Favors, Money, Information, and Action
- Begin with a buffer acknowledging the request.
- Praise the good works of the charity.
- Provide a gentle refusal with or without an explanation.

Figure 9.4 Refusing Donation Request

2. Declining Invitations
- Make a special effort to soften the refusal because responses to invitations are often taken personally.
- Buffer the impact of the request refusal with a compliment.

Figure 9.5 Declining an Invitation

V. Handling Bad News With Customers (p. 268)

A. Damage Control: Dealing with Disappointed Customers

- Call the individual involved.
- Describe the problem and apologize.
- Explain why the problem occurred, what you are doing to resolve it, and how you will prevent it from happening again.
- Follow up with a letter that documents the phone call and promotes goodwill.

Figure 9.6 Bad-News Follow-Up Message
PowerPoint slides 22-28

B. Handling Problems With Orders

- Use the direct pattern if the message has some good-news elements.
- Use the indirect pattern when the news is disappointing.

C. Announcing Rate Increases and Price Hikes

- Explain the reasons.
- Link the increase to benefits.
- Give advance warning of rate increases.

Figure 9.7 Blog Announcing Price Increase With Audience Benefits
PowerPoint slides 29-31

D. Denying Claims

- Use the reasons-before-refusal plan when denying claims.
- Don't blame customers and avoid sounding preachy.
- Use neutral, objective language and an empathetic tone.

Figure 9.8 Denying a Claim

E. Refusing Credit

- Avoid language that causes hard feelings.
- Retain customers on a cash basis.
- Prepare for possible future credit without raising false expectations.
- Avoid disclosures that could cause a lawsuit.

VI. Delivering Bad News Within Organizations (p. 277)

A. Giving Bad News Personally

- Gather all the information.
- Prepare and rehearse.
- Explain: past, present, future.
- Consider taking a partner.
- Think about timing.
- Be patient with the reaction.

B. Refusing Internal Requests

- Start with a buffer that delivers honest praise.
- Provide reasons for the refusal in the middle paragraph.
- Close with a qualified alternative.

Figure 9.9 Refusing an Internal Request
PowerPoint slide 32

C. Delivering Bad News to Groups

- Managers should deliver the news personally or through hard-copy memos.
- Use the indirect strategy and an upbeat buffer.
- Strive to show fairness of the company's position.
- Provide clear, convincing reasons that explain the decision.

Figure 9.10 Announcing Bad News to Employees
PowerPoint slide 33

D. Saying No to Job Applicants

- Use the indirect pattern to lessen the blow.
- Be vague in explaining why the candidate was not selected to avoid charges of discrimination or wrongful actions.

Figure 9.11 Saying No to Job Candidate
PowerPoint slide 34

VII. Presenting Bad News in Other Cultures (p. 281)

- Americans prefer to break bad news slowly and indirectly.
- In Germany and Britain, bad news is revealed directly.
- In China and Japan, straightforwardness is avoided.
- In Latin cultures, bad news may be totally suppressed.
- In Asian cultures, negativism is avoided and hints may suggest bad news.

Lecture Transparencies
(available in a separate packet and at http://www.meguffey.com)

Negative Messages Acetates	Transparency Number
Goals in Communicating Negative News	90
Avoiding Legal Liability in Conveying Negative News	91
Examining the Components of Effective Negative Messages	92
Comparing Strategies	93
Techniques for Delivering Bad News Sensitively	94-95
Damage Control: Dealing with Disappointed Customers	96
"Before"—Ineffective Customer Request Refusal (Activity 10.6)	97
Critical Thinking Questions	98
"After"—Improved Refusal of Request	99

Solution Masters

	Page Number in This Book
Applying Your Skills at Southwest Airlines	563
9.1 Organizational Strategies	564
9.2 Employing Passive-Voice Verbs	564
9.3 Subordinating Bad News	565
9.4 Implying Bad News	565
9.5 Document for Analysis—Revision	566
9.6 Document for Analysis—Revision	567
9.7 Document for Analysis—Revision	568
9.8 Document for Analysis—Revision	569
9.9 Helping Abused Children	570
9.10 Jamba Asks for Juicy Favor	571
9.11 Greening the Office	572
9.12 Rejecting Agent's Appeal for Wireless Devices	573
9.13 Fun Ship Slams Door on Under-21 Crowd	574
9.14 Can't Evict Noisy Tenant	575
9.15 Refusing Refund for Japandroids and Bugskull Concert	576
9.16 She Wants Reimbursement for Her Eyeglasses	577
9.17 Sorry – Smokers Must Pay	578
9.18 The StairClimber or the LifeStep?	579
9.19 University Admission Message Erroneously Welcomes All Who Applied	580
9.20 Rate Increase of Your Choice	581
9.21 Your Credit Card Is Refused	582
9.22 J. Crew Goofs on Cashmere Turtleneck	583
9.24 Worms in Her PowerBars!	584
9.25 Costly SUV Upgrade to a Ford Excursion	586
9.26 Paying Cash at Atlanta Athletic Club	587
9.27 Camcorders for Rudy's Camera Shop	588
9.28 Company Games Are Not Date Nights	589
9.29 We Can't Pay Your Tuition	590
9.30 Negative News in Other Cultures	590

Answers to Chapter Review Questions

1. **When delivering bad news, how can a communicator reduce the bad feelings of the receiver? (Obj. 1)**

   Bad feelings can be reduced if the receiver (a) knows the reasons for the rejection, (b) feels that the news was revealed sensitively, and (c) believes the matter was treated seriously and fairly.

2. What is the most important part of Phase 1 of the writing process for negative messages? (Obj. 1)

The most important part is analyzing the bad news and anticipating its effect on the receiver.

3. When should you use the direct strategy in delivering bad news? (Obj. 2)

Use the direct strategy when the bad news is not damaging, when the receiver may overlook the bad news, when the organization or receiver prefers directness, or when firmness is necessary.

4. When should you use the indirect strategy in delivering bad news? (Obj. 2)

Use the indirect strategy when the bad news is personally upsetting, will provoke a hostile reaction, threatens the customer relationship, or is unexpected.

5. What are the major differences between the direct and indirect strategies in delivering bad news? (Obj. 2)

The major differences depend on whether you start with a buffer and how early you explain the reasons for the negative news. In the direct strategy, you start with a buffer and delay the bad news until after you have presented the reasons.

6. What is a buffer? Name five or more techniques to buffer the opening of a bad-news message. (Obj. 2)

A buffer is a device to reduce shock or pain. Appropriate buffers in bad-news messages might include starting with the best news, a compliment, appreciation, agreement, facts, understanding, or an apology.

7. What is an apology? When should an apology be offered to customers? (Obj. 2)

An apology is admission of blameworthiness and regret for an undesirable event. Apologies should be offered to customer when an organization has erred. Apologies are most effective when they sound sincere and when the writer accepts responsibility.

8. Name four or more techniques that cushion the delivery of bad news. (Obj. 2)

(a) Position the bad news strategically, (b) use the passive voice, (c) accentuate the positive, (d) imply the refusal, and (e) suggest a compromise or alternative.

9. What are some typical requests that big and small businesses must refuse? (Obj. 3)

Requests for money, time, equipment, and support

10. Identify a process used by a majority of business professionals in resolving problems with disappointed customers. (Obj. 4)

A majority of business professionals resolve problems immediately and personally by (a) calling the individual involved; (b) describing the problem and apologizing; (c) explaining why the problem occurred, what is being done to resolve it, and what measure are being taken to prevent its recurrence; and (d) following up with a letter that documents the phone call and promotes goodwill.

11. If you must deny the claim of a customer who is clearly at fault, should you respond by putting the blame squarely on the customer? (Obj. 4)

Even when customers are at fault, businesses should strive to establish goodwill and not blame the customer.

12. What is an effective technique in announcing rate increases and price hikes? (Obj. 5)

In announcing rate and price hikes, most companies strive to relate the increase to improved service, a better product, or other customer benefits.

13. How can a subordinate tactfully, professionally, and safely deliver upsetting news personally to a superior? (Obj. 6)

Gather all the information, prepare and rehearse, explain what happened and how it will be fixed, consider taking a partner, consider timing, and be patient with the reaction.

14. What are some channels that large organizations may use when delivering bad news to employees? (Obj. 5)

Organizations may use e-mail, videos, webcasts, and voice mail. But interoffice memos remain the most effective method because hard-copy memos are more formal and create a permanent record.

15. In Latin countries why may employees sometimes fail to report accurately any negative messages to management? (Obj. 6)

In Latin countries it is considered disrespectful and impolite to report bad news to superiors.

Answers to Critical Thinking Questions

1. **Communication author Dana Bristol-Smith likens delivering bad news to removing a Band-Aid−you can do it slowly or quickly. She thinks that quickly is better, particularly when companies must give bad news to employees. Do you agree or disagree? (Objs. 1−6)**

   Whether to deliver bad news slowly or quickly depends greatly on the situation and audience. Bristol-Smith says that employees want to know the truth, and they are likely to respect the company for telling it like it is. She offers a four-part plan: (1) Tell them what's happening, (2) tell them why it's happening, (3), show empathy, and (4) tell them what's next. However, blunt announcements—even to employees—may be less effective than those that are approached more sensitively.

2. **Respected industry analyst Gartner Research issued a report naming social networking as one of the top ten disruptive influences shaping information technology in the next five years. Should organizations fear Web sites where consumers post negative messages about products and services? What actions can companies take in response to this disruptive influence? (Objs. 1−5)**

   Proactive companies are creating their own Twitter and Facebook accounts and trolling the Web so that they can monitor comments and respond directly to consumers through social networking sites. Tech-savvy staffers search for keywords, complaints, and issues related to their brands. The most progressive companies see social networking as a new channel or communication tool for interacting with consumers. Social networking is indeed a disruptive influence in customer relations, but in a positive manner. These sites provide opportunities for companies to engage their customers directly and quickly.

3. **Consider times when you have been aware that others have used the indirect pattern in writing or speaking to you. How did you react? (Objs. 1–5)**

   Students may indicate that they appreciated the indirect pattern because it was more tactful and made them feel that the communicator cared about their feelings. On the other hand, students may suggest that they felt they were being manipulated and that they distrusted the communicator who was not forthright. Others may say that they were impatient to hear the bottom line. They disliked "beating around the bush."

   Most business communicators feel that using the indirect pattern prepares that individual for bad news or for an important idea. Other communicators contend that the indirect strategy is unethical. However, it is not unethical to make the best presentation possible. To say that something is unethical is to suggest dishonesty. It's not dishonest to delay bad news in an effort to protect the feelings of the receiver. The important point to recognize here is assessment of the receiver's reaction. If you feel that the receiver would prefer to have the news directly, then do just that.

4. **When Boeing Aircraft reported that a laptop containing the names, salary information, and social security numbers of 382,000 employees had been stolen from an employee's car, CEO Jim McNerney wrote this e-mail to employees: *I've received many e-mails over the past 24 hours from employees expressing disappointment, frustration, and downright anger about yesterday's announcement of personal information belonging to thousands of employees and retirees being on a stolen computer. I'm just as disappointed as you are about it. I know that many of us feel that this data loss amounts to a betrayal of the trust we place in the company to safeguard our personal information. I certainly do.* Critics have faulted this apology. With what did they find fault? Do you agree? (Obj. 1)**

   Critics said this apology was counterproductive. The CEO's memo admits that he spent 24 hours reading e-mail complaints instead of immediately working on a letter apologizing to his employees. In other words, he needed hundreds of e-mail complaints to get the point. They also said that equating his hurt feelings with those of 382,000 employees was the worst illustration of shirking his responsibility. Critics complained that he did not take responsibility. But should he assume responsibility for the actions of an employee (who was subsequently fired)? Ask students how his apology could have been improved. ("Rating Apologies," *Networkworld*, March 14, 2007, p. 3.)

5. **Ethical Issue: You work for a large corporation with headquarters in a small town. Recently you received shoddy repair work and a huge bill from a local garage. Your car's transmission has the same problems that it did before you took it in for repair. You know that a complaint letter written on your corporation's stationery would be much more authoritative than one written on plain stationery. Should you use corporation stationery? (Obj. 1)**

   Although the letter might seem more impressive on corporation stationery, it is clearly unethical and possibly illegal to use the stationery for personal business. If the car were owned by the corporation, the situation might be different. Company stationery should never be used for personal matters.

Writing Improvement Exercises

9.1 Organizational Strategies (Objs. 1–5)

a. Direct
b. Indirect
c. Indirect
d. Indirect
e. Indirect
f. Direct
g. Indirect
h. Indirect
i. Direct
j. Indirect

9.2 Employing Passive-Voice Verbs (Obj. 3)

a. Free shipping cannot be offered after January 1.

b. Credit cards in our retail stores will no longer be accepted for purchases under $5.

c. Because more stringent security is required, company tours must be postponed indefinitely.

d. Patients cannot be examined until after their insurance coverage is verified. OR Patients can be examined after verification of their insurance coverage.

e. Large SUVs are not covered by your car rental insurance.

f. Health and dental benefits are offered only after employees have been on the job for 12 months.

9.3 Subordinating Bad News (Obj. 2)

a. Although your cabinet hinge is no longer manufactured, we are sending a replacement that should work for you.

b. Although smoking is not allowed within 5 feet of a state building, the college has set aside 16 outdoor smoking areas.

c. Although we no longer print a complete catalog, we now offer all of our catalog choices at our Web site, which is always current.

d. Although your complete order cannot be shipped at this time, two corner workstations should arrive within five days.

e. Although an employment offer cannot be extended at this time, we appreciate your interest in our organization.

9.4 Implying Bad News (Obj. 2)

a. Although all our present funds are needed to lease equipment and offices for our new branch in Hartford, we hope to be able to support this commendable endeavor in the future.

b. We have your fresh fruit basket ready and will ship it as soon as you call us with your credit card number.

c. Because our billboard space was completely filled during the holidays, we hope to display your message, as promised, next month.

9.5 Document for Analysis: Wedding Request Refusal (Objs. 1–4)

Weaknesses

- Fails to open with a buffer statement before announcing the bad news.
- Uses negative words *(regret, unfortunately).*
- Implies that the writer is not as smart as other brides who booked in advance.
- Does not use subordinate clause to introduce bad news.
- Provides reason for bad news but uses an arrogant rather than sympathetic tone.
- Suggests alternative but fails to make it easy for reader to follow through on the alternative.
- Makes little effort to promote the alternative or develop goodwill for the Napa Valley Inn.
- Does not provide telephone number or helpful encouragement to call.

Revision

Current date

Ms. Sonya Capretta
2459 Sierra Avenue
Fresno, CA 93710

Dear Ms. Capretta:

Thanks for your inquiry regarding weddings at the Napa Valley Inn, one of the most beautiful and romantic settings in the country.

June is our busiest month, and this year is no exception. Although all of the Saturdays in June are booked, we can accommodate your party in midweek if you reserve soon. With unparalleled cuisine and service, along with panoramic Napa Valley and vineyard views, our Inn offers a unique, intimate ambiance in a breathtaking location for your special event.

Let the Napa Valley Inn with its 45 Mediterranean-style rooms and suites, each with its own sun-drenched private terrace, provide the perfect location for you and your guests to celebrate your union. Afternoon ceremonies typically begin at 11 a.m., while evening ceremonies usually begin at 6 p.m. Please call me at 1-800-435-3321 so that I can help you plan a midweek event in June. But act quickly to ensure your reservation.

Sincerely,

9.6 Document for Analysis: Copier Request Refusal (Objs. 1–4)

Weaknesses

- Fails to open with a buffer statement before unloading the bad news.
- Relies on negative words (*impossible, prohibiting, must deny*)
- Does not give reasons before the bad news.
- Makes little effort to retain goodwill of customer.
- Insults reader with haughty language (*if we agreed to proposals such as yours*)
- Fails to present alternative in a way that promotes goodwill and future business.
- Does not make it easy for reader to respond.

Revision

Current date

Mr. Tyler Venable
Great Atlantic Financial Services
105 Washington Avenue
Glassboro, NJ 08071

Dear Mr. Venable:

We're happy to learn that you are enjoying the use of the Sharp CopyCenter C20 you have been leasing for the past 11 months.

Like our many other customers, Mr. Venable, you have discovered that Sharp copiers supply remarkable versatility and reliability. One of the reasons we're able to offer these outstanding copiers at such low leasing rates and equally low purchase prices is that we maintain a slim profit margin. If our program included a provision for applying lease payments toward purchase prices, our overall prices would have to be higher. Although lease payments cannot be credited toward purchase price, we can offer you other Sharp models that are within your price range. The Sharp CopyCenter C15 delivers the same reliability with nearly as many features as the top-of-the-line CopyCenter C20.

Please let us demonstrate the Sharp CopyCenter C15 to your staff in your office, Mr. Venable. Our representative, Leila Sanchez, will call you during the week of April 14 to arrange an appointment.

Sincerely,

9.7 Document for Analysis: Refusing Internal Request for Time Off (Objs. 1-3, 5)

Weaknesses

- Uses flippant tone and doesn't seem to take request seriously.
- Provides brusque and vague subject line.
- Announces refusal bluntly, even though the receiver is probably personally affected by this decision.
- Expresses ideas carelessly and sloppily, as if this note was written hurriedly.
- Employs wordy and redundant expressions (*each and every, due to the fact that, in view of the fact that, return back*).
- Misses opportunity to polish writing with parallel phrasing (Improved version: *we need you to interview clients, make video testimonials, and search for customer success stories).*
- Fails to organize message coherently.
- Does not end pleasantly with goodwill effort or plausible alternative.

Revision

To: Sylvia Greene (sgreene@financialsolutions.com)
From: Chester Goings (cgoings@financialsolutions.com)
Subject: Your Request for Time Off
Cc:
Bcc:

Sylvia,

Everyone here at Financial Solutions appreciates the splendid work you have done for the Newborn Hope Foundation. We admire its goal of making differences in the lives of babies, particularly newborns. In the past we've been able to give you release time to work on its fashion show/luncheon, and we've been able to make a considerable financial contribution to the foundation.

This year, however, is different. As you know, we're suffering from the downturn in the economy and we've even had to reduce our staff. With the remaining bare-bones staff, we need every team member to be here and functioning highly as we prepare the upcoming release of our Planning Guide 5.0. You are one of our most valuable team members. We need you to interview clients, make video testimonials, and search for customer success stories. You are the team member on whom we depend to put the final touches on our new Web content. The truth is that we can't launch this new product on time without you.

Perhaps in the future when the economy rebounds and when our new product is successfully received, we'll be able to return to our former level of community involvement for admirable projects such as Newborn Hope Foundation. In the meantime, please accept our profound thanks for the exceptional service you give us here at Financial Solutions.

Chester
[Full contact information]

9.8 Document for Analysis: Refusing a Job Applicant (Objs. 1, 2, 5)

Weaknesses

- Opens with such enthusiastic language that reader is misled about what will follow.
- Reveals dangerous information that may motivate litigation.
- Shows little respect for reader's feelings.
- Uses many subordinate clauses but not skillfully.
- Includes more negative language than is necessary.

Revision

Current date

Mr. Kent W. Bradshaw
2140 Azalea Avenue
Louisville, KY 40216

Mrs. Lugan and I were pleased to interview you last Thursday and tell you something about Appalacian Technologies and its operations.

We were fortunate to have a number of well-qualified individuals apply for the position of human resources assistant. To fill this position, we hired a graduate of the University of Kentucky who seemed to have the qualities we sought. We wanted to write you immediately to enable you to continue your job search.

You have our best wishes in finding exactly the right position to match your background and education.

Sincerely,

9.9 through 9.22 Solutions in the form of transparency masters are available at the end of this manual.

9.23 Damage Control for Disappointed Customers: No Payroll Checks (Objs. 1-3, 5)

Lead a class discussion centered on the following questions. Consider having two students role play the part of Trenton Hughes, sales manager, and customer Jessica Dyhala.

a. Should Hughes call Dyhala or delegate the task to his assistant?

Hughes is the sales manager and presumably is the main contact that Dyhala has with the printing company; therefore, it is his responsibility to deliver the news. Under some circumstances, it might be appropriate to have someone higher up in the organization, such as the CEO, place the call. Two circumstances that might justify this approach follow: (a) Hughes wants to emphasize that the company is taking this problem seriously and wants to go all out to convince the client that the client is important; and (b) the insurance company is one of the printing company's biggest clients.

b. When should Dyhala be informed of the problem?

Immediately.

c. What is the best procedure for delivering the bad news?

- Call the individual involved.
- Describe the problem and apologize.
- Explain why the problem occurred, what you are doing to resolve it, and how you will prevent it from happening again.

In describing the problem and apologizing, Hughes might say, "We discovered just this morning that your check order will not be printed by the date I originally promised you it would be ready. I apologize for causing a difficult situation for your company."

In explaining how the problem occurred, Hughes might say that the employee who schedules orders to be printed misread the promised delivery date for your checks; therefore, he didn't schedule your printing order early enough for it to be ready when you requested. Hughes might add, "As soon as we discovered the mistake, your order was moved to the front of the production queue and is being printed as we speak. As soon as the checks come out of production, we will ship them to you by FedEx Express SameDay delivery. We will cover the increased shipping cost necessary to get your checks to you more quickly. In addition, we're giving you a 10 percent discount on the cost of this order to compensate you in a small way for the inconvenience we've caused you."

In explaining what is being done to avoid recurrence of the problem, Hughes might say, "We've instituted a new system to keep this problem from happening again. After the employee does the initial scheduling of print jobs, we have designated a second employee to double check that all the print jobs have been scheduled in a timely fashion so that we can meet the delivery dates we've promised our clients."

In concluding his telephone call, Hughes should strive for a positive tone that promotes goodwill: "Your satisfaction is what is important to us, and we're working extra hard to make sure you're satisfied with how we're handling this situation."

d. What follow-up phone call would you recommend to Hughes?

Hughes should write a follow-up letter that documents the phone call and promotes goodwill. In addition, Hughes should keep in close contact with Dyhala until the problem is resolved. Confirm that the air freight delivery arrives when it is supposed to arrive. If the shipment does not arrive on time, track the delivery with the shipping company to determine its status. Confirm the delivery of the remainder of the order that is coming by truck.

9.24 through 9.30 Solutions in the form of transparency masters are available at the end of this manual.

ZOOMING IN Part 1: Passengers LUV Southwest Airlines—Even When Flights Are Late

Critical Thinking

- **Suppose you applied for a job that you really wanted, but the company hired someone else. To notify you of the bad news, the company sends a letter. Should the letter blurt out the bad news immediately or soften the blow somewhat?**

  Revealing bad news slowly usually softens its impact. Most people would prefer to be let down gently.

- **What are some techniques you could use if you have to deliver bad news in business messages?**

  Much depends, of course, on the severity of the bad news and the relationship between you and the receiver. In business messages to customers, you could start with a *buffer*, which is a neutral statement. Then you can offer reasons for the bad news before revealing it in a straightforward manner. You might suggest an alternative, a compromise, or a solution. Finally, you might close with a personal, forward-looking statement that does not repeat the bad news. If you or your company were responsible for inconveniencing or angering the customer, you would also consider whether to deliver an apology.

- **What goals should you try to achieve when you have to give disappointing news to customers, employees, suppliers, or others on behalf of your organization?**

  When delivering negative messages on behalf of your organization, you should remember four key goals. You want the recipient to accept and understand the bad news. At the same time, you want to present a positive image of your organization. Your message should be clear, so that you don't have to spend more time corresponding about the issue. Finally, you must protect your organization from future legal action.

ZOOMING IN Part 2: Southwest Airlines

Critical Thinking

- **What are the advantages to Southwest of its proactive approach to passenger problems?**

  Southwest builds customer loyalty and a positive public image by being prepared to deliver bad news. Having a plan and providing employees with information are the best way to break bad news and prevent later complaints. Customers appreciate having the facts and knowing that the airline takes customer service seriously. They are pleasantly surprised when they receive an unsolicited apology from Southwest.

- **How might Fred Taylor use the four-part plan suggested in this chapter to compose his apology letters to passengers?**

  Mr. Taylor could start the letter with a buffer showing appreciation and giving facts, such as thanking the passenger for flying Southwest and mentioning the number of daily flights the airline operates. Then he would continue with the reasons for the letter, describing the actual situation that led to the passenger's problem. For example, if a passenger missed a connection because an incoming plane was late, he might explain that air traffic controllers slowed down the arrival of flights. Thunderstorms in that area caused many flight delays. He would also apologize for the inconvenience to the customer. If relevant—in the case of lost luggage or a mishandled reservation, perhaps—he could also explain any steps the airline is taking to prevent future mishaps. If appropriate, he would close with a gift to compensate for the inconvenience, such as a voucher for a free flight or a discount coupon. The closing should also state that he hopes that the customer will continue to choose Southwest.

- **Contrast the strategies Taylor would develop to deliver bad news to Southwest's employees and to its passengers.**

  The goals when delivering bad news to employees or customers are similar: acceptance of the bad news while maintaining a positive image and avoidance of legal liability. Taylor would use positive language, be tactful, and start with a buffer. Depending on the severity of the bad news, he might be more direct in bad news to employees. He also has the option of delivering the news in person. In delivering bad news to customers, he would use the indirect method and written correspondence. Reasons and the bad news follow the buffer in both cases, and the closing should be pleasant and friendly. However, customers might receive offers of gifts or other benefits; employees would not.

ZOOMING IN Your Turn:
Applying Your Skills at Southwest Airlines

(Transparency solution available)

Current Date

Ms. Elizabeth Dunbar, Director
Animal Rescue League of Iowa
5452 Northeast 22nd Street
Des Moines, IA 50313

Dear Ms. Dunbar:

The Animal Rescue League of Iowa is to be commended on its excellent efforts to save animals in need. We understand and applaud your ambitious drive to build a new state-of-the-art shelter for the homeless animals of Des Moines.

We at Southwest Airlines are also involved in a number of admirable charitable efforts including the Hispanic Association of Colleges and Universities, the Ronald McDonald House, Junior Achievement, Read Across America, and Parkland Burn Camp. When we receive requests to support fund-raising events, we have two guidelines: (1) The request must arrive 45 days in advance of the charitable event, and (2) the request must not exceed two roundtrip passes for transportation between any two cities Southwest Airlines serves within the continental United States. Although your request does not meet these two guidelines, we would be happy to support a request for two roundtrip passes at a time when you can give us 45 days advance notice.

We extend to you our very best wishes for a successful fundraising drive to build your new animal shelter. If we can offer you two roundtrip tickets for a future raffle, please write to us again.

Sincerely,

Discussion Material for PLUGGED IN:
Using Technology to Personalize Form Letters

Students will find numerous legitimate complaints about products and services. For example, one writer complained that after three months of use, his expensive iPod stopped working. He sent it to Apple for repair and received a form letter telling him to buy a new one—despite a repair policy suggesting that within ten days of their initial purchase, buyers would receive a working iPod. The form letter could have been greatly improved using techniques from this chapter.

Ethics Check Solutions

Ethics Check, Page 264
Apology or Excuse?
District Attorney Mike Nifong apologized to three Duke University lacrosse players that he had indicted on charges of attacking an exotic dancer. How ethical and effective is his apology? "To the extent that I made judgments that ultimately proved to be incorrect, I apologize to the three students that were wrongly accused."

This is a classic example of an unethical, lame excuse rather than an apology. Nifong limits his "apology" with the phrase *to the extent*, thereby negating the following words. By saying that he "made judgments that ultimately proved to be incorrect," he refuses to accept responsibility. This "apology" is insincere and does not accept responsibility when he alone clearly caused egregious harm.

Ethics Check, page 279
Canned by E-Mail
When downsizing, Radio Shack used e-mail to fire about 400 employees at its Fort Worth headquarters. The messages said, "The work force reduction notification is currently in progress. Unfortunately, your position is one that has been eliminated." Is it ethical to send such bad news by e-mail, and how do you feel about the tone of the message?

Management experts find such tactics "dehumanizing" for the employees, and most students would probably agree that it's preferable to break bad news about dismissal in person rather than by e-mail.

Photo Essay Solutions

Photo Essay, p. 260
When accelerator defects threatened Toyota's quality reputation and defied easy diagnosis in Lexus and other models, management took to the Internet to communicate directly with customers. President Akio Toyoda led the public relations blitz with an 800-word letter published at online news outlets, and Internet teams posted recall videos and information for more than 100,000 followers at Toyota's Twitter, Facebook, and YouTube accounts. Is the Internet an appropriate channel for addressing customers negatively affected by product recalls?

As consumers continue to go to the Web to air complaints and seek customer service information, more and more businesses will find online social networking tools to be effective for communicating with the masses. During Toyota's recent worldwide recall, online customer information was both comprehensive and updated daily. Managers fielded customer comments and even countered false rumors using Facebook and Twitter.

Addressing customer complaints online has limits, however. For example, investigative inquiries into the Toyota recall concluded that dozens of traffic deaths were potentially linked to Toyota's acceleration glitches. Life and death issues cannot be handled through blogs and Twitter, but instead require phone calls, personal meetings, and letters addressing customer injuries. Personal communications should aim to describe the problem, explain why it occurred, apologize, and discuss what is being done to resolve the issue and prevent it from happening again.

Photo Essay, Page 270
As the global recession deepens and budget shortfalls spread to all sectors of the economy, city managers are struggling to deliver negative news to workers. Faced with a $522 million annual deficit, San Francisco Mayor Gavin Newsom delivered pink slips to more than 15,000 city workers as part of a plan for "saving people's jobs and city services." In response to criticism over his characterization of the situation, Mayor Newsom replied that he was "lawyered up." How can employers avoid legal liability in conveying bad news?

As the marketplace grows increasingly litigious, business communicators can minimize legal liabilities by avoiding abusive language, careless language, and the "good-guy syndrome." In the case of San Francisco's recent layoffs, 15,000 city workers were left guessing whether or not they were fired or merely facing a reduction in hours. Mayor Newsom fell into the good-guy syndrome for characterizing the layoffs as helping the workers and the public. "The reason I'm doing this is to save people's jobs and to save city services," Newsom was quoted as saying. Moreover, in telling the public that he was "lawyered up" in anticipation of legal liabilities, Newsom was using language that could be perceived as overly casual and careless. Delivering negative news safely requires that communicators choose words carefully and intentionally while avoiding empty promises and extraneous data that might be misused.

Video Resources

Instructors may show the *Bridging the Gap* video from Video Library 2, *BuyCostumes.* Instructors will find a complete discussion guide and activity solution for this video presented in this Instructor's Manual.

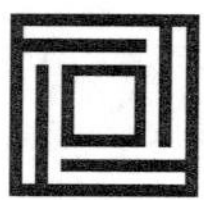

Chapter 10 LECTURE NOTES AND TEACHING SUGGESTIONS

Persuasive and Sales Messages

CHAPTER SYNOPSIS

The ability to use argument or discussion to influence an individual's beliefs or actions is called *persuasion.* The art of persuading someone to take a specific action or change an individual's beliefs is an important skill that requires understanding and practice. This chapter explains the major elements in successful persuasive messages and shows students how to use the 3-x-3 writing process to create effective persuasive requests and marketing messages. To be successful at persuasion, business communicators must be familiar with the products or services they sell and the audiences to whom they promote them. Therefore, this chapter emphasizes how to analyze the purpose of the message, how to adapt it to the audience, and how to appropriately research and organize data. In addition, the chapter emphasizes blending the components of a persuasive message: gaining attention, building interest, reducing resistance, and motivating action.

Students will learn to write practical messages such as those that request favors and action, make claims, and deliver complaints. The chapter also focuses on writing persuasive messages within organizations. The last part of the chapter covers effective and ethical direct-mail and e-mail sales campaigns, as well as comparing persuasive techniques in high- and low-context cultures. Finally, students study basic patterns and techniques in developing persuasive press releases.

LEARNING OBJECTIVES

1. Define the concept of persuasion, identify effective and ineffective persuasive techniques, and apply the 3-x-3 writing process to persuasive messages.
2. Explain the four major elements in successful persuasive messages and how to blend those elements into effective and ethical business messages.
3. Write persuasive messages that request favors and actions, make claims, and deliver complaints.
4. Write persuasive messages within organizations.
5. Write effective and ethical direct-mail and e-mail sales messages.
6. Compare effective persuasion techniques in high- and low-context cultures.
7. Understand basic patterns and techniques in developing persuasive press releases.

WHAT'S NEW IN THIS CHAPTER

- Streamlined chapter by combining related learning objectives and checklists to enhance readability and comprehension.
- Reorganized chapter to combine coverage of persuasive favor requests, claims, and complaints to simplify presentation and allow students to apply similar writing techniques.
- Moved coverage of internal communication (persuasive messages within organization) so that it follows the discussion of external communication (favor requests, claims, and complaints) for a more unified presentation.
- Added model document showing the use of a cover e-mail with an attached memo to help students see how businesspeople combine e-mail and attachments.
- Strengthened coverage of sales messages by adding e-marketing so that readers understand basic techniques for preparing successful e-mail sales messages.
- Illustrated press releases and effective writing techniques with a new model document featuring Hershey's Chocolates.
- Added a new Spotlight on Communicators highlighting Irene Rosenfeld, the persuasive and effective CEO of Kraft Foods.
- Created many new persuasive case studies or Documents for Analysis that engage students in interesting and relevant topics, such as wrapping bananas in plastic at 7-Eleven, adopting a four-day workweek, retaining free apples at an upscale hotel, and reducing health care costs.

LECTURE OUTLINE

I. Understanding Persuasion and How to Use It Effectively and Ethically (p. 295)

PowerPoint slides 1-3

A. What Is Persuasion?

Definition: *Persuasion* is the ability to use argument or discussion in attempting to change an individual's beliefs or actions.

Figure 10.1 Persuasive Action Request
PowerPoint slide 4

B. Effective Persuasion Techniques

1. Establish credibility.
2. Make a reasonable, precise request.
3. Tie facts to benefits.
4. Recognize the power of loss.
5. Expect and overcome resistance.
6. Share solutions and compromise.

PowerPoint slide 5

C. The Importance of Tone

- Avoid sounding preachy or parental.
- Don't pull rank.
- Avoid making threats.
- Soften your words when persuading upward.
- Be enthusiastic.
- Be positive and likeable.

PowerPoint slide 6

II. Applying the 3-x-3 Writing Process to Persuasive Messages (p. 298)

PowerPoint slides 7-9

A. Analyzing the Purpose: Knowing What You Want to Achieve

- Before you start writing your message or planning your presentation, know your purpose and what response you want.

B. Adapting to the Audience by Finding Ways to Make Your Message Heard

- A persuasive message shows how your request helps the receiver fulfill key needs or solve a problem.
- To adapt your request to the receiver, consider these questions that receivers may ask themselves:
  1. Why should I?
  2. What's in it for me?
  3. What's in it for you?
  4. Who cares?

C. Researching and Organizing Data

- Collect data to support your message.
- Organize the message into a logical sequence:
  1. Gain attention.
  2. Build interest.
  3. Reduce resistance.
  4. Motivate action.

III. Blending Four Major Elements in Successful Persuasive Messages (p. 299)

- The key elements in persuasive messages are (a) gaining your audience's attention, (b) building interest by convincing your audience that your proposal is worthy, (c) reducing resistance, and (d) motivating action.

PowerPoint slide 10

A. Gaining Attention

- When mild resistance is anticipated, the opener should be low-key and factual.
- When strong resistance is anticipated, the opening should be provocative and thoughtful.
    1. **Problem description.** Summarize the problem your proposal will help solve.
    2. **Unexpected statement.** Generate interest with a thought-provoking statement.
    3. **Reader benefit.** Promptly communicate reader benefits.
    4. **Compliment.** Offer praise or compliments to entice reader.
    5. **Related facts.** Offer intriguing facts to build interest.
    6. **Stimulating question.** Spark curiosity with a provocative question.

Let's Discuss

An effective sales letter should grab the reader's attention with the opening line. In fact, you have about four seconds to get his or her attention. Which of the following opening lines best captures a reader's attention?

Opener #1: *Our wireless service offers something for every member of your family.*

Opener #2: *Get ready for super-fast Internet connection, unlimited text messaging, and free incoming calls for $14.99 per month.*

Nicastro, Ernest (2007, August 1). Fifteen tips for better sales letters. *Direct (Online Exclusive).* Retrieved September 13, 2007, from Business and Company Resource Center (BCRC) database.

B. Building Interest in Persuasive Messages

- Build interest and reduce resistance with a few paragraphs of explanation.
- Show how your request can benefit the audience directly or indirectly.

C. Reducing Resistance in Persuasive Requests

- Anticipate resistance by asking *What If*?
- Counter resistance by presenting counterarguments in sentences that emphasize benefits.
- Reduce resistance by establishing expertise, referring to credentials, or demonstrating competence.

D. Motivating Action in Persuasive Messages

- Make your recommendations as specifically and confidently as possible.
- Don't sound apologetic and don't supply excuses.

E. Being Persuasive and Ethical

- In a persuasive message, put forth a convincing case but be sure it is based on truth, objectivity, and fairness.

Figure 10.2 Four-Part Plan for Persuasive Messages

IV. Requesting Favors and Actions, Making Claims, and Delivering Complaints (p. 303)

- When requesting a favor or action, think through your purpose and prepare a thoughtful message.
- Use the indirect pattern for persuasive messages that request favors or actions.

Figure 10.3 Persuasive Favor Request

A. Preparing Persuasive Requests for Favors and Actions

Prewrite
- Determine your purpose.
- Anticipate the reaction of your audience.

Gain Attention
- Use the indirect pattern.
- Begin by grabbing attention.

Build Interest
- Develop interest.
- Establish your credibility.
- Support your request.

Reduce Resistance
- Anticipate objections and provide counterarguments.
- Suggest what might be lost.
- Explain how easy it is to respond.

Motivate Action
- Make a precise request.
- Repeat the benefit, provide details, or offer an incentive. Express appreciation.

PowerPoint slides 11-24

B. Writing Persuasive Claims

1. Developing a Logical Persuasive Argument
- Begin with a compliment, point of agreement, statement of the problem, or brief review of the action you have taken to solve the problem.
- Present a logical case with clear facts.
- Enclose documentation that confirms the details of the purchase.

2. Using a Moderate Tone
- Describe your feelings and disappointment without sounding angry, emotional, or irrational.
- Appeal to the reader's fairness, ethical and legal responsibilities, and desire for customer satisfaction.

3. **Composing Effective Complaints**
   - Use a positive opening, a well-documented claim, and a request for specific action in the closing.

Figure 10.4 Claim (Complaint) Letter
PowerPoint slides 25-27

Let's Discuss

What could be included in an effective opening and closing of a claim or complaint message?

The opening should begin with a compliment, point of agreement, statement of the problem, or a brief review of action taken to resolve the problem. The closing should explain exactly what the writer wants done.

V. Writing Persuasive Messages Within Organizations (p. 307)

PowerPoint slides 28-32

A. Persuading Employees: Messages Flowing Downward
- Instructions moving from supervisors to subordinates require little persuasion.
- Messages flowing downward follow the direct pattern with the purpose stated immediately.

Figure 10.5 Persuasive Organizational Message Flowing Downward

B. Persuading the Boss: Messages Flowing Upward
- Messages to managers should emphasize how the proposal saves money or benefits the business.
- Soften your words when persuading upward and avoid sounding pushy.
- Use facts, statistics, examples, and specific details to build a solid foundation for your request.

Figure 10.6 Persuasive E-Mail and Memo Flowing Upward
PowerPoint slides 33-34

C. Checklist for Writing Persuasive Messages Within Organizations

Prewrite
- Know your purpose and state it precisely and concisely.
- Profile the audience.

Gain Attention
- Make the reader aware of a problem.
- Establish your credibility.

Build Interest

- Use facts, examples, and details to build a foundation.
- Strive for a personal but professional tone.
- Soften your words when persuading upwards.

Reduce Resistance

- Recognize any weakness in your proposal and suggest counterarguments.
- In requests flowing upwards, make cost appeals.
- In requests flowing downwards, avoid sounding preachy or authoritarian.

Motivate Action

- State a specific request, including deadline. Suggest ways to make it effortless to respond.
- Repeat a major benefit.
- Include an incentive. Express appreciation if appropriate.

VI. Planning and Composing Effective Direct Mail and E-Mail Sales Messages (p. 311)

PowerPoint slides 35-46

A. Applying the 3-x-3 Writing Process to Sales Messages

1. Analyzing the Product and Purpose for Writing
   - Study the product or service carefully.
   - Identify the central selling points.
   - Determine the purpose of your letter.

2. Adapting to the Audience
   - Tailor the message to a specific audience.
   - Use mailing lists to increase response rate.

B. Crafting Direct-Mail Sales Letters

1. Gaining Attention in Sales Messages
   - Offer
   - Promise
   - Question
   - Quotation or proverb
   - Fact
   - Product feature
   - Testimonial
   - Startling statement
   - Personalized action setting

2. Building Interest With Rational and Emotional Appeals
   - Rational appeal—associated with reason and intellect
   - Emotional appeal—relates to status, ego, and sensual feelings
   - Dual appeal—combines rational and emotional appeals

3. Reducing Resistance and Building Desire
   - When price is an issue, delay mentioning price, show the price in small units, demonstrate how the reader saves money, and compare prices with competitors'.
   - Testimonials
   - Names of satisfied users
   - Money-back guarantee or warranty
   - Free trial or sample
   - Performance tests, polls, or awards

4. Motivating Action at the Conclusion of a Sales Message
   - Offer a gift.
   - Promise an incentive.
   - Limit the offer.
   - Set a deadline.
   - Guarantee satisfaction.

5. Putting Together All the Parts of a Sales Message
   - Because direct mail is expensive, create sales messages that present complete information in a personalized tone for specific audiences.

Figure 10.7 Sales Letter

C. Checklist for Preparing Persuasive Direct-Mail and E-Mail Sales Messages

Prewrite
- Analyze your product or service.
- Profile your audience.
- Decide what you want the audience to do.
- For e-mails, send to only those who opted in.

Gain Attention
- Describe a product, present a testimonial, or show reader in an action setting.
- Offer something valuable.
- Suggest a solution to a problem.

Build Interest
- Describe a product or service.
- Use rational appeals.
- Explain how you can save money, reduce effort, or improve pleasure.

Reduce Resistance
- Counter resistance.
- Build credibility.
- Describe price in small amounts.

Motivate Action

- Close by repeating a central selling point.
- Prompt for action immediately.
- Put strongest motivator in a postscript.
- In e-mails include an opportunity to opt out.

Lecture Tidbit

Extensive research shows that the P.S. is one of the first parts of a letter people read. Restating a key benefit or guarantee here can pull your reader into the body of your letter. It pays to use a P.S.

Nicastro, Ernest (2007, August 1). Fifteen tips for better sales letters. *Direct (Online Exclusive).* Retrieved September 13, 2007, from Business and Company Resource Center (BCRC) database.

VII. Comparing Persuasion in High- and Low-Context Cultures (p. 318)

PowerPoint slides 47-48

A. Being Persuasive in High-Context Cultures

- In high-context cultures, information is not explicit and meaning may be conveyed by clues in the situational context.
- Sales letters, advertisements, Web sites, and other persuasive messages in high-context cultures may be characterized by the following:
  1. Indirectness
  2. Politeness
  3. Soft-sell approach
  4. Relationship appeal
  5. Collectivist view

B. Analyzing High-Context Sales Letters

1. Opens with formal salutation
2. Attempts to build relationship
3. Establishes credibility and respect
4. Uses low-key sales approach
5. No effort is made to develop a "you" view
6. Closes without deadlines, incentives, or postscript
7. Attempts to show respect and harmony

Figure 10.8 Sales Message, High-Context Culture (English translation)

C. Being Persuasive in Low-Context Cultures

- Low-context cultures tend to be logical, linear, and action oriented.
- Sales messages may be characterized as follows:
  1. Directness
  2. Superlatives
  3. Hard-sell approach
  4. Short-term goal (little attempt to develop long-term relationships)
  5. "You" view

VIII. Developing Persuasive Press Releases (p. 321)

- Open with attention-getting lead.
- Include answers to the five *W*s and *H*.
- Appeal to the audience of the target market.
- Present the most important information early, followed by supporting information.
- Make the release visually appealing.
- Look and sound credible.

Figure 10.9 Press Release

Lecture Transparencies (available in a separate packet and at http://www.meguffey.com)

Persuasive and Sales Messages Acetates	**Transparency Number**
Understanding Persuasion and How to Use It Ethically and Effectively	100
Applying the 3-x-3 Writing Process to Persuasive Messages	101
Four Major Elements in Successful Persuasive Messages	102
Requesting Favors and Actions	103–104
"Before"—Ineffective Request	105
Critical Thinking Questions	106
"After"—Improved Request	107–108
How to Write a Good Complaint Letter	109
Persuading Within Organizations	110–111
Preparing Persuasive Direct Mail and E-Mail Sales Messages	112–114
Persuasive Techniques in High- and Low-Context Cultures	115

Solution Masters

	Page Number in This Book
Applying Your Skills at Hands on Miami	591
10.1 Document for Analysis – Revision	593
10.2 Document for Analysis – Revision	594
10.3 Document for Analysis – Revision	596
10.4 Document for Analysis – Revision	598

10.5 Inviting a Speaker 600
10.6 Asking Beijing to Use Excel 601
10.7 Borrowing Suits for Interviews 602
10.8 A Helping Hand for College Expenses 603
10.9 Dear Senator or Representative 604
10.10 School Vending Machines Become Weighty Problem 606
10.11 Overcharged and Unhappy 608
10.12 Legal Costs for Sharing a Slice of Heaven 609
10.13 Botched Print Job 610
10.14 Honolulu Country Club Gets Scammed on Phony Toner Phoner 611
10.15 How About a 4-Day Week? 612
10.16 Providing Handheld GPS Devices to Hotel Guests 614
10.17 An Apple a Day 615
10.18 Keeping Track of Office Projects 616
10.19 Training Telecommuters 617
10.20 Dear Boss 618
10.21 Demanding Mandatory Tipping 619
10.22 Reducing Your Health Insurance Costs 621
10.23 And Now We Want Your Blood! 623
10.24 Cutting Overnight Shipping 627
10.25 Supporting Project H.E.L.P. 628
10.26 Revising Miserable Memo 629
10.27 Curbing Profanity on the Job 630
10.28 Sales Letter Analysis 632
10.29 Weighing In at Work 633
10.30 Adapting From Low Context to High Context 635
10.31 Promoting Your Product or Service 636
10.32 Preparing News for Your Local Newspaper 636
10.33 This Is New! 637

Answers to Chapter Review Questions

1. **What is persuasion? (Obj. 1)**

   Persuasion is the ability to use argument or discussion to change an individual's beliefs or actions.

2. **What four questions are receivers of persuasive messages likely to be asking themselves? (Obj. 2)**

   Receivers are likely to be asking, (1) Why should I? (2) What's in it for me? (3) What's in it for you? (4) Who cares?

3. **What are the four parts of successful persuasive messages? (Obj. 2)**

   (1) Gaining attention, (2) building interest, (3) reducing resistance, (4) motivating action

4. List six ways to gain attention in a persuasive message. (Obj. 2)

a. Describe a problem.
b. Make an unexpected statement.
c. Cite reader benefits.
d. Give a compliment.
e. Provide related facts.
f. Ask a stimulating question.

5. Why is a written favor request or action request more effective than a face-to-face request? (Obj. 3)

A written favor or action request is more effective because it can be more precise and controlled. The writer can think through the purpose and prepare a thoughtful message with carefully chosen words that convey exactly what was intended.

6 Name five or more examples of typical situations requiring persuasive claim messages (Obj. 3)

Persuasive claim messages typically involve damaged products, mistaken billing, inaccurate shipments, warranty problems, return policies, insurance snafus, faulty merchandise, and mistreatment of customers.

7. How can you reduce resistance in requesting favors, making claims, and delivering complaints? (Obj. 3)

Anticipate objections to your request and provide counterarguments. Suggest what might be lost if the request is not granted, but don't make it sound like a threat.

8. When is persuasion necessary in business messages flowing downward in an organization? (Obj. 4)

Directives from management flowing downward to employees may not require persuasion. However, requests that ask employees to participate outside their work roles would require persuasion.

9. When might persuasion be necessary in messages flowing upward? (Obj. 4)

Subordinates might find it necessary to use persuasion in convincing management to adopt a procedure, invest in a product, purchase new equipment, or make any other work-related requests that might be refused.

10. Before composing a letter to sell a product, what should the writer do? (Obj. 5)

The writer should study the product carefully, learning about its design, construction, raw materials, and manufacturing process. The writer should learn about its warranties, service, price, premiums, exclusivity, special appeals, and competition.

11. Name eight or more ways to attract attention in opening a sales message. (Obj. 5)

Present an offer, promise, quotation, proverb, fact, product feature, testimonial, startling statement, or personalized action setting.

12. How can a writer motivate action in a sales letter? (Obj. 5)

A writer can motivate action by offering a gift, promising an incentive, limiting the offer, setting a deadline, or guaranteeing satisfaction.

13. Name four areas of the world where the culture is generally considered to be high context. Name four areas of the world where the culture is generally considered to be low context. (Obj. 6)

Countries in Asia, Africa, South America, and much of the Middle East are considered high-context cultures. Australia and countries in Northern Europe, North America, and Scandinavia are generally considered low-context cultures.

14. How do persuasive messages in high- and low-context cultures differ? (Obj. 6)

In high-context cultures, persuasion is characterized by politeness and indirectness, a soft-sell approach, relationship efforts, and attention to aesthetics. In low-context cultures, persuasion typically includes superlatives and a hard-sell, direct approach.

15. List five or more topics that an organization might feature in a press release. (Obj. 6)

New products, new managers, new facilities, participation in community projects, awards given or received, joint ventures, donations, seminars, demonstrations

Answers to Critical Thinking Questions

1. The word persuasion turns some people off. What negative connotations can it have? (Obj. 1)

Many subconsciously equate persuasion with coercion or force. In fact, both persuasion and coercion share the same continuum of strategies that seek compliance. When done well, however, persuasion answers questions and provides information. Persuasion is nonadversarial. It does not command, force, coerce, or threaten. It uses argument and discussion to change beliefs and to motivate action.

2. What are some of the underlying motivations that prompt individuals to agree to requests that do not directly benefit themselves or their organizations? (Obj. 2)

Many people and organizations agree to requests to donate money, time, equipment, and expertise because they are interested in a project or because they see indirect benefits. For example, computer companies donate equipment to schools hoping that young users will become fans and subsequent customers. At the same time, their donation creates goodwill. Some requests are granted because of ego or feelings of guilt and duty. However, many companies genuinely want to give something back to their communities.

3. Why is it important to know your needs and have documentation when you make requests of superiors? (Obj. 4)

Knowing in concrete terms what is needed and having the documentation to support the request help employees make a favorable impression on superiors. When employees don't think through the situation and the possible negatives involved, they will not be taken seriously and will be considered unprepared and perhaps incompetent.

4. How are direct-mail sales messages and e-mail sales messages similar, and how are they different? (Obj. 5)

Direct-mail sales messages and e-mail sales messages are similar in that both use persuasion to attempt to influence beliefs or motivate action. Many of the techniques of the indirect strategy work for both. Direct mail involves messages delivered by the U.S. Postal Service. These carefully planned marketing campaigns are fairly expensive and often result in low response rates. E-mail sales messages are usually short and far less costly than direct mail. However, they, too, produce a low response rate.

5. Ethical Issue: What is puffery, and how can it be justified in marketing messages? Consider the following: Dr. Phil calls himself "America's most trusted relationship counselor." Rush Limbaugh claims to be "America's anchorman." Sony's Cyber-Shot camera advertisement says "Make time stand still."

Puffery consists of promotional claims that no one takes literally. It would be hard to prove that Dr. Phil is or is not America's most trusted relationship counselor or that Rush Limbaugh is or is not America's anchorman. What's more, everyone knows that Sony can't make time stand still. Such a statement is not considered a fact. It can't be proven true or false. Puffery can come in a variety of forms, such as the exaggerated, blustering, and boasting statements on which no reasonable buyer would rely. How can puffery be justified? Some argue that puffery functions to entertain. Others say it saves time and resources for buyers because it heightens awareness of products. Before consumers can buy products, they must be made aware of them. Advertising creates such awareness. Puffery is one way that advertisers can grab attention.

Activities

10.1 Document for Analysis: Going Bananas at 7-Eleven (Objs. 1-3)

Weaknesses

- Fails to think through what he wants this message to achieve.
- Should begin with a statement of the problem (brown bananas) and the company proposal to wrap them in plastic.
- Did not build interest or develop message in a coherent manner.
- Failed to articulate the request clearly or reduce possible resistance.
- Did not end with clear request or make any attempt to motivate action.
- Did not provide an end date or reason for it.

Revision

To: Members of the 7-Eleven Franchise Owners Association of Chicagoland
From: Nicholas Barajas <nicholas.barajas@hotmail.com>
Subject: Finding a Better Way to Sell Fresh Bananas
Cc:
Bcc:

Fresh Del Monte has suggested that 7-Eleven stores sell fresh bananas wrapped in plastic. Selling more bananas and other fresh foods is helping us build profits lost when cigarette sales declined. Although the wrapper may slow ripening and extend the shelf life of bananas, the wrapping may turn customers off. They may see it as an environmental issue and not like adding a plastic wrapper around something that comes naturally wrapped in the first place.

I suggest that we ask Fresh Del Monte to develop a wrapper that is biodegradable. Until we have a biodegradable wrap, we franchisees should not support the move to plastic-wrapped bananas. At the January 20 meeting of the 7-Eleven Franchise Owners Association of Chicagoland, I propose that we reject the plastic wraps in favor of a biodegradable wrap that could achieve the same purpose.

Please let me know by January 15 whether you agree that a biodegradable wrap would be more attractive to our customers. I look forward to seeing you at the next meeting.

Nick
[Full contact information]

10.2 Document for Analysis: Weak Favor Request (Obj. 3)

Weaknesses

- Fails to impress the reader or gain positive attention in the opening.
- Begins bluntly and directly by revealing favor request in first paragraph.
- Does not build interest with emotional or rational appeals.
- Shows lack of interest and perfunctory attitude by not knowing the exact title of Ms. Watkins' presentation.
- Misses opportunity to build rapport by failing to praise Ms. Watkins' previous presentation.
- Fails to emphasize direct or indirect benefits, such as an enthusiastic audience who would welcome Ms. Watkins' comments.
- Provides easy excuse for declining the request ("We know you are a very busy hospitality professional").
- Makes no attempt to anticipate objections and counter them.
- Sounds flippant and overly casual.
- Does not conclude with specific contact information such as a person and phone number to call.
- Fails to set a deadline coupled with a reason for responding.

Revision

Current date

Mr. Danielle Watkins
The Beverly Hills Hotel
9641 Sunset Boulevard
Beverly Hills, CA 90210

Dear Ms. Watkins:

News of the excellent presentation you made at your local chapter of the National Restaurant Association has reached us here in Los Angeles, and we are very impressed.

Running a successful restaurant operation, as we all know, is tough even on a good day. The intense pace is frenzied, from scrubbing the vegetables early in the morning to latching the front door at day's end. In all this haste, it's easy to lapse into food service faults that can land an operation in big trouble. Your presentation focusing on seven cardinal sins in the food service industry certainly captured our attention.

The LA chapter of the National Restaurant Association asked me to invite you to be the featured speaker at our May 25 dinner on the topic of "Avoiding the Seven Cardinal Sins in Food Service." By sharing your expertise, you can help other restaurant operators recognize and prevent potential problems involving discrimination, workplace safety, hiring practices, and so forth. Although we can offer you only a small honorarium of $200 plus your travel expenses, we can promise you a big audience of enthusiastic restaurateurs eager to hear your presentation.

Our relaxed group doesn't expect a formal address; they are most interested in hearing about best practices and solutions to prospective problems. To make your talk easy to organize, I have enclosed a list of questions our members submitted. Most talks are about 45 minutes long.

Can we count on you to join us for dinner at 7 p.m. on May 25 at the Oak Room of the Westin St. Francis Hotel in San Francisco? Just call me at (213) 351-1220 before March 1 so that I can let our members know you will be joining us.

Sincerely,

Enclosure

10.3 Document for Analysis: Weak Persuasive Memo Flowing Upward (Obj. 4)

Weaknesses

- Fails to provide a descriptive subject line.
- Opening paragraphs sound whining, negative, and critical.
- Fails to begin with an engaging statement or description of existing problem.
- Does not develop logical, focused description of problem or proposal.
- Fails to emphasize savings in highly readable form.
- Does not promote proposal with positive arguments.
- Fails to present counterarguments to possible objections.
- Fails to guide reader to a positive reaction to the proposal or the sample garment.
- Does not put forth a specific recommendation.
- Fails to close with a specific action to be taken and an end date. Omits motivation to act.

Revision

DATE: Current
TO: Bryanna Mazzetta, Vice President, Marketing
FROM: Luke Downey, Exhibit Manager
SUBJECT: Reducing a Major Expense at Trade Shows

At your suggestion, I've been searching for ways to reduce our trade show exhibition costs. One of our major expenses is the booth gift that we present to visitors.

At past trade shows we've given away a nine-color, silk-screened T-shirt designed by a high-priced, outside designer. Each shirt cost $23 to produce. However, I've located a Chinese supplier who can produce good-looking T-shirts, and the cost is only $6 each. Look at the savings:

2,000 silk-screen T-shirts @ $15	$46,000
2,000 cheaper T-shirts @$6	12,000
SAVINGS	$34,000

Please examine the enclosed T-shirt sample. You might expect a cheaper shirt to be less acceptable, but, as you can see, this shirt is quite presentable. What's more, it advertises our name just as well as the more expensive silk-screened T-shirts. We expect folks to wear this shirt when they work out, and the cheaper shirt serves the purpose just as well as the more expensive one.

With increasing travel costs and decreasing trade show budgets, we at Worldclass Trainer have had to look carefully at how we spend our limited funds for exhibitions. We have decreased the number of shows in which we participate, and we take fewer booth staffers. However, here is a significant way in which we can reduce a substantial expense.

To save $34,000 in exhibition costs, please authorize the purchase of 2,000 T-shirts for our next major trade show. If I receive your authorization before April 4, we can be sure of receiving a supply from our Chinese supplier for the September Las Vegas trade show.

Enclosure

10.4 Document for Analysis: Poor Claim Letter (Obj. 3)

Weaknesses

- Fails to open with a compliment, point of agreement, statement of the problem, or brief review of action taken to resolve problem.
- Sounds angry, hostile, and accusatory.
- Does not appeal to the receiver's sense of fairness or responsibility.
- Fails to emphasize benefits to reader (saving the receiver's money, retaining a customer, selling higher-priced model).
- Does not provide a logical explanation of what happened.
- Uses immoderate language (implies that the salesperson lied, calls the transaction a "ripoff").
- Fails to conclude with a specific action request.
- Does not make it easy for the reader to agree or respond.

Revision

Current date

Mr. Jason M. Amato
TEK Copier Solutions
13429 North 59th Avenue
Glendale, AZ 85307

Dear Mr. Amato:

The four Multifunction SX500 photocopiers that we purchased three months ago are inadequate for our volume of copying.

Although we told your salesperson, Gary Kazan, that we average 3,000 copies a day, he recommended the Multifunction SX500. This model appears to have been the wrong choice for our heavy use, and we are disappointed in its performance. Therefore, we would like to trade in our four SX500 copiers (about $2,500 each, as shown on the enclosed invoice) on the purchase of two Multifunction XX800 models (about $13,500 each).

When I discussed this possibility with your district manager, Victor Martineau, he said that we would be charged 50 percent depreciation if we traded in the four SX500 copiers. That amounts to $5,000, a considerable sum for three months of irregular copier use. We think a depreciation rate of 20 percent is more reasonable. Your company would profit in three ways:

- The Multifunction SX500 machines were used a short time, and they can be resold easily.
- You'll be making a sizable profit when we purchase two XX800 copiers.
- Your service technicians will save time by making fewer trips to repair our overworked SX500 machines.

We purchased the Multifunction SX500 copies in good faith on the recommendation of your salesperson. We feel that it is your responsibility to help us secure the proper model for our needs.

Please approve my request to trade in four Multifunction SX500 copiers for a value of $8,000 (allowing for 20 percent depreciation) toward the purchase of two Multifunction XX800 models. Just initial this letter showing your approval, and return it to me in the enclosed envelope before September 1. I'll work out the details of the new purchase with your salesperson.

Sincerely yours,

Enclosure

10.5 through 10.33 Solutions in the form of transparency masters are available at the end of this manual.

ZOOMING IN Part 1: Hands on Miami

Critical Thinking

- **Persuasion is vital to the CEO at Hands on Miami. Who must the CEO effectively persuade to ensure the success of the organization?**

  The CEO must use persuasion—and a bit of psychology—to guide the staff in developing new programs and maintaining current ones with a high level of enthusiasm and efficiency. The CEO must be persuasive in reporting to the board of directors so that it continues to support the organization's projects. To maintain favorable public attention, the CEO must persuade news organizations to present positive coverage of events. The CEO must persuade volunteers to join Hands on Miami and also persuade large and small businesses to sponsor events.

- **In your own career, when might you find it necessary to be persuasive?**

  Career success often depends on how effective you are at persuading people to believe, accept, and act on what you are saying. In your career you will need to be persuasive in many situations including interviewing for jobs, proposing ideas on the job, arguing for or against the ideas of your colleagues or management, justifying a loan for your new business, arguing for a salary increase, asking for flex time, requesting favors of any kind, and demanding adjustments for faulty products or poor service.

- **From your experience, what techniques are effective or ineffective in persuading others to accept your views?**

  Students may suggest that some of the following persuasive techniques are effective for them: laying a good foundation before making a request, waiting for the right time, asking for something small, presenting many facts, appealing to the receiver's emotions, being ready for resistance, offering to compromise, and providing an incentive to act. Ineffective techniques may include being blunt, sounding overbearing, failing to prepare for resistance, making threats, or punishing lack of compliance.

ZOOMING IN Part 2: Hands on Miami

Critical Thinking

- **Do you agree that corporations derive benefits from sponsoring volunteer programs and encouraging employees to participate?**

  Some students may say that they resent companies that coerce employees to "volunteer" for projects outside of work hours. Other students will support the view that socially responsible companies enhance the company's image by participating in community service programs. Students may agree that such programs raise employee morale, foster teamwork and leadership skills, and demonstrate good corporate citizenship.

- **The CEO of Hands on Miami write a letter persuading Miami corporations to use its fee-based Corporate Services Program. What direct benefits could be cited?**

  Direct benefits in a persuasive letter on this topic would be hard to develop. Corporations will receive no monetary profits, and employees receive no direct training or experience that would improve their skills on the job. Students might suggest that a good corporate image will help in the recruiting and retaining of quality employees.

- **In his persuasive letter, what indirect could be cited?**

  Although few direct benefits may be available, a number of indirect benefits can be used to promote the cause:

  1. Demonstration of good corporate citizenship
  2. Enhanced public image
  3. Building better employee work teams
  4. Boosting employee morale and job satisfaction

ZOOMING IN Your Turn: Applying Your Skills at Hands on Miami (Transparency available.)

[Hands on Miami stationery]

Current date

Dear Friends of Miami:

Don't know what to do with your old print cartridges or discarded cell phones? Hold on! Don't toss them out and let them end up in a landfill polluting the environment.

Hands on Miami has a better use for your discards. Donate them, and you can help change lives and strengthen our community. Our volunteer service programs will receive a credit of up to $10 for every used print cartridge and up to $20 for every cell phone your company recycles.

Estimates suggest that nearly 300 million ink cartridges are discarded every year. These cartridges are made of industrial plastics, and they take up to a thousand years to decompose. In North America over 40,000 tons of plastic are saved from landfills every year as a result of cartridge recycling. Cell phones are another item being tossed away. Hundreds of thousands of cell phones are no longer being used as new models flood the marketplace. Instead of letting them gather dust in a drawer, turn them in and help our Community Bridges program.

Why bother? With the money raised from your donations, Hands on Miami will be able to fund many projects that make a difference in our community. Your donations will support the volunteers who feed the homeless at Miami Rescue Mission, read bedtime stories to children at the Salvation Army, clean up Pelican Harbor, and work hard on countless other projects that make Miami a better place to live and work.

It's a win-win solution for everyone! You get rid of used ink cartridges and old cell phones while helping save the environment and the planet. We put to work the credits from your donations in projects that enrich our community's wellbeing. We're both winners!

Participating couldn't be easier. Your cartridges and cell phones may be dropped off at recycling centers, mailed in, or picked up. Just visit www.miamidaderecyling.org or call 1-800-534-9989 for details. Remember, your donation and support will change lives. *

Cordially,

Patrick Morris
President and CEO

* The URL and phone numbers are fictitious.

Discussion Material for ETHICAL INSIGHTS: What's Fair in Persuasion? Avoiding Common Logical Fallacies

This activity will give students a good opportunity to start discussing how ethics come into play when attempting to persuade. Encourage students to consider the three logical fallacies outlined in the Ethical Insights box, and assist students in finding others. You might lead them to the following Web sites:

Stephen's Guide to Logical Fallacies: http://www.datanation.com/fallacies/
The Fallacy Files: http://www.fallacyfiles.org/
Fallacies to Avoid: http://www.lloyd1.com/scsr/Logical.htm
Logical Fallacies Crossword Puzzle: http://www.epistemelinks.com/Humo/LFPuzz.htm
The Adam Smith Institute: http://www.adamsmith.org/logicalfallacies/
Logical Fallacies and the Art of Debate: http://www.csun.edu/~dgw61315/fallacies.html

Ethics Check Solutions

Ethics Check, page 305
Complaint Bullying
As any salesperson will tell you, some customers seem to believe that if they vent their anger and make a scene at the store, they are more likely to get their way by bullying and intimidating a fearful sales representative. Indeed, some sales staff may cave in, wishing to defuse the ruckus. Is it fair to resort to such tactics to get what one wants? Does the end justify the means?

Some students may say yes, anything is fair to obtain the desired result. However, they should be reminded that the saying "You catch more flies with honey" applies no less in business. Even if, say, a bad tempered customer gets his way, the business complies grudgingly and goodwill is lost. As a result, generous policies may be changed to avoid abuse and conflict, harming future customers. Buying and selling is an exchange that should be fair and satisfying to both parties, a win-win situation.

Ethics Check, page 314
Scare Tactics
Direct marketers sometimes resort to scare tactics, for example, to make us purchase alarm systems and subscribe to monitoring services. They may also appeal to our compassion and guilt before the holidays in soliciting money for the less fortunate. Are such emotional appeals ethical?

Perceptive students will realize that such appeals are not unethical, as long as they are executed truthfully, not with the intent to deceive. It is not wrong to invoke recent burglary statistics to make a case for an alarm and monitoring system if these numbers are correct. Similarly, before the holidays when most people take stock of their lives and the year they've had, it's natural to remember charitable giving.

Photo Essay Solutions

Photo Essay, page 296
The effectiveness of the Domino's "pizza turnaround" campaign rests upon the ability to establish credibility and share solutions. When executives openly admitted the pizza had a reputation for blandness, the claim was immediately credible with consumers who had provided that negative feedback for years. Additionally, Domino's used testimonials from customers and expert chefs alike to establish the product's flavorlessness and dire need for new ingredients. Over a two-year period, expert chefs tested dozens of cheeses, sauces, and crust-seasoning blends to remake the pizza. Domino's also let customers provide input and take part in the solution. Allowing others in on the solution promotes greater buy-in and trust that the solution will work. The rebranding effort appears to have paid off, at least for the short term; the Ann Arbor-based pizza chain doubled revenues in the first quarter after unveiling its new core product.

Photo Essay, page 313
Student responses will vary, but research conducted on this highway safety video from the South Wales Police Department was conclusive: the emotional impact of watching a happy occasion turn to injury and death was highly persuasive. A full 86 percent of viewers said the PSA was extremely effective; 80 percent said they would be less likely to text and drive after watching the video. Safety and health organizations use emotional and rational appeals equally well, and safety messages use a mix of staggering statistics and scare tactics to persuade audiences—especially teens. However, a sales letter can never be as effective at making emotional appeals as this terrifyingly realistic video by filmmaker Peter Watkins-Hughes.

Video Resources

Instructors may show the *Bridging the Gap* video from Video Library 2, *Hard Rock Café* or *Innovation, Learning, and Communication: A Study of Yahoo.* Instructors will find a complete discussion guide and activity solution for this video presented in this Instructor's Manual.

Chapter 11 LECTURE NOTES AND TEACHING SUGGESTIONS

Report and Research Basics

CHAPTER SYNOPSIS

An effective flow of information is the life blood of business organizations. Reports serve multiple purposes ranging from simply keeping superiors updated and creating a record to complex studies that are designed to facilitate problem solving and decision making in the organization. Chapter 11 discusses the functions, strategies, writing style, and formats of typical business reports. Students are introduced to collecting data, documenting sources, and integrating data ethically in reports.

Since most research today is conducted electronically, this chapter focuses on online databases, the Web, and other resources for business writers. The chapter addresses primary and secondary sources, and much attention is devoted to avoiding plagiarism. Useful paraphrasing exercises are designed to train students to give credit to sources where credit is due. The chapter also provides tools for creating meaningful and interesting report graphics.

Most workers in business organizations today write some type of report on a regular basis, usually informal short reports, often distributed as a simple e-mail message. Occasionally workers collaborate in teams on larger-scale projects. This is why students need to acquire the considerable skills involved in planning, researching, composing, and presenting business reports. This report and research chapter will help students to develop report writing skills that will impress their future employers.

LEARNING OBJECTIVES

1. Describe basic features of business reports, including functions, strategies (indirect or direct), writing style, and formats.
2. Apply the 3-x-3 writing process to business reports to create well-organized documents that show a firm grasp of audience and purpose.
3. Find, evaluate, and use print and electronic secondary sources.
4. Understand how to generate and use primary data while avoiding researcher bias.
5. Comprehend fast-changing communication technology: the Web, electronic databases, and other resources for business writers and researchers.
6. Recognize the purposes and techniques of documentation in business reports, and avoid plagiarism.

7. Create meaningful and interesting graphics; display numeric information in the appropriate graphic form; and skillfully generate, use, and convert data to visual aids.

WHAT'S NEW IN THIS CHAPTER

- Created a new a real-world three-part business case study illustrating the need for research in business, particularly before launching a startup, to tie chapter concepts to business practice.
- Added new ethics checks highlighting dilemmas posed by research strategies and modern technology to reinforce a strong focus on business ethics.
- Introduced new communicators presented in the spotlight feature to offer students perspectives and comments by business practitioners.
- Expanded the discussion of scope and limitations to clarify for students how to establish the scale and extent of their research assignments.
- Added or changed at least 40 percent of the end-of-chapter activities to provide students and instructors with new and up-to-date examples demonstrating chapter content.

LECTURE OUTLINE

I. Understanding Report Essentials (p. 337)

PowerPoint slides 1-8

A. Report Functions and Types
Informational reports present data without comment or recommendations.
Analytical reports provide data, analysis, and conclusions.

B. Organizational Strategies
The organizational pattern of a business report is determined by the reader's expectations and the content of the report.

Figure 11.1 Audience Analysis and Report Organization
PowerPoint slide 9

1. **Direct Strategy**
The direct pattern places conclusions and recommendations at the beginning of the report.
Informational reports are usually arranged directly.
Analytical reports may be arranged directly if the readers are supportive or familiar with the topic.

Figure 11.2 Informational Report—Letter Format
Figure 11.3 Analytical Report—Memo Format

2. **Indirect Strategy**
The indirect pattern places the conclusions and recommendations at the end of the report.
Use this pattern when readers are unfamiliar with the problem or when readers may be persuaded, disappointed, or hostile toward the report's finding.

Let's Discuss

Is it better to use the direct or indirect pattern for the following business reports?

a. An informational report from a travel agent to a sales executive comparing the costs for a hosting a trade show in three different locations: Las Vegas, Miami, and Toronto.
Direct; the reader is informed, supportive, and eager to have the results first.

b. An analytical report from a city manager to a supportive city mayor recommending a site for a new city park.
Direct; reader is familiar with topic and supportive.

c. An analytical report from a senior manager to subordinate employees presenting cost-reduction strategies to be implemented next month.
Indirect; readers will need to be persuaded and may be unhappy with the recommendations.

C. **Writing Style**
Use a formal writing style for theses, research studies, and controversial or complex reports.
Use an informal writing style for short, routine reports; reports for familiar audiences; noncontroversial reports; and most reports for company insiders.

Figure 11.4 Report-Writing Styles

D. **Report Formats**
Letter format—for short, informal reports addressed outside an organization
Memo and E-mail format—for short, informal reports within organizations
Manuscript format—for longer, more formal reports
Preprinted forms—for repetitive data that can be summarized on preprinted forms with standardized headings
Digital format—for distributing reports in a digital form, not in hard copy

PowerPoint slides 10-15

II. **Applying the 3-x-3 Writing Process to Reports (p. 343)**

PowerPoint slide 16

Step 1: Analyze the problem and purpose.
Step 2: Anticipate the audience and issues.
Step 3: Prepare a work plan.
Step 4: Conduct research.
Step 5: Organize, analyze, interpret, and illustrate the data.

Step 6: Compose the first draft.
Step 7: Revise, proofread, and evaluate.

A. Analyzing the Problem and Purpose
Scope—What issues or elements will be investigated?
Significance—Why is the topic worth investigating at this time?

B. Anticipating the Audience and Issues
1. What do my readers need to know about this topic?
2. What do they already know?
3. What is their educational level?
4. How will they react to this information?
5. Which sources will they trust?
6. How can I make this information readable, believable, and memorable?

Break the major investigative problem into subproblems, called *factoring*.

Let's Discuss

Why is it important to ask the questions shown above about the report's primary and secondary readers?

The answers to these questions determine the direction and depth of your report. They will reveal how much background material to include in your report, how much detail to add, whether to write formally or informally, what tone to use, and how to organize and present the information.

C. Preparing a Work Plan
Statement of the problem (based on key background/contextual information)
Statement of the purpose including scope, significance, and limitations
Research strategy including a description of potential sources and methods of collecting data
Tentative outline that factors the problem into manageable chunks
Work schedule

Figure 11.5 Work Plan for a Formal Report
PowerPoint slide 17

III. Gathering Information From Secondary Sources (p. 349)

Figure 11.6 Gathering and Selecting Report Data

A. Print Resources
1. **Books**
Provide historical, in-depth data
Located through card catalogs and online catalogs

2. **Periodicals**
The Readers' Guide to Periodical Literature offers an index of general-interest magazines.
Electronic indexes, stored in digital databases, include references, abstracts, and full-text articles from magazines, journals, and newspapers.

PowerPoint slide 18

B. Electronic Databases
Begin secondary research with electronic databases.
A database is a collection of information stored electronically so that it is accessible by computer and is digitally searchable.

Figure 11.7 ABI/INFORM (ProQuest) Search Result
PowerPoint slide 19

IV. Gathering Information From Primary Sources (p. 351)

A. Surveys
Select the survey population carefully.
Explain why the survey is necessary
Consider incentives.
Limit the number of questions.
Use questions that produce quantifiable answers.
Avoid leading or ambiguous questions.
Make it easy for respondents to return the survey.
Conduct a pilot study.

Figure 11.8 Preparing a Survey
PowerPoint slide 20

B. Interviews
Locate an expert.
Prepare for the interview.
Maintain a professional attitude.
Make your questions objective and friendly.
Watch the time.
End graciously.

C. Observation and Experimentation
1. **Observations**
Plan ahead.
Arrive early to introduce yourself and set up equipment.
Request permission beforehand.
Take notes on the events, actions, and setting.

2. **Experimentation**
   Valid experiments require research designs and careful attention to matching experimental and control groups.

D. The World Wide Web

- Wikis enable users to create and change Web pages.
- Behind firewalls, many wikis help technical experts and other specialists collaborate.
- Digital content on the Web can be accessed from anywhere using personal digital assistants (PDAs) and browser-enabled smartphones.
- Use specialized tools such as Google, Bing, Yahoo Search, AOL, and Ask.com to search for data effectively.

Figure 11.9 Web Search Tools for Business Writers
Figure 11.10 Business.com
PowerPoint slides 21, 22

1. **Applying Internet Search Strategies and Techniques**
   - Use two or three search tools.
   - Know your search tool.
   - Understand case sensitivity.
   - Use nouns as search words and up to six to eight words in a query.
   - Combine keywords into phrases.
   - Omit articles and prepositions.
   - Use wild cards.
   - Learn basic Boolean search strategies.
   - Bookmark the best.
   - Keep trying.
   - Repeat your search a week later.

2. **Evaluating Web Sources**
   Specific questions to ask as you examine a site:
   1. How current is the information?
   2. Who publishes or sponsors this Web page, and what makes the presenter an authority?
   3. What is the purpose of the content? To entertain, inform, convince, or sell?
   4. How reliable and accurate does the content seem to be?

   PowerPoint slides 23, 24

V. Documenting Information (p. 361)

Definition: *Documentation* is giving credit to your information sources.

PowerPoint slides 25-28

A. Recognizing the Purposes of Documentation

A properly documented report:
Strengthens your argument
Protects yourself against charges of plagiarism
Instructs the reader

B. Distinguishing Between Academic Documentation and Business Practices

College term papers and other academic writing require careful documentation.
Business reports do not require the same level of documentation as academic writing.

C. Learning What to Document

Another person's ideas, opinions, examples, or theory
Any facts, statistics, graphs, and drawings that are not common knowledge
Quotations of another person's actual spoken or written words
Paraphrases of another person's spoken or written words

D. Developing Good Research Habits

1. **Manual Notetaking**

   Record all major ideas on separate note cards.
   Include all publication information and quotations.
   Use one card color for direct quotes and another for paraphrases and summaries.
   Put the original source material aside when you are summarizing or paraphrasing.

2. **Electronic Notetaking**

   Set up a new folder on your hard drive, USB flash drive, CD-RW, or computer disk.
   Create subfolders for major sections.
   Highlight Web material, and paste it into a document in an appropriate folder.
   Include all publication data.
   Consider archiving on a memory stick those Web pages or articles used in your research in case the data must be verified.

E. Practicing the Fine Art of Paraphrasing

Read the original material intently to comprehend its full meaning.
Write your own version without looking at the original.
Avoid repeating the grammatical structure of the original and merely replacing words with synonyms.
Reread the original to be sure you covered the main points but did not borrow specific language.

F. Knowing When and How to Quote

To provide objective background data and establish the severity of a problem as seen by experts
To repeat identical phrasing because of its precision, clarity, or aptness
To duplicate exact wording before criticizing

G. Using Citation Formats

Common citation formats are those presented by the Modern Language Association (MLA) and the American Psychological Association (APA). See Appendix C.

Let's Discuss

You forgot to record the source of some terrific information about leading a focus group you found on the Web and pasted into a Word document. Can you use this information in your report anyway?

No, you can't use this source unless you find the Web site where it came from. Not indicating a source or providing incorrect information would be wrong. You could try finding the Web site again by inserting a string of search terms from the Web page you downloaded into one or more search engines.

VI. Creating Effective Visual Aids (p. 364)

A. Matching Graphics and Objectives

Figure 11.11 Matching Graphics to Objectives

PowerPoint slides 29-33

1. **Tables**
   Place titles and labels at the top of the table.
   Arrange items in a logical order.
   Provide clear headings for rows and columns.
   Identify the units in which figures are given.
   Use *N/A* (not available) for missing data.
   Shade alternate lines or leave a blank line after groups of five.
   Place tables as close as possible to the place where they are mentioned in the text.

Figure 11.12 Table Summarizing Precise Data

2. **Bar Charts**
   Keep the length and width of each bar and segment proportional.
   Include a total figure in the middle of the bar or at its end if the figure helps the reader and does not clutter the chart.
   Start dollar or percentage amounts at zero.
   Place the first bar at some distance (usually half the amount of space between bars) from the y axis.
   Avoid showing too much information, thus producing clutter and confusion.
   Place each bar chart as close as possible to the place where it is mentioned in the text.

Figure 11.13 Vertical Bar Chart
Figure 11.14 Horizontal Bar Chart
Figure 11.15 Grouped Bar Chart
Figure 11.16 Segmented 100% Bar Chart

3. **Line Charts**
Begin with a grid divided into squares.
Arrange the time component horizontally across the bottom
Arrange values for the other variable vertically.
Draw small dots at the intersections to indicate each value at a given year.
Connect the dots and add color if desired.
To prepare a segmented (surface) chart, plot the first value across the bottom; add the next item to the first figures for every increment; for the third item, add its value to the total for the first two items.

Figure 11.17 Simple Line Chart
Figure 11.18 Multiple Line Chart
Figure 11.19 Segmented Line (Area) Chart

4. **Pie Charts**
Make the biggest wedge appear first.
Include the actual percentage or absolute value for each wedge.
Use four to six segments for best results.
Draw radii from the center.
Distinguish wedges with color, shading, or cross-hatching.
Keep all the labels horizontal.

Figure 11.20 Pie Chart

5. **Flowcharts**
Ovals designate the beginning and end of a process.
Diamonds designate decision points.
Rectangles represent major activities or steps.

Figure 11.21 Flowchart

6. **Organization Charts**
Organization charts show chain of command and may illustrate a company's structure.
Organization charts may be organized by the work being performed in each job or by the hierarchy of decision making.

7. **Photographs, Maps, and Illustrations**
Photos add authenticity and provide a visual record.
Maps depict activities or concentrations geographically.
Illustrations indicate how an object looks or operates.

B. Incorporating Graphics in Reports
Evaluate the audience, considering the reader, content, schedule, and budget.
Use restraint and don't overuse color or decorations.
Be accurate and ethical.

Introduce a graph meaningfully. Refer to every graphic in the text and place it close to the point where it is mentioned.
Choose an appropriate caption or title style.

Lecture Transparencies
(available in a separate packet and at http://www.meguffey.com)

Report and Research Basics Acetates	**Transparency Number**
Report Functions and Types	116
Ten Truths You Should Know About Reports	117
Audience Analysis and Report Organization—The Direct Pattern	118
Audience Analysis and Report Organization—The Indirect Pattern	119
Informational Report—Letter Format	120
Analytical Report—Memo Format	121
Analytical Report—Manuscript Format	122
Applying the Writing Process to Reports	123
Getting Information from Secondary Sources	124
Tips for Searching the Web	125
Evaluating Web Resources	126
Documenting Data	127
Creating Effective Visual Aids	128

Solution Masters

Solutions and discussion material for the Chapter 11 activities are found in this lecture outline only. Solution masters are not available.

Answers to Chapter Review Questions

1. **What are the main purposes of business reports? (Obj. 1)**

   Although reports vary in length, content, format, and formality, they all have one or more of these purposes in common: to convey information, answer questions, and solve problems.

2. **Describe the writing style of typical business reports. (Obj. 1)**

   Reports can range from informal to formal, depending on their purpose, audience, and setting. Some consist of mere bulleted lists and are informal, whereas others may be lengthy research reports that tend to be formal. An informal style includes active voice, contractions, and the use of the first person singular or plural. Increasingly, even formal reports are written in an informal writing style, no longer using awkward third-person references to the authors or passive voice.

3. Name five common report formats. (Obj. 1)

Five commonly used report formats include:
1. Letter
2. Memo
3. Manuscript
4. Printed forms
5. Electronic slides

4. List the seven steps in the report-writing process. (Obj. 2)

Seven steps in the report-writing process include:
1. Analyzing the problem and purpose
2. Anticipating the audience and issues
3. Preparing a work plan
4. Researching data
5. Organizing, analyzing, interpreting, and illustrating data
6. Composing first draft
7. Revising, proofreading, and evaluating

5. What is a statement of purpose, and what function does it serve? (Obj. 2)

A statement of purpose is a written statement that defines the focus of a report. It provides a standard that keeps the project on target. Many reports require only a simple statement of purpose, such as *to study recycling options at the company's satellite office*, or *to compare the cost of traveling to the cost of teleconferencing equipment.*

6. Compare primary data and secondary data. Give an original example of each. (Obj. 3)

Primary data are generated from firsthand experience, observation, and experimentation. Secondary data come from reading what others have experienced and observed. Collecting data for a report on selling techniques by watching exceptional sales people results in primary data. Reading about sales techniques produces secondary data.

7. Name at least two of the top four business databases and identify their chief strengths. (Obj. 3, 5)

The four best resources for business writers that you can find in most libraries are, in this order: ABI/INFORM (ProQuest), Factiva (Dow Jones), LexisNexis Academic, and Academic Search Elite (EBSCO). Electronic databases offer unparalleled convenience and feature mostly up-to-date, high-quality journal or newspaper and magazine articles.

8. List four major sources of primary information. (Obj. 4)

1. Surveys
2. Interviews
3. Observation
4. Experimentation

9. How can you ensure that your survey will be effective and appeal to as many respondents as possible? (Obj. 4)

a. Explain why the survey is necessary.
b. Consider incentives.
c. Limit the number of questions.
d. Use question that produce quantifiable answers.
e. Avoid leading or ambiguous questions.
f. Make it easy for respondents to return the survey.
g. Conduct a pilot study.

10. Why are your professors likely to discourage your use of Wikipedia, blogs, and many other sources found on the Web as sources in your reports? (Obj. 5)

The biggest problem with wikis, blogs, and other team-generated content is that they usually don't last and, therefore, are not always verifiable as sources. In contrast to print publications and peer-reviewed journals, the content on the Web is often fleeting. Also, the quality of the contributions is inconsistent at best. In addition, relying on encyclopedias amounts to lazy scholarship and poor research skills.

11. Can any single search engine index all Web pages? How can you optimize your search of Web sources? (Obj. 5)

No single search engine or directory can come close to indexing all pages on the Internet. However, if you try a multiple-search site such as Dogpile, you can save much time because its metasearch technology compares the results of several major search engines, eliminates duplicates, and then ranks the best hits for you.

12. Describe what documentation is, and why it is necessary in reports. (Obj. 6)

Documentation means revealing and crediting sources of information. Careful documentation (a) strengthens the argument of the report, (b) protects the report writer, and (c) instructs the reader so that he or she may undertake additional investigation. (You may want to include a discussion with regard to plagiarism. Students must realize that including direct quotes is acceptable when such quotations strengthen the point being made. But writers must credit the original source.)

13. In what way is documentation of sources in colleges and universities different from business practices? (Obj. 6)

Establishing solid research and documentation habits is important, but in business the handling of sources and citations is not as strict as it is in academic writing. However, be careful to always keep copies of your sources, so that if asked, you can present evidence.

14. Briefly compare the advantages and disadvantages of illustrating data with charts (bar and line) versus tables. (Obj. 7)

Bar and line charts provide a visual overview or impression of trends, but they lack exactness. Tables provide precise figures and values, but important points and trends are not immediately visible.

15. Name five techniques you can use to ensure that visual aids do not distort graphic information. (Obj. 7)

Researchers must not misrepresent data or distort the graphics they create. To provide ethical charts and graphics follow these tips:

1. Pick the right visual aid for the job.
2. Make sure the graphic highlights the most important information.
3. Include all relevant data.
4. Keep your visual information readable by avoiding clutter.
5. Use the correct scale and spacing for your graphics.

Answers to Critical Thinking Questions

1. Howard Schultz, Starbucks president and CEO, has been described as a "classic entrepreneur: optimistic, relentless, mercurial, and eager to prove people wrong." Before Starbucks' latest stumbles, Schultz successfully followed his gut instinct, not established management practices. Unlike other executives, until recently he was not interested in cost control, advertising, and customer research. "I despise research," he said. "I think it's a crutch. But people smarter than me pushed me in this direction, and I've gone along." Starbucks continues to be the most followed company on Facebook. It made $300 million in profit last year.i What do you think Howard Schultz meant when he called consumer research a "crutch"? Can you explain why the corporate maverick hates it so much? (Obj. 4)

Schultz has been called an iconoclast for going against the grain of established business. His unconventional strategy worked as long as Starbucks was expanding at an astounding rate domestically and abroad. Schultz seems to be a hands-on guy who prefers weekly visits to 25 Starbucks stores to consumer surveys. He likes to talk to his baristas, managers, and customers in person. Lately, however, Schultz has been forced to retreat from his past practices and accept the role of a more conventional executive.

2. Why must report writers anticipate their audiences and issues? (Obj. 2)

Reports typically have more than one reader, even though one person may originally have solicited the report. Others in the organizations may eventually read the document, including upper managers and those in other departments. Candid statements to one audience may be offensive to another. Because reports may have primary and secondary audiences, writers must consider what readers need to know; what they already know; how well educated they are; how they will react to the information in the report; which sources they will trust; and how to make their report information readable, believable, and memorable.

3. Is information obtained on the Web as reliable as information obtained from journals, newspapers, and magazines? (Obj. 3)

Information obtained from professional journals and reputable newspapers and magazines has generally been authenticated, edited, and reviewed. Professional journals are also "refereed," which means that the articles have undergone stiff peer review. Thus, the information obtained from these sources is generally considered to be valid, objective, and credible. However, information from the Web is questionable. Anyone can publish on the Web, and the "information" may be propaganda or advertising or worse. It is wise to scrutinize all Web data carefully. Lastly, Web information found today may be gone tomorrow.

4. Some people say that business reports never contain footnotes. If you were writing your first report for a business and you did considerable research, what would you do about documenting your sources? (Obj. 5)

Although some people do assert that business reports never contain documentation, it's dangerous to avoid revealing your sources. The best plan is to check with your supervisor or look in the files to see how previous reports have been documented. If you don't see evidence of sources, it's best to make a list of all your sources and be prepared to submit it should someone ask where the information came from. Even if your company does not have a general documentation style, you should carefully note where your information came from. Another possibility is to note your sources with textual comments, such as this: "According to an article on page B1 in The Wall Street Journal on December 16, 2006, the rate of increase was . . . ." Never assume that giving credit to or documenting your sources is unnecessary.

5. Ethical Issue: You are conducting one-hour-long interviews with high-level banking executives using a questionnaire featuring open-ended questions (qualitative survey) for a market research firm. You receive $75 per completed interview when you deliver legible notes. You tape the talks for accuracy, but then you transcribe the conversations, and you are not required to hand in the tapes. Busy executives are reluctant to sit down with you; you struggle to find the ten top bankers you were contracted to interview. The other interviewer hired for this study tells you that she invented at least two interviews and suggests you do the same. Should you follow her example? Should you not follow her example but stay silent, or should you tell the supervisor that your colleague has been falsifying survey results? (Obj. 4)

Qualitative surveys are expensive and elaborate. Because the sample size is usually small, each interview counts. If even one or two interviews are invented, they skew the results and may invalidate the conclusions. Getting paid for a service not rendered is, of course, unethical. Not only should the example of the dishonest colleague not be followed, but the interviewer should also disclose the nefarious activities of the other interviewer to the supervisor to ensure the integrity of the study.

Activities

11.1 Report Functions, Writing Styles, and Formats (Obj. 1)

a. *Function:* analytical; strategy: indirect; format: manuscript with cover letter

b. *Function:* analytical; strategy: direct or indirect; format: PowerPoint or PDF slide decks, a very condensed new report style formatted as an appealing slideshow to be e-mailed to the client

c. *Function:* informational; strategy: direct; format: memo or e-mail

d. *Function:* analytical; strategy: direct; format: memo or e-mail

e. *Function:* mostly informational; strategy: direct; format: memo or e-mail

f. *Function:* informational; strategy: direct; format: letter

g. *Function:* analytical; strategy: direct; format: manuscript and/or slide deck

11.2 Collaborative Project: Report Portfolio (Obj. 1)

Free, full-text corporate annual reports in PDF format are easy to find on the Web and in electronic databases. Students may want to consult LexisNexis for SEC Filings or Mergent Online for official annual reports to shareholders. On the Web, the SEC provides a searchable database of SEC filings at http://www.secinfo.com; annual reports are also available at http://www.reportgallery.com.

11.3 Data Forms and Questions (Obj. 3)

a. *Data forms:* background or historical, statistical, individual or group opinion *Question:* Will I need to add to the available data?

b. *Data forms*: expert opinion, individual or group opinion, organizational (business Web sites, images retrieved with a search engine on the Internet, business database articles from newspapers and magazines) *Question:* Is the source trustworthy and representative of business customs?

c. *Data form:* statistical *Questions:* Is the source reliable? How were the figures derived? How recent are they?

d. *Data forms:* historical and organizational, expert opinion *Questions:* Are the sources reliable? What are their biases? Are they available?

e. *Data form:* Expert opinion *Questions:* Who are the experts? Are their opinions in print? Can they be interviewed? Do we have in-house experts?

11.4 Problem, Purpose, and Scope Statements (Obj. 2)

a. *Problem question:* Does the introduction of hands-free devices significantly influence traffic accident rates?

   Purpose: To study accident statistics to determine whether hands-free devices lower the incidence of traffic crashes.

   Scope: The report will discuss cell phone bans in the United States and only in jurisdictions where bans are strictly enforced and violators are cited
   Limitations: Statistical information from other nations will be omitted because comparisons between very heterogeneous countries with wildly divergent accident rates would potentially skew the results.

b. *Problem question:* Which persuasive techniques should closers avoid to improve the overall customer ratings of the negotiation process?

   Purpose: To examine current persuasive strategies and improve sales techniques to lower the number of complaints and achieve higher customer ratings in after-sales surveys.

   Scope: This report will focus on those sales strategies that raise the ire of most customers—that is, understating the value of a trade-in, switching between absolute numbers and monthly payments, and hiding the cost of optional accessories.
   Limitations: We will not include after-sale complaints stemming from contacts between customers and financing representatives.

c. *Problem question:* Should the town council consider uprooting the trees and planting a sturdier variety, one that will more likely withstand ice storms and provide more shade for the merchants and their customers?

   Purpose: To recommend whether the town council should invest in uprooting the pecan trees and planting honey locust trees that will be sturdier and provide more shade.

   Scope: In our report we will solely discuss the benefits of the honey locust trees.
   Limitation: We are omitting other types of resilient trees because honey locust trees have already been shown to prosper in our climate and, therefore, will help save us money on additional research and testing of other varieties.

d. *Problem question:* Should Thin Crust hire a laboratory or a consultant to change its food processing and rewrite its package labels to meet new trans fat requirements imposed by the FDA?

   Purpose: To investigate how potential trans fat bans and FDA regulations might affect Thin Crust's food production and package labels. To determine whether a laboratory or a consultant is necessary to comply with the new regulations.

Scope: The report will address only those production processes that include trans fats. Luckily, several of Thin Crust's product lines are already trans fat free.

e. *Problem question:* How can REI train telephone service reps to motivate customers to increase the number of items ordered per call?

Purpose: To investigate and recommend training procedures aimed at motivating telephone service reps to increase the number of items ordered by customers.

Scope: The report will examine several techniques that range from a polite question close to the conclusion of the call to offering incentives such as rebates, discount coupons, and time-sensitive offers.

11.5 Problem and Purpose Statements (Obj. 2)

Sample problem: Our business is losing customers because we are one of the few neighborhood coffee bars that don't offer free Wi-Fi service to our patrons. If the expense for the equipment is not too great and wireless access does not expose us to any liability or security risks, perhaps we could install a broadband connection and routers to blanket the premises with a strong signal.

Problem question: Should we provide free Wi-Fi access to our patrons?

Report purpose: To explore the feasibility of installing a broadband connection and routers.

11.6 Plagiarism, Paraphrasing, and Citing Sources (Obj. 6)

a. *Weakness:* The paraphrased text follows the original too closely in sentence structure and word choice. Only a few words and phrases here and there were changed. The following example is paraphrased correctly. The writer recasts the idea and wording of the original into his or her own language and sentence structure.

Improved Passage: Casual online games offer several advantages compared to games designed for Xbox and similar consoles. They are less risky to develop, cost less to make (below $200,000), and don't require physical copies and packaging. Rather, they allow more creative freedom and shorter production cycles ranging from six to twelve months.

b. *Weakness:* Despite the parenthetical reference (Henderson 44), the passage is plagiarized. It follows the original too closely in sentence structure and word choice. Only a few words here and there were changed.

The following passage is paraphrased correctly. The writer recasts the idea and wording of the original into his or her own language and sentence structure.

Improved Passage: Cellular phone use around the world is increasing rapidly as a result of decreasing computing costs. Half of all new phones are now wireless. Poorer countries are experiencing the most rapid development because they can move straight to cellular without focusing on the outdated technology of landlines (Henderson 44).

c. *Weakness:* The paraphrased text follows the original too closely in sentence structure and word choice. Only a few words here and there were changed.
The following example is paraphrased correctly. The writer recasts the idea and wording of the original into his or her own language and sentence structure.

Improved Passage. Internet users told Yahoo to feature world news on its portal, but in reality during the day visitors to the company's Web site flocked to entertainment news, which was also prominently displayed. In the evening. when they were online to manage their money, users then eagerly accessed financial information.

d. *Weakness:* The paraphrased text follows the original too closely in sentence structure and word choice. Only a few words here and there were changed.
The following example is paraphrased correctly. The writer recasts the idea and wording of the original into his or her own language and sentence structure.

Improved Passage: In offering more upscale fashions, Wal-Mart wanted to rival Target, a large but hip retailer successful in selling both household items and appealing, youthful apparel to its customers. A similar foray into more trendy clothing lines, represented by Metro7 for women, spelled trouble for Wal-Mart after the company tried to duplicate the booming sales it experienced at a few hundred stores in all of its 3,000 outlets.

11.7 Factoring and Outlining a Problem (Obj. 2)

Outline Key

I. Should the Virgin America tour training program be located in Burbank?
  A. Does Burbank have adequate access to air travel?
  B. Does Burbank have available school buildings?
  C. Would Burbank officials cooperate with us?

II. What entertainment areas are available to serve as training sites?
  A. Does NBC offer training seminars, guest speakers, and other resources for tour operators?
  B. Would Magic Mountain allow us to conduct training there?
  C. Would Griffith Park allow tour trainees to practice there?

III. Who could be invited to serve on an advisory committee?
  A. Would representatives of the travel community be interested?
  B. Would executives of other major airlines be willing to serve with JAL people?
  C. How could these people be motivated to participate?

11.8 Developing a Work Plan (Obj. 2)

If your students are writing a long report, you will want to have them complete this exercise as part of their long report assignment.

11.9 Using Secondary Sources (Obj. 3)

The biggest difference will be in the number of relevant retrievals. Much of what search engines produce is marginally or not relevant at all. A metasearch site will list drastically reduced results in thematic clusters that are more likely to be helpful.

11.10 Creating an Online Survey With SurveyMonkey or Zoomerang (Obj. 4)

Students are asked to conduct primary research in the form of online surveys. SurveyMonkey and Zoomerang are user-friendly and will hone students' primary research skills. The goal is to duplicate some of the results of the Sodexo study on campus and to support the recommendations with survey data. An informational memo or e-mail could be assigned summarizing the findings. After students have studied Chapters 12 and 13, they could be asked to complete more analytical tasks such as feasibility reports or proposals.

11.11 Researching Secondary Sources: Debunking Myths About Young People (Obj. Secondary Data: Hot Trends in the Tech Industry (Objs. 3)

The assignment can be a short informational report sent by e-mail or, if additional sources are added, an analytical report. Some useful additional sources are listed in Your Task. The analytical report should suggest ways advertisers could successfully connect with teens, the target population.

11.12 Finding Secondary Data: The Future of Tech (Objs. 3, 5, and 6)

MIT's Technology Review is a treasure trove of business and tech information in a very readable style and format. Any of the topics suggested in this activity are sufficiently represented on the Internet. For example, students should be able to find trade publications and even academic sources on the thumb generation and its use of handheld devices, most notably the worldwide studies on the role of the thumb today by British researcher of cyber culture, Sadie Plant. Business articles about WiMAX and near-field communication also abound. Individual writers could compile separate informational, direct e-mails or memos on each new trend. Alternatively, a team could present three (or more) hot trends they may find in their research in a group memo or e-mail to Jack Holden.

11.13 Researching and Evaluating Data: How Wired Is the World? (Objs. 3, 5)

The first part of the assignment requires students critically to examine statistical information they find on the Web and draw conclusions about its validity and credibility. As for the second part of the assignment, the effort to bring the Internet revolution and computing to developing nations is being waged on a broad front. The United Nations held a conference in Tunisia discussing Internet use in developing countries. Companies such as Google and News Corporation have donated money to develop a low-cost computing device running open-source software Linux.

MIT is working to create a bare-bones device that can be hand-cranked to recharge its battery. Working in teams or individually, students should find ample information on low-cost computer projects. This assignment could be expanded into an informational or analytical report, depending on the knowledge and skill level of the students.

11.14 Researching Data: Target Aims Charitable Giving (Obj. 3, 6, and 7)

This activity lends itself to several options. Potential assignments range from memos summarizing research findings to informational as well as analytical reports after students study Chapters 12 and 13. Corporate social responsibility is a hot topic, and students may find considerable information. Perhaps they could start with CSRwire at **http://www.csrwire.com** and search the Web along with electronic databases for information on charitable giving and corporate philanthropy.

11.15 Gathering Data: Fortune 100 Best Companies to Work For (Objs. 3, 4)

The themes that emerge after studying the winners in *Fortune*'s 100 Best Companies to Work For are the following (not necessarily in order of importance): job security, better-than-average compensation, bonuses, stock options and other financial incentives; fringe benefits such as unlimited sick days, health coverage, child care, and generous vacation leaves; and on-site perks such as gyms, libraries, swimming pools, saunas, and on-duty medical staff.

11.16 Selecting Graphics (Obj. 7)

a. Photo, map
b. Table for exact absolute numbers; line chart for trends
c. Bar chart, possibly pie chart
d. Map
e. Flowchart
f. Map
g. Probably a pie chart; possibly a segmented 100 percent bar chart
h. Organization chart
i. A multiple or segmented line chart would be best for visualizing trends; a grouped bar chart could be used, but it might be confusing; a table would be best for showing exact figures.

11.17 Evaluating Graphics (Obj. 7)

This is another excellent assignment, but it could be time consuming. If you assign this task, you may want students to select an article dealing with the same subject as their written report topic.

11.18 Creating a Bar Chart (Obj. 7)

Talking title: Comparing Tax Rates as Percentage of Gross Domestic Product for Eight Industrial Countries

Functional title: Tax Rates as Percent of Gross Domestic Product

Conclusion: Sweden has the highest and Japan has the lowest tax rate as a percentage of gross domestic product for the industrial countries shown

Emphasize percentages and countries in the graph. In the title emphasize that the numbers represent tax rates as a percentage of gross domestic product.

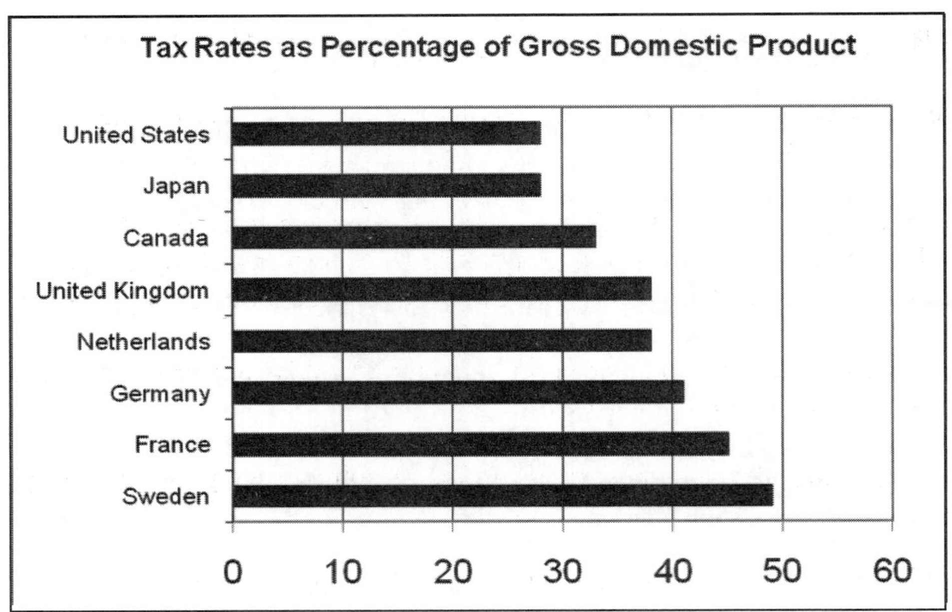

11.19 Creating a Line Chart (Obj. 7)

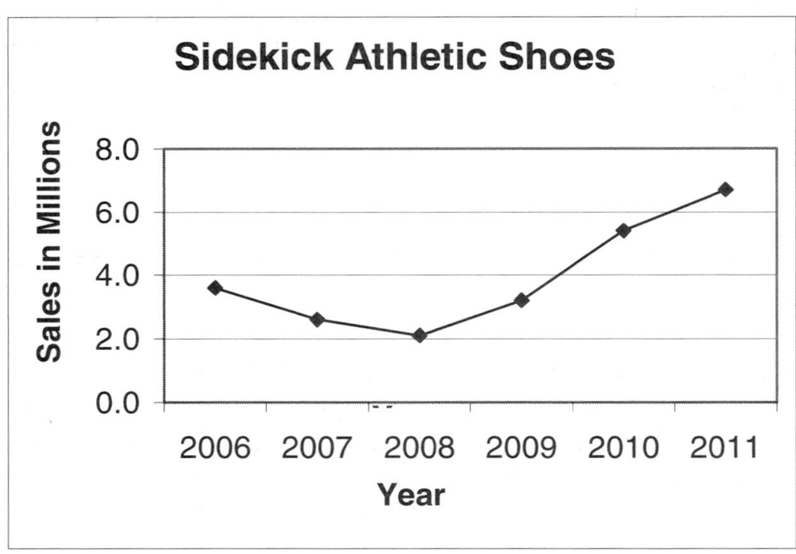

11.20 Studying Graphics in Annual Reports (Obj. 7)

This would be a very informative exercise, especially if students are not going to write a long report. This exercise would be especially beneficial for accounting and finance majors.

11.21 Avoiding Huge Credit Card Debt for College Students (Objs. 3, 5, and 6)

Students are to write a memo information report. They should discuss some of the following information:

- Credit card on parents' account. Parents get the bill and can track spending.
- Secured credit card. A credit line is guaranteed by money in a bank account.
- Unsecured credit card. The credit limits are low for students, allowing them to build a credit record.
- Non-credit card options. Parents can set up a joint checking account with a debit card. They can also fund a prepaid card.

Be sure to require that your students supply a bibliography showing the sources of all data.

11.22 Netflix & Co.: Movies After DVD and Blu-Ray (Objs. 3, 5, and 6)

Answers will vary, but even a casual Web search will reveal solid information, for example, about sales numbers for DVDs and Blue-ray discs (Blue-ray disc sales are up; HD DVD sales are dropping). Searching Google, for example, for the phrase "trends in DVD and Blue-ray market" will yield useful information. CNet News and others discuss the move away from DVDs to Blue-ray discs. Some predict that DVDs and Blue-ray discs will eventually go the way of the VHS tape. Similar search terms could be used to find articles in electronic databases.

ZOOMING IN Part 1: Pet Airways

Critical Thinking

- **Why might a U.S. airline dedicated strictly to traveling pets be an easy sell to the public? Why might it not be?**

  Few topics are as emotional as pets. Americans love and pamper their animals to the point of ascribing decidedly human qualities to them. More than 60 percent of U.S. households include pets, and their owners spend about $45 billion a year on them.[ii] Media stories about pets are popular for their human interest. As the subsequent parts of this case study will show, Pet Airways received significant free promotion from coverage by, among others, Forbes.com, CNNMoney.com, NPR.org, and the George Lopez show.

- **Today's entrepreneurs have many technological resources at their disposal to do research and spread the news when launching a new business. What channels may Dan Wiesel and Alysa Binder have used to explore their business idea and to find potential customers?**

  Without a doubt, Dan and Alysa had to study information on the pet transportation industry and market data. Investigating the potential of a business idea may also involve primary research such as surveys and interviews with pet owners.

  Pet Airways uses a variety of modern communication channels to communicate with the public. A comprehensive company Web site introduces the enterprise, explains its unique nature, describes reservation steps as well as onboard procedures, and allows users to make reservations—for pets on Pet Airways and for humans on typical commercial airlines. The Web site also features a blog, customer testimonials, and press coverage. Visitors to the company blog can subscribe to an RSS feed and share the content on social networking sites such as Facebook, MySpace, and Twitter. Moreover, they can e-mail or bookmark the short blog entries.

- **To hear Dan Wiesel and Alysa Binder tell it on their Web site, before launching Pet Airways, they apparently relied a great deal on anecdotal evidence, a very limited empirical research method. Do you think an entrepreneur's hunch is enough on which to start a business?**

  "Our Story" on the company Web site, is an account authored by Dan and Alysa, the married couple that started Pet Airways. Naturally, articles written for a business Web site are promotional and, hence, may contain an "airbrushed" version of the founding of the enterprise. Simple hunches usually aren't enough to get loans approved or investors interested in a venture. Dan Wiesel and Alysa Binder have publicly revealed only that their start-up has sufficient capital and is financed by a group of investors.

  That said, many successful entrepreneurs say that their business ideas were motivated by simple triggers, often a problem they encountered and wished to solve or a hobby they decided to turn into a profession. However, hunches or instincts must be backed up with persuasive evidence indicating that a potential market, a perceived need, exists for a product or service.

ZOOMING IN Part 2: Pet Airways

Critical Thinking

- **When writing their funding proposal or business plan, do you think Dan and Alysa chose an informational or analytical approach? Why?**

  The two entrepreneurs probably opted for an analytical approach. They had to persuade potential financial backers that their start-up idea had merit and would pay off. They had to analyze the market, the competition, opportunities, and threats. In their business plan or proposal they had to detail how much money they would need to launch and maintain their business.

- **Do you think Dan's and Alysa's proposal was developed directly or indirectly? Why? Should it have been written formally or informally?**

  The entrepreneurs would have done well to adopt a tried-and-true persuasive strategy and choose a formal structure. Most proposals and business plans follow a typical, conventional pattern: gaining attention, building interest, reducing resistance, and motivating action. Students should revisit Chapter 10 to refresh their understanding of the components of a persuasive message. Chapter 13 specifically discusses business plans. Dan and Alysa may have had to persuade potential backers that their business idea represented a viable investment and would turn a profit. To be persuasive, Alysa and Dan would have had to present the problem of pet transportation in cargo as opposed to a comfortable stay aboard in a climate-controlled cabin, and they would have needed to reduce their audience's resistance. One possible angle for reducing resistance would have been to use testimonials from pet owners. Then, they could have continued to build interest by showing how their plan of action had a strong chance of success. Finally, by showing how their business would offer benefits and growth potential, they could have helped to motivate action on the part of financiers.

- **What are some of the questions Dan and Alysa should have asked themselves about their audience before pitching their business idea or writing their proposal?**

  Dan and Alysa should have asked questions such as the following:
  - What do our readers need to know about this type of business?
  - What problem or need will Pet Airways address?
  - How will the problem be solved or the need met?
  - How will the plan be implemented and evaluated?
  - What benefits can we highlight?
  - What personnel and special resources will be needed?
  - What costs will the project generate?

ZOOMING IN Your Turn: Pet Airways

Answers will vary, depending on the continued success of this business model. Before Pet Airways, no carrier existed that would be dedicated solely to ferrying furry critters around in style and comfort, away from the dangers of the cargo hold of airplanes. The Pet Airways Web site is a good starting point for up-to-date company information, for example, about expansion plans and new features of the service. Periodically the airline has been featured in the media. The company's strategic plan involved expanding the service to new cities and also to include animals other than cats and dogs. So far it seems that Pet Airways is well on its way to success.

Discussion Material for PLUGGED IN: Staying on Top of Research Data

This exercise gives students an opportunity to practice using different techniques to record and manage information they find when conducting research online. More important, they will discover the value of using Boolean operators as an effective tool for narrowing a search. Their responses will vary widely depending on the searches they conducted and the techniques they used to save their results.

Discussion Material for ETHICAL INSIGHTS: Making Ethical Charts and Graphics

Any good business researcher knows that statistics can lie. Statistics on charts and graphs can be skewed to present data so that it is interpreted in a specific way. This activity will give students a chance to interpret and analyze data presented in graphics. Most importantly, it gives students a chance to question the data. Consider having students complete this activity in small groups to discuss their findings.

Ethics Check Solutions

Ethics Check, Page 355
Cribbing From References?
Doing last-minute research for a class or work project, you are in a hurry; therefore, you decide to copy some sources from the list of references that you found in an article on your topic to boost your number of works cited. Is it unethical to list sources you have not actually read?

Opinions may vary on whether copying someone else's sources without reading them constitutes cheating. In any case, it is lazy scholarship and shows poor study habits. By relying on paraphrases in secondary articles and not viewing the original piece, the writer risks misunderstanding or misrepresenting the unread source. The reference we find in another article and don't verify could have been misused, which happens more often than report writers realize. Furthermore, each time students seek shortcuts, they shortchange their education. When instructors ask for a minimum of sources, they expect students to search for, read, understand, and skillfully integrate information from those sources into their papers. Merely boosting the number of references does not constitute learning. On the other hand, it is not dishonest to kick off one's research by reviewing the list of references in relevant articles and reading some of them to expand one's grasp of the topic.

Ethics Check, Page 356
Legitimate Gripe or Character Assassination?
Few would deny that customers should have an outlet for reasonable complaints against companies that slighted them. However, today, increasingly anonymous cyber threats against companies often erupt suddenly and turn nasty, leaving firms unsure about how to deal with them, whether to respond, and if so, how. In this light, can we trust the information on the Web?

Students should realize that they need to be critical consumers of information online. Anyone with a computer can act as an opinion leader as long as he or she finds an audience. Electronic media permit the instantaneous, speedy distribution of attacks, and once unleashed, they are difficult to manage. Distinguishing among true, distorted, and plain untruthful information can be difficult. Businesses increasingly hire services to contain the fallout from cyber rumors and put a favorable spin on perceived or genuine wrongdoing. Students may want to consider some of the defensive strategies (damage control) open to companies—when might a business decide to ignore an attack and when should it respond? The ethics of spin as a countermeasure could be discussed alongside the ethics of unsubstantiated rumormongering on the Internet.

Photo Essay Solutions

Photo Essay, Page 345

Unicast reports are written primarily for upper-level management at AOL, NBC, ABC, FOX, Sports Illustrated and other media firms. Managers rely on Unicast's consumer statistics to inform their decisions about Website services and online advertising. The report states that the engagement of NCAA fans online presents "valuable opportunities to publishers and brand marketers looking to reach the primary March Madness audience – male sports fans aged 18-35." However, secondary readers include Internet technology workers, handheld device manufacturers, and applications developers. Communicators who write reports for Unicast must keep all audiences in view when deciding what details to include, which statistics will be the most useful to publishers and advertisers, and whether or not to include jargon.

Photo Essay, Page 355

For scientists, who are specialists in developing primary data, written reports must document peer-reviewed experiments that properly follow the scientific method. The errors in the IPCC Fourth Assessment Report were caused by the inclusion of information derived not from formal scientific research but from non-scientific secondary sources traced to advocacy groups and opinion-based speculation.

As mentioned earlier in the chapter, a report is only as good as its data. To demonstrate valid cause and effect correlations, researchers must test variables in experimental and control groups and guard against researcher bias. The data errors at the IPCC mirrored similar problems encountered by its top research partner, the University of East Anglia, whose Climate Research Unit recently retracted claims about rising sea levels, world CO2 measurements, and overall warming trends.

---

[i] Berfield, S. (2009, August 17). Howard Schultz versus Howard Schultz. *BusinessWeek*, p. 33.

[ii] 2009/2010 National Pet Owners Survey cited by American Pet Products Association. (2010). *APPA.com*. Retrieved January 15, 2010, from http://www.americanpetproducts.org/press_industrytrends.asp

Chapter 12 LECTURE NOTES AND TEACHING SUGGESTIONS

Informal Business Reports

CHAPTER SYNOPSIS

Even a business executive as averse to marketing surveys as Starbucks CEO Howard Schultz has come to acknowledge the advantages of gauging customers' and employees' perceptions and preferences. Surveys are an important part of a company's strategic decision making and often form the basis of reports, both periodic and situational. Chapter 12 focuses on informal reports that help managers track their supervisees' and the company's performance and to make informed decisions.

Students are introduced to statistical techniques to sort and interpret business report data. They learn to tabulate information and, most important, to draw meaningful conclusions from the results and make feasible recommendations. After all, the conclusions and recommendations are the most widely read sections of a report.

The chapter provides guidelines for students to understand when to choose a direct or indirect organizational strategy, depending on the knowledge of the readers and their attitude toward the subject. It cannot be stressed enough that report readers look for road signs such as introductions, transitions, and headings to help them navigate through the information. Students will apply these writing strategies as they prepare informational and analytical reports.

LEARNING OBJECTIVES

1. Tabulate information, use statistical techniques, and create decision matrices to sort and interpret business report data skillfully and accurately.

2. Draw meaningful conclusions and make practical report recommendations after sound and valid analysis.

3. Organize report data logically and provide cues to aid comprehension.

4. Write short informational reports that describe routine tasks.

5. Compose short analytical reports that solve business problems.

WHAT'S NEW IN THIS CHAPTER

- Updated Starbucks three-part business case study to provide students with an opportunity to analyze current business problems.

- Added new ethics checks allowing students to confront the moral dilemmas facing executives, managers, and rank-and-file employees on the job.
- Introduced new spotlight on communicators to provide students with topical insights by business practitioners relevant to the material students are learning in the chapter.
- Replaced at least a third of end-of-chapter activities to present students with fresh activities, cases, and business scenarios.
- Added five new self-contained report tasks that enable instructors to assign business problems accompanied by data sets that require no outside research.
- Introduced a new figure showing a periodic (activity) report in bullet form sent by e-mail to reflect the latest technological trends in workplace communication.

LECTURE OUTLINE

I. Interpreting Data (p. 380)

PowerPoint slides 1-5

A. Tabulating and Analyzing Reponses
Tabulating and statistical techniques simplify, summarize, and classify large amounts of data into meaningful terms.

1. **Tables –** Using systematic columns and rows, tables make quantitative data easier to comprehend and analyze.

Figure 12.1 Converting Survey Data Into Finished Tables

Let's Discuss

When are tables the most appropriate analytical tool and tabulating technique? What types of data are best presented in tables?

Tables are most suitable for numerical data because they help researchers understand quantitative information. The systematic columns and rows in a table enable researchers to summarize and simplify numerical data from surveys and interviews.

2. **The Three Ms: Mean, Median, Mode –** These statistical concepts help you describe data and loosely mean "average."

   Mean – the arithmetic average
   Median – the midpoint in a group of figures
   Mode – the most frequently occurring figure

PowerPoint slides 6-7

3. **Correlations –** Relationships among two or more variables may stimulate investigation and present possible solutions to be explored.

4. **Grids** – Complex verbal information is transformed into concise, manageable data.

Figure 12.2 Grid to Analyze Complex Verbal Data About Building Cash Reserves

5. **Decision Matrices –** These special grids help managers make the best choice among complex options by organizing important criteria in a matrix.

Figure 12.3 Decision Matrix Used to Choose a Laptop for Sales Reps

II. Drawing Conclusions and Making Recommendations (p. 386)

PowerPoint slides 8-13

- The most widely read portions of a report are the sections devoted to conclusions and recommendations.

A. Analyzing Data to Arrive at Conclusions

- Remain objective.
- Use consistent evaluation criteria.
- Avoid exaggerating your findings.

B. Preparing Report Recommendations

- Provide practical recommendations that are agreeable to the audience.
- Make each recommendation a command.
- Avoid conditional statements, such as *maybe* and *perhaps*, that reduce the strength of the recommendations.

Figure 12.4 Report Conclusions and Recommendations.

C. Moving From Findings to Recommendations

- Recommendations evolve from interpretation of the findings and conclusions.

III. Organizing Data (p. 389)

Figure 12.5 Organizational Patterns for Informational and Analytical Reports

PowerPoint slides 14, 15

A. Ordering Information Logically

1. Time – establishing a chronology of events
2. Component – organized by location, geography, division, product, or part
3. Importance – proceeding from the most important to the least important, or vice versa.
4. Criteria – organizing data by criteria
5. Convention – a prescribed plan that everyone understands

B. Providing Reader Cues

- Provide introductions, transitions, and headings to guide readers through the data.

PowerPoint slides 16-19

1. Introduction
   - Tells the purpose of the report
   - Describes the significance of the topic
   - Previews the main points and the order in which they will be developed
2. Transitions
   - Inform readers where ideas are headed and how they relate
3. Headings
   - Use appropriate heading levels.
   - Capitalize and underline carefully.
   - Try to balance headings within levels.
   - For short reports use first-level or first- and second-level headings.
   - Include at least one heading per report page.
   - Keep headings short but clear.

Figure 12.6 Levels of Headings in Reports

IV. Writing Short Informational Reports (p. 394)

- Informational reports describe periodic, recurring activities or nonrecurring events.
- Readers are usually neutral or receptive.
- Use direct organizational pattern.

PowerPoint slides 20-23

A. Summaries

- Present the goal of the document being summarized.
- Highlight the research methods, findings, conclusions, and recommendations.
- Omit illustrations, examples, and references.
- Organize for readability.
- Include an overall evaluation if asked to do so.

B. Periodic (Activity) Reports

- Provide information at regular intervals.
- Help management monitor and remedy business strategies.
- Summarize regular activities performed during the reporting period.
- Describe irregular events deserving management attention.
- Highlight special needs and problems.

Figure 12.7 Periodic (Activity) Report—E-Mail Format

C. Trip, Convention, and Conference Reports

- Begin by identifying the event and previewing the topics to be discussed.
- Summarize three to five main points that might benefit the reader.

- Itemize expenses separately.
- Close by expressing appreciation or synthesizing the value of the trip or event.

Figure 12.8 Conference Report—Memo Format

D. Progress and Interim Reports

- Specify in the opening the purpose and nature of the project.
- Provide background information if the audience requires it.
- Describe the work completed.
- Explain the work currently in progress, including personnel, activities, methods, and locations.
- Describe current problems and anticipate future problems and possible remedies.
- Discuss future activities and provide the expected completion date.

Figure 12.9 Progress Report

E. Investigative Reports

- Provide information without interpretation or recommendations.

V. Checklist for Writing Informational Reports (p. 399)

Introduction

- Begin directly.
- Provide a preview.
- Supply background data selectively.
- Divide the topic.

Body

- Arrange the subtopics logically.
- Use clear headings.
- Determine degree of formality.
- Enhance readability with graphic highlighting.

Summary/Concluding Remarks

- When necessary, summarize the report.
- Offer a concluding thought.

VI. Preparing Short Analytical Reports (p. 401)

- Analytical reports present information but emphasize reasoning, conclusions, and recommendations.

PowerPoint slides 24-35

A. **Justification/Recommendation Reports**

1. **Direct Strategy**
   - Identify the problem or need briefly.
   - Announce the recommendation, solution, or action concisely and with action verbs.
   - Explain more fully the benefits of the recommendation or steps necessary to solve the problem.
   - Include a discussion of pros, cons, and costs.
   - Conclude with a summary specifying the recommendation and necessary action.

Figure 12.10 Justification/Recommendation Report—Memo Format

2. **Indirect Strategy**
   - Make a general reference to the problem, not to your recommendation, in the subject line.
   - Describe the problem or need your recommendation addresses. Use specific examples, supporting statistics, and authoritative quotes to lend credibility to the seriousness of the problem.
   - Discuss alternative solutions, beginning with the least likely to succeed.
   - Present the most promising alternative (your recommendation) last.
   - Show how the advantages of your recommendation outweigh its disadvantages.
   - Summarize your recommendation. If appropriate, specify the action it requires.
   - Ask for authorization to proceed if necessary.

Figure 12.11 Justification/Recommendation Report: Indirect Pattern, MLA Style

Do you recommend that the direct or indirect strategy be used for the following analytical reports?

1. An analytical report written by a consultant recommending that a major U.S. corporation lay off 4,500 workers in a Chinese factory.

Indirect. The consultant needs to gain support for this recommendation by presenting supporting data and providing persuasive reasons before recommending a decision that is sensitive in nature.

2. An analytical report written by the manager of a superstore who recommends to his supportive boss replacing Sony microwaves with Amana microwaves in the appliances section of the store.

Direct. This is a nonsensitive topic being presented to a receptive audience.

B. Feasibility Reports

- Announce your decision immediately.
- Provide a description of the background and problem necessitating the proposal.
- Discuss the benefits of the proposal.
- Describe the problems that may result.
- Calculate the costs associated with the proposal, if appropriate.
- Show the time frame necessary for implementing the proposal.

Figure 12.12 Feasibility Report – Memo Format

C. Yardstick Reports

- Begin by describing the problem or need.
- Explain possible solutions and alternatives.
- Establish criteria for comparing the alternatives; tell how the criteria were selected or developed.
- Discuss and evaluate each alternative in terms of the criteria.
- Draw conclusions and make recommendations.

Figure 12.13 Yardstick Report

VII. Checklist for Writing Analytical Reports (p. 412)

Introduction

- Identify the purpose of the report.
- Describe the significance of the topic.
- Preview the organization of the report.
- Summarize the conclusions and recommendations for receptive audiences.

Findings

- Discuss pros and cons.
- Establish criteria to evaluate alternatives.
- Support the findings with evidence.
- Organize the findings for logic and readability.

Conclusions/Recommendations

- Draw reasonable conclusions from the findings.
- Make recommendations, if asked.

Lecture Transparencies
(available in a separate packet and at http://www.meguffey.com)

Informal Business Reports Acetates	**Transparency Number**
Interpreting Data	129
Mean, Median, Mode	130
Tips for Drawing Report Conclusions	131
Tips for Making Report Recommendations	132
Organizing Information	133
Structural Cues for Reports	134
Levels of Report Headings	135
Informational Report Content	136
Analytical Report Content	137
Typical Informational Reports	138
Typical Short Analytical Reports	139

Solution Masters

Solutions and discussion material for the Chapter 12 activities are found in this lecture outline only. Solution masters are not available.

Answers to Chapter Review Questions

1. **What is cross-tabulation, and when is it useful? (Obj. 1)**

   Cross-tabulation allows researchers to analyze two or more variables together. By cross-tabulating findings, you sometimes uncover data that may help answer your problem question or that may prompt you to explore other possibilities. Resist undertaking cross-tabulation unless it serves more than merely satisfying your curiosity.

2. **Calculate the mean, median, and mode for these figures: 5, 15, 15, 15, 30. (Obj. 1)**

   The mean, or average, is 16 (divide the total by the number of units); the median is 15 (the midpoint in a group of figures arranged in order—either smallest to largest or largest to smallest); the mode is 15 (the number that occurs most frequently).

3. **What are correlations? (Obj. 1)**

   In tabulating and analyzing data, you may see relationships among two or more variables that help explain the findings. For example, a correlation may exist between years of education and starting salary.

4. **Why is a decision matrix a valuable managerial tool? (Obj. 1)**

   A decision matrix is valuable because it establishes criteria and assigns weights to each option. Managers can then see which option ranks highest based on an objective system.

5. Why is the ability to do research and draw conclusions likely to increase your value to your employer? (Obj. 2)

The ability to analyze information logically and show how the data answer questions and solve problems is invaluable because it determines business success.

6. How can you make your report conclusions as objective and bias-free as possible? (Obj. 2)

You can make your report conclusions more objective by using consistent evaluation criteria. For example, when comparing several items or options, you apply the same standards and measures to each. Also, you don't exaggerate your findings.

7. Name five methods for organizing report data. Be prepared to discuss each. (Obj. 3)

Five methods for organizing report data are as follows:

1. Time: Establishing a chronology of events.

2. Component: Organizing data by component such as location, geography, department, division, product, part, and so on.

3. Importance: Beginning with the most important information and proceeding to the least important, or vice versa.

4. Criteria: Establishing criteria that readers can use to judge the information with consistency.

5. Convention: Following a prescribed plan that everyone understands.

8. What three devices can report writers use to prevent readers from getting lost in the text? (Obj. 3)

Report writers can use the following to prevent readers from getting lost:

a. An introduction that explains the report purpose and previews main points
b. Logic markers or transitions (words or expressions such as *consequently* and *on the other hand*)
c. Headings

9. Name at least four guidelines for creating effective headings, and be prepared to explain them. (Obj. 3)

a. Use appropriate heading levels. The position and format of a heading indicate its level of importance and relationship to other points.
b. Capitalize and underline carefully. Most writers identify main titles by opting for all capital letters and choosing to capitalize only the main words in first- and second-level headings.

c. Try to balance headings within levels. Attempt to create headings that are grammatically similar at a given level.
d. For short reports use first-level or first-level and second-level headings. Because most business reports are short documents, using only one or two levels of headings makes sense.
e. Include at least one heading per report page. Headings increase the readability and attractiveness of report pages. Use at least one per page to break up blocks of text.
f. Keep headings short but clear. One-word headings are emphatic but not always clear. Experiment with headings that concisely tell who, what, when, where, and why.

10. How do business writers organize most informational reports, and what can writers assume about the audience? (Obj. 4)

Informational reports describe recurring or one-time events to readers who are receptive or neutral. Because they deliver nonsensitive data, informational reports are organized directly.

11. Describe periodic reports and what they generally contain. (Obj. 4)

Periodic reports describe recurring operations, such as sales, shipments, and customer service calls. They generally contain a summary of regular activities, irregular events, and special needs and problems.

12. What should a progress report include? (Obj. 4)

Progress reports should include the purpose and nature of the project, background information, a description of work in progress, anticipated problems and remedies, future activities, and a completion date.

13. When is the indirect pattern appropriate for justification/recommendation reports? (Obj. 5)

The indirect pattern works best in justification/recommendation reports when delivering sensitive findings to potentially unreceptive audiences.

14. What is a feasibility report? Are such reports generally intended for internal or external audiences? (Obj. 5)

A feasibility report examines the practicality and advisability of following a particular course of action. Feasibility reports are typically internal documents examining a decision in the organization.

15. What is a yardstick report? (Obj. 5)

A yardstick report examines problems with two or more solutions. To evaluate the best solution, the writer establishes criteria by which to compare the alternatives. The criteria then act as a yardstick against which all the alternatives are measured.

Answers to Critical Thinking Questions

1. **When tabulating and analyzing data, you may discover relationships among two or more variables that help explain the findings. Can you trust these correlations and assume that their relationship is one of cause and effect? (Obj. 1)**

   Our intuition sometimes suggests correlations that may or may not be correct. The business researcher who sees a correlation begins to ask why and how the two variables are related. Apparent correlations can stimulate investigation and present possible solutions to explore. In reporting correlations, you should avoid suggesting that a cause-and-effect relationship exists when none can be proven. Only sophisticated research methods can statistically prove cause and effect. Cautious statements followed by explanations will lend you credibility and allow readers to draw their own conclusions.

2. **Researchers can draw various conclusions from a set of data. How do you know how to shape conclusions and recommendations? (Obj. 2)**

   Conclusions and recommendations should reflect the original assignment. What do the data mean in terms of solving the original problem? Conclusions and recommendations may be shaped to agree or disagree with the goals of the person or organization authorizing the report. Generally, researchers strive to be objective. They avoid letting preconceptions color their reasoning. But the conclusions drawn depend greatly on the viewpoint of the researcher and the organization's goals.

3. **How can you increase your chances that your report recommendations will be implemented? (Obj. 2)**

   Reports that consider the audience's needs and offer specific, practical recommendations are most likely to succeed. How specific and forceful your recommendations can be depends on your authorization and status in the organization. Writers must carefully consider both the background and information needs of their audiences. Recommendations that are impractical or unacceptable to those who authorize reports will serve no purpose.

4. **Should all reports be organized so that they follow the sequence of investigation—that is, a description of the initial problem, an analysis of the issues, data collection, data analysis, and conclusions? Why or why not? (Obj. 3)**

   Like letters and memos, reports may be organized directly or indirectly. The reader's expectations and the content of a report determine its pattern of development. Corporate annual reports may have some parts developed directly while other parts are arranged indirectly. Reports should be organized for the convenience of the reader. Determine and then implement the most appropriate pattern for the audience of every report.

5. **What are the major differences between informational and analytical reports? (Objs. 4, 5)**

   Analytical reports differ significantly from informational reports. Although both seek to collect and present data clearly, analytical reports also analyze the data and typically try to persuade the reader to accept the conclusions and act on the recommendations.

6. Ethical Issue: You have learned that drawing conclusions involves subjectivity, although your goal is to remain objective. Even the most even-handed researchers bring their goals, background, and frame of reference to bear on the inferences they make. Consider the contentious issue of climate change. Most mainstream scientists now believe climate change to be real and induced by human activity. However, some scientists cast doubt on the extent to which global warming is human-made and constitutes an imminent threat. How can something objectively measurable be so contentious? (Obj. 2)

The problem with climate change is that it is a very complex issue. Not only does it involve highly complicated scientific data and measurements, but it also raises far-reaching political, social, and economic questions. The climate change debate illustrates nicely that even well-meaning experts introduce their natural biases and agendas into their research. A recent breach of e-mail communication among climatologists revealed that some of these scholars might have attempted to manipulate their results to make them appear more dramatic and urgent. This finding, in turn, became welcome fodder for climate change skeptics and deniers.

Activities

12.1 Tabulation and Interpretation of Survey Results (Obj. 1)

a.

REACTIONS OF SOUTH BAY COLLEGE STUDENTS TO FOUR PROPOSALS ABOUT BOOKSTORE BAGS
Fall 2011
N = 560 students

	Agree	Undecided	Disagree
Provide no bags; encourage students to bring their own bags	73.9%	4.5%	21.6%
Provide no bags; offer cloth bags at a reduced price (about $3)	63.4	3.4	32.9
Continue to provide plastic bags	23.6	3.0	73.4
Give a cloth bag with each major purchase, the cost to be included in registration fees	11.3	2.7	86.1

b. The data could be cross-tabulated by examining each response in terms of number of units carried (did full-time students react differently from part-time students?), by sex, and by major (if those questions had been asked in the survey). However, such examination seems to serve no purpose beyond a curiosity factor. The action taken will not be affected by such knowledge.

c. Three conclusions that could be drawn from the survey:

1. A majority of students are concerned enough about the environment to want to give up plastic bags.
2. Although a majority of students want to eliminate plastic bags, they do not want to replace them with cloth bags financed by their registration fees.
3. Most students seem to prefer bringing their own bags.

d. The following are possible recommendations based upon the data collected:

1. Stop supplying plastic bags with each purchase.
2. Encourage students to bring their own bags to hold purchases. Publicize this change in policy in the campus newspaper and with signs around campus and in the bookstore.
3. Encourage students who want bags to purchase the bargain $3 cloth bag. Put signs in the bookstore to promote cloth bags.
4. Mount an advertising campaign to inform students of the impact on the environment of plastic bags and your effort to reduce pollution.

e. Through this role-play activity, students will polish their presentation and persuasion skills as they present recommendations to Mr. Locke.

12.2 Evaluating Conclusions (Obj. 2)

This is an excellent assignment, but it could be quite time consuming. If you assign this task, you may want students to select an article dealing with the same subject as their written report topic.

12.3 Distinguishing Between Conclusions and Recommendations (Obj. 2)

For each statement below indicate whether it could be classified as a conclusion or recommendation.

a. Red light violations are dangerous offenses. *Conclusion*

b. Red light cameras are an effective traffic safety tool. *Conclusion*

c. Local governments should be allowed to implement red light camera programs. *Recommendation*

d. Although red light camera programs are expensive, they prevent crashes and are, therefore, worthwhile. *Conclusion*

e. The city of Centerville should not implement a red light program because of the program's cost. *Recommendation*

f. Red light programs are not necessarily profitable for local governments. *Conclusion*

12.4 Using Decision Matrices (Objs. 1, 2)

Reflecting the new priority of price, the outcome favors the Acer Aspire Timeline with 80 points. Because it is more expensive, the Dell Inspiron, the winner on battery life, is a close second, with 79 points.

12.5 Buying a Car: Create a Decision Matrix (Objs. 1, 2)

Students should create a decision matrix with two tables that could look something like this:

Table 1: Unweighted Matrix (Scale from 1 to 5; from worst to best)

Features:	Price	Cargo	Fuel	Comfort	Look	Quality	Total
Weights:							
Station wagon	3	4	3	4	1	2	
4-door sedan	4	2	5	3	1	4	
SUV	1	5	1	4	3	2	
Sports car	1	1	1	1	5	4	

Students should decide which relative weights to assign to each feature above and could arrive at the following table after multiplying the factors with the scores in Table 1:

Table 2: Weighted Matrix (Factors range from 1 to 5)

Features:	Price	Cargo	Fuel	Comfort	Look	Quality	Total
Weights:	4	5	3	2	4	3	
Station wagon	12	20	9	8	4	6	59
4-door sedan	16	10	15	6	4	12	63
SUV	4	25	3	8	12	6	58
Sports car	4	5	3	2	20	12	46

This example may surprise students because the "boring" option, the staid family sedan, scores the highest and seems to be the best option for David. Answers may vary, depending on the weights used.

12.6 Organizing Data (Obj. 3)

a. A weekly bulleted activity report sent by e-mail to the supervisor. *Convention. The report is periodic and most likely has standardized, recurring features.*

b. An agenda previewing a week-long management retreat and training program. *Time. Like itineraries, agendas require attention to chronology.*

c. A report comparing three locations for a fast-food company's new restaurant. The report presents data on real estate values, construction costs, traffic patterns, competition, state taxes, labor availability, and population demographics. *Criteria. It is better to discuss findings by criteria than by location site.*

d. A report describing the history of the development of dwarf and spur apple trees, starting with the first genetic dwarfs discovered about 100 years ago and progressing to today's grafted varieties on dwarfing rootstocks. *Time. A history of the tree varieties suggests chronological order.*

e. A report comparing the sales volume among the largest fast-food outlets in the United States. *Component. The data would be grouped by company: McDonald's, Yum Brands (KFC, Pizza Hut, and Taco Bell), Wendy's/Arby's, Burger King, etc.*

f. A recommendation report to be submitted to management presenting four building plans to improve access to your building, in compliance with federal regulations. The plans range considerably in feasibility and cost. *Importance. You would probably want to present the most feasible plan first.*

g. An informational report describing a company's expansion plans in South America, Europe, Australia, and Southeast Asia. *Component. The report will cover each region as part of the whole that constitutes the company.*

h. An employee performance appraisal submitted annually. *Convention. Employee performance appraisals are highly standardized and recur at regular intervals.*

12.7 Evaluating Headings and Titles (Obj. 3)

a. Disadvantages Functional. This heading describes a purpose and may be appropriate in a short report, but it is not very interesting or helpful to the reader.

b. Why Fast Food Has Slowed Down Talking. This heading reveals what follows in the subsequent section, yet it is short enough for easy reading.

c. Discussion Functional. This heading provides minimal information, but in a report covering a sensitive topic that might offend readers, its generic nature may be effective.

d. Balancing Worker Productivity and Social Media Use Talking. This heading clearly prepares the reader for what follows.

e. Case History: Glatfelter's Direct-Mail Campaign Heralds Sustainability Combination. This heading combines talking and function at an appropriate length.

f. Recommendations: Solving Our Applicant-Tracking Problem Combination. This heading combines both talking and function and is short enough.

g. Comparing Costs of Hiring Exempt and Nonexempt Employees Talking. This heading is precise in telling the reader what is coming.

h. Equipment Functional. This functional heading provides minimal information and is not very interesting.

12.8 Writing a Survey: Studying Employee Use of Instant Messaging (Obj. 1)

This is an excellent exercise to help students understand the benefits and risks involved in using IM on the job. You can make it a short in-class exercise and develop a few survey questions together, or you can make it a more complex assignment by having teams develop surveys, fill in fictitious responses, analyze the findings, draw conclusions, and make recommendations to the boss. A sample survey follows:

Anonymous Employee Survey

We understand that some employees are using instant messaging on the job. To help you make the best use of this convenient and economical communication tool, we need more information about how it is currently being used. This survey is anonymous so that you can be candid in your responses.

	Yes	No
1. Do you currently use Instant Messaging on the job?	___	___
2. Do you know of others on the job who are using IM?	___	___
3. Would you like to learn more about how IM can be used on the job?	___	___

If you are NOT currently using IM on the job, please submit this form at this time.

If you are using IM on the job, please continue.

4. What type of IM software have you downloaded?

____

5. Approximately how many IM messages do you send or receive each day?

    ____ 1 ____ 5 ____ 6–10 ____ 11–15 ____ 16–20 ____ 21 or more

6. Approximately how many hours a day do you spend on IM?

    ___ Up to 1 hour ___1–2 hours ___ 3 hours or more

7. For what reasons do you use IM? Check as many items as you wish:

    ___ Helps me obtain company information quickly.

    ___ Avoids the "click, open, read, re-read, click, reply, proof, click, send, and hope for a response sometime soon" process of e-mail.

    ___ Avoids the telephone tag played with voice messaging.

___ Helps me build company morale by keeping in touch.

___ Enables me to be sure that my receiver gets my message.

___ Other reason (Please explain in space below.)

____

8. What problems do you encounter with the workplace use of IM?

____

Please return this form to _____ by _____[date]. Your response is important and appreciated!

12.10 Periodic Report: Filling in the Boss (Obj. 4)

This is an excellent activity to help students relate report writing to their current jobs. If a student is not working, he or she can apply this activity to the classroom. How could students use periodic reports to keep instructors up-to-date on their progress on research projects or term papers.

12.11 Progress Report: Checking In (Obj. 4)

One of the biggest problems students have with any long report assignment is procrastination. Without having to report progress periodically, many students put the work off until the last minute. This activity gives students incentive to stay on track and helps them avoid procrastination. You can have students come up with their own formats for this report, or you can provide a consistent format for all students to use. The periodic, or activity, report in Figure 12.7 is a document style much used in busy workplaces. Students could be encouraged to use this bulleted e-mail report as a model.

12.12 Investigative Report: Ensuring Fair Employment Practices Abroad (Obj. 4)

This subject is well documented, and students should have no problem finding secondary material. The trade press, for example, *BusinessWeek,* recently ran stories about sweatshop conditions among Chinese suppliers. The Fair Labor Association reports on unannounced audits in suppliers' factories. Its studies are freely accessible. Students could investigate the garment trade, but abuses have been documented in other industries as well. The advantage of this assignment is that students become familiar with the fair labor practices of "responsible capitalism" and learn about other cultures, their conduct of business, and the clashes between values.

12.13 Investigative Report: Exploring a Possible Place to Work (Obj. 4)

Encourage students to select a company they would like to work for in the future. They can also use the information they gather when they prepare their employment documents for Chapter 15.

12.14 Investigative Report: Marketing Abroad (Obj. 4)

This is an excellent way to help students increase their cultural awareness. In addition to library materials, students will also find excellent information on the Web. Two useful sites are http://www.executiveplanet.com and http://globaledge.msu.edu/.

12.15 Investigative Report: Expanding Operations Abroad (Obj. 4)

This is an excellent assignment that will help students increase their awareness of culture and gender. In addition to library materials, students will also find excellent information on the Web. Two useful sites are http://www.executiveplanet.com and http://globaledge.msu.edu/.

12.16 Progress Report: Heading Toward That Degree (Obj. 4)

This is another excellent activity to help students stay on track. They could also share this report with their counselors.

12.17 Conference or Trip Report: In Your Dreams (Obj. 4)

Activities 12.17 through 12.23 give students a number of opportunities to create a variety of reports. Many of these activities can be applied to the students' current work or academic situations, giving them even more meaning. These reports can be written individually or collaboratively as part of a small group.

12.20 Justification/Recommendation Report: Developing an Organizational Media Use Policy (Obj. 5)

This assignment allows for great versatility. Because many companies today have e-mail policies and a majority monitor and record traffic on their servers, the focus could shift to policies regulating visits to social networking sites, the use of smartphones on the job, instant messaging, texting, and blogging. Cases of workers fired over inappropriate media use abound; at the same time, increasingly companies are using social networking tools such as Twitter and Facebook to sell their products and create marketing buzz. Moreover, students could investigate guidelines determining the private use of company computers, PDAs, and smartphones. Would voluntary guidelines suffice, or do businesses need strict policies?

12.23 Yardstick Report: Evaluating Equipment (Obj. 5)

This assignment requires careful monitoring as it may invite copying of product descriptions and comparisons from the Internet and little original thinking. To safeguard against plagiarism, determine beforehand the models and specifications for students to compare. Try string searches (using exact word groups from student papers) in Google and other search engines, or find out whether your campus subscribes to the antiplagiarism site Turnitin.com if you encounter texts that sound copied.

12.25 Justification/Recommendation Report: Faster Service at Seguiti Family Pizza's Service* (Obj. 5)

This self-contained problem provides all the data necessary to complete the report without further research. Here are possible conclusions and recommendations that may be derived from the data provided:

CONCLUSIONS

Although a taste test was not conducted and, therefore, the quality of each competitor's pizza cannot be evaluated here, my observations have yielded useful results. Based on the analysis of the data, the following conclusions may be drawn:

1. Tomasia's has the most efficient system for serving customers. The average time it takes a customer to receive an order is half the time it takes at Seguiti Family Pizza.

2. Using an electronic system or calling out the menu item, having customers pick up their orders, and having one cash register per counter person result in a significant reduction in the average time it takes a customer to receive an order.

3. Because preparing the pizza dough in advance saves one minute per order, it makes sense to do that.

4. Because the TurboCrust Model 100 convection oven reduces cooking time by two minutes, it makes sense to consider investing in one. However, a taste and quality test for comparison makes sense.

RECOMMENDATIONS

Some suggestions for making the ordering process more efficient require few expenditures; others may call for a significant investment. The conclusions to the study lead to the following recommendations:

1. Have counter clerks call out orders to the cooks in the short run, and purchase an electronic system for recording orders in the medium to long run.

2. Consider letting customers pick up their own orders.

3. Purchase at least one new cash register.

4. Prepare the pizza dough before the store opens.

5. Consider investing in a TurboCrust Model 100 convection oven after conducting an undercover taste test comparing the products of various pizza ovens.

12.26 Justification/Recommendation Report: Analyzing Service at Sporting World (Obj. 5)

Score: 5 = Excellent, 4 = Very good, 3 = Good, 2 = Fair, 1 = Poor

Customer Survey Data as Percentages	5	4	3	2	1
1. Based on your shopping experience, how would you rate this Sporting World store?	35	32	20	9	4
2. Based on your shopping experience, how would you rate the likelihood that you will return to this Sporting World store?	53	30	14	2	1
3. How would you rate the likelihood that you would recommend this Sporting World store to a friend?	37	28	24	7	4
4. How would you rate the efficiency of checkout at the register?	16	25	45	10	4
5. How would you rate the efficiency of service at the customer service counter?	6	12	40	30	12
6. How would you rate the service staff's handling of problems?	8	30	17	40	5

CONCLUSIONS

Based on the results from customer surveys, the employee survey, and personal observations, the following conclusions may be drawn:

1. Although 67 percent of those surveyed felt that service was good or excellent, Sporting World has many weak areas where it could improve customer service.

2. Service at the cash registers needs to improve significantly, because only 16 percent of its customers rated checkout efficiency as *Excellent*, which is well below Sporting World's goal. Alarmingly, 59 percent of customers rated cash register efficiency as only *Good* or worse.

3. Based on the employee survey and my observations, the likely causes of delays at registers are the security tag removers, the procedure for approvals and overrides, and the volume of customers buying hunting and fishing licenses.

4. Service at the customer service counter needs immediate improvement because only 6 percent of customers rated their service as *Excellent,* 12 percent rated their service as *Very good*, and 42 percent rated their service as *Fair* or *Poor*.

5. Based on my observations, the likely causes of the low customer ratings of service at the customer service counter are (a) understaffing and (b) inadequate communication between the service and technical department staff.

6. After service at the customer service counter, the service needing immediate improvement is the service staff's handling of problems because only 8 percent of customers rated the staff's handling of problems as *Excellent,* 30 percent rated it as *Very good*, and 45 percent rated it as *Fair* or *Poor*.

7. The training to operate cash registers appears adequate, based on the employee survey and my observations.

8. The employee survey data I gathered is reliable, because (a) employees who deal with problems every day generally know what the problems are and (b) my observations support the employee survey results.

9. The fishing and footwear departments are understaffed, and the camping department is overstaffed, based on my observations and sales data.

RECOMMENDATIONS

The following recommendations will improve customer service and register wait times at Sporting World:

1. Repair or replace security tag removers to eliminate the need for employees to leave their registers.

2. Move staff from low-traffic areas such as the camping department to the customer service counter, the fishing department, and the footwear department, especially during peak periods.

3. Equip the customer service counter and technical department staff with headsets so that customer service staff can summon technical department staff without leaving the counter area.

4. Encourage managers to be on hand for customers' concerns, overrides, and check approvals during peak periods. Equip managers with headsets, so they can quickly go to the registers when summoned and monitor communication among other employees.

5. Consider designating a separate register for selling hunting and fishing licenses during peak volume times.

12.27 Yardstick Report: Comparing Textbook Options (Obj. 5)

This self-contained problem provides all the data necessary to complete the report without further research. Here are possible conclusions and recommendations that may result from the data:

CONCLUSIONS

The data gathered were complex and presented a mixed picture until a decision matrix was employed. Based on the analysis of the data, the following conclusions may be drawn:

1. No alternative is a clear winner in all criteria.
2. Renting books and buying books online are solid performers in all criteria.
3. Students should not buy the Fleetfoot Reader for reading college textbooks, because the selection is small and the device is difficult to use.
4. Renting books is cheaper than buying books from the campus bookstore.
5. Buying books from the campus bookstore is unavoidable in some cases, as the campus bookstore is the only outlet for certain titles.

RECOMMENDATIONS

After considering the various options and studying them with our specific priorities in mind, I am happy to make a few cost-saving suggestions. The conclusions drawn from the extensive data lead to the following recommendations:

1. Rent textbooks. Visit bookrentingsite.com first, because this site consistently had the lowest prices.
2. Buy books online that are not available for rental.
3. Buy any remaining books you need at the campus bookstore and return them in as good a condition as possible.

DECISION MATRIX FOR ALTERNATIVES TO BOOK BUYING

	CRITERIA			
OPTIONS	Price	Availability	Readability	**SUMMARY**
Weight	5	3	1	
Campus bookstore	1	5	5	25
Fleetfoot Reader	3	1	2	20
Rent books	5	4	5	42
Buy books online	4	4	5	37
Download e-books	2	2	1	17

12.28 Feasibility Report: Can Rainbow Precision Instruments Afford a Children's Center?

The main problem here is what to do about the Children's Center. The underlying questions are many; some are ethical issues of principle:

- Do companies such as Rainbow Precision Instruments have an ethical obligation to provide daycare for their workers?
- Is RPI responsible to the surrounding community in any way and, conversely, does the community have any reciprocal obligations to employers who feed, care for, and educate local children?
- Can a company like RPI avoid dealing with the ethical problems of daycare by simply hiring men and women past the childbearing years?
- Is there a conflict between the management's responsibility to its shareholders and the obligation to provide safe daycare for employees?
- Since the company allowed children from families not employed by RPI to enter the Children's Center, is it obligated to continue to look after them?

Here are some possible conclusions and recommendations:

CONCLUSIONS

- The total operating budget for the Center is $300,000 per year, so about $100,000 seems to be covered by tuition (the subsidy amounts to $200,000).
- RPI is paying $200,000 annually to keep the Center open while serving 14 employee children (145 is the total number of children served; 10 percent were employee kids in 2007).
- The number of community children reached 137 in 2007.
- The company subsidy per child stands at $1,380 per year. The current tuition of $696 per year covers about one third of the operating budget (multiply $696 times 145, the number of children).
- RPI is losing $2.5 million a year. The Center's subsidy of $200,000 amounts to 8 percent of this loss.
- The number of employee kids has been decreasing at a slightly accelerated rate. In the 5-year period between 2000 and 2005, the drop was 30 percentage points from 55 to 25 percent—6 percent per year. In the two years between 2005 and 2007, the number of employee children diminished 15 percentage points—7.5 percent per year.
- The company would need to charge $2,069 per student annually to operate the facility at cost.
- The intangible benefit of maintaining the goodwill of the community is greater than practical cost considerations.
- Although the company is losing money, the subsidy for the Center is only 8 percent of the total loss. The company needs to tighten cost controls in other areas.
- The company is responsible for providing a daycare facility to the surrounding community because few alternatives exist. RPI invited the local children who now form a 90 percent majority at the Center to join as the number of employee children was shrinking.
- The company is not responsible for providing a daycare facility to the community because it is losing money and its primary responsibility is to its employees, shareholders, and its financial health.
- The current operating hours are generous, covering two shifts from 7 a.m. to 10:30 p.m.
- Having children on the premises of the plant constitutes a liability and a safety risk under any circumstances.

RECOMMENDATIONS

- Explore cost-cutting options while keeping the Center open. Here are two possibilities:
  - Limit the operating hours to one shift.
  - Scale back the educational and curricular standards of the Center to save money on professional instructors.

- Raise the tuition to levels that would make the Center self-sustaining. If parents cannot afford the tuition of at least $2,069 per year, consider closing the facility.
- Try the changes proposed above for one calendar year. If the trends do not improve, close the Center.
- Close the Center immediately for the following reasons:
  - The company could reduce its current annual loss 8 percent by eliminating the facility.
  - The presence of children at the plant represents a liability and an expensive potential insurance risk.
  - Serving a mere 10 percent or 14 children of employees does not justify the high subsidy of $1,380 per child.
- Although an intangible benefit, the goodwill of the community is not worth $200,000 per year, given that the percentage of employee children is steadily decreasing.

12.29 Feasibility Report: Should We Continue to Outsource Personal Computer Manufacturing Jobs to India? (Obj. 5)

CONCLUSIONS

In our evaluation of outsourcing and onshoring, we considered flagging employee morale at Cyberdynamic Systems Corporation and negative public perceptions of outsourcing as well as onshoring.

Based on the analysis of the data, we arrived at the following conclusions:

1. Outsourcing PC manufacturing makes sense from a competitive standpoint. Costs are lowered, while product quality remains high. Profits and market share increased because of outsourcing, which helps to ensure the company's long-term future.

2. Outsourcing jobs is unpopular with the public, but given a choice, stockholders would rather live with an unpopular, but profitable strategy than a popular, but unprofitable one.

3. Although Equal Job appears to be a creative idea, it's a failure, as is onshoring.

4. Operation Web Office is a promising program because of its popularity with employees and significant cost savings. However, it shouldn't be put into widespread use until the company works out the bugs.

RECOMMENDATIONS

The conclusions to the study lead to the following recommendations:

1. Continue to outsource PC manufacturing to India, despite shortcomings.
2. Discontinue Equal Job and onshoring.
3. Increase efforts to make Operation Web Office a success.

The negative public perception of outsourcing is more than offset by hefty profits and shareholder approval. This is why the practice should continue. Eliminating onshoring and Equal Job would go a long way toward restoring employees' trust and, hence, morale. Moreover, getting Operation Web Office online as soon as possible would further this goal.

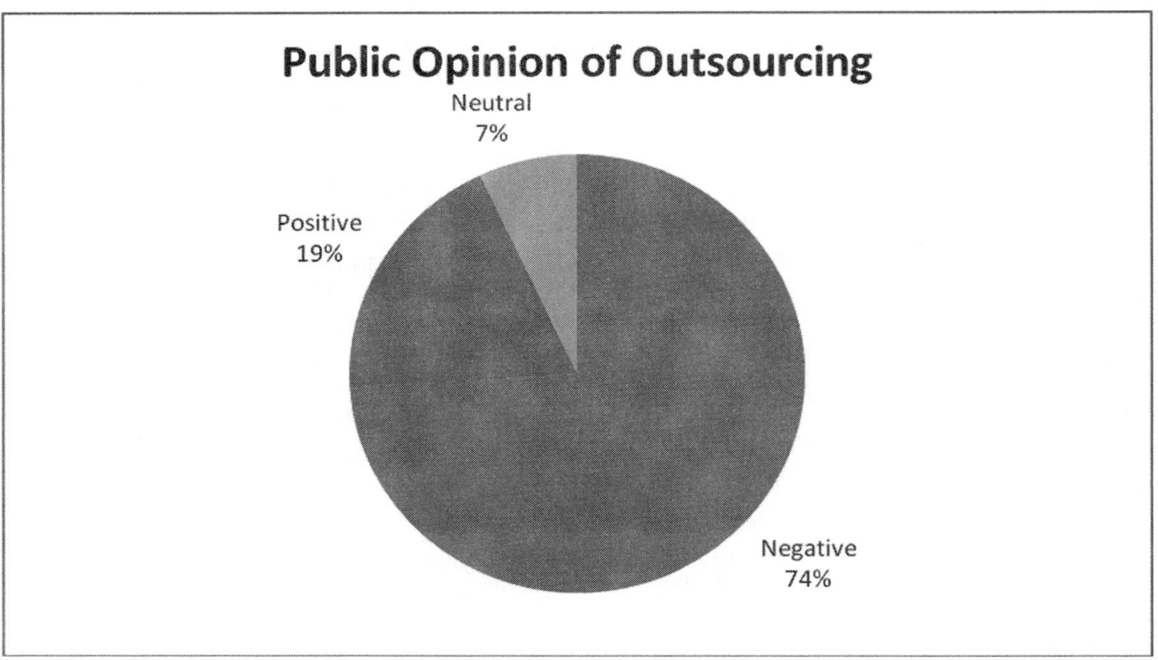

12.30 Yardstick Report: Parking Problem at Caputi's Italian Restaurant (Obj. 5)

CONCLUSIONS

Having thoroughly analyzed all available options, I have arrived at the following conclusions. The decision matrix helped in fleshing out the advantages to the restaurant and the benefits to its customers.

1. Overall, offering valet service is the best solution to the restaurant's parking problem because it ranks highest in the two most important criteria: cost to the restaurant and convenience to the customer.

2. The shuttle service is the least attractive solution and, therefore, should not be implemented.
3. Advertising, although only somewhat effective, is inexpensive and still provides some benefit to the restaurant and its customers.

RECOMMENDATIONS

Based on the preceding conclusions, and after weighing the relative importance of the criteria we discussed, the following recommendations seem the most advisable:

1. Hire a valet service.
2. Advertise parking options on the restaurant's Web site.
3. Avoid advertising parking options at the restaurant, as this strategy will likely confuse customers and anger the valet parking company.

These three recommendations are highly likely to satisfy patrons while also keeping restaurant costs down.

Weighted Decision Matrix						
		Cost to Restaurant	Cost to Customer	Ease of Implementation	Convenience to Customer	Total
	Weights:	10	6	4	8	
Valet		3	1	2	3	68
Shuttle		1	3	1	2	48
Advertising		2	3	3	1	58

ZOOMING IN Part 1: Starbucks Perks Up: Recapturing the Soul of the Coffeehouse

Critical Thinking

- **What kind of information should Starbucks gather to help it decide how closely to locate its stores?**

  Because its location strategy is based on intercepting consumers on their way to work, home, or anywhere in between, Starbucks could collect information about its customers' work and home locations from those willing to disclose such information. In addition, Starbucks could collect information on the length of lines and parking problems at each location, including anything that reduces convenience. In a place where long lines and parking problems occur, Starbucks could consider placing another store nearby.

- **How could Howard Schultz test his impression that the intimate communal coffee-drinking experience is fading at Starbucks?**

  This type of research calls for wide-ranging customer and barista (employee) surveys. First, a small pilot study could help test a standardized questionnaire for a representative survey. In a pilot study, researchers ask open-ended questions to establish key areas of concern. After analyzing trends and establishing clusters of answers, investigators construct a questionnaire for a large representative sample. Howard Schultz may be judging by his own limited experience, also called "anecdotal evidence." To ensure that such narrow judgments are valid, objective and representative surveys must confirm them.

- **How can collected information be transmitted to Starbucks' decision makers?**

  Information collected from surveys and other sources is generally transmitted to organization decision makers in written reports or oral presentations. Staff members collect information, analyze the findings, draw conclusions, and make recommendations, if requested to do so.

ZOOMING IN, Part 2: Starbucks

Critical Thinking

- **How important to Starbucks are the collection, organization, and distribution of up-to-date information regarding food and beverage trends, competition, and product development?**

  The collection, organization, and distribution of current data regarding food and beverage trends, competition, and product development are extremely important to Starbucks. For a company that has single-handedly created the espresso bar culture in this country, Starbucks must stay on the cutting edge in its product offerings and the experience it creates for its customers. Maintaining a position of market leadership takes lots of research. Even then, as evidenced by the failed pursuits cited in the case, no one can predict what will be the next big hit with customers. In large complex organizations, the gathering of information is critical. All this information must be organized into meaningful reports.

- **In what ways could Starbucks use the Internet to monitor its competitors, Caribou Coffee and Dunkin' Donuts?**

  Regular visits to Caribou Coffee's Web site **(http://www.cariboucoffee.com)** would keep Starbucks apprised of Caribou's new coffeehouse locations and new products. In addition, monitoring newswire reports for Caribou Coffee, McDonald's McCafé, and Dunkin' Donuts' stunning variety of caffeinated beverages, along with online resources such as LexisNexis, would also provide valuable information.

- **What kind of reports might be made to management by employees assigned the task of monitoring Starbucks' competition?**

  Employees monitoring Caribou Coffee's growth and McDonald's McCafé's as well as Dunkin' Donuts' bold new take on the market leader would probably write informational reports. If the reports were submitted weekly or monthly, they would be periodic reports and would probably follow a consistent format

ZOOMING IN AT WORK, Your Turn: Applying Your Skills at Starbucks

The first assignment calls for a feasibility report. The researchers could study media coverage and sales data for the new concept stores to evaluate their success. One interesting resource is Yelp, the social networking site that allows users to review local restaurants. Roy Street Coffee & Tea and 15th Ave. Coffee & Tea each has enough entries to gauge customers' opinions. A discussion of Yelp could include reminders to take these community views with a grain of salt and a discussion of the reliability of Web sources. Yelp has been accused of lending itself to manipulation by merchants and customers with an ax to grind.

The second assignment requires a recommendation report. Howard Schultz has repeatedly hinted at wanting to return to the company's core business, which is the selling of caffeinated beverages. Starbucks has recently given up on the Hear Music label, and some of its media selections have flopped. For example, the much-touted film *Akeelah and the Bee* became a box-office and DVD dud. Similarly, the company may face litigation from Carly Simon for lackluster sales of her CD.

Discussion Material for CAREER COACH: The Top Ten Tips for Designing Better Documents

This is an excellent activity for students to work on collaboratively. Have students find additional tips for designing professional documents in books, on Web sites, or on their own through brainstorming. Each group should present its findings to the class. They should then use all the tips presented to analyze the attractiveness and professionalism of annual reports. Students can use hardcopy annual reports or Web-based annual reports for this activity.

Ethics Check Solutions

Ethics Check, Page 381
Good Corporate Citizens
Like many innovative companies, Starbucks wants to be seen as a responsible corporate citizen. On its Web site Starbucks posts its annual corporate social responsibility report. The company also has an "Environmental Mission Statement" and holds suppliers to a "Supplier Code of Conduct." Do ethical considerations affect your opinions of companies or sway your buying decisions?

Students could look at Starbucks' Web site and read the various mission statements, codes of conduct, and annual CSR reports. Ask students if they are aware of other companies that have a strong environmental bent or emphasize corporate social responsibility. Apple Computers, Gap, Google, and others come to mind. Poll the students to find out if they respond to such appeals or if they see them as "gimmicks" to increase sales. The underlying question, of course, is whether companies have a responsibility other than generating profit, a view popularized by the Chicago School of Economics, most notably, Milton Friedman. Most economists today hold a view similar to Friedman's.

Ethics Check, Page 402
Is This $100 Bill Yours?
Purchasing managers at Frito-Lay, Safeway, and B&G Foods have pleaded guilty to taking bribes that led to tainted foods purchased at inflated prices. Company officials relied on false reports and documentation supplied by their managers. How did food suppliers know whom to bribe? New Jersey businessman and food broker Randall Rahal said he could guess who would be susceptible to bribery by dropping a $100 bill on the floor, then picking it up and saying, "You must have dropped this. Is it yours?" Is this a good test?

Most students will probably agree that an inherently dishonest person would see an opportunity to make a buck and claim the $100 bill, whereas really honest people would never dream of claiming something that is not theirs. In this case Mr. Rahal pleaded guilty to racketeering, price fixing, and money laundering. He was accused of bribing ingredient buyers as early as 1998. One buyer was a purchasing manager at Nabisco, who later went to work at Ortega Mexican foods. As many as 55 companies were involved in tainted food shipments. A U.S. attorney in Sacramento said, "If you have a couple of people who are willing to bend the rules and they set that tone from the top, that can spread very quickly in that company and in that niche of the industry, and that's what happened here." [Neuman, W. (2010, February 25). Hidden ingredient: The sweetener. *The New York Times*, pp. B1, B5.]

Photo Essay Solutions

Photo Essay, Page 394
Informational reports, such as periodic reports and progress and interim reports, provide managers with a written record on how a project is developing. Informational reports summarize regular activities while identifying special problems and potential remedies that need to be addressed to keep plans on schedule.

Photo Essay, Page 402
Persuasive justification reports explain fully all the benefits of a recommendation and also anticipate possible reader objections. Effective justification reports often identify a problem or need, list pros and cons of various plans of action, and support recommendations with statistics and authoritative quotes. When crafting a justification report for receptive audiences, writers should utilize a direct pattern. An indirect pattern is recommended for less favorable audiences.

Chapter 13 LECTURE NOTES AND TEACHING SUGGESTIONS

Proposals and Formal Reports

CHAPTER SYNOPSIS

If your course includes a proposal or formal report, you may want to introduce this chapter early in the course. Assigning a long report usually means introducing the topic six to ten weeks before the report is due. Because this chapter outlines all the parts of proposals and formal reports, you can discuss it when you first make the report assignment and return to it when students are completing their reports. If your students do not actually write long reports, they can still benefit by analyzing their structure and seeing the application of the 3-x-3 writing process to longer documents. Once your students are familiar with long reports, they can use this chapter for reference when they need to prepare them for other courses or at work.

Emphasize the differences and similarities of proposals and formal reports. To overcome the sense that some students have that preparing proposals and formal reports is overwhelming, show them how applying Guffey's 3-x-3 writing process divides a large task into manageable steps. Assure them that such reports are written over time and often in teams. Generally, proposals and large reports are not written in isolation. Emphasize that such projects are completed through sufficient preparation and perseverance.

This chapter also introduces the components of a business plan with special emphasis on how it promotes growth potential and establishes confidence in the management team.

LEARNING OBJECTIVES

1. Discuss the general uses and basic components of proposals and grasp their audience and purpose.

2. Discuss formal proposals and how to anticipate a receiver's reaction to your message.

3. Identify the components of typical business plans and ethically create buy-in for your business ideas.

4. Describe the components of the front matter in formal business reports, and show how they further the purpose of your report.

5. Describe the body and back matter of formal business reports and how they serve the purpose of your report.

6. Specify tips that aid writers of formal business reports.

WHAT'S NEW IN THIS CHAPTER

- Updated three-part case study Zooming In to reflect the most current practices in proposal writing.
- Added two new Spotlights highlighting business leaders sharing their insights into proposal and business plan writing.
- Created a photo essay featuring the NBC/Comcast merger to illustrate formal report writing.
- Added a photo essay about an alternative energy source, hydrokinetic power turbines, to demonstrate persuasion in formal proposals.
- Reorganized the content to make the chapter easier to grasp and easier to retain for students.
- Introduced new model documents that provide a glimpse of current business practices in proposal and report writing to readers.
- Added end-of-chapter activities to practice executive summaries as requested by reviewers to meet instructor and student needs.

LECTURE OUTLINE

I. Preparing Informal Proposals (p. 425)

A. Components of Informal Proposals

Figure 13.1 Components of Formal and Informal Proposals
Figure 13.2 Informal Proposal

PowerPoint slides 1-9

1. **Introduction**
   - Hint at extraordinary results with details to be revealed shortly.
   - Promise low costs or speedy results.
   - Mention a remarkable resource (well-known authority, new computer program, well-trained staff) available exclusively to you.
   - Identify a serious problem (worry item) and promise a solution, to be explained later.
   - Specify a key issue or benefit that you feel is the heart of the proposal.

2. **Background, problem, and purpose** – Identify the problem and discuss the goals or purposes of the project.

3. **Proposal, plan, and schedule** – Discuss your plan for solving the problem.

4. **Staffing** – Describe the credentials and expertise of the project leaders.

5. **Budget** – List the proposed project costs.

6. **Authorization Request** – Close with a request for authorization.

II. Preparing Formal Proposals (p. 430)

A. Special Components of Formal Proposals

1. Copy of the RFP
2. Letter of Transmittal
3. Abstract or Executive Summary
4. Title Page
5. Table of Contents
6. List of Illustrations
7. Appendix

B. Checklist for Writing Proposals

Introduction

- Indicate the purpose.
- Develop a persuasive "hook."

Background, Problem, Purpose

- Provide necessary background.
- Introduce the problem.

Proposal, Plan, Schedule

- Explain the proposal.
- Discuss plan management and evaluation.
- Outline a timetable.

Staffing

- Promote the qualifications of your staff.
- Mention special resources and equipment.

Budget

- Show project costs.
- Include a deadline.

Authorization

- Ask for approval.

III. Creating Effective Business Plans (p. 432)

PowerPoint slides 10-15

A. Components of Typical Business Plans

- Letter of transmittal and/or executive summary with mission statement
- Table of contents
- Company description
- Product/service description

- Market analysis
- Operations and management
- Financial analysis
- Appendixes

B. Seeing Sample Business Plans on the Web

- http://www.bplans.com
- http://www.sba.gov/smallbusinessplanner/

Lecture Tidbit

When writing a business plan, leave out the vague and the meaningless babble of business phrases (such as "being the best") because they are simply hype. Remember that the objective of a plan is its results, and for results, you need tracking and follow up. You need specific dates, management responsibilities, budgets, and milestones. Then you can follow up. No matter how well thought out or brilliantly presented, a business plan means nothing unless it produces results.

T. Berry, "Common Business Plan Mistakes." Retrieved October 23, 2007, from http://www.bplans.com/dp/article.cfm/35.

IV. Writing Formal Reports (p. 433)

Figure 13.3 Components of Formal and Informal Reports

PowerPoint slides 16-25

A. Front Matter Components of Formal Business Reports

PowerPoint slides 26-37

1. Cover
2. Title page
3. Letter or memo of transmittal
4. Table of contents
5. List of illustrations
6. Executive summary
   - Summarize key points.
   - Look for strategic words and sentences.
   - Prepare an outline with headings.
   - Fill in your outline.
   - Begin with the purpose.
   - Follow the report sequence.
   - Eliminate nonessential details.
   - Control the length.

7. Introduction
   - Background
   - Problem or purpose
   - Significance
   - Scope
   - Organization

   Also:
   - Authorization
   - Literature review
   - Source and methods
   - Definition of key terms

8. Body
9. Conclusions
10. Recommendations
11. Appendix
12. Work cited or references

V. Final Writing Tips (p. 438)

- Allow sufficient time.
- Finish data collection.
- Work from a good outline.
- Provide a proper writing environment.
- Use the features of your computer.
- Write rapidly; revise later.
- Save difficult sections.
- Be consistent in verb tense.
- Generally avoid *I* and *we*.
- Let the first draft sit.
- Revise for clarity, coherence, and conciseness.
- Proofread the final copy three times.

A. Putting It All Together

Figure 13.4 Model Formal Report With APA Citation Style

B. Checklist for Preparing Formal Reports

Report Process

- Analyze the report and purpose.
- Anticipate the audience and issues.
- Prepare a work plan.
- Collect data.
- Document data sources.
- Interpret and organize the data.

- Prepare graphics.
- Compose the first draft.
- Revise and proofread.
- Evaluate the product.

Report Components

- Title page
- Letter of transmittal
- Table of contents
- List of illustrations
- Executive summary
- Introduction
- Body
- Conclusions and recommendations
- Appendix
- Works Cited or References

Lecture Transparencies
(available in a separate packet and at http://www.meguffey.com)

Proposals and Formal Reports Acetate	Transparency Number
Preparing Proposals	140
Preparing an Effective Business Plan	141-142
Business Reports	143-144
Formal Report Components	145-148
Components in Formal and Informal Reports	149

Solution Masters

Solutions and discussion material for the Chapter 13 activities are found in this lecture outline only. Solution masters are not available.

Answers to Chapter Review Questions

1. **What purpose do proposals serve? (Objs. 1, 2)**

   Proposals are written offers to solve a problem, provide services, or sell equipment.

2. **Who uses requests for proposals (RFPs), and why? (Objs. 1, 2)**

   Government agencies and many firms use requests for proposals (RFPs) to solicit competitive bids on projects. RFPs ensure that bids are comparable and that funds are awarded fairly, using consistent criteria.

3. **What are the six principal components of an informal letter proposal? (Obj. 1)**

   The six principal components of an informal letter proposal are the following: introduction, background, proposal, staffing, budget, and authorization request.

4. **Why is the budget section in a proposal particularly important? (Obj. 2)**

   Because a proposal is a legal contract, the budget must be carefully researched.

5. **Why does an entrepreneur need to write a business plan? (Obj. 3)**

   An entrepreneur needs to write a business plan to secure financial backing and to have a detailed road map to chart the course of the business.

6. **Name eight components of typical business plans. (Obj. 3)**

   Typical business plans generally include the following: letter of transmittal or executive summary, table of contents, company description, product or service description, market analysis, operations and management analysis, financial analysis, and appendixes.

7. **What should a business plan mission statement include and how long should it be? (Obj. 3)**

   A mission statement explains the reasons a business will succeed. It can be as short as a couple of sentences, but ideally it should be one or two short paragraphs.

8. **Why are formal reports written in business? Give an original example of a business related formal report. (Obj. 4)**

   Formal reports represent the end product of thorough investigation and analysis. They provide ordered information to decision makers and are instrumental in solving problems. Example: A study to investigate increasing travel costs within an organization.

9. **What is a letter or memorandum of transmittal? (Obj. 4)**

   A letter or memorandum of transmittal introduces a formal report. The transmittal letter or memo (a) announces the topic and tells how the report was authorized; (b) briefly describes the project; (c) highlights the findings, conclusions, and recommendations, if the reader is expected to be supportive; and (d) ends with appreciation for the assignment, instruction for the reader's follow-up actions, acknowledgment of help from others, or offers of assistance in answering questions.

10. **How long should a typical executive summary be? (Obj. 4)**

    The length of executive summaries is usually 10 percent of the original report or article. A 100-page report could have a 10-page executive summary.

11. Name the steps necessary to write an executive summary in a formal business report. (Obj. 4)

a. Summarize key points.
b. Look for strategic words and sentences.
c. Prepare an outline with headings.
d. Fill in your outline.
e. Begin with the purpose.
f. Follow the report sequence.
g. Eliminate nonessential details.
h. Control the length.

12. What should be included in the introduction to a formal report? (Obj. 4)

The introduction should discuss the background, purpose, significance, and scope of the report. It should preview the report's organization. It may also tell who authorized the report. It could include a literature review, sources, methods, and definitions of key terms.

13. What should the writer strive to do in the body of a formal report? (Obj. 5)

The writer should discuss, analyze, interpret, and evaluate the research findings or the solution to the initial problem. The writer should show how the evidence justifies any conclusions.

14. Why must writers list their sources and identify them in the text? (Obj. 5)
The purpose of references or works cited is to help readers locate the sources of ideas mentioned in a report, to disclose the sources the writer has relied on, and to demonstrate the author's integrity.

15. In your view, what are six of the most important tips for the writer of a formal report? Explain each of your choices. (Obj. 6)

Answers will vary, but students should discuss some of the following:

1. Allow sufficient time.
2. Finish data collection before beginning to write.
3. Work from a good outline.
4. Provide a proper writing environment.
5. Use the features of your computer.
6. Write rapidly; revise later.
7. Save difficult sections to write after you complete easier sections.
8. Be consistent in verb tense.
9. Generally avoid I and we.
10. Let the first draft rest before revising.

Answers to Critical Thinking Questions

1. **Which category of proposal, solicited or unsolicited, is more likely to succeed, and why? (Obj. 1)**

   Sending unsolicited proposals carries a certain degree of risk because the author has to work extra hard to convince the recipient that a problem exists. Solicited proposals respond to invitations to submit bids, which means that the agency or firm posting an RFP acknowledges the problem and calls for solutions. Moreover, proposal writers can rely on the RFP as a road map to help them develop their outline and tailor their approach to the needs of their audience.

2. **Compare and contrast proposals and business plans. (Objs. 1–3)**

   Proposals and business plans are similar in that they both are persuasive messages. A proposal seeks to sell a product or service; a business plan seeks funding for a new business or for expansion of a current business. Both proposals and business plans begin with transmittal letters or memos. Both contain an overview of the proposed plan of operation. Both promote the writer's expertise and qualified staff. Both include a budget. However, a business plan presents a marketing plan, analysis of the competition, and a complete look at the finances of the proposed company. A business plan describes start-up costs and operating costs. Both might include appendixes with supporting documents not integral to the report.

3. **What is the purpose of a business plan, and what should it communicate to investors? (Obj. 3)**

   A business plan is a persuasive document, the purpose of which is to obtain funding. The business plan should be prepared thoughtfully and thoroughly to show that the writer has done his or her homework and has the necessary skills to launch and sustain the start-up. Investors are more likely to buy in to the new business if they see a carefully planned path to success and demonstrated knowledge of the industry.

4. **How do formal reports differ from informal reports? (Objs. 4–6)**

   Formal reports differ from informal reports in length, tone, writing style, and format. The bodies of both would be similar, but the beginning and ending matter would differ.

5. **Ethical Issue: How can a team of writers ensure that each member shoulders an equal or fair amount of the work on an extensive writing project, such as a formal proposal or report?**

   This is a nagging question in college writing teams and, no doubt, in the workplace as well. Answers will vary, but for a productive collaboration and peace of mind in the group, it is essential that all members perceive the shared labor as fairly distributed. Each member must pull his or her weight, whether the group of three or four divides the report into three or four parts, writes together in real time, or designates the strongest writer to pull the findings together.

Activities

13.1 Proposals: Solving a Workplace Problem in an Unsolicited Informal Proposal (Obj. 1)

The advantage of this assignment is that most students have had some workplace or internship experience to draw on. However, one initial difficulty involves identifying a problem that's substantial enough for a proposal. Students tend to bring up problems that are insignificant or don't generate much in savings or earnings—the standard for writing a proposal. Otherwise, why not just *say* it? Students may need help with identifying a problem that would merit writing about it. Another standard for writing a letter or memo proposal is a cost-benefit analysis. The problem must be serious enough to require such an analysis, however informal it may be. Topics could include improved waste management or recycling (switching companies); changing store closing times to adjust to new shopping habits; a new peer-counseling fitness program; and so forth.

13.2 Proposals: Think Like an Entrepreneur (Obj. 1)

Many students dream of owning a business one day; some students even run small businesses while in college. This is why they enjoy activities that provide hypothetical scenarios in entrepreneurship. At the same time, this activity playfully introduces students to important resources, such as the Small Business Administration's Web site.

Finding a service or product to promote may not pose a great problem for students. However, the instructor needs to be aware of potential copying from the Internet. This is why the instructor may want to limit the scope or determine which specific product or service the class will promote and the audience it will target. The more specific features the professor provides, the better the prospects of thwarting any illegitimate work. The assignment calls for a letter proposal. To prepare, the instructor may want to analyze direct mail that students could bring to class. Most of us receive enough "junk mail," so that specimens are easy to come by. Many such letters are excellent, well-written samples of persuasive writing. Examples could include promoting a new dental office, a massage therapist, a gardening service, an iPod song loading business, and so forth.

13.3 Proposals: Comparing Real Proposals (Objs. 1, 2)

This activity encourages students to use the rich resources of the Web to locate actual proposals. Real proposals are too long to include as models in the textbook, but the Web has many examples. Students will find numerous Web sites that are hawking proposal templates or books to sell. This is a good exercise for students to develop their skills in distinguishing marketing sites from authentic resources.

13.4 Proposals: Medicus Associates Solicits Your Proposal (Obj. 1)

This activity was developed as a teaching module by Professor Peggy Brunyansky. You may download her module from http://www.meguffey.com. Look under Teaching Modules, "Team Assignments That Work."

13.5 Proposal and Grant Writing: Learning From the Nonprofits (Objs. 1, 2)

This activity encourages students to use the Web to learn more about writing proposals and grants. You may want to assign this memo report as a research project that lays a foundation for class participation in writing real proposals for local nonprofit organizations.

13.6 Business Plans: Can Your Team Write a Winning Plan? (Obj. 3)

A complete classroom module for developing a business plan as a report-writing assignment is available at http://www.meguffey.com. Look under Teaching Materials, "Teaching the Business Plan."

13.7–13.11.

These activities give students a number of ideas for topics for long reports and proposals. These reports and proposal can be written individually or collaboratively.

ZOOMING IN Part 1: Writing Winning Proposals at Raytheon

Critical Thinking

- **Why are proposals vitally important to a company like Raytheon?**

  As is typical in the aerospace industry, Raytheon's business is largely program-based. Both large and small programs are based on customer evaluations of proposals submitted by contractors. Each company's success in winning such proposals determines:
  - What programs it will have to employ its personnel
  - Which product development efforts will receive the funding needed to make them successful
  - How successful the different business units within the company will be

  Ultimately, the quality of Raytheon's proposals determines its ability to win competitions, and its ability to win competitions determines how much money the company will be able to make.

  Even noncompetitive programs often require proposals to be submitted for such things as (a) follow-up on contracts and (b) spare parts and other kinds of logistic support. Usually these proposals are not competitive and involve mostly cost information. However, they are essential to the company as vehicles for acquiring contracts.

- **How are proposals at Raytheon similar to and different from proposals or long reports written by students?**

  Both student proposals and corporate proposals are:
  - Purpose-driven business documents
  - Persuasive and often sales-oriented
  - Time constrained
  - Audience or customer-focused

  Student proposals are generally shorter and simpler than most corporate proposals. They also are more likely to be written as an exercise by a single person, while corporate proposals, especially the most important, largest corporate proposals are always for real and are likely to be:
  - Critical to the success of the business
  - Written in response to customer requirements documents and requests for proposal
  - Written by teams of writers, not individuals

  Long reports and proposals at Raytheon are similar in format to proposals, and are:
  - Often written by teams of writers
  - Often argumentative or persuasive in their intent
  - Frequently important, customer-focused documents

  Sometimes long reports at Raytheon are addressed not to customers but to a variety of internal audiences. But they are always written to accomplish some serious business purpose that the company believes makes them worth the cost of producing them. As with student proposals, student reports tend to be:
  - Simpler and less complex than most corporate reports
  - Written by individuals rather than teams
  - Often written as exercises rather than for real business purposes

- **How can team members maintain consistency and meet deadlines when writing important, time-constrained, multivolume documents such as this proposal?**

  In developing large, multivolume, team-written documents on tight schedules, many things can go wrong either in the planning and management of the document development process or in developing the content required to make the document a success. The first challenge is to create a document development plan that:
  - Includes everything that must be accomplished to complete the document
  - Schedules all of the events (storyboard and draft reviews, executive reviews, document sign offs, etc.) that must be accomplished
  - Identifies the people needed to write the document and manage the development process and makes sure that they know what they must accomplish and when
  - Enables authors who are not professional writers to develop sections that are accurate, effective, and accomplishable within the time and resource constraints that impact the creation of the document

- Enables these same authors to know what they have to say where, and how to do so at the level of detail and using language that is compatible and consistent with that being used by other authors elsewhere in the document.

The next step is to implement this plan using a structured document development process that provides the management controls and the author support that enables all of the above to be accomplished within the schedule constraints of the project. It is best if the process used is one that involves a formal and structured implementation of the standard three-phased writing process that is used by most writers in developing almost any written document. A disciplined application of such processes under the management of people who understand this process and know how to apply it in complex situations will result in the development of a successful, large, multivolume business document.

ZOOMING IN Part 2: Writing Winning Proposals at Raytheon

Critical Thinking

- **What aspects of Raytheon's proposal writing process can you apply to your own work?**

Basically, Raytheon's proposal process institutionalizes the three phases of the writing process (prewriting, writing, and revising) and provides authors with support and assistance from other team members and from corporate executives as they apply this process to their proposal sections.

The process offers the following to support the prewriting phase of the process:

- Extensive proposal planning (schedules, RFP analyses, win strategy development and documentation, customer and competitor analysis, and the development of detailed technical, management, and cost planning) by the company and proposal team personnel before the intensive writing effort begins
- The selection of authors who are generally experts in their fields, which reduces the amount of extra research and shortens the learning curve as authors prepare to write
- Group meetings attended by authors at which proposal plans are discussed and explained, thereby ensuring that authors understand the big picture issues for the proposal as well as the issues involved in their own areas
- Personal attention and guidance (via face-to-face discussions and storyboard reviews) from the proposal leadership relating to each author's sections as he or she begins to develop them.

During the writing phase additional support is provided as the author's research, plan, and draft their topics.

- All of the materials developed during the prewriting phase of the proposal effort (the RFP, the win strategy, and other related documents, technical management, and cost-planning information, etc.) are made available to authors either in hard copy or online to enable efficient research by authors into these issues.

- Proposal planning meetings explain the proposal development techniques that will be used, the scheduling of events, and the organizational structure of both the proposal and the team, thereby helping the authors to understand the context within which their writing assignments will be completed.
- The storyboard development and review process provides intensive individual guidance relating to each section the author must write, forcing each writer to outline each section to make it fit within the context of the rest of the proposal as a whole.
- The annotated storyboards provide detailed guidance for writing each section as the author composes it, and the proposal schedule forces immediate attention to composition by scheduling management and executive reviews for the drafts.

The revision phase is equally well supported, first by the scheduled draft reviews mentioned above, but also by additional activities that authors must prepare.

- Drafts are maintained (usually hanging on a wall) in the team's proposal room and all team members are encouraged to review and make comments on topics written by other authors.
- Volume managers are responsible for reviewing each author's drafts to ensure that they are responsive to the RFP, implement the comments by the Pink Team and other reviewers, and respond to the guidance provided by the storyboard reviews.
- The formal Red Team review involves a high-level management evaluation of the draft to ensure that it meets the proposal's content and quality standards.
- Author and volume managers make final corrections in response to the Red Team and prepare for final formatting, proofreading, and publication—often by a professional publications organization ensuring that the end product meets corporate publication standards.

Most of the practices outlined above can be implemented in a more informal manner by students, especially if they are working in teams or are encouraged to seek help improving the quality of their writing efforts, particularly for long-term projects. Shorter individual projects offer less opportunity for outside help but can be improved by the students themselves as they follow the steps in the writing process to their work.

- **How do you think the various reviewers and their reviews help ensure the success of a proposal effort?**

The preceding discussion explains many of the ways in which the reviewers and their reviews help the authors to provide quality work. In general, each reviewer offers his or her expertise, both as an expert in the field and as an outside reader striving to understand the author's work. In some cases this expertise will be largely technical and will serve to ensure that the author's technical content is appropriate and accurate. In other cases, it will be managerial, or cost-oriented and will help ensure that the author clearly and accurately represents the company's position on these issues. Some reviewers, particularly the ones who are proposal specialists or editors, will provide important guidance related to writing style and clarity, or will help the authors ensure that their chosen visuals are appropriate to the proposal's purpose and that they are clear.

Using multiple reviewers and extending the reviewing process from the earliest prewriting phase of the author's writing effort until the final formatting and proofreading stage of the process enables even inexperienced or poor writers to gradually improve their product until their final product is likely to be much better than they could have produced by themselves. This extended reviewing process also helps to standardize what might otherwise be individualistic writing styles until they blend together into a corporate standard that extends throughout the proposal. But the most important result of this extended series of reviews is the removal of errors and the shaping of the writing until each piece of the proposal contributes to its ultimate purpose as a sales document that presents the company's case strongly and effectively to the customer.

- **Why do you think Raytheon puts so much effort into proposal executive summaries?**

  The executive summary's importance and the reason Raytheon spends so much time on improving it lies in its audiences. The summary is likely to be the only document in the proposal that is read by every member of the customer's proposal evaluation team. It thus provides an inclusive context within which each evaluator can read the sections of the proposal that they are scoring. Evaluators usually read only those sections of the proposal that relate to their individual areas of expertise, not the whole proposal. This is an important mission of the executive summary.

  But the most important mission of the executive summary is to explain the company's proposal to the most important members of the customer's evaluation team, the executives (often very high-level executives) or the single executive who will make the decision about which proposal wins the competition. For these high-level executives, the executive summary is likely to be the only proposal document they read. As such, it must address their needs and interests and make a strong but concise presentation of the company's proposal. It is for this audience that Raytheon expends a significant amount of time and effort creating high-quality executive summaries for their proposals.

ZOOMING IN Your Turn: Applying Your Skills at Raytheon

Task 1 requires a short (3 to 5 pages) business report recommending a structured writing process to be used for team-written company documents. The following is a suggested outline for this report:

1. Executive Summary summarizing the key points that follow (optional)
2. Introduction identifying the occasion for this report and outlining the need for an improved writing process for team-written company documents
3. Background survey of the characteristics that an effective team-writing process for business documents should have
4. Discussion of possible alternative approaches that might work, identifying the strengths and weaknesses of each
5. Description of your preferred process saying why it is the preferred approach
6. Discussion of the resources needed to implement the selected process

7. Discussion of the likely costs of implementing and using this process
8. Recommendation to management that the company implement and use this process where appropriate and saying why it is a good idea
9. List of references

A storyboard could be prepared providing detailed outlines for each outline entry or could be done for multiple parts of the outline such as Sections 1, 2 and 8; Sections 3 and 4; and Sections 5 through 7. This would work well for a three-person team. Another possibility might be two storyboards, one for the first four sections and another for the last four sections. This would work well for a two-person team.

Task 2 requires a memo evaluating several (two to four) proposal consulting companies that might be able to help Raytheon teams write good, new business proposals when the company's proposal specialists are unavailable.

This memo should be in standard memo (or e-mail) form and should recommend a short list of proposal consultant firms that could be used by Raytheon to help proposal teams build high-quality, new business proposals. It should also provide information about how each of the selected firms could be contacted. The following is a list of several well-known proposal consulting firms providing contact information for each.

- Steve Myer and Associates: http://www.whenyoumustwin.com
- Shipley Associates: http://www.shipleywins.com
- The Marx Group, Federal Proposal.com: http://www.federalproposals.com
- Organizational Communication Inc.: http://www.orgcom.com/proposal-services.html
- The Sant Corporation: http://www.santcorp.com/services/sant_consulting.htm
- The 24 Hour Company (for graphics and publication support): http://www.24hrco.com

Ethics Check Solutions

Ethics Check, Page 433
Honesty Is Key
A business plan's purpose is to help manage a company and raise capital; hence, it is a persuasive document that must be accurate and honest. Whether the goal is to persuade a lender or investors or whether it is the blueprint for running operations, the business plan must be realistic. What are the risks of "fudging" numbers or sugarcoating potential challenges?

To create buy-in from potential investors and to ensure the smooth management of the start-up, solid research and an honest look at the strengths and weaknesses and the opportunities and threats are necessary. After all, among the reasons for the failure of many start-ups are not writing a business plan; creating a weak, unpersuasive document; or implementing a business plan poorly. The business plan is a living document that needs to change as the business evolves yet that creates a solid basis for the entrepreneur. A flawed or dishonest business plan will not lead to long-term success. The chances that a new incorporated business will survive for eight years are about 50 percent.

Ethics Check, Page 407
Cheater on the Team
If one of your teammates cowriting a formal report with you has been found to have plagiarized a portion of your writing project, typically the instructor will punish the entire group, assuming ownership of the entire team. After all, researchers are expected to deliver a product that they have jointly prepared. Is this approach fair?

Answers will probably vary. Most instructors consider the team as a whole guilty of academic dishonesty, whereas many students view their research tasks as work that they divide among themselves and don't perceive it as a coherent whole. Each group member assumes responsibility for an activity—such as researching, writing, or editing—or team members write small sections of the report, say, a third or a quarter each in a three- or four-member team. Such an approach makes cheating nearly undetectable, and the group members have little control over the work individuals do. Anticheating Web sites like Turnitin.com can help students protect themselves against lazy, unskilled, or unethical peers if their instructors allow the submission of drafts or multiple versions. However, even if Turnitin.com is not available, each researcher must take full responsibility for the report. Few instructors are willing or able to play detective to find the guilty party, if indeed only one person cheated or plagiarized.

Photo Essay Solutions

Photo Essay, page 426
Effective proposals include persuasive "hooks" in the introduction that grab the reader's attention. One common strategy for writing hooks is to list some important or unique benefit that the company offers to clients. An effective hook for Hoku Scientific might emphasize the environmental benefits, cost savings, or "green marketing" opportunities related to using Hoku's solar components and materials.

Photo Essay, page 434
Thorough justification for a company's proposed action is found in the body section of a formal report. However, since formal reports are long and redundant at times, brief justification is often expressed in the letter of transmittal, executive summary, introduction, or conclusions sections as well.

Chapter Presentation Ideas and Extras

1. Provide actual business proposals and formal reports for students to examine. Consider putting them on reserve in your library. Being able to examine these closely will help students understand what actually goes into these documents and why. They can examine and evaluate these documents using the explanations and guidelines for preparation that you give them during your class lectures on these topics.

2. Discuss with students the various parts of formal reports and proposals. Be sure they have a general idea of what readers expect to be found in each part. Then discuss what types of

individuals would be most interested in recommendations, conclusions, and executive summaries and why.

3. Has your campus recently been involved in activities that resulted in a formal report to the president or other academic official? Has a local company recently submitted a proposal for management's approval? If possible, have a campus administrator or an outside company representative discuss how their particular project was planned, developed, and prepared so that students will be able to see that these types of projects require a great amount of planning, coordinating, writing, and revising. Students need to perceive how important planning their work and working their plan can be to the successful completion of their projects.

4. It can be difficult to come up with appropriate report and proposal topics. Therefore, students can find a list of suitable business-related report and proposal topics in the student resources at http://www.meguffey.com. These topics are divided into the following categories related to students' major courses of study: accounting, finance, personnel/human resources, marketing, information systems, management, and general business/education/campus issues. Students can gather information for many of these reports by using the Web. You may assign the topics as individual or team projects. Topics are appropriate for business proposals, business plans, or formal reports.

   Students should follow the formats and development plans provided in Guffey's *Business Communication: Process and Product*. You should specify length, format, and emphasis for the topics.

5. One of the most exciting parts of this chapter for many students is the section on business plans. Many students have dreams of opening their own businesses one day, and they should be aware that writing an effective business plan is an essential part of the process. One of the best sources for information about small business is the Web site of the Small Business Administration (http://www.sba.gov). Encourage students to explore this site thoroughly, particularly if they would like to start a business one day.

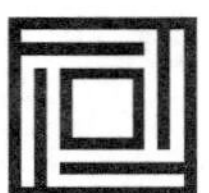

Chapter 14 LECTURE NOTES AND TEACHING SUGGESTIONS

Business Presentations

CHAPTER SYNOPSIS

As the chapter states, the number one predictor of success and upward mobility is how much workers enjoy public speaking and how effective they are at it. On the job, students must be able to present their ideas both informally and formally. Having the opportunity to give oral presentations in college classes, when those presentations will receive constructive criticism, will only help students to become more successful when making them in the business world. The ability to give effective formal and informal presentations to large and small groups alike will set them apart as employees with promotion potential.

Reassure students that they will increase their comfort level and deliver a professional performance if they focus on the following: preparation, organization, audience rapport, visual aids, and delivery. Students will also learn effective techniques for communicating as a team and addressing an intercultural audience. Furthermore, they will be introduced to strategies for improving telephone and voice mail skills.

LEARNING OBJECTIVES

1. Discuss two important first steps in preparing effective business presentations.

2. Explain the major elements in organizing a presentation, including the introduction, body, and conclusion.

3. Identify techniques for gaining audience rapport, including (a) using effective imagery, (b) providing verbal signposts, and (c) sending appropriate nonverbal messages.

4. Discuss designing visual aids, handouts, and multimedia presentations and using presentation technology competently.

5. Specify delivery techniques for use before, during, and after a presentation, and apply reflective thinking skills.

6. Organize team-based written and oral presentations, and understand how to communicate in teams.

7. Explain effective techniques for adapting oral presentations to intercultural audiences, and demonstrate intercultural and diversity understanding.

8. List techniques for improving telephone and voice mail skills to project a positive image.

WHAT'S NEW IN THIS CHAPTER

- Created a brand new three-part Zooming In feature about Steve Jobs at Apple to provide students with a highly relevant, contemporary case study to stimulate analysis and critical thinking.
- Emphasized cutting-edge concepts in presentation software such as those introduced in *Presentation Zen* by Garr Reynolds to demonstrate to students the trend toward less text and more reliance on images.
- Added photo essay discussing the much-anticipated launch of Apple's iPad to illustrate its potential business uses including its benefits for oral presentations.
- Provided authentic coverage from business practitioners such as venture capitalist Guy Kawasaki to create interest and familiarize readers with current best practices in business slide presentations.
- Highlighted prominent communicators whose comments illustrate important chapter concepts, for example, "Telephone Doctor" Nancy Friedman's advice on improving phone and voice mail skills.
- Added end-of-chapter activities to critique PowerPoint clips on YouTube and to evaluate or outline Apple Keynotes to help students understand what makes business presenters successful.
- Created two end-of-chapter activities to practice persuasive speaking skills.
- Devised a unique end-of-chapter activity to teach students how to text professionally.

LECTURE OUTLINE

I. Preparing Effective Oral Presentations (p. 457)

A. Knowing Your Purpose

- Determine whether your goal is to persuade or inform.
- Have a clear idea of what you want your audience to remember.

B. Knowing Your Audience

- Analyze your audience.
- Anticipate the audience's reactions to your presentation.
- Adapt your presentation as needed.

Figure 14.1 Succeeding With Four Audience Types
PowerPoint slides 1-13

Let's Discuss

Assume you must make a presentation to your staff on the company's fourth quarter financial performance. You anticipate your audience to be uninterested and have a short attention span. How do you plan your presentation?

Organizational pattern: Present a maximum of three main points. Focus on the most important facts you want them to remember.
Delivery style: Be enthusiastic and entertaining. Move around and use large gestures. Present financial data using colorful visuals. Demonstrate how their personal job performance affects the company's overall results to make the topic more relevant to them.
Supporting material: Keep the audience tuned in by using humor, cartoons, colorful visuals, or interesting quotations and statistics.

II. Organizing the Content for a Powerful Impact (p. 458)

- **Step 1:** Tell them what you're going to say.
- **Step 2:** Say it.
- **Step 3:** Tell them what you have just said.

A. Capturing Attention in the Introduction

- Capture listeners' attention and get them involved.
- Identify yourself and establish your credibility.
- Preview your main points.

Figure 14.2 Oral Presentation Outline

B. Organizing the Body

- Chronology
- Geography/space
- Topic/function/conventional grouping
- Comparison/contrast (pro/con)
- Journalistic pattern
- Value/size
- Importance
- Problem/solution
- Simple/complex
- Best case/worst case

C. Summarizing in the Conclusion

- Summarize the main themes of the presentation.
- Leave the audience with a specific and memorable "take-away."
- Include a statement that allows you to leave the podium gracefully.

III. Building Audience Rapport Like a Pro (p. 463)

PowerPoint slides 14-19

A. Effective Imagery

- Analogies – a comparison of similar traits between dissimilar items
- Metaphors – a comparison between otherwise dissimilar items without using the words *like* or *as*
- Similes – a comparison that includes the words *like* or *as*
- Personal anecdotes – a personal story that connects you to the audience
- Personalized statistics – memorable statistics directly related to the audience
- Worst- and best-case scenarios – descriptions of worst or best cases that are memorable to the audience

B. Verbal Signposts

- Previewing
- Summarizing
- Switching directions

C. Nonverbal Messages

- Look terrific.
- Animate your body.
- Speak extemporaneously.
- Punctuate your words.
- Get out from behind the podium.
- Vary your facial expressions.

IV. Planning Visual Aids and Multimedia Presentations (p. 465)

A. Types of Visual Aids

Figure 14.3 Pros and Cons of Visual Aid Options
PowerPoint slides 29-33

1. Multimedia slides
2. Overhead transparencies
3. Handouts
4. Speaker's notes

V. Designing an Impressive Multimedia Presentation (p. 466)

A. Applying the 3-x-3 Writing Process to Slide Presentations

1. Analyze the situation.
2. Anticipate your audience.
3. Adapt the text and color selections.
4. Research your PowerPoint options.
5. Organize your slides.
6. Create a template and select a layout.
7. Compose your slideshow.

8. Design for optimal effect.
9. Revise, proofread, and evaluate your slideshow.

Figure 14.4 Revising and Enhancing Slides for Greater Impact
Figure 14.5 Converting a Bulleted Slide Into a Diagram
Figure 14.6 Designing More Effective Slides
Figure 14.7 PowerPoint Slides That Summarize and Illustrate Multimedia Presentations
Figure 14.8 Creating Visually Appealing Slides That Engage Your Audience

B. Using PowerPoint Effectively With Your Audience

C. Practicing and Preparing

- Allow plenty of time to set up and test your equipment.
- Make sure video and Web links are working.
- Bring backups of your presentation (overhead transparencies or handouts) or transfer your presentation to a CD or a USB flash drive to run on any laptop.

D. Keeping Your Audience Engaged

- Know your material.
- Allow the audience time to absorb the information.
- Leave the lights as bright as you can.
- Use a radio remote control so you can move freely.
- Maintain a connection with the audience by using a laser pointer to highlight slide items to discuss.
- Don't leave a slide on the screen when you no longer discuss it.

VI. Analyzing an Effective Presentation (p. 473)

Figure 14.8 Creating Visually Appealing Slides That Engage Your Audience

A. Eight Steps to Making a Powerful Multimedia Presentation

1. Start with the text.
2. Select background and fonts.
3. Choose images that help communicate your message.
4. Create graphics.
5. Add special effects.
6. Create hyperlinks to approximate the Web browsing experience.
7. Engage your audience by asking for interaction.
8. Move your presentation to the Internet.

PowerPoint slides 34-41

VII. Polishing Your Delivery and Following Up (p. 476)

A. Choosing a Delivery Method

- Present extemporaneously (speaking feely without notes).

- Memorize significant parts of your presentation.
- Do not read from your manuscript.

Let's Discuss

Do you feel connected to a speaker when he or she reads from prepared notes?

Probably not. The key to a successful presentation is preparation. Apple CEO Steve Jobs rarely takes his eyes off his audience when he speaks. He never reads from slides, notes, or the text of a speech. To achieve this level of professionalism, Jobs rehearses a presentation for four hours at a stretch. He rehearses every slide, every demo, and every message point out loud. Very few speakers who are considered "charismatic" break eye contact by reading from prepared text. Consider taking a cue from the best, and rehearse your presentations to avoid reading.

Gallo, C. (2006). How to wow 'em like Steve Jobs. *BusinessWeek*. Retrieved October 23, 2007, from http://www.businessweek.com/smallbiz/content/apr2006/sb20060406_865110.htm?chan=search.

B. Combating Stage Fright

- Stage fright is normal.
- You can control stage fright by using the following strategies.

PowerPoint slides 46, 47

C. Before Your Presentation

- Prepare thoroughly.
- Rehearse repeatedly.
- Time yourself.
- Check the room.
- Greet members of the audience.
- Practice stress reduction.

PowerPoint slide 42

D. During Your Presentation

- Begin with a pause.
- Present your first sentence from memory.
- Maintain eye contact.
- Control your voice and vocabulary.
- Put the brakes on.
- Move naturally.
- Use visual aids effectively.
- Avoid digressions.
- Summarize your main points and arrive at the high point of your talk.

PowerPoint slides 43, 44

E. After Your Presentation
- Distribute handouts.
- Encourage questions.
- Repeat questions.
- Reinforce your main points.
- Keep control.
- Avoid *Yes, but* answers.
- End with a summary and appreciation.

PowerPoint slide 45

VIII. Organizing Team-Based Written and Oral Presentations (p. 479)

A. Preparing to Work Together
- Establish ground rules.
- Name a meeting leader, a recorder, and an evaluator.
- Decide if team will reach decisions by consensus or majority rule.
- Recognize the value of conflict.
- Decide how to handle teammates who are slackers.

B. Planning the Document or Presentation
- Record all decisions.
- Establish the purpose and identify the main issues.
- Decide on the format, components, and presentation format.
- Profile the audience and focus on questions audience members will want answered.
- Develop a work plan with assignments and deadlines.

C. Collecting Information
- Double-check facts to be sure they are accurate.

D. Organizing, Writing, and Revising
- Decide on one person to coordinate all parts of the written document or presentation.
- Build smooth transitions between presenters.
- Agree on a consistent style, format, and feel in the final product.

E. Editing, Rehearsing, and Evaluating
- For written reports, assign one person to examine the entire document for consistency, format, and vocabulary.
- For oral presentations, assign one person to ensure files are consistent in design, format, and vocabulary.
- Practice the presentation several times.
- Practice fielding questions.

IX. Adapting Presentations to Intercultural Audiences (p. 481)

PowerPoint slides 48, 49

A. Understand Different Values and Nonverbal Behavior

- Anticipate expectations and perceptions that may differ from what you consider normal.
- Express ideas in small chunks and slow down your presentation for audiences whose English is limited.
- Break your presentation into short, discrete segments.
- Be aware that nonverbal behavior may be misinterpreted.

B. Adjusting Visual Aids to Intercultural Audiences

- Check the audience's understanding by asking questions.
- Avoid deviating from the PowerPoint slides.
- Use visual aids to help communicate your message.
- Provide handouts in English and the target language.
- Never use numbers without projecting or writing them for all to see.

C. Checklist for Preparing and Organizing Oral Presentations

Getting Ready to Speak

- Identify your purpose.
- Analyze the audience.

Organizing the Introduction

- Get the audience involved.
- Establish yourself.
- Preview your main points.

Organizing the Body

- Develop two to four main points.
- Arrange the points logically.
- Prepare transitions.
- Have extra material ready.

Organizing the Conclusion

- Review your main points.
- Provide a strong, final focus.

Designing Visual Aids

- Select your medium carefully.
- Highlight main ideas.
- Try to replace bullets whenever possible.
- Use aids skillfully.

Developing Multimedia Presentations

- Learn to use your software program.
- Select colors based on the light level in the room.
- Use bulleted points for major ideas.
- Include multimedia options that will help you convey your message.
- Make speaker's notes.
- Maintain control.

X. Improving Telephone and Voice Mail Skills (p. 483)

PowerPoint slides 50, 51

A. Making Telephone Calls Efficiently

- Plan a mini-agenda.
- Use a three-point introduction.
- Be brisk if you are rushed.
- Be cheerful and accurate.
- Bring it to a close.
- Avoid telephone tag.
- Leave complete voice mail messages.

B. Receiving Telephone Calls Professionally

- Identify yourself immediately.
- Be responsive and helpful.
- Practice telephone confidentiality.
- Take messages carefully.
- Explain what you are doing when transferring calls.

C. Making the Best Use of Voice Mail

- Announce your voice mail.
- Prepare a warm and informative greeting.
- Test your message.

Lecture Transparencies
(available in a separate packet and at http://www.meguffey.com)

Business Presentations Acetates	Transparency Number
Preparing Effective Oral Presentations	150-151
Methods for Organizing an Oral Presentation	152-153
Building Audience Rapport Like a Pro	154
Nine Techniques for Gaining and Keeping Audience Attention	155
Verbal Signposts, Nonverbal Messages	156
Oral Presentation Outline	157
Planning Visual Aids, Handouts, and Multimedia Presentations	158

Pros and Cons of Visual Aid Options 159
Eight Steps to a Powerful Multimedia Presentation 160-161
Polishing Your Delivery and Following Up 162-163
Improving Telephone and Voice Mail Skills 164

Solution Masters

Solutions to all activities are available in this lecture outline or on the Instructor's Resource CD, not as solution masters.

Answers to Chapter Review Questions

1. **Can speaking skills be improved, or do we have to be "born" communicators? (Obj. 1)**

   Although rhetorical talent undeniably comes in handy, anyone determined to improve his or her speaking skills can become a proficient speaker.

2. **Why are analyzing an audience and anticipating its reactions particularly important before business presentations, and how would you adapt to the four categories of listeners? (Obj. 1)**

   By anticipating your audience, you have a better idea of how to organize your presentation. A friendly audience will respond to humor and personal experiences. A neutral audience requires an even, controlled delivery style. The talk would probably be filled with facts, statistics, and expert opinions. An uninterested audience that is forced to attend requires a brief presentation. Such an audience might respond best to humor, cartoons, colorful visuals, and startling statistics. A hostile audience demands a calm, controlled delivery style with objective data and expert opinion.

3. **In preparing an oral presentation, you can reduce your fears and lay a foundation for a professional performance by focusing on what five areas? (Obj. 1)**

   The five foundational areas are the following:
   1. Preparation
   2. Organization
   3. Audience rapport
   4. Visual aids
   5. Delivery

4. **In the introduction of an oral presentation, you can establish your credibility by using what two methods? (Obj. 2)**

   Two methods that you can use to establish your credibility in the introduction of an oral presentation are to (1) describe what qualifies you to speak (your position, knowledge, or experience) and (2) connect with your audience.

5. **What is Guy Kawasaki's 10/20/30 rule, and what is it good for? (Obj. 2)**
Venture capitalist and angel investor Guy Kawasaki believes that persuasive PowerPoint presentations should be no more than 10 slides long, last 20 minutes at most, and contain 30-point fonts or bigger. Kawasaki is convinced that presentations deviating from this rule will fall short of their purpose, which is typically to reach some type of agreement.

6. **List six techniques for creating effective imagery in a presentation. Be prepared to discuss each. (Obj. 3)**

Six techniques for creating effective imagery:

a. Analogies
b. Metaphors
c. Similes
d. Personal anecdotes
e. Statistics
f. Worst-/best-case scenarios

7. **List suggestions that would ensure that your nonverbal messages reinforce your verbal messages effectively. (Obj. 3)**

a. Look terrific.
b. Animate your body.
c. Speak extemporaneously.
d. Punctuate your words.
e. Get out from behind the podium.
f. Vary your facial expression.

8. **What is the picture superiority effect? (Obj. 4)**

The term picture superiority effect suggests that images have a far greater impact than text does. Very visual business presentations are far more likely to be understood and retained than those lacking visual enhancement.

9. **Name specific advantages and disadvantages of multimedia presentation software. (Obj. 4)**

Speakers use electronic presentation software because it prepares visual aids that are economical, flexible, and easy to make. The slides also make the speaker look professional. However, electronic presentation software limits creativity, hogs the limelight, and is risky to use (because of possible technical failures).

10. **How is the 6-x-6 rule applied in preparing bulleted points? (Obj. 4)**

In making slides, apply the 6-x-6 rule. Use no more than six bullets per screen; six words per bullet, max.

11. What delivery method is most effective for speakers? (Obj. 5)

Speaking from note cards or an outline is probably the most effective delivery method for most speakers. They have their notes to rely on if they lose their train of thought, and they can present their thoughts in an interesting conversational manner.

12. Why should speakers deliver the first sentence from memory? (Obj. 5)

Speakers should deliver their first sentence from memory since they can immediately establish eye contact and will sound confident and knowledgeable.

13. Which five issues should be resolved before a team can collaborate productively? (Obj. 6)

At the outset, the team should (1) name a leader, (2) establish how it will make decisions, (3) create a meeting schedule, (4) discuss the value of conflict, and (5) determine penalties for lack of or poor member contributions.

14. How might presentations before international audiences be altered to be most effective? (Obj. 7)

For international audiences one should speak slowly, use simple English, avoid jargon and clichés, use professional-looking visual aids prepared in both languages, write out numbers, and use short sentences.

15. How can you avoid telephone tag? (Obj. 8)

If someone you are calling is not in, ask when you might be able to reach the individual. If you are directed to leave a voice mail message, say when you will be calling again or when you can be reached. Naturally, make sure that you will actually call at the appointed time or are available at the time you indicated for a call back.

Answers to Critical Thinking Questions

1. Why should even practiced speakers plan their presentations when addressing a business audience instead of just "winging it"? (Obj. 3)

Very few people can speak off the cuff competently. Without a plan, it's very easy to ramble instead of focusing on just a few principal ideas. To avoid overwhelming their listeners, experienced speakers choose just the right kind of information and sort it in a few main ideas that they then emphasize. Because listeners do not have the benefit of written copy with which they could follow along or to which they could return, verbal signposts, transitions, and even a certain redundancy are desirable.

2. **"Communicate—don't decorate." This principle is one of 20 rules that graphic designer and educator Timothy Samara discusses in his 2007 book *Design Elements: A Graphic Style Manual*. How could you apply this principle to the design of your PowerPoint presentations? (Obj. 4)**

Although an image carries more meaning and emotion than text does, this rule suggests that visuals must be functional, not merely decorative or even "cute." The primacy of image over text means that visuals have a greater impact and are more memorable than text, but only if they reinforce and complement the message the speaker wants to convey.

3 **How can speakers prevent multimedia presentation software from stealing their thunder? (Obj. 4)**

Multimedia presentation programs such as PowerPoint can draw all the attention away from the speaker. The speaker, however, must guard against this by remembering that slides merely summarize important points. The speaker must be prepared to offer substantial narration to support each slide. As a presentation is prepared, the speaker should be making extensive notes (perhaps using the "Speaker's Notes" feature) with examples, evidence, and discussion for each slide. Another way to maintain a connection between the speaker and the slides is to use a laser pointer.

4. **Discuss effective techniques for reducing stage fright. (Obj. 5)**

Various techniques help reduce stress. Some speakers use deep breathing to reduce chest stress and to help distract themselves. They think of their sweaty palms and dry mouth as signs of their excitement; they channel their stress into enthusiasm for their topics. They select topics that they know well and that their audiences will appreciate. They use positive self-talk and remind themselves that they know their topic and are well prepared. They shift attention from themselves to their visuals and ignore any stumbles. Another technique that speakers sometimes use is imagining that all the members of their audience are dressed only in their underwear. This is a humorous thought and has the tendency to put the speaker more at ease.

5. **Ethical Issue: Critics of PowerPoint claim that flashy graphics, sound effects, and animation often conceal thin content. Consider, for example, the findings regarding the space shuttle *Challenger* accident that killed seven astronauts. Report authors charged that NASA scientists had used PowerPoint presentations to make it look as though they had done analyses that they hadn't. Overreliance on presentations instead of analysis may have contributed to the shuttle disaster. What lessons about ethical responsibilities when using PowerPoint can be learned from this catastrophe in communication? (Objs. 1, 2, and 4)**

When presenters minimize or ignore altogether the importance of the basics of knowing their purpose and knowing their audience, they can spend too much time preparing an impressive multimedia presentation and end up leaving out important content. In this instance, the scientists missed the mark in accomplishing the purpose of providing complete and accurate information that would result in a safe space shuttle mission. When presenters shift their focus to the medium instead of the message, they are likely to neglect their ethical responsibility to present thorough and truthful information.

Whether it was true in this instance is unknown; however, another ethical responsibility can be learned from this case. Namely, never use presentation technology to camouflage difficult or negative information so that your audience misses or doesn't realize the importance of the negative information.

Activities

14.1 Critiquing a Speech (Objs. 1–4)

If your students are giving oral reports for your class, this would be an effective activity for them, especially if they critique a speech related to their written and oral report requirement.

14.2 Knowing Your Audience (Objs. 1–2)

Be prepared to set your parameters for defining "recent issue" and also for limiting or not limiting the resources students can use. Verbalizing why the topic will appeal to their audience and how it relates to their needs will shift your students' focus from themselves to where it needs to be, on their audience.

14.3 Overcoming Stage Fright (Obj. 5)

This activity could help students come to grips with their fears. After completing this discussion and/or writing memos, students will realize that they all share some of the same anxieties. Stress that all speakers suffer stage fright occasionally and that controlled stress helps you to make a better presentation.

14.4 Investigating Oral Communication in Your Field (Objs. 1, 5)

You may want students to discuss this activity in groups of three or four, and then have one individual from each group give a synopsis of their findings. Requiring students to come to class with a prepared report ready for submission will ensure that all group members will participate in the discussion.

14.5 Outlining Oral Presentations (Objs. 1, 2)

This activity helps students get their thoughts organized. Organized thought leads to an organized and effective oral presentation.

14.6 Critiquing a Satirical Clip Lampooning PowerPoint (Objs. 1–4)

Electrical engineer turned comedian Don McMillan is famous for his humorous critique of PowerPoint misdeeds and other office life. The don'ts in the expanded version, "Life

After Death by PowerPoint 2010," are the following: Too much text, small font size, annoying text animations, poor typeface selection, excessive bullet points, pointless animation of graphs, too many acronyms, and unnecessary charts. McMillan's clips appear on YouTube and on his Web site **http://technicallyfunny.com.**

14.7 Evaluating and Outlining Podcasts of Apple Keynotes (Objs. 1–4)

The podcasts of Steve Jobs' keynotes are easy to access on the Web. They mostly embody the best practices in public speaking. A discussion of Steve Jobs' presentation skills is included in the Zooming In feature of this chapter.

14.8 Creating an Oral Presentation: Outline Your Job Duties (Objs. 1–4)

Students are asked to present a three- to five-minute talk about the duties of a current position or a past job, volunteer activity, or internship. We provide a model of a typical professor's job duties here. This PowerPoint presentation is also available digitally on the Instructor's Resource CD.

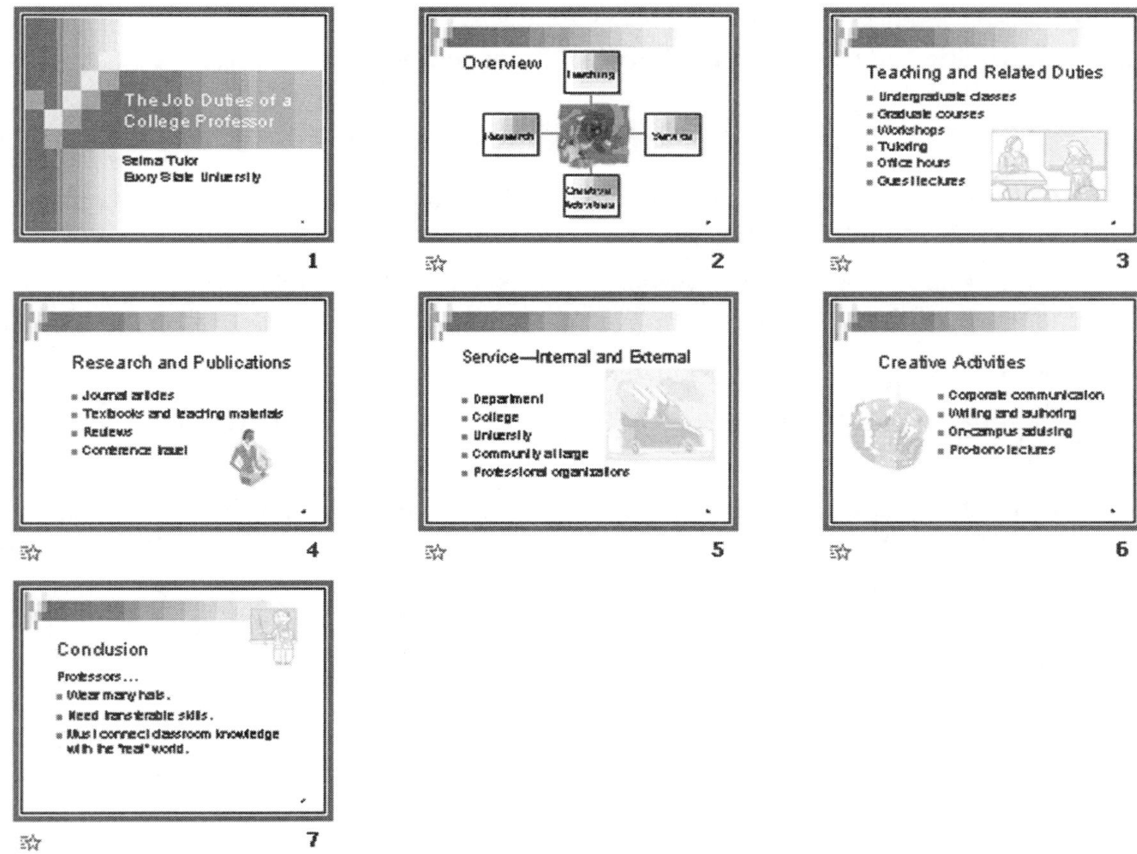

14.9 Creating an Oral Presentation: Pitch to Guy Kawasaki (Objs. 1–4)

Answers will vary. Students typically enjoy assignments that encourage them to discuss their future entrepreneurial endeavors. In each class you will most likely have a few students who want to start their own businesses. This assignment also lends itself to role play: Students could take turns as the future entrepreneurs as well as the angel investor.

14.10 Delivering an Impromptu Elevator Speech (Objs. 1–4)

This activity works best if the particulars of the topic are revealed at the last minute and the student must deliver an impromptu message. Consider taping students if you have that capability.

14.11 Self-Contained Multimedia Activity: Creating a PowerPoint Presentation (No additional research required) (Objs. 2, 3)

Answers will vary. Students should create slides that correctly summarize the text but do so efficiently, without verbosity or cluttered slides.

14.12 Improving the Design and Content of PowerPoint Slides (Objs. 2, 3)

Suggested improvements for the three slides presented in Figure 14.9 follow:

Color choices: The font color gray is too dark to display on dark red background. White font color provides greater contrast.

Font choices—style and point size: The Slide 2 title should be enlarged to equal the font size of the other slide titles.

6-x-6 rule: Slides 1 and 3 violate the rule. See the revision in the following slides.

Listings in parallel grammatical form: Slides 1 and 3 need revising as shown in the following revisions.

Consistent capitalization and punctuation: Slide 1 has inconsistent punctuation. Use periods after bulleted items that are complete sentences. Because commands are complete sentences, they are punctuated with periods.

Graphics and images: Slide 2 uses a clip-art image. A photo would probably look more professional. In Slide 2 a graphic could be created to replace the bulleted list, giving the list more prominence.

Revised Slides: Show here are possible revised slides. These are also available in PowerPoint on the Instructor's Resource CD.

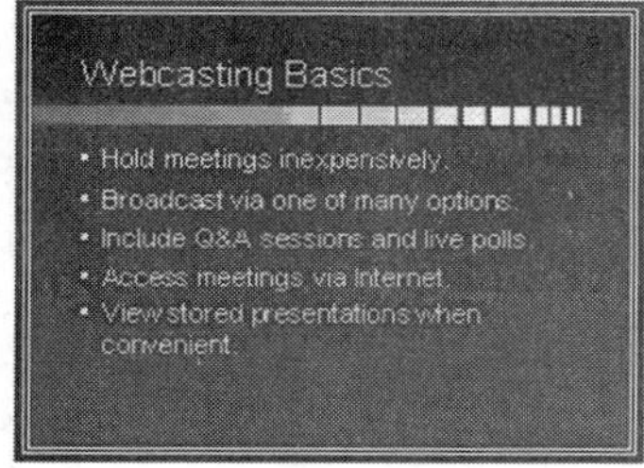

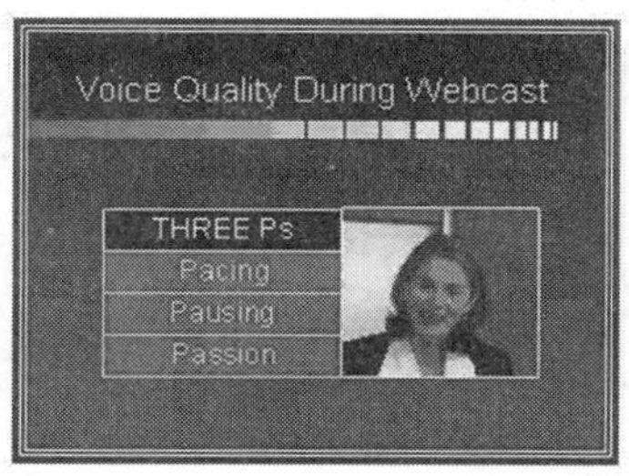

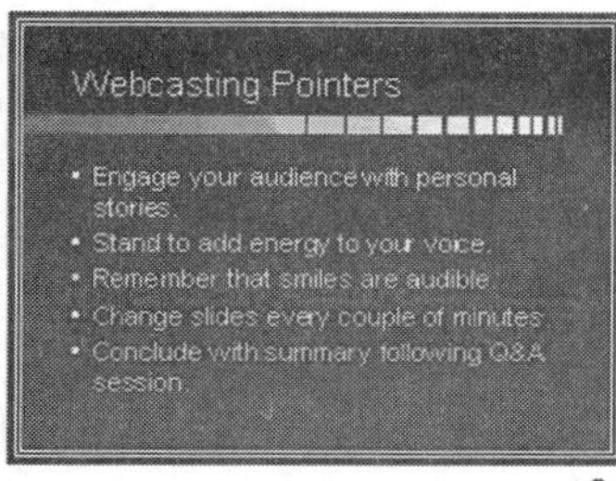

14.13 Researching *Fortune* List Information (Objs. 1–5)

This assignment provides students with an opportunity to broaden their awareness of the best companies in the world. You may want to customize which lists your students may research. Other annual Fortune lists include 100 Fastest Growing Companies, Best Companies for Minorities, Most Powerful Black Executives, China 100, Fortune 40, Blue Ribbon Companies, MBAs' Top 50 Employers, 40 Under 40, Most Powerful Women in Business, and 25 Most Powerful People in Business. You may want to refer students to http://www.fortune.com/fortune/alllists for additional information.

The five lists from this assignment are briefly described below:

a. *Fortune 500.* Since this annual ranking of America's largest corporations based on sales revenues was first published in 1955, 1,857 companies have appeared. Many of them have changed names due to mergers, acquisitions, or bankruptcies. Other companies have gone private or simply changed their names. Only three companies have held the top spot on the FORTUNE 500 since 1955. General Motors and Exxon Mobil were both on the original FORTUNE 500. Wal-Mart made the list for the first time in 1995.

b. *Global 500.* First published in 1995, this list ranks world companies ranked on sales revenues.

c. *100 Best Companies to Work For.* List first published in 1998. Some 46,526 randomly selected employees from 304 candidate companies filled out an employee-opinion survey. Nearly half of them also gave written comments about their workplaces. Each candidate company also filled out a questionnaire detailing its people policies, practices, and philosophies. Each company is evaluated on both the employee surveys and the company questionnaires, with the employees' opinions accounting for two-thirds of the total score.

d. *America's Most Admired Companies.* First published in 1983. For the industry list, the Hay Group started with the ten largest companies by revenue in 64 industries, including foreign firms with large U.S. operations. Then it asked 10,000 executives, directors, and securities analysts to use a scale of one to ten to rate the companies in their own industries on eight criteria (innovation, employee talent, use of corporate assets, social responsibility, quality of management, financial soundness, long-term investment value, quality of products/services).

e. *Global Most Admired Companies.* First published in 1997. The Hay Group conducted the survey of more than 10,000 directors, executives, and analysts. Three hundred forty-six companies (208 of them based outside the U.S.) were divided into 30 industry groups, each with no more than 15 companies. Each respondent was asked to rank the other companies in his or her industry and country lists. Respondents ranked companies in their industry in nine key attributes (innovation, employee talent, use of corporate assets, social responsibility, quality of management, financial soundness, long-term investment value, quality of products/services, globalness) on a scale of one to ten, and a final score was calculated by averaging the nine categories.

14.14 Choosing a Topic for an Oral Presentation (Objs. 1–6)

You can treat 14.5 and this activity as a unit. Students could first be required to submit an outline of their chosen topic. Then they would be expected to prepare a presentation with effective visual aids.

14.15 Consumer: Will Maxing Out My Credit Cards Improve My Credit Rating? (Objs. 1–5)

Researching this topic will reveal many misconceptions about credit scores. Students can test their knowledge of credit scores at www.consumerfed.org/score.

14.16 Improving Telephone Skills by Role-Playing (Obj. 8)

Students' telephone communication skills are often their weakest. This activity will give them much needed practice.

14. 17 Presenting Yourself Professionally on the Telephone and in Voice Mail (Obj. 8)

This activity will help students practice leaving a professional voice mail message.

14.18 Presenting Yourself as a Professional When Texting (Obj. 8)

This activity will help students practice texting in a professional manner.

ZOOMING IN Part 1: Apple's Steve Jobs and His Keynotes

Critical Thinking

- **What kind of oral presentations might you have to make in your chosen career field?**

  This question is meant to stimulate realistic thinking about the need for developing speaking skills. Many students prefer to think that they will never have to make presentations. But students should understand that nearly all jobs today require an individual to present ideas persuasively, either in informal or formal settings. Speaking skills become even more important as one is promoted into management positions, and nearly every college student will eventually be in some kind of supervisory or management role.

- **Why are most people fearful of making presentations?**

  People are naturally fearful because they are self-conscious and worry that they will sound and look bad. But individuals can overcome this fear by learning how to prepare and by doing lots of practicing. You might take this opportunity to talk about the success of Toastmasters, an organization that provides opportunities and encouragement to fledgling speakers.

- **How do you think people become effective speakers?**

  Effective speakers are not born. They become skillful through training and practice. It is no secret that the more presentations one makes, the better he or she gets at it. Many speakers look natural and sound confident, but most of them had ample coaching and practice to achieve these results. Remind students that nothing can make them more visible in the business world than the ability to express themselves effectively before a group.

ZOOMING IN Part 2: Apple's Steve Jobs and His Keynotes

Critical Thinking

- **What can you learn from the speaking style of Steve Jobs?**

  Answers will vary. Students may recognize that they won't always have a "holy smokes moment" to reveal to their audiences, but that it is smart to try to build an element of surprise into their presentations. Similarly, they may not always have a big flashy prop to show off, but it is worth the effort to plan a demo whenever possible. Nor may students be able to identify a villain whom they could use as a foil; however, they can certainly learn to create simple, visually powerful slides and present their idea or product consistently and using simple catch phrases. Finally, the students need to recognize that enthusiasm and emotional involvement sell products. An unenthusiastic presenter will not generate interest and buy-in.

- **Why is simplicity important in an oral presentation?**

  Because humans have trouble retaining complex information just by hearing it or seeing it on-screen, speakers should focus on a few main points and provide internal summaries as well as transitions to help the audience understand the organization of the talk.

  In terms of visuals, simple, effective, and image-driven slides are key. Cluttered slides are confusing and turn off audiences. One of the reasons that text-heavy slides put audiences to sleep is our high reading speed. We can read a lot faster than the speaker can talk. If the entire slide is revealed instantly, we tend to read ahead of the speaker and get bored if the presenter is reading from the screen. Also, apparently, the brain is able to process images we watch while listening to a speaker, but our gray matter has difficulty processing the text we read on-screen while simultaneously trying to listen to a presenter's comments. This fact illustrates that simple, uncluttered graphics make a better visual impact.

- **Communication coach Carmine Gallo says that charismatic speakers such as Steve Jobs are driven by the zeal to make the world a better place and enrich people's lives. If you were an entrepreneur, what would be your sense of mission?**

  Answers will vary. Perhaps some of your students will have already started small businesses and will be able to articulate their philosophies. This question could lead to a discussion of the profit motive and the other powerful motivators in entrepreneurship. Students tend to think that businesspeople are solely driven by the promise of money and that companies' only interest is profit. Students could be asked to consider that although the bottom line is very important in business, it is not the only motivating force. Also, businesses have many stakeholders, in addition to shareholders or investors. The most inspirational and charismatic corporate leaders are those who are able to inspire their subordinates with their drive and passion. That kind of infectious enthusiasm allows them to lead. In Carmine Gallo's words, passion, emotion, and enthusiasm are underestimated in professional business communication, and yet they are powerful ingredients that motivate others.

ZOOMING IN Your Turn: Applying Your Skills at Apple Computer

The Apple iPad, the hot item of 2010, followed the iPhone, which had exceeded expectations since its launch in 2007. Students should research subsequent buzz-worthy gadgets. Apple can be relied on releasing a new and often game-changing electronic toy each January.

Discussion Material for CAREER COACH: The 10/20/30 Rule of PowerPoint

Career Application

This activity requires students to revise and improve an existing PowerPoint presentation. They may want to select one that they had created themselves or download freely available slideshows from a Web site such as SlideShare.

The topics that lend themselves the most to the 10/20/30 rule are relatively straightforward subjects, ones that do not require much technical data and explanations. The best simple, visual presentations rely on images, but most highly specialized, technical, or abstract subjects don't lend themselves to a very visual presentation. In those situations, a more conventional approach, such as the 6-x-6 rules for slides, may be most appropriate.

Discussion Material for CAREER COACH: How to Avoid Stage Fright

Career Application

This activity requires that students interview someone in a business environment about making effective presentations. If this proves to be too time consuming, have students interview each other about making effective presentations. What techniques do they use to give an effective oral presentation in class or at work? What methods do they use to battle stage fright? You may have some excellent ideas right in your own class!

Ethics Check Solutions

Ethics Check, page 481
The Robot Presenter
In one of your courses, you are witnessing a PowerPoint presentation, during which it becomes obvious that the speaker has completely memorized her talk. However, she stumbles badly a few times, struggling to remember her lines. Worse yet, you perceive her accent as nearly impenetrable. How should the instructor and the class handle the evaluation of such a presentation?

This sensitive subject should lead to a lively discussion. Perhaps not surprisingly, nonnative speaker students struggling with English hate public speaking even more than many U.S.-born students do. As a result, they sometimes resort to memorization in the hope of receiving a better presentation grade than if they attempted extemporaneous delivery. In the absence of accent-reduction classes in most colleges and because of the stubborn nature of most accents, it may be unreasonable to expect fast improvement. Hence, commenting on someone's accent may seem pointless. On the other hand, every student needs to be able to present competently and be understood. As for evaluating such a flawed presentation, most instructors would probably shy away from public criticism of the student's language skills but encourage him or her in private to intensify efforts to acquire the language. Some classmates may favor saying openly that they have not understood much of the talk, whereas others may choose to overlook the obvious and comment on some other feature of the presentation.

Ethics Check, page 484
Telling White Lies
Obviously, you wouldn't want to tell callers that your colleague went to the restroom or that your boss is responding to e-mail from a golf course in Hilo, Hawaii. But what about people who, for instance, hide behind voice mail and want you to lie about it? When is it acceptable to tell "white lies" on the phone to maintain confidentiality and decorum, and when is lying for others wrong?

Answers will vary as students may perceive the exact boundaries of propriety and impropriety differently. They may suggest that it depends on the relationship between the caller and the person he or she is trying to reach. They may be more forthcoming toward friends and family, perhaps. Sometimes workers may be avoiding clients if they are behind with their work or if they must disclose something unpleasant. Most would probably agree that covering for a colleague who takes the afternoon off pretending to be sick would be too much of a lie to shoulder.

Photo Essay Solutions

Photo Essay, page 475
For Kiva founder Jessica Flannery, delivering inspirational presentations is about speaking extemporaneously, knowing the topic, and using engaging visuals. Flannery's powerful delivery does not consist in wrote memorization or over-rehearsed lines, but in sharing Kiva's social mission to "connect people through lending for the sake of alleviating poverty." When a communicator connects with the topic, the delivery flows more naturally and is more likely to hold the audience's attention. Presenters should also memorize opening and closing lines and select attractive slides to guide the speech forward.

Video Resources

Instructors may show the *Effective On-the-Job Oral Presentations* from Video Library 1, *Building Workplace Skills*. Students will learn how to apply the writing process to the development of oral presentations. Students see what is meant by anticipating the audience and focusing on a purpose. After viewing the video, students should be prepared to discuss critical-thinking questions.

Chapter Presentation Ideas and Extras

1. *Videotaping Presentations.* Use audio or video recorders to tape students giving three- to five-minute prepared speeches. Have each student bring his or her own tape for later review. The speech should be extemporaneous on topics relevant to the issues of the course. Have students take the tapes home to review and write one-page critiques on their strengths and weaknesses according to the criteria for effective presentation in this chapter. Ask them to note also how they plan to improve their weaknesses. Since many students have never listened to their recorded voices or seen themselves presenting on video, they are surprised, sometimes shocked, at how they sound and look.

   A Note of Caution: Be careful about public critiques of student weaknesses, especially of those inexperienced or reluctant speakers. If the student is shy, the critique may do more harm than good. Usually, reviewing the tape in private with a student is more helpful.

2. *A Speaking Tip.* It is preferable to present the opening line of your speech from memory, but those who memorize run the risk of forgetting. To give yourself added security, write the first two sentences of your speech in your notes and write down the last sentence of your conclusion. The rest of your notes should be in outline form. If you freeze, you know that you always can get on or get off the podium smoothly by reading the appropriate sentences. You probably won't need to look at them, but knowing that your entrance and exit lines are written down will help you feel secure.

3. *A Professional's Advice.* Invite a guest speaker who is a businessperson to the class to speak about the role of presentations in his or her career. Good candidates to invite are job interviewers, salespeople, trainers, or meeting professionals. Many professionals use PowerPoint or other presentation software regularly to make sales pitches to clients, speeches to professional groups, or informational and persuasive presentations to upper management. Students are eager to ask questions after seeing them speak. You can provide your students with a useful glimpse into the realities of mastering excellent communication skills.

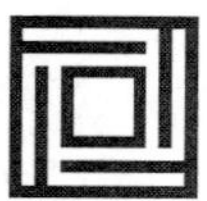

Chapter 15 LECTURE NOTES AND TEACHING SUGGESTIONS

The Job Search, Résumés, and Cover Letters

CHAPTER SYNOPSIS

Chapter 15 shows students how to evaluate their assets, career paths, and the job market in preparation for employment. It presents two kinds of résumés: chronological and functional. Students learn to organize, format, and produce a persuasive résumé for themselves. They also learn to optimize their résumé for today's technologies, including techniques for preparing a scannable résumé, a plain-text résumé, and an e-portfolio. Finally, students study methods for composing customized cover letters. This chapter contains some of the most important topics in the business communication course and deserves ample class time. Even if your school offers employment communication in another course, students will benefit from reading this chapter and the following chapter on interviewing.

Because the job search is so personal, your students will be highly motivated to do these tasks well. If you and your students do a really good job on this chapter, it could make a great deal of difference to them and to you. Nothing is quite so satisfying as having successful students let you know how much your course helped them and what a difference you and your course made to them. Aren't these the types of comments that teachers live for?

LEARNING OBJECTIVES

1. Prepare for a successful job search by identifying your interests, evaluating your assets, recognizing the changing nature of jobs, and choosing a career path.

2. Apply both online and traditional job search techniques.

3. Appreciate the need to customize your résumé, and know whether to choose a chronological or a functional résumé style.

4. Organize your qualifications and information into effective résumé segments.

5. Describe techniques that optimize a résumé for today's technologies, including preparing a scannable résumé, a plain-text résumé, and an e-portfolio.

6. Write a customized cover letter to accompany a résumé.

WHAT'S NEW IN THIS CHAPTER

- Revised the Liz Ryan three-part business case study to include up-to-date information about networking and making oneself memorable during the job search.
- Updated section on today's workplace to provide information about cutting-edge employment trends.
- Added current statistics about the effectiveness of searching for a job online, and modified list of job boards to include those most widely used by today's job seekers.
- Expanded list of employment sites to include social media sites, which are widely used by both employers and job seekers today.
- Added a new section covering tips for conducting a safe and effective online job search, including strategies for avoiding identity theft.
- Expanded tips for using online networking to tap into the hidden job market by adding advice for using Twitter during the job search.
- Created a new photo essay that discusses the ethics of lying on a résumé using Notre Dame's George O'Leary as a model.
- Strengthened section about using technology to optimize one's résumé by including information on the latest trends.
- Organized résumé models into a new Résumé Gallery, and scrutinized every model to ensure each complies with the most up-to-date trends in résumé development.
- Included information about the ethics of using hidden keywords in online résumés.
- Added new end-of-chapter activities that cover using social media during the job search and e-portfolios.

LECTURE OUTLINE

I. **Preparing for a Successful Job Search (p. 495)**
The job market is highly competitive. In order to stand out from your competition, you need to know how to locate available positions and how to prepare persuasive résumés and cover letters. This chapter provides a wealth of information that will help you land your dream job.

Figure 15.1 The Employment Search
PowerPoint slides 1-5

A. **Identifying Your Interests and Goals**
- *What are you passionate about? Can you turn this passion into a career?*
- *Do you enjoy working with people, data, or things?*
- *Would you like to work for someone else or be your own boss?*
- *How important are salary, benefits, technology support, and job stability?*
- *How important are working environment, colleagues, and job stimulation?*
- *Would you rather work for a large or small company?*
- *Must you work in a specific city, geographical area, or climate?*
- *Are you looking for security, travel opportunities, money, power, or prestige?*
- *How would you describe the perfect job, boss, and coworkers?*

Lecture Tidbit

A study conducted by the Families and Work Institute (FWI) revealed that workers born before 1964 tend to make work their top priority. On the other hand, younger workers born after 1964 are more likely to make family their top priority. The results of this study could result in a lively classroom discussion. Do your students agree? How important is it to students to balance their professional and personal lives?

B. Evaluating Your Qualifications

- *What technology skills can you offer?*
- *What other skills have you acquired in school, on the job, or through activities?*
- *Do you work well with people? Do you enjoy teamwork?*
- *Are you a leader, self-starter, or manager?*
- *Do you speak, write, or understand another language?*
- *Do you learn quickly? Are you creative?*
- *Do you communicate well in speech and in writing?*

C. Recognizing Employment Trends in Today's Workplace

- Growing number of small businesses offer employment opportunities.
- Increased use of teams and outsourcing presents challenges.

D. Choosing a Career Path

- Visit your campus career center.
- Search the Web.
- Use your library.
- Take a summer job, internship, or part-time position in your field.
- Interview someone in your chosen field.
- Volunteer with a nonprofit organization.
- Monitor the classified ads.
- Join professional organizations in your field.

Lecture Tidbit

A thorough job search takes patience. A Bureau of Labor Statistics survey found that the average job search now lasts up to 18 weeks. To keep your search as short as possible, Quintessential.com recommends the following:

1. Network.
2. Find job leads from numerous sources.
3. Make cold calls.
4. Apply for jobs on corporate Web sites.
5. Tailor your résumé and cover letter every time.
6. Use a variety of job-search methods.
7. Treat your job search like a full-time job.

II. Conducting a Successful Job Search (p. 498)

A. Searching for a Job Online

- Check the big boards: Monster, CareerBuilder, CareerJournal, College Recruiter, Yahoo.
- Use the big boards for information, but realize that few people actually find jobs on them.
- Look beyond the big boards to corporate Web sites, professional association sites, local employment sites, and niche sites.

Figure 15.2 Using the Web to Search for a Job
PowerPoint slides 6-8

Lecture Tidbit

When searching for a job online, be careful to protect your privacy. You don't want to do anything that could result in your identity being stolen, an influx of spam, or your current employer finding your résumé posted online. Here are some privacy-protection tips from Job-Hunt.org:

1. Before posting anything, read the site's privacy protection policies carefully.
2. Limit your personal contact information on an online résumé; include only what's necessary for an employer to contact you, such as your e-mail address.
3. Post your résumé only on reputable sites.
4. If offered, choose to limit access to your complete résumé.
5. Keep careful records of where and when you posted your résumé online.
6. Never place your social security number on your résumé.

Lecture Tidbit

Some career experts now recommend that job seekers keep blogs. To help job seekers, Jason S. Gorham founded Job Search Blogs (http://www.jobsearchblogs.com). The goal of this site is to "bring job seekers and hiring companies together in order to help fill open job requirements." By creating a free blog on this site, job seekers gain another way to spotlight their talents and qualifications, and employers learn about these talents and qualifications more easily than with more traditional tools. A blog also allows job seekers to provide more detailed information to potential employers. Could this be the wave of the future?

B. Searching for a Job Using Traditional Techniques

- Check classified ads in local and national newspapers.
- Check announcements in publications of professional organizations.
- Contact companies in which you are interested, even if you know of no current opening.
- Sign up for campus interviews with visiting company representatives.
- Attend career fairs.
- Ask for advice from your instructors.
- Develop your own network of contacts.

PowerPoint slides 9-11

III. Creating a Customized Résumé (p. 503)

A customized résumé is designed specifically for each position you want and helps distinguish you from other applicants.

A. Choosing a Résumé Style

- **Chronological:** Focuses on job history with most recent positions listed first
- **Functional:** Focuses on skills

B. Deciding on Length

- Make your résumé as long as needed to sell your skills to recruiters and hiring managers.
- One-page résumé—when you have fewer than ten years of experience, are making a career change, or have had only one or two employers.
- Two-page résumé—when you have more than ten years of experience.
- Three pages or more—when you are a senior-level manager or executive or you have a lengthy history of major accomplishments.

IV. Organizing Your Information Into Effective Résumé Categories (p. 504)

PowerPoint slides 12-24

- **Main Heading**
  List your name, address, phone, and e-mail address.
- **Career Objective**
  Include a career objective for a targeted job.
  Ideally, name job title, area of specialization, and type of company.
- **Summary of Qualifications**
  Present your most impressive skills and accomplishments in a concise list.
- **Education**
  Name your degree, date of graduation, and institution.
  List your major and GPA.
  Give information about your studies, but don't inventory all your courses.
- **Work Experience or Employment History**
  If your work experience is significant and relevant to the position sought, place this section before education.
  Start with the most recent jobs. Include employer's name and city, dates of employment (month, year), and most significant title.
  Use action verbs to summarize achievements and skills relevant to your targeted job.
  Give evidence of communication, management, and interpersonal skills. Employers want more than empty assurances. Try to quantify your skills.
- **Capabilities and Skills**
  Emphasize your proficiencies with the Internet, software programs, office equipment, and communication technology tools.
  Describe proficiencies you have acquired through training and experience.
  Highlight exceptional aptitudes, such as working well under stress or interacting with customers.
  Highlight those talents that are relevant to your targeted job.

- **Awards, Honors, and Activities**
  If you have three or more awards or honors, highlight them by listing them under a separate heading.
  If not, put them with activities or in the education or work experience section, if appropriate.
  Include school, community, volunteer, and professional activities.
  List awards and extracurricular activities, especially if they demonstrate leadership, teamwork, reliability, loyalty, initiative, efficiency, and self-sufficiency.
- **Personal Data**
  Employers are legally barred from asking personal data, such as birth date, health, and marital status. Therefore, omit such items from your résumé. You can include hobbies or interests that might grab the recruiter's attention or serve as conversation starters.
- **References**
  Listing references directly on your résumé takes up valuable space.
  Instead, most recruiters prefer that you bring to the interview a list of individuals willing to discuss your qualifications.
  The best references are instructors, your current employer or previous employers, colleagues or subordinates, and other professional contacts.

Figure 15.3 Action Verbs
Figure 15.4 Use Action Verbs in Statements That Quantify Achievements
Figure 15.5 Sample Reference List
Figure 15.6 Chronological Résumé: Recent College Graduate With Related Experience
Figure 15.7 Chronological Résumé: Current College Student With Limited Experience
Figure 15.8 Chronological Résumé: Current University Student With Limited Relevant Experience
Figure 15.9 Chronological Résumé: University Graduate With Substantial Experience
Figure 15.10 Functional Résumé: College Graduate With Unrelated Part-Time Experience
Figure 15.11 Scannable Résumé

Lecture Tidbit

Yahoo HotJobs researchers surveyed recruiters and hiring managers who use HotJobs to learn what they look for in résumés: Here is what they found:

1. Eighty-three percent of recruiters and hiring managers prefer receiving résumés via e-mail.
2. Eighty-four percent prefer chronological résumés.
3. Fifty-three percent said résumés over one page in length are always acceptable; 41 percent said that résumés over one page are acceptable only for job seekers with extensive experience; and 6 percent said résumés should never be longer than one page.
4. Thirty-eight percent of recruiters consider unsolicited résumés for current openings; 17% throw away unsolicited résumés.

V. Optimizing Your Résumé for Today's Technologies (p. 516)

Today's communication technologies have changed the way we submit résumés to employers. Many employers now prefer that résumés be submitted via e-mail or online, and some employers use software to scan résumés. Therefore, job seekers should know how to prepare résumés formatted in a variety of ways to satisfy technological requirements.

PowerPoint slide 25

A. Designing a Print-Based Résumé

- Use when electronic submission is not required.
- Present in addition to an electronic submission.
- Bring to a job interview.

B. Preparing a Scannable Résumé

- Use a large, well-known font such as 12-point Times New Roman or Arial.
- Avoid unusual typefaces, underlining, and italics.
- Be sure your name is on the first line.
- List each phone number on its own line.
- Use smooth white paper, black ink, and quality printing. Provide white space.
- Avoid double columns.
- Don't fold or staple your résumé.

Figure 15.12 Plain-Text Résumé
PowerPoint slide 26

C. Maximizing "Hits"

- Focus on specific keywords.
- Use accurate names.
- Be careful about abbreviations and acronyms.
- Describe interpersonal traits and attitudes.

D. Preparing a Plain-Text Résumé

- Follow the tips for scannable résumés.
- Reformat with shorter lines.
- Think about using keyboard characters to enhance format (=== or ~~~).
- Move all text to the left.
- Save your résumé in plain text (.txt) or rich text format (.rtf).
- Test your résumé before sending it.

PowerPoint slide 27

E. Showcasing Your Qualifications in an E-Portfolio or a Video Résumé

- An e-portfolio is a collection of digitized materials that provides viewers with a snapshot of a candidate's performance, talents, and accomplishments.
- An advanced portfolio might include links to electronic copies of your artwork, film projects, or blueprints that may be difficult to share with potential employers.
- Video résumés may get you an interview with a targeted employer or connect you with a company in a distant location.

VI. Applying the Final Touches to Your Résumé (p. 520)

A. Polishing Your Résumé

- Study résumé models for ideas on improving your format.
- Remove information that doesn't belong.
- Ensure you have created a professional-looking document.

B. Proofreading Your Résumé

- Proofread for spelling, mechanics, content, and format.
- Enlist a friend or relative to proofread your résumé.

C. Submitting Your Résumé

Formats for submitting your résumé may include the following:

1. Word
2. Plain-text
3. PDF document
4. Company database
5. Fax

PowerPoint slides 28, 29

Let's Discuss

Is it an invasion of privacy if employers use information found in social sites networking in their hiring decisions?

A University of Dayton survey revealed that 42% of 326 employers said they would consider factoring a Facebook profile into their hiring decisions. Some of those employers also said they had rescinded offers because of information and photos they had discovered online.

Stress to students that they must clean up these sites or make them private. Delete messages from friends that are inappropriate or information that is unflattering. Remind students that information in the public domain is fair game and may be damaging in a hiring situation.

D. Checklist for Preparing for Employment and Submitting a Customized Résumé

Preparation

- Research the job market.
- Analyze your strengths.
- Study models.

Headings and Objectives

- Identify yourself.
- Include a career objective for a targeted job.

Education

- Name your degree, date of graduation, and institution.
- List your major and GPA.

Work Experience

- Itemize your jobs.
- Describe your experience.
- Promote your "soft" skills.

Special Skills, Achievements, and Awards

- Highlight your technology skills.
- Show that you are a well-rounded individual.

Final Tips

- Look for ways to condense your data.
- Double-check for parallel phrasing.
- Make your résumé computer friendly.
- Consider omitting references.
- Project professionalism and quality.
- Resist the urge to inflate your qualifications.
- Proofread, proofread, proofread!

Submitting

- Follow instructions for submitting.
- Practice sending plain-text résumés.

Lecture Tidbit

A recent survey by ResumeDoctor.com found that the most common résumé lies include inflated titles, education, salaries, and accomplishments; inaccurate dates, often used to cover up gaps in employment; and inaccurate descriptions of job duties. Jude Werra, an executive search recruiter and author of the *Liars Index*, surveyed 100 companies and found that 95 of them would immediately eliminate a candidate from consideration if he or she claimed to have a degree that was never granted. He tells the story of a man whose claim included an MBA from the University of Maryland on his résumé. After he was hired, he often talked about his life on campus. He was fired when his employer learned that he never attended the University of Maryland but merely tended bar near campus.

VII. Creating a Customized, Persuasive Cover Letter (p. 524)

Although most job listings don't specifically mention a cover letter, a well-written, persuasive cover letter should accompany every résumé you send out. Without it, your résumé may never be read.

A. Gaining Attention in the Opening

1. **Openings for Solicited Jobs**
   - Refer to the name of an employee in the company.
   - Refer to the source of your information precisely.
   - Refer to the job title and describe how your qualifications fit the requirements.

2. **Openings for Unsolicited Jobs**
   - Demonstrate an interest in and knowledge of the reader's business.
   - Show how your special talents and background will benefit the company.

Figure 15.13 Solicited Cover Letter
Figure 15.14 Unsolicited Cover Letter

PowerPoint slide 30

3. **Selling Your Strengths in the Body**
   - Describe your strongest qualifications in relation to the needs of the employer.
   - Discuss your personal traits.
   - Refer the reader to your résumé.

PowerPoint slide 31

4. **Motivating Action in the Closing**
   - Ask confidently for an interview, not the job.

PowerPoint slide 32

5. **Sending Your Cover Letter**
   - Always include a cover letter, even with résumés submitted by e-mail or fax.

Figure 15.15 E-mail Cover Letter

PowerPoint slide 33

6. **Final Tips for Successful Cover Letters**
   - Reduce the number of sentences that start with I. Make activities and outcomes, not yourself, the subject of sentences.
   - Use a traditional letter style, such as block.
   - Print on the quality paper.
   - Proofread carefully.

PowerPoint slides 34-39

B. Checklist for Preparing and Sending a Customized Cover Letter

Opening
- Use the receiver's name.
- Identify your information source, if appropriate.
- Gain the reader's attention.

Body
- Describe what you can do for the reader.
- Highlight your strengths.
- Refer to your résumé.

Closing
- Ask for an interview.
- Make it easy to respond.

Sending
- Include a cover letter with your résumé.
- If you e-mail your cover letter, put your contact information in the signature area.

Lecture Transparencies
(available in a separate packet and at http://www.meguffey.com)

The Job Search, Résumés, and Cover Letters Acetate	**Transparency Number**
The Job Search	165–166
The Customized Résumé	167–169
Poor Résumé	170
Improved Résumé	171
Functional Résumé	172
Chronological Résumé	173
Scannable Résumé	174
Optimizing Your Résumé for Today's Technology	175
Submitting Your Résumé	176
The Customized Cover Letter	177
Sending Your Cover Letter by E-mail	178
Preview Employment Quiz	179
Answers to Preview Employment Quiz	180

Solution Masters

	Page Number in This Book
15.1 Document for Analysis: Résumé – Revision	638
15.2 Document for Analysis: Cover Letter – Revision	640

Answers to Chapter Review Questions

1. **You are about to begin your job search. What should you do first? (Obj. 1)**

   The job search process should begin with identifying your interests and goals and evaluating your qualifications.

2. **What employment trends are occurring in today's workplace? (Obj. 1)**

   a. Companies are employing fewer people in permanent positions.
   b. Other forms of employment, such as temporary teams, are replacing traditional jobs.
   c. Employers are less willing to hire people into jobs with narrow descriptions; instead, they are hiring contingency employees who work temporarily and then leave.
   d. Big companies are no longer the main employers; people work for smaller companies, or they are starting their own businesses.
   e. Employees can't count on a lifelong career with a single company, regular pay raises, promotions, or retirement income.
   f. Workers will need updated, marketable skills as they move from job to job.
   g. To keep up with technology, employees will have to upgrade and retrain themselves constantly.

3. **What sources can you use to help you determine a career path? (Obj. 1)**

   a. Visit a campus career center.
   b. Explore job search Web sites.
   c. Access print and online resources in a library.
   d. Take a summer job, internship, or part-time position in your field.
   e. Interview someone in your field.
   f. Volunteer with a nonprofit organization.
   g. Monitor the classified ads.
   h. Join a professional or student organization in your field.

4. **Using the Web, where should job candidates look in addition to searching the big job board sites? (Obj. 2)**

   a. Company Web sites
   b. Professional organization Web sites
   c. JobCentral National Labor Exchange
   d. Local employment Web sites
   e. Niche Web sites
   f. Social media sites

5. **What are some tips you should follow to ensure a safe and effective online job search? (Obj. 2)**

   a. Use only reputable job sites.

b. Limit the number of sites on which you post your résumé.
c. Use an e-mail address that you set up exclusively for the job search.
d. Limit the amount of personal information you include on your résumé.
e. Post your résumé privately if given the option.
f. Renew your résumé every 14 days, and repost it to a different site after 45 days.
g. Keep careful records and remove your résumé at the end of your job search.
h. Don't post your references online.
i. Don't respond to "blind" job postings.

6. Even with the popularity of online job search sites, traditional job search techniques are still important. What are some traditional sources for finding jobs? (Obj. 2)

a. Checking classified ads in local and national newspapers
b. Checking announcements in publications of professional organizations
c. Contacting companies in which you are interested, even if you know of no current opening
d. Signing up for campus interviews with visiting company representatives
e. Attending career fairs
f. Asking for advice from your instructors
g. Developing a network of contacts

7. What is a customized résumé, and why should you have one? (Obj. 3)

A customized résumé is one that is prepared to respond to a specific job opening or to meet the needs of a targeted organization. It is written for one application. A customized résumé is important today to enable you to stand out in competition with hundreds or thousands of other applicants who may be pursuing the same job opening. You must make yourself immediately appealing to busy recruiters who can quickly see how you can benefit the organization.

8. What is a chronological résumé, and what are its advantages and disadvantages? How does it differ from a functional résumé? (Obj. 3)

A chronological résumé lists a candidate's work history in the order of jobs, starting with the most recent. A chronological résumé is advantageous because recruiters prefer this format. They expect to see it, and it makes their jobs easier. Chronological résumés are easier to write than functional résumés. A chronological résumé, however, is not always the best format for someone who has little experience, a negative employment history, or a desire to change careers. A functional résumé, in comparison, lists skills and accomplishments in special categories. It highlights accomplishments and may be used to de-emphasize a negative employment history. It appeals to candidates who have little experience, employment gaps, or a desire to change careers. Its disadvantages are that recruiters dislike this format and may be suspicious of it, job boards may not accept it, and it is difficult to write.

9. Describe a summary of qualifications, and explain why it is increasingly popular on résumés. (Obj. 4)

A summary of qualifications provides a list of your most impressive accomplishments. It is written to ensure that busy recruiters don't overlook anything important and to compel them to read further. A summary includes approximately three to eight statements, in bulleted list form, that prove you are the ideal candidate for the position.

10. What personal information should be included, and what should be omitted, on a résumé? (Obj. 4)

Some job seekers include personal information about hobbies or interests (such as skiing or photography) that might grab the recruiter's attention or serve as conversation starters. However, job seekers should omit personal data such as birth date, marital status, height, weight, national origin, health, disabilities, and religious affiliation. Such information doesn't relate to genuine occupational qualifications, and recruiters are legally barred from asking for such information.

11. To optimize your résumé for today's technologies, how many versions of your résumé should you expect to make? What are they? (Obj. 5)

You should expect to make three versions: (a) a print-based résumé; (b) a scannable résumé; and (c) a plain-text, ASCII résumé. You may also convert your print-based résumé to a PDF file.

12. What is an e-portfolio? How can having one benefit you? (Obj. 5)

An e-portfolio is a collection of digital files that can be navigated with the help of menus and hyperlinks much like a personal Web site. An e-portfolio provides viewers with a snapshot of your performance, talents, and accomplishments and may include a copy of your résumé, reference letters, commendations for special achievements, awards, certificates, work samples, a complete list of your courses, thank-you letters, and anything else that touts your accomplishments. An e-portfolio might include links to digital copies of your artwork, film projects, videos, blueprints, documents, photographs, multimedia files, and blog entries that might otherwise be difficult to share with potential employers.

E-portfolios have many advantages. On Web sites they can be viewed at an employer's convenience. E-portfolios can also be seen by many individuals in an organization without circulating a paper copy. But the real reason for preparing an e-portfolio is that it shows off your talents and qualifications more thoroughly than a print résumé does.

13. What are the three purposes of a cover letter? (Obj. 6)

A cover letter introduces the résumé, highlights your strengths in terms of benefits to the reader, and strives to gain an interview.

14. What information goes in the body of a cover letter? (Obj. 6)

The body of a cover letter should explain how your preparation and experience fill the requirements for the position. It should stress how your skills can be important to the hiring organization. This content is more important than listing college courses or discussing duties performed in previous jobs.

Answers to Critical Thinking Questions

1. How has the Web changed job searching for individuals and recruiters? Has the change had a positive or a negative effect? Why? (Obj. 1)

The Internet has revolutionized the job search. People used to check the classified ads and were confined primarily to newspapers in their local areas. They prepared gorgeous copies of their résumés and sent them out after seeing jobs advertised. Now nearly half of all job seekers start their search online. They can find job listings for jobs around the country and around the world. Résumés are often submitted online. Candidates can even interview for jobs without being there in person. However, the sad truth is that few applicants actually find jobs online. Some consider it a "black hole" into which résumés disappear. The Internet has changed the job market positively in expanding the breadth of job searching. Candidates know more about what is available and what is required to be hired. Applying for a job is also easier. On the negative side, recruiters are inundated with applicants, and candidates have a harder time being noticed.

2. In regard to hiring, conventional wisdom holds that it's all about whom you know. How can job candidates find an insider to refer them for a job opening? (Obj. 2)

Big companies are increasingly turning to their own employees to find candidates for job openings. For example, in a recent year at Prudential, employee referrals resulted in 48 percent of all new-hires. [See Orgel, M. (2010, February 10). Job seekers aided by employee referral programs. *The Wall Street Journal.* Retrieved March 8, 2010, from http://online.wsj.com/article/BT-CO-20100210-709089.html] Job candidates can increase their opportunities by joining social networking sites, using online alumni databases, and joining professional organizations.

3. Discuss the advantages and disadvantages of unconventional job applications that use gimmicks such as video résumés to get noticed. (Obj. 5)

Creative and unusual job applications that may be acceptable in advertising would be risky in business and should be avoided. Gimmicks can easily backfire, especially if the resulting effect is not clever or has little substance.

Video résumés may quite possibly be the wave of the future, but as at least one recent notorious example shows, the medium has not yet matured and for now should best remain in the hands of artists, actors, and other creative professionals. The most infamous specimen, Aleksey Vayner's preposterous and self-serving video résumé, made the Yale graduate the laughingstock of Wall Street, which he hoped to enter as an investment banker. Students may enjoy viewing this supreme example of puffery and shameless self-promotion on IvyGate. Apparently, YouTube withdrew the notorious video after threats of legal action by Vayner.

4. **Some job candidates think that applying for unsolicited jobs can be more fruitful than applying for advertised openings. Discuss the advantages and disadvantages of letters that "prospect" for jobs. (Obj. 5)**

   The advantage of "prospect" letters is that the competition is reduced. Many people apply for advertised jobs, but few candidates will take the time to write to companies when no job may exist. The disadvantages, of course, are that no job may be available. Moreover, the writer risks alienating the recruiter.

5. **Ethical Issue: Job candidate Karen accepts a position with Company A. One week later she receives a better offer from Company B. She wants very much to accept it. What should she do?**

   Here is Karen's difficulty. She would like to be working for Company B, but she doesn't want to alienate Company A or damage her credibility or reputation. Perhaps notifying Company A immediately that she has a better offer and has changed her mind would give Company B a chance to offer the position to their second-choice candidate.

Activities

15.1 Document for Analysis: Résumé (Obj. 4) Digital versions of the Documents for Analysis appear at http://www.meguffey.com. Students may edit and revise these documents without total retyping. Solutions for these documents are provided in the transparency solutions.

Weaknesses:

a. Omits the area code for the telephone number.
b. Fails to provide a professional e-mail address.
c. Reveals sloppy formatting with headings that are poorly spaced and lack parallel form.
d. Presents information in wordy, dense paragraphs reducing readability.
e. Fails to organize experience chronologically and with easily recognizable job titles, dates of employment, and accomplishments.
f. Includes high school reference, which should be omitted.
g. Does not emphasize computer skills.
h. Has series of words and phrases that are not parallel.
i. Has several typographical errors, punctuation errors, and misspelled words.
j. Looks unprofessional and slapdash.

Revision: A revision of this résumé is available in the transparency solutions in this manual.

15.2 Document for Analysis: Cover Letter (Obj. 6)

Weaknesses:

a. Fails to use the receiver's name in the salutation.
b. Neglects to identify the position, title, and specifically where the announcement appeared.
c. Fails to back up assertions with evidence of qualifications.
d. Offers little to show how the writer's qualifications fill the internship requirements.
e. Fails to promote the writer's experience and special skills.
f. Overworks the pronoun *I*. Nearly every sentence begins with *I*.
g. Fails to refer to her résumé and does not request an interview.
h. Does not make it easy for reader to respond.
i. Has several typographical errors, punctuation errors, and misspelled words.

Revision: A revision of this cover letter is available in the transparency solutions in this manual.

15.3 Identifying Your Employment Interests and Goals (Obj. 1)

Although this assignment takes time, it is invaluable because it encourages the kind of introspection necessary for making valid decisions regarding career paths. Collect the memo and make comments on it but don't grade it. Helping students during the preparation stages makes grading their résumés much easier in the long run.

15.4 Evaluating Your Qualifications (Objs. 1, 2, and 3)

See the comments for Activity 15.3. Be sure to have students prepare theses worksheets. They may resist, but with your encouragement and insistence they will do a good job. You may wish to divide students into groups of three or four to discuss the results. Collect their sheets and give some kind of credit for completing the work. This exercise should be one part of their total employment communication score.

15.5 Choosing a Career Path (Obj. 1)

Many students know amazingly little about the kind of work done in various occupations. Encourage them to find out. Although jobs are changing rapidly, many positions still require basic skills and students should know what these skills are. They should also know what a job description is, even though actual jobs often depart from their job descriptions.

15.6 Locating Salary Information (Obj. 1)

Students should print wage information for their chosen occupations. Discuss with them what the percentages mean: 10 percent of the people in this occupation earn the amount shown in the first column; 25 percent earn the amount in the second column; 50 percent earn the amount shown as "median." What do these percentages indicate? You might want to encourage students to discuss what they learned, in addition to salary data, about this occupation from the site.

15.7 Searching the Job Market (Obj. 1)

Students are to clip or print a job advertisement or announcement from (a) the classified section of a newspaper, (b) a job board on the Web, (c) a company Web site, or (d) a professional association listing. They are to select an advertisement or announcement describing the kind of employment being sought. They should save this advertisement to submit with the résumé and cover letter they will create in Activities 15.9 and 15.10.

15.8 Posting a Résumé on the Web (Obj. 2)

Many, many Web sites encourage the posting of résumés. In class discussion or in team meetings, you might wish to have students discuss those sites that seemed most promising. The primary advantage for posting a résumé to a Web site is wide exposure. But that same exposure can become a disadvantage for a person already employed if his employer sees the employee's posted résumé. Be sure that students also understand the disadvantages to posting a résumé online. Stress the importance of checking the credibility of a site before posting. After all, their résumés contain considerable valuable information.

15.9 Writing Your Résumé (Obj. 4)

Have students submit drafts until their résumés and lists of references are perfect. You might have them bring their completed résumés to class. In small groups have students exchange their résumés. Each reviewer should provide at least two supportive comments and one suggestion for improvement. Students can learn a lot from seeing how other students prepare their résumés. Encourage them to be tactful and offer constructive criticism. Promote this activity as an opportunity to improve their résumés by having multiple proofreaders who can point out weaknesses and strengths.

15.10 Preparing Your Cover Letter (Obj. 6)

Have students revise their cover letters until they are perfect. You might have them bring their completed cover letters to class, along with the job posting. Have students exchange letters. Each reviewer should assume the role of the hiring manager; he or she should read the job posting and then read the letter, offering constructive feedback about its effectiveness. Does the letter capture attention in the beginning? Does it refer specifically to the ad? Does it focus on what the applicant can do for the organization? Does it ask confidently for an interview?

15.11 Using Social Media in the Job Search (Obj. 2)

Social media sites are changing the job search process. This exciting activity will allow students to learn how both employers and employees use these sites. Encourage students to share their findings with their classmates.

15.12 E-Portfolios: Job Hunting in the Twenty-First Century (Obj. 5)

Answers will vary. Students will see highly polished, professional-looking digital portfolios on the one hand and attempts bordering on amateurish work on the other. They will turn up a host of designs and color schemes—as varied as the Web itself. Most e-portfolios resemble multilevel Web sites or blogs. As for instructions, resources abound. The CET site at USC (**http://cet.usc.edu/**) is rich in interesting links and references. This project could be expanded to include having students prepare e-portfolios if your college or university provides the appropriate server space.

ZOOMING IN Part 1: Workplace Expert Liz Ryan Shares Job-Search Tips

Critical Thinking

- **Why is searching for a job both exhilarating and intimidating? How can one overcome the feelings of intimidation?**

  Searching for a job is exhilarating because of all the wonderful possibilities. You feel excited and invigorated because a new world may be opening up to you—new friends, new rewards, new challenges, new avenues for success. However, you can also feel intimidated because of fear of intense competition, poor performance, or rejection. You may feel that you will be misunderstood or that you simply are not good enough. Job searching is indeed intimidating, but knowing what to expect and preparing 110 percent can improve your confidence immensely.

- **Is it easier to search for a job by registering at a big job board or by networking? Which method do you think is more successful?**

  Most students will say that searching for a job online is easier. It's fun to sit at a computer and read job descriptions and fill out an application now and then. But is it successful? Sadly, very few people actually find jobs through big job boards. Recruiters receive so many applications that they are overwhelmed. Chances are slim that your résumé will be selected. However, this chapter will provide advice on finding jobs successfully by using online resources and by networking.

- **Why is it important to be memorable during the job search? What techniques would you use to make yourself memorable?**

  Job seekers will encounter so much competition in today's employment field that being memorable at every step of the job search is essential. Students will list a variety of techniques to make themselves memorable and should be encouraged to share these techniques in class.

ZOOMING IN Part 2: Workplace Expert Liz Ryan Shares Job-Search Tips

- **Compare the advantages and disadvantages of searching for jobs at big board sites, such as *Monster.com*, with searching at company Web sites.**

  A wider selection of jobs is available at the big boards. Application procedures are usually easy. However, applicants at big boards must compete with hundreds and possibly thousands of other applicants. One may never get a response, and few people actually find jobs through the big boards. Company sites have a smaller selection of jobs, and they may not fit a candidate's skill set. However, the chance of success is greater. More applicants actually find jobs through company sites.

- **Why would companies ask job applicants to comment on their newsletter?**

  Companies are deluged with responses to online job ads. They can filter out individuals who are mechanically blasting their résumés out to all job ads. By asking specific questions that require research, they can reduce the number of random applicants considerably. They can also evaluate your writing and thinking skills when they ask you to comment on something at their Web site. Responding well can make a big difference in whether you are in the stack of selected candidates.

- **If recruiters are so pressed for time, why don't they appreciate résumés and cover letters written in the abbreviated style of instant messaging?**

  The abbreviated instant messaging writing style is unclear, unprofessional, and unbusinesslike. Recruiters want to see evidence that applicants can write clear and correct English. Résumés that deviate from correct style are ignored.

ZOOMING IN Your Turn: Applying Your Skills With Liz Ryan

Students are asked to provide Liz Ryan with information for her to use in advice articles and blog items. She posed four questions, which students should be able to answer without research. The challenge is to organize the information well and write coherent paragraphs in their memo reports. Encourage students to follow the checklist for information reports in Chapter 12. The report might begin with, *As you requested, I am submitting this report that discusses . . . .*

Discussion Material for CAREER COACH: Network Your Way to a Job in the Hidden Market

Career Application

This activity will allow students to start putting together a networking list, which can prove to be valuable during a job search. The activity also allows students to learn how mailing lists and discussion boards can help them in their job search. Encourage students to share their findings with the class. Who have they placed on their traditional list of networking contacts? What mailing lists and discussion boards did they find for networking?

Discussion Material for ETHICAL INSIGHTS: Are Inflated Résumés Worth the Risk?

Career Application

This activity offers some excellent questions for students to discuss in class, either as a whole group or in small groups. Because students want to make their résumés look good, many resort to inflating some aspects of it, especially in the area of puff-up accomplishments. They feel they can justify using inflated language to describe work experience. But how much is too much? Have students share their questions, feelings, and experiences. You should also look for related cases in the media to share with the class to prove that it's not worth it to lie on a résumé.

Ethics Check Solutions

Ethics Check, Page 521
Résumé Fibbing
Insecure entry-level workers are not the only job seekers who sometimes feel tempted to fudge the facts. RadioShack's CEO David Edmondson had to resign after it was found that he had incorrectly claimed to have two academic degrees. Are such lies always wrong, or can you imagine extenuating circumstances when, for example, the dishonest employee or executive is highly effective?

Students should realize that lies catch up with any employee at any level and profoundly and permanently destroy the trust in that individual. If students argue that as long as a lie does not cause harm to anyone it is defensible, remind them that trust is fragile and irreparable once lost. If we apply the moral measure of who gets hurt, it is perhaps easy to demonstrate to the class that fakers and liars can cause great harm. Think, for instance, of unqualified professionals such as doctors, lawyers, and, yes, teachers, and the damage they can wreak.

Ethics Check, Page 528
Cover Letter Bloopers
Advice columns and Internet blogs are teeming with cover letter bloopers. Downright lies aside, some candidates simply need a lesson in selling: *P.S. I haven't taken a sick day in years; I don't get sick.* Or consider this candid job board posting: *I have a lot of customer*

service experience, but I am willing to do just about anything. I am in a lot of debt and need a good solid job to help me get out of it. **After reading this chapter, what advice would you give such job seekers?**

The first example is meant to be reassuring to the recruiter, but in reality only the youthful assumption that good health is a guaranteed commodity seems noteworthy. The best advice, of course, would be not to include such a comment in a cover letter. References to physical appearance and health should be omitted as a matter of principle to prevent discrimination. As for the second ill-advised example, the writer should use better judgment and more discretion. Applicants should avoid sounding desperate and never give reasons for wanting a job that are unflattering to themselves.

Photo Essay Solutions

Photo Essay, Page 506
Education is an important component of any résumé. However, applicants with limited education can arrange their résumés in an order that emphasizes work experience, employment history, and skills. This method of emphasizing work experience above education on résumés is both ethical and advised.

Photo Essay, Page 516
Many job seekers create video résumés to show prospective employers who they really are. Unlike print, video is capable of communicating a job applicant's personality. Video has drawbacks, however. Homespun video productions can inadvertently paint a person in an amateurish or even silly light, sabotaging an applicant's chances for an interview. In addition, employers that turn down candidates after viewing video résumés may open a door for discrimination lawsuits.

Video Resources

Instructors may show *The Job Search* from Video Library 1, *Building Workplace Skills*. The video illustrates the job search and is a useful introduction to Chapters 15 and 16. After viewing the video, students should be prepared to discuss critical-thinking questions.

Chapter Presentation Ideas and Extras

1. *Examining Field in the Job Market.* To introduce this chapter, assign students to groups by major or field to examine the job market in accounting, information systems, marketing, management, banking, financial planning, or marketing. Have groups search career databases on the Web for job postings for entry-level positions in their chosen fields, review career materials, read classified ads, and interview personnel at the campus career services or placement office. Direct the groups to cover educational requirements, desired experience, special requirements, and salary range and benefits. Each group can prepare a report collaboratively and present its findings orally to the class. The assignment can enhance students' team skills and their understanding of the job market. They will learn the importance of relocating, quoting realistic salaries, and using targeted versus prospecting résumés.

2. *Employment Quiz.* Another quick way to introduce this chapter and pique interest is to give a short employment test, such as that shown on in Lecture Transparency 179. You can do this orally or you can make a transparency. But do have students write their answers down. The answers to the employment quiz are available on Lecture Transparency 180.

3. *Guest Speaker.* Invite someone from your career center or someone who reads résumés in the business world. Ask that expert to discuss the job market, résumés, application letters, and so on with your students. Students sometimes don't accept everything they read in texts or what their instructors say; therefore, inviting an outside expert to class to share his or her expertise reinforces effectively the messages of the text and the teacher. When the expert repeats what you have said in class, you become a more credible source of information for the students.

4. *Advice for Candidates With Little Work Experience.* When students have little or no work experience, you can help them convert some of their acquired skills into marketable ones. Here are possibilities based on Yana Parker's *The Damn Good Résumé Guide* (Berkeley: Ten Speed Press):

   - Working on a school paper or yearbook (researching, editing, writing, selling ads)
   - Working as a student intern for a business
   - Serving on student government committees
   - Coaching sports or tutoring academic subjects
   - Winning recognition for an exceptionally good essay, report, or project
   - Helping a professor research background information for a textbook
   - Creating photography projects, science projects, marketing projects
   - Helping promote a concert
   - Helping put a band together
   - Helping with church activities
   - Performing leadership roles in a club
   - Developing a Web site

Chapter 16 LECTURE NOTES AND TEACHING SUGGESTIONS

Interviewing and Following Up

CHAPTER SYNOPSIS

This chapter is one of the most important in the book because it focuses on employment, the ultimate goal of all students. Chapter 16 helps students distinguish between two kinds of employment interviews: screening interviews and hiring/placement interviews. It describes how to prepare for both kinds of interviews. Screening interviews may be conducted by telephone or online. Students learn the various types of hiring/placement interviews that they may encounter, including one-on-one, panel, group, sequential, and stress interviews. This chapter teaches students to research the target company, rehearse success stories, clean up digital dirt, and practice answers to possible questions. They also learn how to conduct themselves during such interviews, including controlling nonverbal messages. The major focus of the chapter, however, is on typical questions that are asked during hiring interviews and how students should respond. The chapter discusses how to respond to illegal questions and some behaviors to avoid during interviews. It also describes how to close an employment interview. Finally, students learn what to do after an interview and how to write several follow-up letters and other employment messages.

LEARNING OBJECTIVES

1. Understand the importance of a job interview, its purposes, and its forms, including screening, hiring/placement, one-on-one, panel, group, sequential, stress, and online interviews.

2. Describe what to do before an in-person or online interview, including researching the target company, rehearsing success stories, practicing answers to possible questions, and cleaning up digital dirt.

3. Explain what occurs the day of your interview, including traveling to and arriving at the interview, performing effectively during the interview, sending positive nonverbal messages, and using good techniques in answering questions.

4. Describe how to answer typical interview questions such as those that seek to get acquainted, gauge your interest, probe your experience, explore your accomplishments, look to the future, and inquire about salary expectations.

5. Understand how to close an interview positively, including asking meaningful questions.

6. Outline the activities that take place after an interview, including thanking the interviewer and contacting references.

7. Understand how to complete employment applications and write résumé follow-up, rejection follow-up, job acceptance, and job rejection messages.

WHAT'S NEW IN THIS CHAPTER

- Expanded section on screening interviews to include details about how companies are using virtual tools such as Second Life to conduct virtual job fairs and screening interviews.
- Added information about online interviews, which often take place using webcams.
- Created new photo essay that discusses how to succeed in interviews that take place over meals.
- Expanded the "Before the Interview" section to include tips for ensuring professional telephone techniques and for making the first telephone conversation with a prospective employer impressive.
- Updated company research section to include strategies for using Facebook, Twitter, and other social media sites to gather information about prospective employers.
- Enhanced section on digital dirt to provide specific examples of online information that could be looked at negatively by employers. Also added list of techniques for cleaning up one's online presence.
- Developed new photo essay that discusses tattoos and piercings and how to deal with them during the job search and on the job.
- Expanded the "During the Interview" section to include tips for traveling to and arriving at the job interview.
- Added a new Career Coach feature that provides techniques for fighting fear during the job interview.
- Added a new Ethics Check that looks at layoffs from the employer's perspective.
- Added new end-of-chapter activities that cover using social media sites (Facebook, Twitter, YouTube) for company research, appropriate interview attire, requesting a reference, and evaluating the course.

LECTURE OUTLINE

I. The Job Interview: Understanding Its Importance, Purposes, and Types (p. 537)

PowerPoint slides 1-3

A. Purposes of Employment Interviews

- To convince the employer of your potential
- To find out more about the job and the company
- To expand on the information in your résumé

PowerPoint slide 4

B. Types of Employment Interviews

- **Screening Interviews** – Screen out candidates who fail to meet minimum requirements
- **Hiring/Placement Interviews** – Help recruiters learn how the candidate would fit into their organization
  1. One-on-One Interviews – Meet with one company representative to discuss qualifications
  2. Panel Interviews – Participate in an interview conducted by people who will be your supervisor and colleagues
  3. Group Interviews – Join other candidates in an interview where several applicants are interviewed at one time
  4. Sequential Interviews – Meet with two or more interviewers on a one-on-one basis
  5. Stress Interviews – Test your reactions during nerve-racking situations

PowerPoint slide 5

II. Before the Interview (p. 540)

PowerPoint slides 6-10

A. Ensuring Professional Phone Techniques

1. Invest in a good voice mail service.
2. Ask others to answer the phone professionally.
3. Prevent children from answering the phone.
4. Don't answer your cell phone unless you are in a good location for answering interview questions.
5. Use voice mail to screen calls.

B. Making the First Conversation Impressive

1. Keep list of positions for which you have applied near your phone.
2. Treat any call from an employer just like an interview.
3. Have a copy of your resume available.
4. Be prepared for a screening interview.
5. Take good notes during the phone conversation.
6. Reconfirm date and time of your interview.

C. Researching the Target Company

1. Research the target company prior to the interview.
2. Study its annual report, marketing information, and Weblogs to learn about its products and culture.

Let's Discuss

Does researching a company before an interview make a difference?

Absolutely! Hiring managers at such companies as Yahoo, Advanced Micro Devices, Restoration Hardware, Google, and PG&E stress that job candidates must prepare ahead of time if they want to perform well in an interview. Mark Buxton, vice president of human resources for Del Monte Foods Company, sums it up nicely when he says that the biggest mistake interviewees can make is "coming unprepared. We expect the people we interview to have done research about Del Monte, to have read recent news about what we've been up to and to understand the job they're interviewing for."

B. Preparing and Practicing

1. Rehearse success stories.
2. Practice answers to possible questions.
3. Clean up any digital dirt.
4. Expect to explain problem areas on your résumé.
5. Decide how to dress.
6. Gather items to bring.

Let's Discuss

What do your outgoing messages on your home and cell phones sound like right now? Would they impress an interviewer?

Many students don't think about how their outgoing messages might sound to potential employers. Students will first get a good laugh at what some of their messages sound like. You can then remind them of the importance of having a professional, concise outgoing message. Remind students that messages should be in their own voice and should include their name so that employers know they've reached the right person.

III. During the Interview (p. 545)

PowerPoint slides 11-16

A. Sending Positive Nonverbal Messages and Acting Professionally

- Control your body movements.
- Exhibit good posture.
- Practice appropriate eye contact.
- Use gestures effectively.
- Smile enough to convey a positive attitude.
- Listen attentively.
- Turn off your cell phone.
- Don't chew gum.
- Sound enthusiastic and interested—but sincere.
- Avoid "empty" words.

IV. Answering Typical Interview Questions (p. 546)

Figure 16.1 Twelve Interview Actions to Avoid

A. Questions to Get Acquainted

- Incorporate success stories in your responses.
- Keep the interviewer's needs in mind as you respond.
- Practice a short formula response to each question.

Typical Questions:

1. *Tell me about yourself.*
2. *What are your greatest strengths?*
3. *Do you prefer to work by yourself or with others? Why?*
4. *What was your major in college, and why did you choose it?*
5. *What are some things you do in your spare time? Hobbies? Sports?*

PowerPoint slide 17

B. Questions to Gauge Your Interest

- Recruiters will want to gauge your interest in the position.

Typical Questions:

1. *Why do you want to work for _(name of company)__?*
2. *Why are you interested in this position?*
3. *What do you know about our company?*
4. *Why do you want to work in the _______________ industry?*
5. *What interests you about our products (services)?*

Let's Discuss

How do you fight fear before a job interview?

Students may have other techniques for fighting fear that they can share with the class. Additional techniques may include:

1. Put things in perspective. The worst that can happen is you don't get the job. But you still gain experience interviewing and can apply what you learn to future interviews.
2. Remember that an interview is just a conversation with another person. You do this all the time!
3. Realize that the interviewer may be just as nervous as you are.

C. Questions About Your Experience and Accomplishments

- Focus on your skills and accomplishments when answering these questions.

Typical Questions:

1. *Why should we hire you when we have applicants with more experience or better credentials?*
2. *Describe the most rewarding experience of your career so far.*

3. *How have your education and professional experiences prepared you for this position?*
4. *What were your major accomplishments in each of your past jobs?*
5. *What was a typical workday like?*
6. *What job functions did you enjoy most? Least? Why?*
7. *Tell me about your computer skills.*
8. *Who was the toughest boss you ever worked for and why?*
9. *What were your major achievements in college?*
10. *Why did you leave your last position? OR: Why are you leaving your current position?*

PowerPoint slide 18

D. Questions About the Future

- Your answers to these questions demonstrate that you are goal oriented and ambitious.

Typical Questions:

1. *Where do you expect to be five (or ten) years from now?*
2. *If you got this position, what would you do to be sure you fit in?*
3. *This is a large (or small) organization. Do you think you would like that environment?*
4. *Do you plan to continue your education?*
5. *What do you predict for the future of the ______________ industry?*
6. *How do you think you can contribute to this company?*
7. *What would you most like to accomplish if you were to get this position?*
8. *How do you keep current with what is happening in your profession?*

PowerPoint slide 19

E. Challenging Questions

- Answer these questions truthfully without dwelling on your weaknesses.
- Convert any negative responses into a discussion of your strengths.

Typical Questions:

1. *What is your greatest weakness?*
2. *What type of people do you have no patience for?*
3. *If you could live your life over, what would you change and why?*
4. *How would your former (or current) supervisor describe you as an employee?*
5. *What do you want the most from your job? Money? Security? Power?*
6. *What is your grade-point average, and does it accurately reflect your abilities?*
7. *Have you ever used drugs?*
8. *Who in your life has influenced you the most and why?*
9. *What are you reading right now?*
10. *Describe your ideal work environment.*
11. *Is the customer always right?*
12. *How do you define success?*

F. Questions About Salary

- Defer discussion about salary until later in the interview when you know more about the job.

Typical Questions:

1. *How much money are you looking for?*
2. *How much are you presently earning?*
3. *How much do you think you're worth?*
4. *How much money do you expect to earn within the next ten years?*
5. *Are you willing to take a pay cut from your current (or previous) job?*

PowerPoint slide 20

G. Situational Questions

- Situational questions test your thought process and logical thinking.
- Knowledge of the position and the company culture will help you respond favorably.
- Keep your responses positive.

Lecture Tidbit

Lying is one of the worst things a job candidate can do during an interview. Lisa Stevens, executive vice president and San Francisco Bay Area regional president at Wells Fargo, agrees. According to Ms. Stevens, "We always find out if a candidate's lying." Some interviewers look for nonverbal signals that a candidate may be lying, including coughing nervously, licking the lips, lack of eye contact, blushing, or restricted hand gestures.

H. Behavioral Questions

- Use the STAR technique (Situation or Task; Action; Results).
- Describe only educational and work-related situations.

PowerPoint slide 21

I. Illegal and Inappropriate Questions

- It is inappropriate for interviewers to ask questions related to gender, age, religion, color, race, national origin, disability, or sexual orientation.

Inappropriate questions:

1. *What is your marital status? Are you married? Do you live with anyone?*
2. *Do you have any disabilities? Have you had any recent illnesses?*
3. *Where are you from? What is the origin of your last name?*
4. *Have you ever filed a worker's compensation claim or been injured on the job?*
5. *Have you ever had a drinking problem or been addicted to drugs?*
6. *Have you ever been arrested?*
7. *How old are you?*
8. *Of what country are you a citizen? Where were you born?*
9. *What is your maiden name?*

10. Do you have any religious beliefs that would prevent you from working holidays?
11. Do you have children? Do you plan to have children?
12. How much do you weigh? How tall are you?

- How to respond to inappropriate or illegal questions?
  a. If the question is harmless, answer it.
  b. If answering might damage your chances, try to deflect it. (*Could you tell me how my marital status relates to the responsibilities for this position?)*
  c. Try to determine the reason behind the question, and respond to that. (*Are you concerned about my freedom to travel?*)
  d. You could respond by confronting the interviewer and threatening a lawsuit, but you will not be hired, of course.
  e. Remember that often an illegal or inappropriate question is posed innocently by an inexperienced interviewer.

PowerPoint slides 22, 23

Let's Discuss

Have you ever been asked an inappropriate or illegal question during a job interview? How did you handle it?

Students will enjoy sharing their experiences with the class, and some of the questions they may have been asked will surprise and even shock you. One student reports being asked what type of birth control she was using! This question is sure to result in a lively and educational discussion.

V. Closing the Interview (p. 553)

PowerPoint slides 24-27

A. Asking Your Own Questions

- Be prepared to ask questions about the company or the position.

Typical Questions:

1. What will my duties be (if not already discussed)?
2. Tell me what it's like working here in terms of the people, management practices, workloads, expected performance, and rewards.
3. What training programs are available from this organization? What specific training will be given for this position?
4. Who would be my immediate supervisor?
5. What is the organizational structure, and where does this position fit in?
6. Is travel required in this position?
7. How is job performance evaluated?
8. Assuming my work is excellent, where do you see me in five years?
9. How long do employees generally stay with this organization?

10. What are the major challenges for a person in this position?
11. What do you see in the future of this organization?
12. What do you like best about working for this organization?
13. May I have a tour of the facilities?
14. When do you expect to make a decision?

B. Ending Positively

- Summarize your strongest qualifications, thank the interviewer, and ask for the interviewer's card.
- Find out what action will follow.
- Don't be afraid to say that you want to the job.

VI. After the Interview (p. 554)

PowerPoint slides 28-30

A. Thanking Your Interviewer

- Send you a thank-you letter immediately after the interview.
- Refer to the date of the interview, the exact job title, and specific topics discussed.
- Send a separate letter to each interviewer.

Let's Discuss

Would you send a thank-you letter after a job interview even if you know you don't want the position? Why or why not?

Most students initially say *no* when asked this question. However, you should stress the value of sending a thank-you letter after any interview. Doing so shows good manners and respect for the interviewer's time. Just be sure that the letter isn't misleading.

Let's Discuss

Can sending a thank-you letter make a difference?

Without a doubt! Karen Hansen, columnist for Quintessential Careers, reports that only about 5 percent of interviewees take the time to send thank-you letters following job interviews. Doing so will certainly make a candidate stand out. The most effective thank-you letters are personalized and sent with 24 hours of the job interview.

B. Contacting Your References

- Alert your references that they may be contacted.

Figure 16.2 Interview Follow-Up Letter

C. Following Up

- Call or e-mail the interviewer within five days (or the specified time) to find out how the decision process is going.
- Communicate professionally and courteously.

VII. Other Employment Documents and Follow-Up Messages (p. 557)

Job seekers should be aware of other employment letters they may write and documents they may have to complete. These include interview thank-you, reference contact, application or résumé follow-up, rejection follow-up, job acceptance, job rejection, and resignation letters. In this chapter you will also learn how to effectively complete an application form.

- Application form
- Application or résumé follow-up letter
- Rejection follow-up letter
- Job acceptance and rejection letter
- Resignation letter

Lecture Transparencies
(available in a separate packet and at http://www.meguffey.com)

Interviewing and Follow Up Acetates	Transparency Number
Purposes of Interviews; Types of Interviews	181
Before the Interview	182
Traveling to and Arriving at Your Interview	183-184
Kinds of Interview Questions	185-186
Using the STAR Method to Answer Behavioral Interview Questions	187
Closing the Interview	188-189
Typical Applicant Evaluation Form	190

Solutions Transparencies

Solutions and discussion material for the Chapter 16 activities are found in this lecture outline only. Solution masters are not available.

Answers to Chapter Review Questions

1. **How are the main purposes of a job interview different for the job candidate and for the employer? (Obj. 1)**

   The purposes of a job interview for job candidates are to (a) convince the employer of your potential, (b) find out more about the job and the company, and (c) expand on the information in your résumé.

   The purposes of a job interview for an employer are to (a) assess your abilities in relation to the requirements for the position; (b) discuss your training, experience, knowledge, and abilities in more detail; (c) see what drives and motivate you; and (d) decide whether you would fit into the organization.

2. What is a screening interview, and why is it so important? (Obj. 1)

A screening interview is usually conducted on the telephone. The recruiter seeks to eliminate less qualified applicants. It is supremely important because if the candidate does not impress the recruiter, no in-person interview will follow.

3. Briefly describe the types of hiring/placement interviews you may encounter. (Obj. 1)

One-on-one interviews are most common and require the candidate to sit down with a company representative and talk about the job and his or her qualifications. Panel interviews, also called team interviews, are interviews conducted by teams of two or more people.
Group interviews occur when a company interviews several candidates for the same position at the same time.

Sequential interviews allow a candidate to meet with two or more interviewers on a one-on-one basis over the course of several hours or days. Stress interviews are meant to test the candidate's reactions during nerve-wracking situations. Online interviews, often conducted using webcams, take place when the interviewer and interviewee are in different geographical locations.

4. You have scheduled an interview with a large local company. What kind of information should you seek about this company, and where can you expect to find it? (Obj. 2)

You should research the target company looking for information about its history, products, mission, goals, number of employees, customers, competitors, geographic locations, culture, management structure, names of leaders, reputation in the community, financial condition, strengths and weaknesses, and future plans. You can find this information using the library, the Web, the company's Web site, the company's marketing brochures and annual report, the company's Facebook page or Twitter feeds, and company blogs. You can also talk with company employees.

5. What are success stories, and how can they be used? (Obj. 2)

Success stories are 30-second "sound bites" with specific examples of your educational and work-related experience that demonstrate your accomplishments and achievements. They should be practiced so that they can be used when answering interview questions.

6. What is digital dirt, and what should you do to clean it up during the employment process? (Obj. 2)

Digital dirt is inappropriate information that appears online that might cause an employer to not hire you. Examples include provocative or inappropriate photographs or information; postings about drinking or doing drugs; negative comments about previous employers, colleagues, or clients; and discriminatory comments. You can clean up your online presence by removing incriminating, provocative, or distasteful photos, content, or links; keeping comments positive; being selective about who is on your list of friends; avoiding joining groups or fan pages that may be viewed negatively; and setting up a professional social networking page.

7. **How can you address problem areas on your résumé such as lack of experience, getting fired, or earning low grades? (Obj. 2)**

Lack of experience: Focus on recent training and up-to-date skills.
Getting fired: Accept some responsibility and focus on what you have learned from the experience. Don't badmouth former employers.
Earning low grades: If the grades were low for only one or two terms, point to progress in the next semester, if applicable.

8. **What is your greatest fear of what you might do or what might happen to you during an employment interview? How can you overcome your fears? (Obj. 2)**

Some students fear they will choke and start a coughing fit. Others fear drawing a blank and being unable to answer a question at all. Some worry that they will drop something or stumble or sweat profusely. Students can overcome most fears by preparing thoroughly for the interview, conducting mock interviews, rehearsing answers to typical questions, and practicing deep breathing.

9. **Name at least six interviewing behaviors you can exhibit that send positive nonverbal messages during the job interview. (Obj. 3)**

a. Arrive on time or a little early.
b. Be courteous and congenial to everyone, including the receptionist.
c. Dress professionally.
d. Greet the interviewer confidently with a handshake.
e. Wait for the interviewer to offer you a chair.
f. Control your body movements, keeping your hands, arms, and elbows to yourself.
g. Exhibit good posture.
h. Use appropriate eye contact.
i. Use gestures effectively.
j. Smile enough to convey a positive attitude.
k. Listen attentively.
l. Turn off your cell phone and other electronic devices.
m. Don't chew gum.
n. Sound enthusiastic and interested.
o. Avoid empty words.

10. **Should you be candid with an interviewer when asked about your weaknesses? (Obj. 4)**

Most experts advise against being candid about your weaknesses! No one was ever hired for a job because of his or her weaknesses. If pressed to name a weakness, name a strength disguised as a weakness, identify a corrected weakness, cite an unrelated weakness or a learning objective, or simply state that you have no weaknesses that would affect your ability to perform this job.

11. What should you do if asked a salary question early in an interview? (Obj. 4)

Try to defer discussion of salary until later when you know more about the job and whether it will be offered.

12. How should you respond to questions you feel are inappropriate or illegal? (Obj. 4)

If you feel that question is harmless, answer it. If you think that answering the question would damage your chance of being hired, try to deflect the question tactfully by asking how it relates to the duties of the position. Of course, you could also threaten to sue—but this action would likely prevent you from being hired.

13. What kinds of questions should you ask during an interview? (Obj. 5)

You should ask questions that help you gain information about the position and that will impress the interviewer with your thoughtfulness and interest in the position.

14. List the steps you should take immediately following your job interview. (Obj. 6)

a. Make notes of what was said in case you are called back for another interview.
b. Jot down key points, the names of your interviewers, and other details.
c. Ask yourself what went well and what needs improvement.
d. Note your strengths and weaknesses during the interview so that you can work to improve in future interviews.
e. Send appropriate thank-you letters.
f. Contact your references.

15. If you are offered a position, why is it important to write an acceptance letter, and what should it include? (Obj. 7)

It is important to write an acceptance letter to confirm your acceptance of the position. It should show your enthusiasm, review salary and benefits, and include a specific starting date.

Answers to Critical Thinking Questions

1. What can you do to appear professional when a potential employer contacts you by phone for a screening interview or to schedule a job interview? (Obj. 2)

To appear professional when an employer first contacts you, invest in a good answering machine or voice mail service; tell those who might answer your phone at home about your job search; prevent children from answering the phone; don't answer your cell phone unless you are in a good location to carry on a conversation; and use voice mail to screen calls. To make the first conversation impressive, keep a list near the telephone of positions for which you have applied; use a professional tone and businesslike language; be polite and enthusiastic; be prepared for a screening interview; take good notes during the phone conversation; and reconfirm the date and time of your interview before hanging up.

2. **Why do you think so many employers search for information about job applicants online using Google, Facebook, Twitter, and other online tools? Do you think these kinds of searches are ethical or appropriate? Isn't this similar to snooping? (Obj. 2)**

   Many employers who search for information about a job applicant online say that the information they gather gives them a more accurate picture of the job applicant. Employers might argue that such searches are ethical because the information was made public by the individuals themselves. Their findings often reveal an applicant's communication skills, judgment, and integrity. This question could result in a dynamic classroom discussion as students will have varying opinions about whether such searches are appropriate.

3. **Do you think behavioral questions (such as, Tell me about a business problem you have had and how you solved it) are more effective than traditional questions (such as, Tell me what you are good at)? Why? (Obj. 4)**

   Companies are increasingly using behavioral questions because such questions enable interviewers to predict how the candidate will respond to similar situations in the future. Past behavior is a good indicator of future behavior. Such questions also reveal the candidate's ability to communicate and provide insight into how he or she thinks.

4. **If you are asked an illegal interview question, why is it important to first assess the intentions of the interviewer? (Obj. 4)**

   Most illegal interview questions are asked in true innocence. Inexperienced interviewers are ignorant of the law. They do not know what questions are proper and are unaware of how the information could be used by others in a discriminatory way. Most illegal questions are asked when an untrained interviewer is just trying to be friendly and inquires about the candidate's family or personal life. If you feel the intentions of the interviewer are innocent, you should avoid being tempted to assert your constitutional rights.

5. **Ethical Issue. When asked about his previous salary in a job interview, Jeremy boosts his salary a bit. He reasons that he was about to get a raise, and he also felt that he deserved to be paid more than he was actually earning. Even his supervisor said that he was worth more than his salary. Is Jeremy justified in inflating his previous salary? (Obj. 4)**

   Although it may seem justified, lying about a previous salary is unethical and possibly unlawful. If Jeremy is hired and offered a salary based on false information, he could be fired for giving misinformation. Instead of lying about a previous salary (information that will surely be discovered eventually), Jeremy should make a strong case for the salary he wants. If he is offered a lower salary, he might ask to start at that salary and be considered for a raise as soon as he proves his worth.

Activities

16.1 Researching an Organization (Obj. 2)

This activity will allow students to become familiar with some of the resources that are available for researching company information. It should also help students develop the habit of researching any company before interviewing with it.

16.2 Learning What Jobs Are Really About Through Webblogs (Obj. 2)

Students should enjoy this activity. More and more company blogs are being created every day, and students may be surprised at some of the information employees post on these blogs. Consider having students share their findings and impressions with the class.

16.3 Taking a Look at Corporate Web Videos (Obj. 2)

This activity shows students how employers are using videos for recruiting and other job search purposes. Consider having students share their findings in class, including showing the best videos they located online.

16.4 Building Interview Skills (Objs. 2, 3)

This is an excellent activity to help students think about what employees are looking for in job applicants. The lists students develop for this activity will help them with Activity 16.4.

16.5 Preparing Success Stories (Obj. 2)

Students must learn how important it is to develop success stories in advance of an interview. Consider having students select one of their success stories to share with the class.

16.6 Exploring Appropriate Interview Attire (Obj. 2)

Students need to know more than to wear a suit to an interview. The opportunities for dress code violations are many and involve crucial details—for example, the correct fit of a suit (i.e., proper length of pants and sleeves, matching socks, and so forth). Students may need help in distinguishing between high-end wool or silk ensembles and polyester duds. Quality suits don't need to be expensive, and if chosen carefully, they can last for years. Sales often provide opportunities to pick up a brand-name suit for a fraction of its original price.

Many companies today have introduced dress codes to clarify the fuzzy dividing line between business casual and casual wear. Negotiating such distinctions with ease may ensure students' future interviewing and career success.

16.7 Polishing Answers to Interview Questions (Obj. 4)

This activity could also be done in pairs or small groups. Have students select three questions from each category to ask their partners or teammates.

16.8 Learning to Answer Situational Interview Questions (Obj. 4)

Students will enjoy writing their own situational interview questions and playing the role of both interviewer and interviewee. Be sure to monitor the role playing to make sure that they have developed appropriate situational questions.

16.9 Developing Skill With Behavioral Interview Questions (Obj. 4)

Students should list some of the following skill areas: analytical/problem solving, communication, creativity/innovation, decision making, goal setting, flexibility/adaptability, integrity/honesty, interpersonal, leadership/initiative, organization/time management, strengths/weaknesses, and teamwork. The STAR method involves focusing on a Situation or Task, Action, and Result.

16.10 Creating an Interview Cheat Sheet (Objs. 2–5)

Preparing an interview "cheat sheet" is an excellent strategy, particularly for new job seekers. Once students have prepared their cheat sheets, have them share the sheets with others for feedback. This will also allow students to share ideas.

16.11 Handling Inappropriate and Illegal Interview Questions (Obj. 4)

Students may be confronted with inappropriate or illegal questions in actual interviews. Many students didn't even realize at the time that these questions were inappropriate or illegal. Moreover, most candidates don't know how to properly handle such questions. This activity will help students prepare to handle such questions professionally and tactfully.

16.12 Knowing What to Ask (Obj. 5)

Students are sometimes caught off guard when asked if they have any questions at the end of a job interview. Careful preparation can help students ask appropriate questions that demonstrate their interest in the company and the position.

16.13 Role-Playing in an Mock Interview (Objs. 3, 4)

Students will enjoy this activity and will learn from it. Carefully observe these mock interviews to make sure that students are giving appropriate answers that will reflect positively on them during an interview. Role playing is one of the most effective methods to learn and internalize appropriate responses.

16.14 Recording an Interview (Objs. 3–6)

You may experience some student reluctance to being videotaped, but convince them that doing so will give them valuable feedback that they can use in future interviews.

16.15–16.18, 16.21

These activities enable students to prepare an interview thank-you letter, a refusal letter, and a résumé follow-up letter. Decide which of these activities you would like your students to prepare, and consider having them submit all documents to you in an employment portfolio. The documents in this portfolio can then be used by students as models as they begin their job searches. Also consider having students exchange employment documents so that they can give each other feedback and obtain employment document preparation ideas from others.

16.19 Saying Yes to a Job Offer (Obj. 7)

16.20 Searching for Advice (Obj. 1–7)

The Web is filled with valuable information about the job search. Considering having students share their findings with others in the class.

ZOOMING IN, Part 1: Googling for Jobs

Critical Thinking

- **Before you apply for a job, why must you investigate carefully the background of any company that interests you?**

  Recruiters are impressed by candidates who are knowledgeable about the company. Your research conveys a sincere interest in the company. The more you know abut the company, the better you can tailor your résumé to the company and craft responses to an interviewer's questions that show how your skills and background are a good match for the position.

- **What types of skills and background do you think Google recruiters look for in a candidate?**

  Google recruiters seek job applicants who love technology and its applications, have demonstrated success in prior jobs, are creative thinkers, have held leadership positions on campus, show initiative and an entrepreneurial spirit, and thrive in an unstructured environment.

- **How would you craft a résumé and cover letter so that it would stand out when it arrives at Google?**

  Your résumé and cover letter should address the special qualities that Google seeks in its employees. Consider which form of résumé—chronological or functional—works best to present your technology skills, leadership roles, and other attributes that Google seeks. Make sure to use action verbs. Address your cover letter to a specific person. If you are applying for a posted job, begin by mentioning it and how you learned about it. If you are sending an unsolicited letter, begin with a general statement that shows you are familiar with Google and follow it with information that shows how your special talents and background would benefit Google. Follow either opening by highlighting your qualifications and documenting them with examples.

ZOOMING IN, Part 2: Googling for Jobs

- **Why are online questionnaires and screening interviews useful tools for Google's recruiters?**

  Google receives thousands of job applications each week. Searching through responses to online questionnaires streamlines the process of finding candidates with the specific skills recruiters seek. A screening interview allows the recruiter to learn more about an applicant's suitability for a particular job before inviting him or her to interview in person.

- **How does thorough preparation help a candidate reduce the stress and butterflies that most people feel during an interview?**

  Preparation is essential if you expect to remain calm under the pressure of job interviewing. Knowing that you have done painstaking company research and that you have practiced typical questions along with your success stories will boost your confidence. This self-assurance is a major factor in calming nervousness.

- **How can you prepare in advance for behavioral interview questions?**

  Consider the position for which you are applying and define the key points from your résumé that you wish to highlight. Think about your major accomplishments, your training, and your education. Also make a list of the core competencies—such as *detail oriented, effective multitasker, great team player*—that make you a perfect fit for the job. Prepare at least six success stories for each key point and each core competency. Use these stories as examples when you respond to behavioral questions.

ZOOMING IN, Your Turn: Applying Your Skills at Google

Students should prepare a "cheat sheet" that summarizes Google's business philosophy, corporate culture, products, and other topics of interest. They can obtain this information by consulting the Google site, by visiting http://www.hoovers.com, or by searching other sites that specialize in company data summaries. Their "cheat sheet" should include typical interview questions, such as *Tell me about yourself* and *Why do you want to work for Google*? Students can generate good questions to ask by searching for current Google information as well as by looking over questions provided in this chapter.

Discussion Material for CAREER COACH: Fighting Fear During Your Job Interview

Have two students role-play a short scenario with preliminary interview questions before approaching the salary question. Encourage them to use their imaginations in responding realistically. One student plays the role of the hiring manager, and the other is the candidate. Then they can switch roles and role-play again. You could pair up everyone in the class and have them conduct their role-plays simultaneously. The goal is to encourage students to try their skills at negotiating because practice improves performance.

Discussion Material for CAREER COACH: Let's Talk Money: Salary Negotiation Dos and Don'ts

Taking part in a mock salary negotiation is an excellent way for students to develop their negotiating skills. Encourage students to give each other constructive feedback during this role play activity. You will want to monitor these mock interviews to ensure that all students are participating and that students are following the dos and don'ts presented in the Career Coach box.

Ethics Check Solutions

Ethics Check, Page 543
Just Looking
Like all relationships, the job-search process is about two parties looking to find a good match. Filling a position is costly for employers, and candidates likewise invest time and money in their job hunts. Under the circumstances, is it ethical for a job seeker to accept on-site interviews when not genuinely interested in the prospective employer?

Answers will probably vary. Some students think that it is OK to practice their skills by scheduling interviews in which they are not too interested. Others may claim that in today's competitive climate "anything goes," pointing to companies that fire thousands when they see a need to "downsize." As a result, students may grant some latitude to the interviewee who is often perceived as an underdog to begin with. However, most business professionals would probably agree that accepting an on-site interview without being committed to its positive outcome is not fair. After all, the company inviting applicants has already narrowed the field and is now demonstrating a serious interest in the remaining candidates. The entire interview process rests on trust and on the assumption that each side is sincere.

Ethics Check, Page 552
Human Resources Must Get Firing Right
Former General Electric CEO Jack Welch and his business journalist wife Suzy believe that human resources must execute layoffs fairly: First, the Welches recommend that pink slips be delivered "face-to-face, eyeball-to-eyeball" by the employee's manager, not a stranger. Second, HR must handle severance arrangements evenhandedly. Last, HR has to provide genuine consolation and assist with the transition, the Welches suggest. Do you believe that such attempts at making downsizing more humane are effective?

Without a doubt, to be laid off is a painful, even traumatic experience for most workers. However, the Welches clearly imply that human resources has an important role to play in making the firing of employees fair and dignified. Jack and Suzy Welch state the following: "Being fired is dehumanizing in any event, but to get the news from a 'hired gun' only makes the matters worse." [Welch, J., & Welch, S. (2009, March 23). Layoffs: HR's moment of truth. *BusinessWeek*, p. 104.] Students could be asked to watch *Up in the Air* by director Jason Reitman, a film that describes the evolution of a "hired gun" whose sole job it is to travel around the country and fire employees, and who, in the end, undergoes a transformative experience.

Ethics Check, p. 557
Halfhearted
Assume that you have been offered a job. However, you have gone to several other interviews that seemed to have gone very well, and now you are emboldened by your success and want to wait for a better offer. Is it ethical to accept the present offer while you are waiting, and later turn it down if something better comes along?

The solution to this ethical dilemma *ought* to be simple: The candidate should either request more time to decide or politely decline the offer. However, it is possible that students will advance self-serving arguments. They may point out that a hotly contested candidate has great leverage and negotiating power and should put both to good use, regardless of their effect on the potential employer. More thoughtful students might realize that ethical professionals act responsibly. A good-faith offer should, in turn, be answered with integrity.

Photo Essay Solutions

Photo Essay, Page 539
Interviewing can be stressful enough, but when the interview takes place over a meal, the stress level is even greater. In addition to answering questions, interviewees must also worry about following proper dining etiquette, ordering appropriately, and carrying on a conversation while eating. The most successful candidates prepare ahead of time by studying dining etiquette rules and practicing with a friend who can give constructive feedback.

Photo Essay, Page 543
Despite liberalization of workplace fashions, tattoos and body piercings continue to be a turnoff for many interviewers. Although some bosses are loosening dress codes to attract young talent, many companies have policies that require employees, especially those who have direct contact with the public, to conceal body art. In either case, an interview is never the right place to "go casual." Proper dress for interviews should always be in keeping with professionalism and the desire to appear competent, qualified, and successful.

Video Resources

Instructors may show *The Job Search* from Video Library 1, *Building Workplace Skills*. The video illustrates the job search and is a useful introduction to Chapters 15 and 16. After viewing the video, students should be prepared to discuss critical-thinking questions.

Chapter Presentation Ideas and Extras

Learning to Network: Interviewing a Professional Practitioner. Early in the term ask your students to schedule an interview with a professional in their field to (1) make a professional contact and (2) learn about what is expected on the job. Students can make the appointments through their own contacts or through calling a company and seeking an appointment. Students should explain that they want information and advice from professionals in their fields.

Pre-Interview: Once the appointment is made, have the students prepare interview questions such as

What kinds of duties and responsibilities do you have?

What is a typical day like for you?

How did you get started in this field?

If you could start over, what would you do differently?

What are some of the drawbacks of a career in this field?

What is a typical career path for advancement?

What do you like best about your job? What do you like the least?

What is the average salary for an entry-level position?

What advice can you give that might help me to prepare more adequately for a career in this field?

Can you suggest names of other people who may be willing to give me more information?

Women may want to ask whether or not employment and promotional opportunities are limited for women in this field.

One question required of every student: *In what ways and to what extent do you use your communication skills (reading, writing, speaking, and listening) on the job?*

The Interview: Students must dress professionally for the interview, be prepared, and keep to the time limit agreed on. They need to take good notes (no tape recorders—they need to practice note-taking and listening skills).
Post-Interview: Require students to write an appropriate thank-you note to the person interviewed, citing what things they appreciated about the experience. Students should write memos or make short presentations to the class about their interview results. They should cover what information they learned, how they felt during their interviews, what they gained from their experiences, and how and to what extent the professionals they interviewed use communication skills on the job.

Benefits of the Assignment: Students make valuable contacts, gain confidence in interviewing, and develop insight into the workings of their chosen professions. If students make oral summaries of their interview, the whole class shares advice about career preparation and employment searches from multiple professional sources. Also, since all of the professionals interviewed will stress the importance of effective communication skills, the class will get the message. Finally, some by-products of the experience may be job or internship offers, further contacts with other professionals, and future appointments to learn more about the profession.

SOLUTIONS

Solution masters are provided for all Documents for Analysis and for nearly all of the writing activities appearing in Chapters 1, and 4-10. Answers to end-of-chapter questions and solutions for activities in other chapters appear in the Chapter Teaching Suggestions. Additional teaching transparency masters appear in the Transparency Acetate Packet. Note that students may find copies of all Documents for Analysis at www.meguffey.com so that they do not have to rekey when revising.

1.11 Document for Analysis—Revision

DATE: Current

TO: All Employees

FROM: Albertina Sindaha, Operations Manager

SUBJECT: Improving Our Cleaning Routines

Because of custodial cutbacks, it is necessary for all of us to pitch in to clean up the department before leaving on Friday afternoons. This new procedure was to have started last Friday, but our first effort was not as successful as we had hoped.

Although some individuals cleaned their own areas, few departmental employees helped clean common areas. Once you have cleaned your own area, please help in the following tasks:

- Clean the copy machine area, including emptying waste baskets and organizing paper and toner supplies.
- Clean the office lunch room, including wiping the counters, cleaning the sinks, removing all food from the refrigerator, and cleaning the coffee machine.
- Straighten office supply shelves.

If we can complete these tasks on Friday, we can return to a clean office on Monday. Please cooperate in this cleanup so that individuals do not have to be assigned to a specific cleaning schedule.

4.1 Audience Benefits and the "You" View

a. **To prevent you from losing money in third-party check transactions, our credit union no longer cashes such checks presented by our members.**

b. **To have your orders processed more quickly and efficiently, please fill out your customer information at this Web site.**

c. **You may use your iPhone discount for the next 30 days at our electronics center.**

d. **All your work-related travel expenses will be reimbursed under our new policy.**

e. **Congratulations! You have been selected to enter our management trainee program!**

f. **So that you may continue to buy name brands at discount prices, we offer only store credit on returned merchandise.**

4.2 Conversational but Professional

a. As you requested, we are sending your printer toner and supplies to your Oakdale office.

b. Please tell me whether your representative will be visiting before June 1.

c. Please submit your departmental budget before January 1.

d. Although we've fallen behind somewhat in the schedule, we don't have to begin anew.

e. We urge you to approve the agreement by voting yes.

f. She didn't have the nerve to criticize him to his face.

4.3 Positive and Courteous Expression

a. Customers with membership cards receive a 10 percent discount.

b. We can process your claim if you send us a letter from your doctor showing that he or she treated your injuries.

c. By following each requirement, you will receive your $50 rebate.

d. We will pay you once you complete the job satisfactorily.

e. In the message you left at our Web site, you explain that you returned a headset.

f. The first 25 customers will be able to purchase our special netbook computers.

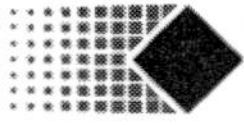

4.4 Bias-Free Language

a. Applicants for firefighter positions must submit medical reports signed by their physicians.

b. All employees are entitled to see their personnel files.

c. All servers are covered under our new benefits package.

d. A salesperson (or Salespeople) would have to be very skillful to sell those condos.

e. Serving on the panel are a veterinarian, a doctor, two businesspeople, and a CPA.

f. All conference participants and their spouses (or partners) are invited to the banquet.

g. How many working hours are required to complete the project?

4.5 Plain Language and Familiar Words

a. Please learn whether we must continue our current contract despite troubling profits.

b. He guessed that the car (or truck) was not working because of a broken gasket.

c. Because we cannot check all cash payments, we must end the contract.

d. The contract requires that management continue the retirement plan.

e. I'll talk with Mark about using (addressing?) his staff.

f. One party cannot leave the contract early without a good reason. (Plain English version)

4.6 Precise, Vigorous Words

a. applaud

b. include, recipient

c. complicated, create

d. glitch, retrieve

e. (a) examining, studying, analyzing (b) useless, deceptive, unethical

f. (a) eliminate, reduce (b) balance, cut, repair

g. (a) explained, declared, suggested (b) qualified, experienced, proficient

4.7 Legal Language

a. reviewed or studied

b. facilitate

c. evaluate, assess, or analyze

4.8 Document for Analysis—Revision

To: All Employees
From: B. A. Cartwright <bacartwright@integrity.com>
Cc:
Subject: Implementing New E-Mail and Internet Policy
Attached: New E-Mail and Internet Policy

Effective immediately we will be implementing a new policy regarding e-mail and Internet use. This policy allows the use of e-mail and the Internet for work-related business and for essential personal messages only.

Our IT managers tell me that our bandwidth is seriously compromised as a result of employee gaming, blogging, shopping, chatting, and downloading of streaming video. These activities are definitely not work-related.

We would like very much to continue to offer the privilege of e-mail use to employees for limited personal messages. To retain that privilege and to be sure you can download your work-related documents and messages quickly, please do not use company computers or bandwidth for anything other than necessary work tasks.

Attached is our revised E-Mail and Internet Policy. Please read it carefully and return the signature form by March 1 so that we can continue to offer e-mail privileges to employees.

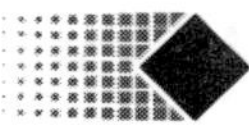

4.9 BURGER KING AND THE $1 DOUBLE CHEESEBURGER

Discussion material for this activity is offered in the Chapter Teaching Suggestions.

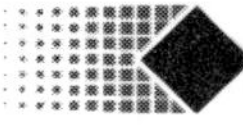

4.10 CHANNEL SELECTION

a. If this request is likely to be refused and you wish to be quite persuasive, talk to Crystal in person. Otherwise, use the telephone. Any other channel would probably be too slow—unless you know that Crystal answers her e-mail immediately.

b. A wiki would work well as an information repository where members can add, remove, and edit content about the progress of the project.

c. If all the team members are online, you could use instant messaging to see whether they are available. Sending an e-mail is also possible, but it is slower and problematic. You won't know whether the message was received.

d. Schedule a personal conversation with each one.

e. Most global transactions such as this are conducted by fax, which is cheap and fast and provides a written record. E-mail would also be appropriate if you have the customer's address.

f. Write a letter because it provides a written record of correspondence sent outside of your organization.

g. As a member of the Information Technology Department, you must collect information about virus protection software for your office computers and make a recommendation to the hands-on company president.

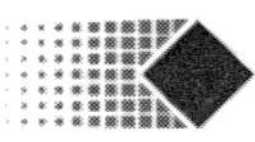

4.11 Analyzing Audiences

a. Because the primary reader is your sales manager, you should know what kind of communication format and content he expects. But he may not know much about the customer and specifically what the customer is demanding. Because the manager is familiar with the business, you can use jargon or references that outsiders might not understand. You can expect the receiver to be receptive to prospective new business; perhaps he's willing to make concessions to please this new customer. However, you should also remember that the sales manager may wish to forward your message to a higher executive, so you should be sure to fill in details and use fairly formal language.

b. The primary reader will probably be a busy human resources director, an educated, experienced individual who may be deluged with applications. Because the job is advertised, you would expect the reader to be neutral or positive toward your letter. Because your relationship is professional, your tone should be formal, yet friendly.

c. The audience will be all municipal water users, with a wide range of language abilities represented. The audience knows little about the technicalities of water chemistry and delivery. You would use plain English, adopt a conversational yet professional tone, and show courtesy.

d. The primary reader is your boss, but a secondary reader may be your boss's superior, if further approval is sought. The relationship is both personal and professional. Because your boss probably has no knowledge of the computer class, you would want to describe the class in detail and explain why your proposal would benefit both the company and you.

e. A targeted audience of executives means that you have some expectations about their income, education, status, and interests. You can use language that educated readers would comprehend. Because readers probably know little about

[4.11 Continued]

shared ownership of jet planes, you will have to provide persuasive arguments and data. You might expect to have to overcome a negative response.

4.12 COPYRIGHT CONFUSION: MYTHS AND FACTS

Discussion material for this activity is offered in the Chapter Teaching Suggestions.

CHAPTER 5 APPLYING YOUR SKILLS AT GAP INC.

Students are to brainstorm, create cluster diagrams, and outline their ideas about ways to turn around Gap's fortunes. Discussion and responses for this activity will vary.

5.1 SENTENCE ELEMENTS

IC = independent clause
DC = dependent clause
P = phrase

a. DC — you
b. IC — interviewer
c. P
d. DC — they
e. IC — results
f. P
g. DC — people
h. P

5.2 SENTENCE FAULTS

a. Fragment. Revision: Because 90 percent of all business transactions involve written messages, good writing skills are critical.

b. Fragment. Revision: The recruiter requested a writing sample even though the candidate seemed to communicate well orally.

c. Comma splice. Revision: Major soft-drink companies considered a new pricing strategy. They tested vending machines that raise prices in hot weather.

d. Run-on. Revision: Thirsty consumers may think that variable pricing is unfair; they may also refuse to use the machine. OR: Thirsty consumers may think that variable pricing is unfair. They may also refuse to use the machine.

[5.2 Continued]

e. Comma splice. Revision: About half of Pizza Hut's 7,600 outlets make deliveries; the others concentrate on walk-in customers. OR: About half of Pizza Hut's 7,600 outlets make deliveries. The others concentrate on walk-in customers.

f. Run-on. Revision: McDonald's sold its chain of Chipotle Mexican Grill restaurants. The chain's share price doubled on the next day of trading.

g. Fragment. Revision: Private equity players are betting they can breathe new life into old brands, which explains why Golden Gate Partners paid millions for defunct retailer Eddie Bauer. Note: This long sentence could also be broken into two shorter sentences.

5.3 Emphasis

a. 2
b. 2
c. 1
d. 1
e. 2
f. 1
g. 1
h. 1
i. 2

5.4 Active Voice

a. The manager gave employees their checks at 4 p.m. every Friday.

b. McDonald's tried new spices and cooking techniques to improve its hamburgers.

c. My boss designed our new company logo.

[5.4 Continued]

d. The CEO commended the managers with the most productive departments.

e. The leader asked all team members to brainstorm for 10 minutes.

5.5 Passive Voice

a. A computational error was discovered [by the auditor] in the company's tax figures.

b. Your order for ten monitors cannot be shipped until June 15. BETTER: Your order for ten monitors will be shipped June 15.

c. The accounting statement was not submitted on time [by Stacy].

d. Deceptive diet advertisements by weight-loss marketers were targeted [by the Federal Trade Commission].

e. Corporate and financial information is being stolen by thieves using data-stealing malware on the Web.

5.6 Dangling and Misplaced Modifiers

a. By advertising extensively, our company filled all open jobs quickly.

b. Correct. The understood subject is you (To apply for early admission, [you] submit your application by November 1.)

c. After leaving the midtown meeting, Angela discovered that her car would not start.

d. Walking up the driveway, the detectives immediately spotted the Hummer parked in the garage.

[5.6 Continued]

e. **No matter how silly they seemed, the manager's rules were to be observed by all staff members.**

f. **To complete the project on time, the team established a new deadline.**

g. **Acting as manager, Mr. Lopez hired several new employees.**

h. **In our boardroom Michelle Mitchell presented a talk about workplace drug problems.**

5.7 PARAGRAPH ORGANIZATION

a. 5
b. 4
c. 1, 2, 3, 6, 7
d. Revision:

The old sports scoreboard should be replaced for many reasons. It is a tired warhorse that was originally constructed in the 1960s. It's now hard to find replacement parts for it when something breaks. In addition, the old scoreboard is not energy efficient. Finally, the old scoreboard shows only scores for football games. Consequently, when we have soccer games or track meets, we're without any functioning scoreboard.

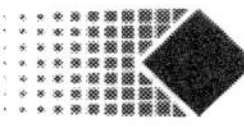

5.8 Paragraph Organization and Revision

a. **Pizza Hut is considering launching a new product called "The Extreme." It will be the largest pizza on the market. With double the cheese and double the toppings, it will target the X and Y Generations. These are the fastest growing segments in the fast-food market. This population segment has been successfully targeted with the "extreme" strategy in other areas. However, we feel that the "extreme" strategy has not been developed fully in the fast-food market. The same target audience that would respond to an extreme product also reacts to low prices. Therefore, we plan to price this new pizza at $19.99.**

b. **A common problem in PowerPoint involves lost sound and video files. When you move the presentation to a network folder or send it to someone else, it has no sound. However, you can solve this problem by keeping your sound and video files together. Create a new folder for your presentation and copy the sound and video files to that folder before you put them in your presentation. When you move the presentation to the network, move the entire folder. As a result, you will always have your sound files ready for use with your presentation.**

c. **A number of high-level positions are available to current employees. These positions are in production, marketing, and administrative support. If you are interested, come to the Human Resources Department to see the list showing positions, qualifications, and job descriptions. Many of the jobs are now open. Therefore, you should apply immediately. Interviews must be scheduled within the next two weeks.**

5.9 Document for Analysis—Revision

Dangling modifiers: Sentences 3, 11, 17
Passive voice: Sentences 1, 4, 5, 11, 12, 13, 17
Fragments: Sentences 8, 14, 16

Suggested Revision

Dear Mr. Gibbons:

[1]You probably chose Body Fitness Center here in Scottsdale because it is one of the top-rated gyms in the Southwest. [2]Our principal goal has always been making your workouts enjoyable. [3]To continue to provide you with the best equipment and programs, we need your feedback.

[4]Body Fitness provides an outstanding program with quality equipment and excellent training programs. [5]However, we could give more individual attention to our customers if we could extend our peak usage time. [6]You have probably noticed that attendance at the gym increases from 4 p.m. to 8 p.m. [7]We wish it were possible to accommodate all our customers on their favorite equipment during those hours. [8]Although we can't stretch an hour, [9]we would like to make better use of the time between 8 p.m. and 11 p.m. [10]With more members coming later, we would have less crush from 4 p.m. to 8 p.m.

[11]To encourage you to stay later, my partner and I are considering adding security cameras for our parking area. [12]We may also add cameras for some inside facilities. [13]We have given this matter a lot of thought, [14]although Body Fitness has never previously had an incident that endangered a member.

[15]Please fill in the attached interactive questionnaire, [16]which will give us instant feedback about scheduling your workouts. [17]By completing this questionnaire, you will help us schedule workouts and training sessions to give you exactly the equipment and trainers you prefer.

Cordially,

5.10 THROUGH 5.15

Discussion material for these activities is offered in the Chapter Teaching Suggestions.

Chapter 6 - Applying Your Skills at Taco Bell —Revised Memo

DATE: Current
TO: Taco Bell Executive Council
FROM: Erin Jackson, Culinary Product Manager
SUBJECT: FAST-FOOD TRENDS AND MENU OPTIONS

As you requested, I am submitting the following ideas based on my observation and research about eating trends in fast-food restaurants. Below is a rough outline of possible concepts to upgrade Taco Bell's menu. This memo summarizes the findings to be presented at our next meeting.

Mexican cuisine is increasingly popular from coast to coast, and in a depressed economy our restaurants can offer value as well as tasty food. From my first-hand experience gained as a chef and from current research, I have observed numerous eating trends. Below are four that are of interest as we rethink the Taco Bell menu.

<u>Current Eating Trends</u>

- <u>Low-fat, healthful choices</u>. With as many as one in five U.S. consumers on a diet, our menu should reflect low-calorie, healthful options that still taste good.

- <u>Spices</u>. Consumers are appreciating more highly spiced foods and hot sauces. Spicy Thai and other ethnic dishes are growing in popularity.

- <u>Freshness</u>. As consumers become more knowledgeable and more discriminating, they are demanding fresher ingredients.

- <u>Tasty food but at low prices</u>. In an economic downturn, consumers are looking for value meals that don't break their budgets.

Taco Bell Executive Council Page 2 Current date

Given the increasing acceptance of Mexican cuisine and the rich array of flavors and textures, we have many possibilities for expanding our menu. Although my full report contains additional trends and menu ideas, I will focus on four significant concepts.

New Menu Concepts

- **Spicy grilled items. Selections might include chicken marinated in lime juice, chipotle-rubbed ahi tuna served with cranberry-mango salsa, and Volcano Beef Burrito served with Lava sauce.**

- **Fresco menu. I suggest that we offer an entire menu of ten or more items that cater to dieters and health-conscious customers. The Fresco menu might include Crunchy Beef Taco, Grilled Steak Taco, Blazing Bean Burrito, and Ranchero Chicken Soft Taco. These, low-fat items will contain fewer than 10 grams of fat but be tasty, filling, and inexpensive.**

- **Self-serve salsa bar. We could offer exotic fresh salsas with bold flavors and textures.**

- **Fruit-flavored frozen drinks. Mango and strawberry-flavored frozen beverages topped with strawberries could be sweetened with sucrose rather than high-fructose corn syrup for an appealing, inexpensive, low-calorie selection.**

I would be happy to discuss these ideas with you in greater detail and to demonstrate them in the kitchen. Thanks for this opportunity to work with you in expanding our menu to ensure that Taco Bell remains tops in Mexican cuisine.

Format note: We underlined headings because boldface is used throughout. However, students may use Roman for the body font and then use boldface for headings.

6.1 Flabby Expressions

a. Although we lost the contract, we must now move forward.

b. Because prices are falling, we will invest soon. [OR: Because prices are falling, we will invest March 1.]

c. We cannot fill the order until payment is received for previous shipments.

d. Generally, we would not accept the return; however, we will probably make an exception in this case.

6.2 Long Lead-Ins

a. I received your e-mail and its attachments.

b. We will observe Monday as a holiday.

c. Your homeowner's coverage expires soon.

d. The loss of laptops endangers company security.

6.3 *There Is/Are* and *It Is/Was* Fillers

a. Many businesses are implementing strict e-mail policies.

b. The CEO must approve the plan.

c. You must update several Web pages.

d. The manager says that many employees did not return the health surveys.

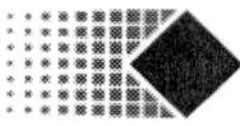

6.4 Redundancies

a. Because the proposals are identical, we need not check each item.
b. All requests for iPods and BlackBerrys were combined in our proposal.
c. The office walls were painted beige.
d. Our supervisor requested that team members return to the office.

6.5 Empty Words

a. He scheduled the meeting for 11 a.m.
b. Because of the surprising response, the company expanded its gift program.
c. I will distribute your proposal immediately.
d. Are you aware that our budget has a deficit of about $100,000?

6.6 Trite Business Phrases

a. As you request, we will no longer send you e-mail offers.
b. Thank you for considering our plea for community support.
c. As you request, we are sending the original copies separately.
d. Enclosed is a check for $700.

6.7 Clichés, Slang, and Wordiness

Note: Acceptable student responses may vary from the suggested responses.

a. Although our last presentation failed, we are sure our new presentation will be well received.

b. Out team must be willing to think creatively when developing marketing ideas that capture attention.

c. As usual, our competitor has made an underhanded claim that we think is unfair [*OR*: devious, false, undeserved].

d. If you refer to the budget, you will see provisions that prevent overspending.

6.8 Buried Verbs

a. Ms. Nelson appraised the home's value.

b. Web-based customer service reduces overall costs.

c. Management recommended abandoning the pilot project.

d. The board of directors will consider the contract at its next meeting.

6.9 Lists, Bullets, and Headings

a. Security Plus specializes in the following preemployment background reports:
   - Professional reference interviews
   - Criminal reports
   - Driving records
   - Employment verification
   - Credit information

[6.9 Continued]

b. A high-powered MBA program costs hundreds of dollars an hour. Our program covers the same information:

- Starting a business
- Business plans
- Taxes
- Marketing feasibility studies
- Employment benefits plans
- Licensing requirements

c. On-site GuruGeek computer technicians provide fast, affordable solutions to residential and small business clients including the following popular offerings:

- Antivirus security. Our GuruGeek technician can protect your computer against viruses, worms, and spyware as well as help you avoid e-mail attacks, identity theft, and malicious hacker programs.
- Wireless networking. We can help you share Internet access through a single wireless router so that many computer users use the same network.
- Data backup and recovery. Our technicians focus on helping small businesses and home users protect their data without investing a lot of time and energy.

6.10 Document for Analysis—Revision

Current date

Mr. Michael Chatham
329 Sycamore Street
Pikeville, KY 41605

Dear Mr. Chatham:

We are changing your World Bank Card Agreement. These changes will be effective for all billing periods beginning on or after February 3.

How Your APR Will Change

We are increasing your variable APR (annual percentage rate) for purchases. Your APR will be identical to the U.S. Prime Rate plus 10.99 percent with a minimum APR of 16.99 percent.

Default APR

All of your APRs on all balances may automatically increase to the default APR if you default under any card agreement you have with us if

- You do not make the minimum payment when due
- You make a payment that is not honored

The default APR takes effect as of the first day of the billing period in which you default. We may lower the APR for new purchases or cash advances if you meet the terms of all card agreements that you have with us for six billing periods.

Mr. Michael Chapman Page 2 Current Date

Right to Opt Out

To opt out of these changes, call or write us by March 31. Include your name, address, and account number in your letter. If you opt out of these changes, you may use your account under the current terms until the end of your current membership year or the expiration date on your card. We will close your account at that time. You must then repay the balance under the current terms.

Please take advantage of your World Bank Card revolving line of credit and all the benefits and services we offer you.

Sincerely,

Note: Based on a real credit card message, this letter definitely employs the direct strategy.

See Chapter 6 Teaching Suggestions for a list of document weaknesses.

6.11 DOCUMENT FOR ANALYSIS—REVISION

To: Marcy Love <marcy.love@sokia.com>
From: Shelton Matthews <shelton.matthews@sokia.com>
Cc:
Subject: Improving Presentation Techniques

Marcy,

As you requested, I attended a seminar about presentation techniques. You suggested that I might learn tips to share with other staff members, especially those who use PowerPoint. The speaker, Gary Dixon, made several important points to help speakers avoid putting listeners to sleep in what he called a "PowerPoint slumber party." Our staff members might consider the following:

- Create the message, not the slide, first. Only after preparing the entire script should you think about how to illustrate it.

- Prepare slides with short lines. Your slides should have only four to six words per line. Short lines encourage people to listen to you and not read the slide.

- Don't put everything on the slide. If you put too much on the slide, your audience will be reading Item C while you are still talking about Item A.

- Think in terms of headlines. What is the main point? What does it mean to the audience?

Please let me know whether you want me to expand on these points after the next staff meeting.

Shelton
[Full contact information]

See Chapter 6 Teaching Suggestions for a list of document weaknesses.

6.12 Document for Analysis—Revision

Current date

Mr. DeJuan Wilson
Fairfield Associates, Inc.
4290 Park Avenue
Fairfield, CT 06435

Dear Mr. Wilson:

At your request I am sending you the attached materials about improving security in your business. To improve your after-hours security, you should first decide what must be protected. You are probably concerned about your electronic equipment and about company data.

Because we feel you will want to protect both equipment and data, we can suggest a number of prudent steps to deter crime. First, install defensive lighting. Our lighting expert can design both outside and inside lighting. Second, post security signs. Amateur thieves are often deterred by signs on windows and doors. Finally, install space alarms. These sensors look down over protected areas. The sensors can activate bells or lights, thus scaring off intruders.

After reading the enclosed materials, please call me at (385) 259-1380 to further discuss protecting your business.

Sincerely,

Enclosure

See alternate version on next page. See Chapter 6 Teaching Suggestions for a list of document weaknesses in the draft.

ALTERNATE REVISION FOR 6.12

Current date

Mr. DeJuan Wilson
Fairfield Associates, Inc.
4290 Park Avenue
Fairfield, CT 06435

Dear Mr. Wilson:

At your request, I am sending you the attached materials about improving security in your business. To improve your after-hours security, you should first decide what must be protected. You are probably concerned about your electronic equipment and about company data.

Because we feel you will want to protect both equipment and data, we suggest the following three steps to deter crime:

1. Install defensive lighting. Our lighting expert can design both outside and inside lighting.

2. Post security signs. Amateur thieves are often deterred by signs on windows and doors.

3. Install space alarms. These sensors look down over protected areas. The sensors can activate bells or lights, thus scaring off intruders.

After reading the enclosed materials, please call me at (385) 259-1380 to discuss further protecting your business.

Sincerely,

Enclosure

Note: Enumerated paragraphs may be indented or typed flush left.

6.13 Document for Analysis—Revision

Current date

Ms. Monique Faria
Grey Wolf BioSolutions
4210 Geddes Road
Ann Arbor, MI 48105

Dear Ms. Faria:

Thank you for your interest in employee leasing through Enterprise Staffing Services. Small businesses like yours can now enjoy powerful personnel tools previously available only to larger firms.

The employee leasing concept allows you to outsource personnel duties so that you can focus on the fundamentals of running your business. You can reduce many administrative burdens such as monthly payroll, quarterly taxes, and personnel records. Expert guidance in the areas of human resources, compliance, and safety is available. Because we have extensive experience, your employer liability can be significantly reduced. You can be assured that our entire staff will assemble a plan that will save you time and money as well as protect you from employee hassles and employer liability.

Whether you offer no benefits or a full benefits package, Enterprise Staffing Services can analyze your needs and help you return to the basics of running your business and improving profits. Please allow me to call you to arrange a time to meet and talk about your specific needs.

Cordially,

See Chapter 6 Teaching Suggestions for a list of draft document weaknesses.

6.14— 6.18 Discussion material and solutions for these activities are found in the Teaching Suggestions for Chapter 6.

7.1 DOCUMENT FOR ANALYSIS—REVISION

To: Greta Targa <greta.targa@gamma.com>
From: Jim Morales <jim.morales@gamma.com>
Subject: Need You to Confirm the Gamma Fall Training Conference Speakers
Cc:
Bcc:

Please send e-mails to the following speakers to confirm their dates and topics for the Gamma Fall Training Conference in Miami:

Date	Speaker	Topic
Tuesday, November 12	Nicole Gold nicole.gold@etc.com	Using E-Mail and IM Effectively
Wednesday, November 13	Anthony Mills tony.mills@sunbelt.net	Leading Groups and Teams

Because we must print the program by September 1, please send me the confirmation information by August 15. Thanks for helping to make this one of the best training sessions ever.

Jim
[Full contact information]

Note: Students may choose a different organization of speaker data such as the following:

> Tuesday, November 12: Nicole Gold (nicole.gold@sunbelt.net) "Using E-Mail and IM Effectively"
>
> Wednesday, November 13: Anthony Mills (tony.mills@sunbelt.net) "Leading Groups and Teams"

See Chapter 7 Teaching Suggestions for a list of draft document weaknesses.

7.2 Document for Analysis—Revision

To: Mitchell Moraga <mitchell.moraga@media.com>
From: Eleanor Hutchinson <ehutchinson@media.com>
Subject: Suggestions for Preventing Workplace Violence
Cc:
Bcc:

Mitchell:

As you requested, I am submitting the following report with suggestions for preventing workplace violence in our organization. These ideas resulted from the November 3 Workplace Issues conference that I attended as our company representative. Kit Adkins, the presenter, provided many excellent ideas, which I will summarize in three categories.

- Prescreen Applicants. Wise companies, said Ms. Atkins, do not offer employment until a candidate's background has been checked. Just the mention of a check often makes a candidate with something to hide withdraw.

- Recognize Red-Flag Behavior. Companies should train managers to recognize signs of possible workplace violence. Some of these include a rise in petty arguments with coworkers; extreme changes in behavior, statements indicating depression over family or financial problems; bullying or harassing behavior; and bringing a firearm to work or exhibiting an extreme fascination with firearms.

- Develop Reporting Procedures. Companies should prepare a good employee handbook that outlines what employees should do when they suspect potential workplace violence. Include a system for anonymous notification.

The recommendation that I think is most feasible is prescreening of job candidates. Please let me know by November 15 whether you want me to do more research on

prescreening techniques and present a full conference report at our December 3 management meeting.

Ellie

[include full contact information]

7.3 Document for Analysis—Revision

This instant messaging exchange is unprofessional, too informal, folksy, and chatty. See the Chapter 7 Teaching Suggestions for further discussion of this exchange.

7.4 Choosing a Holiday Plan

To: All Employees
From: Student's name and e-mail address
Subject: Floating Holiday Options
Cc:
Bcc:

Would you prefer (a) an individual floating holiday or (b) a company-wide uniform floating holiday?

Because we're genuinely interested in developing a holiday plan that pleases as many people as possible, we'd like your response below.

In the past we've allowed 11 holidays plus one floating holiday, agreed on by company-wide ballot. Now, though, we'd like to offer you the possibility of an individual floating holiday. You would be able to choose the date you wish to take, subject to staffing needs within your departments. If several requests are made for the same date, employment seniority would govern.

In your reply e-mail, please return only this part to me, and check the plan of your choice (use an X):

___ I prefer to retain the current policy of a uniform floating holiday.

___ I prefer an individual floating holiday, subject to the provisions described above.

To have your choice counted, return this form to Human Resources by January 25.

Student's name
Student's contact information

 7.5 REACHING CONSENSUS ABOUT BUSINESS ATTIRE

To: Michael Harding <Michael.Harding@schilling-voigt.com>
From: Student's name and e-mail address
Subject: Your Request for Reaction to CEO's Inquiry Regarding Casual Dress
Cc: [Other team members' names and e-mail addresses]
Bcc:

At your direction, our team of interns consulted literature and discussed the casual-dress policy questions posed by CEO Laughton. Here are our reactions to the first five questions in his e-mail request.

Acceptable Wear for Women on Casual-Dress Days. After reading a number of articles and discussing the matter among ourselves, we concluded that acceptable wear for women included the following: slacks, skirts, and ankle-length pants along with coordinating blouses or wool or cotton sweaters and flat leather shoes. To be avoided are leggings, Spandex pants, casual and short shorts, ultra short skirts, camisoles, bared midriffs, halter tops, tank tops, sportswear tee-shirts, jeans, sweats, athletic shoes, and thong-like "flip-flop" sandals.

Acceptable Wear for Men on Casual-Dress Days. For men, business casual means khakis, chinos, or gabardine trousers and a collared shirt, either polo-style or button-down. Ties are optional, with wool or cotton sweaters, trousers, and loafers with dark, coordinated trouser socks. To be avoided are garish print sport shirts, sportswear tee-shirts, sport team jackets, jeans, sweats, athletic "tube" socks, hiking boots, athletic shoes, and sandals.

Restrictions on Body Art and Piercing. We believe that body art and piercing should not be visible. Tattoos covered by clothing are not a problem. In regard to body piercing, we believe that one set of traditional pierced earrings for women is appropriate.

Eyebrow and other piercing to display jewelry of any sort are out of place in a conservative environment such as Schilling & Voigt.

Supervisors Reacting to Inappropriate Clothing. If someone comes to work in offensive, tasteless, revealing, or sloppy clothing, we think that a supervisor has the right to send the employee home to change. We would hope that the dress code is specific enough to prevent this occurrence.

Definition of Casual Attire. Although it is difficult to define "casual attire," we believe that a specific dress code spelling out what is acceptable and what is unacceptable should function as the definition that staff members at Schilling & Voigt understand and follow. It is critical that the dress code define specifics, as we did in our previous remarks.

Advantages and Disadvantages of Dress Code. Proponents of casual dress say that it improves employee communication by removing symbols that dictate differences between people. Casual dress brings comfort, increased camaraderie, and improved productivity. Casual clothes cost less than more formal clothes and therefore represent a saving for employees. As a result, a casual dress policy is a cheap "perk" for companies to offer.

Critics say, however, that casual attire forces employees to have two wardrobes, creates confusion about what is appropriate to wear, contributes to sloppy work, and makes people feel uncomfortable or less presentable in professional situations. Casual dress also damages the image of professionals in the eyes of clients.

Please let us know if you need any more information about business attire.

Best regards,

Student's name
Student's full contact information

7.6 Learning to Write Superefficient Tweets

Examples:

AllComm's customer service is super responsive. They often don't know the answer, but hold times are short. Call center is based in the U.S. (140 characters with spaces)

I'm having Internet problems, and MineNet isn't picking up the phone. Customer service is awful. Anybody having issues with the Internet? (137 characters with spaces)

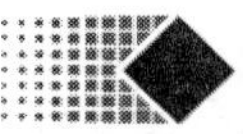

7.7 Practicing Your Professional IM Skills

Examples:

AllComm's customer service is super responsive. They often don't know the answer, but hold times are short. Call center is based in the U.S. (140 characters with spaces)

I'm having Internet problems, and MineNet isn't picking up the phone. Customer service is awful. Anybody having issues with the Internet? (137 characters with spaces)

7.8 Analyzing a Podcast

Example of a Tweet or Brief Text Message:

Excerpted from Grammar Girl, who is attempting a "quick-and-dirty" definition of the object of a sentence:

I love you. You are the object of my affection and my sentence. It's like a Valentine's Day card and grammar mnemonic all rolled into one. (138 characters with spaces)
[See http://grammar.quickanddirtytips.com/who-versus-whom.aspx]

7.9 through 7.15

Discussion material for these activities is offered in the Chapter Teaching Suggestions.

CHAPTER 8—APPLYING YOUR SKILLS AT BEN & JERRY'S

Current date

Ms. Cora Nicol
246 Falls Overlook Drive
Niagara Falls, NY 14109

Dear Ms. Nicol:

Subject: Your Letter About Ben & Jerry's Products

You're absolutely right in expecting an ample number of cookie and chocolate chunks in your Ben & Jerry's ice cream. Like you, we are disappointed when a product doesn't meet your expectations—or ours.

Although we work hard and long to get the right amount of chunks, nuts, and cookies in each pint, our chunking equipment is not always as consistent as we would like it to be. However, you can be sure that I will report your remarks to our production personnel so that they can redouble their efforts to maintain the proper ratio of chunks to ice cream.

You inquire about our dairy operations in Nevada. In an effort to meet the heavy demand for our products from West Coast customers while respecting the environment, we established dairies in Nevada. Doing so enables us to avoid the high energy costs involved in trucking milk from Vermont to the West Coast.

We appreciate learning that you share our concern with milk from cloned cows. We also appreciate your writing so that we can make amends to you. Because your satisfaction is very important to us, we are enclosing a check for $4.49, the estimated cost of a pint of ice cream. We hope that with your next pint we can regain you as a satisfied customer.

Sincerely,

8.1 Direct Openings

a. Liberty Bank would deeply appreciate your answers to a few questions to help us learn about developing an internship program.

b. Please answer the following questions about your voice recognition software program.

c. Yes, we do offer our European-style patio umbrella in the following colors: cream and forest green.

d. Nearly all of the riders in the Honda Superbike Classic in Alabama selected Dunlop Blue Groove hard compound front and rear tires.

e. Yes, I would be happy to talk about online résumés at your business management club May 2.

8.2 Writing Instructions

a. To order from our Web site, follow these steps:

1. Find the items you want in the catalog.
2. Add the items to your shopping cart.
3. Proceed to checkout.
4. Create a new account.
5. Enter a shipping address and shipping method.
6. Provide payment information.
7. Review and submit your order.

b. To make a YouTube video, you should do the following:

1. **Obtain a video recording device such as a cell phone, webcam, or camcorder.**

2. **Decide whether you want to make a video blog, comedy skit, how-to video, or travel video.**

3. **Keep the video to 10 minutes or less for traditional YouTube membership accounts.**

4. **Record in the daytime for good light quality.**

c. To make double-sided copies, do the following:

1. **Place Side 1 of the original face down on the document glass.**
2. **Close the document cover.**
3. **Select the required quantity.**
4. **Press Start.**
5. **Remove Original 1, and insert Original 2 face down on the document glass.**
6. **Close the document cover.**
7. **Remove the copy of Original 1 from the output tray and insert it face down in the paper bypass tray.**
8. **Select the alternate paper tray and press Start.**

8.3 Document for Analysis—Revision

To: Amsoft Manager List
From: Stella Soto <stella.soto@amsoft.com>
Subject: Answering Questions to Address E-Mail Problem
Cc:
Bcc:

Managers,

Please help us address the problem of excessive e-mail by answering the questions below. Your ideas will assist us develop a plan that should benefit your staff, yourself, and our organization.

Everyone expected e-mail to be a huge productivity tool. However, its excessive use cuts into work time. One study found that the average office worker spends three hours a day on e-mail. In our organization we may be spending even more than this. It's difficult to get any work done because of countless e-mails every day. Your responses to the following questions will help us focus on the problem.

1. About how many e-mail messages do you receive and answer personally each day?
2. About how many hours are your staff members spending on e-mail each day?
3. How could we reduce the volume of e-mail within our own organization?
4. Do you think that e-mail is being used excessively by our employees?
5. What do you think of a weekly e-mail-free day, such as Friday?

I look forward to your advice in controlling e-mail and improving productivity. Your written responses to these questions by May 5 will help me prepare for our supervisory committee meeting May 10, when we will discuss this problem. Many thanks!

Stella Soto
Vice President, Operations

Note: See Chapter 8 Teaching Suggestions for document weaknesses.

8.4 Document for Analysis—Revision

MEMORANDUM

Date: March 4, 2010
To: Trevor Kurtz, CEO
From: Emily Lopez-Rush
Subject: Report on Instant Messaging Symposium

Because many of our employees are using instant messaging, you asked me to attend the March 2 Instant Messaging Symposium sponsored by Pixel Link. It was a most informative meeting, and I learned some information that should help us decide how to handle instant messaging in our organization.

The symposium leader, Jason Howard, discussed the benefits, risks, providers, and costs involved in using instant messaging in the workplace. Let me summarize his major points:

- **Instant messaging is here to stay. Over 80 million workers now use it, and the number is increasing steadily.**
- **Its primary advantages are speed, documentation, and cost savings.**
- **Its principal disadvantages are spam, security, control, and possible loss of productivity.**
- **The major IM providers for consumers are AOL Messenger, MSN Messenger, and Yahoo Messenger.**
- **Misuse of IM will result in productivity deterioration, but appropriate use will have positive results.**
- **For maximum security, many organizations are investing in enterprise-level IM systems and adopting employee guidelines.**
- **Costs range from $30 to $100 per user license, depending on functionality.**

I would be happy to elaborate on these points. Please let me know by March 13 whether you want me to make a presentation to the next management council meeting on March 25.

8.5 Document for Analysis—Revision

Current date

Ms. Melanie Cholston, Manager
Nationwide Car Rentals
1325 Commerce Street
Dallas, TX 75202

Dear Ms. Cholston:

Please reimburse my company $49.43. This amount was charged for a tank of premium gasoline when I returned a rental car to your branch in Houston June 26.

On June 23 I rented the car at the Dallas-Ft. Worth International Airport. Because its gas tank was nearly empty, I filled it. I assumed your policy required car rental customers to fill the tanks when they received their cars. Therefore, when I returned the car in Houston, I purposely left the tank nearly empty. However, your attendant filled it up and charged me for it. Surely your company does not provide cars with empty tanks and then expect customers to return them with full tanks.

Enclosed are a copy of the signed rental agreement and a receipt showing my payment of $426.50 (which includes $49.43 for gas). You may either credit my company card, or you may send a check for $49.43 made payable to my company. If you issue a VISA credit, please send a copy to me at Criterion Enterprises, 402 North Griffin Street, Dallas, TX 74105.

We have not regularly used Western Car Rentals in the past, but your good service and competitive rates encourage me to give you our repeat business.

Sincerely,

Enclosure

Note: Students should adjust the spacing between the date and inside address to balance a letter on the page. Because of spacing constraints, however, these acetates will not show that adjustment. See Chapter 8 Teaching Suggestions for document weaknesses.

8.6 Document for Analysis—Revision

To: Sam Oliver <sam.oliver@stcc.edu>
From: Alexandra Tutson <alex.tutson @stcc.edu>
Subject: New Online Instructions for Reporting Equipment Repairs
Cc:
Bcc:

A new procedure for submitting equipment repairs will speed the process by enabling us to better track your request. We are transitioning from using the printed "Equipment Repair Form" to a more efficient online database system. Please begin using the following new procedure immediately:

1. Log on to http://www.BigWebDesk.net.
2. Select the kind of repair you need: AudioVisual, Mac, PC, or Printer.
3. Select "Create New Ticket" to begin the process of data entry for your specific problem.
4. Fill in the information required.
5. Print the ticket and attach it securely to the equipment.

The warehouse truck driver will pick up and deliver the equipment as before. If you have questions, call Sylvia at Extension 255 or write her at *sylvia.freeman@stcc.edu*. We look forward to providing you with efficient pickup and repair service.

Alexandra Tutson, Manager
Operations and Facilities
alex.tutson@stcc.edu
(813) 355-3200, Ext. 230

8.7 Seeking a New Look for the Company Web Site

To: Cole Prewarski <cprewarski@global.net>
From: Your Name <your e-mail address>
Subject: Need Information About Redesigning Web Site
Cc:
Bcc:

Please answer a few questions about possibly redesigning our company Web site to update its appearance and function.

- Do you have any idea how much a complete redesign might cost? How about a partial redesign?
- Have any usability tests been done on the current site?
- Is it possible to add animation, sound, or video? Would you recommend doing so?
- What is the best time to revamp our Web site, should we decide to do so?
- Can you suggest any ways to use our site to increase sales and improve customer service?
- Have users suggested any changes that would improve the functioning of our site?

The Committee on Web Site Redesign would be pleased to have you answer these questions at its meeting April 6 at 2 p.m. in the conference room. Please let me know by April 1 whether you can join us.

Your Name
Your Contact Information

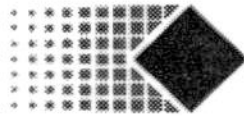

8.8 HEADING TO LAS VEGAS

Current date

Ms. Isabella Cervantes
Manager, Convention Services
Caesars Palace
257 Palace Drive
Las Vegas, NV 87551

Dear Ms. Cervantes:

Can Caesars Palace provide rooms for 85 guests and their families for either April 20-24 or July 10-14?

My company will be hosting a four-day combination sales conference/vacation/retreat for 85 of our engineers, product managers, and marketing staff. Please answer the following questions to help us choose a suitable resort:

- **What are the room rates and room sizes? Is there any discount for off-peak season or for corporate customers?**
- **Do you have three conference rooms available that would accommodate 25 people? We would need these rooms for one and a half days. What size are these rooms?**
- **Do the conference rooms have audio-visual and computer facilities?**
- **What entertainment possibilities are available for the families of our staff?**

Ms. Isabella Cervantes
Page 2
Current date

- **What entertainers will be featured at Caesars Palace at the times of our proposed visit?**

- **Do you have facilities for us to host a banquet for 125 people one evening?**

Your answers to these questions before November 10 will help me make a complete presentation to our CEO, who is eager to select a spectacular resort for this conference.

Sincerely,

8.9 Restaurants Join Obesity Fight

Note: Instructors: To make this activity more challenging, describe the program but require your students to develop the list of criteria to qualify for a Healthy Dining rating. Omit paragraph 4 of the instructions.

Current date

Mr. Adrian Hammersmith
Adrian's Steak House
974 South Cobb Drive
Marietta, GA 30060

Dear Mr. Hammersmith:

Thanks for inquiring about the new Healthy Dining rating system. Your restaurant can attract more customers and help them make healthful food choices by displaying the Healthy Dining rating and by changing your menu to include nutritious options.

Partners for a Healthier Community, in conjunction with the City Health and Human Services Department, has developed a number of criteria that distinguish healthful restaurants. To earn a Healthy Dining rating, your restaurant should meet the following criteria:

- **Offer at least two choices of fruits or vegetables other than potatoes.**
- **Allow substitution of salad or other vegetables for fried potato dishes such as french fries.**
- **Clearly designate low-fat and low-calorie menu items when available.**
- **Offer some dishes in smaller portion sizes, such as half-portion sizes.**
- **Offer 1 percent or skim milk when milk is served as a beverage.**

Mr. Adrian Hammersmith Page 2 Current date

Eating is one of life's best pleasures. Help your restaurant customers increase their enjoyment and contribute to their good health by joining the Healthy Dining program. You can learn more about it and submit an application at www.healthydining.com.

Sincerely,

PARTNERS FOR A HEALTHIER COMMUNITY

Your name
Your title

8.10 RESPONSE: LUXURY HOTELS EMBRACE SIGNATURE SCENTS

Date: Current
To: Michelle Long, CEO
From: Your Name
Subject: Selected Hotels and Their Custom Fragrances

As you requested, I have conducted online research on fragrances used by hotels. Apparently hotel chains (particularly upscale properties) are attempting to forge a connection between pleasant surroundings and signature scents to encourage genuine customer loyalty and repeat business.

Here is a summary of selected hotels and their scents:

- Park Hyatt in Washington, DC, which you visited, fills the lobby with a warm, woodsy scent.
- Omni Hotels uses a lemongrass and green tea scent in the lobby, coconut fragrance near the pool, and is considering citrus (to enhance energy) in its meeting rooms.
- Westin Hotels & Resorts offers a white tea aroma.
- Hotel Costes in Paris presents a complex scent with notes of lavender, bay tree, coriander, white pepper, rose, incense, woods, and musk.
- Naumi Hotel in Singapore offers a refreshing ginger and lime citrus scent with an Asian undertone that complements the hotel's youthful image.
- M Hotel in Singapore favors its guests with a blend of ginger and lily, reflecting the hotel's strong Asian values.

As you can see, many luxury hotels are adopting custom fragrances to encourage guests to associate the hotel's brand with a specific sensory appeal. However, you should also know that one environmental Web site advocates fragrance-free hotels

Memo to Michelle Long Page 2 Current date

that strive for fresh, not perfumed, air. It warns that chemical-based fragrances reduce air quality and increase health problems.

Regardless, the trend among hoteliers is definitely toward enhancing guests' sense of smell with custom fragrances. If you would like to discuss my findings or if you want more research, call me at 238-0784.

8.11 ARRANGING INTERVIEWS FOR ENVIRONMENTAL ARCHITECT/DESIGNER

Date: **Current**
To: **James F. Becker, CEO**
From: **Your Name**
Subject: **Rescheduling Interviews for Environmental Architect/Designer**

As you requested, I have rescheduled three candidates for the position of environmental architect/designer. Here is a summary of the schedule with brief information about their backgrounds:

Day, Time	Candidate	Background
March 28, 10 a.m.	Raul Rameriz	Owner, Green Building Consulting. 10 years' experience with energy efficiency, sustainable materials, domes, and earth-friendly design
March 28, 2 p.m.	Amanda Froescher	M.A., Boise State University. 5 years' experience with sustainable building materials as architect planner for Boise Builders
March 29, 11 a.m.	Scott Hogarth	B.A., University of Southern California. 2 years' experience with SolarPlus, Inc., specializing in passive solar energy

Do you want me to send this summary to Mr. Grafsky so that he can plan to attend? Please let me know by March 15 so that he can plan his schedule.

8.12 New Process for Purchase Requests

Date: Current
To: All Staff Members
From: Your Name, Purchasing Department
Subject: New Purchase Request Procedure to Speed Your Orders

You can fill your purchase requests more rapidly and accurately with a new procedure that will become effective immediately. Follow these steps to submit a purchase request:

1. Download a purchase request form from <http://www.lynch.com>.
2. Complete the form either digitally or manually.
3. Include date, quantities, catalog numbers, complete descriptions, complete vendor mailing information, delivery requirements, and shipping methods (usually f.o.b.).
4. Secure approval from the budget manager.
5. Send the completed original to the Purchasing Department.
6. Keep a copy.

Following this procedure will help us deliver the best possible service to you. Should you have any questions, write [your name] at (your.name@lynch.com).

8.13 CELL PHONE USE AND TEXTING WHILE DRIVING

Date: Current
To: All Capri Sales Representatives
From: Student's Name, Operations Manager
Subject: Using Your Wireless Devices Safely While Driving

Because we know how essential your wireless devices have become to you and because we also know how dangerous they can be, your management council has taken two steps to help you use your wireless phones more safely.

First, we have ordered hands-free devices for all company cell phones. These should arrive within a month and will be installed immediately.

Second, we have done some research and prepared the following list of safety rules that we want every sales rep to follow:

- Never send text messages while driving!
- Whenever possible, pull over to make or receive calls. Dial calls only when you are stopped.
- Never use your cell phone in hazardous driving conditions, such as during heavy traffic, rain, sleet, snow, or icy conditions.
- Allow your voice mail to pick up any calls that come in during inconvenient times.
- Warn callers that you are driving as you speak and that your call may be interrupted.
- Use the hands-free device, which will be installed within a month, so that you can keep both hands on the wheel.
- Do not take notes or look up phone numbers while driving.

All Capri Sales Reps
Page 2
Current date

- **Become familiar with your phone and its features. Memorize the keypad.**
- **Avoid any stressful or emotional conversations while you are driving.**

Following these rules for wireless devices will make your driving much safer. Remember, your life is far more important than completing any call.

8.14 Describing a Workplace Procedure

Messages will vary.

8.15 How to Be Safe at Work

Date: Current
To: Branch Office Managers
From: Kathryn Gossoni, Vice President
Subject: Improving Office Security for Employees

Because we had a scare in one of our branches, I would like to review security measures with you.

A senior associate was working late one evening recently when she heard the front door open and someone enter. The intruder left as soon as he realized an employee was working. Although this encounter ended well, it made me realize that we must do a better job of improving security in our branch offices. Following are steps that each branch should take:

- Pay attention to before-and-after-hours security. If office workers remain beyond regular hours, discuss with them security practices. Anyone who arrives early should ensure that the office doors stay locked until a full complement of staff members arrive. Employees working overtime should make sure the door is locked after most workers have left. Don't open office doors after hours to people you don't know, especially if you are in the office alone.

- Ensure that proper lighting covers all points of entry and parking areas. Sufficient lighting is an inexpensive and easy way to discourage burglars and intruders. If you are currently turning off all lights at night to conserve energy, consider using lights connected to motion detectors. Lighting is particularly important for doors and windows that are out of sight to neighbors or passersby.

[8.15 Continued]

- **Don't display office valuables. Passersby should not be able to look in and see equipment or other valuables. As much as possible, place expensive equipment where it is not visible. Lock up laptop computers and other small portable equipment at night.**

- **Advertise your security system. Most of our branches are guarded by Broadview Security. Make sure their decals are prominently placed on windows and doors so that viewers can see that the premises are electronically protected. Some offices are now displaying "cash-free" decals, which may cause thieves to think twice before breaking and entering.**

Can you suggest other ways to improve office security? Please come to our June 8 quarterly meeting ready to discuss these and other ideas.

8.16 Writing Clear Instructions

Activity A-5

HOW TO OPERATE THE TURBOFAX 3200

The new TurboFax 3200 is now available for your use in the front office. Please use it carefully following the instructions below. Remember that this machine is intended for office work only.

<u>Inserting Documents</u>

- **Place your document face down.**
- **Adjust the guides to your document's width.**
- **Insert the document's leading edge into the feed slot.**
- **If sending two or more sheets, form a slope by lifting the sheets so that the bottom sheet enters first.**

<u>Dialing Phone</u>

- **Pick up telephone handset. When you hear a continuous dial tone, dial the receiving fax number.**
- **Press START key when you hear the fax signal of the answering phone.**
- **Hang up when the start lamp stops glowing.**

[8.16 Continued]

Activity A-6

Instructions for Automobile Club

WHAT TO DO IF YOUR VEHICLE BREAKS DOWN

The following instructions are intended to keep motorists and their vehicles safe in case of vehicle breakdowns.

1. **Move your vehicle as far off the roadway as possible.**
2. **Turn on your four-way flashers.**
3. **Exit from the passenger side.**
4. **Raise the hood.**
5. **Attach a light-colored cloth to the antenna or door handle to indicate distress.**
6. **Stay with your vehicle, if possible, until a uniformed law enforcement officer arrives.**
7. **Do not roll down your window or get out of your vehicle for anyone other than a uniformed law enforcement officer.**
8. **Crack a window if anyone approaches. Request that law enforcement be sent.**
9. **Leave a note if you must walk or accept a ride. Include your name, date, time of leaving, and the direction in which you headed. Include the name and license plate number of anyone who gives you a ride.**

WARNING: Beware of anyone in civilian clothes driving an unmarked car, even if that person shows what appears to be a law enforcement badge.

8.17 PROTESTING UNEXPECTED CHARGES

Current date

Ms. Arletta Sandusky
Customer Services
Premier Promos
2445 Bermiss Road
Valdosta, GA 31602

Dear Ms. Sandusky:

Please credit the account of Rochester Preferred Travel for $258.20. This represents the cost of sample items that were ordered January 11 and returned January 21.

The promotional items that I ordered were not appropriate as gifts for our customers. Because your firm promises that free samples of promotional merchandise may be returned under your "No Surprise" policy, I returned the items expecting a full credit on our account. I called in February and spoke to Virginia, who assured me that a credit would appear on our next statement. When no credit appeared on our March statement, I called again and received a similar promise.

The items were returned promptly. Enclosed is a postal receipt showing the date they were sent. In keeping with your policy of fairness to customers, I am asking that you credit our account immediately. We are hoping that your prompt handling of this matter will enable us to recommend your firm to others in the travel industry.

Sincerely,

Enclosure

8.18 SHORT DOOR FOR TALL PLAYER

Current date

Mr. Michael Medina
Operations Manager
American Custom Wood
140 NE 136 Avenue
Vancouver, WA 98654

Dear Mr. Medina:

Please send a check for $940.50 to cover the cost of rebuilding a door opening. This construction was necessary to adjust the size of the opening to the smaller door we received from American Custom Wood.

In a telephone request on May 17, I ordered an oversized 12-foot mahogany entry door ("Provence"). I asked that the door measure 12 feet 2 inches. However, when it arrived, it measured 11 feet 10 inches. After consulting my carpenter, we decided to rebuild the openings since that was faster than waiting for a new door to be made and shipped. My client wanted the door installed immediately in his living room. Rebuilding the openings also made sense in that it saved the cost of returning the door and making a new custom door. Enclosed are copies of my carpenter's bill for his work and the invoice for the door.

The quality of your products generally complements the quality of service that I give my discerning customers. I would like to continue to use American Custom Wood doors, windows, and hardware for future custom projects. You may credit my account or send a check for $940.50 to my company.

Sincerely,

Enclosures

8.19 The Real Thing

Current date

Ms. Alicia Stevenson
Customer Service Department
Avery Dennison Office Products
Diamond Bar, CA 91765

Dear Ms. Stevenson:

Please send me a new box of laser labels or refund three quarters of the purchase price for a box that will not work in my printer.

On March 3 I purchased a box with 100 sheets of Avery Laser Labels (No. 5166). The cost was $36.99 plus tax. I used 25 sheets immediately, and they worked well in my laser printer. Then I put the box away and didn't need it again until June 14. At that time the labels would not feed through my printer. In fact, some of the labels lifted off their sheets and jammed my printer. Although I was able to get the printer working again, I threw out the remaining labels because I could not risk ruining my printer.

Because I am forced to buy a box with 100 sheets when I need many fewer, I wonder if you have considered packaging these labels in smaller units. Apparently, they do not store well and must be used fairly soon after purchase.

I would appreciate your check for $30 (which is about three quarters of the purchase price) or a replacement of the 75 sheets of Avery address labels that I had to discard. Enclosed is the bar code from the box I purchased.

Sincerely,

Enclosure

8.20 Barking Mad With Happypets.com

To: CustomerServices@Happypets.com
From: Your Name <your e-mail address>
Subject: Credit for Incorrect Order
Cc:

Customer Services:

Please issue me a credit for $107.93. This represents the total for my order number 0095644-1, which did not include any of the items I requested.

I was recently drawn to your site's offer of free shipping on orders over $100 and placed an order for two bottles each of Top Performance UltraCoat Hot Oil Treatment and UltraCoat A-1 Hot Oil Shampoo as well as one Very Berry Bow Canister. The total came to $107.93, which I paid with a credit card. My shipment arrived promptly, but although the packing slip listed the items I had ordered, the carton contained six bottles each of Pet Effects Watermelon and Pear Shampoo and Top Performance Soothing Suds Shampoo.

I realize that the items I ordered were not eligible for return, but I did not receive the products I requested and should not be liable for a mistake made by your shipping department. Because I have had to purchase the products locally to use during my busy holiday season, I do not want to exchange the shipment.

Please credit my account for the full amount of the order. If you want me to return the carton with the items I did not order, please send a shipping label with appropriate postage. I hope that your quick response to my request encourages me to consider ordering from your site again.

Sincerely,

Your Name
[Your contact information]

8.21 BUT IT DOESN'T WORK!

Current Date

Mr. Dennis Garcia
Manager, Digital Depot
2300 Austin Street
Houston, TX 77074

Dear Mr. Garcia:

After purchasing two faulty Panasonic HD TVs (Model TC-P42X1) from your store, I believe you should sell me a similar sized set for a price close to that of the Panasonic.

I recently decided to purchase an HDTV and chose the Panasonic for its features and benefits. I found a great deal at Digital Depot and purchased the set for $599.95 plus tax. I sold my old set and installed the new one, spending considerable time and energy to get it up and running. That evening, the set worked fine, but the next day it didn't turn on. Figuring that I had a faulty set, I packed it up and returned it to your store, which is a 45-minute drive from my home. I brought home another Panasonic and set it up. That evening it worked, but the same problem occurred the following day.

When I returned the second set, I was told I could get another Panasonic. But after the two faulty TVs, hours of my time assembling and repacking the Panasonics, and hours spent driving up and back to your store, I did not want to take another chance. Digital Depot sells a Samsung (model PN42B450B1D) that is the same size as the Panasonic, but it costs more.

Because I am a loyal customer who wants to continue to enjoy the great prices and service Digital Depot offers, please provide me with the necessary approval to purchase the Samsung at the same or nearly the same price I paid for the Panasonic.

Sincerely,

8.22 Responding to Short Doors for Tall Player

Current date

Ms. Erica Adams
Contempo Interiors
2304 River Ridge Road
Indianapolis, IN 46031

Dear Ms. Adams:

Subject: Our Check for $940.50 Requested in Your June 20 Letter

The enclosed check for $940.50 tells you that American Custom Wood takes pride not only in its quality doors but also in its commitment to customer service.

We examined your May 17 order and saw the discrepancy in measurements. Apparently, you requested our Provence mahogany door measuring 12 feet 2 inches. However, our telephone order taker recorded the measurement at 11 feet 10 inches. At the time your order was placed, we had just hired two new telephone clerks. Although I'm not certain that the discrepancy occurred at this point, you can be sure that I will personally investigate our training program for telephone clerks. We want to ensure that measurements for custom orders are verified so that your experience is not repeated. I will also institute a new policy of calling customers to confirm custom measurements.

Over the years we have worked hard to build a reputation as manufacturer of the finest wood doors and frames on the market. Our products combine prime woods, meticulous craftsmanship, award-winning design, and ingenious engineering. Quality products, though, are not enough. We realize that we must also provide service that satisfies our customers.

Ms. Erica Adams Page 2 Current date

Along with your check, we are enclosing a brochure describing our new line of greenhouse windows to brighten the rooms of your discerning customers.

We sincerely hope that we have earned your confidence and that we may look forward to providing you with top-quality custom doors in your future design projects.

Cordially,

Enclosures

8.23 We Can Restretch But Not Replace

To: Charles Huntzinger
<cmhuntzinger@huntzconstruction.com>
From: Your Name
Subject: Your Message Regarding Your ArtWorkOnline Painting
Cc:

Dear Mr. Huntzinger:

We agree that your newly purchased painting for your executive offices should have arrived without sags in the canvas, and we urge you to engage a local framing shop to restretch it.

When any ArtWorkOnline painting is shipped, we encase it in three layers of protection: two layers of convoluted foam and one layer of Perf-Pack foam. These multiple layers work together to provide superior shock absorption and guard your art from bumps and scrapes during shipping. However, the shipper may have laid the package down instead of standing it, thus allowing the canvas of this large painting to sag somewhat. You can be sure that we will review our transport instructions with our shippers so that future deliveries follow our strict guidelines, thus preventing your experience.

ArtWorkOnline takes pride in offering works of art of the highest quality and value to collectors and decorators. Your satisfaction is important to us, and that's why we encourage you to have your new painting restretched at a local framing shop so that you will be completely satisfied with the way your work of art hangs in your executive offices. Please have the bill sent to us at 438 West 84th Street, New York, NY 10024.

To see our latest collection of original fine art at extraordinary prices, please visit www.aartworkonline.com. We appreciate your patronage, and our dedicated staff looks forward to continuing to serve you.

Sincerely,

8.24 Pigeon Problems

Current date

Mrs. Tia Walsh
24 Canyon Lake Shore Drive
Spring Branch, TX 52319

Dear Mrs. Walsh:

You have every right to be upset over the loss of pigeons at the Scottsdale Hilton. We were equally disturbed and immediately halted the use of the chemical Avitrol when we discovered its lethal effects.

Pigeon droppings have been a considerable nuisance to our guests, and we hoped to solve the problem by discouraging the birds. When we approached an exterminator about our pigeon problem, he recommended Avitrol. He promised that this drug would merely disorient the birds and cause them to roost elsewhere. However, we discovered that Avitrol could kill birds and wildlife.

We are now looking into alternative methods to solve our pigeon problem. One method is installing electrical wires that provide a mild shock, thus preventing the pigeons from roosting. Apparently this solution has been successful at the Maricopa County Jail in downtown Phoenix. Another possible solution is the use of netting that forms a transparent barrier preventing birds from entering certain areas.

Rest assured, Mrs. Walsh, that we at the Scottsdale Hilton are committed to providing our guests with luxury facilities in a scenic, natural setting. Moreover, we promise to do that without harming the bird population. We appreciate your patronage and look forward to your next visit.

Sincerely,
Enclosure

8.25 Backing Up "No Surprise" Offer

Current date

Ms. Leticia Vascellaro
Rochester Preferred Travel
245 East Avenue
Rochester, NY 14604

Dear Ms. Vascellaro:

Your account will be credited immediately for $258.20 representing the value of the items you returned in January. We apologize for the delay in crediting your account. More than anything we hate to disappoint our customers. That's why we instituted our "No Surprise" policy some time ago, and that's why you can count on us to honor it.

At the time your returned items were received, our Accounting Department was changing the way it handled returns. For some reason your return was not immediately credited to your account. But I have personally called Accounting and authorized the credit. I was assured that it will appear on your next statement.

To compensate you for your inconvenience and to encourage you to take another look at our promotional items, we are enclosing a sample imprinted travel mug in a gift box and a Coleman 8-quart jug cooler. These items, which you may keep, would make exciting gifts for your clients. For your patience and patronage, we are truly grateful and we look forward to serving you again soon. Remember that Premier Promos is the most reliable source for the lowest-priced imprinted promotional products in the field.

Sincerely,

Enclosure

8.26 THANKS FOR A FAVOR: GOT THE JOB!

6745 West Axel Drive
Kansas City, KS 41126
Current date

Dr. Thomas Hirsch
School of Business
Mt. Carmel College
P.O. Box 410
Carmel, IN 46952

Dear Dr. Hirsch:

Thank you for your teaching and encouragement during my four years of school at Mt. Carmel. Your courses in financial management, advanced investment finance, and international finance helped to prepare me for my new job as a junior financial analyst.

Your supportive recommendation letter was instrumental in helping me obtain a position with Fidelity Investment Services. The company was also impressed with the investment portfolio I compiled in your advanced investment finance course. The portfolio and other assignments helped me to respond knowledgeably when interviewers questioned me about real-world financial situations.

Thank you for writing highly of my work as a student. You were an excellent teacher, and I learned a great deal from your courses.

Sincerely,

8.27 THANKS FOR THE HOSPITALITY: HOLIDAY ENTERTAINING

8332 S. Mountain Trail
Denver, CO 80439
Current date

Mr. and Mrs. Dennis Tran
122 W. Evergreen
Denver, CO 80437

Dear Dennis and Charlene:

Thanks so much for sharing your home and hospitality with all of us last Friday evening.

Your home was decorated beautifully for the holidays, and the roasted turkey was elegantly prepared and served. Everyone remarked at what a pleasure it was to enjoy such a delightful evening sharing good food and conversation with friends. Perhaps we did not resolve the issue of exorbitant salaries for athletes, but we certainly thrashed it out.

We appreciate the opportunity you provided for us to spend time with you and with our co-workers.

Sincerely,

8.28 PERSONALIZING GROUP GREETING CARDS

DATE: Current

TO: Instructor

FROM: Your name

SUBJECT: BON MOTS FOR SPECIAL OCCASIONS

As you requested, I am submitting a list of "bon mots" that are appropriate for use in celebrating office birthdays and retirements. These were located at Web sites such as www.birthdaycelebrations.net and www.geocities.com. Here are selected short quotes for office celebrations:

Birthdays

- "You wear your birthdays well."
- "Age isn't important unless you're a cheese."
- "Aging is bad, but consider the alternative."
- "May you have the gift of a beautiful day."
- "Never regret growing old. Many are denied the privilege."
- "The best things in life are not things—they're people like you."
- "The secret of staying young is to live honestly, eat slowly, and lie about your age."—Lucille Ball
- "Old age is like everything else. To make a success of it, you've got to start young." – Fred Astaire

Retirement

- "Retired but not tired!"
- "Twice as much time; half as much money."
- "Today is your day!"
- "Working people have a lot of bad habits, but the worst of these is work." – Clarence Darrow
- "You're good enough, you're smart enough, and doggone it, people really like you!" – Stewart Smalley, Saturday Night Live

8.29 Responding to Good Wishes: Saying Thank You

Current date

Dear Brad:

I appreciated very much receiving your good wishes at the time of my graduation. It made me feel good to know that you cared enough to write.

Cordially,

8.30 Extending Sympathy: To a Spouse

524 Ivyside Drive
Altoona, PA 16601
Current date

Dear Shirley,

Your many friends and I here at QuadCom, Inc., were deeply saddened to learn of the death of your husband Bob.

I remember when we first met Bob at a company party many years ago. He was extremely entertaining, especially when he affectionately referred to you as "The Maiden of Mirth." You and Bob were a remarkable couple.

Although it's difficult for others to understand what a deep loss you must feel, I hope that your strong faith and your beautiful memories can outlast the pain of your grief. Please know that we share your profound loss and are available to help if you will but call on us.

Fondly,

8.31 NEGOTIATING A COOL DEAL WITH A CHINESE SUPPLIER

To: Michael Zhu <michael.zhu@AmRep.com>
From: Terrance Shaw <tshaw@pioneercable.com>
Subject: Establishing a Good Business Relationship Between Pioneer Cable and AmRep China
Cc:

Thank you for joining in the videoconference held September 14 between representatives of Pioneer Cable and AmRep China. We at Pioneer Cable are grateful for the opportunity to talk with you and look forward to establishing a mutually beneficial relationship.

To make sure that we understand your services as discussed in our videoconference, let me review the points we agreed on. We understand that AmRep China will do the following:

- Seek a suitable cable assembly supplier for our company
- Negotiate in Chinese with suppliers to achieve the best price/quality ratio possible
- Ensure that any supplier adheres to ISO 9001:2000 standards and procedures
- Help manage supplier production and delivery schedules
- Provide continuous data feedback on quality control and technical conformance to the specifications that Pioneer submits

Please let me know in an e-mail response before September 20 that I have understood our discussion correctly. If any of the above statements are inaccurate, please tell me how I might correct them.

We are eager to move forward in our search for a Chinese supplier, and we sincerely hope that you will be able to help us.

Terrance Shaw
CEO, Pioneer Cable
E-Mail: tshaw@pioneercable.com
Phone: (814) 739-2901
FAX: (814) 739-3445

CHAPTER 9 APPLYING YOUR SKILLS AT SOUTHWEST AIRLINES

Current Date

Ms. Elizabeth Dunbar, Director
Animal Rescue League of Iowa
5452 Northeast 22nd Street
Des Moines, IA 50313

Dear Ms. Dunbar:

The Animal Rescue League of Iowa is to be commended on its excellent efforts to save animals in need. We understand and applaud your ambitious drive to build a new state-of-the-art shelter for the homeless animals of Des Moines.

We at Southwest Airlines are also involved in a number of admirable charitable efforts including the Hispanic Association of Colleges and Universities, the Ronald McDonald House, Junior Achievement, Read Across America, and Parkland Burn Camp. When we receive requests to support fund-raising events, we have two guidelines: (1) The request must arrive 45 days in advance of the charitable event, and (2) the request must not exceed two roundtrip passes for transportation between any two cities Southwest Airlines serves within the continental United States. Although your request does not meet these two guidelines, we would be happy to support a request for two roundtrip passes at a time when you can give us advance notice of 45 days.

We extend to you our very best wishes for a successful fundraising drive to build your new animal shelter. If we can offer you two roundtrip tickets for a future raffle, please write to us again.

Sincerely,

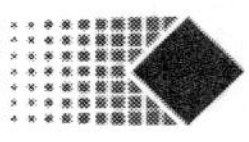

9.1 Organizational Strategies

a. Direct

b. Indirect

c. Indirect

d. Indirect

e. Indirect

f. Direct

g. Indirect

h. Indirect

i. Direct

j. Indirect

9.2 Employing Passive-Voice Verbs

a. Free shipping cannot be offered after January 1.

b. Credit cards in our retail stores will no longer be accepted for purchases under $5.

c. Because more stringent security is required, company tours must be postponed indefinitely.

d. Patients cannot be examined until after their insurance coverage is verified. *OR* Patients can be examined after verification of their insurance coverage.

e. Large SUVs are not covered by your car rental insurance.

f. Health and dental benefits are offered only after employees have been on the job for 12 months.

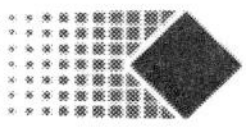

9.3 Subordinating Bad News

a. Although your cabinet hinge is no longer manufactured, we are sending a replacement that should work for you.

b. Although smoking is not allowed within 5 feet of a state building, the college has set aside 16 outdoor smoking areas.

c. Although we no longer print a complete catalog, we now offer all of our catalog choices at our Web site, which is always current.

d. Although your complete order cannot be shipped at this time, two corner workstations should arrive within five days.

e. Although an employment offer cannot be extended at this time, we appreciate your interest in our organization.

9.4 Implying Bad News

a. Although all our present funds are needed to lease equipment and offices for our new branch in Hartford, we hope to be able to support this commendable endeavor in the future.

b. We have your fresh fruit basket ready and will ship it as soon as you call us with your credit card number.

c. Because our billboard space was completely filled during the holidays, we hope to display your message, as promised, next month.

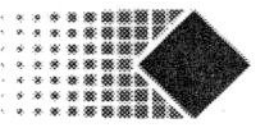

9.5 Document for Analysis—Revision

Current date

Ms. Sonya Capretta
2459 Sierra Avenue
Fresno, CA 93710

Dear Ms. Capretta:

Thanks for your inquiry regarding weddings at the Napa Valley Inn, one of the most beautiful and romantic settings in the country.

June is our busiest month, and this year is no exception. Although all of the Saturdays in June are booked, we can accommodate your party in midweek if you reserve soon. With unparalleled cuisine and service, along with panoramic Napa Valley and vineyard views, our Inn offers a unique, intimate ambiance in a breathtaking location for your special event.

Let the Napa Valley Inn with its 45 Mediterranean-style rooms and suites, each with its own sun-drenched private terrace, provide the perfect location for you and your guests to celebrate your union. Afternoon ceremonies typically begin at 11 a.m., while evening ceremonies usually begin at 6 p.m. Please call me at 1-800-435-3321 so that I can help you plan a midweek event in June. But act quickly to ensure your reservation.

Sincerely,

Note: See the Chapter 9 Teaching Suggestions for a list of document weaknesses.

9.6 Document for Analysis—Revision

Current date

Mr. Tyler Venable
Great Atlantic Financial Services
105 Washington Avenue
Glassboro, NJ 08071

Dear Mr. Venable:

We're happy to learn that you are enjoying the use of the Sharp CopyCenter C20 you have been leasing for the past 11 months.

Like our many other customers, Mr. Venable, you have discovered that Sharp copiers supply remarkable versatility and reliability. One of the reasons we're able to offer these outstanding copiers at such low leasing rates and equally low purchase prices is that we maintain a slim profit margin. If our program included a provision for applying lease payments toward purchase prices, our overall prices would have to be higher. Although lease payments cannot be credited toward purchase price, we can offer you other Sharp models that are within your price range. The Sharp CopyCenter C15 delivers the same reliability with nearly as many features as the top-of-the-line CopyCenter C20.

Please let us demonstrate the Sharp CopyCenter C15 to your staff in your office, Mr. Venable. Our representative, Leila Sanchez, will call you during the week of April 14 to arrange an appointment.

Sincerely,

 9.7 Document for Analysis—Revision

To: Sylvia Greene (sgreene@financialsolutions.com)
From: Chester Goings (cgoings@financialsolutions.com)
Subject: Your Request for Time Off
Cc:
Bcc:

Sylvia,

Everyone here at Financial Solutions appreciates the splendid work you have done for the Newborn Hope Foundation. We admire its goal of making differences in the lives of babies, particularly newborns. In the past we've been able to give you release time to work on its fashion show/luncheon, and we've been able to make a considerable financial contribution to the foundation.

This year, however, is different. As you know, we're suffering from the downturn in the economy and we've even had to reduce our staff. With the remaining bare-bones staff, we need every team member to be here and functioning highly as we prepare the upcoming release of our Planning Guide 5.0. You are one of our most valuable team members. We need you to interview clients, make video testimonials, and search for customer success stories. You are the team member on whom we depend to put the final touches on our new Web content. The truth is that we can't launch this new product on time without you.

Perhaps in the future when the economy rebounds and when our new product is successfully received, we'll be able to return to our former level of community involvement for admirable projects such as Newborn Hope Foundation. In the meantime, please accept our profound thanks for the exceptional service you give us here at Financial Solutions.

Chester
[Full contact information]

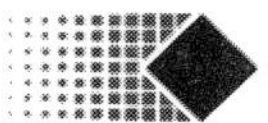

9.8 Document for Analysis—Revision

Current date

Mr. Kent W. Bradshaw
2140 Azalea Avenue
Louisville, KY 40216

Mrs. Lugan and I were pleased to interview you last Thursday and tell you something about Appalachian Technologies and its operations.

We were fortunate to have a number of well-qualified individuals apply for the position of human resources assistant. To fill this position, we hired a graduate of the University of Kentucky who seemed to have the qualities we sought. We wanted to write you immediately to enable you to continue your job search.

You have our best wishes in finding exactly the right position to match your background and education.

Sincerely,

Note: See the Chapter 9 Teaching Suggestions for a list of document weaknesses.

9.9 Helping Abused Children

Current date

Mrs. Olivia Hernandez
3592 Marine Creek Parkway
Fort Worth, TX 76279

Dear Mrs. Hernandez:

Let me commend you on the fine work you are doing as a volunteer with CASA. Its programs to recruit, train, and support volunteers to work with abused children deserve the high praise it receives from local and national communities. My heart goes out to those children who have been mistreated and whose futures are determined by the courts. CASA performs an invaluable service in helping these children find adoptive homes and escape the child welfare system.

In the past my company was able to make generous contributions. This fiscal year, however, has been difficult for us and for many other financial services organizations. Although funds are unavailable for charitable donations this year, we hope to be able to continue our support of CASA when the economy picks up and the future looks brighter.

Sincerely,

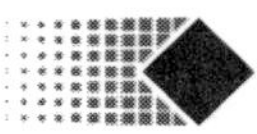

9.10 JAMBA ASKS FOR JUICY FAVOR

Current date

Mr. Joe Wong, Vice President
Product Development
Jamba Inc.
450 Golden Gate Avenue
San Francisco, 94102

Dear Joe:

It's good to learn that Jamba Inc. is expanding its menu with drinks that are more substantial and could substitute for a meal. In today's fast-paced world, people have less time for sit-down meals, and a hearty, healthful smoothie would be perfect for nutrition-conscious folks on the move.

Like you, we at Mainstream Software have been expanding our work force. We have many employees, but we have no dedicated cafeteria. Instead we have a lunchroom where employees may eat lunches they bring from home. It is quite small and offers no amenities such as would be needed to offer the experimental drinks on which you have been working. Although we can't help you by installing a Jamba Juice booth bar here at Mainstream, I am personally interested in sampling your experimental concoctions. Is there any way I could try out some of your drinks and give you my feedback?

I am definitely a Jamba Juice fan and have tried nearly all the drinks you now offer. Please let me know how I can act as a guinea pig for you. Go Jamba!

Sincerely,

9.11 Greening the Office

Current date

Ms. Donna Payne
Society of Commercial Realtors
of Greater Fort Lauderdale
1765 NE 26th Street
Fort Lauderdale, FL 33305

Dear Ms. Payne:

The HinesGo program helps offices identify and implement no-cost and low-cost green alternatives for standard indoor office environments. Bringing this message to the Society of Commercial Realtors in Fort Lauderdale could mean that your group becomes the foremost community leader in developing green workplaces.

Thanks for your invitation to speak to your group. Although my calendar is currently filled, I do have an opening in late January. Is it possible for your group to schedule my program at that time?

I look forward to the opportunity to tell you about the HinesGO program and share cost-effective strategies for office properties in Fort Lauderdale.

Sincerely,

9.12 Rejecting Agent's Appeal for Wireless Devices

Date: Current
To: Jon Tabaldo
From: Warren R. Sims
Subject: Your Request for Wireless Devices

You have put a good deal of time and thought into your request for using wireless devices to speed up information available to agents and clients, and I applaud your professionalism, Jon. After giving serious thought to your proposal, I want to share with you my concerns and suggestions.

I see value in having updated multiple listing information immediately available to agents in the field. Although this technology may not always appeal to us oldtimers, I'm sure it makes sense and would enable agents to be more competitive in tracking customers and managing data.

This software and hardware, however, would cost about $8,000 for the first year and require $15,000 in annual software updates for our staff of 22 agents in three offices. Although this expense cannot be justified for our agency, I do recognize the advantages that this MLS data and Web access offer agents. It seems more reasonable to me, however, that agents make this investment themselves as tools for their advancement and effectiveness in the profession. They would be responsible for keeping the wireless device secure and current. Just as agents purchase their own laptops for use in the field, they should purchase their own handheld devices for such use.

I encourage you to work with other agents in demonstrating the effectiveness of this tool. Once they see its value, the most professional agents will be inspired to acquire it themselves.

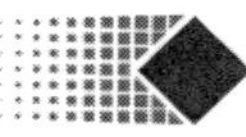

9.13 Fun Ship Slams Door on Under-21 Crowd

Current date

Ms. Elizabeth Neil
Leisure World Travel Agency
636 South Michigan Avenue
Chicago, IL 60605

Dear Ms. Neil:

We at Carnival Cruises genuinely appreciate Leisure World Travel's continued use of the "Fun Ship" line for your holiday tour packages for travelers of all ages.

In the past we have been able to offer fun, sun, and exotic ports of call to a wide range of guests, including high school and college students. More recently, however, some of our younger guests have been loud and disruptive. Last year we raised the drinking age from 18 to 21, but to no avail. Unruly young people still made it impossible for others to fully enjoy their travel aboard our cruise ships. Therefore, we're starting a new policy.

Effective immediately, any passenger under 21 will be accepted only when accompanied by an adult over 25. Although this policy may affect your student tour packages, we hope that you will understand our need to provide a relaxing environment for all our passengers. We encourage you to consider promoting family packages in which students join their families for vacation fun away from the stresses of everyday life.

Your customers have learned to expect carefree, fun-filled cruises from Carnival; and we will not disappoint them. Carnival attracts more guests than any other cruise line in the world, and 98 percent say they are well satisfied. We promise to keep them satisfied. Enclosed is our schedule for spring and summer Caribbean cruises. I will call during the week of January 15 to help you plan tour packages for your New York customers.

Sincerely,

Enclosure

9.14 CAN'T EVICT NOISY TENANT

Current date

Mr. Michael Vazquez, CPA
Suite 230
Peachtree Business Plaza
116 Krog Street
Atlanta, GA 30307

Dear Mr. Vazquez:

Subject: Your Recent Inquiry About a Neighboring Tenant

Thank you for bringing me your concerns about the loud music coming from Mr. Chomko's office. I can understand how frustrating the noise must be, especially when you are conducting business with clients.

Leasing commercial property is frequently a challenge, as the working environments of tenants are invariably diverse. A commercial tenancy is different from a residential tenancy. A lease for an apartment can include specific language regarding issues such as noise, but a standard commercial lease may not. Because Mr. Chomko has not broken any of the covenants in his lease, he is entitled to conduct business in the building.

Mr. Vazquez, as one of my most valued tenants, you can be sure that I will work with you to resolve this matter. I suggest that we meet with Mr. Chomko to discuss an equitable resolution to the problem. We might consider sharing the cost of soundproofing. I will set up a meeting for later this week.

Sincerely,

9.15 Refusing Refund for Japandroids and Bugskull Concert

Current date

Ms. Avianna Jones
2045 Live Oak Drive
Sacramento, CA 95841

Dear Ms. Jones:

We appreciate your letter regarding the July 4 Summertime Slam concert featuring the Japandroids and Bugskull bands. The situation surrounding that concert certainly was unusual.

An independent contractor arranged entertainment for that performance. Although Adventureland agreed to provide the venue and advertising, we had little control over the concert itself. On June 30 the independent contractor left town with all advance payments from financial backers. Only then did Adventureland learn that many of the artists who were supposed to be scheduled were not even planning to attend.

Faced with this difficult dilemma, Adventureland decided to offer a slightly modified version of the event. Radio advertising describing the change in talent began on Thursday, and we posted signs at the entrance of the park and in the parking lot. Moreover, patrons desiring a refund were allowed to return their tickets to the box office before the concert started.

Adventureland Park is committed to providing quality concerts and entertainment for its guests. Although a cash refund cannot be given after a concert takes place, we are enclosing two complimentary passes to Adventureland that will enable you and a friend to enjoy a carefree day at the park. We look forward to entertaining you as our guests.

Sincerely,

Enclosure

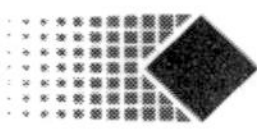

9.16 She Wants Reimbursement for Her Eyeglasses

Current date

Mrs. Annette Boyer-Parker
3560 Veteran Avenue
Santa Monica, CA 90401

Dear Mrs. Boyer-Parker:

We apologize for the loss of your glasses on our flight from Atlanta to Seattle with a stopover at O'Hare in Chicago.

Our flight attendants are instructed to remind passengers that the cabins will be cleaned during brief layovers. Most passengers leave the plane and do not return because they are catching connecting flights. During these brief layovers, cleaning crews must work swiftly as they pass through the cabins picking up discarded newspapers and other items. However, they should have recognized your glasses and given them to an attendant.

We regret your loss, and we will definitely review our instructions to crews about warning passengers to remove their personal belongings if they deplane. Although we can't reimburse you for the loss, we can offer you an equivalent value in travel vouchers on our planes between any destinations they serve.

Thank you for flying American Southern Airline, and we hope to see you soon as you use the enclosed travel vouchers.

Sincerely,

Enclosure

9.17: SORRY—SMOKERS MUST PAY

Current date

Mr. Wilson M. Weber
634 Wetmore Avenue
Everett, WA 98201

Dear Mr. Weber:

Century Park Hotel is committed to providing an attractive setting and comfortable surroundings for every guest's visit. We realize that our guests have high expectations, and to meet or exceed those expectations we recently completed a two-year plan to refurbish many rooms with new carpets, upholstery, finishes, and draperies.

You stayed in one of our renovated nonsmoking rooms. That room was clearly marked as a "Nonsmoking Room." In addition to the notice inside the room, guests are given a handout detailing our nonsmoking policy for selected rooms. The handout says that guests who disregard our nonsmoking policy will have a fee of $150 charged to their accounts.

Your business is very important to us. We hold each guest in the highest regard and are truly thankful for your patronage. On your next visit to the Century Park, we would be happy to reserve for you a smoking room.

Sincerely,

9.18 THE STAIRCLIMBER OR THE LIFESTEP?

Current date

Mr. Greg Waller
New Bodies Gym
3402 Copeland Drive
Athens, OH 45701

Dear Mr. Waller:

Thank you for your order! Your new Lifecycle Trainers, Pro Abdominal Boards, and Tunturi Muscle Trainers have been shipped and should arrive soon via UPS.

The Dual-Action StairClimbers you ordered are a favorite of many of our home customers. StairClimbers offer an enjoyable full-body workout without the harmful impact of running or walking. However, most fitness centers purchase our LifeStep StairClimber, which is designed for the heavy use and varying needs of fitness center customers.

In addition to its sturdier construction, LifeStep offers a choice of workouts that challenge muscles progressively. It provides computer-controlled interval training and electronic monitoring of step height, calories burned, elapsed time, and adherence to fitness levels. Although LifeStep costs a bit more at $2,395, the machine will withstand the constant climbing your customers will give it. With all of its advanced features, your StairClimber is sure to be a favorite among your customers.

Before we ship your StairClimbers, however, I'd like to be sure that we're sending you the equipment that is best for New Bodies Gym. Of course, we're happy to ship the Dual-Action StairClimber if you prefer it. Please call me at 1-800-254-9001 so that we can confirm the StairClimber model and ship this part of your order.

Sincerely,

9.19 University Admission Message Erroneously Welcomes All Who Applied

To: [Student applicant's e-mail address]
From: Mae Brown <mbrown@ucsd.edu>
Subject: Erroneous E-Mail Message
Cc:
Bcc:

Dear UCSD Applicant,

Just a few moments ago we sent you an e-mail message by mistake. It invited those who have been admitted to a campus orientation. That message should have gone only to the 18,000 students accepted by the University of California, San Diego. Through a data coding error, the message was sent to everyone who applied.

I realize how disturbing this message must have been to you, especially since we had already notified many of you that you were not accepted. The Admissions Office has never experienced an error of this magnitude before, and you can be sure that I have ordered a complete review of the notification process so that this kind of mistake will not reoccur.

To ease your mind and confirm your admission status, you may send an e-mail to the Admissions Office at *admissions@ ucsd.com*. We will notify you immediately of your status.

In all humility, I ask that you accept my sincere apologies and those of the University of California, San Diego.

Sincerely,

9.20 Rate Increase of Your Choice

Student messages will vary. Here are portions of an authentic letter announcing a newspaper rate increase.

Dear Home Delivery Subscriber:

Effective February 6, there will be a modest increase in the price of home delivery of ______, the first home delivery price increase in four years. This increase reflects the rising costs of printing and delivery. The new weekly rates are shown in a separate box.

In the four years since our last increase, we have significantly enhanced our coverage of the arts, travel, business, and real estate giving you even richer perspectives on vital aspects of your life and helping you make the most of your free time, investments, and so much more. We introduced new sections, Thursday Styles and Friday's Escapes, to help you discover new looks and new destinations. We also introduced such new features as The Funny Pages and Freakonomics to our Sunday magazine.

The _____ is also rewarding our readers in new ways. Home delivery customers now have free access to a powerful online resource featuring articles going back 25 years, as well as information that's unavailable anywhere else, exclusive multimedia events, blogs, interaction with our columnists, and more.

Home delivery remains the most convenient and reliable way to benefit from all that The ______ has to offer. It continues to be a cost-effective way to stay exceptionally well informed. We thank you for your business and for choosing The _______.

Sincerely,

9.21 Your Credit Card Is Refused

Current date

Ms. Arlene Getz
68 Riverside Drive, Apt. 35
New York, NY 10025

Dear Ms. Getz:

We sincerely apologize for the inconvenience you suffered when you tried to use your Visa card and were refused service.

Your purchase was rejected because it represented an unusual spending pattern. To prevent someone from using your card without your permission, we are now using neural-network technology. This program tracks spending patterns and detects anything unusual. It has been extraordinarily successful in identifying thieves who steal cards and immediately run up huge purchases. Since we started using the technology, our fraud rate dropped from 15 cents to 6 cents per $100. This savings can be passed on to our customers. More important, though, this new technology means that you won't have to suffer the hassle and heartache associated with fraudulent purchases on your card.

The technology, however, is not foolproof. Although we try to call as soon as we detect an unusual purchase, in some cases we cannot reach the cardholder. Because we prefer to err on the side of safety, we freeze any account with unusual purchases not verified by the cardholder.

If you plan to make any unusually large purchases or if you are traveling, it's a good idea to notify us so that our neural-network system isn't sent into action. Call our customer support people at 1-800-553-0321.

Because of our neural-network technology, you can feel safer about using your Visa card. Please be assured that we will continue to look for ways in which we can improve our service to you because we value you and your business.

Sincerely,

 9.22 J. Crew Goofs on Cashmere Turtleneck

To: <e-mail address of J. Crew customer>
From: J. Crew <staff@jcrew.com>
Subject: Your Cashmere Turtleneck Order
Cc:
Bcc:

Dear J. Crew Web Shopper:

At J. Crew we take pride in offering fashionable clothes at affordable prices. Recently at our Web site you ordered a sensational zip turtleneck cashmere sweater at the amazing price of $18.

To ensure accurate pricing, we double-check all copy material before it is posted to our Web site. Occasionally, though, we miss a typo. In the case of this cashmere sweater, that $18 cashmere blew right by our proofreaders. Although this stunning turtleneck should have been listed at $218, because of our error we would like to offer you this sweater for only $118.80 ($130.80 for larger sizes). If you check our current Web listings, you will see that this sweater is now correctly offered at $218.

The $18 sweater has been removed from your recent order, but you may reorder it for $118 (or $130.80) at a special Web address: <www.jcrew.special.html>. Only those J. Crew customers affected by the Web price error are being invited to purchase this sweater at this reduced price. Our big goof becomes your big bargain!

You can be sure we'll redouble our proofreading efforts for all future Web catalog items. Thanks for shopping J. Crew where you always catch terrific bargains.

Sincerely,

9.23 NO PAYROLL CHECKS

See the discussion material in Ch. 9 Teaching Suggestions for this activity.

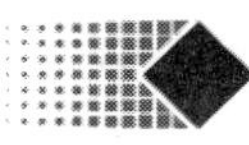

9.24 WORMS IN HER POWERBARS!

Current date

Ms. Kelly Keeler
932 Opperman Drive
Eagan, MN 55123

Dear Ms. Keeler:

Thanks very much for calling us to explain your experience with our PowerBar. Your distress is certainly understandable, and we sincerely apologize for your encounter with the larvae of the Indian meal moth.

This moth is a pantry pest that causes millions of dollars in damage worldwide. It feeds on grain-based products, such as cereal, flour, dry pasta, crackers, dried fruits, nuts, spices, and pet food. The moths fly mostly at night and may enter homes during summer months through open doors or windows. But most "hitchhike" inside of packaged goods and groceries, and they are difficult to control. Moths lay tiny eggs that can remain dormant for some time or hatch quickly into tiny worms that penetrate food wrappers and enter products.
We are extremely vigilant in preventing infestation at our manufacturing facilities. We inspect all incoming grains, supply proper ventilation, and shield all grain-storage areas with screens to avoid entry. We also use light traps and electrocuters to eradicate the moths with the least environmental impact.

Despite our stringent measures, moths may enter our products during the distribution stage. It is rare, however, for infestations

Ms. Kelly Keeler
Page 2
Current date

such as you experienced to occur in our bars. Although entomologists say that the worms are not toxic and will not harm humans, we realize that it is disgusting to find these worms in your food. We promise to redouble our efforts to ensure a clean environment in manufacturing our products.

You can learn more about the Indian meal moth and how to properly store food products in the enclosed brochure titled "Notes About the Indian Meal Moth." We are also enclosing a kit for you to use in sending us your infested PowerBar. Our goal is to analyze it in our Boise, Idaho, laboratories to see what we can learn about this infestation. Finally, we are enclosing a check for $26.85 to reimburse you for your purchase.

Once again, I want to thank you for taking the time to report your experience and for letting us explain how this could happen. We appreciate your patronage and hope that you will continue to use PowerBar, the fuel choice of top athletes around the world.

Sincerely,

Enclosures

9.25 Costly SUV Upgrade to a Ford Excursion

Current date

Mr. Steven Chan
5300 Park Ridge, Apt. 4A
Oakland, CA 93578

Dear Mr. Chan:

Thank you for writing to us about your experience in renting a Ford Excursion at our Oakland office. We can readily understand your concern when you learned that your insurance carrier did not cover the damage incurred during your rental of this vehicle.

Our Budget agents are trained to offer a risk product in the form of insurance to every car rental patron. However, we find it difficult or impossible to keep abreast of the many variations in individual carrier provisions.

We are also keenly aware of the need for speed in delivering vehicles to each of our valued customers. We consistently rank high in customer satisfaction for our swift counter work and efficient paper handling. Although we cannot warn customers about specifics of their own insurance coverage, we strive to provide efficient service and a wide range of risk products and rental vehicles at competitive rates.

Because we value you as a Budget customer and feel that we can offer you an unparalleled rental experience, we are enclosing a coupon for two days' free rental of a full-size sedan on your future trips. We sincerely appreciate your taking the time to share your comments with us, and we look forward to serving you again.

Sincerely,

Enclosure

9.26 PAYING CASH AT ATLANTA ATHLETIC CLUB

Current date

Ms. Cherie Liotta
Apartment 15, Springdale Hills
Sandy Springs, GA 30328

Dear Ms: Liotta:

Thanks for selecting the Atlanta Athletic Club as your workout choice. We appreciate your application for our Extended Membership plan. An Extended Membership in Atlanta Athletic Club qualifies members for all of our testing, exercise, recreation, yoga, and aerobics programs.

This unique multiservice fitness program is expensive for us to offer because it requires that we maintain an extensive staff. As a result, a solid credit rating is required of applicants. Your credit report, which we obtained from Experian, indicates that your credit history makes it impossible for an Extended Membership to be offered at this time. However, you may be interested in our Drop In and Work Out plan. This plan would enable you to use our available facilities on a cash basis. You could sign up for yoga and aerobics classes, space permitting, and reserve space on the racquetball and handball courts.

I suggest that you inquire about your credit report at Experian, where you may receive a free credit report if you mention your application to us. In the meantime, we hope to see you at the Atlanta Athletic Club for Drop In and Work Out sessions soon. Our evening aerobics classes are filling up fast.

Sincerely,

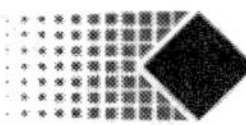 9.27 CAMCORDERS FOR RUDY'S CAMERA SHOP

Current date

Mr. Ron Kasbekar
Rudy's Camera Shop
3016 East Lucas Drive
Beaumont, TX 77657

Dear Mr. Kasbekar:

You've come to the right place for Canon Vixia camcorders! We appreciate your March 13 order. The model that you ordered offers outstanding features including sleek lightweight design, brilliant optical quality, vibrant images, and outstanding image capture in low-light conditions.

Because we would like to see this fine product distributed by Rudy's Camera Shop, we submitted your credit application to Experian, our credit reporting agency. After reviewing its report, we find that credit cannot be extended at this time. To learn more about your credit report, you may call an Experian counselor at (403) 369-3211. When your firm's financial situation improves, we would sincerely like to serve you on a credit basis.

In the meantime, please consider this plan. Order six of the Canon Vixia camcorders today. By paying for this reduced order with cash, you would receive a 2 percent cash discount. After you have sold these fast-moving camcorders, place another cash order through our toll-free order number. We promise to deliver your items immediately so that your inventory is never depleted. In this way, you can obtain the units you want now, you can enjoy cash discounts, and you can replace your inventory quickly.

You and your customers will be happy you decided to stock the popular Canon Vixia camcorder. If we can do business with you now or in the future, please call me at 1-800-896-3233.

Cordially,

9.28 Company Games Are Not Date Nights

Date: Current
To: Staff Members
From: Your Name, Director, Human Resources
Subject: Nonemployees on Intramural Sports Teams

Several employees recently requested that friends and family members be invited to participate in Weyerman Paper Company sports teams. Our intramural sports teams are a popular employee social activity that we hope to continue.

Currently, our intramural teams are open to all employees of Weyerman. The company has eight volleyball, tennis, and softball teams, with over 100 employees participating. Because most team rosters are currently full, adding participants to the teams would require changing the team rosters and game schedules for which employees have already planned. More important, our intramural sports teams give employees regular opportunities to have fun together. Keeping the team rosters "employee-only" ensures that all employees can enjoy the camaraderie of Weyerman teams.

I hope that employees will invite family and friends to participate as spectators at games and to socialize with us afterwards. Our teams always welcome cheering fans!

9.29 We Can't Pay Your Tuition

Date: Current
To: Yasmin Qajar
From: Your Name, Director, Human Resources
Subject: Your Inquiry Regarding Tuition Reimbursement

We appreciate your thoughtful message requesting that Middleton Bank establish a program to reimburse the costs of college expenses such as tuition and books.

You're smart, Yasmin, in striving to further your education by returning to school to take additional courses that improve your career skills. Thriving companies are able to offer tuition reimbursement to selected employees when they return to school. These programs are expensive to an organization because they involve not only the actual cost of tuition and books but also the cost of program administration.

As you know, Middleton Bank is facing stiff competition in the banking industry and our profits have not been strong. Although a tuition-reimbursement program cannot be considered at this time, we are hopeful that it might be possible in the future.

Our CEO Christopher Epley joins me in expressing our appreciation for the fine work you are doing at Middleton Bank. We admire your desire to advance your education and wish you all the best.

9.30 Negative News in Other Cultures

This can be a revealing and instructive exercise for students. Although responses will obviously vary, your students may find that other cultures are quite concerned with saving face. This assignment would make a challenging but interesting long report.

CHAPTER 10 APPLYING YOUR SKILLS AT HANDS ON MIAMI

[Hands on Miami stationery]

Current date

Dear Friends of Miami:

Don't know what to do with your old print cartridges or discarded cell phones? Hold on! Don't toss them out and let them end up in a landfill polluting the environment.

Hands on Miami has a better use for your discards. Donate them, and you can help change lives and strengthen our community. Our volunteer service programs will receive a credit of up to $10 for every used print cartridge and up to $20 for every cell phone your company recycles.

Estimates suggest that nearly 300 million ink cartridges are discarded every year. These cartridges are made of industrial plastics, and they take up to a thousand years to decompose. In North America over 40,000 tons of plastic are saved from landfills every year as a result of cartridge recycling. Cell phones are another item being tossed away. Hundreds of thousands of cell phones are no longer being used as new models flood the marketplace. Instead of letting them gather dust in a drawer, turn them in and help our Community Bridges program.

Why bother? With the money raised form your donations, Hands on Miami will be able to fund many projects that make a difference in our community. Your donations will support the volunteers who feed the homeless at Miami Rescue Mission, read bedtime stories to children at the Salvation Army, clean up Pelican Harbor, and work hard on countless other projects that make Miami a better place to live and work.

Friends of Miami Page 2 Current Date

It's a win-win solution for everyone! You get rid of used ink cartridges and old cell phones while helping save the environment and the planet. We put to work the credits from your donations in projects that enrich our community's wellbeing. We're both winners!

Participating couldn't be easier. Your cartridges and cell phones may be dropped off at recycling centers, mailed in, or picked up. Just visit www.miamidaderecyling.org or call 1-800-534-9989 for details. Remember, your donation and support will change lives.*

Cordially,

President and CEO

***The URL and phone numbers are fictitious.**

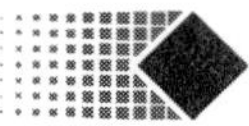

10.1 Document for Analysis—Revision

To: Members of the 7-Eleven Franchise Owners Association of Chicagoland
From: Nicholas Barajas <nicholas.barajas@hotmail.com>
Subject: Finding a Better Way to Sell Fresh Bananas
Cc:
Bcc:

Fresh Del Monte has suggested that 7-Eleven stores sell fresh bananas wrapped in plastic. Selling more bananas and other fresh foods is helping us build profits lost when cigarette sales declined. Although the wrapper may slow ripening and extend the shelf life of bananas, the wrapping may turn customers off. They may see it as an environmental issue and not like adding a plastic wrapper around something that comes naturally wrapped in the first place.

I suggest that we ask Fresh Del Monte to develop a wrapper that is biodegradable. Until we have a biodegradable wrap, we franchisees should not support the move to plastic-wrapped bananas. At the January 20 meeting of the 7-Eleven Franchise Owners Association of Chicagoland, I propose that we reject the plastic wraps in favor of a biodegradable wrap that could achieve the same purpose.

Please let me know by January 15 whether you agree that a biodegradable wrap would be more attractive to our customers. I look forward to seeing you at the next meeting.

Nick
[Full contact information]

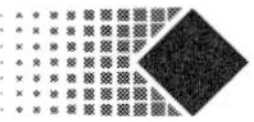

10.2 DOCUMENT FOR ANALYSIS—REVISION

Current date

Mr. Danielle Watkins
The Beverly Hills Hotel
9641 Sunset Boulevard
Beverly Hills, CA 90210

Dear Ms. Watkins:

News of the excellent presentation you made at your local chapter of the National Restaurant Association has reached us here in Los Angeles, and we are very impressed.

Running a successful restaurant operation, as we all know, is tough even on a good day. The intense pace is frenzied, from scrubbing the vegetables early in the morning to latching the front door at day's end. In all this haste, it's easy to lapse into food service faults that can land an operation in big trouble. Your presentation focusing on seven cardinal sins in the food service industry certainly captured our attention.

The LA chapter of the National Restaurant Association asked me to invite you to be the featured speaker at our May 25 dinner on the topic of "Avoiding the Seven Cardinal Sins in Food Service." By sharing your expertise, you can help other restaurant operators recognize and prevent potential problems involving discrimination, workplace safety, hiring practices, and so forth. Although we can offer you only a small honorarium of $200 plus your travel expenses, we can promise you a big audience of enthusiastic restaurateurs eager to hear your presentation.

Our relaxed group doesn't expect a formal address; they are most interested in hearing about best practices and solutions to prospective problems. To make your talk easy to organize, I have enclosed a list of questions our members submitted. Most talks are about 45 minutes long.

Ms. Danielle Watkins Page 2 Current date

Can we count on you to join us for dinner at 7 p.m. on May 25 at the Oak Room of the Westin St. Francis Hotel in San Francisco? Just call me at (213) 351-1220 before March 1 so that I can let our members know you will be joining us.

Sincerely,

Enclosure

10.3 Document for Analysis—Revision

Date: Current
To: Bryanna Mazzetta, Vice President, Marketing
From: Luke Downey, Exhibit Manager
Subject: Reducing a Major Expense at Trade Shows

At your suggestion, I've been searching for ways to reduce our trade show exhibition costs. One of our major expenses is the booth gift that we present to visitors.

At past trade shows we've given away a nine-color, silk-screened T-shirt designed by a high-priced, outside designer. Each shirt cost $23 to produce. However, I've located a Chinese supplier who can produce good-looking T-shirts, and the cost is only $6 each. Look at the savings:

2,000 silk-screen T-shirts @ $15	$46,000
2,000 cheaper T-shirts @$6	12,000
SAVINGS	$34,000

Please examine the enclosed T-shirt sample. You might expect a cheaper shirt to be less acceptable, but, as you can see, this shirt is quite presentable. What's more, it advertises our name just as well as the more expensive silk-screened T-shirts. We expect folks to wear this shirt when they work out, and the cheaper shirt serves the purpose just as well as the more expensive one.

With increasing travel costs and decreasing trade show budgets, we at Worldclass Trainer have had to look carefully at how we spend our limited funds for exhibitions. We have decreased the number of shows in which we participate, and we take fewer booth staffers. However, here is a significant way in which we can reduce a substantial expense.

[10.3 Continued]

To save $34,000 in exhibition costs, please authorize the purchase of 2,000 T-shirts for our next major trade show. If I receive your authorization before April 4, we can be sure of receiving a supply from our Chinese supplier for the September Las Vegas trade show.

Enclosure

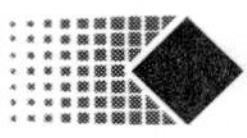

10.4 Document for Analysis—Revision

Current date

Mr. Jason M. Amato
TEK Copier Solutions
13429 North 59th Avenue
Glendale, AZ 85307

Dear Mr. Amato:

The four Multifunction SX500 photocopiers that we purchased three months ago are inadequate for our volume of copying.

Although we told your salesperson, Gary Kazan, that we average 3,000 copies a day, he recommended the Multifunction SX500. This model appears to have been the wrong choice for our heavy use, and we are disappointed in its performance. Therefore, we would like to trade in our four SX500 copiers (about $2,500 each, as shown on the enclosed invoice) on the purchase of two Multifunction XX800 models (about $13,500 each).

When I discussed this possibility with your district manager, Victor Martineau, he said that we would be charged 50 percent depreciation if we traded in the four SX500 copiers. That amounts to $5,000, a considerable sum for three months of irregular copier use. We think a depreciation rate of 20 percent is more reasonable. Your company would profit in three ways:

- **The Multifunction SX500 machines were used a short time, and they can be resold easily.**
- **You'll be making a sizable profit when we purchase two XX800 copiers.**
- **Your service technicians will save time by making fewer trips to repair our overworked SX500 machines.**

Mr. Jason M. Amato Page 2 Current date

We purchased the Multifunction SX500 copies in good faith on the recommendation of your salesperson. We feel that it is your responsibility to help us secure the proper model for our needs.

Please approve my request to trade in four Multifunction SX500 copiers for a value of $8,000 (allowing for 20 percent depreciation) toward the purchase of two Multifunction XX800 models. Just initial this letter showing your approval, and return it to me in the enclosed envelope before September 1. I'll work out the details of the new purchase with your salesperson.

Sincerely yours,

Enclosure

10.5 INVITING A SPEAKER

To: Marion Minter <mminter@temphelp4you.com>
From: <Student's e-mail address>
Subject: Sharing Your Success Story With Business Students
Cc:
Bcc:

Dear Ms. Minter:

As a former [name of school or school's team], I hope you will accept my invitation to be the keynote speaker at the Business and Accounting Association's annual kick-off meeting.

Because of our club's focus on business and your success as an entrepreneur, you would be the perfect speaker to get our club off to a great start this year. Your expertise as well as your history with our campus will make your talk a big draw for our members. With their business and accounting backgrounds, some students in our club may even be potential employees at TempHelp4You.

The meeting will be held on Wednesday, September 10, 2008, from noon until 1:30 p.m. in Branford Hall. We would like you to speak for about 30 minutes and then take questions from the audience. On the day of the event, we would provide you with lunch and a complimentary parking permit, which you could pick up at the information kiosk at the main entrance to the campus.

Please let me know if you can speak at our meeting by August 20 so I can make the appropriate arrangements. You can phone me at [student phone] or e-mail me at [student e-mail] if you have any questions. We hope you will share your success story with us in September!

Sincerely,

10.6 Asking Beijing to Use Excel

Date: Current
To: Zhu Chen, Regional Sales Manager, Beijing
From: Mario Franchini, Regional Sales Manager, Seattle
Subject: Submitting Sales Figures

Although we have not corresponded recently, I hope you are well and that your staff continues to enjoy strong sales.

My staff here in Seattle has requested that I ask a favor of you. It would help us greatly if you would submit your sales figures in Excel spreadsheets. If you could grant this kindness for us, we would be able to integrate your sales figures more easily into our records. The Excel software is available on the company intranet so that it is immediately available. Using Excel is simple and would make it easier for you to track your quarterly sales figures for the Beijing branch. An excellent tutorial for Excel is available should you or your staff need it.

If you would be able to submit your September quarterly sales figures in Excel spreadsheets, it would be most helpful to our staff here in Seattle. We appreciate the solid sales your branch is generating, and we congratulate your staff on its success.

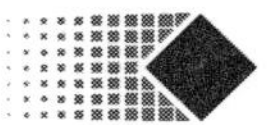

10.7 Borrowing Suits for Interviews

Current date

Dean John Smith
College of Business Administration
North Central College
111 Main Street
Anytown, MA 02106

Dear Dean Smith:

Our students are well trained, smart, and have spotless résumés. However, they may not fare well on the job market if they aren't dressed properly.

Perhaps North Central could find a way to provide a "Suitable Suits" program similar to that at Barnard College. Its Office of Career Development keeps a closet filled with 21 crisp black suits that students can borrow for job interviews. Being professionally dressed for a job interview can make all the difference in the world to the confidence and success of the candidate.

Barnard's program was funded by a grant from Goldman Sachs. I realize that we would not have such a grant, but other possibilities can be explored for developing such a program. Perhaps local department stores would be interested in helping create and support the program. Perhaps thrift stores could provide appropriate garments. Perhaps graduates could contribute clothing or ideas for supporting the project.

I don't have all the answers, but I think it's a topic that deserves investigation. May I see you during the week of November 10 to discuss the possibility of developing a Suitable Suits program for North Central? Please call me at 455-9802 or send a message to me at <jlbrown@aol.com>.

Sincerely,

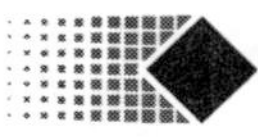

10.8 A Helping Hand for College Expenses

Date: Current
To: [Your boss]
From: Student's name
Subject: Improving Employee Productivity, Morale, and Recruiting

We employees here at First Federal think that the two most important elements in workplace productivity are skills and high morale.

Both of these elements can be boosted through an employer-sponsored tuition-reimbursement program. Here's how the program works. Employees attend evening or online college classes. If they finish approved courses with a *C* or better, they are reimbursed for the costs of books and fees.

Many local employers—such as Bank of America, Chase, GE, and Computer Associates—already have such programs in operation. Enclosed are several articles and printouts describing such programs. These employers consider tuition-reimbursement programs a smart investment because employees improve their skills and create a strong pool for promotion. Surveys show that such programs improve morale and loyalty. Moreover, companies with tuition-reimbursement programs are more attractive to quality job candidates.

My colleagues and I have done research on these programs at other companies. In a meeting before April 1, we'd like to show you our data and discuss the possibility of such a program here at First Federal. Please call me at Ext. 348 to arrange a time.

Enclosure

 10.9 Dear Senator or Representative

460 South Superior Street
Denver, CO 80202
Current date

Honorable Wayne Allen
716 Hart Senate Office Building
Washington, DC 20510

Dear Senator Allen:

Subject: Bill S.8 Superfund Cleanup Acceleration Act of 2008

As a Colorado resident, I appreciate the clean air, clean water, and undisturbed natural lands that most of Colorado offers. Therefore, I was disturbed to hear of Senate Bill S.8, the Superfund Cleanup Acceleration Act. This bill does not benefit our environment or the Colorado communities that are affected by Superfund sites. I hope you will oppose S.8 when it comes to the Senate floor next month.

S.8 attempts to give grants to local governments, Indian tribes, redevelopment agencies, and other eligible entities. The grants will be used to assess and respond to "brownfields," or abandoned industrial sites polluted with hazardous wastes. Although I support the cleanup of these Superfund sites, I'm concerned about the S.8 bill because it does the following:

- Allows polluters to control clean-up. According to the Sierra Club Action Alert #24, "polluters would be allowed to write their own cleanup plans, and the EPA has only 180 days to review the plans." If the Agency is unable to review the plans during this time, the plan becomes fully authorized by default.

Honorable Wayne Allen
Page 2
Current date

- Repeals the liability for polluters to pay for waste cleanup at "co-disposal" sites. Hundreds of co-disposal sites include industrial as well as municipal waste. Yet S.8 would give the burden of hazardous waste cleanup to municipalities, not polluters.

- Limits protection of ground water supplies. The bill states that "groundwater protection criteria are applicable to cost-effective remedial action plans, considering actual or future use of the resource." In other words, if ground water is not considered as a future drinking water source, cleanup plans may not be required to protect it.

You have often voted in favor of industries when environmental votes are taken, Senator Allen. However, I know that you want all the residents of Colorado to benefit from legislation you endorse. I am appealing to you personally to help me and my family continue to enjoy clean air and water in my home state.

Please consider the details of The Superfund Act and vote no when it is brought to the floor. Colorado deserves a thorough and careful solution to the cleanup of its Superfund sites.

Sincerely,

10.10 SCHOOL VENDING MACHINES BECOME WEIGHTY PROBLEM

Current date

Board of Directors
Gresham-Barlow School District
P.O. Box 310
Gresham, OR 97033

Dear Directors:

Recent surveys show that approximately one third of U.S. children aged 6 to 19 are overweight, and this obesity epidemic threatens the health of current and future generations. Obesity is known to be associated with diabetes, heart disease, high blood pressure, and arthritis.

Although many factors including lack of exercise contribute to the obesity problem, a significant element is poor nutrition. The American Academy of Pediatrics says that cutting out soda pop would help to reduce obesity among school-age children. Cans of sugar-loaded, carbonated drinks provide empty calories and should not be readily available to our children. For this reason, the PTA strongly opposes an extension of the Coca-Cola vending machine contract now under consideration.

A school should provide a healthy learning and living environment. Vending machines with soda and snacks fail to accomplish these goals. We applaud the school boards in the nation's two largest public school districts—New York City and Los Angeles—for banning soda vending during school hours. We believe, however, that vending machines have no place on a school campus at any time—before, during, and after school. Some argue that children will just go off campus to purchase drinks and snacks, and that the school is needlessly losing a revenue source.

Gresham-Barlow School District Page 2 Current date

As parents, however, we know that the consumption of soda pop and snacks will be greatly reduced if the temptation is not readily available. We are doing our students no favor by selling out their health to the perks that come from vending machine sales. Schools must assume a more active role in providing nutritious food and in limiting access to foods of minimal nutritional value to children in their care.

We realize that the district has come to depend on vending machine sales to provide extra funds for equipment and school activities. As a PTA, we will do everything possible to raise funds to help replace this lost revenue. We urge you to refuse this Coca-Cola contract and join with us in finding alternate revenue sources that will free us from the burden of vending machine evils.

Sincerely,

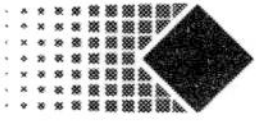

10.11 Overcharged and Unhappy

Current date

Customer Service
Country Inn, Inc.
428 Church Street
Nashville, TN 37219

Dear Customer Service Representative:

In recent years my company has recommended that its traveling employees use the Country Inn in Nashville because we have been pleased with your accommodations, rates, and especially with your service. That's why I'm sure you will want to reverse a charge that I believe was made in error to our account.

On May 4 and 5 two employees and I attended a conference in Nashville. We spent the evening of May 4 at your hotel and had breakfast May 5 in the Atrium. Because this was a weekend, we understood that we were being charged the weekend special rate, which included a full hot breakfast—in the restaurant. I realize that many weekend guests, as part of your special rate, are given a continental breakfast in a lounge on their floor. However, when we made the reservations, we were told that a hot breakfast in the restaurant was included.

I was surprised to see on our credit statement a charge for $114 for three champagne buffet breakfasts at the Atrium for the morning of May 5. By the way, we arrived at the restaurant so early that the Sunday buffet had not yet been set up, and we were served no champagne at all.

Enclosed is a statement showing this erroneous charge. Please remove this charge and restore our faith in your hotel.

Sincerely,

Enclosure

10.12 Legal Costs for Sharing a Slice of Heaven

Current date

Mr. Henry Giordano
Attorney at Law
Giordano, Murphy, and Associates
254 Sherborn Street
Boston, MA 02215

Dear Mr. Giordano:

Mystic Pizza® has a reputation for excellent pizzas made from its secret recipes. Naturally, when Mystic Pizza was asked to distribute its product in grocery and convenience stores, the company sought only excellent legal advice for doing so.

Giordano, Murphy, and Associates drew up contracts regarding the use of Mystic Pizza's name and quality standards for the distributed product. The bill we received included 38 hours of attorney preparation at $400 per hour. Surely experienced attorneys like yours would not require so many hours to prepare such contracts. Could an error have been made in the billing hours? Moreover, when I checked with other businesses, I learned that competing law firms charge half your rate, only $200 per hour.

We would like to continue working with your prestigious firm, Mr. Giordano. However, we expect accurate billing statements and competitive rates. Please adjust the billing hours and rate to reflect a reasonable assessment of your services. Since we would like to send you a check before our fiscal year closes June 30, your response before June 20 would be greatly appreciated.

Sincerely,

10.13 Botched Print Job

Current date

Mr. Howard Moscatelli
Jiffy Printers
3402 South Main Street
Rochester, NY 14634

Dear Mr. Moscatelli:

On October 15 I took a complex print job to Jiffy Printers in Brighton. Although I explained carefully what was to be done, the resulting print job was unsatisfactory. Some of the pages were on the wrong paper, the photos and graphics turned out poorly, and many of the sheets were poorly or improperly cut.

Because my company, Holiday Travel, needed that print job immediately, I allowed the Brighton shop to repeat the job. This time Jiffy used its paper instead of the special paper that I brought for the first job. The repeat of the job turned out fairly well, and I appreciate that. We were able to use the brochures to complete our mailing. However, they were not done on the paper I preferred, and the mailing was delayed.

I feel that some adjustment should be made to the charge of $782, shown on the enclosed invoice copy. At the minimum, my company should be credited for the loss of $100 worth of distinctive paper. We have used Jiffy Printers for many printing tasks, and I would like to continue to do so. Please restore my faith in your company by allowing a generous adjustment to the amount we were charged.

Sincerely,

Enclosure

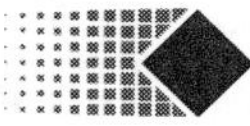

10.14 Honolulu Country Club Gets Scammed on Phony Toner Phoner

Current date

Copy Machine Specialists
4320 Admiralty Way
Honolulu, HA 96643

Ladies and Gentlemen:

SUBJECT: Returning Two Bottles of Toner

Your telephone marketer misrepresented himself in a recent call to the Waialae Country Club. As a result, our assistant ordered two bottles of inferior toner. With this letter, we are returning those bottles.

This toner is inferior to the Xerox Toner Model 1313 that we normally order from Island Office Supply. In addition to its inferior quality, the enclosed product is exorbitantly priced at over $400 a bottle. Our normal toner costs $129 a bottle.

You misrepresented yourself as our supplier, which you are not. We feel no obligation to pay any part of your $960.43 bill. Please stop billing us and cease all telephone solicitations. Any further reminders received from you will be sent to the state attorney general as well as to the local Better Business Bureau.

Yours truly,

Enclosure

10.15 How About a 4-Day Week?

Date: Current
To: Skin Essentials Management Council
From: Student names
Subject: Saving Energy, Reducing Costs, and Pleasing Employees

Skin Essentials has always been an employee-centric company with an emphasis on environmental stewardship, and we would like to suggest a program that meets those goals and reaps other impressive benefits.

Many companies and municipalities are switching to a four-day workweek to save energy, reduce their carbon footprint, help recruit and retain employees, reduce operational costs, improve air quality, and boost employee morale. A group of managers here at Skin Essentials has met to discuss this possibility, and we would like to submit a proposal to the management council.

A four-day workweek would involve 10-hour days for employees. By coming to work only four days, employees would reduce the number of cars on the road and help meet the county's Trip Reduction Program aimed at improving air quality. Fewer trips means that employees are using less fuel, thus saving money for them, reducing air pollution, and reducing the need for importing gas.

Many municipalities have already implemented a four-day workweek. In Avondale, Arizona, the city ran a pilot program known as "Green Friday," to save energy and reduce overall costs. The summer-long pilot program was a huge success with more than 80 percent of employees and residents in favor of the schedule. Avondale also reduced its annual janitorial costs by $10,000 and reduced its electricity use by $45,000.

[10.15 Continued]

Researchers at the Romney Institute of Public Management at Brigham Young University studied the effects of a compressed workweek in more than 150 cities in 38 states. Their findings revealed that four-day employees reported lower levels of work-family conflict and increased productivity compared with traditional workers. In our own small survey of Skin Essentials employees, we found that 80 percent favored a compressed workweek. Such a flexible workweek has innumerable benefits for employees and could also improve efficiency.

Changing the workweek at Skin Essentials represents a serious move, but it could be tried in a pilot program over the summer to test its effectiveness. Our committee of managers strongly urges the Management Council to consider a compressed workweek. May we present our recommendation at the next council meeting on March 5? Please respond by February 20 so that we can prepare our presentation.

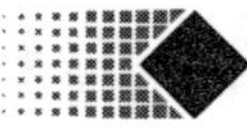

10.16 PROVIDING HANDHELD GPS DEVICES TO HOTEL GUESTS

Date: Current
To: Martin Zatari, Manager, Biltmore West
From: Student's Name, Assistant Manager
Subject: Attracting and Pleasing Guests With a Useful but Chic Perk

Our guests here at Biltmore West frequently ask the concierge Stephen for directions to The Golden Oyster, the China Pavilion, or countless other places. He patiently tells them how to get there, but often they get lost. Instead of frustrating our guests, we could give them a device that leads them right to their destination and back again with a minimum of instruction and frustration.

I'm suggesting that Biltmore West invest in one or two handheld GPS devices that guests could borrow for their excursions. The Carlyle in Manhattan and The Mansion on Turtle Creek in Dallas both offer GPS devices to their guests. A concierge plugs in the desired location, hits "go," and then the GPS takes over. A gentle voice directs guests on foot or in their cars to the destination. If guests are out jogging or sightseeing and lose their way, the GPS takes them back to the hotel from anywhere. As a perk for our guests, these GPS devices could give us a distinct marketing advantage in attracting upscale visitors. What's more, Martin, you could be the first manager in our chain who offers this chic yet useful perk to attract guests!

For our purposes I recommend the Garmin nuvi 260. It's a good buy for $250 at TigerDirect.com. Although the price may seem high, if it attracts just two more guests per month we will have made up the cost in no time at all. To keep costs down, we might start out with one or two GPS navigators as a trial to see how effectively they work.

May I talk with you and show you literature about this GPS device before August 1? We could begin featuring this attraction for our fall season guests if we act quickly.

10.17 An Apple a Day

Current date

Mr. Richard Johnson
Vice President, Omni Hotels
420 Decker Drive
Irving, TX 75062

Dear Mr. Johnson:

As an Omni associate, I am grateful to be employed by a luxury chain known for its high rankings of guest satisfaction and its many amenities. I am also pleased to be trained in The Power of One, and I enjoy the encouragement it provides to associates in offering their opinions regarding the hotel's mission and its four-diamond services.

I understand that Omni is considering giving up its practice of offering free apples in its lobbies. In my opinion, this is not the best way to cut costs. Yes, I know that hotels, like other businesses, are looking for ways to reduce expenses. However, cutting apples is a step in the wrong direction. In addition to looking wholesome and inviting, apples provide quick, healthful nourishment for tired travelers. Arriving guests often need a light bite to hold them over until they can reach the restaurant or until they can call room service. Guests passing through the lobby can always pick up an apple for a snack on the way to the pool or to a business appointment.

Surely our excellent managers can find other ways to cut costs that have less impact on guest perceptions and expectations. Some hotels are buying food in larger quantities, streamlining restaurant menus, or reducing the hours of lobby cafes.

A bowl of Granny Smith or Red Delicious apples lifts the spirit and says, "Welcome!" Bowls of apples provide an immediate nonverbal greeting to guests and quickly put them in a good mood. Please do not remove our apple greetings.

Sincerely,

10.18 Keeping Track of Office Projects

To: Mike.Kuryia@walters_inc.com
From: YourName@your_e-mail.com
Cc:
Subject: Improving Communication and Project Support
Bcc:

Hi, Mike,

Our company is fortunate to have so many successful projects underway. However, keeping track of them, assigning support staff, and communicating with all of the project managers in remote locations is increasingly difficult.

To keep the lines of communication open and to ensure that your project is fully supported, I am proposing that we install a dry erase board in our office. On this board we would list every project, its location, and its status. That way, we can see at a glance where everyone is and be able to direct messages to you and schedule support more efficiently. The cost of a plain dry erase board is negligible, and I can pick one up at Wal-Mart. What's more, I will be happy to keep the board current with the information you provide me.

If a majority of project managers approve, I will purchase a board and have it installed. Then I will need your help in keeping it up-to-date. If you agree that this is a good plan to improve communication and project support, let me know by July 1 before everyone leaves on vacations.

Best,

Your Name
[Full contact information]

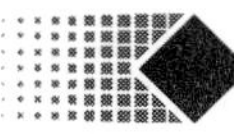

10.19 Training Telecommuters

To: Victor Vasquez <victor.vasquez@beta.com>
From: Your Name <your e-mail>
Cc:
Re: Improving Training for Telecommuters and Their Managers

An increasing number of our employees are becoming telecommuters. Although working at home or at remote locations promised reduced overhead costs and higher productivity, not all telecommuting has been successful. Many teleworkers do not succeed because they and their managers have not been trained in effective procedures.

Currently we have 83 telecommuters, and an increasing number are asking for permission to work at remote locations. These workers and their managers could be more effective if we better prepared them for the telecommuting experience.

Some of the problems that telecommuters typically face are lack of face time, resentment among other office workers, difficulty in coordinating projects, lost creativity from lack of stimulation, and unmet expectations. They assume that somehow home is going to be a friendlier, easier, and quieter place to work than the office—and that is not always the case.

A good training program, according to one consultant, integrates four key issues:

- How to set good objectives and measure productivity
- How to develop performance management skills
- How to enhance communication with people in the office
- What to expect when you are a telecommuter

[10.19 Continued]

Although we could develop our own in-house training program, I believe we would be better served by hiring an experienced consultant or agency that specializes in offering telecommuting programs for large companies.

May I have your permission to arrange a meeting with a consultant to explore a telecommuting training course for our employees? Please give me your response before November 5 when we will be developing our budget for the next year.

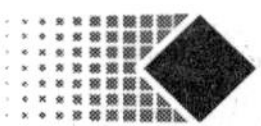

10.20 Dear Boss

Solutions will vary depending on the situation.

10.21 Demanding Mandatory Tipping

Current date

Mr. Nicholas Ruiz, General Manager
Bayside Inn Golf and Beach Resort
9300 Emerald Coast Parkway West
Sandestin, FL 32550-7268

Dear Mr. Ruiz:

Even when servers have given good service, some customers leave no tip. This is a serious problem for the servers in the Dolphin Watch. Many of us have gotten together and decided to bring the problem—and a possible solution—to your attention in this letter.

Restaurants such as the famous Coach House Restaurant in New York now add a 15 percent tip to the bill. Other restaurants are printing gratuity guidelines on checks. In fact, American Express now provides a calculation feature on its terminals so that restaurants can choose the tip levels they want printed. In Europe a service charge of 10 to 15 percent is automatically added to a check.

We servers feel that a mandatory tip printed on checks would work well here at the Dolphin Watch. We know that we give good service, but some customers forget to tip. By printing a suggested tip on the check, we remind them so that they won't forget. A printed mandatory tip also does the math for them, which is an advantage for customers who are not too good with figures.

Printing mandatory tips on checks not only helps customers but also proves to the staff that you support them in their goal to receive decent wages for the hard work they do. A few

Mr. Nicholas Ruiz
Page 2
Current date

customers might resist, but these customers can always cross out the printed tip if they wish. If you have any doubts about the plan, we could try it for a six-month period and monitor customer reactions.

We urge you to begin printing a mandatory 15 percent tip on each customer's bill. Our American Express terminals are already equipped to do this. Please let us know your feelings about this proposal within two weeks because it is a serious concern to us.

Sincerely,

10.22 Reducing Your Health Insurance Costs

Date: Current
To: All Employees
From: Melissa Mendoza, Human Resources
Subject: Reducing Your Healthcare Costs and Improving Your Health

If you would like to reduce your insurance deductible by up to $2,000 and improve your health at the same time, we have an exciting offer to make.

We know that all employees suffered when our health insurance deductible rose last year from $500 to $2,500. Now, however, we've worked out a plan with our carrier to help you reduce your deductible. For every health benchmark you reach, you can reduce your deductible by $500. The benchmarks involve these categories:

- Cholesterol
- Body mass index
- Blood pressure
- Tobacco use

For each benchmark that you reach, your deductible decreases by $500. If you are a nonsmoker, for example, you receive a $500 decrease right away. What are the benchmarks? The enclosed brochure explains the health goals you can reach to earn the lower deductible charges. In addition to reducing your out-of-pocket expenses, this plan brings you long-term health benefits that can mean a happier, healthier, and longer life for you. If you are worried about how you can meet the benchmarks, we have literature, fitness programs, and counselors to help you meet your goals. The first step is signing up for a session with our fitness counselor to map out a plan customized for you.

[10.22 Continued]

Let's work together to reduce your healthcare costs and boost your fitness. Please return the enclosed application for a counselor's visit before January 15 so that you can get started immediately on the road to a healthier you and enjoy an extra $2,000 in your pocket. Send your application to Melissa Mendoza, Human Resources. Call Extension 488 if you have questions.

Enclosure

10.23 AND NOW WE WANT YOUR BLOOD!

Message 1

To: Christine Davis <christine.davis@colman.com>
From: Your Name <yourname@colman.com>
Subject: Decisions About a "Healthier You" Program
Cc:
Attached: "Healthier You" Information

As you requested, our intern team mapped out a proposed health assessment program for Colman. We suggest calling the program "Healthier You," which emphasizes benefits to employees. Here is a summary of our decisions regarding the program.

WHAT? We propose that Colman initiate a "Healthier You" program that enables employees to fill out health assessment questionnaires and take blood tests. The success of such a program depends on positive promotion from the entire Colman management team.

WHEN? American Healthways will conduct the blood tests 9 to 4 on Thursday and Friday, April 14 and 15.

WHERE? The blood tests will be done on site, probably in our company meeting room.

WHY? Colman has a vested interest in the health of its employees. Healthy employees make good business sense. "Healthy people are appreciating assets, and healthy people make healthy companies," said Robert Allen, President and CEO, AT&T. "It is also a business priority because a healthy, growing, competitive enterprise depends on the health, vitality, and energy of individuals." Healthy people also reduce health care costs for themselves and their employers. They live longer, richer lives. A health-risk assessment program is the first step in controlling chronic and expensive health problems such as

[10.23 Message 1 Continued]

diabetes, obesity, and tobacco addiction. Simple, nearly painless blood tests are critical in early detection of many diseases and conditions. The earlier a problem is detected, the more likely it is to be treatable.

HOW? Our "Healthier You" program involves filling out a health assessment questionnaire and taking a simple blood test on site. Employees will receive test results within a month, and they learn how their blood work compares with their own assessments. We would assure employees that only they receive individual results. Aggregate results would come to the company. To announce the program, we suggest notifying employees through an initial hard-copy memo so that they have a formal, permanent written notice to think about. Our message will focus on direct benefits to employees (healthier lifestyle with fewer disease risks, overall wellbeing, lower health insurance costs) and indirect benefits (a more productive, viable company as a result of its healthy employees). Because some people fear blood tests, we will stress that the procedure is quick and relatively painless. One or two e-mail messages could follow up as program reminders.

INCENTIVES? Our team feels that positive rather than negative incentives are more effective. We propose giving employees a $20 monthly discount on their health care costs if they follow through with the complete program.

Attached is our proposed announcement of the program. Please send your reactions and suggest revisions, if any, to me <your name@colman.com>.

Format Note: We show these side headings in all caps, but they could also be boldfaced or underlined.

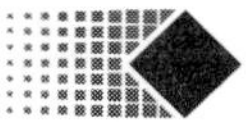

10.23 AND NOW WE WANT YOUR BLOOD!

Message 2

Date: Current
To: All Colman Employees
From: Christine Davis, Vice President, Human Resources
Subject: "Healthier You": Good for You and Your Pocketbook!

In an effort to help you reduce your health care costs and improve your health and wellbeing at the same time, Colman is launching "Healthier You." The purpose of this program is to help you avoid chronic and expensive health problems such as diabetes, obesity, and tobacco addiction.

What Is "Healthier You"?

"Healthier You" is a simple health assessment program that can make a big difference in your life. It involves a questionnaire that you fill out about your perception of your current health status. The program also includes an on-site blood test, which is practically painless and takes only a few minutes. You will receive results of the test within a month so that you can see how closely your questionnaire assessment matches the blood test results. Only you will see your test results. Colman will receive the aggregate totals for all employees, but not specific results for individuals. The blood tests screen for cholesterol, diabetes, hypertension, body fat, liver function, and nicotine.

Why Participate?

Just as other companies have experienced, Colman has seen its health care insurance costs skyrocket. You don't like to shell out an increasing chunk of your salary for insurance costs, and neither do we. Other companies using health assessment

[10.23 Message 2 Continued]

programs with blood tests have seen their health care costs drop from $300 to $1,400 per participant. More important, however, is that you can be healthier and happier if you learn about your current health status and how to reduce your risks. Health statistics reveal that many Americans are overweight, don't exercise, and are at risk for many chronic health problems. You can take an important first step in improving your health by participating in "Healthier You." Because we are so convinced of the benefits of this program, Colman will reduce your monthly health care premiums by $20 if you agree to participate. This means you can save money at the same time you are saving your health.

We need your good health to maintain our vital, high-energy company. You need your good health to enjoy a satisfying, productive, and long life to spend with your family. Resolve now to take the first step toward a healthier you! Let us help you reach your goal with the "Healthier You" assessment program. Remember, you will be saving $20 every month if you choose to participate.

How Can You Participate?

American Healthways will be here at Colman from 9 to 4 on Thursday and Friday, April 14 and 15, to conduct the blood tests. Please reserve your spot by calling Karen at Ext. 3589 before April 1. Karen will make sure that you receive the health assessment form, which you should fill out and bring with you to the blood test.

Format Note: Side headings may be formatted in boldface or underlined. We show them underlined because the entire message is in boldface.

10.24 Cutting Overnight Shipping

Date: Current
To: All Employees
From: Your Name, Manager
Subject: Reducing Overnight Delivery Costs

Overnight delivery services are wonderful, but they are costing us a bundle! To avoid rigid future restrictions imposed by the CEO, I'm asking you to voluntarily reduce your use of these delivery services by 50 percent in the next two months.

Rather than face a ban on all overnight services, let's work together to reduce our costs. Here are some suggestions:

- Ask yourself whether the recipient will really use the information immediately. If not, use a cheaper method.

- Send messages by fax or e-mail. A long-distance fax costs only about 35 cents and local messages cost nothing. E-mail messages are equally inexpensive.

- Use the FedEx or UPS account number of the recipient whenever possible.

- Plan ahead so that you can use FedEx or UPS ground service. These ground services take about three to five days.

Some overnight shipments, of course, are critical. To retain our budget for those shipments, we must cut our overall use by one half—before March 1. If you can think of other ways to reduce overnight shipments, please call me at Ext. 455. I appreciate your ideas and your help in solving this problem.

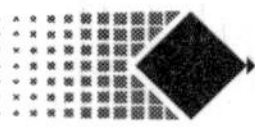

10.25 Supporting Project H.E.L.P.

To: Staff <staff_list@prudential.com>
From: Your name <your_name@prudential.com>
Subject: Project H.E.L.P.
Cc: wp@prudential.com; cms@prudential.com; mc@prudential.com; library@prudential.com
Bcc:

Would you like to increase your commitment to your community and improve your job skills? Project H.E.L.P. is an opportunity for employees to train and encourage local students. You can also improve your own supervisory and interpersonal skills.

Project H.E.L.P. joins major corporations and their employees with the Newark Unified School District to give young people on-the-job training. This semester 12 Prudential employees will share their expertise with 600 students who need on-the-job experience. Students will serve in Claims, Word Processing, Corporate Media Services, Marketing, Communications, Library, and Administrative Support departments. Company employees from those departments will supervise and instruct students for four hours per week at the Prudential Newark facility.

As they instruct, lead, and supervise students, Project H.E.L.P. volunteers will gain the opportunity to hone their own supervisory, speaking, and interpersonal skills. With two hours of release time per week to work with students, employees are supported by the company as they improve their own skills. Most of all, however, employees will enjoy knowing that they have helped students gain real-world business experience.

Prudential employees who have worked with Project H.E.L.P. know that being a Project H.E.L.P. volunteer is satisfying and rewarding. If you would like to be a part of this worthwhile project, please reply to this e-mail by August 6.

10.26 REVISING MISERABLE MEMO

Date: Current
To: All Managers and Employees
From: Rita Nelson, CEO
Subject: SCHEDULING EMPLOYEE MEETINGS

To save your time and to reduce your frustration, we are suggesting that anyone who schedules employee meetings in the future give serious thought to these questions:

- **Is a face-to-face meeting absolutely necessary?**
- **Could you achieve your purpose with a telephone, video, or e-mail conference?**

If you decide that a meeting is absolutely necessary, please follow these suggestions:

- **Meet at a place where most of the participants work or at a central location.**
- **Schedule the meeting at times that avoid rush-hour traffic.**
- **Travel together, if possible.**

None of you should have to spend three or more hours of your valuable time traveling to and from a meeting. Following these suggestions should avoid unnecessary travel and meeting time.

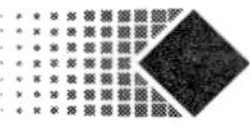

10.27 CURBING PROFANITY ON THE JOB

Date: Current
To: Sales Associates
From: Your Name, Sales Manager
Subject: Use of Professional Language in the Workplace

It's the one thing Oprah Winfrey really dislikes about herself. Maybe it's something you would also like to change about yourself. Oprah says, "I agree that swearing is terrible, and I'm going to quit."

What's so bad about swearing? It depends on why, when, and where you are swearing. Cursing is sometimes humorous but can also be rude, crude, and offensive. It can help vent anger or provoke it. It can relieve stress or cause it. It can be clever and flirtatious or sexist and intimidating. Consequently, be aware of when and where you swear. Control it, tame it, time it; and while at work, eliminate it.

Why is swearing not appropriate at work? Profanity gives a bad impression; it doesn't demonstrate respect for yourself or others. Worse yet, it can create a negative workplace in which fellow employees feel embarrassed, intimidated, or demoralized. It can lead to a legal charge against the firm for allowing a hostile work environment. It can also get you fired.

How can you control swearing? Swearing, like any other undesirable habit, can be broken with determination and alternate behaviors. You may want to visit the Cuss Control Academy at www.cusscontrol.com. The site gives numerous suggestions for curbing your use of inappropriate language. These suggestions are summarized in the attachment, which you are encouraged to post in your office.

Sales Associates Page 2 Current date

When should you stop swearing at work? TODAY. Effective December 1, the following policy becomes part of the company's Employee Handbook as Section P.3.2:

> **The use of vulgar, profane, or demeaning language, whether written or oral, while on company premises or when representing the company in any capacity is expressly prohibited. Violations will result in punitive actions, including possible suspension or termination.**

Thanks for your attention to this important issue and for your efforts toward "cleaning up" our work environment. Together, we can assure that our company projects a professional image that makes us all proud.

Attachment

***Based on DuFrene, D. D., & Lehman, C. M. (2002, March). Persuasive appeal for clean language. *Business Communication Quarterly*, 65(1), 48-55. Reprinted with permission of Association for Business Communication.**

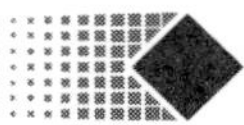

10.28 Sales Letter Analysis

Analyze a sales letter by answering these questions:

a. **What techniques capture the reader's attention?**

b. **Is the opening effective? Explain.**

c. **What are the central selling points?**

d. **Does the letter use rational, emotional, or a combination of appeals? Explain.**

e. **What reader benefits are suggested?**

f. **How does the letter build interest in the product or service?**

g. **How is price handled?**

h. **How does the letter anticipate reader resistance and offer counterarguments?**

i. **What action is the reader to take? How is the action made easy?**

j. **What motivators spur the reader to act quickly?**

10.29 WEIGHING IN AT WORK

Current date

Ms. Carol Wong
Director, Human Resources
Prophecy Financial Services
790 Lafayette Boulevard
Bridgeport, CT 06604

Dear Ms. Wong:

Would Prophecy Financial Services like to reduce its medical costs by over $1,000 per employee per year?

To control surging medical costs, companies such as Prophecy are installing economical on-site fitness centers designed by Fitness for Life, one of the country's leading fitness operators. By helping employees shed excess pounds through proper exercise, an on-site fitness center can significantly reduce employee medical costs at Prophecy Financial Services. Health research shows that companies can save as much as $1,200 per employee per year if employees shed excess weight.

On-site fitness centers from Fitness for Life reduce medical costs by making it convenient for employees to exercise, lose weight, and improve overall health. Your employees will love working out before or after work right at the office. In addition, improved employee health can reduce absenteeism and increase productivity.

Fitness for Life provides everything you need to open an on-site fitness center. Our fitness experts will design a facility suited to the needs of Prophecy for Financial Services, install ready-to-use exercise equipment, and design appropriate fitness programs. Best of all, the one-time start-up fee of $30,000 is typically offset with cost savings in just one year.

Ms. Carol Wong
Page 2
Current date

For an additional fee, Fitness for Life will conduct employee fitness assessments and train employees on proper equipment use. We can even clean and manage the facility.

To learn more about how Prophecy can start reducing medical costs and increasing productivity right now, check out the enclosed brochure detailing Fitness for Life centers. Then please call me at (414) 961-0082 so that I can meet with you personally. I would like to answer your questions and begin planning Prophecy Financial Service's fitness center.

Sincerely,

Enclosure

P.S. Open your fitness center before December 1 and receive a free fitness assessment for every Prophecy employee!

10.30 Adapting From Low Context to High Context

Six factors and techniques typify this low-context sales letter:

a. **Directness**. The letter speaks directly to the reader and openly presents a sales pitch for a credit card.

b. **Tone**. The letter is conversational and informal. It might be considered presumptuous and overly familiar in assuming the reader is one *who appreciates convenience and value.* The tone is almost accusatory: *Realistically, how could you pass up these attractive opportunities?*

c. **Superlatives**. The letter uses superlatives (*absolutely FREE, unsurpassed card protection, exceptional personal customer service).*

d. **Hard-sell approach**. The letter uses pushy, hard-sell techniques including a deadline for responding and a P.S. offering additional incentives to act quickly.

e. **"You" view**. Throughout, the letter emphasizes specific benefits aimed at the reader. The writer also uses *I* instead of the collectivist *we, our.*

f. **Short-term goal.** The letter has only one purpose—selling the Citibank credit card. It makes no attempt to develop a long-term relationship.

The letter could be made more appealing to a high-context audience by being more formal in tone and less aggressive in its appeals. It should begin with a softer opening that suggests respect for the reader. The tone throughout the letter should be more polite, modest, and humble. A high-context sales letter would probably be less specific and use more general terms in describing the product.

10.31 Promoting Your Product or Service

Solutions will vary.

10.32 Preparing News for Your Local Newspaper

FOR IMMEDIATE RELEASE

Contact: Cindy Eikenberg
(410) 847-9420

BIG MACS GO GREEN WITH POTATO-STARCH CLAMSHELL CONTAINERS

Santa Barbara, CA, current date. In an effort to use biodegradable packaging, McDonald's has approved a new sandwich container for its Big Mac. Over 300 McDonald's stores will begin handing out its most popular sandwich in an environmentally friendly clamshell container made from potato starch, limestone, and 100 percent post-consumer recycled fiber.

The new container, produced by EarthShell, is whipped up out of renewable starch that is reclaimed from the commercial processing of potatoes and French fries. It also uses natural limestone, cellulose fiber (from post-consumer recycled school milk cartons and juice boxes), biodegradable protective coatings, manufacturing release agents, water, and a thickener. The mixture is blended into a batter and then placed between two heated mold plates. Water in the mixture turns to steam, expanding the blend that eventually cools into a waffle-like form.

The miraculous EarthShell product is surprisingly strong, yet economical and biodegradable. It meets industry requirements for rigidity, insulation, stacking, consumer usage properties, and graphic capabilities. Using low-cost raw materials processed in conventional machinery, EarthShell packaging requires less total energy to make than polystyrene or paper products. What's more, EarthShell products are competitively priced.

EarthShell Press Release
Page 2

Many fast-food restaurants have turned to paper after consumer groups insisted on banning polystyrene packaging, which is almost indestructible when discarded. But paper packaging is expensive and offers reduced performance. EarthShell offers a better solution.

EarthShell Corporation is engaged in the licensing and commercialization of proprietary composite material technology for the manufacture of disposable food-service packaging, such as cups, plates, bowls, hinged-lid containers, and sandwich wraps. EarthShell packaging is designed to be cost and performance competitive compared to other food-service packaging materials. However, it also provides important environmental advantages.

For more information, visit its Web site at www.EarthShell.com.

# # #

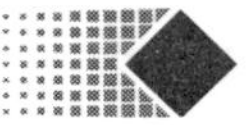

10.33 THIS IS NEW!

Solutions will vary.

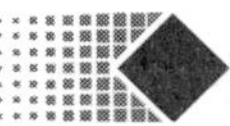

Chapters 11-14

Solutions and discussion material for selected activities in Chapters 11-14 are found in the Teaching Suggestions for each chapter.

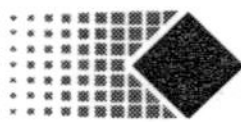

15.1 Document for Analysis: Résumé—Revision

Janet P. Garza

530 North Comanche Street, Apartment B
San Marcos, TX 78666
Phone: (512) 396-5182 E-mail: JGarza@gmail.com

OBJECTIVE: General bookkeeping position with a large accounting firm where my accounting education and financial consulting experience can help the firm achieve its goals.

SUMMARY OF QUALIFICATIONS

- Expect BA degree with accounting major/marketing minor in June 2011
- AA degree/certificate of completion in accounting
- Have on-the-job practical experience including financial consulting in the mortgage industry
- Developed people, team, and leadership skills as line manager for Home Depot
- Trained in PowerPoint, Excel, and database management
- Able to work well in stressful situations

EDUCATION

Texas State University, San Marcos, TX

- BA to be conferred in December 2011
- Major: Accounting; Minor: Finance
- Completed 90 units including courses in Analysis and Application of Accounting Data and Financial Reporting
- Dean's Honor List, Fall 2010

Austin Community College, San Marcos, TX

- AA degree, Accounting, December 2009
- Earned Certificate of Completion, Entry-Level Accounting, June 2009

15.1 Document for Analysis: Résumé—Revision [Continued]

EXPERIENCE

Primerica Financial Services, San Marcos, Texas
Financial Consultant, January 2010 to present

- Assist clients in obtaining mortgages, and consolidating current mortgage loans
- Assess clients' life insurance needs
- Praised by supervisor for reliability and painstaking work

Home Depot, Kyle, Texas
Line Manager, September 2004-March 2008

- Supervised 50 cashiers and front-end associates
- Prepared weekly work schedules
- Conducted annual performance reviews
- Issued disciplinary action notices as needed
- Maintained change drawer and monetary exchanges with 100 percent accuracy
- Substituted for manager as necessary, overseeing entire store
- Named Line Manager of the Month, September 2006 and August 2005

Penn Foster Career School, Scranton, Pennsylvania
Teacher, August 2003-September 2004

- Taught courses in flower design to classes with an average of 25 students each
- Supervised 15 florists
- Made floral arrangements and delivered them to customers
- Maintained inventory of flowers and all necessary supplies

ACTIVITIES

- American Accounting Association (AAA), Chair, January-December 2009
- Movimiento Estudiantil Chicano de Aztlán (M.E.Ch.A), Webmaster, January-May 2010

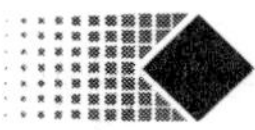

15.2 DOCUMENT FOR ANALYSIS: COVER LETTER—REVISION

530 North Comanche Street, Apt. B
San Marcos, TX 78666
May 4, 2011

Ms. Susan L. Winter
Director, Human Resources
Cook & Associates, P.C.
2018 Hunter Road
San Marcos, TX 78666

Dear Ms. Winter:

Please accept my application for the accounting internship position that I saw listed on the Cook & Associates Web site on May 3.

My business coursework and work experience permitted me to develop the skills and qualifications that are listed on the Web site for this position. Over 90 units of college work at Texas State University, including eight courses in accounting, have helped me build a firm foundation for a career in this field. My special interest is in accounting and finance.

Working as a financial consultant with Primerica Financial Services, where I assist clients with obtaining mortgages, consolidating current mortgages, and assessing life insurance needs, has taught me to be painstaking and detail-oriented. As a line manager with Home Depot, I honed my managerial and teamwork skills by effectively supervising 50 cashiers and front-end associates. My position as a floral design teacher with Penn Foster Career School helped develop interpersonal and leadership skills. As you can see, I am able to juggle multiple responsibilities including school and work.

15.2 Document for Analysis: Cover Letter—Revision [Continued]

Ms. Susan L. Winter
Page 2
May 4, 2011

To discuss how I could contribute to the Cook & Associates workforce, please review the enclosed résumé. Because I recognize this as a genuine opportunity to gain experience and also to make a contribution to an industry-leading accounting firm, I am eager to talk with you. Please call me at (512) 396-5182.

Sincerely,

Janet P. Garza

Enclosure

NOTE: See Chapter 15 Teaching Suggestions for a list of document weaknesses for Activities 15.1 and 15.2.

NOTE: See Chapters 15 and 16 Teaching Suggestions for discussion material for remaining activities in Chapters 15 and 16.